BEHAVIORAL FINANCE, INDIVIDUAL INVESTORS, AND INSTITUTIONAL INVESTORS

CFA® Program Curriculum
2016 • LEVEL III • VOLUME 2

CFA Institute | **WILEY**

Please visit our website at
www.WileyGlobalFinance.com.

WILEY

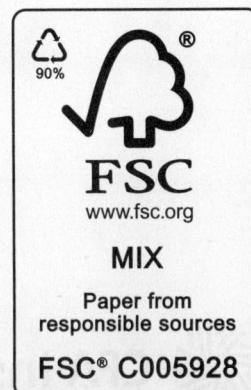

CONTENTS

◙ indicates an optional segment

🔘 indicates an optional segment

◙ indicates an optional segment

◙ indicates an optional segment

How to Use the CFA Program Curriculum

Congratulations on reaching Level III of the Chartered Financial Analyst (CFA®) Program. This exciting and rewarding program of study reflects your desire to become a serious investment professional. You are embarking on a program noted for its high ethical standards and the breadth of knowledge, skills, and abilities it develops. Your commitment to the CFA Program should be educationally and professionally rewarding.

The credential you seek is respected around the world as a mark of accomplishment and dedication. Each level of the program represents a distinct achievement in professional development. Successful completion of the program is rewarded with membership in a prestigious global community of investment professionals. CFA charterholders are dedicated to life-long learning and maintaining currency with the ever-changing dynamics of a challenging profession. The CFA Program represents the first step toward a career-long commitment to professional education.

The CFA examination measures your mastery of the core skills required to succeed as an investment professional. These core skills are the basis for the Candidate Body of Knowledge (CBOK™). The CBOK consists of four components:

- A broad outline that lists the major topic areas covered in the CFA Program (www.cfainstitute.org/cbok);

- Topic area weights that indicate the relative exam weightings of the top-level topic areas (www.cfainstitute.org/level_III);

- Learning outcome statements (LOS) that advise candidates about the specific knowledge, skills, and abilities they should acquire from readings covering a topic area (LOS are provided in candidate study sessions and at the beginning of each reading); and

- The CFA Program curriculum, which contains the readings and end-of-reading questions, that candidates receive upon exam registration.

Therefore, the key to your success on the CFA examinations is studying and understanding the CBOK. The following sections provide background on the CBOK, the organization of the curriculum, and tips for developing an effective study program.

CURRICULUM DEVELOPMENT PROCESS

The CFA Program is grounded in the practice of the investment profession. Beginning with the Global Body of Investment Knowledge (GBIK), CFA Institute performs a continuous practice analysis with investment professionals around the world to determine the knowledge, skills, and abilities (competencies) that are relevant to the profession. Regional expert panels and targeted surveys are conducted annually to verify and reinforce the continuous feedback from the GBIK collaborative website. The practice analysis process ultimately defines the CBOK. The CBOK reflects the competencies that are generally accepted and applied by investment professionals. These competencies are used in practice in a generalist context and are expected to be demonstrated by a recently qualified CFA charterholder.

The Education Advisory Committee, consisting of practicing charterholders, in conjunction with CFA Institute staff, designs the CFA Program curriculum in order to deliver the CBOK to candidates. The examinations, also written by charterholders, are designed to allow you to demonstrate your mastery of the CBOK as set forth in the CFA Program curriculum. As you structure your personal study program, you should emphasize mastery of the CBOK and the practical application of that knowledge. For more information on the practice analysis, CBOK, and development of the CFA Program curriculum, please visit www.cfainstitute.org.

ORGANIZATION OF THE CURRICULUM

The Level III CFA Program curriculum is organized into 10 topic areas. Each topic area begins with a brief statement of the material and the depth of knowledge expected.

Each topic area is then divided into one or more study sessions. These study sessions—18 sessions in the Level III curriculum—should form the basic structure of your reading and preparation.

Each study session includes a statement of its structure and objective and is further divided into specific reading assignments. An outline illustrating the organization of these 18 study sessions can be found at the front of each volume of the curriculum.

The readings and end-of-reading questions are the basis for all examination questions and are selected or developed specifically to teach the knowledge, skills, and abilities reflected in the CBOK. These readings are drawn from content commissioned by CFA Institute, textbook chapters, professional journal articles, research analyst reports, and cases. All readings include problems and solutions to help you understand and master the topic areas.

Reading-specific Learning Outcome Statements (LOS) are listed at the beginning of each reading. These LOS indicate what you should be able to accomplish after studying the reading. The LOS, the reading, and the end-of-reading questions are dependent on each other, with the reading and questions providing context for understanding the scope of the LOS.

You should use the LOS to guide and focus your study because each examination question is based on the assigned readings and one or more LOS. The readings provide context for the LOS and enable you to apply a principle or concept in a variety of scenarios. The candidate is responsible for the entirety of the required material in a study session, which includes the assigned readings as well as the end-of-reading questions and problems.

We encourage you to review the information about the LOS on our website (www.cfainstitute.org/programs/cfaprogram/courseofstudy/Pages/study_sessions.aspx), including the descriptions of LOS "command words" (www.cfainstitute.org/programs/Documents/cfa_and_cipm_los_command_words.pdf).

FEATURES OF THE CURRICULUM

OPTIONAL
SEGMENT

Required vs. Optional Segments   You should read all of an assigned reading. In some cases, though, we have reprinted an entire chapter or article and marked certain parts of the reading as "optional." The CFA examination is based only on the required segments, and the optional segments are included only when it is determined that they might help you to better understand the required segments (by seeing the required material in its full context). When an optional segment begins, you will see an icon and a dashed vertical bar in the outside margin that will continue until the optional segment ends, accompanied by another icon. *Unless the material is specifically marked as optional, you should assume it is required.* You should rely on the required segments and the reading-specific LOS in preparing for the examination.

END OPTIONAL
SEGMENT

End-of-Reading Problems/Solutions　　*All problems in the readings as well as their solutions (which are provided directly following the problems) are part of the curriculum and are required material for the exam.* When appropriate, we have included problems within and after the readings to demonstrate practical application and reinforce your understanding of the concepts presented. The problems are designed to help you learn these concepts and may serve as a basis for exam questions. Many of these questions are adapted from past CFA examinations.

Glossary and Index　　For your convenience, we have printed a comprehensive glossary in each volume. Throughout the curriculum, a **bolded** word in a reading denotes a term defined in the glossary. The curriculum eBook is searchable, but we also publish an index that can be found on the CFA Institute website with the Level III study sessions.

Source Material　　The authorship, publisher, and copyright owners are given for each reading for your reference. We recommend that you use the CFA Institute curriculum rather than the original source materials because the curriculum may include only selected pages from outside readings, updated sections within the readings, and problems and solutions tailored to the CFA Program.

LOS Self-Check　　We have inserted checkboxes next to each LOS that you can use to track your progress in mastering the concepts in each reading.

DESIGNING YOUR PERSONAL STUDY PROGRAM

Create a Schedule　　An orderly, systematic approach to exam preparation is critical. You should dedicate a consistent block of time every week to reading and studying. Complete all reading assignments and the associated problems and solutions in each study session. Review the LOS both before and after you study each reading to ensure that you have mastered the applicable content and can demonstrate the knowledge, skill, or ability described by the LOS and the assigned reading. Use the LOS self-check to track your progress and highlight areas of weakness for later review.

As you prepare for your exam, we will e-mail you important exam updates, testing policies, and study tips. Be sure to read these carefully. Curriculum errata are periodically updated and posted on the study session page at www.cfainstitute.org. You can also sign up for an RSS feed to alert you to the latest errata update.

Successful candidates report an average of more than 300 hours preparing for each exam. Your preparation time will vary based on your prior education and experience. For each level of the curriculum, there are 18 study sessions. So, a good plan is to devote 15–20 hours per week for 18 weeks to studying the material. Use the final four to six weeks before the exam to review what you have learned and practice with topic and mock exams. This recommendation, however, may underestimate the hours needed for appropriate examination preparation depending on your individual circumstances, relevant experience, and academic background. You will undoubtedly adjust your study time to conform to your own strengths and weaknesses and to your educational and professional background.

You will probably spend more time on some study sessions than on others, but on average you should plan on devoting 15–20 hours per study session. You should allow ample time for both in-depth study of all topic areas and additional concentration on those topic areas for which you feel the least prepared.

An interactive study planner is available in the candidate resources area of our website to help you plan your study time. The interactive study planner recommends completion dates for each topic of the curriculum. Dates are determined based on study time available, exam topic weights, and curriculum weights. As you progress through the curriculum, the interactive study planner dynamically adjusts your study plan when you are running off schedule to help you stay on track for completion prior to the examination.

CFA Institute Topic Exams   The CFA Institute topic exams are intended to assess your mastery of individual topic areas as you progress through your studies. After each test, you will receive immediate feedback noting the correct responses and indicating the relevant assigned reading so you can identify areas of weakness for further study. For more information on the topic tests, please visit www.cfainstitute.org.

CFA Institute Mock Exams   The three-hour mock exams simulate the morning and afternoon sessions of the actual CFA examination, and are intended to be taken after you complete your study of the full curriculum so you can test your understanding of the curriculum and your readiness for the exam. You will receive feedback at the end of the mock exam, noting the correct responses and indicating the relevant assigned readings so you can assess areas of weakness for further study during your review period. We recommend that you take mock exams during the final stages of your preparation for the actual CFA examination. For more information on the mock examinations, please visit www.cfainstitute.org.

Preparatory Providers   After you enroll in the CFA Program, you may receive numerous solicitations for preparatory courses and review materials. When considering a prep course, make sure the provider is in compliance with the CFA Institute Prep Provider Guidelines Program (www.cfainstitute.org/utility/examprep/Pages/index.aspx). Just remember, there are no shortcuts to success on the CFA examinations; reading and studying the CFA curriculum is the key to success on the examination. The CFA examinations reference only the CFA Institute assigned curriculum—no preparatory course or review course materials are consulted or referenced.

SUMMARY

Every question on the CFA examination is based on the content contained in the required readings and on one or more LOS. Frequently, an examination question is based on a specific example highlighted within a reading or on a specific end-of-reading question and/or problem and its solution. To make effective use of the CFA Program curriculum, please remember these key points:

1   All pages of the curriculum are required reading for the examination except for occasional sections marked as optional. You may read optional pages as background, but you will not be tested on them.

2   All questions, problems, and their solutions—found at the end of readings—are part of the curriculum and are required study material for the examination.

3   You should make appropriate use of the topic and mock examinations and other resources available at www.cfainstitute.org.

4 Use the interactive study planner to create a schedule and commit sufficient study time to cover the 18 study sessions, review the materials, and take topic and mock examinations.

5 Some of the concepts in the study sessions may be superseded by updated rulings and/or pronouncements issued after a reading was published. Candidates are expected to be familiar with the overall analytical framework contained in the assigned readings. Candidates are not responsible for changes that occur after the material was written.

FEEDBACK

At CFA Institute, we are committed to delivering a comprehensive and rigorous curriculum for the development of competent, ethically grounded investment professionals. We rely on candidate and member feedback as we work to incorporate content, design, and packaging improvements. You can be assured that we will continue to listen to your suggestions. Please send any comments or feedback to info@cfainstitute.org. Ongoing improvements in the curriculum will help you prepare for success on the upcoming examinations and for a lifetime of learning as a serious investment professional.

Portfolio Management

STUDY SESSIONS

This volume includes Study Sessions 3–6.

TOPIC LEVEL LEARNING OUTCOME

The candidate should be able to prepare an appropriate investment policy statement and asset allocation; formulate strategies for managing, monitoring, and rebalancing investment portfolios; evaluate portfolio performance; and analyze a presentation of investment returns for consistency with Global Investment Performance Standards (GIPS®).

3

Behavioral Finance

Behavioral Finance is introduced in the first study session on portfolio management because all market participants, regardless of expertise, may be subject to behavioral biases. An understanding of emotional and cognitive behavioral biases provides insight into how these biases may influence individuals' perceptions and investment decisions. As a consequence, knowledge of behavioral biases may help in understanding client goals, in constructing investment portfolios, and in identifying inconsistencies in investment decision making. Behavioral finance also provides insights into issues such as market anomalies. The readings argue that integration of behavioral and traditional finance may lead to a better outcome than either approach used in isolation.

READING ASSIGNMENTS

Reading 5	The Behavioral Finance Perspective by Michael M. Pompian, CFA
Reading 6	The Behavioral Biases of Individuals by Michael M. Pompian, CFA
Reading 7	Behavioral Finance and Investment Processes by Michael M. Pompian, CFA, Colin McLean, FSIP, and Alistair Byrne, PhD, CFA

Note: The readings in this study session use widely recognized terminology. Nevertheless, readers should be aware that writers on behavioral finance vary in their choice of terminology.

The Behavioral Finance Perspective

by Michael M. Pompian, CFA

Michael M. Pompian, CFA (USA)

LEARNING OUTCOMES

Mastery	The candidate should be able to:
☐	**a.** contrast traditional and behavioral finance perspectives on investor decision making;
☐	**b.** contrast expected utility and prospect theories of investment decision making;
☐	**c.** discuss the effect that cognitive limitations and bounded rationality may have on investment decision making;
☐	**d.** compare traditional and behavioral finance perspectives on portfolio construction and the behavior of capital markets.

INTRODUCTION

1

Behavioral finance attempts to understand and explain observed investor and market behaviors. This differs from traditional (standard) finance, which is based on hypotheses about how investors and markets should behave. In other words, behavioral finance differs from traditional finance in that it focuses on how investors and markets behave in practice rather than in theory. By focusing on actual behavior, behavioral researchers have observed that individuals make investment decisions in ways and with outcomes that differ from the approaches and outcomes of traditional finance. As Meir Statman so succinctly puts it, "Standard finance people are modeled as "rational," whereas behavioral finance people are modeled as "normal."[1] Normal people behave in a manner and with outcomes that may appear irrational or suboptimal from a traditional finance perspective. As a result of identified divergence between observed and theoretically optimal decision making, the global investment community has begun to realize that it cannot rely entirely on scientific, mathematical, or economic models to explain individual investor and market behavior.

---

[1] Statman (1999).

As behavioral finance gains acceptance, efforts to understand what drives individual investor and market behavior will increase. Complete understanding will never be possible, however, because human behavior cannot be predicted with scientific precision or fully explained by a simple "unifying theory." In fact, trying to predict economic behavior, and by extension market behavior, has been likened to trying to predict the weather.

> Like weather forecasters, economic forecasters must deal with a system that is extraordinarily complex, that is subject to random shocks, and about which our data and understanding will always be imperfect. In some ways, predicting the economy is even more difficult than forecasting the weather, because the economy is not made up of molecules whose behavior is subject to the laws of physics, but rather of human beings who are themselves thinking about the future and whose behavior may be influenced by the forecasts that they or others make. To be sure, historical relationships and regularities can help economists, as well as weather forecasters, gain some insight into the future, but these must be used with considerable caution and healthy skepticism.

US Federal Reserve Chairman Ben Bernanke[2]

At its core, behavioral finance is about understanding how people make decisions, both individually and collectively. By understanding how investors and markets behave, it may be possible to modify or adapt to their behaviors in order to improve economic outcomes. In many instances, this may entail identifying a behavior and then modifying the behavior so it more closely matches that assumed under the traditional finance models. In other instances, it may be necessary to adapt to an identified behavior and to make decisions that adjust for the behavior. The integration of behavioral and traditional finance has the potential to produce a superior economic outcome; the resulting financial decision may produce an economic outcome closer to the optimal outcome of traditional finance, while being easier for an investor to adhere to in practice.

To provide a framework for understanding the implications of the decision-making process for financial market practitioners, throughout this reading we will use an approach developed by decision theorist, Howard Raiffa. Raiffa (1997) discusses three approaches to the analysis of decisions that provide a more accurate view of a "real" person's thought process. He uses the terms normative analysis, descriptive analysis, and prescriptive analysis. Normative analysis is concerned with the rational solution to the problem at hand. It defines an ideal that actual decisions should strive to approximate. Descriptive analysis is concerned with the manner in which real people actually make decisions. Prescriptive analysis is concerned with practical advice and tools that might help people achieve results more closely approximating those of normative analysis. We can think of the traditional finance assumptions about behavior as normative, behavioral finance explanations of behaviors as descriptive, and efforts to use behavioral finance in practice as prescriptive.

In order to use behavioral finance in practice, it is important to understand how behavioral finance differs from traditional finance and some of the theoretical perspectives that are relevant to the understanding of the differences. Section 2 compares and contrasts behavioral and traditional perspectives of investor behaviors. Section 3 discusses theories that relax the assumptions about investor behavior that are inherent

---

2 Bernanke (2009).

in traditional finance. Section 4 compares and contrasts traditional and behavioral finance perspectives of market behaviors and portfolio construction. A summary and practice problems conclude the reading.

BEHAVIORAL VERSUS TRADITIONAL PERSPECTIVES

2

Traditional finance is grounded in neoclassical economics. Within traditional finance, individuals are assumed to be risk-averse, self-interested utility maximizers. Investors who behave in a manner consistent with these assumptions are referred to as rational. Traditional finance further hypothesizes that, at the market level, prices incorporate and reflect all available and relevant information. Markets that behave in a manner consistent with this hypothesis are described as efficient.

Behavioral finance is largely grounded in psychology. The term behavioral finance—generally defined as the application of psychology to finance—appears regularly in books, magazine articles, and investment papers; however, a common understanding of what is meant by behavioral finance is lacking. This may be because of a proliferation of topics resembling behavioral finance that examine investor behavior: These include behavioral economics, investor psychology, behavioral science, experimental economics, and cognitive psychology. Such emerging subjects as neuro-economics and adaptive finance (also known as evolutionary finance) are making their way into the conversation and provide another perspective on investor behavior. The variety of approaches taken to examine investor behavior adds to the confusion about what is meant by behavioral finance.

Behavioral finance attempts to understand and explain observed investor and market behaviors and bases its assumptions on observed financial behavior rather than on idealized financial behavior. Behavioral finance neither assumes that people act rationally and consider all available information in decision making nor that markets are efficient. To make behavioral finance easier to understand—and to differentiate the study of individual investor behavior from collective market behavior—behavioral finance in this reading is classified as either behavioral finance micro (BFMI) or behavioral finance macro (BFMA). Behavioral finance micro examines behaviors or biases that distinguish individual investors from the rational actors envisioned in neoclassical economic theory. Behavioral finance macro considers market anomalies that distinguish markets from the efficient markets of traditional finance. Whether BFMI or BFMA is of greater interest to practitioners depends on many factors, including the job held. For example, the primary focus of wealth managers and investment advisers to individual clients is BFMI (i.e., the behavior of individuals), while the primary focus of fund managers and economists is BFMA (i.e., the behavior of markets).

Regardless of whether BFMI or BFMA is of primary interest, it is critical to understand that much of traditional financial theory is based on the assumptions that individuals act rationally and consider all available information in the decision-making process and that markets are efficient. Behavioral finance challenges these assumptions. BFMI questions the perfect rationality and decision-making process of individual investors, and BFMA questions the efficiency of markets.

BFMI suggests that behavioral biases impact the financial decisions of individual investors. Behavioral biases can be categorized as cognitive errors or emotional biases. Cognitive errors stem from basic statistical, information-processing, or memory errors; cognitive errors may be considered to result from reasoning based on faulty thinking. Emotional biases stem from impulse or intuition; emotional biases may be considered to result from reasoning influenced by feelings. Behavioral biases, cognitive or emotional, may cause decisions to deviate from the rational decisions of traditional finance. BFMA suggests that markets are subject to behavioral effects. These behavioral effects may cause markets to deviate from the efficient markets of traditional finance.

Meir Statman, a prolific contributor to behavioral finance research, states comprehensively, "Standard finance is the body of knowledge built on the pillars of the arbitrage principles of Miller and Modigliani, the portfolio principles of Markowitz, the capital asset pricing theory of Sharpe, Lintner, and Black, and the option pricing theory of Black, Scholes, and Merton."[3] Statman's point is that traditional (standard) finance theory is designed to provide mathematically elegant explanations for financial questions that, when posed in real life, are often complicated by imprecise conditions. The traditional finance approach relies on assumptions that tend to oversimplify reality and are challenged by behavioral finance.

Sections 2.1, 2.2, and 2.3 focus on assumptions about investor behavior (BFMI). Section 2.1 provides an overview of the traditional finance perspective of individual behavior; section 2.2 discusses the behavioral finance challenges to the traditional finance perspective of individual behavior; and section 2.3 briefly introduces neuro-economics and its potential role in explaining individual investor behavior. Following section 2 and its discussions of traditional finance and behavioral finance perspectives, section 3 primarily addresses theories developed in response to apparent deviations from the assumptions of traditional finance regarding decision making.

2.1 Traditional Finance Perspectives on Individual Behavior

Traditional finance concepts may be thought of as normative, indicating how people and markets should behave. Investors are assumed to be rational; investors make decisions consistent with utility theory and revise expectations (update beliefs) consistent with Bayes' formula. They are further assumed to be self-interested and risk-averse, to have access to perfect information, and to process all available information in an unbiased way. Each of these underlying assumptions will be discussed further in the following subsections.

2.1.1 Utility Theory and Bayes' Formula

In **utility theory**, people maximize the present value of utility subject to a present value budget constraint.[4] **Utility** may be thought of as the level of relative satisfaction received from the consumption of goods and services. Decision makers choose between risky or uncertain prospects by comparing their expected utility values. They maximize their expected utility—the weighted sum of the utility values of outcomes multiplied by their respective probabilities—subject to their budget constraints. It is important to note that the determination of the value of an item is not based on its price, but rather on the utility it yields. The price of an item is dependent only on the characteristics of the item and is equal for everyone; the utility, however, is dependent on the particular circumstances and preferences of the person making the estimate of utility.

For our purposes, it is not important to understand fully the mathematical aspects of the expected utility model, which assumes that it is possible to quantify exactly how much utility an individual will derive based on the uncertain outcome of an economic decision and that the individual can and will choose between various options to arrive at an optimal decision that maximizes the individual's expected utility. Normatively, this is how people *should* make economic decisions; it is important to understand expected utility theory conceptually.

---

3 Statman (1999).
4 See, for example, Samuelson (1937).

There are some basic axioms of utility theory.[5] It is assumed that a rational decision maker follows rules of preference consistent with the axioms and that the utility function of a rational decision maker reflects the axioms. From any set of alternatives, a *rational* decision maker makes decisions consistent with the axioms of utility theory and chooses the combination of decisions that maximizes expected utility. The basic axioms of utility theory are completeness, transitivity, independence, and continuity.

- *Completeness* assumes that an individual has well-defined preferences and can decide between any two alternatives.

  Axiom (Completeness): Given choices A and B, the individual either prefers A to B, prefers B to A, or is indifferent between A and B.

- *Transitivity* assumes that, as an individual decides according to the completeness axiom, an individual decides consistently.

  Axiom (Transitivity): Transitivity is illustrated by the following examples. Given choices A, B, and C, if an individual prefers A to B and prefers B to C, then the individual prefers A to C; if an individual prefers A to B and is indifferent between B and C, then the individual prefers A to C; or, if an individual is indifferent between A and B and prefers A to C, then the individual prefers B to C.

- *Independence* also pertains to well-defined preferences and assumes that the preference order of two choices combined in the same proportion with a third choice maintains the same preference order as the original preference order of the two choices.

  Axiom (Independence): Let A and B be two mutually exclusive choices, and let C be a third choice that can be combined with A or B. If A is preferred to B and some amount, x, of C is added to A and B, then A plus xC is preferred to B plus xC. This assumption allows for additive utilities. If the utility of A is dependent on how much of C is available, the utilities are not additive.

- *Continuity* assumes there are continuous (unbroken) indifference curves such that an individual is indifferent between all points, representing combinations of choices, on a single indifference curve.

  Axiom (Continuity): When there are three lotteries (A, B, and C) and the individual prefers A to B and B to C, then there should be a possible combination of A and C such that the individual is indifferent between this combination and the lottery B. The end result is continuous indifference curves.

If the individual's decision making satisfies the four axioms, the individual is said to be rational. Put another way, if an individual is to maximize utility, he or she will choose one alternative over another if and only if the expected utility of one alternative exceeds the expected utility of the other alternative. The utility of any choice may be expressed as a function of the utility of the possible outcomes of the choice and their respective probabilities. If an individual believes a choice has possible outcomes, x_i, each with a utility of $u(x_i)$ and a subjective probability of $P(x_i)$, then the individual's subjective expected utility is $\Sigma u(x_i)P(x_i)$.[6] The completely rational individual makes decisions based on the axioms of utility theory in order to maximize expected utility.

The rational decision maker, given new information, is assumed to update beliefs about probabilities according to Bayes' formula. **Bayes' formula** is a mathematical rule explaining how existing probability beliefs should be changed given new information. In other words, Bayes' formula expects people to update old beliefs in a certain manner when given new information. Bayes' formula is essentially an application of conditional

---

5 See von Neumann and Morgenstern (1944).
6 See Savage (1954).

probabilities. This formula is valid in all common probability interpretations. In order to develop the calculation, all possible events must be mutually exclusive and exhaustive events with known probabilities.

Bayes' formula shows how one conditional probability is inversely related to the probability of another mutually exclusive outcome. The formula is:

$$P(A|B) = [P(B|A)/P(B)] \ P(A)$$

where:

> P(A|B) = conditional probability of event A given B. It is the updated probability of A given the new information B.
>
> P(B|A) = conditional probability of B given A. It is the probability of the new information B given event A.
>
> P(B) = prior (unconditional) probability of information B.
>
> P(A) = prior probability of event A, without new information B. This is the base rate or base probability of event A.

EXAMPLE 1

Example of Bayes' Formula

You have two identical urns, U1 and U2. U1 has 2 red balls (R) and 3 white balls (W). U2 has 4 red balls and 1 white ball. You randomly choose one of the urns to pick out a ball. A red ball is pulled out first. What is the probability that you picked U1, based on the fact that a red ball was pulled out first, P(U1|R)?

Solution:

P(R|U1) is the conditional probability of a red ball being pulled out, given U1 is picked:

> 2 red balls/5 balls = 40%

P(U1) is the probability of picking U1:

> 1 urn/2 urns = 50%

P(R) is the probability of a red ball being picked regardless of which urn is picked:

> 2 red balls in U1 + 4 red balls in U2 = 6 red balls
>
> 6 red balls/10 balls = 60%

P(U1|R) is the objective of the exercise. Based on the above formula, we calculate:

> P(U1|R) = [P(R|U1)/P(R)] P(U1) = [40%/60%]50% = 33.3%

This solution can also be shown using a probability tree. In Exhibit 1, we can see that the probability of U1 being picked and a red ball being chosen is P(U1) × P(R|U1) = (0.5 × 0.4) = 0.20. The probability of picking a red ball if either urn is picked is P(R) = (0.20 + 0.40) = 0.60. Therefore, because we know that a red ball was picked, we can find the probability of having chosen U1 by dividing the probability of choosing both U1 and a red ball by the probability of choosing a red ball. This gives us 0.333 or 33.3% [= 0.20/0.60].

Exhibit 1　Probability Tree

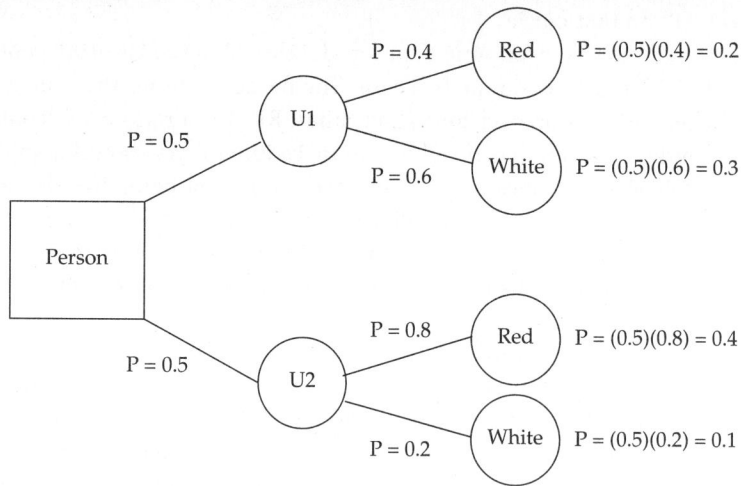

```
                                    P = 0.4    ( Red )    P = (0.5)(0.4) = 0.2

                          ( U1 )
              P = 0.5               P = 0.6    ( White )  P = (0.5)(0.6) = 0.3

    ┌────────┐
    │ Person │
    └────────┘
                                    P = 0.8    ( Red )    P = (0.5)(0.8) = 0.4
              P = 0.5     ( U2 )
                                    P = 0.2    ( White )  P = (0.5)(0.2) = 0.1
```

Different people may make different decisions because they may have different utility functions or different beliefs about the probabilities of different outcomes.

In a perfect world, when people make decisions under uncertainty, they are assumed to do the following:

1　Adhere to the axioms of utility theory.

2　Behave in such a way as to assign a probability measure to possible events.

3　Incorporate new information by conditioning probability measures according to Bayes' formula.

4　Choose an action that maximizes the utility function subject to budget constraints (consistently across different decision problems) with respect to this conditional probability measure.

Is it reasonable, however, to think that ordinary people perform Bayesian updating on a consistent basis or make decisions as if they perform Bayesian updating? Bayesian updating requires the ability to perform complicated statistical calculations. People have cognitive limitations not accounted for in expected utility theory. Behavioral finance proponents argue that it seems highly unlikely that people actually take each of these steps as a matter of procedure every time they make a decision or that the decisions of people are consistent with those that would be made on the basis of Bayesian updating.

2.1.2 *Rational Economic Man*

Traditional finance assumes that after gathering information and analyzing it according to Bayes' formula, individuals will make decisions consistent with the decisions of homo economicus or **rational economic man** (REM). REM will try to obtain the highest possible economic well-being or utility given budget constraints and the available information about opportunities, and he will base his choices only on the consideration of his own personal utility, not considering the well-being of others except to the extent this impacts REM's utility. Using indifference curve analysis, rational economic man will determine the choices that will combine to give him the highest utility. REM will construct curves of consumption bundles amongst which he is indifferent because each bundle gives the same utility. The curve that is within budget constraints and furthest from the origin gives the highest utility. Choices made by REM will fall on that curve.

The notion of rational economic man was developed in the late 19th century as a simple model of human economic behavior. The model assumes that humans make perfectly rational economic decisions at all times. REM is a rational, self-interested, labor-averse individual who has the ability to make judgments about his subjectively defined ends. REM also strives to maximize economic well-being by selecting strategies contingent on predetermined, utility-optimizing goals on the information that he possesses as well as on any other postulated constraints. REM tries to achieve discretely specified goals to the most comprehensive, consistent extent possible while minimizing economic costs.

The amount of utility that REM associates with any given outcome is represented by the output of his algebraic utility function. Predicting how REM will negotiate complex trade-offs, such as the pursuit of wages versus leisure, entails the use of mathematical models using calculus. REM ignores social values unless adhering to them will give him pleasure (i.e., provide utility) or failing to adhere to them will cause him pain (i.e., create disutility). Principles of perfect rationality, perfect self-interest, and perfect information govern REM's economic decisions.

2.1.3 *Perfect Rationality, Self-Interest, and Information*

REM is assumed to maximize utility and make complex deductions toward that end. He is capable of thinking through all possible outcomes and choosing the course of action that will result in the best possible outcome. Perfect rationality assumes that REM is a perfectly rational thinker and has the ability to reason and make beneficial judgments at all times. In reality, however, rationality is not the sole driver of human behavior. At times, it is observed that the human intellect is subservient to such human emotions as fear, love, hate, pleasure, and pain. Moreover, people often use their intellects to achieve or avoid these emotional outcomes.

Perfect self-interest is the idea that humans are perfectly selfish. For every economic decision, REM ensures that he is getting the highest possible utility and will never concede anything to his opponent in a transaction. Many studies have shown that people are not perfectly self-interested. If they were, philanthropy would not exist. Religions prizing selflessness, sacrifice, and kindness to strangers would also be unlikely to thrive as they have over millennia. Perfect self-interest would preclude people from performing unselfish deeds, such as volunteering, helping the needy, or serving in the military. If behaving in an apparently altruistic manner generates utility for the giver, however, then such behavior is consistent with self-interest and may be viewed as rational.

Some people may possess perfect or near-perfect information on certain subjects. A doctor or dentist, for example, should be impeccably versed in her field. It is impossible, however, for every person to enjoy perfect knowledge of every subject. In the world of investing, there is nearly an infinite amount to learn and know, and even the most successful investors don't master all disciplines. In microeconomics, a state of perfect information is assumed in some models of perfect competition. That is, assuming all agents are rational and have perfect information, they will choose the best products; the market will then reward those who make the best products with higher sales accordingly. Perfect information would mean that all consumers know all things about all products at all times; therefore, they would always make the best decision regarding purchases. In competitive markets, unlike in game-theory models, perfect competition does not require that agents have complete knowledge about the actions of others. Rather, in competitive markets, it is assumed that all relevant information is reflected in prices.

2.1.4 *Risk Aversion*

Expected utility theory generally assumes that individuals are risk-averse. This means that an individual may refuse a fair wager (a wager with an expected value of zero), and also implies that his utility functions are concave and show diminishing marginal utility of wealth. Given two choices—investing to receive an expected value with certainty or investing in an uncertain alternative that generates the same expected value—someone who prefers to invest to receive an expected value with certainty rather than invest in the uncertain alternative that generates the same expected value is called risk-averse. Someone who is indifferent between the two investments is called risk-neutral. Someone who prefers to invest in the uncertain alternative is called risk-seeking. In traditional finance, individuals are assumed to be risk-averse.

Following is an example that demonstrates risk neutrality, risk aversion, and risk-seeking. Let's assume a person is given the choice between two scenarios. In the guaranteed scenario, the person receives $100. In the uncertain scenario, a coin is flipped to decide whether the person receives $200 or nothing. The expected payoff for both scenarios is $100. A person who is insensitive to risk or risk-neutral will be indifferent between the guaranteed payment and the coin flip. A person is risk-averse if he or she would accept a payoff of less than $100 with certainty rather than take the coin flip. A person is risk-seeking (or risk-loving) if the guaranteed payment has to be more than $100 to induce him to take the guaranteed option rather than the coin flip, where he could possibly win $200.

An alternative example to demonstrate risk aversion, risk neutrality, and risk-seeking involves determining how much a person is willing to pay to participate in the uncertain scenario. If the person is willing to pay $100 (the expected payoff), the person is risk-neutral. If the person is willing to pay less than $100, the person is risk-averse. If the person is willing to pay more than $100, the person is risk-seeking.

Given an opportunity to participate or to forgo to participate in an event for which the outcome, and therefore his or her receipt of a reward, is uncertain, the **certainty equivalent** is the maximum sum of money a person would pay to participate or the minimum sum of money a person would accept to not participate in the opportunity. The difference between the certainty equivalent and the expected value is called the risk premium. Certainty equivalents are used in evaluating attitudes toward risk.

Risk attitudes toward wealth are reflected in the curvature of the individual's utility function of wealth. As shown in Exhibit 2, risk-neutral individuals have linear utility functions; risk-averse individuals have concave utility functions; and risk-seeking individuals have convex utility functions. A linear utility function means that utility increases at a constant rate with increases in wealth; the risk-neutral individual has a constant marginal utility of wealth. A concave utility function means that utility increases at a decreasing rate with increases in wealth; the risk-averse individual has a diminishing marginal utility of wealth. A convex utility function means that utility increases at an increasing rate with increases in wealth; the risk-seeking individual has an increasing marginal utility of wealth. The degree of risk aversion can be measured by the curvature of the utility function.

Exhibit 2	Utility Function of Wealth

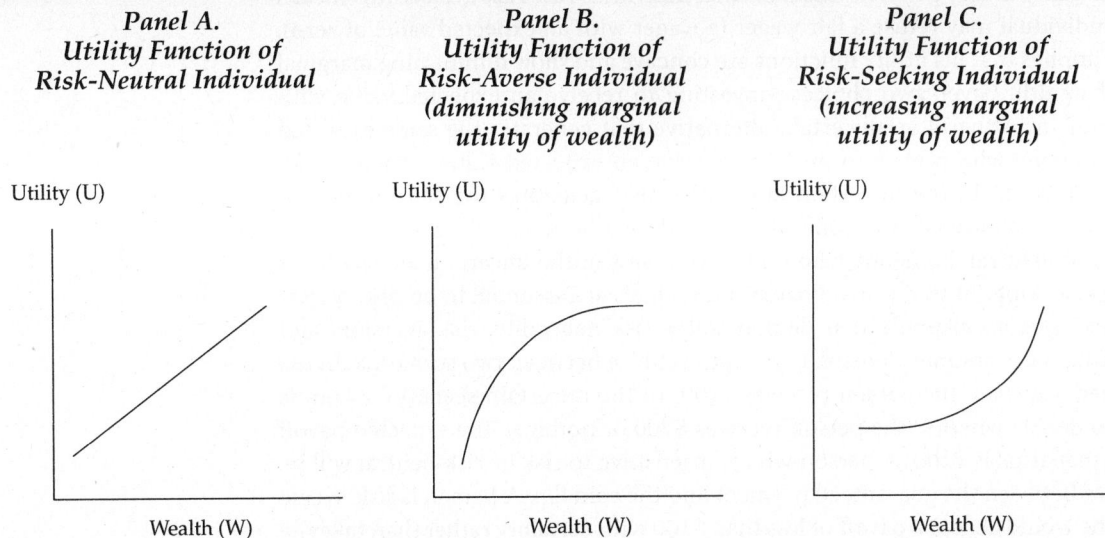

| Panel A. Utility Function of Risk-Neutral Individual | Panel B. Utility Function of Risk-Averse Individual (diminishing marginal utility of wealth) | Panel C. Utility Function of Risk-Seeking Individual (increasing marginal utility of wealth) |

Utility (U)   Utility (U)   Utility (U)

Wealth (W)   Wealth (W)   Wealth (W)

As stated previously, expected utility theory generally assumes that individuals are risk-averse. This implies that utility functions are concave and exhibit diminishing marginal utility. A commonly cited example to demonstrate diminishing marginal utility is a favorite food or beverage. The first taste may give great pleasure (high utility), but each subsequent taste may generate less pleasure; in fact, excessive consumption may lead to discomfort (disutility). Although there may be no discomfort associated with increasing wealth, one can imagine a situation in which an incremental increase to wealth generates less increased utility than a previous increase to incremental wealth. For example, sufficient wealth to pay for housing has a very positive utility, but the extra wealth to pay for a third or fourth home may have a much smaller positive impact on utility. Thus, assuming that individuals are risk-averse and that utility curves are concave and exhibit diminishing marginal utility seems reasonable.

2.2 Behavioral Finance Perspectives on Individual Behavior

Behavioral finance challenges the assumptions of traditional finance based on observed behaviors. The assumptions of traditional finance with respect to the behaviors of individuals are not universally observed to hold true. Investors do not necessarily make decisions consistent with utility theory and revise expectations (update beliefs) consistent with Bayes' formula. They may exhibit behavior that is not self-interested or risk-averse. They do not have access to perfect information and may not process all available information.

In contrast to ideas of perfect rationality or utility maximization, behavioral finance attempts to identify and learn from human psychological phenomena at work within individual market participants. The impact of psychological phenomena on individual market participants may then, in turn, impact financial markets. Behavioral finance, like traditional finance, is guided by basic precepts and assumptions. However, behavioral finance grounds its assumptions in observed financial behavior rather than in idealized financial behavior. For example, behavioral finance examines mental processes, such as the fear of loss or the human tendency to overestimate low-probability events. Some of the behavioral challenges to the assumptions of traditional finance are discussed in the following sections.

2.2.1 Challenges to Rational Economic Man

The validity of rational economic man (REM) has been the subject of much debate since the model's introduction. Those who challenge REM do so by attacking the basic assumptions of perfect information, perfect rationality, and perfect self-interest. Keynes (1936) contends that no human can be fully informed of "all circumstances and maximize his expected utility by determining his complete, reflexive, transitive, and continuous preferences over alternative bundles of consumption goods at all times." Keynes acknowledges the inherent limitations of people in making decisions.

Bounded rationality (discussed further in section 3.2) is proposed as an alternative to the assumptions of perfect information and perfect rationality. It relaxes the assumptions of expected utility theory and perfect information to more realistically represent human economic decision making. Bounded rationality assumes that individuals' choices are rational but are subject to limitations of knowledge and cognitive capacity. Bounded rationality is concerned with ways in which final decisions are shaped by the decision-making process itself.

A shortcoming of the theory of rational economic man is that it disregards the inner conflicts that real people face. For instance, rational economic man does not account for the fact that people can have difficulty prioritizing short-term versus long-term goals (e.g., spending versus saving) and do not behave with perfect self-interest. People instead seem to try to reconcile short-term and long-term goals with individual goals and societal values. This may result in inner conflicts, and these conflicts may lead to behavior that is not rational as defined in traditional finance.

Perhaps the strongest criticisms of REM challenge the underlying assumption of perfect information. It is intuitively obvious that many economic decisions are made in the absence of perfect information. For example, some economic theories assume that people adjust their buying habits based on the monetary policy of central banks. Although some people may know how to find the central bank data, interpret it, and apply it, many do not even know the roles of central banks. This one example demonstrates the implausibility of the idea that all participants in financial markets possess or act as if they possess perfect information.

The concept of rational economic man is appealing to financial theorists for two primary reasons. First, assuming decision making by REM simplifies economic models and analysis, because it is easier to model human behavior given this assumption. Second, this allows economists to quantify their findings, making their work easier to understand. If humans are perfectly rational and self-interested and possess perfect information, then quantifying their behavior may be feasible. However, human rationality covers a spectrum from that which appears perfectly rational to that which appears irrational. Individuals are neither perfectly rational nor perfectly irrational; instead, they possess diverse combinations of rational and irrational characteristics and benefit from different degrees of knowledge. The extent to which any one individual appears to be behaving rationally can vary between decisions depending on a variety of factors, including the type of decision, the extent of the individual's knowledge, and the particular circumstances. Even if individuals do not behave rationally, the idea of REM is useful because it is normative and helps define an optimal outcome.

2.2.2 Utility Maximization and Counterpoint

A useful way to assess the validity of rational economic theory is to use indifference curves. The aim of indifference curve analysis is to demonstrate, mathematically and graphically, the basis on which a rational consumer substitutes certain quantities of one good for another. For example, it is possible to model the effects of a wage adjustment on a worker's allocation of hours to work versus leisure. **Indifference curve analysis** may incorporate budget lines or constraints, which represent restrictions on consumption that stem from resource scarcity. In the work-versus-leisure model, for example, workers may not allocate any sum exceeding 24 hours per day. The number of hours available for work and leisure may be lower than 24 hours depending on other demands on their time.

An indifference curve, as shown in Exhibit 3, depicts all of the possible combinations of two goods amongst which an individual is indifferent.[7] This individual appears to have a constraint of 10 hours available for work and leisure. Consuming any bundle on the curve shown yields the same level of utility for the individual. In Exhibit 3, the individual would achieve equal satisfaction with four hours of work and six hours of leisure or with seven hours of work and three hours of leisure. The indifference curve shows the marginal rate of substitution, or the rate at which a person is willing to give up one good for another, at any point. If the two items are perfect substitutes, then the individual is willing to trade one for the other in a fixed ratio; then, the indifference curve is a line with a constant slope reflecting the marginal rate of substitution. If the two items are perfect complements, then the curve would be L-shaped. An additional amount of either good adds no extra utility because the goods are only used in combination.

Exhibit 3   Trade-Off between Work and Leisure

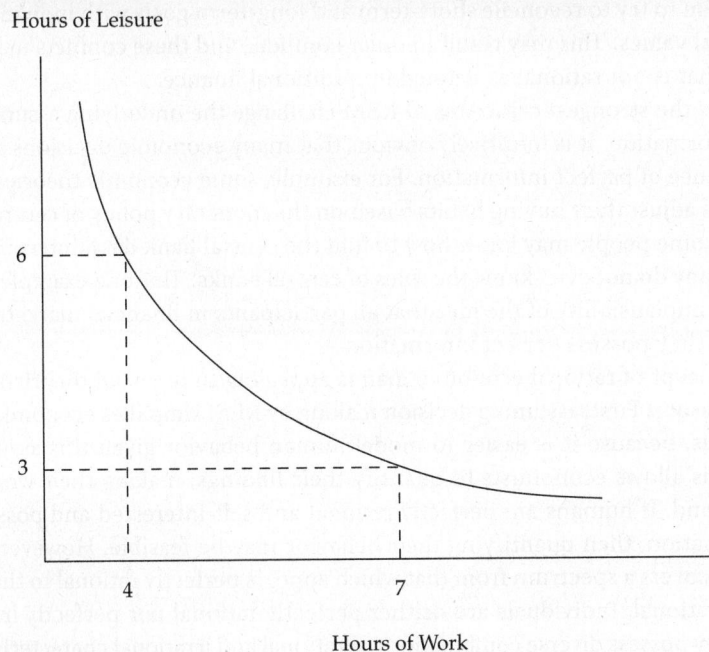

Utility theory should also consider such other factors as risk aversion, probability, size of the payout, and the different utility yielded from the payout based on the individual's circumstances. For example, in a period of high unemployment, an individual may be competing with many others for a job. Under these circumstances, the individual may be willing to work 10 hours a day with no leisure. The trade-off between work and leisure hours is impacted by exogenous factors.

Although indifference curve analysis is theoretically sound, is an individual likely to calculate and perform mathematical equations to determine the trade-off between work and leisure on an ongoing basis? Some might, but many would not. The failure to consider exogenous factors in rational utility analysis is also problematic. Furthermore,

---

7 Note that the intercept of the axes as shown (the origin) is not (0, 0).

risk needs to be accounted for. What is this individual's risk of job loss if he or she does not work eight hours a day? Risk plays an important part in making utility-maximizing decisions. Risk aversion is an assumption underlying actions taken by REM.

2.2.3 Attitudes Toward Risk

Assuming that individuals are risk-averse and that utility curves are concave and exhibit diminishing marginal utility seems reasonable, but observed behaviors are not always consistent with the assumption of an individual who is constantly risk-averse. For example, anyone who has ever purchased a lottery ticket has displayed risk-seeking behavior that is inconsistent with the rational risk-averse behavior assumed in traditional finance. Friedman and Savage (1948) discuss behaviors that seem to contradict the traditional finance beliefs that individuals always seek to maximize the utility of their money and are risk-averse. They cite examples, such as buying lottery tickets and buying insurance, in which expected utility is low but people (even with low incomes) participate in the purchase. The authors find that generally people must be paid a premium to be induced to take moderate risks. However, if an investment offers a few extremely large prizes, its attractiveness is increased far beyond the aggregate value of the prizes. They also find a difference between individuals at different income levels. Those with less income prefer either certainty or a risk that offers a small chance of a large gain to a risk that is moderate. Middle-income people are more likely to be attracted by small, fair gambles.

Perhaps the most important concept we can learn here is that risk evaluation is reference-dependent, meaning risk evaluation depends in part on the wealth level and circumstances of the decision maker. Friedman and Savage indicate that it is not necessarily true that an individual's utility function has the same curvature consistently: There may be levels of wealth, for instance, at which an investor is a risk-seeker and levels of wealth where the investor is risk-neutral. Also, circumstances may vary. As shown in Exhibit 4, the Friedman–Savage **double inflection utility function**, $u(z)$, is concave up to inflection point B, then becomes convex until inflection point C, after which it becomes concave again. Thus, at low income levels (between the origin and z_B), agents exhibit risk-averse behavior; they are also risk-averse at high income levels (above z_C). However, between the inflection points B and C, agents are risk-loving.

Double Inflection Utility Function—A utility function that changes based on levels of wealth.

Exhibit 4   Friedman–Savage Double-Inflection Utility Function

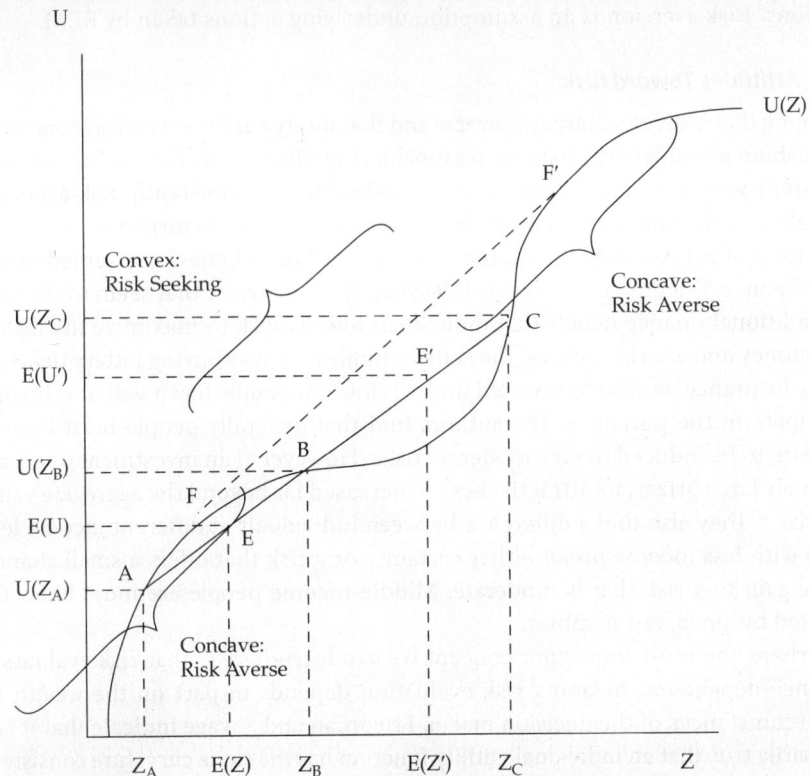

Friedman and Savage try to explain why people may take low-probability, high-payoff risks (e.g., lottery tickets), while at the same time insuring against low risks with low payoffs (e.g., flight insurance). To see this, presume one is at inflection point *B* between risk-averse and risk-seeking. Suppose one faces two lotteries, one yielding *A* or *B*, another yielding *B* or *C*. These lotteries are captured by the solid line segments between the respective payoffs *AB* and *BC*. Expected utility of the first gamble is notated as *E(u)* and is depicted in Exhibit 4 at point *E*—where, obviously, *E(u)* is less than the utility of the expected outcome of the first gamble, *u[E(z)]*. Consequently, a risk-averse agent would pay a premium to avoid it. The second gamble yields expected utility *E(u′)* at point *E′* on the *BC* segment, which is greater than the utility of the expected outcome *u[E(z′)]*. A risk-seeking agent would *pay* a premium to undertake this gamble. Thus, we can view risk-averse behavior with regard to *AB* as a case of insurance against small losses and the risk-seeking behavior with regard to *BC* as a case of purchasing lottery tickets.

Prospect theory (discussed further in section 3.3) has been proposed as an alternative to expected utility theory.[8] Prospect theory assigns value to gains and losses (changes in wealth) rather than to final wealth, and probabilities are replaced by decision weights. In prospect theory, the shape of a decision maker's value function is assumed to differ between the domain of gains and the domain of losses. The value function is defined by deviations from a reference point and is normally concave for gains (implying risk aversion), convex for losses (risk-seeking), and steeper for losses than for gains (loss aversion). Decision weights are generally lower than the corresponding probabilities, except in the range of low probabilities.

---

8 See Kahneman and Tversky (1979).

It appears that the assumptions of traditional finance with respect to the behaviors of individuals are not universally observed to hold true. Investors do not necessarily make decisions consistent with utility theory and revise expectations (update beliefs) consistent with Bayes' formula. They may exhibit behavior that is not self-interested or risk-averse. They may not have access to perfect information and may not process all available information.

2.3 Neuro-economics

Behavioral finance, drawing on psychology, observes behaviors in an attempt to understand and explain how investors and markets behave. Neuro-economics combines neuroscience, psychology, and economics in attempting to explain how humans make economic decisions. Neuro-economics is an emerging field of study relevant to understanding how people make economic decisions under uncertainty. Neuro-economics attempts to explain investor behavior based on the functioning of the brain.

Neuro-economics uses imaging of brain activity and other techniques in combination with experimental economics to study the neural basis of economic decision making. By comparing the blood flow to and activity in different parts of the brain before, during, and after a task, it is possible to associate certain regions of the brain with performance of the task. In addition, chemical levels in the brain are studied to gain insights into responses to events and activities. Neuro-economics attempts to bridge the gap between research on decision behavior and economic theory by understanding the brain activity of judgment and making choices.

Glimcher (2003) described the goal of his research as follows: "The long-term goal of my research is to describe the neural events that underlie behavioral decision making. Our approach to this problem consolidates mathematical economic approaches to decision making with traditional neurobiological tools. By using these tools in our physiological analyses of the brainstem, cortex, and the basal ganglia, we hope to develop a coherent view of how the brain makes decisions."[9]

By observing brain activity, neuro-economics attempts to answer such questions as, "How do emotions affect judgment and decision making? How do people perceive uncertainty? How does risk affect human decision making?" Traditional finance attempts to answer similar questions by making simplifying assumptions. Behavioral finance attempts to answer similar questions by observing behaviors and inferring the basis for the behavior. These approaches each potentially provide insights into financial decision making and should not be viewed as mutually exclusive.

Critics of neuro-economics claim that, although the results of neuro-economics may be interesting, there have been few insights from neurobiological studies that constrain economic theory. Gul and Pesendorfer (2008) argue that neurobiological measurements, per se, are entirely outside the scope of economics. Economic theory makes predictions about behavior, and the actual functioning of the brain during decision making is irrelevant. In short, they argue that insights into biological mechanisms, such as brain activity or chemical levels in the brain, are unlikely to have an impact on economic theory.

Perhaps some of the more interesting insights result from examining chemical levels in the brain. Dopamine and serotonin are chemicals naturally produced in the body. Dopamine functions as a neurotransmitter and is commonly associated with the pleasure system, providing feelings of enjoyment and reinforcement to motivate people to do or continue certain activities. A reduction in serotonin in the body is often linked to such emotional and behavioral problems as anxiety, depression, impulsiveness, and irritability.

---

9 Glimcher (2003).

Dopamine is released in response to both a reward and the expectation of a reward. The release of dopamine after an expected or unexpected reward and the desire for dopamine release may explain risk-taking behavior. The prospect of a euphoric effect may inhibit people from focusing on the more logical thought of how small the odds of a reward (positive outcome) actually are. In this context, it is not difficult to imagine that dopamine may explain such behavioral biases as overconfidence and may also play a role in market overreaction to short-term results.

If an expected reward fails to arrive, dopamine is not released and dopamine levels decline, which may result in a depressed state. Further, unfulfilled expectations depress brain serotonin levels. The resulting emotional state may impact investors in a variety of ways: It may prevent the investors from taking further actions that involve assuming risk or it may cause investors to become impulsive and attempt to recoup losses by employing high-risk investing strategies (usually resulting in excessive trading).

Research focusing on the roles played by areas of the brain also provides insights into human behavior. For example, the amygdala plays a key role in emotions, such as fear and pleasure. It is the amygdala that creates a "fight or flight" response during a sudden event or trauma. For investors, the amygdala may be responsible for a panicked response rather than an analytical response to a dropping market. Although neuro-economics research is interesting and may provide further insights into individual economic decision making, its effect on economic theory remains to be seen.

3   DECISION MAKING

This section examines behavioral theories developed in response to the relaxing of particular assumptions about individual behavior with respect to decision making. Prospect theory relaxes the assumptions of expected utility theory and risk aversion. Bounded rationality relaxes the assumption that all available information is used to arrive at a wealth-maximizing decision. Before discussing prospect theory and bounded rationality, which are based on observations of how people actually do seem to make decisions, we will discuss theories of how people should make decisions. Prospect theory and bounded rationality are descriptive, describing how people *do* behave and make decisions. Expected utility and decision theories are normative, describing how people *should* behave and make decisions.

3.1 Decision Theory

Decision theory is concerned with identifying values, probabilities, and other uncertainties relevant to a given decision and using that information to arrive at a theoretically optimal decision. Decision theory is normative, meaning that it is concerned with identifying the ideal decision. As such, it assumes that the decision maker is fully informed, is able to make quantitative calculations with accuracy, and is perfectly rational. The practical application of decision theory is prescriptive. It analyzes decisions and attempts to provide tools and methods to help people make better decisions.

From a historical perspective, the initial focus of decision theory was on expected value. The first person to record explorations of expected value was Blaise Pascal, a French mathematician and philosopher in the 1600s who is also known for his wager on the existence of God.[10] In 1670, Pascal discussed expected value and choice in this way: "When faced with a number of actions, each of which could give rise to more than one possible outcome with different probabilities, the rational procedure is to identify all possible outcomes, determine their values (positive or negative) and the probabilities that will result from each course of action, and multiply the two to give an expected value. The action to be chosen should be the one that gives rise to the highest total expected value."[11]

Bernoulli (1954) describes the difference between expected utility and expected value.[12] Expected value of an item is based on its price, which is the same for everyone because the price depends only on the item itself. Expected utility of an item is based on the worth assigned to it by the person making the estimate; as a result, it may vary from person to person because it depends on each person's circumstances. Bernoulli's theory of expected utility, which includes the premise that utility increases at a decreasing rate with increases in wealth, is one of the theories that supports traditional finance perspectives.

Frank Knight (1921) makes important distinctions between risk and uncertainty. He defines risk as randomness with knowable probabilities and uncertainty as randomness with unknowable probabilities. Knight argues that situations with risk, such as decision making with unknown outcomes but known ex-ante probability distributions, differ from situations with uncertainty, such as decision making with unknown outcomes and probabilities. He contends that situations in which decision-making rules, such as maximizing expected utility, can be applied differ in a substantial way from those in which they cannot, such as when the probability distribution of a random outcome is unknown. Risk is measurable, but uncertainty is not.

von Neumann and Morgenstern (1944) posit that a rational decision maker makes decisions consistent with the axioms of utility theory and chooses the combination of decisions that maximize expected utility. Savage (1954) introduces subjective expected utility (SEU). The theories of von Neumann and Morgenstern and Savage extend the scope of expected utility theory to situations in which only subjective probabilities are available. SEU theory extends the conditions of perfect utility-maximizing rationality to a world in which the probability distributions of all relevant variables can be provided by the decision makers.

In order to take SEU theory and apply it to actual decision making, prescriptive theories of choice should consider the empirical evidence as to how people actually make decisions. Prescriptive approaches based on SEU theory consider empirical evidence as to the limits on human rationality. These limitations are imposed by the complexity of the world we live in, the incompleteness and inadequacy of human knowledge, the computational inadequacy of people, the inconsistencies of individual preference and beliefs, and the conflicts of value among individuals and groups.

Descriptive analysis of problem solving and decision making are centrally concerned with how people manage to reduce complicated problems to a cognitively manageable size, with how they approximate and heuristically handle complexity. Descriptive analyses make it possible to develop theories and practices that account for the unrealistic parts of SEU theory. These theories illustrate how people respond

---

10 "Pascal's wager" is a classic example of a choice under uncertainty. The uncertainty is whether God exists. Belief or non-belief in God is the choice to be made. Pascal argues that the reward for belief in God if God actually does exist is infinite, while the cost of believing in God if God actually does not exist is low. Therefore, the expected value of belief exceeds that of non-belief, so Pascal contends that it is prudent to believe in God.

11 Pascal's Pensées by Blaise Pascal (1670).

12 Bernoulli's article was originally published in 1738. The 1954 version is a re-publication.

to complexity and limitations, while striving to achieve results that approximate the ideal (i.e., the results of normative theories). Bounded rationality and prospect theory are examples of such theories.

Bounded rationality theory relaxes the assumptions that perfect information is available and that all available information is processed according to expected utility theory. Bounded rationality acknowledges that individuals are limited in their abilities to gather and process information. Prospect theory relaxes the assumptions that individuals are risk-averse and make decisions consistent with expected utility theory. Prospect theory assumes that individuals are loss-averse.

3.2 Bounded Rationality

Simon (1957) proposed the notion of **bounded rationality**, recognizing that people are not fully rational when making decisions and do not necessarily optimize but rather satisfice (defined below) when arriving at their decisions. People have informational, intellectual, and computational limitations. Even supplementing the capabilities of individuals with computers, humans may not be able to make fully informed and rational decisions. Simon introduced the terms *bounded rationality* and *satisfice* to describe the phenomenon where people gather some (but not all) available information,[13] use heuristics to make the process of analyzing the information tractable, and stop when they have arrived at a satisfactory, not necessarily optimal, decision. In contrast to rational economic man making decisions according to expected utility theory, Simon describes individuals who are satisfied to gather what they deem to be enough information, who will process the information in ways they deem adequate, who are prone to identify with sub-goals and limited objectives rather than try to achieve an optimum, and who will stop when they have a decision that fits within parameters they deem satisfactory.[14]

Bounded rationality sets parameters on how much will be done in making a decision and within which decisions will be deemed as satisfactory. The term **satisfice** combines "satisfy" and "suffice" and describes decisions, actions, and outcomes that may not be optimal, but they are adequate.[15] To satisfice is to find a solution in a decision-making situation that meets the needs of the situation and achieves the goals of the decision maker. Satisficing is finding an acceptable solution as opposed to optimizing, which is finding the best (optimal) solution. The optimal solution is the one that maximizes the utility realizable from the situation. Individuals lack the cognitive resources to arrive at optimal solutions. For example, individuals typically do not know the relevant probabilities of the potential outcomes, can rarely identify or evaluate all outcomes, and have weak and unreliable memories.

Decision makers may choose to satisfice rather than optimize because the cost and time of finding the optimal solution can be very high. In these circumstances, satisficing creates a stop rule to the decision process and allows the cost incurred and time taken to be limited. Another reason for decision makers to use satisficing is that even when people can continue evaluating exhaustive alternatives and cost is not a factor, they still need to find new alternatives and their expected outcomes. This search for an optimum will often become so complicated and time consuming that it is eventually infeasible. The empirical evidence in Simon's studies suggests that consumers, employees, and business people typically satisfice rather than optimize.

---

13 Heuristics are mental shortcuts based on experience and knowledge that simplify decision making. They are sometimes called "rules of thumb."
14 See Simon (1991).
15 See Simon (1996).

The reason behind this is bounded rationality. It is infeasible to generate all possible alternatives, estimate the probability of each possible outcome of each alternative, and define consistent utility functions for every alternative prior to making a decision.

Instead of looking at every alternative, people set constraints as to what will satisfy their needs. These constraints indicate what is aspired to. This is not a minimum acceptable outcome but a satisfactory acceptable outcome. Simon refers to these constraints as aspiration levels. Aspiration levels are set based on experiences and on comparisons with what other individuals have achieved. People tend to aspire for a future that is better than the past. When aspirations are reached, people tend to adjust the aspirations upward; when aspirations are not reached, people tend to adjust downward.

When searching for alternative solutions to an issue or problem, decision makers may use heuristics to guide their search. Although using heuristics may simplify the search for alternatives, they also may result in alternatives being missed (not identified). Rather than taking a holistic approach, heuristics may use more of an incremental approach. An example of heuristics is means-ends analysis, where the problem solver is at a current state and decides on the goal state. Rather than looking for alternatives to achieve the goal, the decision maker moves toward the goal in stages. Decisions are made progressively until the goal state is achieved: The first decision is made to get one step closer to the goal state, the next decision results in getting still closer to the goal, and decisions continue to be made until the goal state is met. Another example is the divide-and-conquer procedure, where a problem or issue is divided into components. In this case, rather than attempt to find alternatives to solve the issue or problem, the decision makers attempt to find satisfactory solutions for each sub-problem.

An accepted principle of decision making is to attend to only the most important aspects of the situation. When evaluating alternatives, an investor needs to be aware of the surrounding economic and political environment. An investor needs to have an in-depth understanding of the aspiration levels and satisficing heuristics of business people, government officials, and other investors. One is rarely able to use optimization to determine what is best for a portfolio. Alternatives are almost infinite, and accurately estimating an outcome for each alternative is extremely difficult and both cost and time prohibitive. Because investors have only a limited capacity to assess alternatives and outcomes, they act within the constraints of bounded rationality. Thus, portfolio decisions are based on a limited set of factors, such as economic indicators, deemed most important to the end goal. When the alternatives are limited, a person can dedicate more time to evaluating the most likely outcomes to help make decisions that will satisfice the investment goals.

A decision maker is said to exhibit bounded rationality when he violates some commonly accepted precept of rational behavior but nevertheless acts in a manner consistent with the pursuit of an appropriate set of goals or objectives. Although this definition specifies neither the precept being violated nor conditions under which a set of goals may be considered appropriate, it is still usable.

EXAMPLE 2

Bounded Rationality

Harry Timmons has cash that he wishes to earn interest on, have accessible, and protect against loss. He is aware that the amount of cash to be deposited will be fully insured by a corporation backed by the government if it is deposited in an eligible account at an insured member institution. He has decided to deposit the funds in a checking account at the bank down the street. The bank clearly posts on its door that it is a member institution and only offers eligible accounts. The account will pay 0.25 percent.

Explain how this decision has violated rational behavior but is consistent with bounded rationality.

Solution:

Timmons did not behave totally rationally because he did not gather full information to identify a listing of insured members and what types of accounts are eligible. There may be other institutions that offer eligible accounts that pay higher interest. Further, he did not search for alternatives to depositing in an eligible account with a member institution that met his criteria.

Timmons' behavior is boundedly rational because his decision meets the criteria specified but is not necessarily optimal. Although the decision is undoubtedly suboptimal because higher returns may have been possible, it satisfices within the totality of the investor's decision-making environment. Timmons may have decided he had neither the time nor the resources to research all alternatives. Given the investor's apparently limited knowledge of alternatives, and considering time constraints and the three criteria (interest, accessibility, and loss protection), depositing in a fully insured checking account at 0.25 percent may be reasonable.

3.3 Prospect Theory

Kahneman and Tversky (1979) introduce prospect theory as an alternative to expected utility theory. Prospect theory describes how individuals make choices in situations in which they have to decide between alternatives that involve risk (e.g., financial decisions) and how individuals evaluate potential losses and gains. Prospect theory considers how prospects (alternatives) are perceived based on their framing, how gains and losses are evaluated, and how uncertain outcomes are weighted.

In prospect theory, based on descriptive analysis of how choices are made, there are two phases to making a choice: an early phase in which prospects are framed (or edited) and a subsequent phase in which prospects are evaluated and chosen. The framing (editing phase) consists of using heuristics to do a preliminary analysis of the prospects, often yielding a simpler representation of these prospects. More specifically, people decide which outcomes they see as economically identical and then establish a reference point to consider where these prospects rate. Outcomes below the reference point are viewed as losses, and those above the reference point are gains. In the second phase, the edited prospects are evaluated and the prospect of highest perceived value is chosen.

During the editing or framing stage, alternatives are ranked according to a basic heuristic that was identified and chosen by the decision maker. This contrasts with the elaborate algorithms of expected utility theory. Framing refers to the way a choice option or prospect can be affected by the way in which it is presented. Understanding that how choices are presented or framed impacts the final choice is a critical aspect of prospect theory. In many situations, a decision maker does not know all the options available. Depending on the number of prospects, there may be up to six operations in the editing process: codification, combination, segregation, cancellation, simplification, and detection of dominance. In the process, individuals identify their options, and choice can be affected by how that identification is done. The ultimate purpose behind editing is to simplify the evaluation of choices available by reducing the choices to be more thoroughly evaluated. People use editing when making choices because of cognitive constraints.

The following are examples of six operations in the editing process.[16] Some editing operations will permit or prevent others from being carried out. The sequence of editing operations is likely to vary with the offered set and the format of the display. In the editing phase, a decision maker organizes and reformulates the available options to simplify the choice.

- *Codification*: People perceive outcomes as gains and losses rather than final states of wealth or welfare. A gain or loss is, of course, defined with respect to some reference point. The location of the reference point affects whether the outcomes are coded as gains or losses. Prospects are coded as (gain or loss, probability; gain or loss, probability; ...) such that the probabilities initially add to 100 percent or 1.0.

- *Combination*: Prospects are simplified by combining the probabilities associated with identical gains or losses. For example, a prospect initially coded as (250, 0.20; 200, 0.25; 200, 0.15; 150, 0.40) will be simplified to (250, 0.20; 200, 0.40; 150, 0.40).

- *Segregation*: The riskless component of any prospect is separated from its risky component. For example, a prospect initially coded as (300, 0.8; 200, 0.2) is decomposed into a sure gain of (200, 1.0) and a risky prospect of (100, 0.8; 0, 0.20). The same process is applied for losses.

The above operations are applied to each prospect separately. The following operations are applied to two or more prospects:

- *Cancellation*: Cancellation involves discarding common outcome probability pairs between choices. For example, the pairs (200, 0.2; 100, 0.5; 20, 0.3) and (200, 0.2; 300, 0.4; −50, 0.4) are reduced to (100, 0.5; 20, 0.3) and (300, 0.4; −50, 0.4).

- *Simplification*: Prospects are likely to be rounded off. A prospect of (51, 0.49) is likely to be seen as an even chance to win 50. Also, extremely unlikely outcomes are likely to be discarded or assigned a probability of zero.

- *Detection of Dominance*: Outcomes that are strictly dominated are scanned and rejected without further evaluation.

Preference anomalies may arise from the act of editing. An example of a preference anomaly is the isolation effect. This results from the tendency of people to disregard or discard outcome probability pairs that the alternatives share (cancellation) and to focus on those which distinguish them. Because different choice problems can be decomposed in different ways, this can lead to inconsistent preferences.

The following is an example of the isolation effect.[17] Experimental subjects were given the choice of Gambles A and B.

- Gamble A: A 25 percent chance of receiving $3,000 and a 75 percent chance of receiving nothing.

- Gamble B: A 20 percent chance of receiving $4,000 and an 80 percent chance of receiving nothing.

Sixty-five percent of the experimental subjects chose Gamble B. The expected value of Gamble B is $800 compared to an expected value of $750 for Gamble A, so it is not surprising that the majority of subjects chose Gamble B.

---

16 Readers should note that there is ongoing work in the area of prospect theory. There have been many papers written on this theory that include examples of the editing and evaluation phases. The examples here are merely presented as an overview.

17 This example comes from the Experimental Economics Center at Georgia State University in Atlanta.

Next, the experimental subjects were given a two-stage gamble. The first stage involves a 0.75 probability of ending the game without winning or losing anything and a 0.25 probability of moving to the second stage. The second stage involves a choice between Gambles C and D. The choice of Gamble C or D had to be made prior to the first stage.

- Gamble C: A 100 percent chance of receiving $3,000.

- Gamble D: An 80 percent chance of receiving $4,000 and a 20 percent chance of receiving nothing.

Seventy-eight percent of the experimental subjects chose C.

The fact that 65 percent of the subjects chose B in the first gamble and 78 percent chose C in the second gamble is viewed as surprising. It is surprising because the true probabilities and expected values of Gambles C and D in the two-stage gamble are respectively the same as those of Gambles A and B in the first gamble. In the two-stage gamble, the majority of subjects chose the gamble with the lower expected value.

- Gamble C: 0.25 × 1.0 = 25 percent chance of receiving $3,000 and a 75 percent chance of receiving nothing.

- Gamble D: 0.25 × 0.8 = 20 percent chance of receiving $4,000 and an 80 percent chance of receiving nothing.

Clearly, how the prospects were framed had an effect on the choice. Kahneman and Tversky interpret this finding in the following manner: To simplify the choice between alternatives, people frequently disregard components that the alternatives share and instead focus on those that distinguish them. Because different choice problems can be decomposed in different ways, inconsistent preferences can result, as above. They call this phenomenon the isolation effect.

3.3.1 *The Evaluation Phase*

In the evaluation phase of prospect theory, people behave as if they compute a value (utility) function based on the potential outcomes and their respective probabilities and then choose the alternative that has a higher utility. For this evaluation process, Kahneman and Tversky assume the following formula:

$$U = w(p_1)v(x_1) + w(p_2)v(x_2) + \ldots$$

where $x_1, x_2 \ldots$ are the potential outcomes and $p_1, p_2 \ldots$ their respective probabilities; v is a function that assigns a value to an outcome; and w is a probability-weighting function. The probability-weighting function expresses the fact that people tend to overreact to small probability events but underreact to mid-sized and large probabilities. The value function (see Exhibit 5), which passes through the reference point, is s-shaped; moreover, as its asymmetry implies, given the same variation in absolute value there is a bigger impact of losses than of gains (loss aversion). People are not risk-averse but rather are loss-averse.

Exhibit 5	Value Function

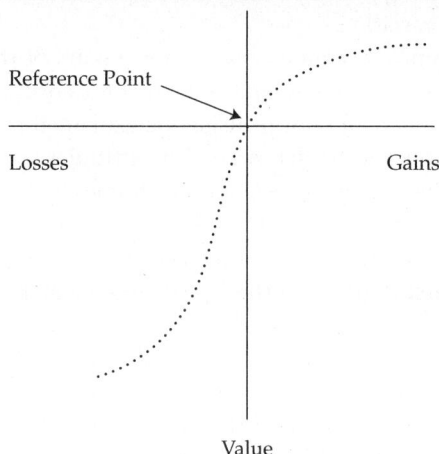

A quantitative illustration of the evaluation process is complex and not necessary to review here. What is important to know is that the quantitative elements resemble those of expected utility theory, although there are some important differences. Values are attached to changes rather than final states, and the decision weights need not coincide with probabilities. Experimental evidence shows that most people reject a gamble with even chances to win and lose, unless the amount of the possible win is at least twice the amount of the possible loss. In contrast to expected utility theory, the prospect theory value function measures gains and losses but not absolute wealth and is reference-dependent. Reference dependence is incompatible with the standard interpretation of expected utility theory. Reference dependence is a feature of prospect theory and is central to prospect theory's perspective on how people make decisions under uncertainty.

Kahneman and Tversky illustrate reference dependence with an example. People are presented with the following two situations and asked to make choices.

Situation 1   Given a 50 percent probability of winning $150 and a 50 percent probability of losing $100, is an individual likely to take this gamble? Is the individual's choice likely to change if overall wealth was lower by $100?

There will be few takers of the gamble because experimental evidence shows that most people reject a gamble with even chances to win and lose, unless the possible win is at least twice the size of the possible loss. In this case, the answer to the second question is negative.

Situation 2   Given the choice of losing $100 with certainty and a gamble with a 50 percent probability of winning $50 and a 50 percent probability of losing $200, which is an individual likely to choose? Would the individual's choice change if overall wealth were higher by $100?

In situation 2, the gamble may appear more attractive than the sure loss. Experimental results indicate that risk-seeking preferences are held by a large majority of respondents in choices of this kind. Here again, a change of $100 in total wealth is unlikely to alter preferences. Situations 1 and 2 evoke different preferences, but the difference is caused by a framing effect. In both cases, the gamble compared to the certain position provides an expected net gain of $25 {Situation 1 = E[gain of gamble] − E[certainty] = $25 − $0 = $25; Situation 2 = −$75 − (−$100) = $25}. The situations differ only in that all values are lower by $100 in situation 2. This should be an inconsequential variation.

Kahneman and Tversky examined many choice pairs of this type early in their explorations of risky choice, and they concluded that the abrupt transition from being risk-averse to risk-seeking could not plausibly be explained by a utility function for wealth. Preferences appear to be determined by attitudes toward gains and losses, which are defined relative to a reference point that frames the situation. The discarding of components that are common to all prospects (outcomes) may lead to inconsistent preferences depending on the framing of the choice.

Kahneman and Tversky's prospect theory explains apparent deviations in decision making from the rational decisions of traditional finance. These deviations result from overweighting low probability outcomes, underweighting moderate and high probability outcomes, and having a value function for changes in wealth (gains and losses) that is in general concave for gains, convex for losses, and steeper for losses than for gains. As a result, people are risk-averse when there is a moderate to high probability of gains or a low probability of losses; they are risk-seeking when there is a low probability of gains or a high probability of losses. This is consistent with people simultaneously buying lottery tickets and insurance while investing money conservatively.

4	## PERSPECTIVES ON MARKET BEHAVIOR AND PORTFOLIO CONSTRUCTION

Traditional finance assumes that, at the market level, prices incorporate and reflect all available and relevant information. Markets that behave in a manner consistent with this assumption are referred to as efficient. Portfolios constructed in accordance with traditional finance assumptions are referred to as optimal. Section 4.1 provides an overview of the traditional finance perspectives of market behavior. Section 4.2 provides a brief overview of the traditional finance perspectives on portfolio construction. Section 4.3 discusses behavioral finance alternatives to the traditional finance perspective of market behavior and portfolio construction.

4.1 Traditional Perspectives on Market Behavior

Much of modern investment theory and practice is predicated on the efficient market hypothesis:

> Markets fully, accurately, and instantaneously incorporate all available information into market prices.

However, the efficient market hypothesis (EMH) is not universally accepted. In this section, we will discuss the EMH and explore some of the evidence supporting and opposing it.

Writing in the *Financial Times*, Thaler (2009) comments on two aspects of the EMH. He terms these "The Price is Right" and "No Free Lunch." The *price is right* assumes that asset prices fully reflect available information and that securities' prices can be used as a means to allocate resources. Accepting the EMH as fact, and noting the random nature (unpredictability) of prices, some economists infer that prices are indeed right. Robert Shiller calls this inference "one of the most remarkable errors in the history of economic thought."[18] The price is right is a fallacy because mere randomness does not ensure that the prices are not wrong.[19]

No free lunch assumes that it is difficult for any investor to consistently outperform the market after taking risk into account given the inherent unpredictability of prices. Thaler notes that a myriad of studies over several decades have resulted in the same basic conclusion: There is no free lunch. With the exception of some apparent anomalies, the market is hard to beat. In fact, many of the investment strategies that seemed to beat the market did not do so once risk was more accurately measured.

Thaler concludes that the risks of investments are more correlated than previously thought, that high returns based on high leverage may be transitory and an illusion, and that revealed price distortions challenge the assumption of the price is right. Further, the acceptance of the price is right has led to significant misallocations of resources. However, Thaler leaves us with a quandary: If we abandon the efficient market hypothesis and its assumption that the price is right, how do we allocate resources? Thaler suggests that regulation may serve a useful function in the process of allocating resources.

4.1.1 *Review of the Efficient Market Hypothesis*

An efficient market is a market wherein prices fully reflect available information because of the actions of a large number of rational investors (the population of investors). Underlying market efficiency is the assumption that market participants are rational economic beings, always acting in their own self-interest and making optimal decisions by trading off costs and benefits weighted by statistically correct probabilities and marginal utilities. The efficient market hypothesis requires that agents have rational expectations. This means that, in aggregate, the population is correct, even if no one person is. Also, whenever new relevant information appears, the population updates its expectations. Another key assumption is that relevant information is freely available to all participants. Competition among participants results in a market wherein prices of individual investments always reflect the total effect of all information—including information about events that have already happened and events that the market expects to happen in the future. In sum, at any given time in an efficient market, the price of a security will match that security's intrinsic value. If markets are efficient, then no market participant should be able to consistently earn excess returns.

Grossman and Stiglitz (1980) argue that prices must offer a return to information acquisition, otherwise information will not be gathered and processed. If information is not gathered and processed, the market cannot be efficient. This is known as the Grossman–Stiglitz paradox. They conclude that in equilibrium, if markets are to be efficient, a return should accrue to information acquisition. A market is inefficient if, after deducting such costs, active investing can earn excess returns. An investor or researcher should consider transaction costs and information acquisition costs when evaluating the efficiency of a market.

Fama (1970) proposes three forms of market efficiency: the weak form, the semi-strong form, and the strong form. Weak-form market efficiency assumes that all past market price and volume data are fully reflected in securities' prices. Thus, if a market is weak-form efficient, technical analysis will not generate excess returns. Semi-strong-form market efficiency assumes that all publicly available information, past and present, is fully reflected in securities' prices. Thus, if a market is semi-strong-form efficient, technical and fundamental analyses will not generate excess returns. Strong-form

---

18 Quoted in Fox (2009).
19 See Lamont and Thaler (2003).

market efficiency assumes that all information, public and private, is fully reflected in securities' prices. Thus, if a market is strong-form efficient, even insider information will not generate excess returns.

4.1.2 *Studies in Support of the EMH*

The idea of efficient markets goes back to the turn of the 20th century. In 1900, a French mathematician named Louis Bachelier submitted a PhD dissertation to the Sorbonne titled "The Theory of Speculation" which describes market movements as random. The opening paragraphs show his early insights: "Past, present, and even discounted future events are reflected in market price, but often show no apparent relation to price changes....if the market, in effect, does not predict its fluctuations, it does assess them ... mathematically." Many studies have been conducted that support the EMH. Typically, a study tests either the weak form or semi-strong form of efficiency with respect to a particular market. It is more difficult to test the strong form of efficiency. Extensive support for the weak-form and semi-strong forms of market efficiency has been published.

4.1.2.1 Support for the Weak Form of the EMH

Initially, most statistical research of the stock market focused on the weak form of market efficiency and tested whether security prices are serially correlated (i.e., whether trends exist in stock prices) or whether they are random (i.e., whether prices of securities, on any given day, are as likely to go up as they are to go down). A number of studies conclude that the path of securities' prices cannot be predicted based on past prices. For example, Roberts (1959) plots the results of a series of randomly generated numbers to see whether any patterns identified by technical analysts are visible. Roberts notes that it is virtually impossible to tell whether his plots are generated using random numbers or actual stock market data. Roberts writes: "If the stock market behaved like a mechanically imperfect roulette wheel, people would notice the imperfections and, by acting on them, remove them."

Several other researchers have studied stock price movements. Fama (1965) concludes that daily changes in stock prices had nearly zero positive correlation. He proposes that the stock market works in a way that allows all information contained in past prices to be incorporated into the current price. In other words, markets efficiently process the information contained in past prices. Samuelson (1965) emphasizes the randomness of stock prices. Like Roberts, he finds that market prices follow random patterns and that future stock prices are unpredictable. Samuelson begins with the observation that "in competitive markets there is a buyer for every seller. If one could be sure that a price would rise, it would have already risen." Samuelson asserts that "we would expect people in the marketplace, in pursuit of avid and intelligent self-interest, to take account of those elements of future events that in a probability sense may be discerned to be casting their shadows before them." By presenting his proof in a general form, Samuelson adds strength to the idea that markets are efficient.

Malkiel (1973) provides credence to the idea of random stock price movements. He performed a test in which he gave students a fictional stock that was initially worth $50. The closing stock price for that stock was determined by a coin flip. If the result was heads, the price would close a half point higher; if the result was tails, it would close a half point lower. Thus, each time, the price had a fifty–fifty chance of closing higher or lower than the previous day. The results of the coin flips were assembled into a chart and graph form. Malkiel took his results in chart and graph form to a chartist (now known as a technical analyst), whom he defined as a person who "seeks to predict future movements by seeking to interpret past patterns on the assumption that 'history tends to repeat itself.'" The chartist told Malkiel that he needed to buy the stock immediately. When Malkiel told him it was based purely on flipping a coin, the chartist was very unhappy. Malkiel argues that this indicates that the market and stocks can be just as random as flipping a coin. These studies of random stock price movements support the weak form of the EMH.

4.1.2.2 Support for the Semi-Strong Form of the EMH   Several studies attempt to test the semi-strong form of market efficiency. These tests are typically event studies. An event study looks at a sample of similar events that occurred to different companies at different times and determines what effect(s) these events had on the stock price (on average) of each company. For example, Fama et al. (1969) study the stock market reaction to stock splits. The study finds that the market begins to anticipate a stock split more than two years before it actually happens and incorporates the consequences of the split the day it is announced. As may be seen in Exhibit 6, stock prices are shown to rise pre-split. This price action is a matter of some debate because stock splits do not technically add any value to a company. Fama et al. find that 72 percent of firms in their sample announced above-average dividend increases in the year after the split and proposed that stock splits signaled that dividend increases were on the horizon. On average, they find that stocks increased sharply prior to the split, but returns after the split were very stable. These results indicate that the implications of a stock split appear to be reflected in price immediately following the *announcement* of the split and not the event itself. This research supports the semi-strong form of market efficiency, because investors would not earn abnormal returns after the stock split information is publicly available. Numerous subsequent event studies also provide support for the semi-strong form of market efficiency.

Exhibit 6   Stock Split Event Study

Cumulative Average Residual

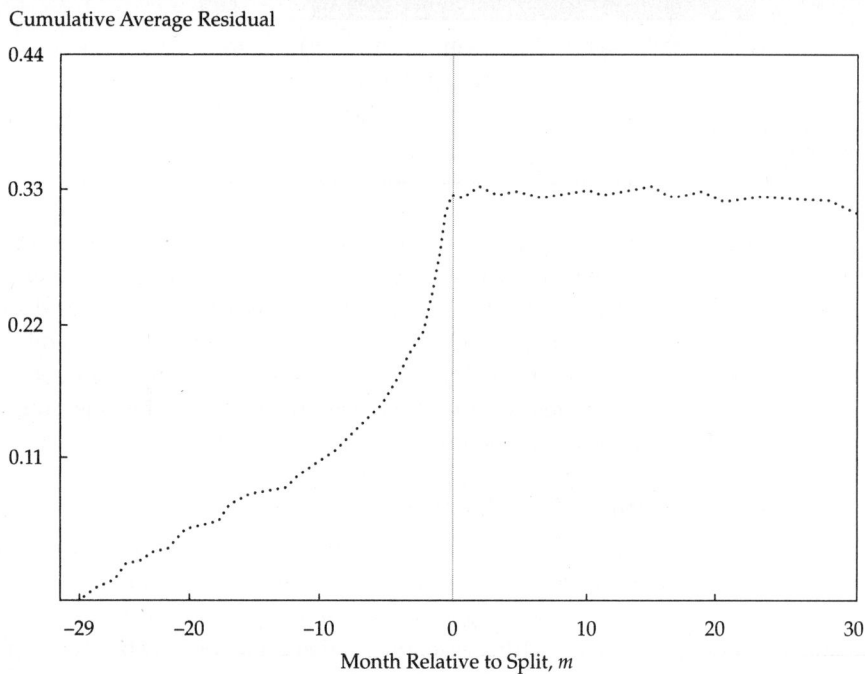

Month Relative to Split, *m*

Source: Fama et al. (1969).

Other studies investigate returns to active management. The absence of positive returns to active management is taken as evidence of market efficiency. For example, Alfred Cowles (1933) analyzes thousands of stock selections made by investment professionals from 1928 to 1933 and finds no evidence to suggest that professional investors are able to outperform the market. Jensen (1967) investigates whether mutual fund managers had the skill to outperform the overall market over the long term. Using fund returns after fees but ignoring sales loads, he examines annual return data for the Standard and Poor's (S&P) 500, which he uses as a proxy for the market portfolio, and 115 mutual funds. He uses regression analysis to determine whether mutual funds in his data set generated positive alphas. His estimated alphas for all 115 mutual funds are summarized in Exhibit 7.

Exhibit 7   Estimated Alphas for 115 Mutual Funds

Frequency

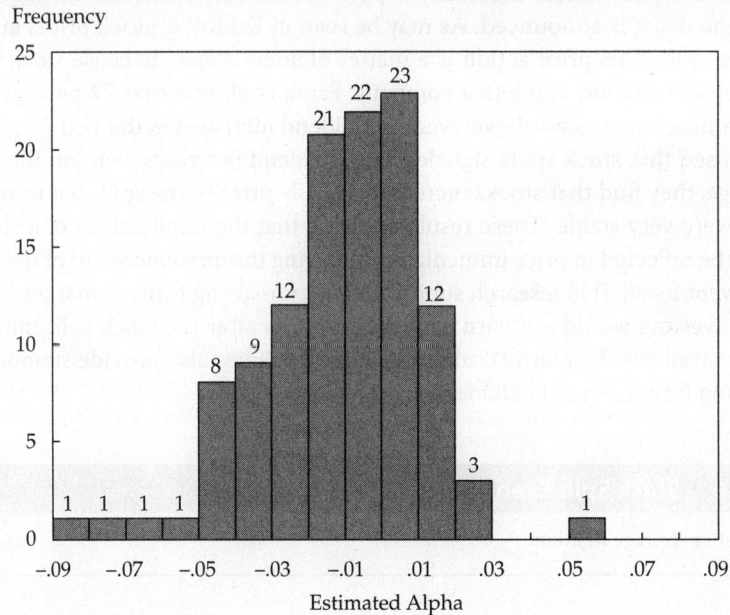

Source: Jensen (1967).

Jensen finds that the majority have estimated alphas below zero. The average fund's alpha is −0.011, or −1.1%. This means that after fees, but not including sales loads, the average fund underperforms the overall market by 110 basis points per year during the examination period. Examining the returns gross of fees, the results are marginally better. A majority still have negative alphas, with the average being −0.4%. Studies that demonstrate the ineffectiveness of professional investors, like this one, support the semi-strong form of market efficiency.

4.1.3 *Studies Challenging the EMH: Anomalies*

Some studies find evidence that appears to contradict market efficiency. These studies mainly describe apparent market anomalies or deviations from the efficient market hypothesis. A market anomaly must persist for a lengthy period to be considered evidence of market inefficiency. Otherwise, the market anomaly may be attributable to the sample period and a strategy that provided abnormal returns in the past may not provide abnormal returns in the future. Exhibit 8 provides a partial list of the studies that claim to identify market anomalies.

		Exhibit 8 Selected Research Studies on Market Anomalies	
Year	**Authors**	**Article or Study Title**	**Anomalies Discovered**
1968	Ball and Brown	"An Empirical Evaluation of Accounting Income Numbers"	Post earnings announcement drift
1976	Rozeff and Kinney	"Capital Market Seasonality: The Case of Stock Market Returns"	January effect: January stock returns were higher than in any other month
1981	Gibbons and Hess	"Day of the Week Effects and Asset Returns"	Monday effect: Stock prices tended to go down on Mondays
1981	Shiller	"Do Stock Prices Move Too Much to Be Justified by Subsequent Changes in Dividends?"	Excess volatility
1982	Rendleman, Jr., Jones, and Latane	"Empirical Anomalies Based on Unexpected Earnings and the Importance of Risk Adjustments"	Earnings surprises and their effect on the stock price
1985	De Bondt and Thaler	"Does the Stock Market Overreact?"	Stock market overreacts to bad news
1991	Ritter	"The Long-Run Performance of Initial Public Offerings"	Negative long-run performance of IPOs
1992	Fama and French	"The Cross-Section of Expected Stock Returns"	Value investing
1993	Jegadeesh and Titman	"Returns to Buying Winners and Selling Losers; Implications for Stock Market Efficiency"	Momentum

There are three main types of identified market anomalies: fundamental, technical, and calendar. There is, however, disagreement about whether these are actual anomalies or the result of incomplete models being used in the testing. In effect, the test is often a joint test of market efficiency and the pricing model being used to test for it. We will now review some of the primary anomalies in each category.

4.1.3.1 Fundamental Anomalies   A fundamental anomaly is an irregularity that emerges when one considers a stock's future performance based on a fundamental assessment of the stock's value. Examples of fundamental anomalies are the performance of small-capitalization companies and value companies compared to large-capitalization companies and growth companies, respectively. The effect of company size on performance has been documented in a number of studies.[20]

Value and growth investing inherently assume that anomalies from the efficient market hypothesis exist. Value investors attempt to identify stocks that are priced below their intrinsic values in order to earn excess returns. Growth investors attempt to identify stocks with high growth opportunities, which are not yet reflected in current market prices, in order to earn excess returns. Value companies typically have, on a per share basis, lower than average price-to-earnings, price-to-book value, and price-to-sales ratios and higher than average dividend yields. Growth companies typically have, on a per share basis, higher than average price-to-earnings, price-to-book value, and price-to-sales ratios and lower than average dividend yields. A large body of evidence supports the premise that investors consistently overestimate the prospects of growth companies and underestimate the prospects of value companies. As a result, value stocks appear to generate anomalously high returns compared to growth stocks.

---

20 For example, Banz (1981) and Fama and French (1992).

Numerous studies show that low price-to-book value ratios (high book value to price ratios) are reasonably consistent predictors of future value.[21] A low price-to-earnings ratio (P/E) is another attribute that tends to correlate anomalously with outperformance. Several studies show that low P/E stocks outperform both high P/E stocks and the market in general.[22] Securities with low price-to-sales ratios also appear to exhibit fundamentally anomalous performance. O'Shaughnessy (1996) demonstrates that stocks with low price-to-sales ratios outperform stocks with high price-to-sales ratios as well as stocks in general. He believes that the price-to-sales ratio is the strongest single determinant of excess return. These studies appear to support the existence of a market anomaly.

However, other studies, including Fama and French (1995, 2008), contend that the studies on value investing do not identify anomalies but rather are a function of incomplete models of asset pricing. Fama and French, for example, propose a three-factor model as a more complete model than the capital asset pricing model (CAPM) to predict stock returns. The proposed model includes a market risk premium as in the CAPM, size of the firm based on equity market value, and the ratio of the firm's book value of equity to market value of equity. The latter two factors proxy for sensitivity to risk, and thus their inclusion is consistent with the rational pricing of stocks. The apparent size and value stock anomalies may be a function of incomplete models being used in testing for inefficiency rather than actual anomalies.

4.1.3.2 Technical Anomalies

A technical anomaly is an irregularity that emerges when one considers past prices and volume levels. Technical analysis encompasses a number of techniques that attempt to forecast securities prices by studying past prices and volume levels. Common technical analysis strategies are based on relative strength and moving averages, as well as on support and resistance. For example, Brock, Lakonishok, and LeBaron (1992) analyze moving averages and trading range breaks on the Dow Jones Industrial Index from 1897 to 1985. The technical rules addressed in the study are:

- *Moving Averages.* Buy and sell signals are generated by the crossing of a short moving average with a long moving average. When the short moving average moves above (below) the long moving average, the signal is to buy (sell). They test long moving averages of 50, 150, and 200 days with short moving averages of 1, 2, and 5 days.

- *Trading Range Break (Support and Resistance).* A buy signal is generated when the price penetrates the resistance level, and a sell signal is generated when the price penetrates the support level. Brock et al. test support and resistance based on past 50, 150, and 200 days with signals generated when a maximum or minimum is violated by 1 percent. They then compute 10-day holding period returns following the buy and sell signals.

The authors conclude that the "results are consistent with technical rules having predictive power." However, they warn that transaction costs may reduce the benefits of trading based on technical anomalies. Numerous other researchers dispute the validity of technical analysis. These researchers believe that prices adjust rapidly to new stock market information and that technical analysis is unlikely to provide any advantage to investors who use it. However, proponents of technical analysis continue to argue the validity of certain technical strategies.

---

21 For example, Stattman (1980); Rosenberg, Reid, and Lanstein (1985); Chan, Hamao, and Lakonishok (1991); Fama and French (1992); and Lakonishok, Shleifer, and Vishny (1994).
22 See Ball (1978); Basu (1983); Jaffe, Keim, and Westerfield (1989); Chan, Hamao, and Lakonishok (1991); and Fama and French (1992).

4.1.3.3 Calendar Anomalies   A calendar anomaly is an irregularity identified when patterns of trading behavior that occur at certain times of the year are considered. A well known calendar anomaly is the January effect. Historically, stocks in general—and small stocks, in particular—have delivered abnormally high returns during the month of January. Haugen and Jorion, two researchers on the subject, note that "The January Effect is, perhaps, the best known example of anomalous behavior in security markets throughout the world."[23] The January effect is particularly interesting because it has not disappeared despite being well known for 25 years. Arbitrage theory tells us that anomalies should disappear as traders attempt to exploit them in advance.

Some studies have shown that stocks earn higher returns on the last day and first four days of each month—the turn-of-the-month effect. Hensel and Ziemba (1996) examined returns of the S&P 500 over a 65-year period and found that US large-cap stocks consistently generate higher returns at the turn of the month. In fact, they found "that the total return from the S&P 500 over this sixty-five-year period was received mostly during the turn of the month." The study implies that investors making regular stock purchases may benefit by scheduling those purchases prior to the turn of the month.

4.1.3.4 Anomalies: Conclusion   Support exists for both efficient markets and anomalous markets. Studies that claim to identify anomalies are often critiqued for their use of an assumed pricing model. When an assumed pricing model is used, it is impossible to say if the observed results are indicative of a true anomaly or simply a consequence of using an incorrect pricing model. In reality, markets are neither perfectly efficient nor completely anomalous; market efficiency is not black or white, but rather gray. In markets exhibiting substantial inefficiency, sophisticated investors may be able to outperform less savvy participants. Many analysts believe that such US large-capitalization stocks as GE and Microsoft are quite efficient, but US small-capitalization and international stocks offer more opportunities for outperformance. Alternative investment markets, such as real estate and venture capital markets, may be less efficient. They lack fluid and continuous prices, and information asymmetries may exist between market participants. This may restrict arbitrage from pricing away market inefficiencies.

4.1.3.5 Limits to Arbitrage   Shleifer and Vishny (1997) develop a theory of limited arbitrage. They assume that implicit restrictions are placed on a fund's ability to arbitrage by investors' ability to withdraw their money. The potential for withdrawal of money imposes limits on the ability of the fund to take advantage of arbitrage situations in which two securities are not rationally priced (priced at intrinsic or fundamental value based on all available information), because securities' prices may remain in a non-equilibrium (irrational) state for long periods of time. In other words, when a firm or portfolio manager is viewed as incompetent or simply wrong about a trade, because certain securities remain irrationally priced for extended periods of time, investors may withdraw their money before the irrational pricing corrects itself and the position may have to be closed prematurely. In his 2010 book "The Big Short," Michael Lewis describes the situation where a hedge fund manager, Michael Burry, was criticized for years by his investors and backers for holding credit default swaps on sub-prime mortgages (effectively shorting the sub-prime housing market) only to have the investment pay off handsomely in the end. His ability to impose restrictions on withdrawal of money from his fund was the only reason he was able to make his investment strategy pay off.

Shleifer and Vishny's theory of limited arbitrage is in stark contrast to the EMH, which assumes that whenever mispricing of a publicly traded stock occurs, an opportunity for arbitrage profit is created for rational traders who should act on those opportunities, resulting in rational pricing (efficient markets). Why might rational traders

---

23 Haugen and Jorion (1996).

choose not to act on observed opportunities? If market participants are engaged in highly leveraged arbitrage trades and prices move against them and stay there for an extended time before returning to intrinsic value, they may eventually need to liquidate prior to realizing the gains expected to result from the prices moving to intrinsic value. In the professional money management business, clients may demand liquidity before a manager's strategy is fully implemented and a successful outcome is realized. To deliver funds, the manager may have to sell or close out positions at a loss. The possibility of an extended period of mispricing and the potential need for liquidity makes market participants less prone to take advantage of arbitrage opportunities. This action has the tendency to exacerbate the problem of pricing inefficiency.

Implicit in the limits to the arbitrage idea is that the EMH does not hold. Specifically, if market participants are engaged in highly leveraged arbitrage trades and prices move against them and stay there irrationally before returning to fundamental value, they may eventually need to liquidate prior to realizing the gains expected to result from the prices moving to fundamental value. Rational traders often work for professional asset management firms and invest other peoples' money. If they engage in arbitrage in reaction to a stock mispricing and the mispricing persists for an extended period, clients of the money management firm can (and do) withdraw their funds. The clients are not willing to wait for the manager's expectations to be met. To deliver funds, the manager must unwind positions at a loss. This is a reason for the restrictions placed on hedge fund withdrawals (i.e., lock-up periods).

4.2 Traditional Perspectives on Portfolio Construction

From a traditional finance perspective, a "rational" portfolio is one that is mean–variance efficient. The appropriate portfolio for an investor is constructed holistically by considering the investor's tolerance for risk, investment objectives, investment constraints, and investor circumstances. An investor will typically take or administer a risk tolerance questionnaire, document financial goals and constraints, and then adopt the output of a mean–variance model (optimized using software or human judgment) that matches the investor's risk tolerance category and accomplishes the investor's financial goals. In the case of institutional investors, they will consider these items from the perspective of the entity they are acting on behalf of. An investment adviser will consider these items from the perspective of the client when developing investment policy statements and asset allocations. Subject to investment objectives and constraints, a suitable portfolio is chosen from the opportunity set of mean–variance efficient portfolios. The output of the mean–variance model may be considered as a "rational" or optimal portfolio allocation.

However, this approach to portfolio construction implicitly assumes that investors (or their advisers) have perfect information and that investors behave rationally in forming their portfolios. If these assumptions do not apply, then portfolios may be constructed using other approaches resulting in portfolios that have too much or too little risk when compared to the optimal portfolio. Further, although a portfolio based on mean–variance optimization may be theoretically sound, it may fail to meet the needs of the investor because of behavioral considerations.

4.3 Alternative Models of Market Behavior and Portfolio Construction

The traditional finance perspective of market behavior may not satisfactorily explain observed market behavior and portfolio construction, but a significant challenge also exists for behavioral finance. There is no single unifying theory of behavioral finance to explain the observed market behaviors. In the absence of such a theory, supporters of traditional finance perspectives contend that the traditional finance perspectives remain superior to behavioral finance perspectives. A number of behavioral models have been advanced, but none has yet been accepted as presenting a complete or unifying description of market behavior. Four of the behavioral models advanced to explain market behavior and portfolio construction are discussed in the following sections. None of these models has yet achieved the kind of general acceptance among finance practitioners and academics that the EMH and mean–variance portfolio construction models have.

4.3.1 *A Behavioral Approach to Consumption and Savings*

Shefrin and Thaler (1988) propose an alternative to the traditional life-cycle model in which people are assumed to spend and save money rationally to achieve an optimal short-term and long-term consumption plan. They developed a behavioral life-cycle theory that incorporates self-control, mental accounting, and framing biases. In the traditional life-cycle model, self-control allows people to pursue long-term goals rather than focus on short-term satisfaction. In behavioral finance, the self-control bias recognizes that people may focus on short-term satisfaction to the detriment of long-term goals. Mental accounting is the phenomenon whereby people treat one sum of money differently from another sum of money even though money is fungible (interchangeable). Framing bias results in different responses based on how questions are asked (framed).

Shefrin and Thaler suggest that people classify their sources of wealth into three basic accounts: current income, currently owned assets, and the present value of future income. This mental accounting exists even though money is fungible. Mental accounting is a partial response to the issue of self-control. By classifying some wealth so that it is considered less available, it is less likely to be consumed in the short-term. People are assumed to be most likely to spend from current income (high marginal propensity to consume) and least likely to spend based on expectations of future income (low marginal propensity to consume). In other words, people lack self-control when it comes to current income. Any current income that is saved is reclassified as current assets or future income. The portion saved will increase with income. As Shefrin and Thaler indicated, "To the poor, saving is a luxury." Mental accounting and framing help people accommodate the competing goals of short-term gratification and long-term benefits. Rather than viewing money (their wealth) as fungible, people tend to frame their expenditure decisions taking into account the source of the wealth.

Individuals are hypothesized to first spend current income, then to spend based on current assets, and finally to spend based on future income. These propensities to consume have a variety of implications. For example, people may save a higher proportion of bonus income because they may classify bonus income as a current asset rather than current income and thus have a lower marginal propensity to consume it. If a government cuts taxes but does not reduce withholding rates, the ensuing tax refunds may be treated as current assets rather than current income. This may result in greater savings than if the tax reduction had been treated as current income. When spending from current assets, liquidity and maturity are taken into account. Basically, such short-term liquid assets as cash and checking accounts are liquidated first to finance current expenditures. Long-term, less-liquid assets, such as homes and retirement savings, are less likely to be used to finance current expenditures. However, individuals who view home equity as part of current assets are more likely to take out loans based on their home's value to finance current consumption than individuals who view their home as part of their retirement assets or future income. Similarly, individuals who classify pension assets as current assets rather than as a source of future retirement income are more prone to take loans against or spend their pension assets.

Shefrin and Thaler hypothesize that individuals will spend, for current consumption, most of their current income, varying portions of their currently owned assets, and very little based on their expectations of future income. The consumption/saving (investment) decisions made when individuals are subject to self-control, mental accounting, and framing biases differ from those of the rational economic individuals of traditional finance. Although mental accounting and framing will result in some saving for long-term goals, the outcome will not necessarily match the optimal short-term and long-term consumption plan of traditional life-cycle models. As a result, individuals will not achieve their theoretically optimal short-term and long-term consumption opportunities. Knowledge of behavioral propensities may help people move closer to the optimal solutions of traditional finance.

4.3.2 A Behavioral Approach to Asset Pricing

Some researchers believe that market behaviors are better explained from a behavioral perspective than a traditional perspective, which assumes that perfectly rational investors make wealth-maximizing decisions at all times using all available information. They find the traditional perspective difficult to accept because they observe investors displaying biased behaviors that lead to less-than-optimal decisions.

Shefrin and Statman (1994) begin to develop an alternative to the classic capital asset pricing model. Shefrin (2005, 2008) develops the idea further and proposes a behavioral approach to asset pricing using models, which Shefrin terms behavioral stochastic discount factor-based (SDF-based) asset pricing models. Shefrin, based on the results of empirical tests, concludes that investors do not make their decisions in an unbiased way. The stochastic discount factor to reflect this bias is a function of investor sentiment relative to fundamental value. The model focuses on market sentiment as a major determinant of asset pricing, which in turn is derived from systematic errors in judgment committed by investors. Shefrin asserts that sentiment causes asset prices to deviate from values determined using traditional finance approaches.

In order to have a tractable behavioral approach to asset pricing, it is necessary to have a well-defined measure of sentiment with an impact that can be traced on market prices and risk premiums. Shefrin (2005) proposes that the dispersion of analysts' forecasts serves as a proxy for the sentiment risk premium in the model. In support of this theory, he cites Ghysels and Juergens (2004), who determine that dispersion of analysts' forecasts is statistically significant in a Fama–French multi-risk-factor framework. Alternatively, the dispersion of analysts' forecasts may be a systematic risk factor not accounted for by other factors in the model. Doukas, Kim, and Pantzalis (2004) find that value stocks earn higher returns than growth stocks because the dispersion of analysts' forecasts is greater for value stocks—which supports dispersion of opinion as a measure for a source of risk.

Shefrin develops a stochastic process for sentiment and a fundamental SDF-based asset-pricing equation. The price of an asset is the expected value of its discounted payoffs. The discount rate captures the effects of the time value of money, fundamental risk, and sentiment risk. Sentiment pertains to erroneous, subjectively determined beliefs. If an investor's subjective beliefs about the discount rate match those of traditional finance, the investor is said to have zero risk sentiment. If an investor's subjective beliefs about the discount rate do not match those of traditional finance, the investor's beliefs are said to include risk sentiment. Thus, the discount rate on a security is the sum of the risk-free rate and fundamental premiums (corresponding to efficient prices) and a sentiment premium (reflecting sentiment-based risk).[24]

---

24 See Shefrin (2008).

Although Shefrin cites evidence that investors commit errors that result in inefficient prices in the aggregate, it is important to determine if these errors are either systematic or essentially random in nature. If they are systematic, then the errors may be predicted and exploited to earn excess returns. A logical assumption, in that case, is that rational and informed investors—however few in number—would act on these inefficiencies and thereby limit the scope of the pricing errors. If investors' errors are random in nature, however, then observing and modeling them presents a formidable challenge, as indicated in the original work by Shefrin and Statman (1994).

4.3.3 *Behavioral Portfolio Theory*

Shefrin and Statman (2000) extend their 1994 work to develop behavioral portfolio theory (BPT). BPT uses a probability-weighting function rather than the real probability distribution used in Markowitz's portfolio theory (1952). The optimal portfolio under BPT can differ from the perfectly diversified portfolio of Markowitz. In Markowitz's portfolio theory, risk-averse investors construct diversified portfolios based on mean–variance analysis and consideration of the covariance between assets. They are concerned about the expected return and variance of the portfolio as a whole. In behavioral portfolio theory, however, investors construct their portfolios in layers and expectations of returns and attitudes toward risk vary between the layers. The resulting portfolio may appear well-diversified, but diversification is incidental to and not necessarily an objective of the portfolio construction.

Shefrin and Statman contend that portfolio construction is primarily a function of five factors. First, the allocation to different layers depends on investor goals and the importance assigned to each goal. For example, if high importance is assigned to an upside potential goal, then the allocation of funds to the layer with the highest upside potential will be greater than if high importance is attached to minimizing potential downside losses. Second, the allocation of funds within a layer to specific assets will depend on the goal set for the layer. If a higher goal is set, then the assets selected for the layer are likely to be riskier or more speculative in nature. Third, the number of assets chosen for a layer depends on the shape of the investor's utility function. Risk-averse individuals have concave utility functions, meaning that utility increases at a decreasing rate with increases in wealth (diminishing marginal utility of wealth). The greater the concavity of the utility curve, the earlier the satiation for a specific security. Thus, the greater the concavity of the utility curve, the greater the number of securities included in a layer. Fourth, concentrated positions in some securities may occur if investors believe they have an informational advantage with respect to the securities. Fifth, investors reluctant to realize losses may hold higher amounts of cash so that they do not have to meet liquidity needs by selling assets that may be in a loss position. Further, the portfolios of investors reluctant to realize losses may continue to hold some securities not because of the securities' potential, but rather because of the investor's aversion to realize losses. Although the resulting portfolios may appear well-diversified, they may not, in fact, be well-diversified from a mean–variance perspective. In other words, the portfolio may not be mean–variance efficient.

Shefrin and Statman explain how BPT is consistent with the apparently irrational behavioral tendency of many people to purchase insurance policies and also buy lottery tickets, as discussed in Friedman and Savage (1948). A BPT investor maximizes expected wealth subject to the constraint that the probability of the wealth being less than some aspirational level cannot exceed some specified probability. A BPT investor can tolerate failure to achieve at least the aspirational level of wealth but only with a small probability. In other words, the investor maximizes expected wealth on a particular portfolio subject to a safety constraint. As a result, the optimal portfolio of a BPT investor is a combination of bonds or riskless assets and highly speculative assets. The BPT investor is essentially constructing a portfolio equivalent to an insurance policy and a lottery ticket.

In the first layer, the investor seeks safety by buying bonds or riskless assets in order to insure his aspirational level of wealth with a small maximum chance of failure. In the second layer, the investor is willing to take risk with the residual wealth. In consequence, a BPT-optimal portfolio can differ from the rational diversified portfolio that is mean–variance efficient. In the BPT model, risk aversion is taken into account by the constraint that limits the risk of failing to achieve the aspirational level of wealth.

EXAMPLE 3

Behavioral Portfolio Theory

Two BPT investors are developing portfolios. The portfolios will contain at most three layers: a layer of riskless investments, a layer of moderately risky investments, and a layer of highly risky speculative investments. The riskless investments (layer 1) are expected to return 1 percent; the moderately risky investments (layer 2) are expected to return −3 percent with 10 percent probability, 5 percent with 80 percent probability, and 9 percent with 10 percent probability; and the speculative investments (layer 3) are expected to return −50 percent with 15 percent probability, 12 percent with 50 percent probability, and 75 percent with 35 percent probability.

The first BPT investor has 2,000,000 euros and an aspirational level of 2,000,000 euros with a probability of 100 percent. In other words, this BPT investor will not tolerate any loss in wealth. The second BPT investor has 2,000,000 euros and an aspirational level of 2,100,000 euros with a probability of 80 percent. Further, this investor can tolerate some potential loss in wealth but cannot tolerate the portfolio declining below 1,800,000 euros. Construct the BPT optimal portfolio for each investor.

Solution:

The first BPT investor's portfolio will be approximately 100 percent in the layer of riskless investments given the inability to tolerate any losses. The second BPT investor has an aspirational level of return of 5 percent (100,000 euros). Given the safety level and a maximum potential loss of 50 percent on the speculative assets, the investor may put approximately 1,568,627 euros in layer 1 and 431,373 euros in layer 3. This portfolio will result in an expected return of 6.123 percent.

	Allocation	Expected Return	Portfolio Return
Layer 1	78.43%	1.00%	0.784%
Layer 2	0.00%	4.60%	0.000%
Layer 3	21.57%	24.75%	5.339%
Total	100.00%		6.123%

This portfolio will result in 1,800,000 euros with 15 percent probability, 2,067,451 euros with 50 percent probability, and 2,339,216 euros with 35 percent probability. The safety objective is met, but the portfolio is short of the aspirational goal. The portfolio will result in at least 2,067,451 euros with 85 percent probability rather than 2,100,000 euros with 80 percent probability. Based on risk tolerance, the investor may decide this is acceptable or may decide to lower her safety level objective.

(*Note*: The resulting portfolios are not necessarily mean–variance efficient because no consideration is given to the covariance of the investment layers.)

4.3.4 *Adaptive Markets Hypothesis*

Lo (2004) proposes the **adaptive markets hypothesis** (AMH). The AMH applies principles of evolution—such as competition, adaptation, and natural selection—to financial markets in an attempt to reconcile efficient market theories with behavioral alternatives. Similar to factors that influence an ecological system, markets are influenced by competition for scarce resources and the adaptability of participants. The greater the competition for scarce resources or in markets for profits and the less adaptable the participants, the greater the likelihood of not surviving. Following are two examples that have been simplified but serve to demonstrate the ideas behind the AMH. In a natural example, pandas are extremely non-adaptable, eating only bamboo. This reduces the likelihood of pandas surviving in significant numbers outside of protected settings. In a financial example, Long-Term Capital Management (LTCM) was faced with increasing competition that used the same arbitrage techniques as LTCM did. Rather than adapting and changing techniques, LTCM increased leverage and ultimately faced the possibility of non-survival.

Lo notes that biases identified by those researching in behavioral finance may be consistent with the AMH. These biases are simply the result of applying previously learned heuristics to a changed environment where they no longer work. The successful participant will adapt to the changed environment and develop new heuristics. Success is defined as survival rather than as having maximized expected utility.

Behavior of market participants is not necessarily that of a REM, but is rather behavior that is perceived to result in less-than-optimal rational outcomes. Lo discusses this in the context of Simon's notions of bounded rationality and satisficing.[25] As a result of informational, intellectual, and computational limitations, individuals use judgment to gather sufficient information, to adequately process the information, to identify with satisfactory sub-goals and limited objectives rather than try to achieve an optimum, and to make decisions that meet these sub-goals and objectives. Applying an evolutionary perspective to Simon's framework provides useful insights. For example, the choice of satisfactory goals is determined through trial and error, which can be viewed as equivalent to a process of natural selection. As experience increases, individuals learn and the heuristics they apply to a situation evolve. As these heuristics based on past experiences are applied to new situations, they may or may not be appropriate and additional learning takes place.

The AMH is a revised version of the EMH that considers bounded rationality, satisficing, and evolutionary principles. Under the AMH, individuals act in their own self-interest, make mistakes, and learn and adapt; competition motivates adaptation and innovation; and natural selection and evolution determine market dynamics. Five implications of the AMH are: 1) The relationship between risk and reward varies over time (risk premiums change over time) because of changes in risk preferences and such other factors as changes in the competitive environment; 2) active management can add value by exploiting arbitrage opportunities; 3) any particular investment strategy will not consistently do well but will have periods of superior and inferior performance; 4) the ability to adapt and innovate is critical for survival; and 5) survival is the essential objective. In other words, recognizing that things change, the survivors will be those who successfully learn and adapt to changes.

---

25 See Simon (1957).

SUMMARY

With its simplifying assumption of rational investors and efficient markets, traditional finance has gained wide acceptance among academics and investment professionals as a guide to financial decision making. Over time, however, the limitations of traditional finance have become increasingly apparent. Individual decision making is not nearly as objective and intellectually rigorous, and financial markets are not always as rational and efficiently priced as traditional finance assumes. To bridge this gap between theory and practice, behavioral finance approaches decision making from an empirical perspective. It identifies patterns of individual behavior without trying to justify or rationalize them.

A practical integration of behavioral and traditional finance may lead to a better outcome than either approach used in isolation. By knowing how investors should behave and how investors are likely to behave, it may be possible to construct investment solutions that are both more rational from a traditional perspective and, because of adjustments reflecting behavioral insights, easier to accept and remain committed to. Although these behavioral insights will not lead easily or automatically to superior results, it is hoped that they will help many improve their investment approach and enhance risk management.

Among the points made in this reading are the following:

- Traditional finance assumes that investors are rational: Investors are risk-averse, self-interested utility-maximizers who process available information in an unbiased way.

- Traditional finance assumes that investors construct and hold optimal portfolios; optimal portfolios are mean–variance efficient.

- Traditional finance hypothesizes that markets are efficient: Market prices incorporate and reflect all available and relevant information.

- Behavioral finance makes different (non-normative) assumptions about investor and market behaviors.

- Behavioral finance attempts to understand and explain observed investor and market behaviors; observed behaviors often differ from the idealized behaviors assumed under traditional finance.

- Behavioral biases are observed to affect the financial decisions of individuals.

- Bounded rationality is proposed as an alternative to assuming perfect information and perfect rationality on the part of individuals: Individuals are acknowledged to have informational, intellectual, and computational limitations and as a result may satisfice rather than optimize when making decisions.

- Prospect theory is proposed as an alternative to expected utility theory. Within prospect theory, loss aversion is proposed as an alternative to risk aversion.

- Markets are not always observed to be efficient; anomalous markets are observed.

- Theories and models based on behavioral perspectives have been advanced to explain observed market behavior and portfolio construction.

- One behavioral approach to asset pricing suggests that the discount rate used to value an asset should include a sentiment risk premium.

- Behavioral portfolio theory suggests that portfolios are constructed in layers to satisfy investor goals rather than to be mean–variance efficient.

- The behavioral life-cycle hypothesis suggests that people classify their assets into non-fungible mental accounts and develop spending (current consumption) and savings (future consumption) plans that, although not optimal, achieve some balance between short-term gratification and long-term goals.

- The adaptive markets hypothesis, based on some principles of evolutionary biology, suggests that the degree of market efficiency is related to environmental factors characterizing market ecology. These factors include the number of competitors in the market, the magnitude of profit opportunities available, and the adaptability of the market participants.

- By understanding investor behavior, it may be possible to construct investment solutions that will be closer to the rational solution of traditional finance and, because of adjustments reflecting behavioral insights, easier to accept and remain committed to.

REFERENCES

Ball, R. 1978. "Anomalies in Relationships between Securities' Yields and Yield-Surrogates." *Journal of Financial Economics*, vol. 6:103–126.

Banz, R.W. 1981. "The Relationship between Return and Market Value of Common Stocks." *Journal of Financial Economics*, vol. 9:3–18.

Basu, Sanjoy. 1983. "The Relationship between Earnings Yield, Market Value, and Return for NYSE Common Stocks: Further Evidence." *Journal of Financial Economics*, vol. 12:129–156.

Bernanke, Ben S. 2009. Commencement of the Boston College School of Law. Newton, MA (22 May).

Bernoulli, Daniel. 1954. (originally published in 1738). "Exposition of a New Theory on the Measurement of Risk." *Econometrica: Journal of the Econometric Society*, vol. 22, no. 1:23–36.

Brock, William, Josef Lakonishok, and Blake LeBaron. 1992. "Simple Technical Trading Rules and the Stochastic Properties of Stock Returns." *Journal of Finance*, vol. 47, no. 5 (December):1731–1764.

Chan, L., Y. Hamao, and Josef Lakonishok. 1991. "Fundamentals and Stock Returns in Japan." *Journal of Finance*, vol. 46, no. 5 (December):1739–1764.

Cowles, Alfred. 1933. "Can Stock Market Forecasters Forecast?" *Econometrica: Journal of the Econometric Society*, vol. 1:309–324.

Doukas, John, Chansog (Francis) Kim, and Christos Pantzalis. 2004. "Divergent Opinions and the Performance of Value Stocks." *Financial Analysts Journal*, vol. 60, no. 6:55–64.

Fama, Eugene F. 1965. "Random Walks in Stock Market Prices." *Financial Analysts Journal*, vol. 21, no. 5 (September/October):55–59.

Fama, Eugene F., M. Jensen, L. Fisher, and R. Roll. 1969. "The Adjustment of Stock Prices to New Information." *International Economic Review*, vol. 10, no. 1 (February):1–21.

Fama, Eugene F. 1970. "Efficient Capital Markets: A Review of Theory and Empirical Work." *Journal of Finance*, vol. 25, no. 2 (May):383–417.

Fama, Eugene F., and Kenneth R. French. 1992. "The Cross-Section of Expected Stock Returns." *Journal of Finance*, vol. 47, no. 2 (June):427–465.

Fama, Eugene F., and Kenneth R. French. 1995. "Size and Book-to-Market Factors in Earnings and Returns." *Journal of Finance*, vol. 50:131–155.

Fama, Eugene F., and Kenneth R. French. 2008. "Average Returns, B/M, and Share Issues." *Journal of Finance*, vol. 63:2971–2995.

Fox, Justin. 2009. *The Myth of the Rational Market*. New York: HarperCollins.

Friedman, M., and L. J. Savage. 1948. "The Utility Analysis of Choices Involving Risk." *Journal of Political Economy*, vol. 56, no. 4 (August):279–304.

Ghysels, E., and J. Juergens. 2004. "Do Heterogeneous Beliefs Matter for Asset Pricing?" Working Paper, University of North Carolina.

Glimcher, Paul. 2003. *Decisions, Uncertainty, and the Brain: The Science of Neuroeconomics*. Cambridge, MA: MIT Press.

Grossman, Sanford J., and Joseph E. Stiglitz. 1980. "On the Impossibility of Informationally Efficient Markets." *American Economic Review*, vol. 70, no. 3:393–408.

Gul, F., and W. Pesendorfer. 2008. "The Case for Mindless Economics." In *The Foundations of Positive and Normative Economics*. A. Caplin and A. Schotter, eds. New York: Oxford University Press.

Haugen, Robert, and Philippe Jorion. 1996. "The January Effect." *Financial Analysts Journal*, vol. 52, no. 1 (January/February):27–31.

Hensel, C., and W. Ziemba. 1996. "Investment Results from Exploiting Turn-of-the-Month Effects." *Journal of Portfolio Management*, vol. 22, no. 3 (Spring):17–23.

Jaffe, J., D. Keim, and R. Westerfield. 1989. "Earnings Yields, Market Values, and Stock Returns." *Journal of Finance*, vol. 44, no. 1 (March):135–148.

Jensen, Michael C. 1967. "The Performance of Mutual Funds in the Period 1945–1964." *Journal of Finance*, vol. 23, no. 2:389–416.

Kahneman, Daniel, and Amos Tversky. 1979. "Prospect Theory: An Analysis of Decision under Risk." *Econometrica: Journal of the Econometric Society*, vol. 47, no. 2 (March):263–291.

Keynes, John Maynard. 1936. *The General Theory of Employment, Interest, and Money*. New York: Harcourt, Brace.

Knight, Frank. 1921. *Risk, Uncertainty, and Profit*. Boston: Beard Books.

Lakonishok, Josef, Andrei Shleifer, and Robert W. Vishny. 1994. "Contrarian Investment, Extrapolation, and Risk." *Journal of Finance*, vol. 49, no. 5:1541–1578.

Lamont, Owen A., and Richard H. Thaler. 2003. "Can the Market Add and Subtract? Mispricing in Tech Stock Carve-Outs." *Journal of Political Economy*, vol. 111, no. 2:227–268.

Lewis, Michael. 2010. *The Big Short*. New York: W.W. Norton & Company.

Lo, Andrew. 2004. "The Adaptive Markets Hypothesis." *Journal of Portfolio Management*, vol. 30, no. 5 (30th anniversary issue):15–29.

Malkiel, Burton. 1973. *A Random Walk Down Wall Street*. New York: W.W. Norton & Company.

Markowitz, Harry. 1952. "Portfolio Selection." *Journal of Finance*, vol. 7, no. 1:77–91.

O'Shaughnessy, James P. 1996. *What Works on Wall Street*. Columbus, OH: McGraw-Hill.

Raiffa, Howard. 1997. *Decision Analysis: Introductory Readings on Choices under Uncertainty*. Columbus, OH: McGraw-Hill.

Roberts, Harry V. 1959. "Stock-Market 'Patterns' and Financial Analysis: Methodological Suggestions." *Journal of Finance*, vol. 14, no. 1.

Rosenberg, B., K. Reid, and R. Lanstein. 1985. "Persuasive Evidence of Market Inefficiency." *Journal of Portfolio Management*, vol. 11:9–17.

Samuelson, Paul A. 1937. "A Note on Measurement of Utility." *Review of Economic Studies*, vol. 4, no. 2 (February).

Samuelson, Paul A. 1965. "Proof That Properly Anticipated Prices Fluctuate Randomly." *Industrial Management Review*, vol. 6, no. 2:41.

Savage, L.J. 1954. *The Foundation of Statistics*. New York: John Wiley.

Shefrin, Hersh. 2005. *A Behavioral Approach to Asset Pricing*. Burlington, MA: Elsevier.

Shefrin, Hersh. 2008. "Risk and Return in Behavioral SDF-Based Asset Pricing Models." *Journal of Investment Management*, vol. 6, no. 3:1–18.

Shefrin, Hersh, and Meir Statman. 1994. "Behavioral Capital Asset Pricing Theory." *Journal of Financial and Quantitative Analysis*, vol. 29:323–349.

Shefrin, Hersh, and Meir Statman. 2000. "Behavioral Portfolio Theory." *Journal of Financial and Quantitative Analysis*, vol. 35, no. 2.

Shefrin, Hersh, and Richard Thaler. 1988. "The Behavioral Life-Cycle Hypothesis." *Economic Inquiry*, vol. 26, no. 4:609–643.

Shleifer, Andrei, and Robert W. Vishny. 1997. "The Limits of Arbitrage." *Journal of Finance*, vol. 52, no. 1 (March):35–55.

Simon, Herbert A. 1957. *Models of Man: Social and Rational*. New York: John Wiley and Sons.

Simon, Herbert A. 1991. *Models of My Life*. New York: Basic Books.

Simon, Herbert A. 1996. *The Sciences of the Artificial*. 3rd ed. Cambridge, MA: MIT Press.

Statman, Meir. 1999. "Behavioral Finance: Past Battles and Future Engagements." *Financial Analysts Journal*, vol. 55, no. 6 (November/December):18–27.

Stattman, D. 1980. "Book Values and Stock Returns." *The Chicago MBA: A Journal of Selected Papers*, vol. 4:25–45.

Thaler, Richard. 2009. "Markets Can Be Wrong and the Price Is Not Always Right." *Financial Times* (4 August).

von Neumann, John, and Oskar Morgenstern. 1944. *Theory of Games and Economic Behavior*. Princeton, NJ: Princeton University Press.

PRACTICE PROBLEMS

The following information relates to Questions 1–6

Mimi Fong, CFA, a private wealth manager with an asset management firm, has been asked to make a presentation to her colleagues comparing traditional and behavioral finance. She decides to enliven her presentation with statements from colleagues and clients. These statements are intended to demonstrate some key aspects of and differences between traditional and behavioral finance.

Statement 1   (from a colleague): "When new information on a company becomes available, I adjust my expectations for that company's stock based on past experiences with similar information."

Statement 2   (from a client): "When considering investments, I have always liked using long option positions. I like their risk/return tradeoffs. My personal estimates of the probability of gains seem to be higher than that implied by the market prices. I am not sure how to explain that, but to me long options provide tremendous upside potential with little risk, given the low probability of limited losses."

Statement 3   (from a client): "I have always followed a budget and have been a disciplined saver for decades. Even in hard times when I had to reduce my usual discretionary spending, I always managed to save."

Statement 4   (from a colleague): "While I try to make decisions analytically, I do believe the markets can be driven by the emotions of others. So I have frequently used buy/sell signals when investing. Also, my 20 years of experience with managers who actively trade on such information makes me think they are worth the fees they charge."

Statement 5   (from a colleague): "Most of my clients need a well-informed advisor to analyze investment choices and to educate them on their opportunities. They prefer to be presented with three to six viable strategies to achieve their goals. They like to be able to match their goals with specific investment allocations or layers of their portfolio."

Statement 6   (from a client): "I follow a disciplined approach to investing. When a stock has appreciated by 15 percent, I sell it. Also, I sell a stock when its price has declined by 25 percent from my initial purchase price."

Statement 7   (from a client): "Overall, I have always been willing to take a small chance of losing up to 8 percent of the portfolio annually. I can accept any asset classes to meet my financial goals if this constraint is considered. In other words, an acceptable portfolio will satisfy the following condition: Expected return − 1.645 × Expected standard deviation ≥ −8%."

1   Which of the following statements is *most* consistent with expected utility theory?

   A   Statement 1.

   B   Statement 2.

   C   Statement 3.

2   Which of the following statements *most likely* indicates a belief that technical anomalies exist in the capital markets?

   A   Statement 2.

   B   Statement 4.

   C   Statement 6.

3   Statement 4 is *most* consistent with:

   A   the adaptive markets hypothesis.

   B   a behavioral approach to asset pricing.

   C   Savage's subjective expected utility theory.

4   The clients of Statement 5 *most likely* exhibit:

   A   loss-aversion.

   B   bounded rationality.

   C   mental accounting bias.

5   The client of Statement 6 is *most likely* behaving consistently with:

   A   prospect theory.

   B   expected utility theory.

   C   behavioral portfolio theory.

6   The client of Statement 7 would *most likely* agree with which of the following statements?

   A   I strive for a mean–variance efficient portfolio.

   B   I construct my portfolio in layers to meet my goals.

   C   I am loss-averse and have a value function that is steeper for losses than gains.

SOLUTIONS

1 C is correct. Statement 3 is most consistent with expected utility theory. The client exhibits self-control and is able to defer consumption. This client is considering short-term and long-term goals and attempting to maximize the present value of utility. In Statement 1, beliefs are being updated using heuristics rather than Bayes' formula. Statement 2 is consistent with prospect theory; the client is overweighting the probability of a high financial impact outcome (gains on options) and underweighting the probability of a loss (the option premium cost).

2 B is correct. Statement 4 indicates the belief that buy/sell signals can be used to earn excess returns.

3 B is correct. Statement 4 indicates that markets can be influenced by the emotions of others (sentiment). This is consistent with a behavioral approach to asset pricing that includes sentiment such as the behavioral stochastic discount factor-based asset pricing model proposed by Shefrin.

4 C is correct. The clients discussed in Statement 5 exhibit mental accounting bias because they consider their portfolio by matching its layers to goals. The clients may not have time themselves to examine the investment universe and arrive at optimal solutions, but they rely on their adviser to do this for them. Thus, they do not exhibit bounded rationality.

5 C is correct. The client of Statement 6 is behaving consistently with behavioral portfolio theory. The client sells and holds a stock not because of the stock's potential, but rather from a fear of the stock declining in value and gains dissipating and an aversion to realizing losses. Loss-aversion in prospect theory is discussed from a different perspective.

6 A is correct. The client is expressing a portfolio goal that considers expected return and standard deviation. This is consistent with traditional finance and the client is likely to prefer a mean–variance efficient portfolio. There is nothing in the statement that indicates loss-aversion as opposed to risk-aversion or a preference for constructing a portfolio in layers.

The Behavioral Biases of Individuals

by Michael M. Pompian, CFA

Michael M. Pompian, CFA (USA)

LEARNING OUTCOMES

Mastery	The candidate should be able to:
☐	**a.** distinguish between cognitive errors and emotional biases;
☐	**b.** discuss commonly recognized behavioral biases and their implications for financial decision making;
☐	**c.** identify and evaluate an individual's behavioral biases;
☐	**d.** evaluate how behavioral biases affect investment policy and asset allocation decisions and recommend approaches to mitigate their effects.

INTRODUCTION

1

Much of traditional economic and financial theory is based on the assumptions that individuals act rationally and consider all available information in the decision-making process and that markets are efficient. Behavioral finance challenges these assumptions and explores how individuals and markets actually behave. To differentiate the study of individual investor behavior from the study of collective market behavior, the subject of behavioral finance can be classified as **Behavioral Finance Micro** (BFMI) and **Behavioral Finance Macro** (BFMA).

BFMI examines the behavioral biases that distinguish individual investors from the rational decision makers of traditional finance. BFMA detects and describes market anomalies that distinguish markets from the efficient markets of traditional finance. In this reading, we focus on BFMI and the behavioral biases that individuals may exhibit when making financial decisions. BFMI attempts to observe and explain how individuals make financial decisions. This approach is in contrast to traditional theories of financial decision making that describe how people *should* make decisions under uncertainty.

Many prominent researchers have demonstrated that when people are faced with complex decision-making situations that demand substantial time and effort, they have difficulty devising completely rational approaches to developing and analyzing various courses of action. Facing uncertainty and an abundance of information to process, individuals may not systematically describe problems, record necessary data, or synthesize information to create rules for making decisions. Instead, individuals may follow a more subjective, suboptimal path of reasoning to determine a course of action consistent with their basic judgments and preferences.

A decision maker may have neither the time nor the ability to arrive at a perfectly optimal decision. Individuals strive to make good decisions by simplifying the choices available, using a subset of the information available, and discarding some possible alternatives to choose among a smaller number. They are content to accept a solution that is "good enough" rather than attempting to find the optimal answer. In doing so, they may unintentionally bias the decision-making process. These biases may lead to irrational behaviors and decisions.

By understanding behavioral biases, investment professionals may be able to improve economic outcomes. This may entail identifying behavioral biases they themselves exhibit or behavioral biases of others, including clients. Once a behavioral bias has been identified, it may be possible to either moderate the bias or adapt to the bias so that the resulting financial decisions more closely match the rational financial decisions assumed by traditional finance. Knowledge of and integration of behavioral and traditional finance may lead to superior results.

Section 2 describes and broadly characterizes behavioral biases. Sections 3 and 4 discuss specific behavioral biases within two broad categories: cognitive errors and emotional biases. The discussion will include a description of the bias, potential consequences of the bias, detection of the bias, and guidance on moderating the effects of the bias. Section 5 considers the implications of behavioral biases for investment policy development and asset allocation decisions. A summary and practice problems conclude the reading.

2 CATEGORIZATIONS OF BEHAVIORAL BIASES

Dictionary definitions of bias include the following: a statistical sampling or testing error caused by systematically favoring some outcomes over others; a preference or an inclination, especially one that inhibits impartial judgment; an inclination or prejudice in favor of a particular viewpoint; an inclination of temperament or outlook, especially a personal and sometimes unreasoned judgment. In the context of this reading, we are considering biases that result in irrational financial decisions caused by faulty cognitive reasoning or reasoning influenced by feelings. The first dictionary definition of bias is consistent with faulty cognitive reasoning; the other three definitions are more consistent with reasoning influenced by feelings or emotions.

The simple categorization of distinguishing between biases based on faulty cognitive reasoning (**cognitive errors**) and those based on reasoning influenced by feelings or emotions (**emotional biases**) is used in this reading. Although researchers in the field of psychology have developed many different classifications and identifying factors to categorize and better understand biases, it is possible to see how each of these fit within the two categories. For example, psychologists' factors include cognitive information-processing shortcuts or heuristics, memory errors, emotional and/or motivational factors, and such social influences as family upbringing or societal culture. The first two are cognitive; the last two are emotional. Some biases identified by psychologists are understood in relation to human needs, such as those identified by Maslow (e.g., physiological, safety, social, esteem, and self-actualizing). In satisfying these needs, people will generally attempt to avoid pain and seek pleasure. The avoidance of pain can be as subtle as avoiding acknowledging mistakes in order to maintain a positive self-image. The biases that help to avoid pain and produce pleasure may be classified as emotional. Other biases found by psychologists are attributed to the particular way the brain perceives, forms memories, and makes judgments; the inability to do complex mathematical calculations, such as updating probabilities; and the processing and filtering of information. These can be classified as cognitive.

In summary, cognitive errors stem from basic statistical, information-processing, or memory errors; cognitive errors may be considered the result of faulty reasoning. Emotional biases stem from impulse or intuition; emotional biases may be considered to result from reasoning influenced by feelings. Behavioral biases, regardless of their source, may cause decisions to deviate from the assumed rational decisions of traditional finance.

2.1 Differences between Cognitive Errors and Emotional Biases

In this reading, behavioral biases are classified as either cognitive errors or emotional biases. This distinction is not only simple and easily understood, but it also provides a useful framework for understanding how effectively biases can be corrected for. If we think of decision making as occurring along a spectrum from the totally rational decision making of traditional finance to purely emotional decision making, cognitive errors are basic statistical, information-processing, or memory errors that cause the decision to deviate from the rational decisions of traditional finance. Emotional biases arise spontaneously as a result of attitudes and feelings that can cause the decision to deviate from the rational decisions of traditional finance.

Cognitive errors are more easily corrected than emotional biases. Individuals are better able to adapt their behaviors or modify their processes if the source of the bias is logically identifiable, even if not completely understood. For instance, an individual may not understand the complex mathematical process to update probabilities but may comprehend that the process initially used was incorrect. Cognitive errors can also be thought of as "blind spots" or distortions in the human mind. Cognitive errors do not result from emotional or intellectual predispositions toward certain judgments, but rather from subconscious mental procedures for processing information. Because cognitive errors stem from faulty reasoning, better information, education, and advice can often correct for them. Thus, most cognitive biases can be "moderated"—to moderate the impact of a bias is to recognize it and attempt to reduce or even eliminate it within the individual.

Because emotional biases stem from impulse or intuition—especially personal and sometimes unreasoned judgments—they are less easily corrected. It is generally agreed that an emotion is a mental state that arises spontaneously rather than through conscious effort. Emotions are related to feelings, perceptions, or beliefs about elements, objects, or relations between them and can be a function of reality or the imagination. In the world of investing, emotions can cause investors to make suboptimal decisions. Emotions may be undesired to the individual feeling them; he or she may wish to control them but often cannot. Thus, it may only be possible to recognize an emotional bias and "adapt" to it. When a bias is adapted to, it is accepted and decisions are made that recognize and adjust for it (rather than making an attempt to reduce or eliminate it).

The cognitive–emotional distinction will help us determine when and how to adjust for behavioral biases in financial decision making. However, it should be noted that specific biases may have some common aspects and that a specific bias may seem to have both cognitive and emotional aspects. Researchers in financial decision making have identified numerous specific behavioral biases. This reading will not attempt to discuss all identified biases. Rather, this reading will discuss some of the more publicized and recognized biases within the cognitive–emotional framework. This framework will be useful in developing an awareness of biases, their implications, and ways of moderating their impact or adapting to them. The intent is not to develop a list of biases to be memorized but rather to create an awareness of biases so that financial decisions and resulting economic outcomes are potentially improved.

In Sections 3 and 4, specific behavioral biases will be discussed. Cognitive errors will be discussed in Section 3 and emotional biases in Section 4. For each bias we will 1) describe the bias, including evidence supporting the existence of the bias; 2) describe the consequences of the bias; and 3) offer guidance on detecting and overcoming the bias. We will limit our focus to gauging the presence or absence—not the magnitude—of each bias discussed. That is, we will not try to measure how strongly the bias is exhibited, but rather we will describe the behavioral bias, its potential consequences, and the detection of and correction for the behavioral bias. In detecting a bias, we will identify statements or thought processes that may be indicative of the bias. Diagnostic tests of varying degrees of complexity are available to detect biases but are beyond the scope of this reading.[1]

3   COGNITIVE ERRORS

We will now review nine specific cognitive errors, their implications for financial decision making, and suggestions for correcting for them. We classify cognitive errors into two categories. The first category contains "belief perseverance" biases. In general, belief perseverance is the tendency to cling to one's previously held beliefs irrationally or illogically. The belief continues to be held and justified by committing statistical, information-processing, or memory errors. A second category of cognitive error has to do with "processing errors," describing how information may be processed and used illogically or irrationally in financial decision making.

The belief perseverance biases discussed are conservatism, confirmation, representativeness, illusion of control, and hindsight. The processing errors discussed are anchoring and adjustment, mental accounting, framing, and availability.

In this reading, the individuals of interest are "financial market participants" ("FMPs") engaged in financial decision making. These include both individual investors and financial services professionals.

3.1 Belief Perseverance Biases

Belief perseverance biases are closely related to the psychological concept of **cognitive dissonance**. Cognitive dissonance is the mental discomfort that occurs when new information conflicts with previously held beliefs or cognitions. To resolve this dissonance, people may notice only information of interest (selective exposure), ignore or modify information that conflicts with existing cognitions (selective perception), or remember and consider only information that confirms existing cognitions (selective retention). Aspects of these behaviors are contained in the biases categorized as belief perseverance.

3.1.1 *Conservatism Bias*

Conservatism bias is a belief perseverance bias in which people maintain their prior views or forecasts by inadequately incorporating new information. This bias has aspects of both statistical and information-processing errors. Academic studies have demonstrated that conservatism causes individuals to overweight initial beliefs about

---

1 Some diagnostic tests are included in *Behavioral Finance and Wealth Management* by Pompian (2006).

probabilities and outcomes and under-react to new information; they fail to modify their beliefs and actions to the extent rationally justified by the new information. In Bayesian terms, they tend to overweight the base rates[2] and underweight the new information, resulting in revised beliefs about probabilities and outcomes that demonstrate an underreaction to the new information. As a result of conservatism bias, FMPs may underreact to or fail to act on new information and continue to maintain beliefs close to those based on previous estimates and information.

EXAMPLE 1

Conservatism in Action

James Montier writes, "The stock market has a tendency to underreact to fundamental information—be it dividend omissions, initiations or an earnings report."[3] When discussing the behavior of security analysts, Montier explains, "People tend to cling tenaciously to a view or a forecast. Once a position has been stated, most people find it very hard to move away from that view. When movement does occur, it does so only very slowly. Psychologists call this conservatism bias. The chart below shows conservatism in analysts' forecasts. We have taken a linear time trend out of both the operating earnings numbers, and the analysts' forecasts. A cursory glance at the chart reveals that analysts are exceptionally good at telling you what has just happened. They have invested too heavily in their view, and hence will only change it when presented with indisputable evidence of its falsehood."[4] The chart accompanying Montier's analysis (2002b) appears as Exhibit 1. Discuss Montier's analysis in the context of biases of individuals.

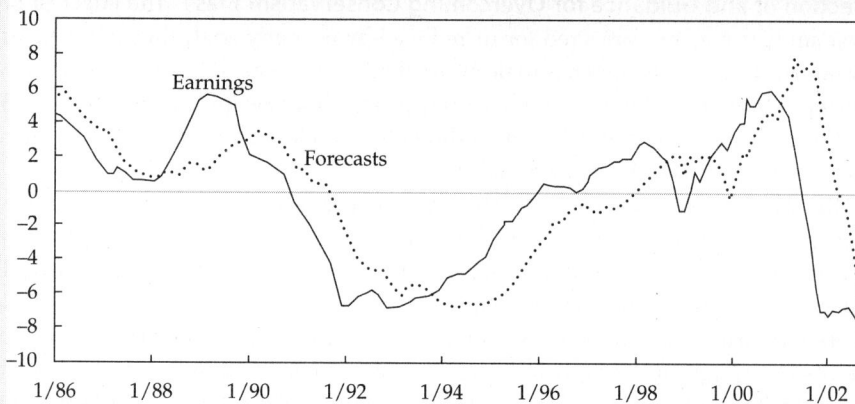

Exhibit 1   Analysts Lag Reality

---

2 The base rate is the probability of the event without the new information.
3 Montier (2002a).
4 Montier (2002b).

Solution:

In relating conservatism to security analysts, Montier provides clear evidence of the conservatism bias in action: The analysts maintain their forecasts even when presented with new information. The behavior observed in security analysts can logically be extended to individual investors who are likely to engage in similar behavior when managing their own investment portfolios.

Consequences of Conservatism Bias   As a result of conservatism bias, FMPs may do the following:

- Maintain or be slow to update a view or a forecast, even when presented with new information. For example, if an investor purchases a security of a pharmaceutical company based on the belief that the company is about to receive regulatory approval for a new drug, and then the company announces that it is experiencing problems getting the approval, the investor may cling to his initial valuation of the company and fail to respond or respond slowly to the new information. As a result, the investor may hold the security longer than a rational decision maker would.

- Opt to maintain a prior belief rather than deal with the mental stress of updating beliefs given complex data. This behavior relates to an underlying difficulty in processing new information. For example, if an investor purchases a security based on the belief that the company is entering a period of significant earnings growth, and then the company announces its growth rate may appear lower than expected because of a number of difficult-to-interpret accounting changes, the investor may maintain the prior belief rather than attempt to decipher the fundamental impact, if any, reflected in the accounting changes. As a result, the investor may hold the security longer than a rational decision maker would.

Detection of and Guidance for Overcoming Conservatism Bias   The effect of conservatism bias may be corrected for or reduced by properly analyzing and weighting new information. The first step is to be aware that a bias exists. If FMPs find themselves ignoring new information or not adequately processing new information on the basis that the information is not relevant, is difficult to understand, or would not change beliefs, a conservatism bias may exist.

Hirshleifer (2001) provides evidence that the processing of new information and the updating of beliefs are inversely correlated with the effort involved in processing the information and updating the beliefs. He terms this effort cognitive cost. The higher the cognitive cost, the less likely information will be processed and beliefs updated. Information that is abstract and statistical is cognitively costly, and it thus receives less weighting. As a result, the base rate is overweighted. Information that is cognitively inexpensive (easily processed) may receive a higher weighting. As a result, individuals may overreact to information that is easily processed and may even underweight base rates. The costly processing idea can explain base rate overweighting and underweighting.

When new information is presented, the FMP should ask such questions as, "How does this information change my forecast?" or "What impact does this information have on my forecast?" Specifically, FMPs should react decisively to new information and avoid retaining old forecasts by disregarding new information. This reaction does not imply action before analysis. FMPs should conduct careful analysis incorporating the new information and then respond appropriately. When an appropriate course of action becomes clear, even if it deviates from the course of action based on previous information and beliefs, it should be implemented without hesitation.

When investors are ignoring information because it is difficult to interpret or understand, they should seek advice from a professional who can either explain how to interpret the data or can explain the action implications of the data to the satisfaction of the investor. Otherwise, investors may fail to make appropriate financial decisions. Inappropriate decisions may include making or failing to make investments because they are poorly understood.

3.1.2 *Confirmation Bias*

Confirmation bias is a belief perseverance bias in which people tend to look for and notice what confirms their beliefs, and to ignore or undervalue what contradicts their beliefs. This behavior has aspects of selective exposure, perception, and retention and may be thought of as a selection bias. It is an all too natural response to cognitive dissonance and reflects an ability to convince ourselves of what we want to believe by giving more weight to evidence that supports our beliefs and to ignore or modify evidence that conflicts with our beliefs.

Numerous studies have demonstrated that people generally place excessive weight on confirmatory information; that is, they place greater weight on information that supports their beliefs. Information is considered positive if it supports their beliefs and negative if it fails to support or refutes their beliefs. Thomas Gilovich, a researcher in the field of human psychology, notes that, "The most likely reason for the excessive influence of confirmatory information is that it is easier to deal with cognitively."[5] Researchers are sometimes guilty of confirmation bias when they set up experiments or frame their data in ways that tend to confirm their hypotheses. They compound the problem by proceeding in ways that avoid dealing with data that would contradict their hypotheses.

All FMPs—whether individual investors, analysts, investment advisers, or fund managers—may, after making an investment decision, tend to notice and consider information in a manner consistent with resolving cognitive dissonance. They may notice and consider only confirmatory information and ignore or modify contradictory information. Most experienced private wealth advisers have dealt with a client who conducts some research and insists on adding a particular investment to his portfolio. Unfortunately, the client may have failed to consider how the investment fits in his portfolio, as well as evidence of its fundamental value. This type of client may insist on continuing to hold the investment, even when the adviser recommends otherwise, because the client's follow-up research seeks only information that confirms his belief that the investment is still a good value. The confirmation bias is not limited to individual investors; all FMPs should be wary of the potential confirmation biases within themselves.

Consequences of Confirmation Bias   In the investment world, confirmation bias is exhibited repeatedly. As a result of confirmation bias, FMPs may do the following:

- Consider only the positive information about an existing investment and ignore any negative information about the investment.

- Develop screening criteria and ignore information that either refutes the validity of the screening criteria or supports other screening criteria. As a result, some good investments that do not meet the screening criteria may be ignored; conversely, some bad investments that do meet the screening criteria may be made.

---

5 Gilovich (1993).

- Under-diversify portfolios, leading to excessive exposure to risk. FMPs may become convinced of the value of a single company and its stock. They ignore negative news about the company and its stock, and they gather and process only information confirming that the company is a good investment. They build a large position and eventually own a poorly diversified portfolio.

- Hold a disproportionate amount of their investment assets in their employing company's stock because they believe in their company and are convinced of its favorable prospects. Favorable information is cited, and unfavorable information is ignored. If the employee was to acknowledge unfavorable information, the associated mental discomfort might make work very difficult for the employee.

Detection of and Guidance for Overcoming Confirmation Bias   The effect of confirmation bias may be corrected for or reduced by actively seeking out information that challenges your beliefs. The conscious effort to gather and process negative information (information that challenges a belief), as well as positive information, provides more complete information on which to base a decision. Even well-informed decisions can lead to unfavorable results; however, making the extra effort to gather complete information, positive and negative, will likely result in better decisions.

Another useful step is to get corroborating support for an investment decision. For example, if investment selections are based on criteria confirming an existing belief, such as stocks breaking through their 52-week highs, it is usually advisable to obtain supporting information (e.g., fundamental research on the company, industry or sector information) to assure that a good investment is being made. Accepting an investment idea unquestioningly and confirming it through purchases is not a proven investment strategy. Additional research is highly recommended.

3.1.3 Representativeness Bias

Representativeness bias is a belief perseverance bias in which people tend to classify new information based on past experiences and classifications. They believe their classifications are appropriate and place undue weight on them. This bias occurs because people attempting to derive meaning from their experiences tend to classify objects and thoughts into personalized categories. When confronted with new information, they use those categories even if the new information does not necessarily fit. They rely on a "best fit" approximation to determine which category should provide a frame of reference from which to understand the new information.

Although this perceptual framework provides an expedient tool for processing new information, it may lead to statistical and information-processing errors. The new information superficially resembles or is *representative* of familiar elements already classified, but in reality it can be very different. In these instances, the classification reflex deceives people, producing an incorrect understanding that often persists and biases all future thinking about the information. *Base-rate neglect* and *sample-size neglect* are two types of representativeness bias that apply to FMPs. In Bayesian terms, FMPs tend to underweight the base rates and overweight the new information—resulting in revised beliefs about probabilities and outcomes that demonstrate an overreaction to the new information.

Base-Rate Neglect   In **base-rate neglect**, the base rate or probability of the categorization is not adequately considered. For example, an FMP attempting to determine the potential success of an investment in Company ABC might use a familiar, easy to understand classification scheme and categorize Company ABC as a "growth stock." This classification is based on some information about ABC that is consistent with the FMP's beliefs about growth companies, but it ignores the base probability that a company is a growth company. The FMP draws conclusions about ABC's risks and rewards based on that categorization. FMPs often follow this erroneous path because it is an easy alternative to the diligent research actually required when evaluating investments. To rephrase this error, some FMPs rely on *stereotypes* when making investment decisions without adequately incorporating the base probability of the stereotype occurring.

Sample-Size Neglect   A second type of representativeness bias is **sample-size neglect**. In sample-size neglect, FMPs incorrectly assume that small sample sizes are *representative* of populations (or "real" data). Some researchers call this phenomenon the "law of small numbers." This bias reflects erroneous beliefs about the laws of probability; they mistakenly believe that a small sample is representative of or similar in characteristics to the population. When people do not initially comprehend a trend or pattern reflected in a series of data, they may make assumptions relying on only a few data points. Individuals prone to sample-size neglect are quick to treat properties reflected in small samples as properties that accurately describe large pools of data. They overweight the information in the small sample.

EXAMPLE 2

Representativeness

APM Company is a large, 50-year old auto parts manufacturer having some business difficulties. It has previously been classified as a value stock. Jacques Verte is evaluating the future prospects of the company. Over the 50-year life of APM, there have been few failures of large auto parts manufacturers even given periods of difficulty. There have been a number of recent headlines about auto parts manufacturers having business and financial difficulty and potentially going out of business. He is considering two possibilities:

A APM will solve its difficulties, the company's performance will revert to the mean, and the stock will again be a value stock.

B APM will go out of business, and the stock will become valueless.

1 Is Scenario A or B more likely? Explain why.

2 If Verte is subject to representativeness bias, is he more likely to classify APM into A or B? Explain why.

Solution to 1:

Scenario A. It is more likely that APM will solve its difficulties, the company's performance will revert to the mean, and the stock will again be a value stock. The base rate, based on 50 years of data, is that more auto parts companies revert to the mean rather than go out of business.

Solution to 2:

Verte is likely to classify APM as B, predicting that it will go out of business because he read some headlines about other auto parts manufacturers going out of business. Verte, in classifying APM as likely to go out of business, may be guilty of both base-rate neglect and sample-size neglect. He has potentially ignored the base-rate information that far more auto parts manufacturers revert to the mean rather than go out of business, and he has assumed that the small sample of failing auto parts manufacturers is representative of all auto parts manufacturers.

Consequences of Representativeness Bias   A wide variety of FMP behaviors indicate susceptibility to the premise of the representativeness bias: FMPs often overweight new information and small samples because they view the information or sample as representative of the population as a whole. As a result of representativeness bias, FMPs may do the following:

- Adopt a view or a forecast based almost exclusively on new information or a small sample. For example, when evaluating investment managers, FMPs may place undue emphasis on high returns during a one-, two-, or three-year period, ignoring the base probability of such a return occurring. As a result, the investor may hire an investment manager without adequately considering the likelihood of such returns continuing. This situation may also result in high investment manager turnover as the investor changes investment managers based on short-term results.

- Update beliefs using simple classifications rather than deal with the mental stress of updating beliefs given complex data. This issue relates to an underlying difficulty (cognitive cost) in properly processing new information. For example, if an investor purchases a security based on the belief that the company is entering a period of significant earnings growth, and then the company announces that its growth rate may appear lower than expected because of a number of difficult-to-interpret accounting changes, the investor may simply reclassify the stock rather than attempt to decipher the fundamental impact, if any, reflected in the accounting changes. As a result, the investor may sell the security when fundamentals would not justify such a decision.

Detection of and Guidance on Overcoming Representativeness Bias   In both base-rate neglect and sample size neglect, investors ignore the laws of probability to satisfy their need for patterns. FMPs need to be aware of statistical mistakes they may be making and constantly ask themselves if they are overlooking the reality of the investment situation being considered.

For example, an FMP might conclude that a mutual fund manager possesses remarkable skill based on performance over a short time period, such as one, two, or three years. However, over a short time period, a manager's track record may benefit as much from luck as from skill. Several studies demonstrate this concept.

A study conducted by Vanguard Investments Australia (2004), later released by Morningstar, analyzes the five best-performing funds from 1994 to 2003. The results of the study are as follows:

- Only 16 percent of top five funds made it to the following year's list.
- Top five funds averaged 15 percent lower returns the following year.
- Top five funds barely beat the market the following year (by 0.3 percent).
- 21 percent of all top five funds ceased to exist within the following 10 years.

Barras, Scaillet, and Wermers (2010) evaluate the skill of active managers. Their study was intended to make general statements about the mutual fund industry rather than about any single mutual fund. They evaluate performance over the full set of mutual funds and separate them into three categories—skilled (generating positive alpha), unskilled (generating negative alpha), and zero-alpha. They add to previous research by explicitly accounting for skill and luck. Earlier empirical work either assumes no luck or full luck, thus producing biased conclusions about the prevalence of truly skilled and truly unskilled fund managers. Barras et al. conclude that 75.4 percent of the 2,076 funds analyzed were zero-alpha funds over their lifetimes. Of the remainder, only 0.6 percent were skilled and 24.0 percent were unskilled. In sum, Barras et al. conclude that the majority of actively managed domestic equity mutual funds have generated at most zero alpha after adjusting for luck, trading costs, and fees.

DALBAR's 2008 *Quantitative Analysis of Investor Behavior*[6] demonstrates that investors tend to buy into a fund immediately following rapid price appreciation. They seem to categorize the funds as good investments based on this recent information. These periods tend to precede a subsequent decline in the fund's performance. Then, when prices fall, FMPs sell their holdings and search for the next hot fund. Based on an analysis of actual investor behavior over the 20 years ended 31 December 2007, the average equity fund investor earned an annualized return of just 4.48 percent— underperforming the S&P 500 by more than 7 percent and outpacing inflation by a mere 1.44 percent. Fixed-income investors fared far worse, losing an average of 1.49 percent in purchasing power per year. Asset allocation fund investors did a bit better, beating inflation by 0.41 percent per year.[7]

These results are consistent with Bogle (2005). Bogle illustrates that returns earned by a group of investors must fall short of the reported market returns or mutual fund returns by the amount of the aggregate costs the investors incur. Thus, we can conclude that the additional costs of moving in and out of funds and lack of performance persistence will generally result in returns lower than those expected by investors. Moving in and out of investments based on categorizations that place undue reliance on recent performance and new information is likely to result in excessive trading and inferior performance results.

Prudent methods for identifying appropriate long-term investments exist. Use an asset allocation strategy to increase the likelihood of better long-term portfolio returns. Invest in a diversified portfolio to meet financial goals, and stick with it. The following questions should help FMPs avoid the futility of chasing returns and also help them select appropriate investments.

1 How does the fund under consideration perform relative to similarly sized and similarly styled funds?

2 What is the tenure of the managers and advisers at the fund?

3 Are the managers well-known and/or highly regarded?

4 Has the fund consistently pursued its strategy, or has its style drifted during different market conditions?

To counteract the effects of the representativeness bias when considering returns, many practitioners use what has become known as the "periodic table of investment returns," as shown in Exhibit 2.

---

6 DALBAR has conducted its annual *Quantitative Analysis of Investor Behavior* since 1994. The analysis measures the effect of investor decisions to transact into and out of mutual funds on returns. The results consistently show that the average investor earns less than indicated on mutual fund performance reports. www.QAIB.com

7 Average stock investor, average bond investor, and average asset allocation investor performance results are calculated using data supplied by the Investment Company Institute. Investor returns are represented by the change in total mutual fund assets after excluding sales, redemptions, and exchanges. This method of calculation captures realized and unrealized capital gains, dividends, interest, trading costs, sales charges, fees, expenses, and any other costs. After calculating investor returns in dollar terms, two percentages are calculated for the period examined: total investor return rate and annualized investor return rate. Total return rate is determined by calculating the investor return dollars as a percentage of the net of the sales, redemptions, and exchanges for the period.

Exhibit 2	Sample of a Periodic Table of Investment Returns									
	1999	**2000**	**2001**	**2002**	**2003**	**2004**	**2005**	**2006**	**2007**	**2008**
Highest Return	Emer. Mkts 66%	Commodity 32%	Small Value 14%	Commodity 26%	Int'l Small 58%	Real Estate 33%	Emer. Mkts 35%	Real Estate 36%	Emer. Mkts 40%	Fixed Inc. −3%
	Int'l Large 27%	Real Estate 31%	Real Estate 12%	Fixed Inc. 10%	Emer. Mkts 56%	Int'l Small 28%	Int'l Small 24%	Emer. Mkts 32%	Commodity 15%	Small Value −29%
	Commodity 24%	Small Value 23%	Fixed Inc. 10%	Real Estate 4%	Small Cap 47%	Emer. Mkts 26%	Commodity 21%	Int'l Large 27%	Int'l Large 12%	Small Cap −34%
	Small Cap 21%	Fixed Inc. 9%	Small Cap 2%	Emer. Mkts −6%	Small Value 46%	Small Value 22%	Int'l Large 14%	Small Value 23%	Fixed Inc. 6%	Commodity −36%
	S&P 500 21%	Large Value 7%	Emer. Mkts −2%	Diversified −6%	Int'l Large 39%	Int'l Large 21%	Diversified 13%	Large Value 22%	S&P 500 5%	Diversified −36%
	Diversified 18%	Diversified 4%	Diversified −4%	Int'l Small −10%	Diversified 37%	Diversified 19%	Real Estate 13%	Diversified 20%	Diversified 5%	Large Value −37%
	Int'l Small 18%	Small Cap −3%	Large Value −6%	Small Value −11%	Real Estate 36%	Small Cap 18%	Large Value 7%	Small Cap 18%	Int'l Small 2%	S&P 500 −37%
	Large Value 7%	Int'l Small −9%	S&P 500 −12%	Int'l Large −16%	Large Value 30%	Large Value 16%	S&P 500 5%	Int'l Small 17%	Large Value 0%	Real Estate −39%
	Fixed Inc. 0%	S&P 500 −9%	Int'l Small −14%	Large Value −16%	S&P 500 29%	S&P 500 11%	Small Cap 5%	S&P 500 16%	Small Cap −2%	Int'l Large −43%
	Small Value −1%	Int'l Large −14%	Commodity −20%	Small Cap −20%	Commodity 24%	Commodity 9%	Small Value 5%	Fixed Inc. 4%	Small Value −10%	Int'l Small −47%
Lowest Return	Real Estate −3%	Emer. Mkts −31%	Int'l Large −21%	S&P 500 −22%	Fixed Inc. 7%	Fixed Inc. 4%	Fixed Inc. 1%	Commodity 2%	Real Estate −18%	Emer. Mkts −53%

Source: Dimensional Fund Advisors and Thomson Financial.

Exhibit 2 shows that asset class returns are highly variable. Many FMPs fail to heed the advice offered by the chart—namely, that it is nearly impossible to accurately predict which asset class will be the best performer from one year to the next. Thus, diversification is prudent (note how the diversified portfolio consistently appears near the center of each column). Practitioners would be wise to present this chart when establishing asset allocations with new clients to emphasize the advantages of diversification over return chasing.

When FMPs sense that base-rate or sample-size neglect may be a problem, they should ask the following question: "What is the probability that X (the investment under consideration) belongs to Group A (the group it resembles or is considered representative of) versus Group B (the group it is statistically more likely to belong to)?" This question, or a similar question, will help FMPs think through whether they are failing to consider base-rate probabilities or neglecting the law of small numbers and thus inaccurately assessing a particular situation. It may be necessary to do more research to determine if a statistical error has indeed been made. In the end, this process should improve investment decisions.

3.1.4 Illusion of Control Bias

Illusion of control bias is a bias in which people tend to believe that they can control or influence outcomes when, in fact, they cannot. Langer (1983) defines the illusion of control bias as the "expectancy of a personal success probability inappropriately higher than the objective probability would warrant." Langer finds that choices, task familiarity, competition, and active involvement can all inflate confidence and generate such illusions. For example, Langer observed that people permitted to select their own numbers in a hypothetical lottery game were willing to pay a higher price per ticket than subjects gambling on randomly assigned numbers. Since this initial study, many other researchers have uncovered similar situations, where people perceived themselves as possessing more control than they did, inferred causal connections where none existed, or displayed surprisingly great certainty in their predictions for the outcomes of chance events.

Consequences of Illusion of Control As a result of illusion of control bias, FMPs may do the following:

- Trade more than is prudent. Researchers have found that traders, especially online traders, believe that they have "control" over the outcomes of their investments. This view leads to excessive trading, which may lead to lower realized returns than a strategy where securities are held longer and traded less frequently.

- Lead investors to inadequately diversify portfolios. Researchers have found that some investors prefer to invest in companies that they may feel they have some control over, like the companies they work for, leading them to hold concentrated positions. In fact, most investors have almost no control over the companies they work for. If the company performs poorly, the investor may experience both the loss of employment and investment losses.

Detection of and Guidelines for Overcoming Illusion of Control Bias There are some useful guidelines to help investors detect and overcome illusion of control bias. The first and most basic idea is that investors need to recognize that successful investing is a probabilistic activity. The first step on the road to understanding illusion of control bias is to be aware that global capitalism is highly complex, and even the most powerful investors have little control over the outcomes of the investments they make.

Second, it is advisable to seek contrary viewpoints. As you contemplate a new investment, take a moment to ponder any considerations that might weigh against the trade. Ask yourself: Why am I making this investment? Is this investment part of an overall plan? What are the downside risks? What might go wrong? When will I sell? These important questions can help you logically evaluate an investment decision before implementation.

Finally, it is critical to keep records. Once you have decided to move forward with an investment, an effective way to prevent illusions of control is to maintain records of your transactions, including reminders outlining the rationale behind each trade. Write down some of the important features of each investment that you make, and emphasize those attributes that you have determined to be in favor of the investment's success.

Rationally, we know that returns on long-term investments are not impacted by the short-term beliefs, emotions, and impulses that often surround financial transactions. Success, or the lack thereof, is usually a result of such uncontrollable factors as corporate performance or general economic conditions. During periods of market turmoil, it can be difficult to keep this fact in mind. One of the best ways to prevent your biases from affecting your decisions is to keep the rational side of your brain as engaged as possible. Investing success is ultimately achieved by those who can conquer the daily psychological challenges and maintain a long-term perspective.

3.1.5 Hindsight Bias

Hindsight bias is a bias with selective perception and retention aspects. People may see past events as having been predictable and reasonable to expect. This behavior is based on the obvious fact that outcomes that did occur are more readily evident than outcomes that did not occur. Also, people tend to remember their own predictions of the future as more accurate than they actually were because they are biased by the knowledge of what has actually happened. To alleviate the discomfort associated with the unexpected, people tend to view things that have already happened as being relatively inevitable and predictable. This view is often caused by the reconstructive nature of memory. When people look back, they do not have perfect memory; they tend to "fill in the gaps" with what they prefer to believe. In doing so, people may prevent themselves from learning from the past.

In a classic example of hindsight bias, Fischhoff (1975) describes an experiment in which he asked subjects to answer general knowledge questions from almanacs and encyclopedias. Next, he gave his subjects the correct answers and asked them to recall their original ones. Fischhoff found that, in general, people overestimate the quality of their initial knowledge and forget their initial errors. Hindsight bias is a serious problem for historically minded market followers. Once an event is part of history, there is a tendency to see the sequence that led to it as inevitable, as if uncertainty and chance were banished. As Posner (1998) notes, outcomes exert irresistible pressure on their interpretations. In hindsight, poorly reasoned decisions with positive results may be described as brilliant tactical moves, and poor results of well-reasoned decisions may be described as avoidable mistakes.

Consequences of Hindsight Bias   As a result of hindsight bias, FMPs may do the following:

■ Overestimate the degree to which they predicted an investment outcome, thus giving them a false sense of confidence. For example, when an investment appreciates for unforeseen reasons, FMPs may rewrite their own memories to reflect those reasons. The hindsight bias may cause FMPs to take on excessive risk, leading to future investment mistakes.

■ Cause FMPs to unfairly assess money manager or security performance. Based on their ability to look back at what has taken place in securities markets, performance is compared against what has happened as opposed to expectations. For example, a given manager may have followed his or her strategy faithfully, and possibly even ranked near the top of the relevant peer group, but the investment results may be disappointing compared to another segment of the market or the market as a whole.

Detection of and Guidelines for Overcoming Hindsight Bias   Once understood, hindsight bias should be recognizable. FMPs need to be aware of the possibility of hindsight bias and ask such questions as, "Am I re-writing history or being honest with myself about the mistakes I made?" Achieving success with investments requires investors to recognize and come to terms with mistakes. This approach is contrary to human nature. However, understanding how markets work and why investments go wrong is critical to achieving investment success.

To guard against hindsight bias, FMPs need to carefully record and examine their investment decisions, both good and bad, to avoid repeating past investment mistakes. In addition, FMPs should constantly remind themselves that markets move in cycles and that good managers stay true to their strategies through good times and bad. Expectations must be managed; there will inevitably be periods when even good managers underperform the broader market. Education is critical here. It is important that all investment managers be evaluated relative to appropriate benchmarks and peer groups.

3.2 Information-Processing Biases

The second category of cognitive errors includes information-processing errors or biases. Information-processing biases result in information being processed and used illogically or irrationally. As opposed to belief perseverance biases, these are less related to errors of memory or in assigning and updating probabilities and more to do with how information is processed.

3.2.1 Anchoring and Adjustment Bias

Anchoring and adjustment bias is an information-processing bias in which the use of a psychological heuristic influences the way people estimate probabilities. When required to estimate a value with unknown magnitude, people generally begin by envisioning some initial default number—an "anchor"—which they then adjust up or down to reflect subsequent information and analysis. Regardless of how the initial anchor was chosen, people tend to adjust their anchors insufficiently and produce end approximations that are, consequently, biased. This bias is closely related to the conservatism bias. In the conservatism bias, people overweight past information compared to new information. In anchoring and adjustment, people place undue weight on the anchor. People anchor and adjust because they are generally better at estimating relative comparisons than absolute figures.

For example, FMPs exhibiting this bias are often influenced by purchase "points," or arbitrary price levels or price indexes, and tend to cling to these numbers when facing questions like, "Should I buy or sell this security?" or "Is the market overvalued or undervalued right now?" This approach is especially prevalent when the introduction of new information regarding the security further complicates the situation. Rational investors treat these new pieces of information objectively, and they do not reflect upon purchase prices or target prices in deciding how to act. Investors with an anchoring and adjustment bias, however, perceive new information through a warped lens. They place undue emphasis on statistically arbitrary, psychologically determined anchor points. Decision making therefore deviates from neo-classically prescribed "rational" norms. Readers interested in academic research on anchoring and adjustment behavior should see Slovic and Lichtenstein (1971), Joyce and Biddle (1981), and Butler (1986), among other studies.

Consequences of Anchoring and Adjustment Bias As a result of anchoring and adjustment bias, FMPs may stick too closely to their original estimates when new information is learned. For example, if the FMP originally estimates next year's earnings for a company as $2.00 per share and the company experiences difficulties during the year, FMPs may not adequately adjust the $2.00 estimate given the difficulties. They remain "anchored" to the $2.00 estimate. This mindset is not limited to downside adjustments; the same phenomenon occurs when companies have upside surprises. In another example, FMPs may become anchored to the "economic states" of countries or companies. In the 1980s, Japan was viewed as a model economy, and many FMPs believed it would remain dominant for decades. It took many FMPs a significant period to revise their beliefs about Japan when its growth slowed. FMPs can similarly anchor on beliefs about companies.

Detection of and Guidelines for Overcoming Anchoring and Adjustment Bias The primary action FMPs can take is to consciously ask questions that may reveal an anchoring and adjustment bias. Examples of such questions include, "Am I holding onto this stock based on rational analysis, or am I trying to attain a price that I am anchored to, such as the purchase price or a high water mark?" and "Am I making this market or security forecast based on rational analysis, or am I anchored to last year's market levels or ending securities prices?"

It is important to remember that past prices, market levels, and reputation provide little information about an investment's future potential and thus should not influence buy-and-sell decisions to any great extent. This advice is particularly relevant when analyzing the recommendations of securities' analysts. FMPs should look at the basis for any recommendations to see whether they are anchored to previous estimates or based on an objective, rational view of changes in company fundamentals.

3.2.2 *Mental Accounting Bias*

Mental accounting bias is an information-processing bias in which people treat one sum of money differently from another equal-sized sum based on which mental account the money is assigned to. Richard Thaler (1980) describes mental accounting as a process in which people code, categorize, and evaluate economic outcomes by grouping their assets into any number of non-fungible (non-interchangeable) mental accounts. This method contradicts rational economic thought because money is inherently fungible. Mental accounts are based on such arbitrary classifications as the source of the money (e.g., salary, bonus, inheritance, gambling) or the planned use of the money (e.g., leisure, necessities). According to traditional finance theory, FMPs should consider portfolios holistically in a risk/return context.

Consequences of Mental Accounting Bias   A potentially serious problem that mental accounting creates is the placement of investments into discrete "buckets" without regard for the correlations among these assets. Meir Statman (1999) contends that the difficulty individuals have in addressing the interaction of different investments leads investors to construct portfolios in a layered pyramid format. Statman (2008) also notes that behavioral portfolio theory is a goal-based theory. Each layer of the portfolio addresses a particular investment goal (such as money for retirement) that is independent of other investment goals (such as college funds). Investors may target such low-risk investments as cash and money market funds to preserve wealth, bonds and dividend-paying stocks to provide income, and such risky investments as emerging market stocks and initial public offerings (IPOs) in an attempt to get rich.

As a result of mental accounting bias, FMPs may do the following:

- Neglect opportunities to reduce risk by combining assets with low correlations. Inefficient investing may result from offsetting positions in the various layers (Shefrin and Statman 1984). This approach can lead to suboptimal aggregate portfolio performance (Kroll, Levy, and Rapoport 1988).

- Irrationally distinguish between returns derived from income and those derived from capital appreciation. Although many people feel the need to preserve capital appreciation (principal), they focus on the idea of spending income that the principal generates. As a result, many FMPs chase income streams, unwittingly eroding principal in the process. Consider a high-yield or "junk" bond that pays a high dividend but can suffer significant loss of principal if the company issuing the bond experiences financial difficulties. Mental accounting can make such instruments appear tremendously appealing, but it is also possible that the original investment could shrink, ultimately reducing or even eliminating income payments.

Detection of and Guidelines for Overcoming Mental Accounting Bias   An effective way to detect and overcome mental accounting behavior that causes investors to place money in discrete investment "buckets" is to recognize the drawbacks of engaging in this behavior. The primary drawback is that correlations between investments are not taken into account when creating an overall portfolio. FMPs should go through the exercise of combining all of their assets onto one spreadsheet or other summary document to see the true asset allocation of various mental account holdings. This exercise often produces information that is surprising when seen as whole, such as higher cash balances than expected. Going through this process will show the suboptimal nature of the portfolio constructed using mental accounting. The logical next step would be to create a portfolio strategy taking all assets into consideration.

With regard to the income versus total return issue, an effective way to manage the tendency of some FMPs to treat investment income and capital appreciation differently is to focus on total return. FMPs should learn the benefits of integrating the two sources of return, allocating sufficient assets to lower income investments to allow principal to continue to grow even after inflation.

3.2.3 *Framing Bias*

Framing bias is an information-processing bias in which a person answers a question differently based on the way in which it is asked (framed). How information is processed is dependent upon how the question is framed. In actual choice contexts, a decision maker has flexibility in how to think about a problem. A decision frame is the decision maker's subjective conception of the acts, outcomes, and contingencies associated with a particular choice. The frame that a decision maker adopts is controlled partly by the formulation of the problem and partly by the norms, habits, and personal characteristics of the decision maker. It is often possible to frame a given decision problem in more than one way.

A framing effect results in a change of preferences between options as a function of the variation of frames, perhaps through variation of the formulation of the decision context. For example, a decision may be presented within a *gain* context (25 percent of the people with disease X given medicine Z will survive) or within a *loss* context (75 percent of the people with disease X will die even if given medicine Z). In the first presentation, people with disease X tend to adopt a positive outlook based on a gain frame of reference and are generally less likely to engage in risky behavior; they are risk-averse because they view themselves as having a potential to gain (survive in this case). In the second presentation, people with disease X tend to adopt a negative outlook based on a loss frame of reference; they may seek risk because they view themselves as having nothing to lose (likely to die in this case).

Narrow framing occurs when people evaluate the information to make a decision based on a *narrow frame* of reference. People lose sight of the big picture and focus on one or two specific points. For example, a consumer considering an automobile purchase might focus on style or design but overlook safety features, fuel economy, and reliability. FMPs may exhibit similar behaviors when choosing securities.

EXAMPLE 3

Effect of Framing

Decision-making frames are quite prevalent in the context of investor behavior. Risk tolerance questionnaires can demonstrate how framing bias may occur in practice and how FMPs should be aware of its effects.

Suppose an investor is to take a risk tolerance questionnaire for the purpose of determining which "risk category" he or she is in. The risk category will determine asset allocations and the appropriate types of investments. The following information is provided to each questionnaire taker:

> Over a 10-year period, Portfolio ABC has averaged an annual return of 10 percent with an annual standard deviation of 16 percent. Assuming a normal return distribution, in a given year there is a 67 percent probability that the return will fall within one standard deviation of the mean, a 95 percent probability that the return will fall within two standard deviations of the mean, and a 99.7 percent probability that the return will fall within three standard deviations of the mean. Thus, there is a 67 percent chance that the return earned by Portfolio ABC will be between –6 percent and 26 percent, a 95 percent chance

that the return will be between −22 percent and 42 percent, and a 99.7 percent chance that the return will be between −38 percent and 58 percent.

The following two questions focus on hypothetical Portfolio ABC, DEF, and XYZ. The risk and return for each portfolio is the same in each of the two questions, but the presentation of information differs. Will an investor choose the same portfolio or different portfolios when asked Question 1 compared to Question 2? Explain your answer.

1   Based on the chart below, which investment portfolio fits your risk tolerance and desire for long-term return?

   A   Portfolio XYZ.

   B   Portfolio DEF.

   C   Portfolio ABC.

Portfolio	95% Probability Return Range	10-Year Average Return
XYZ	0.5% to 6.5%	3.5%
DEF	−18.0% to 30.0%	6.0%
ABC	−22.0% to 42.0%	10.0%

2   Based on the chart below, which investment portfolio fits your risk tolerance and desire for long-term return?

   A   Portfolio XYZ.

   B   Portfolio DEF.

   C   Portfolio ABC.

Portfolio	10-Year Average Return	Standard Deviation of Returns
XYZ	3.5%	1.5%
DEF	6%	12%
ABC	10%	16%

Solution:

An investor may choose different portfolios when asked Question 1 compared to Question 2. Portfolio XYZ may appear more attractive in the first question, where two standard deviations are used to define the range of returns and show the risk, than in the second, where only the standard deviations are shown. Also in the second question, the returns are presented first and the measure of risk second. Thus, how questions are framed and the order in which questions are presented can have a significant impact on how they are answered. FMPs should be acutely aware of how framing can affect investment choices.

Consequences of Framing Bias   FMPs' willingness to accept risk can be influenced by how situations are presented or framed. Similar to what we saw in the standard deviation example previously presented, a common framing problem occurs when investment questions are posed positively or negatively. For example, suppose Mrs. Ang has a choice of Portfolio A or Portfolio B, which are identical in terms of expected risk and return. Mrs. Ang is told that Portfolio A offers a 70 percent chance of attaining her financial goals, and Portfolio B offers a 30 percent chance of falling short of her financial goals. Mrs. Ang is likely to choose Portfolio A because of the positive way the question was framed.

As a result of framing bias, FMPs may do the following:

- Misidentify risk tolerances because of how questions about risk tolerance were framed; may become more risk-averse when presented with a gain frame of reference and more risk-seeking when presented with a loss frame of reference. This may result in suboptimal portfolios.

- Choose suboptimal investments, even with properly identified risk tolerances, based on how information about the specific investments is framed.

- Focus on short-term price fluctuations, which may result in excessive trading.

Detection of and Guidelines for Overcoming Framing Bias   Framing bias is detected by asking such questions as, "Is the decision the result of focusing on a net gain or net loss position?" As discussed above, an investor who has framed the decision as a potential net loss is more likely to select a riskier investment; however, if the decision is framed as a potential net gain, the investor is more likely to go with a less risky investment. When making decisions, FMPs should try to eliminate any reference to gains and losses already incurred; instead, they should focus on the future prospects of an investment.

Regarding susceptibility to the positive and negative presentation of information, investors should try to be as neutral and open-minded as possible when interpreting investment-related situations. This approach can eliminate biased responses, help FMPs create better portfolios, and give FMPs a better chance of meeting long-term financial objectives.

3.2.4 *Availability Bias*

Availability bias is an information-processing bias in which people take a heuristic (sometimes called a rule of thumb or a mental shortcut) approach to estimating the probability of an outcome based on how easily the outcome comes to mind. Easily recalled outcomes are often perceived as being more likely than those that are harder to recall or understand. People often unconsciously assume that readily available thoughts, ideas, or images represent unbiased estimates of statistical probabilities. People decide the probability of an event by how easily they can recall a memory of the event. The basic problem is that there are biases in our memories. For instance, recent events are much more easily remembered and available.

There are various sources of availability bias. We will examine the four most applicable to FMPs: retrievability, categorization, narrow range of experience, and resonance. Each of these categories will be described, and then we will review examples of each as applied to FMPs.

Retrievability   If an answer or idea comes to mind more quickly than another answer or idea, the first answer or idea will likely be chosen as correct even if it is not the reality. For example, Tversky and Kahneman (1973) performed an experiment in which subjects listened to a list of names and were then asked to judge if the list contained more men or women. In reality, the list contained more women than men, but the list of men included famous names. As availability theory would predict, most of the subjects concluded that the list contained more men than women because they immediately recalled the names of the famous men.

Categorization   When solving problems, people gather information from what they perceive as relevant search sets. Different problems require different search sets, which are often based on familiar categorizations. If it is difficult to come up with a search set, the estimated probability of an event may be biased. For example, if an American is asked to come up with a list of famous baseball players and a list of famous soccer players, the list of soccer players is likely to be quite short. This assignment might lead the American to erroneously conclude that there are fewer famous soccer players than baseball players.

Narrow Range of Experience   This bias occurs when a person with a narrow range of experience uses too narrow a frame of reference based upon that experience when making an estimate. For example, assume that a CFA charterholder goes to work for a hedge fund. Because this person encounters other CFA charterholders every day at her own and other hedge funds, she is likely to overestimate the proportion of CFA charterholders who work for hedge funds. She is also likely to underestimate the proportion of CFA charterholders who work in other areas, such as private wealth management, because that is not within her frame of reference. In reality, a small percentage of CFA charterholders work for hedge funds.

Resonance   People are often biased by how closely a situation parallels their own personal situation. For example, jazz music lovers are likely to overestimate how many people listen to jazz music. On the other hand, people who dislike jazz music are likely to overestimate the number of people who dislike jazz music.

Clearly, overlap exists between the sources of availability bias. For instance, a person's range of experience will affect his search sets, what information is retrieved, and what resonates with him. The critical aspect is not to be able to identify the specific source of bias, but rather to know the sources of bias in order to detect and overcome the availability bias. The questions to ask can be much more specific and helpful when based on the sources of availability bias rather than on the more general definition of availability bias.

Consequences of Availability Bias   FMPs' investment choices may be influenced by how easily information is recalled. As a result of availability bias, FMPs may do the following:

- Choose an investment, investment adviser, or mutual fund based on advertising rather than on a thorough analysis of the options. For instance, when asked to name potential mutual fund companies to invest with, many people will name only the funds that do extensive advertising. In reality, many mutual fund companies do little or no advertising. The choice of mutual fund should be based on a variety of factors that make it a good fit given the investor's objectives and risk/return profile. Choices based on advertising are consistent with retrievability as a source of availability bias.

- Limit their investment opportunity set. This may be because they use familiar classification schemes. They may restrict investments to stocks and bonds of one country or may fail to consider alternative investments when appropriate.

- Fail to diversify. This may be because they make their choices based on a narrow range of experience. For example, an investor who works for a fast-growing company in a particular industry may overweight investments in that industry.

- Fail to achieve an appropriate asset allocation. This consequence may occur because they invest in companies that match their own personal likes and dislikes without properly taking into account risk and return.

Detection of and Guidelines for Overcoming Availability Bias   To overcome availability bias, investors need to develop an appropriate investment policy strategy, carefully research and analyze investment decisions before making them, and focus on long-term results. A disciplined approach will prevent the investor from overemphasizing the most recent financial events based on easy recall. It will also help establish suitable asset allocations based on return objectives, risk tolerances, and constraints. It should also help assure that the portfolio of investments is adequately diversified and not affected by the availability bias from any source. FMPs need to recognize that it is a human tendency to overemphasize the most recent financial events because of easy recall.

When selecting stocks, it is crucial to consider your availability bias. Such questions as, "Did you hear about the stocks on Bloomberg, read about them in the *Wall Street Journal*, see them on CNBC, or receive a sell-side research report?" and "Am I buying or selling a group of investments because of some recent market event or trend without doing adequate analysis?" focus on retrievability. A valuable study done by Gadarowski (2001) found that stocks with the highest press coverage underperformed in the subsequent two years.

Such additional questions as, "How did you decide which investments to consider? Did you choose investments based on your familiarity with the industry or country?" and "Did you choose your investments because you like the companies' products?" help identify issues of categorization, narrow range of experience, and resonance as sources of availability bias.

It is also important to realize that humans generally disregard or forget about events that happened more than a few years ago. For example, if you were in a car accident last week, it would be natural for you to drive more cautiously than you normally would for a period of time. However, as time passed, you would likely resume your normal driving behavior. Availability bias causes investors to *overreact* to market conditions, whether positive or negative. An excellent illustration is the technology bubble in the late 1990s. Investors got caught up in technology mania, causing them to disregard the risks. It is natural for people to be influenced by current events.

Another problem is that much of the information we receive is inaccurate, outdated, or confusing. The information may be based on opinions that are not based on sound analysis. Availability bias causes people to think that events that receive heavy media attention are more important than they may actually be. Many FMPs ignore the fact that they lack the training, experience, and objectivity to interpret the massive amount of investment information available.

3.3 Cognitive Errors: Conclusion

Cognitive errors are statistical, information-processing, or memory errors that result in faulty reasoning and analysis. The individual may be attempting to follow a rational decision-making process but fail to do so because of cognitive errors. For example, the person may fail to update probabilities correctly, properly weigh and consider information, or gather information. If these errors are drawn to the attention of an individual attempting to follow a rational decision-making process, he or she is likely to be receptive to correcting the errors.

Individuals are less likely to make cognitive errors if they remain vigilant to the possibility of their occurrence. A systematic process to describe problems and objectives; to gather, record, and synthesize information; to document decisions and the reasoning behind them; and to compare the actual outcomes with expected results will help reduce cognitive errors.

EMOTIONAL BIASES

4

We will now review six emotional biases, their implications for investment decision making, and suggestions for managing the effects of these biases. Although emotion has no single universally accepted definition, an emotion may be thought of as a mental state that arises spontaneously rather than through conscious effort. Emotions may be undesired to the individuals feeling them; although they may wish to control the emotion and their response to it, they often cannot. Emotional biases are harder to correct for than cognitive errors because they originate from impulse or intuition rather than conscious calculations. In the case of emotional biases, it may only be possible to recognize the bias and adapt to it rather than correct for it.

Emotional biases can cause investors to make suboptimal decisions. Because emotions are rarely identified and recorded in the decision-making process—they have to do with how people feel rather than what and how they think—fewer emotional biases have been identified. The six emotional biases discussed are loss aversion, overconfidence, self-control, status quo, endowment, and regret aversion. In the discussion of each of these biases, some related biases may also be discussed.

4.1 Loss-Aversion Bias

Loss-aversion bias was identified by Daniel Kahneman and Amos Tversky in 1979 while they were working on developing prospect theory.[8] In prospect theory, loss-aversion bias is a bias in which people tend to strongly prefer avoiding losses as opposed to achieving gains. A number of studies on loss aversion suggest that, psychologically, losses are significantly more powerful than gains. When comparing absolute values, the utility derived from a gain is much lower than the utility given up with an equivalent loss.

Rational FMPs should accept more risk to increase gains, not to mitigate losses. However, paradoxically, FMPs tend to accept more risk to avoid losses than to achieve gains. Loss aversion leads people to hold their losers even if an investment has little or no chance of going back up. Similarly, loss-aversion bias leads to risk avoidance when people evaluate a potential gain. Given the possibility of giving back gains already realized, FMPs lock in profits, thus limiting their upside profits.

Kahneman and Tversky describe loss-averse investor behavior as the evaluation of gains and losses based on a reference point. A value function that passes through this reference point is seen in Exhibit 3. It is s-shaped and asymmetric, implying a greater impact of losses than of gains for the same variation in absolute value. This utility function implies risk-seeking behavior in the domain of losses (below the horizontal axis) and risk avoidance in the domain of gains (above the horizontal axis). An important concept embedded in this utility representation is what Shefrin and Statman (1985) coined the *disposition effect*: the holding (not selling) of investments that have experienced losses (losers) too long, and the selling (not holding) of investments that have experienced gains (winners) too quickly. The resulting portfolio may be riskier than the optimal portfolio based on the risk/return objectives of the investor.

---

8 Kahneman and Tversky (1979).

Exhibit 3   Value Function of Loss Aversion

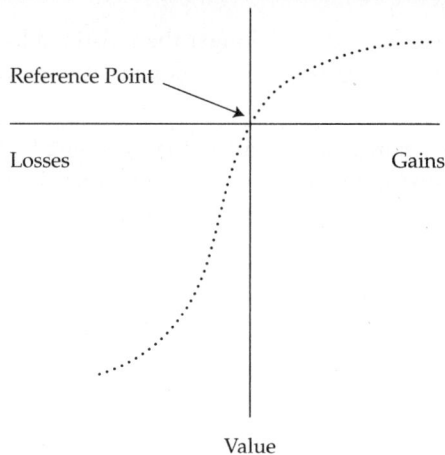

EXAMPLE 4

Effect of Loss-Aversion Bias

Loss-aversion bias, executed in practice as the *disposition effect*, is observed often by wealth management practitioners. The classic case of this bias is when an investor opens the monthly account statement and scans the individual investments for winners and losers. Seeing that some investments have lost money and others have gained, discuss how the investor is likely to respond given a loss-aversion bias.

Sample Solution:

The investor is likely to respond by continuing to hold the losing investments. The idea of actually losing money is so painful that the first reaction is to hold the investment until it breaks even. The investor is acting based on emotions, not cognitive reasoning. In this case, if the investor did some research, he or she might learn that the company in question is experiencing difficulty and that holding the investment actually adds to the risk in the portfolio (hence the term risk-seeking in the domain of losses).

Conversely, the winners are making money. Loss-averse FMPs have a tendency to sell these investments and realize their gains to avoid any further risk. In this case, if the investor did some research, he or she might learn that the company in question actually improves the risk/return profile of the portfolio. By selling the investment, not only is the potential for future losses eliminated, but the potential for future gains is also eliminated. Combining the added risk of holding the losers with the elimination of potential gains from selling the winners may make investors' portfolios less efficient than portfolios based on fundamental analysis.

Consequences of Loss Aversion   As a result of loss-aversion bias, FMPs may do the following:

- Hold investments in a loss position longer than justified by fundamental analysis. FMPs hold losing investments in the hope that they will return to break even.

- Sell investments in a gain position earlier than justified by fundamental analysis. FMPs sell winning investments because they fear that their profit will erode.

- Limit the upside potential of a portfolio by selling winners and holding losers.

- Trade excessively as a result of selling winners. Excessive trading has been shown to lower investment returns.

- Hold riskier portfolios than is acceptable based on the risk/return objectives of the FMP. This is caused by the sale of investments that are winners and the retention of investments that are losers. FMPs may accept more risk in their portfolios than they would if they had based their decision on risk/return objectives and fundamental analysis.

Further, framing and loss-aversion biases may affect the FMP simultaneously, and is a potentially dangerous combination. When people have suffered losses, they may view risky alternatives as a source of opportunity; when people have gained, they may view choices involving additional risk as a threat. For example, an investor who has a net loss is more likely than average to choose the riskier investment, while a net gainer is more likely to go with a less risky alternative.[9] A caveat to this basic principle is that once money is made through a profitable trade, some investors may view the profit differently from other money and decide to engage in additional risky behavior with it. Richard H. Thaler of the University of Chicago refers to this as the "house money effect," which is based on the willingness of gamblers to engage in increasingly risky gambles with previous winnings. The gamblers view themselves as risking someone else's money; in the case of the gambler, it is the casino or house's money they view as at risk.[10]

Special Application: Myopic Loss Aversion   As a possible explanation for the *equity premium puzzle*, a phenomenon that describes the anomalously higher historical real returns of stocks over government bonds, Benartzi and Thaler (1995) conceived *myopic loss aversion*. This combines aspects of time horizon-based framing, mental accounting, and loss-aversion biases. Investors presented with annual return data for stocks and bonds tend to adopt more conservative strategies (lower allocation to equities) than those presented with longer-term return data, such as 30-year compound returns. Investors place stocks and bonds into separate mental accounts rather than thinking of them together in a portfolio context; they seem to be more concerned with the potential for short-term losses than with planning for the relevant time horizon and focusing on long-term results. Benartzi and Thaler use the term *myopic loss aversion* in reference to this behavior. They argue that investors evaluate their portfolios on an annual basis and as a result overemphasize short-term gains and losses and weigh losses more heavily than gains. The overemphasis on short-term losses results in a higher than theoretically justified equity risk premium.

Paul A. Samuelson (1963) presented an example that is illustrative of myopic loss aversion (this was written before the term myopic loss aversion had been introduced). Samuelson offered a colleague the following bet: Flip a coin; if it comes up heads you

---

9 Depending on the incentive structure, an investment manager may be especially prone to this. In essence, having experienced losses, the investment manager may having nothing further to lose by choosing risky investments; or having experienced gains, the investment manager may be motivated to lock in those gains.
10 Thaler and Johnson (1990).

win $200, and if it comes up tails you pay or lose $100. The distribution of outcomes of this bet can be shown as {$200, 0.50; –$100, 0.50}. Samuelson reports that his colleague turned this bet down but said that he would be happy to take 100 such bets. Samuelson then proved that this pair of choices is irrational. That is, someone should not be willing to play a bet many times if he is not willing to play it just once. Of more interest is the explanation offered by the colleague for turning down the bet: "I won't bet because I would feel the $100 loss more than the $200 gain." This view is consistent with loss aversion. A simple utility function that would capture this notion is the following:

(1) $U(x) = x$, when $x \geq 0$ and

$U(x) = 2.5x$, when $x < 0$,

where x is a change in wealth relative to the status quo.

With this loss-averse utility function, the utility of a single play of the gamble is negative (less than the status quo of not playing). The expected utility is -25 [$= 0.5(200) + 0.5(2.5(-100))$]. However, with two plays, you have a 25 percent chance of winning $400, a 50 percent chance of winning $100, and a 25 percent chance of losing $200. The distribution of outcomes created by the portfolio of two bets {$400, 0.25; $100, 0.50; –$200, 0.25} yields a positive expected utility of 25 [$= 0.25(400) + 0.5(100) + 0.25(2.5(-200))$]. Whether a decision maker accepts taking the gamble twice depends on mental accounting. A myopic decision maker will first determine whether he likes the prospect of the initial gamble in the series, will conclude that he does not, and consequently will reject the entire series. Samuelson's friend was evidently loss averse, but he was not myopic because he was willing to accept the series. He did not focus on the short term but considered the long term.

The argument developed by Benartzi and Thaler (1995) is that the price of financial assets reflects the preferences of FMPs who are both loss averse and myopic. To appreciate the effect of myopia on risk attitudes, consider an investor with the utility function defined above who must choose between a risky asset that pays an expected 7 percent per year with a standard deviation of 20 percent (like stocks) and a safe asset that pays a sure 1 percent per year. According to the logic we applied to Samuelson's colleague, the attractiveness of the risky asset depends on the time horizon of the investor. An investor who is prepared to wait a long time before evaluating the outcome of the investment as a gain or a loss will find the risky asset more attractive than another investor (equally loss averse, but more myopic), who expects to evaluate the outcome soon. Furthermore, FMPs who differ in the frequency with which they evaluate outcomes will not derive the same utility from owning stocks. The probability of observing a loss is higher when the frequency of evaluation is high. If losses cause more mental anguish than equivalent gains cause pleasure, the experienced utility associated with owning stocks is lower for the more myopic investor (Kahneman, Wakker, and Sarin, 1997). Over time, the myopic investor is expected to gravitate to a lower level of risk.

Detection of and Guidelines for Overcoming Loss Aversion A disciplined approach to investment based on fundamental analysis is a good way to alleviate the impact of the loss-aversion bias. It is impossible to make experiencing losses any less painful emotionally, but analyzing investments and realistically considering the probabilities of future losses and gains may help guide the FMP to a rational decision.

4.2 Overconfidence Bias

Overconfidence bias is a bias in which people demonstrate unwarranted faith in their own intuitive reasoning, judgments, and/or cognitive abilities. This overconfidence may be the result of overestimating knowledge levels, abilities, and access to information.

For example, people generally do a poor job of estimating probabilities; still, they believe they do it well because they believe that they are smarter and more informed than they actually are. This view is sometimes referred to as the *illusion of knowledge bias*. Overconfidence may be intensified when combined with *self-attribution bias*. Self-attribution bias is a bias in which people take credit for successes and assign responsibility for failures. In other words, success is attributed to the individual's skill, while failures are attributed to external factors. Illusion of knowledge and self-attribution biases contribute to the overconfidence bias.

Overconfidence bias has aspects of both cognitive and emotional errors but is classified as emotional because the bias is primarily the result of emotion. It is difficult to correct for because it is difficult for people to revise self-perceptions of their knowledge and abilities. The concept of overconfidence has been derived from a large number of psychological experiments and surveys in which subjects overestimate both their own predictive abilities as well as the precision of the information they have been given.

There are two basic types of overconfidence bias rooted in the illusion of knowledge: *prediction overconfidence* and *certainty overconfidence*. Both types have cognitive and emotional aspects; both types demonstrate faulty reasoning combined with "gut feel" and such emotional elements as hope. Hope frequently underpins the probabilities assumed when investment decisions are made in an overconfident state. When the FMP feels lucky and bases probabilities on that luck rather than on the actual likelihood of an event, the resulting financial decision is likely to generate results less than those expected by the FMP.

Prediction overconfidence occurs when the confidence intervals that FMPs assign to their investment predictions are too narrow. For example, when estimating the future value of a stock, overconfident FMPs will incorporate far too little variation—using a narrower range of expected payoffs and a lower standard deviation of returns—than justified based on historical results and fundamental analysis. As a result of underestimating risks, particularly downside risks, FMPs may hold poorly diversified portfolios.

Certainty overconfidence occurs when the probabilities that FMPs assign to outcomes are too high because they are too certain of their judgments. This certainty is often an emotional response rather than a cognitive evaluation. For example, having decided that a company is a good investment, people may become blind to the prospect of a loss and predict high returns with virtual certainty. When the results are less than expected, the FMPs are surprised and disappointed. In response, they are likely to sell the investment and look for a replacement that they feel is certain to generate high returns. People susceptible to certainty overconfidence often trade too frequently.

Self-attribution bias is the tendency of individuals to ascribe their successes to innate personal traits, such as talent or foresight, while blaming failures on exogenous factors, such as bad luck. It can be broken down into two subsidiary biases: *self-enhancing* and *self-protecting*. Self-enhancing bias describes people's propensity to claim too much credit for their successes. Self-protecting bias describes the denial of personal responsibility for failures. The need for self-esteem affects the attribution of task outcomes; people protect themselves psychologically as they attempt to comprehend their successes and failures.

EXAMPLE 5

Prediction and Certainty Overconfidence

Prediction Overconfidence:

Clarke and Statman (2000) demonstrated prediction overconfidence when they asked investors the following question: "In 1896, the Dow Jones Industrial Average, which is a price index that does not include dividend reinvestment, was at 40. In 1998 it crossed 9,000. If dividends had been reinvested, what do you think the value of the DJIA would be in 1998? In addition to that guess, also predict a high and low range so that you feel 90 percent confident that your answer is between your high and low guesses." In the survey, few responses reasonably approximated the potential 1998 value of the Dow, and no one estimated a correct confidence interval. (The 1998 value of the DJIA, under the conditions posed in the survey, would have been 652,230!)

Certainty Overconfidence:

People display certainty overconfidence in everyday life situations, and that overconfidence carries over into the investment arena. People have too much confidence in the accuracy of their own judgments. As people learn more about a situation, the accuracy of their judgments may increase but their confidence may increase even more; as a result, they may fallaciously equate the quantity of information with its quality. Confidence also tends to increase if people are given incentives to perform. Overconfidence is greatest when accuracy is near chance levels, and reduces as accuracy increases from 50 percent to 80 percent. Slovic, Fischhoff, and Lichtenstein (1982) gave subjects a general knowledge test and then asked them how sure they were of their answer. Subjects reported being 100 percent sure when they were actually only 70 percent to 80 percent correct.

Consequences of Overconfidence Bias   As a result of overconfidence bias, FMPs may do the following:

- Underestimate risks and overestimate expected returns.
- Hold poorly diversified portfolios.
- Trade excessively.
- Experience lower returns than those of the market.

Many overconfident FMPs claim above-average aptitude for selecting stocks, with little supporting evidence. Barber and Odean (2001) found that after trading costs and before taxes, the average investor underperformed the market by approximately 2 percent per year.

Barber and Odean also found that the average subject's annual portfolio turnover was 80 percent (slightly less than the 84 percent averaged by mutual funds). The least active quintile of participants, with an average annual turnover of 1 percent, earned 17.5 percent annual returns, outperforming the 16.9 percent garnered by the S&P during this period. The most active 20 percent of FMPs averaged a *monthly* turnover of over 9 percent, but they realized pre-tax returns of only 10 percent annually. The authors of the study do, indeed, seem justified in labeling frequent trading as hazardous.

Many overconfident FMPs also believe they can pick mutual funds that will deliver superior future performance. The market-trailing performance of the average mutual fund is proof that most mutual fund clients also fail in this endeavor. Worse yet, FMPs tend to trade in and out of mutual funds at the worst possible times, chasing returns with poor results, as we learned in the previously referenced DALBAR study.

Detection of and Guidelines for Overcoming Overconfidence Bias   FMPs should review their trading records, identify the winners and losers, and calculate portfolio performance over at least two years. Investors with an unfounded belief in their own ability to identify good investments may recall winners and their results but underestimate the number and results of their losers. A conscious review process will force them to acknowledge their losers, because a review of trading activity will demonstrate not only the winners but also the losers. This review will also identify the amount of trading. When FMPs engage in too much trading, they should be advised to keep track of every investment trade and then calculate returns. This exercise will demonstrate the detrimental effects of excessive trading. Because overconfidence is also a cognitive error, more complete information can often help FMPs understand the error of their ways.

It is critical that investors be objective when making and evaluating investment decisions. There is an old Wall Street adage, "Don't confuse brains with a bull market," that warns about self-attribution. It is advisable to view the reasoning behind and the results of investments, winning and losing, as objectively as possible. Unfortunately, most people have difficulty being objective about their own behavior. This can lead to self-attribution and overconfidence biases and result in repeating the same mistakes: overtrading and chasing returns to the detriment of actual realized returns.

To stay objective, it is a good idea to perform post-investment analysis on both successful and unsuccessful investments. When did you make money? When did you lose money? Mentally separate your good money-making decisions from your bad ones. Then, review the beneficial decisions and try to discern what, exactly, you did correctly. Did you purchase an investment at a particularly advantageous time based on fundamentals, or did you luck out by timing a market upswing? Similarly, review the decisions that you categorized as poor. Did you make an investment aptly based on fundamentals and then make an error when it came time to sell, or was the market going through a correction? When reviewing unprofitable decisions, look for patterns or common mistakes that perhaps you were unaware you were making. Note any such tendencies that you discover, and try to remain mindful of them by brainstorming a rule or reminder such as: "I will do X in the future" or "I will not do Y in the future." Being conscious of these rules will help overcome any bad habits you may have acquired, and it can also reinforce your reliance on strategies that have served you well.

4.3 Self-Control Bias

Self-control bias is a bias in which people fail to act in pursuit of their long-term, overarching goals because of a lack of self-discipline. There is an inherent conflict between short-term satisfaction and achievement of some long-term goals. Money is an area in which people are notorious for displaying a lack of self-control, but it is not the only one. Attitudes toward weight loss, smoking, and studying provide other examples. A person who is 100 pounds overweight is told by a doctor that weight loss is essential to long-term good health. Despite this knowledge, the individual may fail to cut back on food consumption. The short-term satisfaction of eating conflicts with the long-term goal of good health. Similarly, smokers may continue to smoke even though they are aware of the long-term health risks involved. People pursuing the CFA charter may fail to study sufficiently because of short-term competing demands on their time. Rational behavior would suggest that people would do whatever was necessary to achieve their long-term goals—whether to stay healthy or become a CFA charterholder—but it often does not happen.

When it comes to money, people may know they need to save for retirement, but they often have difficulty sacrificing present consumption because of a lack of self-control. The apparent lack of self-control may also be a function of hyperbolic discounting. Hyperbolic discounting is the human tendency to prefer small payoffs now compared to larger payoffs in the future. Sacrifices in the present require much greater payoffs in the future; otherwise, people will not be willing to make current sacrifices. People seem to have temporal short-sightedness or temporal myopia, focusing on the present and discounting the future. They spend today rather than save for tomorrow. This behavior can lead to high short-term utility and disastrous long-term utility.

Consequences of Self-Control Bias As a result of self-control bias, FMPs may do the following:

- Save insufficiently for the future.

  Upon realizing that their savings are insufficient, FMPs may do the following:

- Accept too much risk in their portfolios in an attempt to generate higher returns. In this attempt to make up for less than adequate savings, the capital base is put at risk.

- Cause asset allocation imbalance problems. For example, some FMPs prefer income-producing assets in order to have income to spend. This behavior can be hazardous to long-term wealth because income-producing assets may offer less total return potential, particularly when the income is not reinvested, which may inhibit a portfolio's ability to maintain spending power after inflation. Other FMPs may favor equities over bonds simply because they like to take risks. Asset allocations should be based upon a variety of factors, including level of risk tolerance, but they should not be entirely driven by risk tolerance.

Detection of and Guidelines for Overcoming Self-Control Bias People have a strong desire to consume today, which can be counterproductive to attaining long-term financial goals. FMPs should ensure that a proper investment plan is in place and should have a personal budget. Investing without planning is like building without a blueprint. Planning is the key to attaining long-term financial goals; plans need to be in writing, so that they can be reviewed regularly. Failing to plan is planning to fail. FMPs need to maintain a proper balance in asset allocations to attain their long-term financial goals. Adhering to a saving plan and an appropriate asset allocation strategy are critical to long-term financial success.

4.4 Status Quo Bias

Status quo bias, coined by Samuelson and Zeckhauser (1988), is an emotional bias in which people do nothing (i.e., maintain the "status quo") instead of making a change. People are generally more comfortable keeping things the same than with change and thus do not necessarily look for opportunities where change is beneficial. Given no apparent problem requiring a decision, the status quo is maintained. Further, if given a situation where one choice is the default choice, people will frequently let that choice stand rather than opting out of it and making another choice. Thus, the process in presenting choices can influence decisions. For example, companies that enroll employees in defined contribution pension plans but give the employees the ability to opt out of the plan have a much higher participation rate than companies where employees have to opt in to the plan.

Status quo bias is often discussed in tandem with endowment and regret-aversion biases (described later) because the outcome of the biases, maintaining existing positions, may be similar. However, the reasons for maintaining the existing positions differ among the biases. In the status quo bias, the positions are maintained largely because of inertia rather than conscious choice. In the endowment and regret-aversion biases, the positions are maintained because of conscious, but possibly incorrect, choices. When endowment bias exists, ownership imbues an investment with intangible value beyond the true value to the holder. Endowment bias creates a preference for no change or the status quo. With regard to regret aversion, an FMP presented with two investment choices may opt for the status quo rather than potentially experience the regret of selling shares that then went up in price. When status quo, endowment, and regret-aversion biases are combined, people will tend to strongly prefer that things stay as they are, even at some personal cost.

Consequences of Status Quo Bias   As a result of status quo bias, FMPs may do the following:

- Unknowingly maintain portfolios with risk characteristics that are inappropriate for their circumstances.
- Fail to explore other opportunities.

Detection of and Guidelines for Overcoming Status Quo Bias   Status quo bias may be exceptionally strong and difficult to overcome. Education is essential. FMPs should quantify the risk-reducing and return-enhancing advantages of diversification and proper asset allocation. For example, with a concentrated stock position, showing what can happen to overall wealth levels if the stock collapses may persuade an FMP to diversify.

4.5 Endowment Bias

Endowment bias is an emotional bias in which people value an asset more when they hold rights to it than when they do not. Endowment bias is inconsistent with standard economic theory, which asserts that the price a person is *willing to pay* for a good should equal the price at which that person would be *willing to sell* the same good. However, psychologists have found that when asked, people tend to state minimum selling prices for a good that exceed maximum purchase prices that they are willing to pay for the same good. Effectively, ownership "endows" the asset with added value. Endowment bias can affect attitudes toward items owned for long periods of time or can occur immediately when an item is acquired. Endowment bias may apply to inherited or purchased securities.

FMPs may irrationally hold on to securities they already own, which is particularly true regarding their inherited investments. For example, a child or grandchild may hold an outsized inherited stock position because of an emotional attachment, despite the risk of a sizable loss if the stock stumbles. These investors are often resistant to selling even in the face of poor prospects. Again using the example of an inheritance, an FMP may hold an inherited municipal bond portfolio because of an emotional attachment, when a more aggressive asset mix may be more appropriate.

Samuelson and Zeckhauser (1988) aptly illustrate investor susceptibility to endowment bias and the resulting status quo bias. They performed trials in which subjects were told that they had inherited a large sum from their uncle and had four portfolios in which they could invest the sum. The portfolios bore various risks and rates of return. A second trial was performed with a single difference: subjects were told that the uncle had already invested the sum in a moderate risk company (one of the portfolio options in the previous trial). Subjects were presented with the same four portfolio options as in the first trial. The first trial had no status quo; the alternatives were all new. In the second trial, however, the moderate risk company portfolio was the status quo. Subjects chose the moderate risk company portfolio more often when it was in the status quo position than when it was not. Similarly, outcomes occurred for the other options when they (and not the moderate risk company portfolio) held the role of the status quo. This is a classic case of endowment and status quo biases combining. Many wealth management practitioners have encountered clients who are reluctant to sell securities bequeathed by previous generations. Often in these situations, investors cite feelings of disloyalty associated with the prospect of selling inherited securities, general uncertainty in determining the right choice, and concerns with tax issues. Although the latter may be a rational concern, the tax implications are most likely not being considered rationally. Sometimes the appropriate action may be to pay taxes and alter the investment portfolio.

Consequences of Endowment Bias   As is the case with status quo bias, endowment bias may lead FMPs to do the following:

- Fail to sell off certain assets and replace them with other assets.

- Maintain an inappropriate asset allocation. The portfolio may be inappropriate for investors' levels of risk tolerance and financial goals.

- Continue to hold classes of assets with which they are familiar. FMPs may believe they understand the characteristics of the investments they already own and may be reluctant to purchase assets with which they have less experience. Familiarity adds to owners' perceived value of a security.

Detection of and Guidelines for Overcoming Endowment Bias   Inherited securities are often the cause of endowment bias. In the case of inherited investments, an FMP should ask such a question as, "If an equivalent sum to the value of the investments inherited had been received in cash, how would you invest the cash?" Often, the answer is into a very different investment portfolio than the one inherited. It may also be useful to explore the deceased's intent in owning the investment and bequeathing it. "Was the primary intent to leave the specific investment portfolio because it was perceived to be a suitable investment based on fundamental analysis, or was it to leave financial resources to benefit the heirs?" Heirs who affirm the latter conclusion are receptive to considering alternative asset allocations.

When financial goals are in jeopardy, emotional attachment must be moderated; it cannot be accepted and adapted to. Several good resources are available on "emotional intelligence." FMPs should familiarize themselves with the topic so they can help themselves or their clients work through emotional attachment issues.

An effective way to address a desire for familiarity, when that desire contradicts good financial sense, is to review the historical performance and risk of the unfamiliar securities in question and contemplate the reasoning underlying the recommendation. Rather than replacing all familiar holdings with new, intimidating ones, start with a small purchase of the unfamiliar investments until a comfort level with them is achieved.

4.6 Regret-Aversion Bias

Regret-aversion bias is an emotional bias in which people tend to avoid making decisions that will result in action out of fear that the decision will turn out poorly. Simply put, people try to avoid the pain of regret associated with bad decisions. This tendency is especially prevalent in investment decision making. Regret aversion can cause FMPs to hold onto positions too long. They are reluctant to sell because they fear that the position will increase in value and then they will regret having sold it.

Regret aversion can also keep FMPs out of a market that has recently generated sharp losses or gains. Having experienced losses, our instincts tell us that to continue investing is not prudent. Yet periods of depressed prices may present great buying opportunities. Regret aversion can persuade us to stay out of the stock market just when the time is right for investing. On the upside, fear of getting in at the high point can restrict new investments from taking place.

Regret bias can have two dimensions: actions that people take and actions that people *could have* taken. More formally, regret from an action taken is called an *error of commission*, whereas regret from an action not taken is called an *error of omission*. Regret may be distinguished from disappointment in that regret includes strong feelings of responsibility for the choice that has been made. Regret is more intense when the unfavorable outcomes are the result of an error of commission versus an error of omission. Thus, no action becomes the preferred decision.

Koening (1999) argues that regret aversion can initiate herding behavior. Regret aversion causes FMPs to avoid the pain of regret resulting from a poor investment decision, whether the loss comes from an investment that goes down or a "loss" resulting from a stock that went up that they did not own. It is not just the financial loss they regret; it is also the feeling of responsibility for the decision that gave rise to the loss. In order to avoid the burden of responsibility, regret aversion can encourage FMPs to invest in a similar fashion and in the same stocks as others. This herding behavior alleviates some of the burden of responsibility. As John Maynard Keynes (1936) writes in Chapter 12, "Worldly wisdom teaches that it is better for reputation to fail conventionally than to succeed unconventionally."

Consequences of Regret-Aversion Bias   As a result of regret-aversion bias, FMPs may do the following:

■ Be too conservative in their investment choices as a result of poor outcomes on risky investments in the past. FMPs may wish to avoid the regret of making another bad investment and decide that low-risk instruments are better. This behavior can lead to long-term underperformance and potential failure to reach investment goals.

■ Engage in herding behavior. FMPs may feel safer in popular investments in order to limit potential future regret. It seems safe to be with the crowd, and a reduction in potential emotional pain is perceived. Regret aversion may lead to preference for stocks of well-known companies even in the face of equal risk and return expectations. Choosing the stocks of less familiar companies is perceived as riskier and involves more personal responsibility and greater potential for regret.

Detection of and Guidelines for Overcoming Regret-Aversion Bias   In overcoming regret-aversion bias, education is essential. FMPs should quantify the risk-reducing and return-enhancing advantages of diversification and proper asset allocation. Regret aversion can cause some FMPs to invest too conservatively or too riskily depending on the current trends. With proper diversification, FMPs will accept the appropriate level of risk in their portfolios depending, of course, on return objectives. To prevent investments from being too conservative, FMPs must recognize that losses happen to everyone and keep in mind the long-term benefits of including risky assets in portfolios. Recognizing that bubbles happen and keeping in mind long-term objectives will prevent a client from making investments that are too risky. Efficient frontier research can be quite helpful as an educational tool. Investing too conservatively or too riskily can potentially inhibit the ability to reach long-term financial goals.

4.7 Emotional Biases: Conclusion

Emotional biases stem from impulse, intuition, and feelings and may result in personal and unreasoned decisions. When possible, focusing on cognitive aspects of the biases may be more effective than trying to alter an emotional response. Also, educating about the investment decision-making process and portfolio theory can be helpful in moving the decision making from an emotional basis to a cognitive basis. When biases are emotional in nature, drawing these to the attention of an individual making the decision is unlikely to lead to positive outcomes; the individual is likely to become defensive rather than receptive to considering alternatives. Thinking of the appropriate questions to ask to potentially alter the decision-making process is likely to be most effective.

Such questions as, "If an equivalent sum to the value of the investments inherited had been received in cash, how would you invest the cash?" or "Was the primary intent to leave the specific investment portfolio because it was perceived to be a suitable investment based on fundamental analysis, or was it to leave financial resources to benefit the heirs?" are unlikely to elicit defensiveness. These types of questions are likely to open the way to a more rational investment approach.

INVESTMENT POLICY AND ASSET ALLOCATION
5

Behavioral biases can and should be accounted for by investors and their advisers in the investment policy development and asset allocation selection process. Behavioral finance considerations may have their own place in the constraints section of the investment policy statement along with liquidity, time horizon, taxes, legal and regulatory environment, and unique circumstances. Responses to such questions as the following may help develop the behavioral finance considerations that have an impact on investment decisions and the resulting portfolio.

1   Which biases does the client show evidence of?

2   Which bias type dominates (cognitive or emotional)?

3   What effect do the client's biases have on the asset allocation decision?

4   What adjustment should be made to a "rational" (risk tolerance-based) asset allocation that can account for the client's behavioral make-up?

    A   When should behavior be *moderated* to counteract the potentially negative effects of these biases on the investment decision-making process?

    B   When should asset allocations be created that *adapt* to the investor's behavioral biases so the investor can comfortably abide by his or her asset allocation decisions?

    C   When is it appropriate to design a *behaviorally modified asset allocation* (referred to as a modified portfolio, for convenience) for an investor?

    D   Once the decision is made to recommend a modified portfolio, what quantitative parameters should be used when putting the recommendation into action?

At the end of this section, we will review two case studies to help demonstrate these concepts. A variety of approaches exist to incorporate behavioral finance considerations into an investment policy statement and portfolio—including the use of a goals-based investing approach that is consistent with loss aversion (prospect theory) and mental accounting. Goals-based investing involves identifying an investor's specific goals and the risk tolerance associated with each goal. Investments are chosen considering each goal individually. Thus, a portfolio is constructed in layers rather than using the holistic approach to portfolio construction of modern portfolio theory (MPT). In goals-based investing, a portfolio is evaluated in terms of attaining financial goals and risk management focuses on the size and likelihood of potential losses. Investors are assumed to be loss averse, not risk averse.

Investment portfolios are managed and updated based on changing circumstances and goals of the client. This approach may be attractive to investors who are more focused on wealth preservation (i.e., minimizing losses) than on wealth accumulation (i.e., maximizing returns). This approach can also be useful in highlighting the consequences of selecting an asset allocation that is riskier than is appropriate for the investor. Taking a goals-based investment approach to asset allocation is helpful in terms of keeping financial goals in mind and understanding how much risk can be taken when creating a portfolio. Exhibit 4 illustrates a goals-based investing approach. Such an approach matches many investors' natural desire to put money in separate mental accounts and to focus on loss as a measure of risk.

Exhibit 4   Goals-Based Investing Approach

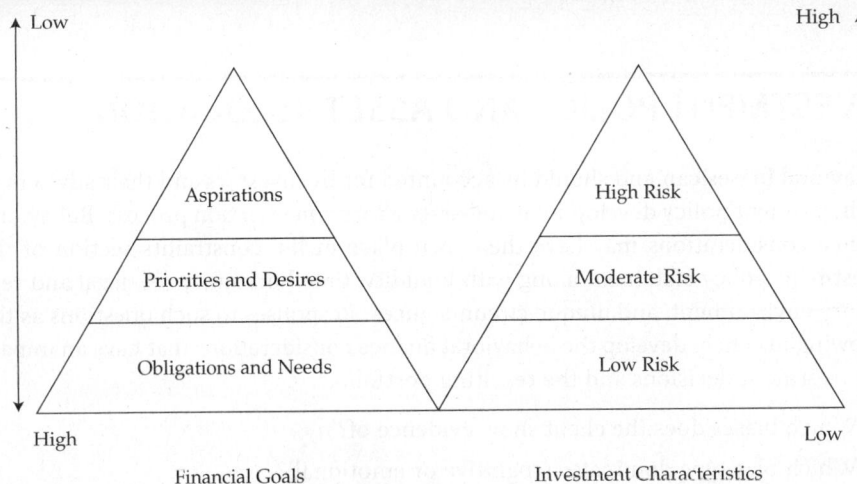

Financial advisers using this approach will typically first get their clients to consider their obligations and needs. The advisers will then estimate how much should be invested in low-risk (capital preservation) assets to meet those needs and obligations. Next, riskier assets are considered to attain priorities and desires. Finally, even riskier assets are added to meet aspirational goals. Typically, investors will end up having a diversified portfolio using this approach, but the resulting portfolio may not be efficient from a traditional finance perspective. The lack of efficiency is because the components of the portfolio are individually justified rather than based on modern portfolio theory that considers correlations between investments. However, risk may be better understood by the investor using this methodology. As a result, investors may find it easier to adhere to investment decisions and portfolio allocations made using this approach.

In the following sections, we will discuss the use of another approach that begins with the rational portfolio and makes modifications to accommodate behavioral finance considerations. The concept of *behaviorally modified asset allocation* is introduced, and guidelines for creating such an allocation are discussed.

5.1 Behaviorally Modified Asset Allocation

When designing a standard asset allocation program, an investor, often working with an adviser, will typically answer a risk tolerance questionnaire, document financial goals and constraints, and then adopt the output of a portfolio optimization model that matches the investor's risk tolerance category and accomplishes the investor's financial goals. In the case of institutional investors, they will consider these items from the perspective of the entity they are acting on behalf of. An investment adviser will consider these items from the perspective of their clients when developing investment policy statements and asset allocations. The output of the portfolio optimization model will be referred to as a "rational" portfolio allocation.

The process described above takes into account risk tolerance and financial goals but fails to take into account behavioral biases. For example, in response to major short-term market movements, some investors, individual and institutional, may change their asset allocations to the detriment of the long-term investment plan. This behavior may be the result of a bias, such as the regret-aversion bias, that may lead to herding behavior or simply loss aversion. An investor's interest may be better served by the adoption of an asset allocation that suits the investor's natural psychological preferences—and it may not be one that maximizes expected return for a given level of risk. For example, one investor's behaviorally modified asset allocation (modified portfolio) may be a modest, lower-returning, long-term investment program compared to the rational portfolio allocation. This modified asset allocation is one to which the investor can comfortably adhere. Another investor with similar natural psychological tendencies may be persuaded of the merits of taking on more risk and as a result have a riskier modified portfolio. In both cases, the investor must be comfortable with the modified portfolio.

In creating a modified portfolio, it is critical to distinguish between emotional and cognitive biases and to consider the level of wealth of the investor in question. Individual biases should primarily be assessed for the purpose of identifying which type of biases dominate (cognitive or emotional) and what actions should be taken in response to observed behaviors while considering the investor's overall wealth level. The basic actions are to adapt to a bias or to moderate the impact of the bias. When a bias is adapted to, it is accepted and decisions are made that recognize and adjust for the bias rather than making an attempt to reduce the impact of the bias. The resulting portfolio represents an alteration of the rational portfolio; the alteration responds to the investor's biases while considering financial goals and level of wealth. To moderate the impact of a bias is to recognize the bias and to attempt to reduce or even eliminate the bias within the individual rather than to accept the bias. The resulting portfolio is similar to the rational portfolio, and a program is adopted to reduce or eliminate the investor's biases.

The next section will examine guidelines for determining a modified portfolio, including an explanation of how to assess wealth level. The perspective taken in the next section is that of a private wealth manager working with an individual client. The approach can be used with modification in other situations.

5.1.1 *Guidelines for Determining a Behaviorally Modified Asset Allocation*

Pompian and Longo (2005) offer two guidelines for helping a private wealth manager identify a behaviorally modified asset allocation for a client.

Guideline I	The decision to moderate or adapt to a client's behavioral biases during the asset allocation process depends fundamentally on the client's level of wealth. Specifically, the wealthier the client, the more the practitioner should adapt to the client's behavioral biases. The less wealthy, the more the practitioner should moderate a client's biases.
Rationale	A client's outliving his or her assets constitutes a far graver investment failure than a client's inability to accumulate wealth. The likelihood of a client outliving his or her assets is a function of the level of wealth. If a bias is likely to endanger a client's standard of living, moderating is an appropriate course of action. If a bias will only jeopardize the client's standard of living if a highly unlikely event occurs, adapting may be more appropriate. However, the potential impact of low-probability, high-impact events should be discussed with the client.

(continued)

Guideline II   The decision to moderate or adapt to a client's behavioral biases during the asset allocation process depends fundamentally on the type of behavioral bias the client exhibits. Specifically, clients exhibiting cognitive errors should be moderated, and those exhibiting emotional biases should be adapted to.

Rationale   Because cognitive errors stem from faulty reasoning, better information and advice can often correct them. Conversely, emotional biases originate from feelings or intuition rather than conscious reasoning, and thus they are more difficult to correct.

Naturally, the determination of high wealth level and low wealth level is a subjective one that must be determined by the adviser in concert with the client. In this context, wealth is determined in relation to lifestyle, not just based on the level of assets. Some people have high levels of assets but also have an extravagant financial lifestyle to match, implying a "low" level of wealth; in other words, some people have a lot of assets but also spend accordingly. This behavior is related to *standard of living risk*. Standard of living risk (SLR) is the risk that the current or a specified acceptable lifestyle may not be sustainable. For example, individuals with modest assets and modest lifestyles that they do not wish to alter may not have a standard of living risk; as such, they might be viewed as having a moderate to high level of wealth. On the other hand, individuals with a high level of assets and extravagant lifestyles that they wish to maintain may have a standard of living risk; these individuals, regardless of level of assets, might be viewed as having a low to moderate level of wealth.

Guidelines I and II may, for some clients, yield a blended recommendation. For instance, a less wealthy client with strong emotional biases should be both adapted to and moderated. Exhibit 5 illustrates when to moderate and when to adapt.

Exhibit 5   Visual Depiction of Guideline I and Guideline II

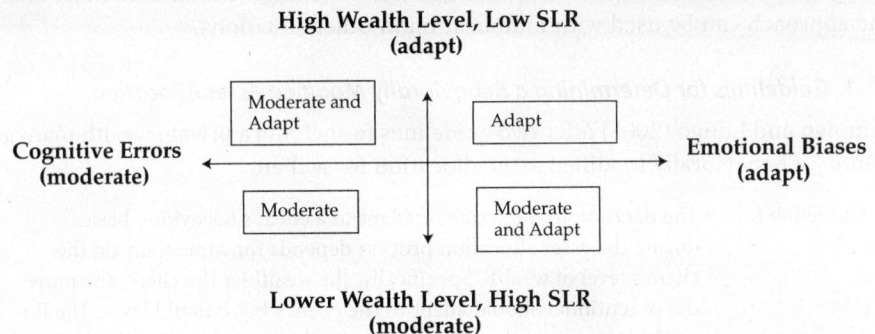

5.1.2 *How Much to Moderate or Adapt*

A key concept in creating a behaviorally modified asset allocation is to decide how much it should deviate from the "rational" allocation of traditional finance. Exhibit 6 offers useful guidelines for helping to determine how much to adjust an allocation for behavioral bias.

Exhibit 6	Deviations from a "Rational" Portfolio	
	Bias Type: Cognitive	Bias Type: Emotional
High Wealth Level/Low SLR	Modest Asset Allocation Change Suggestion: +/− 5 to 10% Max Per Asset Class	Stronger Asset Allocation Change Suggestion: +/− 10 to 15% Max Per Asset Class
Low Wealth Level/High SLR	Close to the Rational Asset Allocation Suggestion: +/− 0 to 3% Max Per Asset Class	Modest Asset Allocation Change Suggestion: +/− 5 to 10% Max Per Asset Class

Note that the percentages listed in the chart are *suggested* percentage adjustments from the "rational" allocation to asset classes based on behavioral bias. In terms of the magnitude of the suggested changes, to some these ranges may appear too narrow or too small in absolute terms, while others may see them as reasonable. The amount of change appropriate to modify an allocation will in large part depend on the number of asset classes used in the allocation. A 5 percent change in 10 asset classes, for example, could yield a substantial tilt to or away from risky assets; however, for an asset allocation with 4 asset classes, 5 percent would not be enough.

It is important to recognize the *relative* differences between these cases. The case requiring the least adjustment to the rational portfolio is a low wealth level client with cognitive bias. Here, the low wealth investor needs to modify his or her behavior to reach his or her financial goals, and with appropriate education and information, he or she should be able to adjust behavior to match the rational allocation. If an adjustment is needed, a +/− 0 to 2 percent maximum asset class adjustment is suggested. We will see an example of this case in the case studies later. The case that will likely require the most adjustment per asset class is emotional bias at high wealth level. Here, a +/− 10 percent maximum adjustment per asset class is suggested. The rationale for such a potentially high adjustment is that a wealthy investor with emotional bias may need substantial flexibility because emotional biases are difficult to correct; a high wealth level permits flexibility. The "middle of the road" cases are the high wealth level with cognitive biases and the low wealth level with emotional biases. With these two cases, a suggested maximum asset class adjustment is +/− 5 percent. The rationale for this adjustment is that there is a need to both adapt to and moderate behavioral biases, and the offsetting that takes place likely requires a modest adjustment. Naturally these are only conceptual guidelines; actual client situations will likely require additional customization.

Through the following case studies, we will identify an investor's behaviorally modified asset allocation. Thus equipped, investors and their advisers can more effectively apply behavioral finance research to investing activities. Institutional investors and money managers are not immune to behavioral biases. They should be particularly wary of cognitive errors. They should attempt to accept their knowledge limits and avoid belief perseverance and information-processing errors. Overconfidence is an emotional bias to which they may be particularly susceptible.

As discussed earlier, designing a standard asset allocation program with a client involves the following steps: 1) Advisers first administer a risk tolerance questionnaire; 2) Advisers discuss the client's financial goals and constraints; 3) Advisers typically recommend the output of a mean–variance optimization from any number of financial planning software programs. This approach may work better for institutional and individual investors who are familiar with financial theory, but institutional and individual investors and investment advisers, along with other financial market participants, are all susceptible to behavioral biases.

In a scenario familiar to investment advisers, in response to short-term market movements, a client may request that his or her asset allocation be changed—to the detriment of the long-term investment plan. Kahneman and Riepe (1998) describe financial advising as "a prescriptive activity whose main objective should be to guide investors to make decisions that serve their best interest." Serving the best interest of the client may be the recommendation of an asset allocation that suits the client's natural psychological preferences; it may not be the rational asset allocation (one that maximizes expected return for a given level of risk). More simply, a client's most appropriate behaviorally modified portfolio may be the long-term allocation recommendation that the client can comfortably adhere to. Conversely, another client's recommended portfolio may be one that goes against his or her natural psychological tendencies, but the client may be well served to accept more risk than he or she might otherwise be comfortable with in order to attain a higher return for that level of risk. Note here that allocation recommendations do not necessarily need to be inefficient; they can still be on the efficient frontier. They can move up or down it based on the client's behavioral make-up. However, even if the portfolio is on the efficient frontier, it may be inefficient considering transaction costs and the financial objectives of the investor.

5.2 Case Studies

The following case studies involve two hypothetical investors, Mr. Renaldo and Mrs. Maradona, and their adviser, Mr. Bobby Moore. Considering two dimensions, level of wealth and type of dominant biases, these case studies will consider two extreme examples: an investor with high wealth and emotional biases (Mr. Renaldo) and an investor with lower wealth and cognitive biases (Mrs. Maradona). Because of space constraints, we will not be able to review the two other extreme examples: an investor with high wealth and cognitive biases and an investor with lower wealth and emotional biases. Still, readers should understand that these cases will likely fall in between the two cases presented here in terms of behavioral adjustments to "rational" portfolio allocations.

These case studies were designed to answer four key questions in determining an investor's modified portfolio.

1 Which biases does the client show evidence of?

2 What effect do the client's biases have on the asset allocation decision?

3 What action should Mr. Moore take: moderate or adapt to these biases?

4 What is the appropriate behaviorally modified asset allocation for each client?

In the real world of investing, each client and each adviser is different; therefore, these case studies illustrate an approach to diagnosing and devising strategies for behaviorally biased clients rather than specific strategies. In each case, put yourself in the role of the adviser, Mr. Bobby Moore, and consider how you (Moore) should deal with the client and the given situation and approach the issues presented. The case studies will contain the following format, which is a simulation of the approach that advisers might encounter with a client:

- Introductory description of the case
- Identification of behavioral finance biases
- Effect of biases on asset allocation decision
- Action to be taken in response to identified biases (moderate or adapt)
- Recommendation of the behaviorally modified asset allocation

These cases involve hypothetical investors and are not intended to represent all investor types. Each client is unique and will differ from the clients described in these case studies. What is important is to follow the process that is being described on how to identify biases, how to determine what the appropriate course of action is for dealing with the biases, and how to adjust or not adjust the rational mean–variance portfolio recommendation for biased behavior.

Capital Markets Assumptions: For each of the case studies, assume that for the last three years, the stock market has experienced moderate and steady increases and interest rates have been stable. For simplicity, we will assume that the investors in the case studies will be limited to investing in three asset classes: stocks, bonds, and cash. Diagnosis for biases is done in two steps in the following way. First, a basic questionnaire (Exhibit 7) is given that assesses the 15 biases presented in this reading per the following list. *Note that the choice of responses would normally be in a multiple choice format, but in the interest of length, only the questions are shown here.* The questions do not follow the order of presentation of biases in the reading but instead intersperse emotional, belief perseverance, and information-processing biases. The question order can be altered, but it is advisable to not cluster questions about similar types of biases. Second, after reviewing the responses, the adviser focuses on biases identified by the questionnaire and delves further into them with the client to help create a modified portfolio.

Exhibit 7	Basic Diagnostic Questions for Behavioral Bias
Behavioral Bias	**Diagnostic Question**
Loss Aversion	Imagine you make an investment that drops 25 percent in the first six months. You are unsure if it will come back. What would you normally do (NOT what you *think* you should do; what you *would* do)?
Endowment	How would you describe your emotional attachment to possessions or investment holdings?
Status Quo	How would you describe the frequency of your trading?
Anchoring	You purchase a stock at $50 per share. It goes up to $60 in a few months, and then it drops to $40 a few months later. You are uncertain what will happen next. How would you respond to this scenario?
Mental Accounting	Generally, do you categorize your money by different financial goals, or do you look at the bigger financial picture?
Regret Aversion	Have you ever made an investment that you have regretted making? How did that affect your future investing decisions?
Hindsight	Do you believe investment outcomes are generally predictable or unpredictable?
Framing	Assume you have agreed to a financial plan created by your adviser that has a projected return of 9 percent and an annual standard deviation of +/–15% (a typical plan). Would it surprise you to know that statistically in the worst case, the plan's return could be negative 36 percent or more in one year out of 100? Would this information cause you to rethink your risk tolerance?
Conservatism	Assume you make an investment based on your own research. An adviser presents you with information that contradicts your belief about this investment. How would you respond?
Availability	Do you ever make investment decisions (such as selecting a mutual fund or online broker) based on word-of-mouth or name recognition?
Representativeness	Have you ever made a new investment because of its apparent similarity to a past successful investment (e.g., a tech stock or value stock) without doing research to validate the new investment's merits?

(continued)

Exhibit 7	(Continued)

Behavioral Bias	Diagnostic Question
Overconfidence	Suppose you make a winning investment. How do you generally attribute the success of your decision?
Confirmation	Suppose you make an investment based on your own research. The investment doesn't move up as much as you thought it might. How are you likely to respond?
Illusion of Control	You are offered two free lottery tickets. You may either select your own numbers or have a machine do it. What would you do?
Self-Control	Do you tend to save or spend disposable income?

5.2.1 Case Study #1: Mr. Renaldo (High Wealth Level, Emotional Biases)

Mr. Renaldo ("Mr. R") is a single, 58-year-old, hard-working, international corporate lawyer (an employee of a large multinational company). He earns a salary of £600,000 annually. He has residences in both London and New York and generally lives within his annual income net of taxes. He occasionally spends more than his net income, but in other years he saves and invests. His current portfolio is worth approximately £3,500,000. It reached this value primarily because of some successful high risk oil and technology investments as well as stock options granted by his employer. Mr. R has no plans for marriage or children. He had a mild heart attack last year, but he has made a full recovery. His primary financial goal is to retire comfortably at age 65 with a reduced spending level of £150,000 and to bequeath any assets remaining at his death to his alma mater, Oxford University. Mr. R's financial adviser, Mr. Bobby Moore, has been working with Mr. R for less than a year. During that time, Moore has proposed a comprehensive financial plan. Despite Moore's recommendations, however, Mr. R's asset allocation has remained the same at nearly 80 percent equities, with 40 percent in his employing company's publicly traded stock. Still, Moore has developed a good working relationship with Mr. R.

Moore believes that Mr. R. is a well-grounded, fairly rational person, but he also believes that Mr. R has some behavioral issues to address. In Moore's view, the most important issue is that Mr. R has not taken action yet on the new, more conservative allocation that Moore proposed months ago of 60 percent stocks, 30 percent bonds, and 10 percent cash. Moore worries about the lack of diversification in Mr. R's portfolio. Moore's concern is that a severe downward market fluctuation or drop in Mr. R's employing company's stock may cause him to sell assets irrationally, affecting his long-term financial plan. Moore's financial plan demonstrates that even with a somewhat less aggressive portfolio, Mr. R could still meet his primary financial objectives if he could save just £25,000 annually. Moore believes that one of the issues is that Mr. R thinks of himself as a very savvy investor because of some risky bets that worked out well for him in the past. Moore suspects that Mr. R hasn't changed his allocation because he thinks Moore's allocation recommendation is too conservative. Moore also notices that Mr. R constantly worries about missing out on hot stocks that go up because he was not aggressive enough. Moore decides that the appropriate course of action is to ask Mr. R to take a behavioral bias diagnostic questionnaire. When Moore gets the answers to the questionnaire, he decides to delve further into three biases: *regret aversion, overconfidence, and self-control.* Moore asks Mr. R further questions on these three biases. Exhibit 8 shows Mr. R's answers to these questions in **bold**.

Exhibit 8   Mr. Renaldo's Bias Diagnostic Tests

Regret-Aversion Diagnostic Test

Question 1:

Suppose you make an investment in Stock ABC, and over the next six months, ABC appreciates by your target of 15 percent. You contemplate selling but then come across an item in the *Financial Times* that rehashes the company's recent successes and also sparks new optimism. You wonder whether ABC could climb even higher. Which answer describes your likeliest response given ABC's recent performance and the FT article?

A   I think I'll hold off and wait to see what happens. I'd really "kick" myself if I sold now and ABC continued to go up.

B   I'll probably sell because ABC has hit the target I set, and I try to stick to the targets I set.

Question 2:

Suppose you have decided to invest £10,000 in one individual company stock, and you have narrowed your choice down to two companies: Blue, Inc., and Red, Inc. Blue is a well-followed, eminently established company whose shareholders include many large pension funds. Red is newer but has performed well; it has not garnered the same kind of public profile as Blue, and it has few well-known investors. According to your calculations, both stocks are expected to have equal risk and return payoffs. Which answer most closely matches your thought process in this situation?

A   I would probably feel indifferent between the two investments, because both generated the same expected parameters with respect to risk and return.

B   I will most likely invest in Blue because if I invested in Red and my investment failed, I would feel foolish. Few well-known investors backed Red, and I would really regret going against their informed consensus only to discover that I was wrong.

C   I will most likely invest in Blue because I feel safe taking the same course as so many respected institutional investors. If Blue does decline in value, I know I won't be the only one caught by surprise. With so many savvy professionals sharing my predicament, I could hardly blame myself for poor judgment.

Scoring Guidelines:

People answering A in Question 1 and/or B or C in Question 2 may harbor susceptibility to regret-aversion bias.

Overconfidence Bias Diagnostic

Question 1:

How easy do you think it was to predict the collapse of the housing market in the United States in 2007–2008?

A   Easy.

B   Somewhat easy.

C   Somewhat difficult.

D   Difficult.

(continued)

Exhibit 8   (Continued)

Question 2:

Assume that from 1926 through 2006, the compound annual return for equities was 10 percent. In any given year, what returns do you expect your equity investments to produce?

A Below 10 percent.

B About 10 percent.

C Above 10 percent.

D **Well above 10 percent.**

Question 3:

How much ability do you believe you have in picking investments that will outperform the market?

A Absolutely no ability.

B Little if any ability.

C Some ability.

D **A fair amount of ability.**

Scoring Guidelines:

Answering A or B in Question 1, answering C or D in Question 2, or answering C or D in Question 3 indicates susceptibility to overconfidence bias.

Self-Control Bias Diagnostic

Question 1:

Suppose that you are in need of a new automobile. You have been driving your current car for seven years, and it's time for a change. Which of the following approaches are you most likely to take?

A I would typically "under spend" on a car because I view a car as transportation and I don't need anything fancy. Besides, I can save the extra money I might have spent on a fancy car and put it away in my savings accounts.

B I would typically purchase a medium-priced model, with some fancy options, simply because I enjoy a nice car. I may forego other purchases in order to afford a nice car. I would not purchase anything extravagant, but a nice car is something that I value to an extent and am willing to spend money to obtain.

C **When it comes to cars, I like to indulge myself. I'd probably splurge on a top-of-the-line model and select most or all available luxury options. Even if I must purchase this car at the expense of saving money, for the long term, I believe that it's vital to "live in the moment." This car is simply my way of living in the moment.**

Question 2:

How would you characterize your retirement savings patterns?

A I consult my advisers and make sure that every tax-favored investment vehicle is "maxed out" (e.g., 401(k), IRA), and I will often save additional funds in taxable accounts.

Exhibit 8   (Continued)

B   I will usually take advantage of most tax-favored investment vehicles, though in some cases I'm sure that details may have escaped my attention. I may or may not save something in taxable investment accounts.

C   **I hardly ever save for retirement. I spend most of my disposable income, so very little remains available for savings.**

Scoring Guidelines:

People answering B or C to Questions 1 or 2 may be susceptible to self-control bias. Lack of self-control is very common.

Through this process, Moore finds that Mr. R is indeed susceptible to the following emotional biases:

- **Regret-aversion bias** (the tendency to avoid making a decision for fear the decision may cause regret later).
- **Overconfidence bias** (the tendency to overestimate one's investment savvy).
- **Self-control bias** (the tendency to spend today rather than save for tomorrow).

As part of the original financial planning process, Moore administered a risk tolerance questionnaire to Mr. R for the purpose of generating a mean–variance optimization portfolio recommendation. When Moore generated the optimization recommendation, Mr. R's proposed asset allocation was 60 percent stocks, 30 percent bonds, and 10 percent cash. Moore's job is now to answer the following three questions:

- What effect do Mr. R's biases have on the asset allocation decision?
- Should Moore moderate or adapt to Mr. R's biases?
- What is an appropriate behaviorally modified asset allocation for Mr. R?

Solutions to Mr. Renaldo Case Study

Effect of Biases   Mr. Renaldo has emotional biases that provide a clear indication of what allocation he would naturally prefer, which is one dominated by equities. Mr. Renaldo's overconfidence leads him to be more comfortable with equities than may be appropriate. This overconfidence, as well as a potential endowment bias, may explain why he has chosen to hold a substantial part of his portfolio in his employing company's stock. Additionally, Mr. R is likely to experience regret if he misses a major market move. On the other hand, he has a high need for current income that supplements his "spend today" mentality (self-control bias), and he may need the "ballast" of fixed-income investments in the event of a market downturn. Because his level of wealth is high, however, he does have some flexibility with his allocation to favor equity over fixed income.

Moderate or Adapt?   When considering level of wealth, Mr. Renaldo clearly does not run a "standard of living" risk, which argues for adapting to his biases. Additionally, his behavioral biases are principally emotional (overconfidence, regret aversion, self-control). Given these facts, and given that he naturally prefers an allocation favoring equity, Moore now has the information with which to make the following graph and the "moderate, adapt, or both moderate *and* adapt" recommendation.

Exhibit 9   Illustration of Mr. Renaldo's Case Study Information

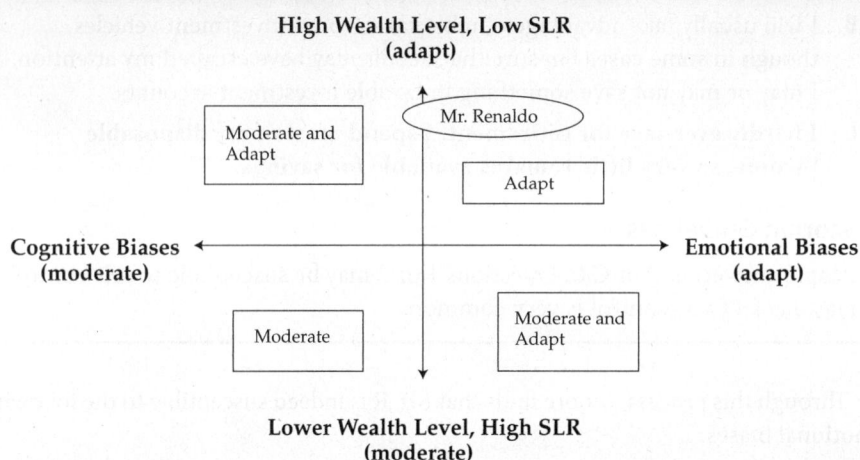

High Wealth Level, Low SLR
(adapt)

Mr. Renaldo

Moderate and
Adapt

Adapt

Cognitive Biases ← — — — — — — — — — — — — → Emotional Biases
(moderate)   (adapt)

Moderate

Moderate and
Adapt

Lower Wealth Level, High SLR
(moderate)

Moore decides that the appropriate recommendation is to *adapt* to Mr. R's biases and create a more aggressive portfolio that Mr. R can adhere to and be comfortable with. Moore also recommends that Mr. R reduce his company stock position by 50 percent and reduce spending, if possible. At the same time, Moore will run a cash flow analysis to ensure that in the event of a market downturn, Mr. R's living expenses will not be at risk. Moore also advises a comfortable cash reserve.

Behaviorally Modified Portfolio Decision   The mean–variance optimizer's recommended allocation was **60 percent stocks, 30 percent bonds, and 10 percent cash**. Using guidelines presented earlier in the reading for emotional biases at a high wealth level, in Moore's judgment, an appropriate behaviorally modified asset allocation is an allocation of **70 percent stocks, 20 percent bonds, and 10 percent cash**. When Moore checks his financial planning software to make sure that this allocation will statistically ensure that Mr. R will have adequate living expenses in the event of a market downturn, it shows that the behaviorally modified asset allocation indeed works. Thus, Moore recommends this allocation to Mr. R, explaining how he arrived at that particular allocation recommendation.

5.2.2 *Case Study #2: Mrs. Maradona (Lower Wealth Level, Cognitive Biases)*

Mrs. Maradona ("Mrs. M") is a 75-year-old widow from the United States with a modest lifestyle and no income beyond what her investment portfolio of $1,500,000 generates (about $90,000 per year) and a small government pension of $10,000 annually. Her adviser, Mr. Bobby Moore, has known Mrs. M for about five years. Although Mrs. M did not clearly articulate her investment goals when Moore first started working with her, over time Moore has learned that Mrs. M's primary investment goals are 1) to not lose money and 2) to maintain the purchasing power of her assets after fees and taxes. Her desire to not lose money stems from the fact that she recalls that her parents lost money in the US market crash of 1929; she has a "Depression Era" mentality. One of her tendencies is to spread her money around many different banks, and she speaks regularly about various "pots" of money—such as one for generating her income, one for her grandson's education, and one for paying her bills. Moore has been challenged by the fact that Mrs. M is quite stubborn in her opinions and rarely, if ever, listens to Moore when he recommends that she change her way of thinking about her investment money and portfolio allocation. Her knowledge of financial concepts is limited, but she is willing to meet regularly and discuss issues with Moore over tea.

Moore is concerned that she is too conservative in her approach and will not accomplish one of her key goals, keeping her purchasing power, because she only invests in government bonds and cash. By taking this approach, her portfolio will not keep up with her spending after inflation and taxes in the long run; therefore, she is putting herself at risk to outlive her assets. As Moore reflects one day on his relationship with Mrs. M, he realizes that the only recommendation she has accepted is to buy investment-grade corporate bonds to slightly increase her returns. Moore suspects that behavioral biases are influencing Mrs. M and not permitting her to feel comfortable with changing her portfolio. Moore asks her if she will take a 15-question assessment to examine her investor personality. She agrees. Based on the answers to the assessment, Moore decides to delve further into three biases: *anchoring, mental accounting, and loss aversion.* Moore provides Mrs. M with additional questions on these three biases. Exhibit 10 shows Mrs. M's answers in **bold**.

Exhibit 10   Mrs. Maradona's Bias Diagnostic Tests

Anchoring Bias Diagnostic

Question 1:

Suppose you own a five-bedroom house and have decided it is time to "down-size" to a smaller house. You are not in a rush to sell your house, but taxes and general expenses on your home are significant and you want to sell it as soon as possible. Your real estate agent, who you have known for many years and trust, lists your home for sale at $500,000. You only paid $125,000 for the house 10 years ago, so you are thrilled. The house has been on the market for several months, and you have not had any serious offers. One day, you get a phone call from your agent saying he needs to come over right away. When he arrives, he tells you that Books-Direct, a major employer in town, just declared bankruptcy and 1,000 people are out of work. He has been in meetings all week with his colleagues, and they estimate that real estate prices are down about 10 percent across all types of homes in your area. He says that you must decide at what price you now want to list your home based on this new information. You tell him that you will think it over and get back to him shortly. Please select one of the following that would be your answer:

A You decide to keep your home on the market for $500,000.

B **You decide to lower your price by 5 percent to $475,000.**

C You decide to lower your price by 10 percent to $450,000.

D You decide to lower your price to $425,000 because you want to be sure you get a bid on the house.

Scoring Guidelines:

Mrs. M chose B, and thus she may be susceptible to anchoring bias. It is clear that if she wants to sell her home, she should lower her price by 10 percent. Mrs. M demonstrates that she is "anchored" to $500,000 and will not fully adjust to the updated information.

Mental Accounting Bias Diagnostic Test

Question 1:

How do you tend to think about your money?

A I tend to think about my money as one "pot," and money is spent out of that one pot.

(continued)

Exhibit 10   (Continued)

B   I tend to segregate my money into various accounts, such as money for paying bills, money for traveling, and money for bequeaths.

C   I tend to segregate my money based on its source, such as pension, interest income, or capital gains.

Scoring Guidelines:

Mrs. M selected B. People who select B or C may be susceptible to mental accounting bias.

Loss-Aversion Diagnostic Test

Question 1:

Suppose you are presented with the following investment choices. Please choose between the following two outcomes:

A   **An assured gain of $400.**

B   A 25 percent chance of gaining $2,000 and a 75 percent chance of gaining nothing.

Question 2:

You are then asked to choose between the following two outcomes:

A   An assured loss of $400.

B   **A 50 percent chance of losing $1,000, and a 50 percent chance of losing nothing.**

Scoring Guidelines

Question 1:

Loss-averse investors are likely to opt for the assurance of a profit in A, even though the expected value of B is $500.

Question 2:

Loss-averse investors are more likely to select B even though the expected value in B is −$500 and the loss in A is only $400.

By making both these choices, Mrs. M appears to exhibit loss aversion.

Moore's suspicions are confirmed. Mrs. M is subject to the following biases:

- **Loss-aversion bias** (the tendency to feel the pain of losses more acutely than the pleasure of gains).

- **Anchoring and adjustment bias** (the tendency to believe that current market levels are "right"; up or down directional estimates are made from the current level).

- **Mental accounting bias** (the tendency to segregate money into different "accounts.")

As part of the original asset allocation process, Moore also administered a risk tolerance questionnaire to Mrs. M for the purpose of generating a mean–variance optimization portfolio recommendation. When Moore generated the optimization recommendation, Mrs. Maradona's "rational" asset allocation was 70 percent bonds, 20 percent stocks, and 10 percent cash; her actual allocation is 100 percent bonds.

Moore is convinced that Mrs. M needs to have a riskier portfolio than the one she currently has and that the reason she is invested so conservatively is primarily because of behavioral biases. Moore's job is now to answer the following three questions:

- What effect do Mrs. M's biases have on the asset allocation decision?
- Should Moore moderate or adapt to Mrs. M's biases?
- What is an appropriate behaviorally modified asset allocation for Mrs. M?

Solutions to Mrs. Maradona Case Study

Effect of Biases   Mrs. Maradona's biases are consistent and demonstrate to Moore a clear allocation preference for bonds. Because Mrs. Maradona does not want to put her principal at risk (which is manifested by loss-aversion bias) and separates her money into mental accounts (mental accounting), she would naturally prefer the safe and secure asset allocation of 100 percent bonds that she now has. Additionally, because the stock market rises and falls regularly, she will likely make irrational conclusions about what the "right" level of the overall stock market should be (anchoring bias); as a result, she will be wary of any exposure to equities. Thus, if Moore as her adviser presented her with an allocation of 100 percent bonds, she would be likely to immediately agree with that recommendation. However, Moore understands that she has a bias toward such an allocation.

Moderate or Adapt?   Mrs. Maradona's level of wealth—which, while not low, is not high—puts her at a relatively high standard of living risk (SLR). If Moore *adapts* to her biases and recommends an allocation of 100 percent bonds, Moore's financial planning software tells him that Mrs. Maradona runs the risk of outliving her assets, a clearly unacceptable outcome. Moore needs to help her understand that she would be at risk if she accepted a 100 percent bond portfolio. Because her biases are principally cognitive (mental accounting, anchoring), and these types of biases can be corrected with education and advice, Moore is confident he can help her make changes. Moore now has the information needed to make the following table.

Exhibit 11   Illustration of Mrs. Maradona's Case Study Information

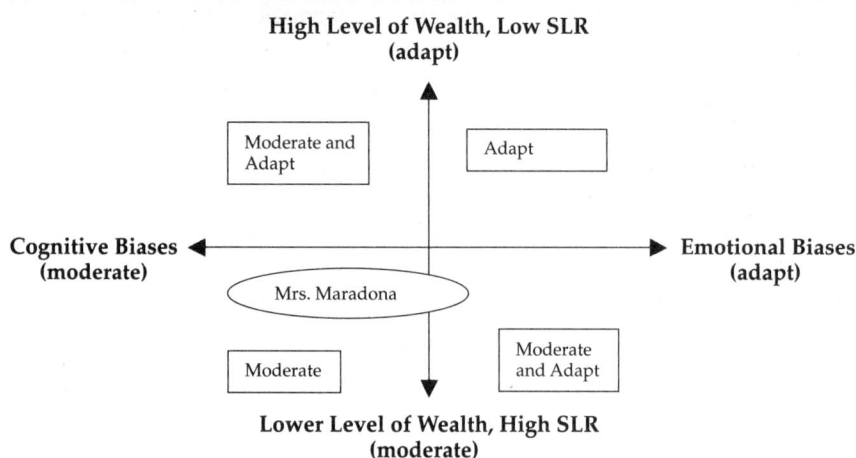

Behaviorally Modified Portfolio Decision   Moore decides that an appropriate course of action is to *moderate* Mrs. M's bias preferences, so he recommends that she accept some risk in her portfolio. Moore reasons that an appropriate moderation of Mrs. M's biases will result in the "rational" allocation of **70 percent bonds, 20 percent equity, and 10 percent cash** (the mean–variance recommendation). Moore checks his financial planning software to make sure that this allocation will statistically ensure that Mrs. M will not outlive her money. The software shows that this allocation is acceptable. Moore explains to Mrs. M how an allocation based on her biases may have led to an allocation such that her resources would have likely been depleted before her death. Thus, Moore recommends the **70 percent bonds, 20 percent equity, and 10 percent cash** allocation to Mrs. M. Also, Moore will continue a program of investor education on the risk of outliving one's assets.

SUMMARY

Behavioral biases potentially affect the behaviors and decisions of financial market participants. By understanding behavioral biases, financial market participants may be able to moderate or adapt to the biases and as a result improve upon economic outcomes. These biases may be categorized as either cognitive errors or emotional biases. The type of bias influences whether the impact of the bias is moderated or adapted to.

Among the points made in this reading are the following:

- Individuals do not necessarily act rationally and consider all available information in the decision-making process because they may be influenced by behavioral biases.

- Biases may lead to sub-optimal decisions.

- Behavioral biases may be categorized as either cognitive errors or emotional biases. A single bias may, however, have aspects of both with one type of bias dominating.

- Cognitive errors stem from basic statistical, information-processing, or memory errors; cognitive errors typically result from faulty reasoning.

- Emotional biases stem from impulse or intuition; emotional biases tend to result from reasoning influenced by feelings.

- Cognitive errors are more easily corrected for because they stem from faulty reasoning rather than an emotional predisposition.

- Emotional biases are harder to correct for because they are based on feelings, which can be difficult to change.

- To adapt to a bias is to recognize and accept the bias and to adjust for the bias rather than to attempt to moderate the bias.

- To moderate a bias is to recognize the bias and to attempt to reduce or even eliminate the bias within the individual.

- Cognitive errors can be further classified into two categories: belief perseverance biases and information-processing biases.

- Belief perseverance errors reflect an inclination to maintain beliefs. The belief is maintained by committing statistical, information-processing, or memory errors. Belief perseverance biases are closely related to the psychological concept of cognitive dissonance.

- Belief perseverance biases include conservatism, confirmation, representativeness, illusion of control, and hindsight.

- Information-processing biases result in information being processed and used illogically or irrationally.

- Information-processing biases include anchoring and adjustment, mental accounting, framing, and availability.

- Emotional biases include loss aversion, overconfidence, self-control, status quo, endowment, and regret aversion.

- Understanding and detecting biases is the first step in overcoming the effect of biases on financial decisions. By understanding behavioral biases, financial market participants may be able to moderate or adapt to the biases and as a result improve upon economic outcomes.

REFERENCES

Barber, Brad M., and Terrance Odean. 2001. "Boys Will Be Boys: Gender, Overconfidence, and Common Stock Investment." *Quarterly Journal of Economics*, vol. 116, no. 1:261–292.

Barras, Laurent, Olivier Scaillet, and Russell Wermers. 2010. "False Discoveries in Mutual Fund Performance: Measuring Luck in Estimated Alphas." *Journal of Finance*, vol. 65, no. 1 (February):179–216.

Benartzi, Shlomo, and Richard H. Thaler. 1995. "Myopic Loss Aversion and the Equity Premium Puzzle." *Quarterly Journal of Economics*, vol. 110, no. 1:73–92.

Bogle, John C. 2005. "The Relentless Rules of Humble Arithmetic." 2005. *Financial Analysts Journal*, vol. 61, no. 6 (November/December):22–35.

Butler, Stephen A. 1986. "Anchoring in the Judgmental Evaluation of Audit Samples." *Accounting Review*, vol. 6, no. 1:101–111.

Clarke, Roger G., and Meir Statman. 2000. "The DJIA Crossed 652,230." *Journal of Portfolio Management*, vol. 26, no. 2 (Winter):89–92.

Fischhoff, Baruch. 1975. "Hindsight Is Not Equal to Foresight: The Effect of Outcome Knowledge on Judgment under Uncertainty." *Journal of Experimental Psychology. Human Perception and Performance*, vol. 1, no. 3 (August):288–299.

Gadarowski, Christopher. 2001. "Financial Press Coverage and Expected Stock Returns." Working paper, Cornell University.

Gilovich, Thomas. 1993. *How We Know What Isn't So: The Fallibility of Human Reason in Everyday Life*. New York: Free Press.

Hirshleifer, David. 2001. "Investor Psychology and Asset Pricing." *Journal of Finance*, vol. 56, no. 4:1533–1597.

Joyce, Edward G., and Gary C. Biddle. 1981. "Anchoring and Adjustment in Probabilistic Inference in Auditing." *Journal of Accounting Research*, vol. 19, no. 1:120–145.

Kahneman, Daniel, and Mark Riepe. 1998. "Aspects of Investor Psychology." *Journal of Portfolio Management*, vol. 24, no. 4:52–65.

Kahneman, Daniel, and Amos Tversky. 1979. "Prospect Theory: An Analysis of Decision under Risk." *Econometrica: Journal of the Econometric Society*, vol. 47, no. 2:263–291.

Kahneman, Daniel, Peter P. Wakker, and Rakesh Sarin. 1997. "Back to Bentham? Explorations of Experienced Utility." *Quarterly Journal of Economics*, vol. 112, no. 2:375–405.

Keynes, John Maynard. 1936. *The General Theory of Employment, Interest, and Money*. New York: Harcourt, Brace.

Koening, J. 1999. "Behavioral Finance: Examining Thought Processes for Better Investing." *Trust & Investments*, vol. 60, (May/June):17–23.

Kroll, Yoram, Haim Levy, and Amnon Rapoport. 1988. "Experimental Tests of the Separation Theorem and the Capital Asset Pricing Model." *American Economic Review*, vol. 78, no. 3:500–519.

Langer, Ellen. 1983. *The Psychology of Control*. Beverly, CA: Sage Publications.

Montier, James. 2002a. *Behavioural Finance: Insights into Irrational Minds and Markets*. West Sussex, England: John Wiley & Sons.

Montier, James. 2002b. "Equity Research." Research report, Dresdner Kleinwort Wasserstein.

Pompian, Michael. 2006. *Behavioral Finance and Wealth Management*. Hoboken, NJ: John Wiley & Sons.

Pompian, Michael, and John Longo. 2005. "Incorporating Behavioral Finance into Your Practice." *Journal of Financial Planning*, vol. 18, no. 3:58–63.

Posner, Richard. 1998. "Rational Choice, Behavioral Economics, and the Law." *Stanford Law Review*, vol. 50, no. 5:1551–1575.

Samuelson, Paul A. 1963. "Risk and Uncertainty: A Fallacy of Large Numbers." *Scientia*, 6th Series, 57th year (April–May):108–113.

Samuelson, William, and Richard Zeckhauser. 1988. "Status Quo Bias in Decision Making." *Journal of Risk and Uncertainty*, vol. 1, no. 1:7–59.

Shefrin, Hersh, and Meir Statman. 1984. "Explaining Investor Preference for Cash Dividends." *Journal of Financial Economics*, vol. 13, no. 2:253–282.

Shefrin, Hersh, and Meir Statman. 1985. "The Disposition to Sell Winners Too Early and Ride Losers Too Long: Theory and Evidence." *Journal of Finance*, vol. 40, no. 3:77–90.

Slovic, Paul, and Sarah Lichtenstein. 1971. "Comparison of Bayesian and Regression Approaches to the Study of Information Processing in Judgment." *Organizational Behavior and Human Performance*, vol. 6, no. 6:649–744.

Slovic, Paul, Baruch Fischhoff, and Sarah Lichtenstein. 1982. "Why Study Risk Perception?" *Risk Analysis*, vol. 2, no. 2:83–93.

Statman, Meir. 1999. "Behavioral Finance: Past battles and Future Engagements." *Financial Analysts Journal*, vol. 55, no. 6 (November/December):18–27.

Statman, Meir. 2008. "What is Behavioral Finance?" In *Handbook of Finance*. Edited by Frank Fabozzi. Hoboken, NJ: John Wiley & Sons.

Thaler, Richard H. 1980. "Toward a Positive Theory of Economic Choice." *Journal of Economic Behavior & Organization*, vol. 1, no. 1:39–60.

Thaler, Richard H., and Eric J. Johnson. 1990. "Gambling with the House Money and Trying to Break Even: The Effects of Prior Outcomes on Risky Choice." *Management Science*, vol. 36, no. 6:643–660.

Tversky, Amos, and Daniel Kahneman. 1973. "Availability: A Heuristic for Judging Frequency and Probability." *Cognitive Psychology*, vol. 5, no. 2 (September):207–232.

Vanguard Investments Australia. 2004. "Fund Performance May Be Luck Not Skill New Study Shows." News Release (Sydney) Vanguard Investments LTD/Morningstar (27 April).

The following information relates to Questions 1–5

Luca Gerber recently became the chief investment officer for the Ludwigs Family Charity, a mid-size private foundation in Switzerland. Prior to assuming this role, Gerber was a well-known health care industry analyst. The Ludwigs' family fortune is primarily the result of entrepreneurship. Gerhard Ludwigs founded ABC Innovations (ABC), a biotech company dedicated to small cell lung cancer research. The foundation's portfolio is fifteen percent invested in ABC.

Gerber initially feels that fifteen percent investment in ABC is high. However, upon review, he decides it is appropriate based on Ludwigs' involvement and their past success with similar ventures. Gerber makes a mental note to himself to closely monitor the investment in ABC because he is not familiar with small-cap startup companies. The remaining 85 percent of the foundation's portfolio is invested in equity of high quality large-cap pharmaceutical companies. Gerber deems this allocation appropriate and is excited that he is able to continue to use his superior knowledge of the health care industry.

For the past two years, ABC has been dedicated to Project M, an effort directed at developing a drug for the treatment of relapses in small cell lung cancer. Project M has delayed its Phase Two trials twice. Published results from Phase One trials have raised some concerns regarding the drug. In its last two quarterly investors' conference calls, ABC's CEO was very cautious in discussing expectations for Project M. ABC's stock price decreased by over 20 percent during the past six months. Gerber believes that the research setbacks are temporary because of ABC's past success with projects. He expects that ABC will begin Phase Two within a year, and also believes that once Project M goes into Phase Two, ABC's stock price should reach a new 52-week high of CHF 80.

Soon after deciding to hold the stock, Gerber reads an article by ABC's chief scientist in which certain scientific results from Project M are detailed. As a conclusion, the article states: "Although we still have some major obstacles to overcome, the Project M team has seen positive signs that a treatment for small cell lung cancer is achievable." While Gerber has difficulty interpreting the scientific results, he feels reassured after reading the concluding statement.

Today, ABC announces the news that it will no longer pursue Project M, citing early signs of failure of the project. As a result of the announcement, the stock price drops by 50 percent. Gerber is stunned. He reviews the company's history and notes that ABC has been up front about its struggles to solve the Project M issues. Gerber now realizes that he has been ignoring all the signs and feels a tremendous regret for not having sold the foundation's investment in ABC earlier.

1   **Discuss** how Gerber displayed availability bias with *one* example. **Determine** the implications of availability bias for financial decision making and **describe** *one* way Gerber could overcome the bias.

2   **Discuss** how Gerber displayed overconfidence bias and **cite** *one* example to support this statement. **Distinguish** between the availability bias and the overconfidence bias.

3   **Discuss** how Gerber displayed conservatism bias. **Cite** three examples from the reading.

4   **Determine** whether Gerber displayed confirmation bias when reviewing the chief scientist's article. **Justify** your answer with one reason.

Answer Question 4 in the template provided below:

Determine whether Gerber displayed confirmation bias when reviewing the chief scientist's article. (circle one)	**Justify** your answer with one reason.
Agree	
Disagree	

5   **Indicate** which bias is illustrated by Gerber's focus on the achievement of a 52-week high of CHF 80. **Discuss** how Gerber could have mitigated its impact.

The following information relates to Questions 6–12

Tiffany Jordan is a hedge fund manager with a history of outstanding performance. For the past 10 years, Jordan's fund has used an equity market neutral strategy (long/short strategy that strives to eliminate market risk; i.e., beta should be zero) which has proved to be effective as a result of Jordan's hard work. An equity market neutral strategy normally generates large daily trading volume and shifts in individual security positions. Jordan's reputation has grown over the years as her fund has consistently beaten its benchmark. Employee turnover on Jordan's team has been high; she has a tendency to be quick to blame, and rarely gives credit to team members for success. During the past twelve months, her fund has been significantly underperforming against its benchmark.

One of Jordan's junior analysts, Jeremy Tang, is concerned about the underperformance and notes the following:

Observation 1   Certain positions are significantly under water, have much higher risk profiles, and have been held for much longer than normal.

Observation 2   The trading volume of the fund has decreased by more than 40 percent during the past year.

Observation 3   The portfolio is more concentrated in a few sectors than in the past.

Tang is worried that the portfolio may be in violation of the fund's Investment Policy Statement (IPS). Tang brings this to Jordan's attention during a regular weekly team meeting. Jordan dismisses Tang's analysis and tells the team not to worry because she knows what she is doing. Jordan indicates that since she believes the pricing misalignment will correct itself, the portfolio will not be able to take advantage of the reversion to the mean if she sells certain losing positions. She reassures the team that this strategy has performed well in the past and that the markets will revert and the fund's returns will return to normal levels.

Tang tactfully suggests that the team review the fund's IPS together, and Jordan interrupts him and reminds the team that she has memorized the IPS by heart. Tang contemplates his next step. He is concerned that Jordan is displaying behavioral biases which are affecting the fund's performance.

6 By taking credit for successes but assigning blame for failures, Jordan is *most likely* demonstrating:

    A loss-aversion bias.

    B self-attribution bias.

    C illusion of knowledge bias.

7 Which of Tang's observations is *least likely* to be the consequence of Jordan demonstrating loss-aversion bias?

    A Observation 1.

    B Observation 2.

    C Observation 3.

8 Which of Jordan's actions *least* supports that she may be affected by the illusion of control bias?

    A Her dismissal of Tang's analysis.

    B Her routine of holding weekly team meetings.

    C Her comment on market turnaround and current holdings.

9 How does Jordan *most likely* demonstrate loss-aversion bias?

    A Telling the team not to worry.

    B Reducing the portfolio turnover this year.

    C Deciding to hold the losing positions until they turn around.

10 Which of the following emotional biases has Jordan *most likely* exhibited?

    A Endowment.

    B Regret aversion.

    C Overconfidence.

11 Which one of the following biases did Jordan *not* demonstrate?

    A Self-attribution.

    B Representativeness.

    C Illusion of knowledge.

12 Which of Tang's findings is *not* a typical consequence of self-control bias?

    A Failure to explore other portfolio opportunities.

    B Asset allocation imbalance problems in the portfolio.

    C A higher risk profile in the portfolio due to pursuit of higher returns.

SOLUTIONS

1   Availability bias, a cognitive error, is an information-processing bias. Individuals exhibiting this bias will assess the likelihood of an outcome based on how easily they can recall the information. Gerber exhibits this bias in two ways:

● Although Gerber felt the foundation's investment in ABC was high, he decided that Ludwigs' involvement and their past success justified the investment in ABC. The information on the past success of Ludwigs' investments came easily to mind.

● Gerber believed 100 percent of the foundation's portfolio in the health care industry was appropriate, most likely because of his past experience as an analyst in the industry. It is easier for Gerber to recall information from his past than to develop a diversified investment portfolio. Investors who exhibit availability bias may limit their investment opportunity set, may choose an investment without doing a thorough analysis of the stock, may fail to diversify, and may not achieve an appropriate asset allocation. Gerber exhibits all of these tendencies when he is evaluating the foundation's portfolio.

The implications of this bias lead the portfolio to be undiversified, and as a result, the portfolio holds assets that may not be appropriate. Gerber is only investing in pharmaceutical companies. The following is a summary of issues with the foundation's portfolio:

● No thorough analysis regarding investment in ABC.

● A limited investment opportunity set; invested only in the health care sector.

● An undiversified portfolio.

● An inappropriate asset allocation; invested only in equity.

Gerber could overcome this bias by developing an appropriate investment policy strategy, with a focus on appropriate goals (short- and long-term), and having a disciplined approach to investment decision making. An investment policy statement would help provide discipline and would alert Gerber and his team that he really has only considered investments that he is familiar with. Further, Gerber and his investment team should consider the asset allocation within the portfolio.

2   Gerber displayed overconfidence bias by having too much faith in his "superior knowledge of the health care industry." Overconfidence bias and the related illusion of knowledge bias result when individuals overestimate their knowledge levels and abilities. Overconfidence bias has aspects of both cognitive and emotional errors but is classified as emotional because the emotional aspect dominates. Emotional biases, which stem from impulse or intuition, may be considered to result from reasoning influenced by feelings. These biases are difficult to correct.

Overconfidence is primarily an emotional bias and is thus different from availability bias which is an information-processing bias and a cognitive error. Cognitive errors result from faulty reasoning and analysis. The individual may be attempting to follow a rational decision-making process but fails to do so because of cognitive errors. Gerber perceives the foundation's investment allocation and stock selection as appropriate, and does not process all of the information available to him. He notes that ABC should be monitored closely because of the fact he is not familiar with startup companies; however, he does not process information that goes beyond his knowledge base to see that the investment itself is problematic. Although the overconfidence and availability biases are clearly related, Gerber can make better investment decisions by focusing on the cognitive error aspects of his behavior. Cognitive biases are easier to correct for than emotional biases, which are based on how people feel.

3 Conservatism bias, a cognitive error, is a belief perseverance bias in which people maintain their prior views or forecasts by inadequately incorporating new information. This cognitive error has aspects of both statistical and information-processing errors. Gerber displayed conservatism bias by maintaining his prior views on ABC without adequately incorporating new information. There are several examples of new information that was either ignored or inadequately considered:

- the delays in initiation of Phase Two trials;
- the discouraging results from Phase One;
- the cautionary language from the CEO; and
- the chief scientist's statement indicating that there were "major obstacles to overcome."

Gerber disregarded all the negative news and cautionary language that was released by ABC. Gerber failed to incorporate the new information into his analysis of ABC. The impact was a loss to the foundation, which could have been reduced had Gerber incorporated the information into his analysis and adjusted the foundation's holdings of ABC.

4

Determine whether Gerber displayed confirmation bias when reviewing the chief scientist's article. (circle one)	**Justify** your answer with one reason.
(Agree) Disagree	Confirmation bias, a cognitive error, is a belief perseverance bias. Individuals who exhibit this bias look for confirmation of their belief and ignore any information which contradicts their belief. Gerber displayed confirmation bias by selectively placing more weight on the portion of the statement "the Project M team has seen positive signs that treatment for small cell lung cancer is achievable" in the article, even though the positive results mentioned in the article appeared to be a general statement. Gerber ignored the comment on the major obstacles which the team had encountered because it was contrary to his belief in Project M.

5 Gerber demonstrated anchoring bias by placing high hope in ABC stock reaching a new 52-week high of CHF 80. Anchoring is an information-processing bias which influences the way people estimate probabilities. When required to estimate a value with unknown magnitude, people generally begin by

envisioning some initial default number—an "anchor"—which they then adjust up or down to reflect subsequent information and analysis. Despite setbacks and new information, Gerber did not adjust his view of CHF 80, but continued to cling to this anchor or belief even after reviewing the chief scientist's report. He perceived new information through a warped lens; thus, the decision making deviated from rational reasoning.

To overcome anchoring bias, Gerber should consciously ask questions that may reveal an anchoring and adjustment bias: "Am I holding on to this stock based on rational analysis, or am I trying to attain a price that I am anchored to, such as the purchase price or a high water mark?" He should look at the basis for his decision to hold ABC to determine if it is anchored to a price target (a new 52-week high) or based on an objective, rational view of the company's fundamentals. Gerber should have periodically reviewed his decision-making process to determine if his analysis of ABC's prospects was appropriate, focusing more on the company's fundamentals rather than the price target.

6 B is correct. Self-attribution is a bias in which people take credit for successes and assign responsibilities for failure. Jordan attributes successful decisions to herself while poor decisions are attributed to the team. Her self-esteem affects how she looks at success and failure. Self-attribution and illusion of knowledge biases contribute to overconfidence bias, which Jordan clearly demonstrates later when she tells the team that she knows what she is doing.

7 C is correct. Loss aversion by itself may cause a sector concentration; however, a market neutral strategy tends to focus on individual stocks without regard to the sector. The sector exposure would be mitigated with the balancing of the individual long and short positions.

8 B is correct. Holding weekly team meetings, which would indicate a willingness to listen to feedback from others, is not representative of the illusion of control bias. The illusion of control bias is one in which people believe they can control outcomes. Individuals exhibiting this bias display great certainty in their predictions of outcomes of chance events and ignore others' viewpoints. Jordan is sure that the market will turn around even though it is out of her control. She chooses not to listen to Tang who is questioning her viewpoint.

9 C is correct. Jordan's behavior is a classic example of loss aversion: When a loss occurs, she holds on to these positions longer than warranted. By doing so, Jordan has accepted more risk in the portfolio. Loss-aversion bias is one in which people exhibit a strong preference to avoid losses versus achieving gains. One of the consequences of loss aversion bias is that the financial management professional (in this case, Jordan) may hold losing investments in the hope that they will return to break-even or better.

10 C is correct. Jordan exhibits overconfidence in several ways. She ignores the analysis done by Tang. This may be because Jordan believes she is smarter and more informed than her team members, which is typical of an individual with an illusion of knowledge bias. The certainty she demonstrates that the market will revert is evidence of overconfidence. Her overconfidence is intensified by her self-attribution bias, which is demonstrated through her dealings with her team when she blames them for losses while taking credit for the gains. Finally, her portfolio's underperformance against the benchmark is a consequence of overconfidence bias.

11 B is correct. Nowhere in the scenario did it mention that Jordan classified certain information into a personalized category. Representativeness bias is a cognitive bias in which people tend to classify new information based on past experiences and classifications. Jordan is not relating the certainty about the future or her decision to hold losing positions back to something she has done or experienced in the past.

12 A is correct. Failing to explore other opportunities is a demonstration of status quo bias, not self-control. Self-control bias occurs when individuals deviate from their long-term goals, in this case, the investment policy statement, due to a lack of self-discipline. Jordan is not adhering to the strategy which has been successful in the past. The consequences of self-control bias include accepting too much risk in the portfolio (C) and asset allocation imbalance problems (B) as Jordan attempts to generate higher returns.

Behavioral Finance and Investment Processes

by Michael M. Pompian, CFA, Colin McLean, FSIP, and
Alistair Byrne, PhD, CFA

Michael M. Pompian, CFA (USA). Colin McLean, FSIP (United Kingdom). Alistair Byrne, PhD, CFA, is at Campion Asset Management (USA).

LEARNING OUTCOMES

Mastery	*The candidate should be able to:*
☐	**a.** explain the uses and limitations of classifying investors into personality types;
☐	**b.** discuss how behavioral factors affect adviser–client interactions;
☐	**c.** discuss how behavioral factors influence portfolio construction;
☐	**d.** explain how behavioral finance can be applied to the process of portfolio construction;
☐	**e.** discuss how behavioral factors affect analyst forecasts and recommend remedial actions for analyst biases;
☐	**f.** discuss how behavioral factors affect investment committee decision making and recommend techniques for mitigating their effects;
☐	**g.** describe how behavioral biases of investors can lead to market characteristics that may not be explained by traditional finance.

INTRODUCTION

1

Much of current economic and financial theory is based on the assumptions that individuals act rationally and consider all available information in the decision-making process.[1] Behavioral finance challenges these assumptions. The relaxing of these assumptions has implications at both the individual and market levels. It is important to note that, at the individual level, all market participants, whether they

---

1 Investors are assumed to be rational; investors make decisions consistent with utility theory and revise expectations (update beliefs) consistent with Bayes' formula. They are further assumed to be self-interested and risk-averse, to have access to perfect information, and to process all available information.

are less knowledgeable individual investors or experienced money managers, may act irrationally; in other words, all market participants may deviate from the behavior that is assumed in traditional financial theory. Some of these deviations have been identified and categorized as behavioral biases. In addition, individual behavioral biases may be reinforced in a group setting, which further complicates rational investment processes.

This reading focuses on understanding individual investor behavior and how it affects adviser–client relationships and portfolio construction, as well as on the analyst-, committee-, and market-level impact of behavioral biases. Section 2 discusses how investors may be classified by type based on the biases and other behaviors they display and explains the uses and limitations of classifying investors into types. Section 3 discusses how behavioral factors affect adviser–client relationships. Section 4 examines the potential effects of behavioral biases on portfolio construction. Section 5 discusses how behavioral biases affect the work of analysts, looking specifically at their forecasts, and explores remedial actions for analyst biases. Section 6 examines committee decision making and how behavioral biases may be amplified or mitigated in a group setting, and discusses steps to make committees more effective. Section 7 discusses how behavioral finance influences market behavior by examining market anomalies and observed market behavior. A summary and practice problems conclude the reading.

2 THE USES AND LIMITATIONS OF CLASSIFYING INVESTORS INTO TYPES

2.1 General Discussion of Investor Types

In recent decades, financial service professionals and researchers have been attempting to classify investors by their psychographic characteristics—in other words, by personality, values, attitudes, and interests—rather than classifying simply based on demographic characteristics. Psychographic classifications are particularly relevant with regard to individual strategy and risk tolerance. An investor's background, past experiences, and attitudes can play a significant role in decisions made during the asset allocation process. If investors fitting specific psychographic profiles are more likely to exhibit specific investor biases, then practitioners can attempt to recognize the relevant behavioral tendencies before investment decisions are made. It is important to note that because psychology is involved, no exact diagnosis can be made of any individual or situation. Although there are limitations to this type of analysis, if financial market participants can gain an understanding of their behavioral tendencies, the result is likely to be better investment outcomes.

We will now review two models of investor psychographics from the 1980s. One model was proposed in Barnewall (1987) and the other in Bailard, Biehl, and Kaiser (1986). We will then move to more recent models of investor behavior.

2.1.1 Barnewall Two-Way Model

One of the oldest and most prevalent psychographic investor models, based on the work of Marilyn MacGruder Barnewall and intended to help investment advisers interface with clients, distinguishes two relatively simple investor types: passive and active. Barnewall notes that "passive investors" are defined as those investors who have become wealthy passively—for example, by inheritance or by risking the capital of others rather than risking their own capital (managers who benefit when their companies do well are examples of the latter category). Passive investors have a greater need for security than they have tolerance for risk. Occupational groups that tend to have passive investors include corporate executives, lawyers with large regional firms, certified public accountants (CPAs) with large CPA companies, medical and dental non-surgeons, small business owners who inherited the business, politicians, bankers, and journalists. Further, the smaller the economic resources an investor has, the more likely the person is to be a passive investor. The lack of resources gives individuals a higher security need and a lower tolerance for risk.

"Active investors" are individuals who have been actively involved in wealth creation through investment, and they have risked their own capital in achieving their wealth objectives. Active investors have a higher tolerance for risk than they have need for security. Related to their high risk tolerance is the fact that active investors prefer to maintain control of their own investments. Their tolerance for risk is high because they believe in themselves. When active investors sense a loss of control, their risk tolerance drops quickly. They are involved in their own investments to the point that they gather tremendous amounts of information about the investments. By their involvement and control, they feel that they reduce risk to an acceptable level, which is often fallacious (Barnewall 1987).

Barnewall's work suggests that a simple, non-invasive overview of an investor's personal history and career record could signal potential pitfalls to guard against in establishing an advisory relationship. Her analysis also indicates that a quick, biographic glance at a client could provide important context for portfolio design.

2.1.2 *Bailard, Biehl, and Kaiser Five-Way Model*

The Bailard, Biehl, and Kaiser (BB&K) model features some of the principles of the Barnewall model, but by classifying investor personalities along two axes—level of confidence and method of action—it introduces an additional dimension of analysis. Bailard, Biehl, and Kaiser (1986) provide a graphic representation of their model (Exhibit 1). Kaiser (1990) explains:

> The first (aspect of personality) deals with how confidently the investor approaches life, regardless of whether it is his approach to his career, his health, or his money. These are important emotional choices, and they are dictated by how confident the investor is about some things or how much he tends to worry about them. The second element deals with whether the investor is methodical, careful, and analytical in his approach to life or whether he is emotional, intuitive, and impetuous. These two elements can be thought of as two "axes" of individual psychology; one axis is called the "confident–anxious" axis and the other is called the "careful–impetuous" axis.

Exhibit 1   Bailard, Biehl, and Kaiser Model

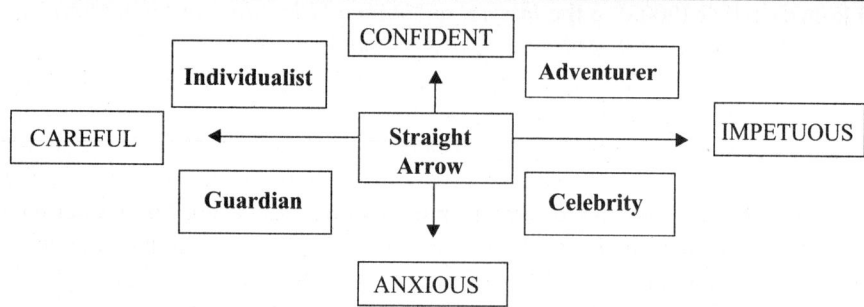

Exhibit 2 includes a synopsis of BB&K's descriptions of each of the five investor personality types that the model generates (Kaiser 1990).

Exhibit 2   BB&K Classifications

- The **Adventurer**: Adventurers may hold highly undiversified portfolios because they are confident and willing to take chances. Their confidence leads them to make their own decisions and makes them reluctant to take advice. This presents a challenge for an investment adviser.

- The **Celebrity**: Celebrities like to be the center of attention. They may hold opinions about some things but to a certain extent recognize their limitations and may be willing to seek and take advice about investing.

- The **Individualist**: Individualists are independent and confident, which may be reflected in their choice of employment. They like to make their own decisions but only after careful analysis. They are pleasant to advise because they will listen and process information rationally.

- The **Guardian**: Guardians are cautious and concerned about the future. As people age and approach retirement, they may become guardians. They are concerned about protecting their assets and may seek advice from those they perceive as being more knowledgeable than themselves.

- The **Straight Arrow**: Straight arrows are sensible and secure. They fall near the center of the graph. They are willing to take on some risk in the expectation of earning a commensurate return.

Although this model may be useful, it is possible that investors do not approach all parts of their life with equal confidence or care. It is important to focus on the approach to investing rather than placing undue focus on evidence from other aspects of their life. In addition, a limitation of all categorization schemes is that an individual's behavior patterns may change or lack consistency.

2.1.3 *New Developments in Psychographic Modeling: Behavioral Investor Types*

In recent years, there have been additional developments in the practical application of behavioral finance. Pompian (2008) identifies four behavioral investor types (BITs). The objective of this categorization scheme, similar to BB&K and Barnewall, is to help advisers and investors better understand investor behavior in an effort to make better investment decisions. However, the approach suggested by Pompian differs from some of the earlier approaches. This section will review the basics of developing investment plans that incorporate behavioral finance. It will build on key concepts in Pompian and Longo's article (2005) in the *Journal of Financial Planning*, and Pompian's book, *Behavioral Finance and Wealth Management* (2006).

These early works outline a method of applying behavioral finance to private clients in a way that Pompian refers to as "bottom up." This term means that for an adviser or investor to diagnose and treat behavioral biases, he or she must first test for all behavioral biases in the client. This testing is done to determine which biases a client has before being able to create an appropriate investment policy statement and a behaviorally modified asset allocation like those presented in the reading, "The Behavioral Biases of Individuals." Pompian and Longo (2005) explain how to plot bias type and wealth level information on a chart to create a "best practical allocation" or "best behaviorally modified allocation" for the client. However, some advisers may find this bottom-up approach too time-consuming or complex.

Pompian (2008) introduces a behavioral alpha (BA) approach. It is a "top-down" approach to bias identification that may be simpler and more efficient than a bottom-up approach. The BA approach is essentially a shortcut that may more efficiently identify biases for the purpose of determining which type of bias dominates. Using the BA approach, advisers and investors can test for the behavioral biases they are likely to encounter based on the psychological profile of clients and consider how to correct for or adapt to the biases.

The Behavioral Alpha Process: A Top-Down Approach

Step 1: Interview the client and identify active or passive traits and risk tolerance. Most advisers begin the planning process with a client interview, which consists mainly of a question-and-answer session intended to gain an understanding of the objectives, constraints, tolerance for accepting risk in the portfolio, and past investing practices of a client. Part of this process should also include the adviser determining whether a client is an *active* or *passive* investor, building on the work of Barnewall (1987). Through this process, the adviser is trying to determine whether the client has in the past (or does now) put his or her capital at risk to build wealth.[2] Understanding the characteristics of active and passive investors is important because they have tendencies toward different biases. Following is an example of a test created by Pompian (2008) to probe the risk tolerance and active/passive nature of a client. Predominantly "a" answers indicate higher risk tolerance and/or active investor traits, whereas "b" answers indicate lower risk tolerance and/or passive investor traits. Note that a traditional risk tolerance questionnaire is an appropriate way to evaluate the risk tolerance level of a client, but it may fail to address the active/passive nature of a client.

Test for Risk Tolerance and Active/Passive Traits

1 Have you risked your own capital in the creation of your wealth?

   A Yes.

   B No.

2 Which is stronger: your tolerance for risk to build wealth or the desire to preserve wealth?

   A Tolerance for risk.

   B Preserve wealth.

3 Would you prefer to maintain control over your investments or prefer to delegate that responsibility to someone else?

   A Maintain control.

   B Delegate.

4 Do you have faith in your abilities as an investor?

   A Yes.

   B No.

5 If you had to pick one of two portfolios, which would it be?

   A 80 percent stocks/20 percent bonds.

   B 40 percent stocks/60 percent bonds.

6 Is your wealth goal intended to continue your current lifestyle, or are you motivated to build wealth at the expense of current lifestyle?

---

2 It is important to make a distinction between investing in a diversified portfolio and risking capital. Risking capital involves doing such things as building companies (big or small), investing in speculative real estate using leverage, or working for oneself rather than for a large company.

A   Build wealth.

B   Continue current lifestyle.

7   In your work and personal life, do you generally prefer to take initiative by seeking out what needs to be done and then doing it, or do you prefer to take direction?

A   Take initiative.

B   Take direction.

8   Are you capital preservation oriented or are you willing to put your capital at risk to build wealth?

A   Capital at risk.

B   Capital preservation oriented.

9   Do you believe in the concept of borrowing money to make money/operate a business or do you prefer to limit the amount of debt you owe?

A   Borrow money.

B   Limit debt.

Step 2: Plot the investor on the active/passive and risk tolerance scale.   Once the adviser has classified the investor as active or passive and determined risk tolerance, the next step is to begin the process of identifying which one of the four BITs, identified by Pompian (2008) and shown in Exhibit 4, that the client falls into. The adviser's task at this point is to determine where the client falls on the risk scale in relation to how the client falls on the active/passive scale. The expectation is that active investors will rank medium to high on the risk tolerance scale whereas passive investors will rank medium to low on the risk scale. Naturally, this division will not always be the case. If there is an unexpected outcome, then the adviser should defer to the risk tolerance as the guiding factor in determining which biases to test for (see next section for more details on bias testing). Without further analysis, the expected relationship between risk and active/passive responses is shown in Exhibit 3.

Exhibit 3	Risk Tolerance and Active/Passive Scale		
General Type:	PASSIVE	ACTIVE	
Risk Tolerance:	Low	Medium	High

Step 3: Test for behavioral biases.   The last step in the process is to confirm the expectation that the client has certain behavioral biases associated and consistent with a specific BIT. Exhibit 4 provides an overview of the characteristics of each BIT, and Exhibit 5 illustrates the entire diagnostic process. An expanded description of each BIT and advice for dealing with each BIT follows Exhibit 5.

Exhibit 4 Biases Associated with Each Behavioral Investor Type

General Type	PASSIVE		ACTIVE	
Risk Tolerance Investment Style	Low ⟵			⟶ High
	Conservative	Moderate	Growth	Aggressive
Bias Types	Primarily emotional	Primarily cognitive	Primarily cognitive	Primarily emotional
BITs	Passive Preserver (PP)	Friendly Follower (FF)	Independent Individualist (II)	Active Accumulator (AA)
Biases				
Emotional	Endownment Loss aversion Staus quo Regret aversion	Regret aversion	Overconfidence and self-attribution	Overconfidence Self-control
Cognitive	Mental accounting Anchoring and adjustment	Availability Hindsight Framing	Conservatism Availability Confirmation Representativeness	Illusion of control

One of the key observations from Exhibit 4 is that at either end of the passive/active scale are clients who are susceptible to *emotional* biases and in the middle are clients affected mainly by *cognitive* biases or errors.[3] This division makes intuitive sense when the investor types are considered. Passive Preservers are conservative investors with low risk tolerance. They have a high need for security, they are highly emotional about losing money, and they become uneasy during times of stress or change. Similarly, aggressive investors with a high risk tolerance, called Active Accumulators, are also emotionally charged. They typically suffer from a high level of overconfidence and have an illusion of control; they mistakenly believe they can control the outcomes of their investments to a greater extent than they can. In between these two extremes are the Friendly Followers and the Independent Individualists who suffer mainly from cognitive biases and need education and information to make better decisions. Importantly, clients who are emotional about their investing need to be advised differently from those who make mainly cognitive errors. When advising emotionally biased investors, advisers should focus on explaining how the investment program being created affects such issues as financial security, retirement, or future generations rather than focusing on such quantitative details as standard deviations and Sharpe ratios. Quantitative measures work better with cognitively biased investors.

Step 4: Classify investor into a behavioral investor type.   Once the adviser finds that the client has certain behavioral biases associated and consistent with a specific behavioral investor type, he or she will classify the client into the appropriate BIT. Exhibit 5 demonstrates the process of classifying investors into a BIT. For example if an investor is passive, the risk tolerance questionnaire reveals a low risk tolerance, and the investor has biases associated with a *Passive Preserver* as shown in Exhibit 4, the investor is then classified as a PP. Note that investors may exhibit some traits similar to the BITs shown beside them in Exhibit 5. Judgment is required in determining which classification best fits an investor.

---

3 Cognitive biases or cognitive errors are errors resulting from faulty reasoning; cognitive errors stem from basic statistical, information-processing, or memory errors. Emotional biases are biases resulting from reasoning influenced by feelings; emotional biases stem from impulse or intuition.

| **Exhibit 5** | **The Behavioral Investor Type Diagnostic Process** |

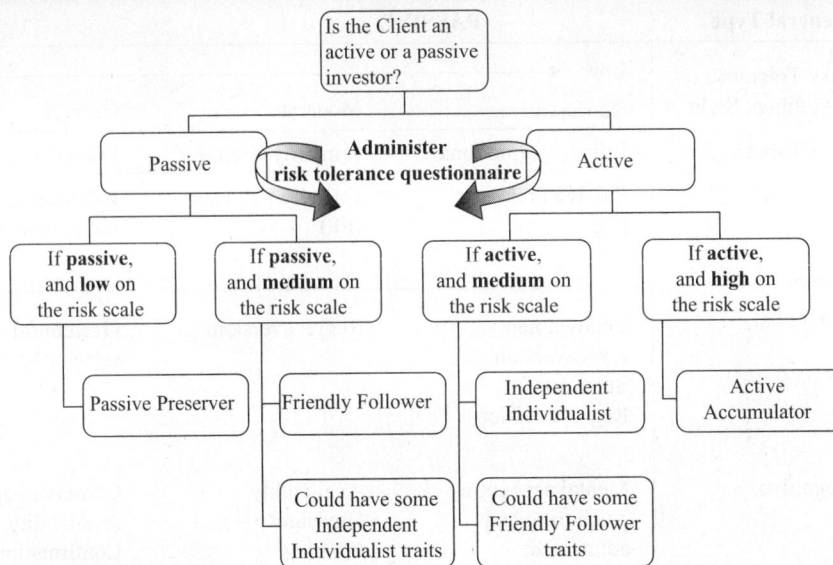

Passive Preserver (PP)

Basic type: Passive

Risk tolerance level: Low

Primary biases: Emotional

Passive Preservers, as the name implies, are investors who place a great deal of emphasis on financial security and preserving wealth rather than taking risks to grow wealth. Many have gained wealth through inheritance or by receiving high compensation at work. Because they have gained wealth without risking their own capital, PPs may not be financially sophisticated. Some PPs are "worriers"; they obsess over short-term performance and are slow to make investment decisions because they are not comfortable with change. This behavior is consistent with the way they have approached their professional lives, being careful not to take excessive risks. Many PPs are focused on taking care of their family members and future generations, especially funding life-enhancing experiences such as education and home buying. Because the focus is on family and security, PP biases tend to be emotional rather than cognitive. This BIT becomes more common as investors' age and wealth level increase. The emotional biases most common to PPs are endowment, loss aversion, status quo, and regret aversion. They may also exhibit cognitive errors, such as anchoring and adjustment and mental accounting.

Advising Passive Preservers: Passive Preservers may be difficult to advise because they are driven mainly by emotion. Although this characterization is true, PPs still need good financial advice. Advisers should take the time to consider the implications of the behavioral biases of their PP clients. PPs are more receptive to "big picture" advice that does not dwell on such details as standard deviations and Sharpe ratios. Because PPs are emotionally biased, providing excessive cognitive detail will lose their attention. Advisers should focus on what the money will accomplish, such as family legacy goals, education, and so on. PPs need to be persuaded about the soundness of their adviser's general philosophy first, and then, as trust is gained, PPs will respond to advice and take action. After a period of time, Passive Preservers are likely to become an adviser's best clients because they value greatly the adviser's professional expertise and objectivity in helping make the right investment decisions.

Friendly Follower (FF)

Basic type: Passive

Risk tolerance level: Low to medium

Primary biases: Cognitive

Friendly Followers are passive investors with a low to medium risk tolerance who tend to follow leads from their friends, colleagues, or advisers when making investment decisions. They often want to be in the latest, most popular investments without regard to current market conditions or the suitability of the investment to the FFs long-term goals. One of the key challenges in working with FFs is that they often *overestimate their risk tolerance.* Advisers need to be careful not to suggest too many "hot" ideas—FFs will likely want to invest in all of them because they may regret it if others make money and they do not. FFs generally comply with professional advice when they get it, and they educate themselves financially. At times, however, FFs can be difficult because they do not enjoy or have an aptitude for the investment process. Biases of FFs tend to be cognitive. Their decisions typically are influenced by availability, hindsight, and framing biases. Resolution of cognitive dissonance is an important factor to FFs. Regret aversion, as it relates to herding behavior, is an emotional bias with a significant impact.

Advising Friendly Followers: Friendly Followers may be difficult to advise because they often overestimate their risk tolerance. Risky trend-following behavior occurs in part because FFs often convince themselves that they "knew it all along" when an investment works out well, which increases future risk-taking behavior. Advisers need to handle FFs with care because they are likely to say yes to advice that makes sense to them without adequately considering the risk involved. Advisers need to guide them to take a hard look at behavioral tendencies that contribute to overestimating risk tolerance. Because FF biases are mainly cognitive, education on the benefits of portfolio diversification is usually the best course of action. Advisers should challenge FF clients to be introspective and provide data-backed support for recommendations. Offering education in clear, unambiguous ways is helpful so that FFs have the opportunity to understand the implications of investment choices. If advisers take the time, this steady, educational approach will generate greater client loyalty and adherence to long-term investment plans from Friendly Followers.

Independent Individualist (II)

Basic type: Active

Risk tolerance: Medium to high

Primary Biases: Cognitive

An Independent Individualist is an active investor with medium to high risk tolerance who is strong-willed and an independent thinker. IIs are self-assured and "trust their gut" when making decisions; however, when they do research on their own, they may be susceptible to acting on information that is available to them rather than getting corroboration from other sources. Sometimes advisers find that an II client made an investment without consulting anyone. This situation can be problematic; because of their independent mindset, these clients maintain the opinion they had when they made the investment, even when market conditions change. They enjoy investing and are comfortable taking risks, but often resist following a financial plan.

Of all behavioral investor types, IIs are the most likely to be contrarian, which can benefit them. II biases are typically cognitive. Conservatism, availability, confirmation, and representativeness biases are common to IIs. Overconfidence and self-attribution biases are the emotional biases that IIs sometimes exhibit.

Advising Independent Individualists: Independent Individualists may be difficult clients to advise because of their independent mindset, but they are usually willing to listen to sound advice when it is presented in a way that respects their intelligence. IIs have faith in themselves and their decisions, but may be unaware of their tendency to take a contrarian position. As with Friendly Followers, education is essential to changing their behavior because their biases are predominantly cognitive. A good approach is to have regular educational discussions during client meetings. In this way, the adviser does not point out unique or recent failures, but rather educates regularly and can incorporate concepts that he or she feels are appropriate for the Independent Individualist client.

Active Accumulator

> *Basic type: Active*
>
> *Risk tolerance: High*
>
> *Primary Biases: Emotional*

The Active Accumulator is the most aggressive behavioral investor type. These clients are entrepreneurial and often the first generation to create wealth; and they are even more strong-willed and confident than Independent Individualists. At high wealth levels, AAs often have controlled the outcomes of non-investment activities and believe they can do the same with investing. This behavior can lead to overconfidence in investing activities. AAs often have high portfolio turnover rates, which normally is a drag on investment performance. AAs are quick decision makers but may chase higher risk investments that their friends or associates are suggesting. If successful, they enjoy the excitement of making a good investment. Some AAs do not accept or follow basic investment principles such as diversification and asset allocation. They are often "hands on," wanting to be heavily involved in the investment decision-making process. AA biases are typically overconfidence, self-control, and illusion of control. As a result of these biases, they may be overly optimistic about their investment choices.

Advising Active Accumulators: Active Accumulators may be the most difficult clients to advise. They like to control, or at least get deeply involved in, the details of investment decision making. They tend to be emotional and display overconfidence, which often manifests itself as optimism. They are convinced that their investments will do well, even if that optimistic attitude is irrational. Some AAs need to be monitored for excessive spending, because they may lack self-control. This spending can inhibit performance of a long-term portfolio. The best approach to dealing with these clients is to take control of the situation. If advisers let the AA client dictate the terms of the advisory engagement, the client's emotionally oriented decision making will dominate and the result will likely be an unhappy client and an unhappy adviser. Advisers need to prove to the client that they have the ability to make wise, objective, and long-term decisions and can communicate these results in an effective way. Advisers who take control are more likely to have Active Accumulator clients listen to and accept their advice.

2.2 Limitations of Classifying Investors into Various Types

The challenge that all financial market participants face is that behavior patterns are not consistently demonstrated. An individual may normally behave one way but at times may behave in an unexpected manner. Different and irrational behaviors are exhibited at random times, usually during periods of financial market or personal stress. Because of inconsistencies in behavior, financial decision making is not always predictable or expectations of financial decision making are not always reliable. Therefore, it is important for readers to understand that whatever system is used to classify or otherwise understand individual investor behavior, there will be limitations to its effectiveness. The limitations of behavioral models include the following:

1 *Individuals may exhibit both cognitive errors and emotional biases.* Unfortunately, the same individual may exhibit both cognitive errors and emotional biases. Either may result in behavior that appears irrational. It may be possible to determine whether cognitive errors or emotional biases dominate, which is the heart of creating a behaviorally modified portfolio, but most people experience both faulty reasoning and feelings. Therefore, it may not be appropriate in most cases to classify a person as either an emotionally biased person or a cognitively biased person.

2 *Individuals may exhibit characteristics of multiple investor types.* Each behavioral investor type has unique characteristics. Unfortunately, people may engage in behaviors that are representative of multiple types. Therefore, users of investor classification models should not look for people to fit neatly into one "box" or type.

3 *Individuals will likely go through behavioral changes as they age.* As people age their behaviors may change. The most widely recognized example is that as people age their tolerance for risk (i.e., losses) generally decreases. They may become more emotional about their investing as well. It is important for BIT users to recognize this limitation and keep a close watch for changes in behavior as their clients age or experience changes in responsibilities or circumstances.

4 *Individuals are likely to require unique treatment even if they are classified as the same investor type because human behavior is so complex.* Even if two people fit the profile of a certain BIT, it is unlikely that one would treat those two people exactly the same. For example, one Passive Preserver may be more emotional or less risk tolerant than another. The classifications should not be taken as absolutes.

5 *Individuals act irrationally at different times and without predictability.* Life would be easier if we knew exactly when we or our clients would act irrationally. Because we do not, it is important to recognize that placing people into classifications may be more challenging at certain points, for example, during periods of market or personal stress compared with times of relative calm or even personal exuberance.

HOW BEHAVIORAL FACTORS AFFECT ADVISER–CLIENT RELATIONS

3

As behavioral finance gains credibility and acceptance by the investment community, advisers and investors are increasingly likely to include behavioral considerations in a client's investment policy statement (IPS). By adding behavioral factors to the IPS, a number of benefits can be realized. There is no doubt that an understanding of investor psychology will generate insights that benefit the advisory relationship. The key result of a behavioral finance–enhanced relationship will be a portfolio to which the adviser and client can comfortably adhere while fulfilling the client's long-term goals. This result has obvious advantages: advantages that suggest behavioral finance will continue to play an increasingly influential role in portfolio structure.

However, because behavioral finance is a relatively new concept as applied to individual investors, investment advisers may be reluctant to accept its validity. Moreover, advisers may not feel comfortable asking their clients psychological or behavioral questions to ascertain biases, especially at the beginning of the relationship. This reluctance should not deter an adviser from considering behavioral factors. Inclusion of behavioral finance considerations in the client–adviser relationship will likely result in a more satisfactory relationship and in investment decisions that are closer to those of traditional finance while being easier for the client to accept and adhere to.

Wealth management practitioners have different ways of measuring the success of an advisory relationship, but few would dispute that every successful relationship shares a few fundamental characteristics, including the following as outlined by Pompian (2006):

1 The adviser understands the client's financial goals and characteristics. These are considered when developing the investment policy statement.

2 The adviser maintains a systematic (consistent) approach to advising the client.

3 The adviser invests as the client expects. Results are communicated on a regular basis and in an effective manner that takes into account the client's characteristics.

4 The relationship benefits both client and adviser.

Behavioral finance can enhance these areas as shown in the following sections.

3.1 Formulating Financial Goals

Experienced financial advisers know that defining financial goals is critical to creating an investment program appropriate for the client. To best define financial goals, it is helpful to understand the psychology and emotions involved in the decisions underlying the goals. Behavioral finance helps advisers discern why investors set the goals they do. Such insights equip the adviser to deepen the bond with the client, thus producing a better relationship and a better investment outcome.

3.2 Maintaining a Consistent Approach

Most successful advisers maintain a consistent approach to delivering wealth management services. Incorporating behavioral finance can become part of that discipline without requiring large-scale changes in the adviser's methods. Behavioral finance can also add professionalism and structure to the relationship, allowing advisers to better understand the client before delivering any investment advice. Clients will appreciate this step, and it will make the relationship more successful.

3.3 Investing as the Client Expects

Addressing client expectations is essential to a successful relationship; in many unfortunate instances, the adviser does not deliver on the client's expectations because the adviser does not understand them. Perhaps no other aspect of the advisory relationship could benefit more from behavioral finance. Behavioral finance provides a context in which the adviser can "take a step back" and attempt to explore the motivations of the client. With a more thorough understanding of the client's expectations, the adviser is better equipped to help satisfy them.

3.4 Ensuring Mutual Benefits

Measures resulting in happier, more satisfied clients will also improve the adviser's practice and work life. Incorporating insights from behavioral finance into the advisory relationship will enhance that relationship and its results. Those in the individual investor advisory business should be aware that factors other than investment results may be considered when clients seek new advisers. Practitioners may lose clients because clients do not feel as though their advisers understand them and/or their financial objectives. Likewise, practitioners may gain clients because clients feel as though their advisers understand them and/or their financial objectives. The primary benefit that behavioral finance offers is the ability to develop a stronger bond between clients and advisers. By "getting inside the head" of the client and developing a comprehensive grasp of his motives and fears, the adviser can help the client better understand why a portfolio is designed the way it is and why it is an appropriate portfolio for him or her, regardless of what happens day-to-day in the markets.

3.5 Limitations of Traditional Risk Tolerance Questionnaires

Today, a dizzying variety of sources supply financial advice. To standardize processes, financial services firms often administer, and require their advisers to administer, risk tolerance questionnaires to clients and prospects prior to drafting any asset allocation. In the absence of any other diagnostic analysis, this methodology is certainly helpful and can generate important information. However, it is important to recognize the limitations of risk tolerance questionnaires. Aside from ignoring behavioral issues, an aspect we will examine shortly, risk tolerance questionnaires can also generate dramatically different results when administered repeatedly to the same individual, but with slight variations. Such imprecision arises primarily from variations in wording. Additionally, many risk tolerance questionnaires are administered once, and may not be revisited despite the fact that an IPS should be reviewed at least annually to measure not only a client's ability to take risk but also their willingness to take risk. Risk tolerance can vary as a result of changing life stages or events so it is critical to re-evaluate it periodically. Another critical drawback of risk tolerance questionnaires is that many advisers interpret their results too literally. For example, some clients might indicate that the maximum loss they would be willing to tolerate in a single year would equal 20 percent of their total assets. Does that mean that an ideal portfolio would place such a client in a position to lose 20 percent? No! Advisers should set portfolio parameters that preclude a client from incurring the maximum specified tolerable loss in any given period. For these reasons, risk tolerance questionnaires provide only broad guidelines for asset allocation, and should be used in concert with other behavioral assessment tools.

From the behavioral finance perspective, risk tolerance questionnaires may work better as a diagnostic tool for institutional investors compared with individual investors. This difference is because institutional investors are familiar with mean–variance optimization and think about risk. For them, risk analysis is a cognitive process. Individual investors are more likely to have feelings about risk, and for them risk analysis is an emotional process. Thus, risk tolerance questionnaires may fail emotionally biased individuals. An asset allocation generated and executed based on mean–variance optimization may result in a scenario in which a client demands, in response to short-term market fluctuations and to the detriment of the investment plan, that his or her asset allocation be changed. Moving repeatedly in and out of an allocation can have serious long-term negative consequences. Behavioral biases should be identified before the allocation is executed, so that such problems can be avoided. By doing so, the IPS that includes behavioral factors may result in decisions that the investor can adhere to. The IPS can be re-evaluated on a regular basis and updated for changes in the investor's circumstances and risk tolerance.

4 HOW BEHAVIORAL FACTORS AFFECT PORTFOLIO CONSTRUCTION

Behavioral biases may affect how investors construct portfolios from the securities available to them. One way to consider this issue is to analyze the actual portfolios investors construct and compare them with the portfolios implied by traditional portfolio theory. Some useful evidence on the portfolio selection decisions of individual investors comes from defined-contribution (DC) pension plans. In particular, investment decisions in US 401(k) plans have been investigated in a number of studies.[4]

4.1 Inertia and Default

Consistent with the status quo bias,[5] a key finding is that most DC plan members show inertia and tend not to change their asset allocations through time, even though it might be assumed that their tolerance for risk and other circumstances would be changing. For example, Samuelson and Zeckhauser (1988) and more recently Arneriks and Zeldes (2000) find the majority of investors in their samples made zero fund switches during the sample period in spite of there being no transaction costs associated with altering allocations among funds.[6]

There is also substantial evidence that shows inertia leads plan participants to stick with default options in terms of contribution rates and investment funds. In many cases, the default funds will be cash or money market funds, which are arguably too conservative for long-term savings, with low risk but also low rates of return (for example, see Madrian and Shea 2001).

Some companies have introduced "autopilot" strategies to counteract the inertia that plan participants frequently exhibit. For example, target date funds automatically switch from risky assets to fixed-income assets as the plan member nears the intended retirement date. The member does not need to take any action to achieve the reduction in risk. Although target date funds can be helpful in countering investor inertia, the potential disadvantage is that they are a "one size fits all" solution that may not match the needs of specific investors.

---

4 A 401(k) plan is a type of pension (retirement savings) plan named after the section of the US Internal Revenue Code in which it appears. A company sponsors the plan but each participant has his or her own account and makes investment decisions for that account.
5 The status quo bias is an emotional bias in which people do nothing or maintain the status quo instead of making a change.
6 The investors sampled held defined-contribution plans through TIAA-CREF in the United States. TIAA-CREF has been helping those in the academic, medical, cultural, and research fields plan for retirement for over 90 years.

EXAMPLE 1

Target Date Fund Glide Path

Target date funds are designed to deal with investor inertia. As the investor approaches the intended retirement date, the fund manager reduces the proportion of risky assets in the fund. The reduction in risky assets is because plan members close to retirement have little time to recover losses or make adjustments to their circumstances if their risky investments incur losses. Investors with longer to retirement are typically more able to bear investment risk.

Although investors could do this kind of risk management for themselves, in practice many would not get around to making the allocation changes. The target date fund manager provides an autopilot solution for them. The diagram below shows the asset allocation "glide path" that T Rowe Price suggests for a 45-year-old investor. As shown, the allocation to stocks will decline (glide down) over time, whereas the allocation to fixed income and short-term income will increase. Similar programs are offered by other investment management companies.

Discuss factors that might make this one-size-fits-all solution inappropriate.

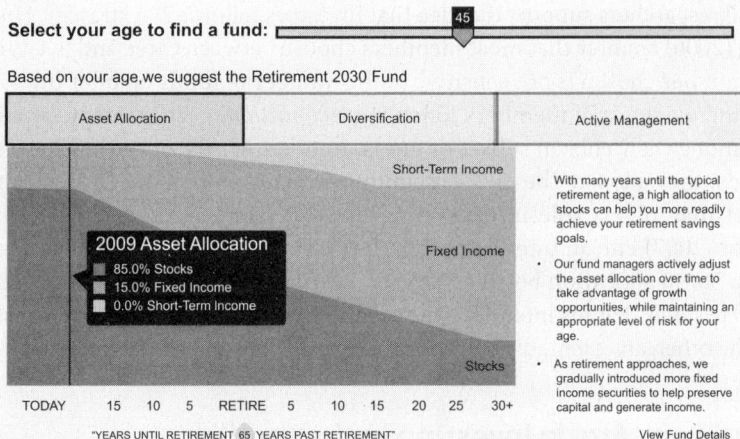

Source: www.troweprice.com.

Solution:

The entire investment portfolio of the investor should always be considered. Where tax treatment differs among types of returns or assets, assets that are expected to generate higher taxable returns may be held in tax-deferred retirement funds. An investor with significant amounts invested in non-retirement funds might prefer to tax shelter some assets in their retirement funds.

An investor with significant wealth and no children may be willing to take more risk. They may be less loss- and risk-averse than another investor of the same age with less wealth and parental responsibilities.

An investor with a preference for active portfolio management might prefer to have different allocations to asset classes based on his or her expectations and market conditions. For example, if interest levels are historically low, the investor might prefer to invest in stocks anticipating that interest rates will rise and the fixed-income portion will decline in value.

These are some of the factors that might be discussed.

4.2 Naïve Diversification

When DC plan members do make active fund choices, some of the decisions appear to be the result of behavioral biases. For example, there is evidence of investors using simple heuristics to allocate among available funds and of framing bias. Benartzi and Thaler (2001) cite evidence of plan members using a "1/n" naïve diversification strategy—dividing contributions equally among available funds irrespective of the underlying composition of the funds. In one experiment conducted by Benartzi and Thaler, one group of subjects is given the choice between a stock (equities) fund and a bond fund and a second group of subjects is given a choice between a stock fund and a balanced (50 percent stock, 50 percent bond) fund. The average asset allocation to equities is higher for the second group because in each group, the mode is to allocate assets evenly between the two funds available for selection. The use of a heuristic and framing bias appear to have impacted the choices. In a real life example studied by Benartzi and Thaler, by comparing allocations of a plan with five stock funds and one bond fund and a second plan with one stock fund and four bond funds, they find average equity allocation is very different. In the first plan, the average equity allocation is 75 percent, and in the second plan, the average equity allocation is only 34 percent. This example demonstrates the impact of framing bias.

Not all researchers support the idea that investors follow a 1/n strategy. Huberman and Jiang (2006) counter that most members choose between three and five funds, and that the number chosen is not sensitive to the number of funds on offer (n). However, they do find evidence of members following a *conditional* 1/n strategy, by allocating equally among their chosen subset of funds. In other words, once they have selected their funds, they allocate the invested amount equally among the chosen funds.

Regret may play a role in explaining naïve diversification strategies. Benartzi and Thaler (2007) cite an interview with Harry Markowitz in which he notes that he selected a 50/50 allocation between stocks and bonds in his TIAA-CREF retirement account. He states that his intention was to minimize future regret from one asset class beating the other, an essentially behavioral explanation, and perhaps an emotional one.

4.3 Company Stock: Investing in the Familiar

A very graphic example of potentially inappropriate portfolio construction approaches in DC plans comes in the form of high levels of investment in the stock of the sponsoring company. Many US 401(k) plans offer the employer's stock as an investment option and many also make employer matching contributions in employer stock, in some cases with restrictions on subsequent sale.

Benartzi (2001) notes that one-third of 401(k) assets are invested in participants' own employer's stock, and in some plans the proportion is more than 90 percent. In many cases, the account balances are comprised in significant part by the employees' *discretionary* allocations. Vanguard (2006) notes that although only 12 percent of plans offer employer's stock as a choice, these are larger plans. As a result, 43 percent of participants have employer's stock as a choice and one-fifth of all participants have more than 20 percent of their account balance in employer's stock. Fifteen percent of participants have more than 80 percent of their account balance in their employer's stock. Balances in employer's stock remain high despite such high profile disasters as WorldCom and Enron.[7]

---

7 Choi, et al (2005) note that at the end of 2000, 62 percent of the $2 billion of assets in Enron's 401(k) plan accounts was invested in Enron stock.

Explanations given for investment in employer's stock include the following:

- *Familiarity and overconfidence effects*: Employees underestimate risk because of familiarity with the employing company and overconfidence in their estimates of the company's performance. A John Hancock (2003) survey shows investors assigning an average risk score of 3.1 to company stock, in comparison with 3.6 for domestic stock funds and 4.1 for global stock funds. Huberman (2001) argues this enthusiasm for own company investment springs from the same familiarity bias that leads to home bias in geographic allocations. The familiarity bias also led US investors to invest more in their local phone company than in other telephone companies. It could be that employees do have an informational advantage that justifies their high holdings in their employer's stock, but evidence on returns (e.g., Benartzi 2001) casts doubt on this view and points to overconfidence as an explanation.

- *Naïve extrapolation of past returns*: Plan members at companies whose stock has done well in the past may expect this performance to continue and hence wish to hold company stock in their account. Benartzi (2001) sorts companies into quintiles based on 10-year past performance of the employing company's stock. Employees at the worst-performing companies on average allocate 10 percent of contributions to company stock; for the best-performing companies, the figure is 40 percent. Subsequent stock performance does not validate this difference in allocation.

- *Framing and status quo effect of matching contributions*: Benartzi (2001) shows that employees who can choose where the employer match is invested allocate 18 percent of their own funds to employer's stock. Where the match is in employer's stock, employees allocate 29 percent of their *own* contributions. Employees may be taking the company's decision to contribute stock to their plan as *implicit advice.*

- *Loyalty effects*: Employees may be willing to hold employer's stock to assist the company, as they perceive it. For example, employees may be encouraged to hold employer's stock as assistance in a takeover defense. Companies with high levels of employee stock holdings may be harder to take over.

- *Financial incentives*: Employees might rationally invest in employer's stock when there are financial incentives for them to do so. These could include being able to purchase stock at a discount to market price, or beneficial tax treatment. Although these explanations are possibilities, most studies show substantial holdings of employer's stock exist in the absence of such incentives. However, this finding may be the result of inertia and employees continuing to hold employer's stock once any restrictions on selling have lapsed.

4.4 Excessive Trading

The evidence of member inertia in DC plans is in contrast to evidence of individuals with retail investment accounts. Investors with retail accounts appear to be more active traders. Barber and Odean (1999) summarize evidence from their studies of investors with discount brokerage accounts. The main findings are that investors trade too much—damaging returns—and tend to sell winners and hold on to losers—the disposition effect.

A winning position, in which current price is above the purchase price, is 1.5 times more likely to be sold in any month than a corresponding losing position. This behavior may be driven by fear of regret. Winners sold subsequently outperform the losers that remain in the portfolio. Excessive trading appears to be driven by overconfidence. Overconfident investors may falsely think that they have the knowledge and insight to make profitable trades, and trade actively to benefit from these insights. The researchers' initial expectation that frequent traders would be worse off because of their transaction costs is not confirmed; in fact, the outcome was even worse than expected in that stocks sold do better than stocks bought by about 3.5 percent over the following 12 months. The frequent traders not only had higher transaction costs because of excessive trading but also experienced opportunity losses because of the disposition effect. Performance is negatively related to turnover levels. Young males are found to trade the most and earn the lowest net returns.

The difference between the findings on trading in the discount brokerage and the 401(k) pension plan accounts may stem from self-selection of individuals (keen traders) into brokerage accounts and the differing levels of investment choice (i.e., choice is generally restricted in 401(k) plans).

4.5 Home Bias

Portfolio diversification represents another dimension in which investors must make a choice. Members can diversify internationally as well as across asset classes. A large body of literature exists showing that many investors maintain a high proportion—often 80 percent or more—of their investments in securities listed in their own country (for example, see French and Poterba 1991; Kang and Stulz 1997). There have been attempts to offer rational explanations for this feature, for example, as a result of information costs. However, there are also behavioral explanations, such as availability, confirmation, illusion of control, endowment, and status quo biases. Familiarity with a country may lead investors to own high concentrations of domestic assets. This choice is closely related to the idea that a similar type of familiarity could lead investors to own excessive amounts of employer stock.

4.6 Behavioral Portfolio Theory

Shefrin and Statman have published a number of articles on behavioral portfolio theory (e.g., Shefrin and Statman 2000; Statman 1999, 2004). The theory is intended to reflect how investors actually form portfolios rather than how traditional theory suggests they should. Shefrin and Statman argue that portfolios, affected by behavioral biases, are formed as layered pyramids in which each layer is aligned with an objective. As a result of a mental accounting bias in which people treat one sum of money differently from another sum based on which mental account the money is assigned to, investments are allocated to discrete layers without regard for the correlations among these investments. For example, a base layer of low risk assets may be intended as "protection from poverty," whereas a higher layer of risky assets represents "hopes for riches." Behavioral investors do not consider the correlation between the layers in the way that modern portfolio theory would suggest they should. Clients can have several layers or mental accounts in their portfolios. The layered approach can explain observed features, such as undiversified stock portfolios (hopes for riches), and the reluctance of investors to invest in foreign stocks despite the seemingly obvious diversification benefits. This latter feature reflects failure to consider the diversification benefits of stocks with a low correlation with the domestic portfolio. The failure to consider diversification benefits is an implication of the mental accounting bias.

An important point to note is that investors do not have a single attitude toward risk. They have multiple attitudes toward risk depending on which part of their wealth is being considered. Hence, in a behavioral context it might make sense for investors to say they are prepared to take a lot of risk with some of their money, even though such a statement makes little sense in a conventional mean–variance portfolio theory framework.

Advisers and portfolio managers constructing an investment policy statement for or with a client may wish to consider behavioral portfolio theory. For example, they can clarify which mental accounts the client has and what attitude toward risk prevails for each one. Exhibit 6 compares the structure of a mean–variance portfolio and a behavioral portfolio (Statman 1999).

Exhibit 6   Structures of Mean–Variance and Behavioral Portfolios

Mean–Variance Portfolio
Mean–variance portfolios are constructed as a whole, and only the expected return and the variance of the entire porefolio matter. Covariance between assets is crucial in determination of the variance of the portfolio.

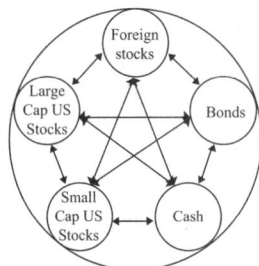

Behavioral Portfolio
Behavioral portfolios are constructed not as a whole but layer by layer, where each layer is associated with a goal and is filed with securities that correspond to that goal. Covariance brtween assets is overlooked.

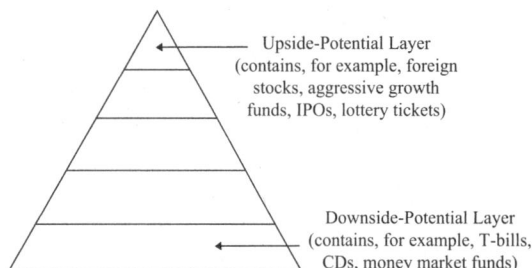

Upside-Potential Layer
(contains, for example, foreign stocks, aggressive growth funds, IPOs, lottery tickets)

Downside-Potential Layer
(contains, for example, T-bills, CDs, money market funds)

Source: Statman (1999).

BEHAVIORAL FINANCE AND ANALYST FORECASTS

5

Sections 2, 3, and 4 focus on understanding individual investor behavior and how it affects the adviser–client relationship and portfolio construction. Sections 5, 6, and 7 focus on how behavioral factors impact security analysts, investment committees, and markets.

Studies have shown that experts in many fields persistently make forecasting errors arising from their behavioral biases. Investment analysts are subject to these biases, and need to be aware of the potential for biases to compromise their professional judgment. When qualified, analysts possess a range of techniques to research companies and securities, yet their superior skills surprisingly place them at greater risk of some types of error. One key issue for all experts is recognizing the occasions when they lack the information or insight to make a good professional judgment. Even possessing good analytical skills, investment professionals' judgment can be limited by human failings and the environment in which they operate. Judgment can be improved if an individual understands the limits to his or her knowledge.

The biases that can adversely impact analysis are not confined to analysts' behavior. The way in which information is presented in company management presentations, reports, and accounts can reflect human biases in corporate executives. To achieve good forecasts or decisions, analysts need to be alert to the potential impact of biases.

Section 5.1 describes the effect of *behavioral biases* on analysts and their work. *Cognitive errors* or failures of reasoning create the potential for errors of judgment, and include memory- and probability-based errors. *Emotional biases* are biases resulting from reasoning influenced by feelings; emotional biases stem from impulse or intuition. *Cognitive dissonance* arises when new information conflicts with previously held beliefs or cognitions. To resolve the dissonance, people may notice only information of interest, may ignore or modify information that conflicts with existing beliefs, may remember and consider only information that confirms existing beliefs, and/or may modify beliefs. The work of analysts, which includes research, judgment, forecasts, decisions, and conclusions, may be affected by behavioral biases and cognitive dissonance. In other words, analysts are not immune to behavioral biases and exhibiting irrational behavior.

5.1 Overconfidence in Forecasting Skills

Overconfidence is a key behavioral bias relevant to investment analysts. Overconfidence bias is a bias in which people demonstrate unwarranted faith in their own intuitive reasoning, judgments, and/or cognitive abilities. This overconfidence may be the result of overestimating knowledge levels, abilities, and access to information. For example, people generally do a poor job of estimating probabilities but believe they do it well because they believe that they are smarter and more informed than they actually are. This behavior is sometimes referred to as the *illusion of knowledge bias*. Overconfidence may be intensified when combined with *self-attribution bias*. Self-attribution bias is a bias in which people take credit for successes and assign responsibility for failures. In other words, success is attributed to the individual's skill whereas failures are attributed to external factors. Illusion of knowledge and self-attribution biases contribute to the overconfidence bias.

Analysts frequently show excessive confidence on the likely correctness of their forecasts. Studies have identified that 90 percent *confidence intervals* for forecasts, which should leave only 10 percent error rates, turn out to be wrong as much as 40 percent of the time (Russo and Schoemaker 1992). The actual error rate is the result of a calibration issue about how sure an expert is about his or her judgment.

Overconfidence can be the result of placing too much emphasis on specific characteristics of a company or what is being examined and neglecting to fully consider the impact of the economic environment and other information. Studies have suggested individuals are more confident when making contrarian predictions that counter the consensus. That is, overconfidence can arise when forecasting what others do not expect or predict (Dunning, Griffin, Milojkovic, and Ross 1990). Overconfidence has been shown to be particularly evident for strategists, rather than for individual stock or industry analysts. Stock analysts are typically more confident about earnings forecasts than target prices.

A key bias linked to overconfidence is the illusion of knowledge. Analysts believe that by acquiring information, they can know more than others and obtain an edge. In other words, information will result in analysts being more knowledgeable and thus more accurate in their forecasts compared with others. As a result, they may collect too much information. Although forecasting is driven by information, additional data that is not adding material content tends not to increase the accuracy of a forecast, but instead reinforces an analyst's confidence in that forecast.

Additional information may contribute to the cognitive bias of representativeness, in which analysts judge the probability of a forecast being correct by considering how much the outcome resembles overall available data (Kahneman, Slovic, and Tversky 1982 and more recently, Shefrin 2007). Typically, this simplification combines probabilities incorrectly. Additional information or detail may appear to conform to the overall scenario being forecast, even if it is largely irrelevant, and so add to confidence in the forecast. The **availability bias** is a cognitive bias that involves individuals giving undue weight to more accessible, readily recalled information. Availability and representativeness can each encourage overreaction to rare events.

Attempting to collect more information can also contribute to the cognitive bias of **illusion of control**, which is a tendency of analysts to try to control what cannot be controlled. Inherently, uncertain outcomes relating to business or the economy cannot have all forecasting risk removed. Risk in a model and the modeling process cannot be eliminated by an excess of information. The illusion of control can lead to analysts forecasting complex patterns of business performance or stock price behavior, or being confident about unlikely combinations of short- and long-term recommendations, price targets, and earnings forecasts.

Overconfidence and the illusion of control can be encouraged by *complex models*. Many analytical problems will require modeling and extensive use of data. More complex models usually fit a particular data set better but prove less robust in a range of different environments. The data set used may be more relevant to a particular economic or business environment or may be influenced by some outlying or atypical observations. Mathematical rigor and spurious precision of models can conceal underlying weaknesses in the models and assumptions. Analysts should avoid modeling that overly focuses on a single set of historical data, which risks optimization on that data set rather than achieving robustness of modeling. Robustness reflects a model's ability to perform well out of sample.

Even when analysts are not managing portfolios of securities, **self-attribution bias** can adversely influence their analyses and contribute to overconfidence in their forecasts. Self-attribution bias is a bias in which people take personal credit for successes and attribute failures to external factors outside the individual's control. Self-attribution bias may reflect a desire to preserve self-esteem while people protect themselves psychologically as they attempt to comprehend successes and failures. Self-attribution bias may be evident in *skewed forecasts*, in which the confidence interval is not symmetric around a central forecast. People may appear to exhibit self-attribution bias as a result of misdirected financial incentives. In this case, it is not true self-attribution bias but a deliberate attempt to gain credit for successes and assign responsibility for failures for financial as opposed to psychological reasons.

Experts often use other self-esteem or ego defense mechanisms, such as **hindsight bias**. Hindsight bias is also called the "I knew it all along" effect. Forecasts are evaluated with hindsight, and that additional knowledge can be combined with a human tendency to see past events as having been predictable. Also, people tend to remember their own predictions of the future as more accurate than they actually are because they are biased by the knowledge of what has actually happened. Hindsight bias is more prevalent when forecasts are ambiguous. Individuals tend to misinterpret past data, which can lead to overconfidence and insufficient adjustment in future forecasts. Hindsight bias can make analysts blind to future risks or the full breadth of the range of outcomes.

Hindsight bias can involve both cognitive and emotional bias. It is a result of the process of integrating new information with prior beliefs. A source of error in calibrating earlier forecasts typically arises from selective recall, in which individuals remember showing greater foresight than proved to be the case. Typically, an outcome is viewed as more likely, in the sense of being capable of being repeated, once it has occurred than is expected before that.

EXAMPLE 2

Analyst Case Study

Based on a company's sales and earnings per share growth over the past 10 years, an analyst has concluded that its high rate of growth will continue in the future. Before the report is completed, the analyst reads in a newspaper that the company's chief executive has made an apparently very profitable personal investment in another unrelated business. The analyst believes that this profitable outcome is evidence of the chief executive's entrepreneurism and dynamism, and that it is additional confirmation of the analyst's assessment of the company in the report. Supported by the additional information, the analyst now feels more confident with the forecasted growth rates and in fact increases the average forecasted earnings growth rate and decreases the dispersion of the forecasted growth rates. He includes the additional information about the chief executive in the report.

Discuss flaws in the analyst's approach and possible biases of the analyst.

Solution:

The value of the additional information is difficult to quantify, and it may not have been collected systematically. The analyst may not have looked as rigorously for evidence of how representative the successful investment was among the chief executive's total portfolio of personal investments; other investments might have shown poor returns but received less publicity. Newspaper coverage can be selective. Thus, the new information might reflect *availability bias*. The chief executive may even have been motivated to diversify his investments by concern about the outlook for the company's stock. The analyst's judgment might have been adversely affected by *overconfidence*, with faulty reasoning contributing to the issue. Further, the analyst might have seen the additional information as being *representative* of a mental picture of the characteristics of a growth business.

5.1.1 *Remedial Actions for Overconfidence and Related Biases*

Dealing with overconfidence is difficult, but *prompt and accurate feedback* combined with a *structure that rewards accuracy* can help analysts to re-evaluate their processes and self-calibrate. Most people calibrate better and reduce overconfidence if they know that the result of their forecast will be known and reflected to them very quickly.

Effective methods of providing incentives need not necessarily be in the form of financial reward. Good motivation can also be achieved if an individual is directly accountable for accuracy to supervisors or clients. An appreciation of stock market history and economic cycles, as well as rigorous self-appraisal, can help improve future forecasts and correct confidence intervals given by analysts. Where resources and organizational structure permit, *appraisal by colleagues, superiors, or systems* can also help calibrate forecasts and control overconfidence.

Well-structured feedback can also reduce hindsight bias. An analyst should document a decision or forecast and the reasons for that judgment. A written record helps make the later evaluation more objective. Documenting the reasons for the judgment not only allows the accuracy to be assessed later, but also why it was right or wrong. The data used should be recorded to allow subsequent assessment. Unambiguous forecasts are less vulnerable to hindsight bias. Where possible, numbers should be included, and it can be helpful to document any consensus or base rates that exist, to compare with the analyst's judgment and for later assessment purposes.

To address hindsight bias and other biases, analysts should make the conclusion as explicit as possible, although this documenting should not be confused with showing greater confidence or adding extraneous detail. What is required is sufficient detail to allow subsequent evaluation of its accuracy. In subsequently evaluating a forecast after the outcome is known, the record of the prediction can be assessed by reviewing the data, assumptions, and model. Feedback or a systematic review process can assist future accuracy and help control overconfidence and reduce hindsight bias.

Some outcomes or sources of forecasting error can be overlooked. Analysts should be thorough in their search for unconsidered outcomes that might have been missed initially and attempt to evaluate those. One method that can help reduce overconfidence is for an analyst to be required to provide at least one counterargument in the report. If the documentation of the research includes one good reason why the conclusion might turn out to be wrong, forecasting accuracy can be improved and confidence be better calibrated. When listing evidence for and against a conclusion, it is the evidence against that does the most good in countering overconfidence.

To counter the risk of inaccuracy and excess confidence based on specific characteristics of the subject of the analysis, analysts should consider whether the sample size is too small. Ensuring that a search process includes only *comparable data* is also helpful to reducing overconfidence. Additional data that cannot be analyzed in the same way as the comparable data set are more likely to add to confidence than accuracy, via the bias of illusion of knowledge.

Bayes' formula is a mathematical rule that explains how existing probability beliefs should be changed given new information. In other words, Bayes' formula expects people to update old beliefs in a certain manner when given new information. Bayes' formula is essentially an application of conditional probabilities.[8] Ideally, analysts should incorporate additional information with a Bayesian approach to calculate probabilities, recognize underlying base rates, and link probabilities conditionally.

Using Bayes' formula, the initial position (prior probability) typically matters less, and more importance can be given to a sequence of useful evidence. Because the starting assumptions are typically less important than collecting and incorporating new information, Bayes' formula can be a useful tool for analysis, reducing the risk of behavioral biases in incorporating new information.

However, base rates—the underlying averages or background frequencies—should be recognized if the data is available. Indeed, in some cases the base rates can be clear and powerful. In some investment analyses the base rate of likely outcomes may be statistically significant, but there is much less information that allows discrimination between investments. For example, there may be insufficient data to determine accurately stock betas in a model. The analysis may be more robust if calculated assuming all the stock betas are equal to 1 (the overall average or base rate).

In Example 3, the correlations and similarity of previous performance between stocks, which can be high within some sectors, demonstrate the difficulty of discriminating between stocks in the short term. Against this background—where it seems quite likely that short-term performance of the two stocks will be similar—achieving a successful recommendation requires a higher hurdle in terms of further evidence and quality of analysis.

---

8 Bayes' formula shows how one conditional probability is inversely related to the probability of another mutually exclusive outcome. The formula is:

P(A|B) = [P(B|A) / P(B)]P(A)

where

P(A) = the prior probability of event A, without new information B. It is the base rate or base probability of event A.

P(A|B) = the conditional probability of event A. It is the updated probability of A given the new information B.

P(B|A) = the conditional probability of B given A. it is the probability of the new information B given event A.

P(B) = the prior (unconditional) probability of information B.

EXAMPLE 3

Analyst Recommendation and Base Rate Case Study

The chief investment officer (CIO) of an investment institution is presented with research by an analyst on his team. The analyst is recommending a switch from the stock of one major integrated oil company, XYZ plc, into another major integrated oil company, ABC plc. Over the previous three years, the stock prices of the two companies had a correlation of 88 percent. On the basis of this high correlation and also the fact that over the period the performance of the two stocks had diverged little, the CIO concludes that the probability of switching costs exceeding the difference in prospective returns over the next 12 months is 80 percent (base rate or prior probability). The CIO estimates the cost of the switch at 4 percent because tax costs are involved. The analyst's judgment is correct 60 percent of the time, in line with the average for the team. How should the CIO evaluate the analyst's recommendation?

Solution:

Exhibit 7	Bayes' Formula Demonstrated Using Natural Frequencies

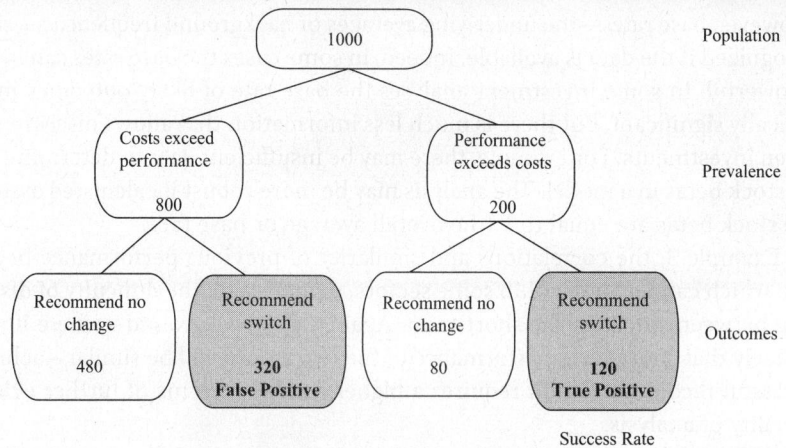

The information in Exhibit 7 is summarized in Exhibit 8.

Exhibit 8			
	Switching Is Worthwhile	Switching Is Not Worthwhile	Total
Analyst recommends a switch	120	320	440
Analyst recommends no change	80	480	560
Total	200	800	1000

P(A) = Probability switching is worthwhile = 1 − 0.8 = 0.2 (given), or 200/1000 = 0.2

P(B) = Probability analyst recommends a switch = 440/1000 = 0.44

P(B|A) = Probability analyst recommends a switch given switching is worthwhile = 0.6 (given), or 120/200 = 0.6

If a population of 1000 outcomes is used, on average in 800 (= 0.8 × 1000) outcomes there will be less than 4 percent annualized difference between the stocks. On the other 200 (= 0.2 × 1000) outcomes, it would be worth switching.

The analyst's 60 percent rate of being correct means on average that he can be expected to identify correctly 120 (= 0.6 × 200) of the useful switching opportunities. But his 40 percent failure rate means that he will not predict the remaining 80 (= 0.4 × 200) outcomes when switching would prove right (false negatives).

Of the 800 outcomes in which switching would not be worthwhile, the analyst will correctly recognize 480 of the outcomes (= 0.6 × 800). But he will wrongly predict a switch on the remaining 320 outcomes in which there is no meaningful difference between the stocks (false positives).

Exhibit 8 indicates that the analyst will make 440 calls to switch (= 120 + 320), of which just 120 can be expected to be correct. The analyst's expected success ratio in calling a profitable switch between two closely correlated stocks is 27 percent (= 120/440) or calculated using Bayes' formula: P(A|B) = [P(B|A)/P(B)]P(A) = [(0.6)/(0.44) × 0.2] = 1.36 × 0.2 = 0.27

The CIO would need more information about time frames and predicted magnitude of performance difference between the stocks before making a decision. However, in these circumstances, the base rate—the similar prior performance of the two stocks—is hard to beat. (Switching costs and the possibility that some outcomes represent an unexpected outperformance of XYZ may even add to the risks.) Where a base rate or prior is very strong, a decision counter to the base rate can only be made with a strong proven ability to discriminate.

Remedial actions include giving prompt, well-structured, and accurate feedback; developing explicit and unambiguous conclusions; having a systematic review process and a structure that rewards accuracy; conducting regular appraisals by colleagues and superiors; providing counterarguments; and documenting comparable data.

5.2 Influence of Company's Management on Analysis

The information that is presented by company management and the way the information is presented can affect external analysts. Analysts should remember that company management is also susceptible to behavioral biases.

Framing, **anchoring and adjustment**, and availability are important cognitive biases. Framing is a cognitive bias in which the same problem is assessed differently depending on how information or a question is presented. Humans assume that the frame or context is providing additional information when it may not be. It can involve anchoring, in which some information is given undue importance in decision making. Anchoring means that the framework for interpreting and analyzing the available information can be influenced disproportionately by an initial, default position or "anchor." This anchor can be chosen in a variety of ways. For example, it may be based on initial information, prominent and vivid data, or recent data. Adjustments from the anchor tend to insufficiently incorporate new information. Availability is a cognitive bias that involves individuals giving undue weight to more accessible, readily recalled information.

For example, a management presentation describing specific successes or selecting favorable comparisons for business performance could anchor an analyst's view of the business results as successful. Subsequent less favorable metrics or explanations might not be given the appropriate consideration or weight. Typically, management presentations and annual reports begin with a summary of results and achievements. Analysts should recognize the risk of this information being given undue importance in the analysis relative to the analyst's own ratios and metrics.

The extent to which company management can be excessively optimistic is shown in Exhibit 9, which analyzes the report of a bank that subsequently moved into significant loss. Analysts reviewing a company report that lacks balance in the language need to consider the potential for their favorable initial impression of reporting language to adversely affect an objective analysis of numbers, via the influence of framing bias.

Exhibit 9   Framing Bias

Consider this text analysis of the chairman's statement and business review in the 2007 annual report of a major European bank published in 2008, a few months before the bank was rescued by the government.

		Occurrences of:	
Negative words		**Positive words**	
Disappoint/disappointed	0	Good	55
Bad/badly	0	Excellent	12
Poor	0	Success/successful	35
Weaker/weakening	7	Improvement	23
Slowdown	6	Strong/stronger/strongly	78

Source: Royal Bank of Scotland plc, Annual Report and Accounts 2007, SVM Analysis.

Analysts should also recognize the possibility of a self-attribution bias in company executives that arises from the impact of incentive compensation on company reporting. Incentive compensation for both company management and for analysts can be too large, creating errors of reasoning and judgment because of preoccupation with specific factors. Company management and analysts can be influenced by optimism. This optimism may be influenced by overconfidence and illusion of control biases. As a result, there is a systematic tendency to overestimate the likelihood of favorable outcomes, and underestimate the likelihood of negative events (Lench and Ditto 2008). Optimism can be evident in company reporting.

Framing and setting expectations may be influenced by companies presenting recalculated earnings. This recalculation may happen if management believes earnings are temporarily or artificially depressed; typically, the recalculation does not comply with generally agreed accounting practice presentation. Usually, the recalculated earnings are more favorable and given greater prominence in company reporting. Because these adjustments can affect valuation, apparent growth rates, and the smoothness of earnings progression (earnings quality), analysts need to consider whether the adjustment is unreasonably influencing their perception of the business in terms of profitability, growth, or riskiness.

5.2.1 Remedial Actions for Influence of Company's Management on Analysis

Analysts can best deal with cognitive biases in the interpretation of information by maintaining a disciplined and systematic approach. Focusing on metrics and comparable data, rather than what is descriptive or unverifiable, can assist forecast accuracy and consistency of approach across research. Calibration of likely accuracy can be improved by framing the issue appropriately, gathering information, and recognizing underlying base rates.

5.3 Analyst Biases in Conducting Research

Although cognitive biases may be the most significant behavioral problem for analysts, there is usually also an emotional component to judgment. Emotional responses are a significant factor in the real-time processing of financial information. Emotional perception of information is not necessarily rational; emotions can improve or disrupt decision making. However, even before an analysis is complete, the model or judgment can only be as good as the data used. The search process for information is an important element of successful analysis, and the optimal stopping point in that search may not be clear. It is possible to collect too much information.

Specific biases can be more prevalent in company analysis. Collecting too much unstructured information may not only lead to illusions of knowledge and control, contributing to overconfidence, but can also expose analysts to the risk of representativeness. Additional information can feed representativeness.

More detail collected from companies can feed confidence. An indicator that a conclusion has been driven by extraneous detail may be that the conclusion is presented as a *story*. A story involves explaining evidence with a story or scenario that fits, and then making a decision that matches the specific scenario. A story may not be based on a thorough analysis but can be compelling because of how it is presented.

Confirmation bias, a cognitive bias, is the tendency for people to misread evidence as additional support for an initial hypothesis. Confirmation bias is a form of resolving cognitive dissonance that describes the tendency to search for, or interpret, information in a way that confirms the analyst's prior beliefs. The additional information may not be analyzed in a rigorous way, but it can nevertheless appear to make the judgment or forecast more likely by sharing some of its general characteristics. An example is when probabilities of independent events are combined inappropriately, such as additively or some variation of adding, to support a belief. This example highlights the conjunction fallacy. The probability of two independent events occurring in conjunction is never greater than the probability of either event occurring alone. In fact, the probability of two independent events occurring together is equal to the multiplication of the probabilities of the independent events.

The **gamblers' fallacy**, a misunderstanding of probabilities in which people wrongly project reversal to a long-term mean, is a related cognitive bias (Shefrin 2007). Investment professionals, and strategists in particular, can suffer from this cognitive bias. It reflects a faulty understanding about the behavior of random events, expecting reversals to occur more frequently than actually happens. With the gamblers' fallacy, the analyst is expecting a pattern that has diverged from the long-term average to reverse within a specific period of time. Another fallacy, common to gamblers and many others, is the hot hand fallacy. People affected by this fallacy wrongly project continuation of a recent trend. Both of these fallacies demonstrate a lack of understanding of statistical independence.

Similar to endowment bias, assets may be endowed with additional value based on an emotional response to them. Analysts can associate financially sound companies with good or safe characteristics, although the external economic environment or high stock price for the company can make it risky. This view can also reflect a confirmation bias. Analysts may look for and notice what confirms their beliefs, and ignore or undervalue what contradicts their beliefs. Studies have suggested that analysts have biases favoring growth over value. Earnings growth records themselves can be seen as representative of a growth business, and naively extrapolated. The tendency of analysts to recommend high-growth and low-yield stocks typically reflects a failure to incorporate the base rate or effect of the environment in which a company operates. This situation may reflect a **representativeness bias**.

EXAMPLE 4

Investment Manager Case Study

It is August. An investment manager has just signed a charitable organization (charity) as a new client. The charity currently holds primarily cash and liquid assets. The directors of the charity would like to move some money not required to fund short- or medium-term activities of the charity into stocks. They expect stocks to earn higher returns than the returns of the assets currently held. They have asked the investment manager to advise them on the timing of entry into the stock market.

The manager advises them that she expects stock to rise over the next 12 months but advises deferring investment in stocks for a month or two. She thinks stocks will decline in the near future because each month for the last six months stocks have risen more than the average monthly increase for the last 25 years. She anticipates a correction that will reduce the increase to the long-term average. She suggests waiting to enter the market until after the anticipated correction.

She states that the probability of a market fall in any September is 0.55 and that the probability of a market increase over a 12-month period is 0.7. She uses these probabilities to support her advice to defer investment for a month or two.

Assume that the probabilities are correct and that the events are independent. What behavioral biases might be evident with this advice? How might the investment manager address these?

Solution:

The expectation of a market reversal—a fall coming after a rising trend—could reflect the gamblers' fallacy. The investment manager is expecting the stocks that have diverged from the long-term average to reverse within a specific period of time. She has not done a thorough analysis but has instead told a compelling story. She may be susceptible to a representativeness bias, in which analysts judge the probability of a forecast being correct by considering how much the outcome resembles overall available data. Frequently, this simplification combines probabilities incorrectly. Additional information or detail may appear to conform to the overall scenario being forecast, even if it is largely irrelevant, and so add to confidence in the forecast. Further, the manager may be anchoring incorrectly on the long-run average. If she believes in a further gain in the stock market, then phased investment over a period of weeks or months may reduce the impact of volatility on timing investment on any single day or month.

Combining this event—a stock market fall in September—with an expectation of a rise in subsequent months to support the manager's belief inappropriately combines probabilities and reflects the **conjunction fallacy**. The probability of two independent events occurring in conjunction is never greater than the probability of either event occurring alone. The probability of a market fall in September is 0.55, the probability of a market rise over the subsequent 12 months is 0.7, and the two events are independent. Therefore, the probability of the two events occurring in the outlined scenario is just 0.385 (= 0.55 × 0.7). This probability is lower than the probability of either individual event. However, the investment manager and the client may suffer from a confirmation bias that makes the additional detail appear supportive of her belief. The information is not being analyzed in a rigorous way. Essentially, the proposal to the client is a sequence of apparently connected events (a story). The added detail in actuality suggests that the assumed scenario is less likely than she asserts, but offers misleading vividness and detail that is being misinterpreted.

5.3.1 Remedial Actions for Analyst Biases in Conducting Research

Given the errors and overconfidence in forecasts, analysts should focus on more objective data such as trailing earnings. However, even reported earnings may be affected by operating and accounting choices made by management. In making forecasts, analysts should *evaluate previous forecasts* and be wary of anchoring and adjustment.

Emotional biases are difficult to deal with and can impact the search process, thereby compromising any subsequent analysis. The solution is to *collect information in a systematic way* and, where possible, use metrics and ratios that allow comparability—comparability in both analysis with previous calculations and also, where possible, benchmarked against current similar calculations. Information should be questioned and assessed relative to its context. It is important when gathering information to use a *systematic approach* with prepared questions. Information should be gathered before analysis is done and a conclusion has been made. In conducting analysis, CFA Institute members and candidates are expected to comply with Standard V of the *Standards of Practice Handbook*.

An analyst should attempt to *assign probabilities*, particularly to underlying base rates of prevalence. It is a human failing to assume that some outcomes are either impossible or certain. Once base rates or events are assessed with other than 0 or 100 percent likelihood, a Bayesian approach to combining evidence will force the conclusion away from unlikely scenarios.

Analysts need to *consider the search process*, the limits of information, and the context of the information. A *structured process* for information gathering and processing can help analysts deal with search biases. A search process should involve *seeking contrary facts and opinions*. Online data gathering or news services can be set to provide information that avoids some search biases. Without structure in the search for information, it is possible for analysts simply to collect more confirmatory evidence while overlooking contradictory information. Clear unambiguous forecasts can help address this shortcoming; confirmatory bias may be greater with complex forecasts that can be easier to appear to confirm.

Having a structured search process and a clear way of *incorporating evidence sequentially*, either as decision rules (trees) or using Bayes' formula, can encourage much faster adaptation of forecasts. *Prompt feedback* not only allows re-evaluation but also helps analysts to gain knowledge and experience that can be drawn on in the future, either consciously or unconsciously (intuitively).

Identifying faulty searches or stories (an excess of representative but less relevant information) is difficult. However, experts' arguments should include some contrary evidence. In a report or forecast, this evidence may be introduced by the use of such words as "however" rather than words that simply reinforce a belief or conclusion, such as "moreover." Vivid and specific illustration in support of an argument may indicate representativeness and availability biases, whereas many good analysts' reports will admit to some abstract unknowns and admit some contrary evidence.

Although analysts should *document* their decision making to assist later evaluation, some of the documentation may be best done once the analysis is complete. Studies suggest that the process of providing explanations can diminish an expert's ability to draw on his or her intuition. Stories can also overwrite nuances and actual knowledge, and they may represent less creative solutions. The amount of knowledge that can be conveyed in a written or spoken answer is small compared with the store of knowledge and decision rules stored in one's head. Spoken and written language can encourage linear thinking, whereas actual decision making is a more complex weighting of different unconnected factors. The nuances of judgment can be hard to verbalize.

Remedial actions include using consistent data, evaluating previous forecasts, taking a systematic and structured approach, assigning probabilities, seeking contrary facts and opinions, incorporating evidence sequentially, having prompt feedback, and documenting the process.

6　HOW BEHAVIORAL FACTORS AFFECT COMMITTEE DECISION MAKING

Many investment decisions are made by groups or committees rather than by individuals acting alone. Examples include analyst stock recommendations that need to be approved by research committees and the asset allocation and fund manager selection decisions of a pension plan made by a board of trustees or some other group of fiduciaries. Often, the motivation for using a group decision is the idea that "two heads are better than one." More formally, the application to a task of a number of individuals, each with different skills and experiences, can be expected to allow for more effective decision making.

Individual decision making is affected by behavioral biases, and a variety of behavioral biases are relevant to investment decisions made by individuals whether they are private or professional investors. Individuals can be overconfident in their information and their ability to forecast earnings or pick winning investments. They can be anchored by irrelevant values, such as past stock prices, or too conservative in updating beliefs in the face of new information, such as earnings forecasts. They can be loss averse and reluctant to close out a position at a loss, even if on an objective basis the future prospects of the investment have deteriorated. As we consider investment committee decision making, we need to evaluate the implications of these individual biases for group decision making. The group process may mitigate a bias or it may exacerbate it. We also need to consider whether the group decision-making process creates additional biases.

Analysts will often work with research teams, and the group environment can have an impact on their own research. Although this arrangement can set standards for good professional work, and provide a cultural and analytical framework for that work, individuals are subject to biases that can compromise their research.

Social proof is a bias in which individuals are biased to follow the beliefs of a group. Analysts may wrongly favor the judgment or endorsement of others, often without being fully aware that they are doing so. This behavior can adversely affect analytical work. For example, a buy-side analyst's investment view might be influenced by his or her team's investment position.

Groups may also amplify individual behavioral biases. The process of reaching a consensus will usually narrow the range of views. If a group-decision process does not encourage private information held by individual analysts to be shared fully with others before a decision is made, the decision may fail to combine the collective wisdom of the group. Group judgments are potentially better than individual ones, but biases mean that the group may not perform optimally. Typically, a group will have more confidence in its decisions after discussion that leads to an overconfidence bias.

6.1 Investment Committee Dynamics

All of the biases present in individuals can be present in investment committee decisions. A group environment may increase them. Wood (2006) cites an example in which his investment recommendation to a committee of a purchase of Ford Motor Company shares was rejected because of the chair's own poor experience with the company's products. Other committee members immediately supported and reinforced the chair's view despite it being based on weak anecdotal evidence:

> ... the rest of the committee chimed in to support the chair's verdict. Any disagreement with people in power is reflected by the Japanese proverb, "the nail that sticks up gets hammered down." Prior experience with group behavior teaches most members to preserve consensus or face the consequences. (p. 30)

There is little evidence in this instance of two heads being better than one. In essence, the committee merely acted to support the judgment of one head, the chair. In general, decision makers are most likely to learn to control harmful behavioral biases in situations where the decision makers have repeated attempts at the decision and there is good quality feedback on prior outcomes. It follows that investment committee decision making should be improved by carefully analyzing and learning from past decisions. Wood (2006) argues that this rarely happens, and changing committee membership is particularly unhelpful in this regard:

> Committees notoriously do not learn from experience. Feedback is a learning mechanism, but feedback from most decisions, when available, is often slow and generally inaccurate. Committees rarely keep track of decisions well enough or long enough to identify systematic biases that creep into their deliberations. Without feedback, people struggle to understand what works and what does not. (p. 32)

6.2 Techniques for Structuring and Operating Committees to Address Behavioral Factors

We might ask why the logic of "two heads are better than one" often fails to apply in committees in practice. Wood (2006) makes an important distinction between crowds and committees. A crowd is a random collection of individuals. For example, in the TV game show "Who Wants to Be a Millionaire?" contestants can opt to ask the studio audience to help identify the correct multiple choice answer to a question. The majority opinion of the audience (a crowd) has been correct 91 percent of the time (Surowieki 2004). Most investment committees fall well short of a 91 percent hit rate.

The main difference is that crowds are diverse, with individuals having varied backgrounds and experiences. Furthermore, in situations like asking the audience, members of the crowd give their own best opinion without consulting, and thus potentially avoid being influenced by other crowd members. In contrast, committees are often made up of individuals with similar backgrounds who are likely to approach decisions in a similar way. Committee decisions are discussed and debated, and as a result, individuals may moderate their own views to fit in with the consensus or may feel pressure to agree with views expressed by powerful individuals on the committee. It follows that committee decision making is likely to be enhanced when a committee is made up of members from diverse backgrounds who are independent enough to express and support their own views rather than falling into line with the views of others. However, assembling and managing such diverse and opinionated committees is likely to be challenging.

The chair of a committee has an important role in ensuring the effectiveness of the committee's decision making. As noted earlier, this responsibility includes assembling a diverse group of individuals with relevant skills and experiences and creating a culture in which members can express dissenting views. The chair is also responsible for ensuring that the committee sticks to the agenda and making sure a clear decision is reached after the various opinions have been heard. The chair should actively encourage alternative opinions so that all perspectives are covered. In turn, committee members have a responsibility to actively contribute their own information and knowledge and not simply fall into line with the consensus for the sake of harmony.

Teams that are diverse in skills, experience, and culture may be less prone to social proof bias. Different perspectives and contrary views are more likely to emerge in a diverse group. Ensuring professional respect between all members of the group and maintaining analysts' self-esteem can help each member contribute to group judgment, even if the views expressed are contrary to group norms. An individual expressing strong contrarian views within the group can help in avoiding too quick of a move to consensus before all the evidence is discussed. The risk of suppressed privately held information by individuals can be reduced if a group leader collects some of the individual views in advance of a discussion.

7 HOW BEHAVIORAL FINANCE INFLUENCES MARKET BEHAVIOR

Much of the day-to-day work of investment professionals will be within the framework of efficient markets. This framework provides a useful set of tools for investment analysis, portfolio management, and risk management. Over time, academic papers have broadened the understanding of market efficiency. However, this understanding still does not explain some persistent market patterns. Behavioral finance does offer some explanation of these exceptions to market efficiency, and this reading focuses on the biases that contribute to these anomalies. Investment professionals should view an understanding of these biases as complementary to their knowledge of market efficiency, thus allowing a greater range of stock market and investor behavior to be explained.

7.1 Defining Market Anomalies

Efficient markets should not deliver abnormal returns. Research has documented a number of puzzles or persistent features of market behavior that appear to contradict the efficient markets hypothesis. On closer examination, not all necessarily contradict the efficient market hypothesis. Note that the hypothesis does not rule out small abnormal returns before fees and expenses are taken into account. Closed-end fund discounts, for example, typically do not offer a profitable strategy to trade when transaction costs are allowed for.

Anomalies (apparent deviations from the efficient market hypothesis) are identified by persistent abnormal returns that differ from zero and are predictable in direction. However, calculating what constitutes normal returns relative to the risk incurred depends on the asset pricing model used. Anomalous behavior can be indicative of shortcomings in the underlying asset pricing model. When high returns persist on a particular class of securities, or relative to a specific factor in valuation, it might simply be a compensation for excess risk rather than genuinely anomalous. Fama (1998) states that if a reasonable change in the method of estimating abnormal returns causes an anomaly to disappear, then it is reasonable to suggest that it is an illusion. He includes in this category apparently low returns following initial public offerings (called the "IPO puzzle") and the positive abnormal returns apparent in the 12 months after a stock split.

Some apparent anomalies may be explained by the small samples involved, a statistical bias in selection or survivorship, or data mining that overanalyzes data for patterns and treats spurious correlations as relevant. The magnitude of any over- or underperformance depends critically on the choice of benchmark, which can make it hard to interpret results. The risk with data mining is that the anomaly may not persist out of sample. From 1967 to 1997, the Super Bowl indicator,[9] a spurious correlation, correctly "predicted" the direction of two out of three US market indices 27 out of 30 times. But it then indicated wrongly 4 times in a row, delivering an accurate result in just 7 out of the next 13 years. Since any correlation between the outcome of a sporting event and stock market performance cannot be rationally explained, it is not surprising that the Super Bowl indicator has turned out to be an inaccurate predictor.

Also, from time to time, markets can present *temporary disequilibrium behavior*, unusual features that may survive for a period of years but ultimately disappear. Publication of the anomaly, which draws attention to the pattern, can start the arbitrage that removes the behavior. For example, the small company January effect, part of the turn-of-the-year effect, does not appear persistent once appropriate adjustment for risk is made. The weekend effect, involving lower stock market returns on Mondays, appears to have reduced in the United States and United Kingdom. However, the market anomalies discussed in this section reflect behavior that has been identified and analyzed in a number of markets around the world and at different time periods. The patterns have been documented in many academic studies, with broadly similar conclusions.

Some of these market features may be attributed to rational behavior that is not captured by accepted pricing models. Investor response to the effect of taxes might be an example of this issue. But for other patterns of questionable rationality, behavioral finance has provided good explanations by identifying persistent cognitive biases or emotional affect. In general, the biases that are harder to rectify are emotional, with cognitive biases typically being easier to correct. However, there is no single unified underlying model of investor psychology. Despite the challenges, the efficient market hypothesis provides a base from which anomalies can be identified, and against which specific cognitive biases can be measured.

---

9 Supposedly if the winner of the United States' National Football League Super Bowl comes from the NFC division, the stock market will increase for the coming year, and if the winner comes from the AFC division, the stock market will decrease for the coming year.

7.2 Momentum

Studies have documented, in a range of markets globally, *momentum* or *trending effects* in which future price behavior correlates with that of the recent past (Jegadeesh and Titman 1993; Dimson, Marsh, and Staunton 2008). Typically in the short term, up to two years, there is a positive correlation, but for longer periods of two to five years returns are negatively correlated and revert to the mean.

Individual investors may make what they believe is a rational decision to imitate the decisions of others, but the sum of the individual decisions can be irrational behavior. This behavior may not necessarily lead to bubbles or crashes, but it could explain the fat tail distribution of stock market returns, in which extreme moves occur more frequently than a normal statistical distribution would predict. The phenomenon is more common in illiquid asset categories in which trading may not be continuous and investors believe that changes in prices may capture private information.

Herding occurs when a group of investors trade on the same side of the market in the same securities, or when investors ignore their own private information and act as other investors do. Herding reflects a low dispersion of opinion among investors about the interpretation of the information, and it may involve following the same sources of information. Herding may be a response to cognitive dissonance. It may give reassurance and comfort to investors to be aligned with the consensus opinion.

Exhibit 10   The Momentum Effect: London Business School Study

The study involves buying the top 20 percent of a performance-ranked list of stocks and selling short the bottom 20 percent. In the 52 years to 2007 in the UK market, the stocks that had outperformed the market most in the previous 12 months went on to generate an annualized return of 18.3 percent, whereas the market's worst underperformers rose by 6.8 percent on average. Over that period, the market as a whole rose by 13.5 percent a year. In a subsequent study using data from 2000 to 2007, the momentum effect was also evident in each of the 16 other international markets researched.

The authors noted "The momentum effect, both in the United Kingdom and globally, has been pervasive and persistent. Though costly to implement on a standalone basis, all investors need to be acutely aware of momentum. Even if they do not set out to exploit it, momentum is likely to be an important determinant of their investment performance."

Source: Dimson, Marsh, and Staunton (2008).

Momentum can be partly explained by short-term underreaction to relevant information, and longer-term overreaction. Investors' bias to sell winners reflects *anchoring* on the purchase price. Investors' willingness to sell winners may also be the result of a belief that a price rise has brought increased risk, irrespective of whether intrinsic value has also increased. The belief in mean reversion can cause investors to underreact to positive news, and stock prices to take time to reflect fully more favorable news or earnings upgrades.

Studies have identified faulty learning models within traders, in which reasoning is based on their recent experience. Behaviorally, this is *availability bias*. The availability bias in this context is also called the *recency effect*, which is the tendency to recall recent events more vividly and give them undue weight. In such models, if the price of an asset rises for a period of time, investors may simply extrapolate this rise to the future. Recency bias causes investors to place too much emphasis on samples that are small or that provide an imperfect picture, but they are favored because the information is recently available. Research points to a tendency for individual private investors to extrapolate trends and to suffer more from recency bias, whereas many investment professionals expect reversion to the mean.

Regret is the feeling that an opportunity has been missed, and is typically an expression of *hindsight bias*. Hindsight bias reflects the human tendency to see past events as having been predictable, and regret can be particularly acute when the market is volatile and investors feel they could have predicted the significant market moves and thereby increased profit or reduced loss. Faced with regret at not owning a mutual fund or stock when it performed in the previous year, investors may be driven emotionally to remedy this regret. These behavioral factors can explain short-term year-on-year trending, and contribute to overtrading.

This response creates a *trend-chasing effect*. In terms of selecting investments, investors have a bias to buy investments they wish they had owned the previous year. This bias reflects the availability bias in projecting a recent trend, and also the innate human focus on searching for patterns, both true and illusory.

However, there is some evidence of price reversals, or a mean reversion, at longer periods of three to five years. The **disposition effect**, which includes an emotional bias to loss aversion, will encourage investors to hold on to losers, causing an inefficient and gradual adjustment to deterioration in fundamental value (Shefrin and Statman 1985). The disposition effect is emotional. Even investors who do not own a poorly performing stock, and are not thus emotionally affected by ownership, may be showing an irrational belief in short-term mean reversion in the form of a price recovery (*gamblers' fallacy*).

The disposition effect has been identified from trading records (Odean 1998). This research identified that investors with US discount brokerage accounts sold winners more readily than losers, a behavior consistent with the emotional bias of loss aversion and the cognitive bias of believing that their winners and losers will revert to the mean. Emotional biases and an irrational belief in mean reversion encourage market trending patterns.

7.3 Bubbles and Crashes

Stock market bubbles and crashes present a challenge to the concept of market efficiency. Periods of significant overvaluation or undervaluation can persist for more than one year, rather than rapidly correcting to fair value. The efficient market hypothesis implies the absence of such bubbles. The frequent emergence of bubbles in history was documented in *Extraordinary Popular Delusions and the Madness of Crowds* (Mackay 1841). The book captures the concept of extremes of sentiment and apparent mass irrationality. Bubbles and crashes appear to be panics of buying and selling. A continuous rise in an asset price is fuelled by investors' expectations of further increase; asset prices become decoupled from economic fundamentals.

A more objective modern definition specifies periods when a price index for an asset class trades more than two standard deviations outside its historic trend. Statistically, if returns are normally distributed, such periods should not represent more than 5 percent of total observations. However, for some stock markets and asset classes, these extremes of valuation account for more than 10 percent.

Exhibit 11   UK House Price Average Multiple of Average Family Income

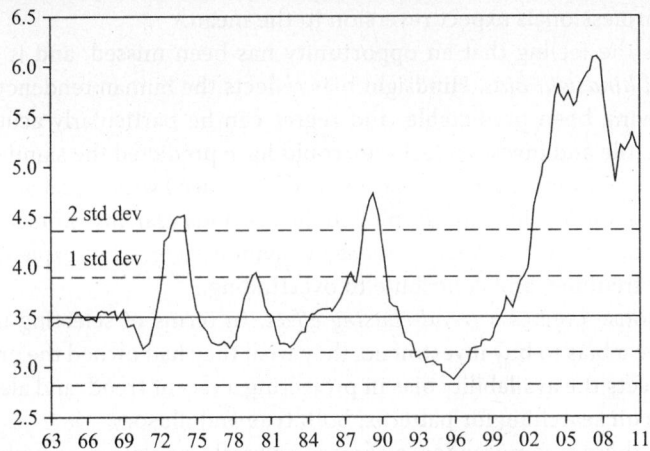

Source: Datastream.

Bubbles and crashes are, respectively, periods of unusual positive or negative asset returns because of prices varying considerably from or reverting to their intrinsic value. Typically during these periods, price changes are the main component of returns. Bubbles typically develop more slowly relative to crashes, which can be rapid. This asymmetry points to a difference in the behavioral factors involved. A crash would typically be a fall of 30 percent or more in asset prices in a period of several months. Some bubbles and crashes will reflect rapid changes in economic prospects that investors failed to anticipate. The global oil price shock of the 1970s and the Japanese asset price bubble of the late 1980s, in which real estate and stock prices rose dramatically, would be examples. Initially in a bubble, some participants may view the trading and prices as a rational response—for example, to easy monetary conditions or a liquidity squeeze—but this view is typically followed by doubts about whether prices reflect fundamental values.

These bubbles have been observed in most decades and in a wide range of asset classes. Recent examples are the technology bubble of 1999–2000 and the residential property boom of 2005–2007, evident in a range of economies globally including the United States, the United Kingdom, and Australia. They appear to be periods of collective irrationality, but can be analyzed in more detail as representing some specific behavioral characteristics of individuals. Behavioral finance does not yet provide a full explanation for such market behavior, but a number of specific cognitive biases and emotional biases prevalent during such periods can be identified.

First, it should be noted that there can also be rational explanations for some bubbles. Rational investors may expect a future crash but not know its exact timing. For periods of time, there may not be effective arbitrage because of the cost of selling short, unwillingness of investors to bear extended losses, or simply unavailability of suitable instruments. These were considerations in the technology and real estate bubbles. Investment managers incentivized on, or accountable for, short-term performance may even rationalize their participation in the bubble in terms of commercial or career risk.

The extent to which investors may rationalize their behavior during bubbles is evident in Exhibit 12. Both managers appear to have misunderstood risks and exhibited the illusion of control bias. The manager of Fund A believed he could exit a bubble profitably by selling near the top. The manager of Fund B may not have recognized the potential scale of a bubble, or client perspectives on a period of relative under-performance while not participating in the bubble.

Exhibit 12   Investor Behavior in Bubbles

Consider the differing behavior of two managers of major hedge funds during the technology stock bubble of 1998–2000:

The manager of Hedge Fund A was asked why he did not get out of internet stocks earlier even though he knew by December 1999 that technology stocks were overvalued. "We thought it was the eighth inning, and it was the ninth. I did not think the NASDAQ composite would go down 33 percent in 15 days." Faced with losses, and despite a previous strong 12-year record, he resigned as Hedge Fund A's manager in April 2000.

The manager of Hedge Fund B refused to invest in technology stocks in 1998 and 1999 because he thought they were overvalued. After strong performance over 17 years, Hedge Fund B was dissolved in 2000 because its returns could not keep up with the returns generated by technology stocks.

In bubbles, investors often exhibit symptoms of *overconfidence*; overtrading, under-estimation of risks, failure to diversify, and rejection of contradictory information. With overconfidence, investors are more active and trading volume increases, thus lowering their expected profits. For overconfident investors (active traders), studies have shown that returns are less than returns to either less active traders or the market while risk is higher (Barber and Odean 2000). At the market level, volatility also often increases in a market with overconfident traders.

The overconfidence and excessive trading that contribute to a bubble are linked to *confirmation bias* and *self-attribution bias*. In a rising market, sales of stocks from a portfolio will typically be profitable, even if winners are being sold too soon. Investors can have faulty learning models that bias their understanding of this profit to take personal credit for success. This behavior is also related to *hindsight bias*, in which individuals can reconstruct prior beliefs and deceive themselves that they are correct more often than they truly are. This bias creates the feeling of "I knew it all along." Selling for a gain appears to validate a good decision in an original purchase and may confer a sense of pride in locking in the profit. This generates overconfidence that can lead to poor decisions. Regret aversion can also encourage investors to participate in a bubble, believing they are "missing out" on profit opportunities as stocks continue to appreciate.

Overconfidence involves an *illusion of knowledge*. Investors would be better off not trading on all the available information, which includes noise or non-relevant information. Asset prices provide a mix of information, both facts and the mood of the crowd. But in a stock market bubble, noise trading increases and overall trading volumes are high. Noise trading is buying and selling activity conducted in the absence of meaningful new information, and is often based on the flow of irrelevant informa-tion. A manager increasing trading activity in a rising stock market can misinterpret the profitability of activity, believing it is trading skill rather than market direction delivering profits.

The disposition effect recognizes that investors are more willing to sell winners, which can encourage excess trading. There can also be a confirmation bias to select news that supports an existing decision or investment. Indeed, search processes may focus almost exclusively on finding additional confirmatory information. Investors may be uncomfortable with contradictory information and reject it. Investors can also have a bias to buy stocks that *attract their attention*, and pay more attention to the market when it is rising. For short-term traders who may derive entertainment from the market, monitoring rising stock prices is more entertaining and instills more pride. Entertainment and pride are emotional effects.

As a bubble unwinds, there can be underreaction that can be caused by anchoring when investors do not update their beliefs sufficiently. The early stages of unwinding a bubble can involve investors in cognitive dissonance, ignoring losses and attempting to rationalize flawed decisions. As a bubble unwinds, investors may initially be unwilling to accept losses. In crashes, the disposition effect encourages investors to hold on to losers and postpone regret. This response can initially cause an underreaction to bad news, but a later capitulation and acceleration of share price decline. This situation will only apply to stocks already held by investors, with hedge funds that can sell stock short being more inclined to react first to bad news in a downturn. In crashes, there may be belief that short sellers know more and have superior information or analysis.

7.4 Value and Growth

A number of studies have identified outperformance of value stocks relative to growth stocks over long periods of time. Fama and French (1998) note that value stocks (high book-to-market equity) outperformed growth stocks (low book-to-market equity) in 12 of 13 major markets during the 1975–1995 period. Value stocks are typically characterized by low price-to-earnings ratios, high book-to-market equity, and low price-to-dividend ratios. Growth stock characteristics are generally the opposite of value stock characteristics. For example, growth stocks are characterized by low book-to-market equity, high price-to-earnings ratios, and high price-to-dividend ratios. Some subsequent studies have included additional factors, such as low price-to-cash flow and low historic growth, to characteristics of value stocks. Fama and French (1998) also identified that small-capitalization stocks outperformed large-cap stocks in 11 of 16 markets.

Fama and French incorporate additional factors in their asset pricing model to explain this anomaly and other apparent anomalies. The Fama and French (1992) three-factor model claims to explain these effects by incorporating additional factors, size and value, alongside market beta. Fama and French show that earnings and size variables capture much of the cross-sectional variation in US stock returns from 1963 to 1990, and this finding has also been documented for a number of non-US markets. Fama and French claim the value stock anomaly disappears in their three-factor model. They believe that the size and book-to-market effects are not mispricing, but are associated with such risk exposures as the greater potential of companies with these characteristics to suffer distress during economic downturns.

A number of other studies have offered behavioral explanations, presenting the anomalies as mispricing rather than risk. These studies recognize emotional factors involved in appraising stocks. The **halo effect**, for example, extends a favorable evaluation of some characteristics to other characteristics. A company with a good growth record and good previous share price performance might be seen as a good investment, with higher expected returns than its risk characteristics merit. This view is a form of representativeness that can lead investors to extrapolate recent past performance into expected returns. Overconfidence can also be involved in predicting growth rates, potentially leading growth stocks to be overvalued.

Studies have also identified that emotions play a role in estimating risk and expected return of stocks. The impact of emotional biases may be greater with less sophisticated or retail investors, but it has also been identified as a bias in analysts and professional investors. The emotional attraction of a stock can be enhanced by personal experience of products, the value of the brand, marketing expenditures, and the proximity of the headquarters to the analyst or investor. This last issue reflects the **home bias** anomaly, by which portfolios exhibit a strong bias in favor of domestic securities in the context of global portfolios. The effect has also been noted within geographical boundaries, favoring companies headquartered nearer the investor. This bias may reflect a perceived relative informational advantage, a greater feeling of comfort with the access to company executives that proximity brings (either personal or local brokerage), or a psychological desire to invest in a local community.

To the extent to which less sophisticated investors are influenced by emotions, they may value growth companies more highly. Statman, Fisher, and Anginer (2008) found that stock returns of funds that are rated as popular in a *Fortune* magazine survey are subsequently low. A more positive emotional rating in a company leads investors to perceive the company's stock as less risky. Although the capital asset pricing model assumes risk and expected return are positively correlated, many investors behave as if the correlation is negative, expecting higher returns with lower risk.

One behavioral theory set out by Shefrin (2008) recognizes the tendency of investors to need downside protection to avoid negatively skewed returns. This investor preference displays excessive risk relative to likely outcomes. Securities that embody significant downside risks in an adverse economic environment, therefore, reflect this risk aversion and offer a premium. An optimal portfolio, taking advantage of behavioral biases, would recognize the extent to which stocks reflect this risk aversion premium, and thus offer returns in excess of true risk. Writing (selling) out-of-the-money put options on securities or indices would be one way to reflect this risk.

Some apparent anomalies disappear over time, possibly being arbitraged away. However, some anomalies persist and may genuinely reflect rational behavior that is not captured by accepted pricing models. The most persistent market anomalies and characteristics that challenge the efficient market hypothesis are the momentum effect and bubbles and crashes. These effects can be created by biases that cause underreactions at times but overreaction on other occasions. Although group behavior can be a factor in these market anomalies, the origins of many anomalies lie in individual biases. The biases that create some of the unusual market behavior include both cognitive biases and emotional effects.

SUMMARY

This reading includes suggestions on how to include behavioral considerations in financial decision making. The effects of including behavioral considerations in adviser–client relationships and portfolio construction are discussed. Finally, the reading considers the effect of behavioral factors on analyst forecasts, committee decision making, and market behavior. It is important to remember that all market participants, regardless of expertise, may exhibit behavior that differs from that assumed in traditional finance. Among the points made in this reading are the following:

- Classifying investors into investor types based on their characteristics, including level of risk tolerance, preferred approach to investing, and behavioral characteristics and biases, is useful for providing insight and financial decision making but should be used with some caution.

- Adviser–client relations and financial decisions will be more effective and satisfying if behavioral factors are taken into account.

- Including behavioral factors in portfolio construction may result in a portfolio that is closer to the efficient portfolio of traditional finance, while being easier for the client to understand and accept as suitable. By considering behavioral biases, it is possible to moderate their effects.

■ All market participants, even those with significant knowledge of and experience in finance, may exhibit behavioral biases. Analysts are not immune. Analysts, in general, are prone to overconfidence, representativeness, availability, illusion of control, and hindsight biases. Awareness of their biases and their potential influences can help analysts put in place measures to help moderate the effect of these biases.

■ Analysts interpreting information provided by management should consider and adjust for the biases that analysts and management teams are typically susceptible to, including framing, anchoring and adjustment, availability, and overconfidence. Management biases can affect both the choice of information presented and how it is presented. These may have an effect on the analysis.

■ Committees often have the responsibility for making investment decisions and are subject to behavioral biases. It is important to implement procedures to alleviate the effect of behavioral biases and improve committee decision making.

■ Behavioral finance has the potential to explain some apparent deviations from market efficiency (market anomalies).

REFERENCES

Ameriks, John, and Stephen P. Zeldes. 2000. "How do Household Portfolio Shares Vary with Age?" TIAA-CREF Working Paper.

Bailard, Thomas E., David L. Biehl, and Ronald W. Kaiser. 1986. *Personal Money Management*, 5th ed. Chicago: Science Research Associates.

Barber, Brad M., and Terrance Odean. 1999. "The Courage of Misguided Convictions." *Financial Analysts Journal*, vol. 55, no. 6:41–55.

Barber, Brad M., and Terrance Odean. 2000. "Trading is Hazardous to Your Wealth: The Common Stock Investment Performance of Individual Investors." *Journal of Finance*, vol. 55, no. 2:773–806.

Barnewall, Marilyn. 1987. "Psychological Characteristics of the Individual Investor." in *Asset Allocation for the Individual Investor*. Charlottesville, VA: The Institute of Chartered Financial Analysts.

Benartzi, Shlomo. 2001. "Excessive Extrapolation and the Allocation of 401(k) Accounts to Company Stock." *Journal of Finance*, vol. 56, no. 5:1747–1764.

Benartzi, Shlomo, and Richard H. Thaler. 2001. "Naive Diversification Strategies in Defined Contribution Saving Plans." *American Economic Review*, vol. 91, no. 1:79–98.

Benartzi, Shlomo, and Richard H. Thaler. 2007. "Heuristics and Biases in Retirement Savings Behavior." *Journal of Economic Perspectives*, vol. 21, no. 3:81–104.

Choi, James, David Laibson, and Brigitte Madrian. 2005. "Are Empowerment and Education Enough? Underdiversification in 401(k) Plans." *Brookings Papers on Economic Activity*, vol. 36, no. 2:151–213.

Dimson, Elroy, Paul Marsh, and Mike Staunton. 2008. *Global Investment Returns Yearbook 2008*. London, UK: ABN AMRO Bank NV.

Dunning, David, Dale Griffin, James Milojkovic, and Lee Ross. 1990. "The Overconfidence Effect in Social Prediction." *Journal of Personality and Social Psychology*, vol. 58, no. 4:568–581.

Fama, Eugene. 1998. "Market Efficiency, Long-Term Returns, and Behavioral Finance." *Journal of Financial Economics*, vol. 49, no. 3:283–306.

Fama, Eugene F., and Kenneth R. French. 1992. "The Cross-Section of Expected Stock Returns." *Journal of Finance*, vol. 47, no. 2:427–465.

Fama, Eugene F., and Kenneth R. French. 1998. "Value versus Growth: The International Evidence." *Journal of Finance*, vol. 53, no. 6:1975–1999.

French, Kenneth R., and James M. Poterba. 1991. "Investor Diversification and International Equity Markets." *American Economic Review*, vol. 81, no. 2:222–226.

Huberman, Gur. 2001. "Familiarity Breeds Investment." *Review of Financial Studies*, vol. 14, no. 3:659–680.

Huberman, Gur, and Wei Jiang. 2006. "Offering versus Choice in 401(k) Plans: Equity Exposure and Number of Funds." *Journal of Finance*, vol. 61, no. 2:763–801.

Jegadeesh, Narasimhan, and Sheridan Titman. 1993. "Returns to Buying Winners and Selling Losers: Implications for Stock Market Efficiency." *Journal of Finance*, vol. 48, no. 1:65–91.

John Hancock. 2003. *Eighth Defined Contribution Plan Survey*. Boston, MA: John Hancock Financial Services.

Kahneman, Daniel, Paul Slovic, and Amos Tversky. 1982. *Judgment under Uncertainty: Heuristics and Biases*. Cambridge, UK: Cambridge University Press.

Kaiser, Ronald. 1990. "Individual Investors." In *Managing Investment Portfolios: A Dynamic Process*, 2nd ed. Boston, MA: Warren, Gorham & Lamont.

Kang, Jun-Koo, and Rene Stulz. 1997. "Why Is There a Home Bias? An Analysis of Foreign Portfolio Ownership in Japan." *Journal of Financial Economics*, vol. 46, no. 1:3–28.

Lench, Heather C., and Peter H. Ditto. 2008. "Automatic Optimism: Biased Use of Base Rate Information for Positive and Negative Events." *Journal of Experimental Social Psychology*, vol. 44:631–639.

Mackay, Charles. 1841. *Extraordinary Popular Delusions and the Madness of Crowds*. 1st ed. United Kingdom: Harriman House Publishing. (New edition published September 2003.)

Madrian, Brigitte, and Dennis Shea. 2001. "The Power of Suggestion: Inertia in 401(k) Participation and Savings Behavior." *Quarterly Journal of Economics*, vol. 116, no. 4:1149–1187.

Odean, Terrance. 1998. "Are Investors Reluctant to Realise Their Losses?" *Journal of Finance*, vol. 53, no. 5:1775–1798.

Pompian, Michael. 2006. *Behavioral Finance and Wealth Management*. Hoboken, NJ: John Wiley & Sons.

Pompian, Michael. 2008. "Using Behavioral Investor Types to Build Better Relationships with Your Clients." *Journal of Financial Planning*, October:64–76.

Pompian, Michael, and John Longo. 2005. "Incorporating Behavioral Finance into Your Practice." *Journal of Financial Planning*, vol. 18, no. 3:58–63.

Russo, J.E., and P.J.H. Schoemaker. 1992. "Managing Overconfidence." *Sloan Management Review*, vol. 33, no. 2:7–17.

Samuelson, William, and Richard Zeckhauser. 1988. "Status Quo Bias in Decision Making." *Journal of Risk and Uncertainty*, vol. 1, no. 1:7–59.

Shefrin, Hersh. 2007. "Behavioral Finance: Biases, Mean–Variance Returns, and Risk Premiums." *CFA Institute Conference Proceedings Quarterly*, vol. 24, no. 2 (June):4–12.

Shefrin, Hersh. 2008. "Risk and Return in Behavioral SDF-Based Asset Pricing Models." *Journal of Investment Management*, vol. 6, no. 3:1–18.

Shefrin, Hersh, and Meir Statman. 1985. "The Disposition to Sell Winners Too Early and Ride Losers Too Long: Theory and Evidence." *Journal of Finance*, vol. 40, no. 3:77–90.

Shefrin, Hersh, and Meir Statman. 2000. "Behavioral Portfolio Theory." *Journal of Financial and Quantitative Analysis*, vol. 35, no. 2:127–151.

Statman, Meir. 1999. "Foreign Stocks in Behavioral Portfolios." *Financial Analysts Journal*, vol. 55, no. 2 (March/April):12–16.

Statman, Meir. 2004. "The Diversification Puzzle." *Financial Analysts Journal*, vol. 60, no. 4 (July/August):44–53.

Statman, Meir, Kenneth Fisher, and Deniz Anginer. 2008. "Affect in a Behavioral Asset Pricing Model." *Financial Analysts Journal*, vol. 64, no. 2 (March/April):20–29.

Surowieki, James. 2004. *The Wisdom of Crowds*. New York: Random House.

Vanguard. 2006. *How America Saves 2006*. Vanguard Group.

Wood, Arnold. 2006. "Behavioral Finance and Investment Committee Decision Making." *CFA Institute Conference Proceedings Quarterly*, vol. 23, no. 4 (December):29–37.

PRACTICE PROBLEMS

The following information relates to Questions 1–7

Ian Wang, CFA, is a financial advisor at Garnier Brothers, a US money management firm. He became a financial advisor several years ago after receiving his CFA charter and currently has three high-net-worth individuals as clients. Wang is conducting his annual review of each client's investment policy statement along with their recently completed risk tolerance questionnaires. He is reflecting on their varying psychographic characteristics:

- Michael Perez is a successful 45-year-old investment banker. Wang describes Perez as a passive investor who is sensible and secure. Perez exhibits low to medium risk tolerance but often overestimates his risk tolerance. His biases include hindsight, framing, and regret aversion. On his questionnaire, Perez indicated a desire for wealth preservation while wanting to invest a significant portion of his assets in his employer's stock.

- Sarah Johnson is an independent-minded 45-year-old real estate developer who has historically utilized significant amounts of financial leverage. Prior to becoming a Garnier client, Johnson managed her own investment portfolio, which was concentrated in just a few stocks. Johnson exhibits a great deal of confidence and high risk tolerance. Johnson's biases include illusion of control and overconfidence. On her questionnaire, Johnson indicated a desire for wealth accumulation and an aversion to investing in non-US equities. In addition, she indicated that her risk tolerance toward a stock investment would increase significantly if she knew that more than one of Garnier's research analysts supported it.

- Neal Patel is a 66-year-old billionaire who accumulated his wealth by starting a successful retail business. Wang describes Patel as cautious and concerned about the future. Patel is concerned about protecting his assets and often seeks advice from those he perceives as being more knowledgeable than himself. Patel exhibits low risk tolerance. Patel's biases include endowment, loss aversion, and status quo. Patel indicated that his risk tolerance would increase significantly if he knew that an investment had the unanimous support of Garnier's Private Wealth Investment Committee.

There was one common observation that Wang noted in all three questionnaires: All three clients indicated that they would perceive a company with a good growth record and good previous share price performance as a good investment.

Once Wang completes his annual review, he revises the investment policy statement for the client's approval. After the client approves the revised policy statement, the portfolio for the client will be reviewed to determine any necessary reallocations. Wang is limited by Garnier as to the specific investment options that can be placed in a client's portfolio; only securities that are covered by Garnier's research analysts and approved by the Private Wealth Investment Committee can be placed in a client's portfolio. Garnier is confident that its analysts provide superior forecasts and ratings because they use a Bayesian approach. Garnier is also proud of its investment approval process. The Private Wealth Investment Committee regularly meets to discuss and debate each security and then votes on which will be approved.

Wang is scheduled to meet with his supervisor next week to discuss the results of his annual review and recommended portfolio reallocations.

1 When advising his clients, Wang is *least likely* to:

   A educate Perez on the benefits on portfolio diversification.

   B limit Johnson's role in the investment decision-making process.

   C provide Patel with details like standard deviations and Sharpe ratios.

2 A traditional risk tolerance questionnaire is *most likely* to be effective as a diagnostic tool for:

   A Patel.

   B Perez.

   C Johnson.

3 Which of the following behavioral biases would be *most* relevant in constructing a portfolio for Johnson?

   A Home bias.

   B Overconfidence.

   C Inertia and default.

4 Which investment portfolio is *least likely* to deviate from the mean–variance portfolio?

   A Patel.

   B Perez.

   C Johnson.

5 With regard to Johnson's comment relating to Garnier's research analysts, which of the following biases is *most likely* to be present in the analysts' data?

   A Confirmation bias.

   B Availability bias.

   C Self-attribution bias.

6 Patel's comment in his risk tolerance questionnaire regarding the Private Wealth Investment Committee fails to recognize which bias?

   A Social proof.

   B Confirmation bias.

   C Gambler's fallacy.

7 The clients' common observation in their risk tolerance questionnaires is *least likely* indicative of:

   A herding.

   B home bias.

   C halo effect.

The following information relates to Questions 8–15

Empire & Associates, an investment management firm, has been in operation since 1974. Empire utilizes a proprietary valuation model based on fundamental analysis to select individual stock and bonds, and also employs technical analysis to help identify market anomalies and momentum effects. They use the output of their fundamental and technical analyses to actively manage clients' accounts. Empire also recognizes the effects of investors' background and past experiences on investors' behaviors and decision making, and uses a behavioral alpha process to classify its clients into behavioral investor types.

Anthony Rodriguez, investment adviser, has been tasked with transitioning three new clients' investment portfolios. Rodriguez has reviewed for each completed new client questionnaire, current portfolio, and some notes on the client. He prepares the following summaries:

- Christine Blake is a 35-year old free-lance writer of several successful children's books. Her primary source of income is royalty payments. She has accumulated a portfolio with a current value of $3.6 million. Blake has always self-managed the portfolio and has confidence in her investment abilities. Blake would like to be able to make independent decisions when opportunities arise. On several occasions, Blake has found herself holding positions with sizable losses and she has been reluctant to sell when a security declines. Because of these losses and the general size of her portfolio, she is seeking professional help. She is willing to consider higher risk investments if her research identifies an attractive opportunity. Her current portfolio consists of 15 equity positions of equal dollar value, diversified across eight industries and four different countries.

- Margaret Neilson is a 59 year old senior vice president of marketing for a highly successful, plastic injection corporation. Neilson has little investment experience and currently holds an $800,000 investment portfolio. Neilson has come to Empire because 80% of her portfolio is invested in the plastic injection corporation's shares that were obtained through an employee stock ownership plan. Neilson is nearing retirement and is worried about a weakening economy and the potential effect it could have on the plastic injection corporation's share price. Neilson wishes to avoid high risk situations.

- Thomas Williamson is a 47 year old surgeon; he is considered one of the world's best in his specialty, and earns several million dollars each year. Williamson recognizes that he has limited investment expertise and considers himself a low to moderate risk taker. Williamson established a brokerage account several years ago and funded it with $4 million. He has made no withdrawals from and no additional payments into the account. He selected investments by acting on the advice of other doctors and friends. This advice led him to purchase many popular stocks, and his portfolio is currently worth $3.55 million. Because he was so busy, he felt he mistimed buying and selling stocks. His current portfolio is concentrated in shares of eight US healthcare companies.

Rodriguez is meeting with Ian Carter, portfolio manager and Lila Suzuki, investment strategist, later in the week to establish an investment plan for each client. Rodriguez has worked with Carter and Suzuki on other client accounts. To facilitate discussion at the meeting, Rodriguez has emailed the summary on each client and asked that they provide some preliminary views prior to the meeting.

Carter is a senior portfolio manager with an excellent performance record. He has expressed concern about the use of investor type classification models due to their many limitations. Carter believes that Empire's fundamental approach to analysis provides great value. However, he believes the technical analysis department is compatible with sound investment practices.

Suzuki tends to rigidly adhere to asset selections based on the proprietary valuation model. She has stated, "Sure it's a complex model, but it incorporates hundreds of different pieces of data relevant to a company; therefore, it's more thorough than any other analysis." With respect to Empire's technical analysis, Suzuki believes that the identified opportunities are not 'true' market anomalies but rather they are associated with higher risk exposures.

In establishing the portfolios for these new accounts, Rodriguez would like to address a recent memo from the technical analysis department that recommended overweighting clients' portfolios in the technology and consumer goods sectors. The memo's conclusion stated, "These sectors are depressed below their ten-year average levels. Every time that this has occurred in the past, these sectors have recovered to their mean in a short period of time." Rodriguez believes that technical analysis has the potential to uncover opportunities where there are over- or under-reactions to relevant information.

8 Which new client would most likely be identified as a friendly follower?

   A Blake.

   B Neilson.

   C Williamson.

9 Carter's statement regarding behavioral classifications is *most likely* justified because individual investors generally:

   A exhibit characteristics of multiple investor types.

   B retain the same emotional biases as they become older.

   C exhibit primarily emotional or cognitive biases, but not both.

10 Given Neilson's behavioral investor characteristics, the *most* effective approach in advising her would include providing her with:

   A frequent reports of the portfolio return and risk measures.

   B information detailing how Empire selects individual securities.

   C information about how Empire will help her meet her investment goals.

11 Blake's portfolio would *most likely* indicate which behavioral bias?

   A Home bias.

   B Loss aversion.

   C Investing in the familiar.

12 Suzuki's rigid adherence to the proprietary valuation model *most likely* exhibits overconfidence in Empire's fundamental analysis due to:

   A availability bias.

   B self-attribution bias.

   C an illusion of control.

13 The recent technical analysis department memo is *most likely* evidence of:

   A anchoring.

   B a confirmation bias.

   C the gambler's fallacy.

14 Blake's portfolio *least likely* reflects:

    A home bias.

    B a disposition effect.

    C naïve diversification.

15 Whose statement regarding the technical analysis department is most accurate?

    A Carter.

    B Suzuki.

    C Rodriguez.

SOLUTIONS

1   C is correct. This would not be an effective way to advise Patel. Given Patel's information, he is likely to be more receptive to "big picture" advice that does not dwell on details like standard deviations and Sharpe ratios. He is emotionally biased and providing excessive cognitive detail will lose his attention. He needs to be convinced of his advisor's general philosophy first and then, as trust is gained, he will respond to advice and take action. (Patel is a Passive Preserver.)

2   B is correct. Perez exhibits primarily cognitive rather than emotional biases. Although risk tolerance questionnaires may fail for emotionally biased individuals and work best for institutional investors, they are generally effective for cognitive-based individuals.

3   A is correct. Home bias is evident in Johnson's questionnaire. Johnson has expressed an aversion to investing in non-US equities. Familiarity with their country may lead investors to own high concentrations of domestic assets and ignore the benefits of international diversification.

4   B is correct. Perez has primarily cognitive error biases. Accordingly, it is likely that, with education, the impact of these biases can be reduced or even eliminated. Because cognitive biases dominate, Wang should seek to moderate the effect of these biases and adopt a program to reduce or eliminate the bias rather than accept the bias. The result will be a portfolio that is similar to the mean–variance portfolio.

5   A is correct. Confirmation bias, a cognitive bias, is the tendency for people to misread evidence as additional support for an initial hypothesis. Confirmation bias is a potential bias for analysts conducting research. It is a form of resolving cognitive dissonance that described the tendency to search for, or interpret, information in a way that confirms the analyst's prior beliefs. The additional information may not be analyzed in a rigorous way, but it can nevertheless appear to make the judgment or forecast more likely by sharing some of its general characteristics.

6   A is correct. Social proof is a belief in which individuals are biased to follow the beliefs of a group. The structure of Garnier's Private Wealth Investment Committee indicates that they may be susceptible to a social proof bias. The committee meets to discuss and debate each security and then votes on which will be approved. Committee members may wrongly favor the judgment of others, often without being fully aware that they are doing so. The process of reaching a consensus will usually narrow the range of views. If a group decision process does not encourage private information held by individual committee members to be shared fully with others before a decision is made, the decision may fail to combine the collective wisdom of the group. There is no evidence that this committee encourages private information.

7   B is correct. Home bias occurs when investors exhibit a strong bias in favor of domestic securities in the context of global portfolios. There is no evidence of a home bias in the clients' common observation.

8   C is correct. Friendly followers are passive investors with low to moderate risk tolerance. Friendly followers tend to follow leads from their friends, colleagues, or advisors. They often want to be in the latest, most popular investments without regard to suitability for long-term goals. Rodriguez's notes indicate

Williamson considers himself to be a low to moderate risk taker. In addition, he admits following the advice of colleagues and this advice resulted in purchase of latest, popular stocks without consideration of goals.

9 A is correct. A limitation of behavioral models is that individual investors do frequently exhibit characteristics of multiple investor types. This is a limitation of behavioral models and justifies Carter's concern. Users of these models should not look for people to fit neatly into one "box" or type.

10 C is correct. Neilson would be classified as a guardian or passive-preserver investment type and these investors are more receptive to "big picture" advice. Passive preservers display predominantly emotional biases and the focus of advice should be on addressing these emotions. Describing how the investment relationship will help her to accomplish her retirement goals would seem most appropriate.

11 B is correct. Loss aversion is a bias in which people tend to strongly prefer avoiding losses as opposed to achieving gains. The disposition effect, which includes an emotional bias to loss aversion, will encourage investors to hold on to losers, causing an inefficient and gradual adjustment to deterioration in fundamental value. On several occasions, Blake has found herself holding positions with sizable losses, and she has been reluctant to sell when a security declines. This suggests that Blake may exhibit loss aversion bias.

12 C is correct. An illusion of control is a behavioral bias of someone who believes that he or she can know more than others simply by acquiring information. This may result in collection of too much information. While this data may not add to the accuracy of the forecast, it does reinforce the confidence placed in that forecast. Suzuki's endorsement of the complex valuation model which relies on large amounts of data most likely would give her an illusion of control.

13 C is correct. The gambler's fallacy is a cognitive behavioral bias in which an analyst wrongly projects a reversal to a long-term trend. This reflects a faulty understanding about the behavior of random events. The analyst expects a pattern that has diverged from the long term average to reverse within a specific period of time. The memo's statement that technology and consumer goods sectors should rebound within a short time period demonstrates the gamble's fallacy.

14 A is correct. Home bias occurs when an investor exhibits an emotional attraction to a stock that may be enhanced by the proximity of the headquarters to the investor. This creates portfolios that show strong bias in favor of domestic equities in the context of global portfolios. Blake's portfolio is diversified among four different countries and therefore would not indicate a home bias.

15 C is correct. Momentum can be partly explained by short-term under-reaction to relevant information, and longer term over-reaction and thus supports Rodriguez's view that the technical analysis department has value.

Private Wealth Management (1)

This study session addresses the process of private wealth management and the construction of an investment policy statement for the individual investor. The investment policy statement (IPS) is a blueprint for investing client assets. The IPS identifies the needs, goals, and risk tolerance of the investor, as well as constraints under which the investment portfolio must operate. The adviser then formulates an investment strategy to tax-efficiently reconcile these potentially conflicting requirements.

Because taxes and regulations vary from locality to locality, tax-efficient strategies for portfolio construction and wealth transfer are necessarily specific to the locality in which the investor is taxed. The study session focuses on investment strategies applicable across a wide range of localities. Although illustrations of such strategies may be presented from a country-specific perspective, candidates should focus on the underlying investment principles and be able to apply them to other tax settings.

READING ASSIGNMENTS

Managing Individual Investor Portfolios

by James W. Bronson, CFA, Matthew H. Scanlan, CFA, and
Jan R. Squires, DBA, CFA

James W. Bronson, CFA, is at Northern Trust Company (USA). Matthew H. Scanlan, CFA, is at RS Investments (USA). Jan R. Squires, DBA, CFA, is at CFA Institute (USA).

LEARNING OUTCOMES

Mastery	The candidate should be able to:
☐	**a.** discuss how source of wealth, measure of wealth, and stage of life affect an individual investors' risk tolerance;
☐	**b.** explain the role of situational and psychological profiling in understanding an individual investor's attitude toward risk;
☐	**c.** explain the influence of investor psychology on risk tolerance and investment choices;
☐	**d.** explain potential benefits, for both clients and investment advisers, of having a formal investment policy statement;
☐	**e.** explain the process involved in creating an investment policy statement;
☐	**f.** distinguish between required return and desired return and explain how these affect the individual investor's investment policy;
☐	**g.** explain how to set risk and return objectives for individual investor portfolios and discuss the impact that ability and willingness to take risk have on risk tolerance;
☐	**h.** discuss the major constraint categories included in an individual investor's investment policy statement;
☐	**i.** prepare and justify an investment policy statement for an individual investor;
☐	**j.** determine the strategic asset allocation that is most appropriate for an individual investor's specific investment objectives and constraints;
☐	**k.** compare Monte Carlo and traditional deterministic approaches to retirement planning and explain the advantages of a Monte Carlo approach.

Managing Investment Portfolios: A Dynamic Process, Third Edition, John L. Maginn, CFA, Donald L. Tuttle, CFA, Jerald E. Pinto, CFA, and Dennis W. McLeavey, CFA, editors. Copyright © 2007 by CFA Institute.

1 INTRODUCTION

In the context of portfolio management, the terms "private client," "high-net-worth investor," and "individual investor" are used virtually interchangeably to reference the unique challenges of managing personal or family assets. Although a more precise definition of the individual investor is elusive, the basic need to properly manage one's financial affairs is self-evident, and the precedent for seeking professional management is well established. Indeed, Anglo-Saxon law has recognized the role of trustee, responsible for managing assets on behalf of others, as far back as the Middle Ages.

Private asset management has only recently begun to receive greater attention from the academic community and financial press. In contrast to large, tax-exempt institutional portfolios that are typically assumed to operate in perpetuity, the universe of private investors is heterogeneous, burdened by taxes, and less well suited to the simplifying assumptions of modern financial theory. Individual investors have diverse investment objectives, time horizons, and perceptions of risk, all subject to tax schedules that have varying degrees of stability and logic.

The increasing attention to private asset management reflects both a rising demand for financial services and an increased interest in empirical investor behavior. Net wealth in individually managed portfolios increased rapidly in the 1990s and beyond, creating a growth market for personalized financial services. At the same time, increased personal responsibility for investing retirement assets, evidenced by the growth in the self-directed segment of defined contribution pensions and savings plans, as well as the portability of fully vested retirement assets, has further increased the need for professional investment management at the individual level.

With the help of a case study, this reading examines the portfolio management process for individual investors. The Ingers are typical of a successful multigenerational family, with most of their wealth generated by a family business. Now that a cash sale of the business is imminent, they must reassess their financial situation and set appropriate guidelines for their soon-to-be large investment portfolio. The Ingers' goal is to create an investment policy statement (IPS) that recognizes their investment goals and constraints and then establishes consistent parameters for investing portfolio assets. The IPS should serve as the fundamental point of reference for both the Inger family and their investment advisors.

2 CASE STUDY

Victoria Jourdan, CFA, works for an investment firm that manages private client accounts. Both Jourdan and the Inger family reside in a politically stable country whose currency trades at a fixed exchange rate of 1:1 with the Euro. Real GDP growth and inflation both average about 3 percent annually, resulting in nominal annual growth of approximately 6 percent.

The country in which the Ingers reside maintains a flat tax of 25 percent on all personal income and a net capital gains tax (based on the sale of price-appreciated assets) of 15 percent, with no distinction between short- and long-term holding periods. Also incorporated into the tax code is a wealth transfer tax. Any asset transfer between two parties, whether as a gift or family inheritance, is taxed at the flat rate of 50 percent.

The country maintains a national pension plan, but that plan's long-term viability has been called into question because of an unfavorable demographic trend toward older, retirement-age recipients. Public debate has grown about how to assure the financial security of future retirees, and among this debate's chief outcomes has been the creation of self-contributory, tax-advantaged investment accounts for individuals. Taxpayers may annually contribute up to €5,000 of *after-tax* income to a Retirement Saving Account (RSA), which they then control. RSA investment returns are exempt from taxation, and participants may begin making tax-free withdrawals of any amount at age 62.

The Inger Family

Jourdan has been asked to manage the Inger family account, which is a new relationship for her firm. Jourdan observes that the Inger family has no stated investment policy or guidelines, and she arranges for a meeting with Peter and Hilda Inger, who have been married for 37 years, plus their two children, Christa and Hans, aged 25 and 30, respectively. Peter, Hilda, and Hans accept the invitation, but Christa, who currently resides a considerable distance away from her parents, cannot attend.

Peter Inger, 59, is a successful entrepreneur who founded a boat manufacturing business, IngerMarine, when he was 23 years old. He has worked compulsively to build the company into a producer of luxury pleasure boats sold worldwide, but he is now considering a business succession plan and retirement. Peter is eager to "monetize" his equity stake in IngerMarine and believes he will be able to sell his company within the next three months. He is already evaluating three separate bids that indicate probable proceeds, net of taxes on gains, of approximately €55 million to the Inger family in total. The four Inger family members are the sole IngerMarine shareholders, and any sale proceeds will accrue to the four family members in proportion to their percentage ownership in IngerMarine. Peter believes that everyone in his family is financially secure and wishes to preserve that security; he recognizes the family's need for a coherent investment plan.

Hilda Inger, 57, comes from a wealthy family. Since her marriage to Peter, she has been a housewife and mother to Christa and Hans. Hilda is the beneficiary of a trust established by her family. Throughout her lifetime, the trust will distribute to her an inflation-indexed annual payment (currently €75,000), which is taxed as personal income. At her death, payments will stop, and the trust's remaining assets will be transferred to a local charity.

Both Hans and Christa are unmarried. Hans currently works as a senior vice president at IngerMarine and specializes in boat design. Peter has tried to involve Christa in the family business but she has resisted, instead achieving moderate recognition and financial success as an artist. Christa has a 5-year-old son, Jürgen, whom she has chosen to raise alone.

The meeting with Peter, Hilda, and Hans and several telephone discussions with Christa result in the following financial and personal details for the Inger family:

Table 1 Inger Family Data	
Income (Annual)	
Peter salary[a]	€500,000
Hans salary	100,000
Hilda trust payout	75,000
Christa (art sales)	50,000
Peter Personal Assets	
Home (fully paid for, held jointly with Hilda)	€1,200,000
IngerMarine company equity[b]	60,000,000
Diversified equity securities	750,000

(continued)

Table 1   (Continued)

Income (Annual)

Fixed income securities	1,000,000
Cash (money market fund)	1,000,000
Gold bullion	500,000
RSA[c]	50,000

Hilda Personal Assets

IngerMarine company equity[b]	€1,200,000

Hans Personal Assets

Home (net of mortgage)	€200,000
IngerMarine company equity[b]	2,400,000
Diversified equity securities	200,000
Cash (money market fund)	100,000

Christa Personal Assets

IngerMarine company equity[b]	€1,200,000
Balanced mutual funds	75,000
Cash (money market fund)	25,000

[a] Peter expects to receive a fixed annual payment of €100,000 (taxable as income) from the IngerMarine pension plan, beginning five years from now.

[b] IngerMarine equity values are pretax market values; the equity has a zero cost basis for purposes of taxation on capital gains. The company stock pays no dividend.

[c] Beginning at age 62, Peter plans to take a fixed annual distribution of approximately €5,000 (tax exempt).

BOX 1 JOURDAN'S FINDINGS AND PERSONAL OBSERVATIONS

Peter

Personality

Peter is a perfectionist and likes to maintain control. Now that he has attained financial success, he seems intent on preserving his wealth. He has consistently been averse to risk, leverage, and change, both in his company and in his personal life. IngerMarine has followed policies of low debt and slow growth, focusing on earnings stability. Like many of his countrymen, Peter holds a portion of his liquid assets in gold bullion. He believes that gold provides a viable hedge against catastrophic economic surprises and plans to maintain his current holding (€500,000) for the foreseeable future. By his own admission, Peter has been slow to adopt a succession plan—he has always believed that he was the best person to run IngerMarine. Although he now wants to sell IngerMarine and retire, in the past he resisted various purchase offers for the company.

Goals

Peter wants to maintain the standard of living that he and Hilda currently enjoy. In fact, he is actively investigating real estate for a second home, and he desires that the new home "make a statement." Hilda hopes the home will ultimately be featured in a magazine and anticipates that it will cost approximately €7 million.

Peter also wants to get to know his grandson better. Since Jürgen's birth, Peter has been estranged from his daughter and he wants to restore the relationship. He would like to provide financial support for Jürgen's health- and education-related expenses, and he plans to begin a gifting program for Jürgen next year; the gifts will be €15,000 per year, increasing with inflation.

Peter has a passion for photography and anticipates purchasing a minority interest (€5 million) in *Exteriors*, a noted photography magazine. The purchase would reflect his desire to support the magazine's high-quality work and might also lead to a post-retirement consulting opportunity. Because the investment is unlikely to produce meaningful current income, Peter does not intend to make any additional investment in *Exteriors*. Finally, Peter also has a strong desire to ensure his family's financial security and feels he will have accumulated enough wealth through the sale of IngerMarine to realize this goal. He does not, however, have a formal estate plan for transferring assets to his children and grandchildren.

Hilda

Personality

Hilda has intentionally removed herself from the family business. She has been a major factor, however, in Peter's decision to retire and have a second home closer to their daughter and grandson. In light of the major changes about to take place, Hilda wants to become more knowledgeable and active in managing the family's wealth.

Goals

Hilda has a strong interest in interior design and two years ago founded a small, sole-proprietorship design company. She is eager to apply her talents to designing and building the Ingers' new home and desires complete freedom in determining the home's interior design. Her company currently operates on a breakeven basis, with revenues approximately matching expenses.

Hans

Personality

Hans appears to be somewhat of a gambler. He has always felt financially secure, and is much more willing than his father Peter to engage in riskier investment opportunities. He sees his father as overly conservative and believes that IngerMarine would be in a more commanding position if Peter had only leveraged the company to expand production and marketing efforts. He drives a very expensive sports car.

Goals

Hans does not want to stay in the boat business and would prefer a career that allows him more free time. He has wanted to participate with college friends in various real estate projects, but his father has steadfastly refused to underwrite the investments. Consistent with his attitudes about risk, Hans prefers high-return investments, believing that he has enough time in his life to recover from any occasional losses. Although Hans is in no hurry to marry and have children, he believes he will ultimately do so and has been looking for a new, larger home, in the €500,000 to €700,000 price range. Finally, Hans is considering a minority investment (estimated to be €550,000, with no further investment planned) in a nightclub scheduled to open in his city.

Christa

Personality

Christa has been estranged from the family for several years. She has resisted pressure to enter the family business, deciding instead to pursue a career in art. She has also elected to raise her son Jürgen without family support, which has created tension within the family. She is very self-reliant but admits to having limited financial expertise. Her relations with the family have recently improved, and she is looking forward to increased contact with her parents.

Goals

Christa is hoping to take a more proactive role in her financial affairs. She recognizes the need for a coordinated family financial plan, yet she does not wish to rely solely on the family's wealth to provide for her son's future. She would like to move into a larger apartment that would afford her the opportunity to create a painting studio. Rents are expensive, however, and she needs an assured source of income so that she may focus on her art career.

3   INVESTOR CHARACTERISTICS

A distinguishing characteristic of private asset management is the wide range of personal concerns and preferences that influence the decision-making process. Often unaccounted for in traditional models of "rational investor" behavior, such factors as personality, life experiences, and personal circumstances can play an important role in determining the framework for addressing financial decisions. An investment approach that begins with consideration of the Ingers' biases, preferences, and perceptions of risk paves the way for a meaningful discussion of portfolio objectives and may result in a stronger, more enduring client relationship than if such consideration were not given.

3.1 Situational Profiling

Many useful attempts have been made to categorize individual investors by stage of life or by economic circumstance. Such "situational" profiling runs the risk of oversimplifying complex behavior and should be used with a measure of caution—individual investors are unique and likely to exhibit characteristics that cut across arbitrary lines of categorization. Nonetheless, situational profiling can serve as a useful first step in considering an investor's basic philosophy and preferences, facilitating the discussion of investment risk by anticipating areas of potential concern or special importance to the investor. Examples of situational profiling include approaches based on source of wealth, measure of wealth, and stage of life.

3.1.1 *Source of Wealth*

Some classification schemes presume that the manner in which an individual investor has acquired wealth offers insight into that investor's probable attitude toward risk. Successful entrepreneurs, such as Peter Inger, who have created their wealth by personally taking business or market risks, are assumed to exhibit a higher level of risk tolerance than those who have been more passive recipients of wealth. "Self-made" investors may have greater familiarity with risk-taking and a higher degree of confidence in their ability to recover from setbacks. Such self-made investors, however, often have a strong sense of personal control over the risks that they assume. Despite their demonstrated willingness to take entrepreneurial risk, they can be very reluctant to cede control to a third party or to accept investment volatility over which they have no influence. Peter's slowness to adopt a succession plan and his largely conservative investment decisions typify such behavior.

In contrast, more-passive recipients of wealth may be associated with reduced willingness to assume risk. Such investors may have inherited their wealth; received a large, one-time payment; or simply accumulated savings during a period of secure employment. Because of the relatively passive nature of their wealth accumulation, these investors are assumed to have less experience with risk-taking, less understanding of what taking risk means, and less confidence that they can rebuild their wealth should it be lost. Christa Inger may be an example of such an investor.

3.1.2 *Measure of Wealth*

Given the subjective nature of financial well-being, it is difficult to categorize investors based on portfolio size (net worth). A portfolio that one individual considers large and ample to meet future needs may be insufficient in the eyes of another individual. All the same, it is not unreasonable to consider that investors who *perceive* their holdings as small may demonstrate lower tolerance for portfolio volatility than investors who perceive their holdings as large. A portfolio whose returns do not easily support the investor's lifestyle might be considered small. If the investor's ongoing needs are so well covered that succession and estate planning issues have become important, the portfolio might be considered "large."

3.1.3 *Stage of Life*

In life-stage classifications, investment policy, and particularly risk tolerance, are determined by one's progress on the journey from childhood to youth, adulthood, maturity, retirement, and death. Theoretically, a person's ability to accept risk should begin at a high level and gradually decline through his lifetime, while willingness to assume risk should be driven largely by cash flow considerations (income versus expenses). The human financial condition is driven by additional factors, however, such as life experiences, living conditions, starting point on the scale of wealth, and personal abilities and ambitions. For the sake of illustration, an individual's investment policy can be viewed as passing through four general phases: foundation, accumulation, maintenance, and distribution.

During the *foundation* phase of life, the individual is establishing the base from which wealth will be created. This base might be a marketable skill, the establishment of a business, or the acquisition of educational degrees and certifications. During the foundation phase, the individual is usually young, with a long time horizon, which normally would be associated with an above-average tolerance for risk. Risk tolerance should certainly be above-average in the foundation stage if the individual has inherited wealth. Lacking such wealth, the foundation phase may be the period when an individual's investable assets are at their lowest and financial uncertainty is at its highest. A young entrepreneur may have substantial expenses in establishing a business, resulting in a liquidity need that overrides all other considerations. Marriage and the arrival of children may create a desire for more-rapid wealth accumulation that is not yet matched by either ability or willingness to assume risk.

Ironically, at the point in life when individuals should theoretically be ready to assume risk, many are either unwilling or unable to do so. Christa, because of her desired independence, has many of the financial stresses associated with the foundation phase and may still be building the foundation of her ultimate career as an artist. Her son Jürgen is in the earliest days of this phase as he begins his childhood education.

In the *accumulation* phase, earnings accelerate as returns accrue from the marketable skills and abilities acquired during the foundation period and gradually reach their peak. In the early years of the accumulation phase, income rises and investable assets begin to accumulate. Expenses also rise during this period, through the establishment of family, purchase of homes, and care and education of children. In the middle and later years of wealth accumulation, expenses typically begin to decline as children reach adulthood, educational needs are fulfilled, and home purchases are completed. Income generally continues to rise as the individual reaches peak productivity. If an individual's personal spending habits do not change, the gap between income and expenses may widen throughout the accumulation phase, allowing for an increase in savings.

Some individuals may forgo investing their growing wealth and instead increase spending on luxury items or perhaps make gifts to relatives or charities. For investors, however, the accumulation phase is characterized by increased risk tolerance, driven by their increasing wealth and a still long-term time horizon. Hans is in the early years of this phase and is clearly willing to assume high risk to achieve his wealth and lifestyle goals.

During the *maintenance phase*, the individual has moved into the later years of life and usually has retired from daily employment or the pressures of owning a business. This phase focuses on maintaining the desired lifestyle and financial security. Preserving accumulated wealth begins to increase in importance, while the growth of wealth may begin to decline in importance. Risk tolerance will begin to decline; not only is the individual's time horizon shortening but his confidence in the ability to replace capital or recover from losses is often diminished.

In the maintenance phase, investors will typically reduce exposure to higher-volatility asset classes, such as common stocks, and increase exposure to lower-volatility investments, such as intermediate-term bonds. Because the individual now has less time to recover from poor investment results, portfolio stability becomes increasingly important. In this phase, the challenge is to achieve a desired level of portfolio stability and maintain an exposure to risky assets sufficient to preserve the portfolio's purchasing power. Investors who become too conservative too soon after retirement may reach an elderly age with assets that have suffered significant declines in purchasing power. With the imminent sale of IngerMarine, Peter is about to enter the maintenance phase.

In the *distribution phase*, accumulated wealth is transferred to other persons or entities. For many, this phase begins when the individual is still reaping the benefits of the maintenance phase and retirement. For most, the phase involves a conscious decision to begin transferring wealth. Dealing with tax constraints often becomes an important consideration in investment planning, as investors seek to maximize the after-tax value of assets transferred to others. Although asset distribution may take place in the later stages of life, planning for such transfers can begin much earlier.

For individuals with substantial wealth, the distribution phase should be a well-planned program executed during the course of several years. Efficient wealth transfers take advantage of market conditions, tax laws, and various transfer mechanisms. An individual may consider various transfer strategies: He might establish trusts or foundations for heirs or charities, make outright gifts of cash or assets, modify the legal ownership structure of certain assets, and make advance provisions for care in the event of health problems and to pay wealth transfer taxes.

Although the progression from accumulation to distribution may be linear, it is not necessarily so. Individuals in the accumulation phase may become dissatisfied with a career choice and return to the foundation phase. Some may be forced to make such a move as demand for their skills diminishes. A sudden illness or accident may move an individual unexpectedly to the distribution phase.

In each of the above phases, personal circumstances are a driving force in how an individual responds to each cycle of life. The foundation phase will be different for those who enter life with a base of inherited wealth than it will for those who come from families of modest means. The distribution phase can become increasingly complicated for the very wealthy but remain quite basic for those with little wealth. Because of obligations and lifestyle, some investors never leave the accumulation phase. For others, the stress of an adverse life experience, such as living through an economic calamity or war, may override all phases and never allow them to properly match their willingness and ability to assume risk in a suitable investment program.

Situational assessments allow investment advisors to quickly categorize potential clients and explore investment issues likely to be of greatest importance to them. We must note, however, that investors seldom fall easily into just one category, and clearly a dynamic relationship exists among the above considerations. Peter and Hilda, for example, have a multigenerational planning perspective and a portfolio sufficiently large to maintain a long-term investment time horizon—their risk tolerance is not necessarily diminished because of their age. Although Hans may be moving into the accumulation phase, he clearly retains elements associated with the foundation phase (e.g., above-average risk tolerance). Similarly, Christa's circumstances most directly mirror the accumulation phase, although she has the financial ability to develop a long-term investment plan. Source of wealth considerations play an obvious role in the Inger family situation and are colored by stage-of-life issues. One recipient of inherited wealth (e.g., Hans) in a later life stage may view his or her portfolio as sufficiently large to assume additional risk, but a second recipient in an earlier stage (e.g., Christa), with less experience and lower confidence, may exhibit less willingness to take risk. The value of situational paradigms, therefore, lies more in their general insights into human behavior and less in their ability to fully interpret individual circumstances. Investment advisors should emphasize the *process* of gathering and assessing relevant situational information rather than the specific category in which an individual investor may fall. The advisor who recognizes familiar patterns is better able to anticipate areas of potential concern and to structure a discussion of portfolio policy in terms relevant to the client.

3.2 Psychological Profiling

A determinant of individual investing that has generally received less focus than other, more objective influences is the psychological process by which an individual establishes his or her investment preferences. Clearly, every individual brings to the investment decision-making process an objective set of financial circumstances, goals, and constraints that will strongly influence the set of investment alternatives from which he chooses. Yet underlying behavioral patterns and personality characteristics often also play an important role in setting individual risk tolerance and return objectives. Psychological profiling, sometimes referred to as personality typing, bridges the differences between "traditional finance" (economic analysis of objective financial circumstances) and what has come to be defined as "behavioral finance."

3.2.1 *Traditional Finance*

Much of the standard history of economic and financial theory rests on the philosophy that financial market participants are rational, information-based investors with dispassionate objectives that maximize the expected utility of wealth.

In models of traditional, or standard, investment decision making, investors are assumed to:

- exhibit risk aversion;
- hold rational expectations; and
- practice asset integration.

Risk aversion implies that investors with otherwise equivalent investment options will prefer the investment with the lowest volatility. They will choose an investment with a certain outcome over an investment with an uncertain outcome that has the same expected value.

Rational expectations assume that investors are coherent, accurate, and unbiased forecasters. Their forecasts will reflect all relevant information, and they will learn from their past mistakes.

Asset integration refers to the process by which investors choose among risky investments. Investors practice asset integration by comparing the portfolio return/ risk distributions that result from combining various investment opportunities with their existing holdings. Assets are evaluated in the context of their impact on the aggregate investment portfolio, not as stand-alone investments.

As a consequence of the traditional assumptions about individual economic behavior, traditional models of the portfolio building process have historically relied on the following tenets:

- Asset pricing is driven by economic considerations such as production costs and prices of substitutes.

- Portfolios are constructed holistically, reflecting covariances between assets and overall objectives and constraints.

3.2.2 *Behavioral Finance*

A growing body of research points to differences in behavior caused by differences in how individuals approach uncertain situations. In these studies, psychological considerations appear to play an important role in guiding investor behavior, especially during periods of stress. Work done by Daniel Kahneman, Meir Statman, Richard Thaler, Robert Shiller, Amos Tversky, and others has firmly established the field of "behavioral finance," and several investment firms currently incorporate behavioral finance as a cornerstone of their investment philosophy. These decision-making models attempt to incorporate the principles of behavioral finance, in which individual investors are recognized to:

- exhibit loss aversion;

- hold biased expectations; and

- practice asset segregation.

Loss aversion is demonstrated when investors evaluate opportunities in terms of gain or loss rather than in terms of uncertainty with respect to terminal wealth. Faced with the choice between a) a certain loss or b) an uncertain outcome that might produce a smaller loss but whose expected value is a larger loss, investors are likely to exhibit loss aversion by choosing the uncertain alternative. Choosing the uncertain outcome actually demonstrates risk-seeking behavior—traditional finance predicts that investors, being risk averse, should choose the certain loss over an alternative whose expected loss is larger.

In their discussion of "prospect theory," Kahneman and Tversky (1979) found that individuals place different weights on gains and losses. Their studies yielded evidence that most people are more distressed by prospective losses than they are pleased by the prospect of equivalent gains. Further, individuals responded differently to equivalent probabilistic scenarios, depending on whether the outcomes resulted in gains or losses. Kahneman and Tversky found that when subjects were presented with a choice between a sure gain of $500 or a 50/50 chance to either gain $1,000 or receive nothing at all, respondents overwhelmingly chose the "sure gain." Correspondingly, when another group was asked to choose between a sure loss of $500 or a 50/50 chance to lose either $1,000 or nothing at all, a majority gravitated to the uncertain alternative. It appears to be human nature to prefer an uncertain loss to a certain loss but to prefer a certain gain to an uncertain gain.

Biased expectations result from cognitive errors and misplaced confidence in one's ability to assess the future. Examples of cognitive errors include mistaking the skills of the average manager for those of a particular manager; overestimating the significance of low-probability events; and overestimating the representativeness of one asset compared with another asset.

Asset segregation is the evaluation of investment choices individually, rather than in aggregate. Related behavior includes reference dependence, in which economic behavior is shaped by the frame of reference or the context in which choices are presented, and mental accounting (organizing investments into separate psychological accounts depending on purpose or preference).

According to behavioral models of individual decision making, portfolio construction takes place under a more complex set of assumptions than those given previously:

- Asset pricing reflects both economic considerations, such as production costs and prices of substitutes, and subjective individual considerations, such as tastes and fears.

- Portfolios are constructed as "pyramids" of assets, layer by layer, in which each layer reflects certain goals and constraints.

Within this behavioral framework, individuals also have characteristics that either sharpen or blunt the human tendencies for risk avoidance. The process of "personality typing" seeks to identify and categorize these characteristics to facilitate the discussion of risk and risk tolerance. We emphasize, however, that the primary value of any personality typing approach is to provide both the investor and the manager with a framework for thinking about the influence of personality on investment decision-making, not to neatly categorize investors into arbitrarily defined personality types.

3.2.3 *Personality Typing*

Generally, all investors have unique, complex personality dimensions shaped by socioeconomic background, personal experience, and current wealth status. These diverse factors make it difficult to precisely categorize investors into types. Yet by combining studies of historical behavior with surveys and scenario analysis, we can broadly classify investors into types. Through "personality typing," investment advisors can better understand the behavioral drivers that lead to an individual's goal setting, asset allocation, and risk-taking decisions, and thus advisors can better manage client expectations and behavior.

Personality typing can assist investment advisors in determining an individual investor's propensity for risk taking and his decision-making style in seeking returns. By assigning values to the factors that successfully identify an individual's propensity to assume risk in the investment process, the advisor can obtain very useful information on the client's risk tolerance.

Generally, two approaches to personality classification exist. Often the default option within investment firms is an ad hoc evaluation by the investment advisor, who categorizes the investor based on personal interviews and a review of past investment activity. Although experienced managers may claim proficiency in their ability to profile investor personalities, subjective assessments are difficult to standardize, and their terms often mean different things to different people. Even when the assessment is generally correct, the degree of an individual investor's risk tolerance is difficult to gauge.

Reflecting a discomfort with this ad hoc approach, a growing number of investment firms now employ short client questionnaires to gain insight into the investor's propensity to accept risk and the decision-making style used in pursuing investment returns. These questionnaires address investment topics but may also include self-evaluative statements that have no direct investment context. A hypothetical example of such a questionnaire is presented in Exhibit 1. The classification scheme blends the Bailard, Biehl, and Kaiser approach[1] with the analytical psychology of Carl Jung.[2] The questionnaire is representative but certainly not definitive or exhaustive; it is intended to reflect the process and content typically employed by investment firms and consultants engaged in more or less formal personality typing of clients.

---

1 See Bailard, Biehl, and Kaiser (1986).
2 See, for example, Berens (2000).

Exhibit 1   Decision-Making Style and Risk Tolerance Questionnaire

Decision-Making Style Questions	Does Not Apply	Somewhat Applies	Generally Applies	Always Applies
1 I keep all my mail. I never throw anything out.	0	1	2	3
2 My favorite subject in school was mathematics.	0	1	2	3
3 I would rather sit in front of the television than organize one of my closets.	0	1	2	3
4 I would rather work by myself than in groups.	0	1	2	3
5 I consider myself to be independent.	0	1	2	3
6 When asked out to dinner or a movie, I generally organize the event.	0	1	2	3
7 I am bothered by people who don't work hard.	0	1	2	3
8 I never leave anything unfinished.	0	1	2	3
9 I generally drive very fast.	0	1	2	3
10 I enjoy competitive sports.	0	1	2	3
11 I rarely worry about finances.	0	1	2	3
12 I like seeing scary movies.	0	1	2	3
13 I am always eager to meet new people.	0	1	2	3
14 I sometimes become impatient waiting for an elevator.	0	1	2	3
15 People accuse me of having a "quick temper."	0	1	2	3

Risk Tolerance Questions	Does Not Apply	Somewhat Applies	Generally Applies	Always Applies
16 I become nervous when flying.	0	1	2	3
17 I don't like contact sports like football.	0	1	2	3
18 When arguing with friends, I am usually the one who concedes.	0	1	2	3
19 I never had a strong bond with my parents.	0	1	2	3
20 I wish I could be more expressive with my feelings.	0	1	2	3
21 I never raise my voice.	0	1	2	3
22 I don't like to discuss personal items with friends.	0	1	2	3
23 I like art.	0	1	2	3
24 I would classify my political beliefs as liberal.	0	1	2	3
25 I am not easily excitable.	0	1	2	3
26 I don't swim in the ocean.	0	1	2	3
27 I am afraid of public speaking.	0	1	2	3
28 If offered a bigger house, I would pass because I don't like the hassle of moving.	0	1	2	3
29 I have had many relationships with the opposite sex.	0	1	2	3
30 I often wear cutting-edge new fashions.	0	1	2	3
31 I will always take the initiative when others do not.	0	1	2	3

The critical question that must be answered with respect to client questionnaires is whether the results consistently assign respondents to risk-taking and decision-making styles that explain the respondents' actual behavior. In addition, there must be a meaningful link between the survey results and the ultimate personality typing. To obtain the appropriate linkage between investor survey responses and ultimate investment behavior, a stratified sample can be drawn to replicate the overall demographic characteristics of investors. A stratified random sample involves independent sampling from subgroups that, when combined, represent a population's overall characteristics. Results from the sample questions (each question addresses a specific category of investor risk tolerance and decision-making style) are tabulated and used to identify systematic differences in decision-making style and risk tolerance. Continuing with the example from Exhibit 1, raw scores are portrayed across the two dimensions of decision-making style and risk tolerance. Based on these measures, four investment personality types are established. The types are consistent with distinct style/risk tradeoffs and may provide predictive insight into an individual's ultimate investment behavior.

Cautious Investors   Cautious investors are generally averse to potential losses. This aversion may be a consequence of their current financial situation or of various life experiences, but most exhibit a strong need for financial security. Cautious investors usually desire low-volatility investments with little potential for loss of principal. Although these individuals generally do not like making their own decisions, they are not easily persuaded by others and often choose not to seek professional advice. Cautious investors dislike losing even small amounts of money and seldom rush into investments. They often miss opportunities because of overanalysis or fear of taking action. Their investment portfolios generally exhibit low turnover and low volatility.

Methodical Investors   This group relies on "hard facts." Methodical investors may intently follow market analysts or undertake research on trading strategies. Even when their hard work is rewarded, they typically remain on a quest for new and better information. Their reliance on analysis and database histories generally keeps them from developing emotional attachments to investment positions, and their discipline makes them relatively conservative investors.

Spontaneous Investors   Spontaneous investors are constantly readjusting their portfolio allocations and holdings. With every new development in the marketplace, they fear a negative consequence. Although spontaneous investors generally acknowledge that they are not investment experts, they doubt all investment advice and external management decisions. They are over-managers; their portfolio turnover ratios are the highest of any personality type. Although some investors in this group are successful, most experience below-average returns. Their investment profits are often offset by the commission and trading charges generated by second-guessing and frequent adjustment of portfolio positions. Spontaneous investors are quick to make decisions on investment trades and generally are more concerned with missing an investment trend than with their portfolio's level of risk.

Individualist Investors   This group has a self-assured approach to investing. Individualists gain information from a variety of sources and are not averse to devoting the time needed to reconcile conflicting data from their trusted sources. They are also not afraid to exhibit investment independence in taking a course of action. Individualist investors place a great deal of faith in hard work and insight, and have confidence that their long-term investment objectives will be achieved.

An advisor can use questionnaire results to plot an investor's risk/style score, as Exhibit 2 illustrates. Clearly, the more extreme investor personality types will plot farther away from the center of the graph.

Exhibit 2	Personality Types	

	Decisions based primarily on thinking	*Decisions based primarily on feeling*
More risk averse	Methodical	Cautious
Less risk averse	Individualist	Spontaneous

As mentioned earlier, a predictive link must exist from the questionnaire responses to the resulting personality typing that is derived, and to the subsequent investment behavior that occurs. If the correlation is high between the personality dimensions outlined in the questionnaire and the individual's ultimate portfolio selections, then the exercise has predictive value. If the results are uncorrelated, then the questionnaire must be revised. In the example above, a stratified sample of clients would complete the questionnaire, and the raw scores would be used to identify subgroups. Each subgroup would then be associated with a specific investment style. A "Methodical" subgroup might be expected to maintain a "value" equity portfolio of very stable stocks, along with a substantial commitment to highly rated fixed income securities.

Correlation analysis can be used to assess a questionnaire's usefulness. By assigning ranks to personality types (1 = Methodical, 2 = Cautious, 3 = Individualistic, 4 = Spontaneous) and to the riskiness of respondents' existing portfolios, standard statistical methods can be used to evaluate whether personality types are correlated with investor behavior, especially risk-taking. If a significant positive correlation exists, the questionnaire may have predictive value and be of practical use to advisors. Note that because questionnaire design and analysis is a specialized area, advisors would be wise to have their classification scheme validated by a psychometrician; the style/risk personality typing example presented here should be viewed as only suggestive of those actually used in practice.

The Inger Family   In trying to classify the Inger family using the above approach, Jourdan asks each family member to complete the investor style/risk survey. Based on their responses, Jourdan classifies the family members as shown in Exhibit 3.

Exhibit 3	Inger Family Personality Types

	Decisions based primarily on thinking	*Decisions based primarily on feeling*
More risk averse	Methodical ●	Cautious ★
Less risk averse	■ Individualist	Spontaneous ◆

- ● Peter Inger
- ■ Hilda Inger
- ◆ Hans Inger
- ★ Christa Inger

The symbols represent the family member's composite survey score. The position of the symbol relative to the box represents the strength or polarization of the personality type. For example, Hilda scored fairly evenly in all categories with a slight bias toward an "individualist" personality, while Hans' score demonstrates a strong bias toward a "spontaneous" investor.

After reviewing the results of the Inger family's questionnaires, Jourdan notes that their scores are generally consistent with her initial observations. Her only mild surprise is that Christa was positioned as a "cautious" investor, which does not fully coincide with what some would see as a relatively aggressive or adventurous decision to ignore the family business and support her child through a career in art.

The survey scores reflect each family member's appetite for risk in his or her individual portfolio, but the challenge remains of integrating these diverse personalities and goals into a coordinated family investment program.

INVESTMENT POLICY STATEMENT

4

The investment policy statement is a client-specific summation of the circumstances, objectives, constraints, and policies that govern the relationship between advisor and investor. A well-constructed IPS presents the investor's financial objectives, the degree of risk he or she is willing to take, and any relevant investment constraints that the advisor must consider. It also sets operational guidelines for constructing a portfolio that can be expected to best meet these objectives while remaining in compliance with any constraints. Finally, the IPS establishes a mutually agreed-upon basis for portfolio monitoring and review.

Constructing an IPS is a dynamic process in which an individual and his investment advisor must identify and then reconcile investment objectives, portfolio constraints, and risk tolerance. The exercise should produce realistic investment goals and, equally important, a common vocabulary for advisor and investor to discuss risk and return.

The process of writing a thorough policy statement ultimately gives the individual investor greater control over her financial destiny. To the extent that drafting the IPS has been an educational process, the investor emerges better able to recognize appropriate investment strategies and no longer needs to blindly trust the investment advisor. Further, an IPS is portable and easily understood by other advisors. If a second opinion is needed, or if a new investment advisor must be introduced, the IPS facilitates a thorough review and ensures investment continuity.

Finally, the IPS serves as a document of understanding that protects both the advisor and the individual investor. If management practices or investor directions are subsequently questioned, both parties can refer to the policy statement for clarification or support. Ideally, the review process set forth in the IPS will identify such issues before they become serious.

4.1 Setting Return and Risk Objectives

Establishing portfolio objectives for return and risk is a systematic process applicable for institutional as well as individual investor portfolios. As one reconciles investment goals with risk tolerance, however, client-specific investment parameters emerge. Both the general process and client-specific results are illustrated as Jourdan continues to work with the Inger family.

4.1.1 Return Objective

The process of identifying an investor's desired and required returns should take place concurrently with the discussion of risk tolerance. In the end, the IPS must present a return objective that is attainable given the portfolio's risk constraints.

It is important at the outset to distinguish between a return requirement and a return desire. The former refers to a return level necessary to achieve the investor's primary or critical long-term financial objectives; the latter denotes a return level associated with the investor's secondary goals. In the case of Peter and Hilda, it appears that their current needs are mostly being met by Peter's salary of €500,000. If IngerMarine is sold, they may *require* a return that replaces Peter's salary (a critical objective) and *desire* a return that will accommodate their major acquisitions and still leave their children financially secure (important but less critical objectives).

Return requirements are generally driven by annual spending and relatively long-term saving goals. Historically, these goals have often been classified as *income* requirements and *growth* requirements, with the presumption that portfolio income (dividends, interest, and rent) is used for current spending, and portfolio gains (from price appreciation) are reinvested for growth. Income needs, therefore, are met with income-producing securities, primarily bonds, and growth objectives are pursued with stocks and other equity-oriented investments.

"Growth" and "income" are intuitively appealing descriptors, and the terms remain in use. The terms are flawed, however, in that they blur the distinction between an investor's return requirements and risk tolerance. Portfolios classified as income-oriented are typically biased toward a lower-risk, heavily fixed-income asset allocation. Conversely, growth-oriented portfolios are biased toward equities, with little direct consideration of risk tolerance.

Return requirements are often first presented in real terms, without adjustment for inflation. When an investor's current spending and long-term savings goals are expressed in terms of purchasing power, however, it becomes clear that even income-oriented portfolios require a considerable element of nominal growth.

As an alternative to "growth" and "income," a "total return" approach to setting return requirements looks first at the individual's investment goals and then identifies the annual after-tax portfolio return necessary to meet those goals. That required return must then be reconciled with the individual's separately determined risk tolerance and investment constraints. With the notable exception of tax considerations, it is typically less important whether the total investment return stems from income or price appreciation.

When an investor's return objectives are inconsistent with his risk tolerance, a resolution must be found. If the investor's return objectives cannot be met without violating the portfolio's parameters for risk tolerance, he may need to modify his low- and intermediate-priority goals. Alternatively, he may have to accept a slightly less comfortable level of risk, assuming that he has the "ability" to take additional risk. An individual, for example, who discovers that his retirement goals are inconsistent with current assets and risk tolerance may have to defer the planned date of retirement, accept a reduced standard of living in retirement, or increase current savings (a reduction in the current standard of living).

If the investment portfolio is expected to generate a return that exceeds the investor's return objectives, there is the luxury of dealing with a surplus. The investor must decide whether to a) protect that surplus by assuming less risk than she is able and willing to accept or b) to use the surplus as the basis for assuming greater risk than needed to meet the original return goals, with the expectation of achieving a higher return.

To calculate the required return and to fully understand the cumulative effects of anticipated changes in income, living expenses, and various stage-of-life events, an advisor may wish to incorporate a cash flow analysis. The statement of cash flows in Exhibit 4 simplistically highlights a five-year horizon for Peter and Hilda Inger based on information gleaned by Jourdan from interviews and background examination.

Exhibit 4	Peter and Hilda Inger Five-Year Statement of Cash Flows					
	Current	**1**	**2**	**3**	**4**	**5**
Inflows	€	€	€	€	€	€
Salary: Peter (taxed as income)	500,000					
Trust payment: Hilda[a] (taxed as income)	75,000	77,250	79,568	81,955	84,413	86,946
Pension: Peter[b] (taxed as income)	—	—	—	—	—	100,000
RSA: Peter[b] (tax-free)	—	—	—	5,000	5,000	5,000
Sale of company (taxed as gain)	—	61,200,000	—	—	—	—
Total inflows	575,000	61,277,250	79,568	86,955	89,413	191,946
Outflows						
Income tax (25%)	(143,750)	(19,313)	(19,892)	(20,489)	(21,103)	(46,737)
Gains tax (15%)		(9,180,000)				
Second home	—	(7,000,000)	—	—	—	—
Investment in magazine	—	(5,000,000)	—	—	—	—
Support for Jürgen[a]	—	(15,000)	(15,450)	(15,914)	(16,391)	(16,883)
Transfer tax on support payment (50%)		(7,500)	(7,725)	(7,957)	(8,196)	(8,442)
Living and miscellaneous expenses[a]	(500,000)	(515,000)	(530,450)	(546,364)	(562,754)	(579,637)
Total expenses	(643,750)	(21,736,813)	(573,517)	(590,724)	(608,444)	(651,699)
Net additions/withdrawals	(68,750)	39,540,437	(493,949)	(503,769)	(519,031)	(459,753)

[a] Assumed to increase with inflation at 3% annually.
[b] Fixed annual payments.

Net cash flows for Peter and Hilda conveniently stabilize in Year 2 and decline in Year 5. Consequently, we can estimate their after-tax return objective in Exhibit 5 by dividing projected needs in Year 2 (€493,949) by their net investable assets at the end of Year 1 (€42.3 million). We find that €493,949/€42,300,000 = 1.17 percent. Adding the current annual inflation rate of 3.00 percent to 1.17 percent results in an approximate after-tax nominal return objective of 4.17 percent. [Note: Strictly speaking, the inflation rate should be adjusted upward by the portfolio's average tax rate. For ease of presentation, we have simply added 3 percent inflation.]

Exhibit 5	Peter and Hilda Inger Investable Assets, Net Worth, and Required Return	
Investable Assets	**Amount**	**Percent of Net Worth**
Year 1 cash flow	€39,540,437	77
Stock holdings	750,000	1
Fixed-income holdings	1,000,000	2
Cash equivalents	1,000,000	2
RSA account	50,000	0
Total	€42,340,437	83
Real Estate		
First home	€1,200,000	2
Second home	7,000,000	14
Total	€8,200,000	16
Gold	€500,000	1
Net Worth	€51,040,437	100
Return Objective		
Distributions in Year 2	€ 493,949	= 1.17
Divided by investable assets	€42,340,437	
Plus expected inflation	3%	= 4.17

4.1.2 *Risk Objective*

An individual's risk objective, or overall risk tolerance, is a function of both ability to take risk and willingness to take risk.

Ability to Take Risk   Assessing an individual's ability to take risk is suited to quantitative measurement. It is generally the investment advisor who defines the terms of the analysis and then must explain the results. Although approaches to the analysis will vary, all must address the following questions:

1   What are the investor's financial needs and goals, both long term and short term?

    An investor's ability to take risk is determined by his financial goals relative to resources and the time frame within which these goals must be met. If the investor's financial goals are modest relative to the investment portfolio, clearly he has greater ability, all else equal, to accommodate volatility and negative short-term returns.

As the investment portfolio grows or as its time horizon lengthens, the ability to recover from intermediate investment shortfalls also increases. All else equal, longer-term objectives allow the investor greater opportunity to consider more-volatile investments, with correspondingly higher expected returns.

Peter and Hilda Ingers' investment objectives are primarily short to intermediate term in nature:

- support for current lifestyle;
- construction of second home;
- investment in *Exteriors*;
- support for Jürgen's education;
- expansion of Hilda's design company.

Longer term, Peter and Hilda wish to preserve the financial security that their family currently enjoys. Preserving purchasing power is apparently more important to them than creating further wealth.

2 How important are these goals? How serious are the consequences if they are not met?

Critical goals allow lower margin for error and reduce the portfolio's ability to accommodate volatile investments. Financial security and the ability to maintain current lifestyle are generally among the investor's highest priorities; luxury spending, however defined, is least critical.

Beyond assuring their financial security, the Ingers' investment goals appear *important* but perhaps not *critical*. The second home is important to both Peter and Hilda and will play a major role in defining their future lifestyle. Similarly, Peter's investment in *Exteriors* is not driven by economic need, but it will play an important role in his life after the sale of IngerMarine.

3 How large an investment shortfall can the investor's portfolio bear before jeopardizing its ability to meet major short-term and long-term investment goals?

The limit of a portfolio's ability to accept risk is reached when the probability of failing to meet a high-priority objective becomes unacceptably high. The investment advisor can provide guidance with probability estimates and identify clearly unrealistic expectations, but the ultimate determination of "acceptable" will also depend on the investor's general willingness to accept risk.

Willingness to Take Risk   In contrast to ability to take risk, investor willingness involves a more subjective assessment. No absolute measure of willingness exists, nor does any assurance that willingness will remain constant through time. Psychological profiling provides estimates of an individual's willingness to take risk, but final determination remains an imprecise science. It may, in fact, be necessary that investors have personal experience with significant losses as well as gains before a productive discussion of risk tolerance with them is possible.

Peter Inger's case illustrates both nuances in his willingness to take risk and a tension between willingness and ability. Peter's risk-taking has clearly centered on the business risk of IngerMarine. He has retained ownership of the company for many years, demonstrating tolerance for business risks that he may feel he controls. In other areas, including company debt policy and expansion plans, Peter has shown less willingness to take risk. His personal debt policy and low-volatility investment portfolio also indicate a conservative approach to finances. When asked what he would consider to be bad portfolio performance, Peter at first answered "any loss greater than 5 percent is unacceptable." After being reminded of his ability to take risk, however, he revised his answer to no loss greater than 10 percent.

4.2 Constraints

The IPS should identify all economic and operational constraints on the investment portfolio. Portfolio constraints generally fall into one of five categories:

- liquidity;
- time horizon;
- taxes;
- legal and regulatory environment;
- unique circumstances.

4.2.1 *Liquidity*

Liquidity refers generally to the investment portfolio's ability to efficiently meet an investor's anticipated and unanticipated demands for cash distributions. Two trading characteristics of its holdings determine a portfolio's liquidity:

- **Transaction Costs**

    Transaction costs may include brokerage fees, bid–ask spread, price impact (resulting, for example, from a large sale in a thinly traded asset), or simply the time and opportunity cost of finding a buyer. As transaction costs increase, assets become less "liquid" and less appropriate as a funding source for cash flows.

- **Price Volatility**

    An asset that can be bought or sold at fair value with minimal transaction costs is said to trade in a highly liquid market. If the market itself is inherently volatile, however, the asset's contribution to portfolio liquidity (the ability to meet cash flow needs) is limited. Price volatility compromises portfolio liquidity by lowering the certainty with which cash can be realized.

Significant liquidity requirements constrain the investor's ability to bear risk. Liquidity requirements can arise for any number of reasons but generally fall into one of the following categories:

- **Ongoing Expenses**

    The ongoing costs of daily living create a predictable need for cash and constitute one of the investment portfolio's highest priorities. Because of their high predictability and short time horizon, anticipated expenses must be met using a high degree of liquidity in some portion of the investment portfolio.

- **Emergency Reserves**

    As a precaution against unanticipated events such as sudden unemployment or uninsured losses, keeping an emergency reserve is highly advisable. The reserve's size should be client specific and might cover a range from three months to more than one year of the client's anticipated expenses. Individuals working in a cyclical or litigious environment may require a larger reserve than those in more stable settings. Although the timing of emergencies is by definition uncertain, the need for cash when such events do occur is immediate.

- **Negative Liquidity Events**

    Liquidity events involve discrete future cash flows or major changes in ongoing expenses. Examples might include a significant charitable gift, anticipated home repairs, or a change in cash needs brought on by retirement. As the time horizon to a major liquidity event decreases, the need for portfolio liquidity rises.

For the sake of completeness, positive liquidity events and external support should also be noted in the policy statement. In the case of a multigenerational family plan, positive liquidity events might include anticipated gifts and inheritance; the advisor should note, however, that inheritance planning is a sensitive and potentially divisive topic among family members.

Significant liquidity events facing the Ingers include the sale of IngerMarine and subsequent loss of Peter's salary, the purchase of a second home, and the investment in *Exteriors*. As the potential need for cash distributions increases, so too must the investment portfolio's commitment to assets that can be easily sold at predictable prices. Peter and Hilda have agreed on a normal liquidity reserve equal to two years of Peter's current salary (2 × €500,000) but will maintain an above-average reserve during their transition into retirement.

Illiquid Holdings   To ensure that all parties have a complete understanding of portfolio liquidity, the IPS should specifically identify significant holdings of illiquid assets and describe their role in the investment portfolio. Examples might include real estate, limited partnerships, common stock with trading restrictions, and assets burdened by pending litigation.

The home or primary residence, often an individual investor's largest and most illiquid asset, presents difficult diversification and asset allocation issues. Unfortunately, this asset defies easy classification, having investment returns in the form of psychological and lifestyle benefits as well as the economic benefits of shelter and potential price appreciation.

The emotions attached to the primary residence will vary from individual to individual, and investment advisors must be sensitive to their clients' long-term view of the "home." Some investors may view their residence as part of their overall investment portfolio; others may view it as a "homestead" or sanctuary where life is lived, children are raised, and retirements are planned. Whether the primary residence is viewed objectively or with emotional attachment, the fact remains that it generally represents a significant percentage of an individual investor's total net worth. As such, the IPS should address the investment role of the primary residence.

It is not uncommon to exclude the residence from the asset allocation decision, under the premise that the home is a "sunk cost," a "legacy" or "private use" asset that is not actively managed as an investment. A similar approach treats the home as a long-term investment that will be used to meet equally long-term housing needs or estate planning goals. Somewhat analogous to cash-flow matching or bond defeasance, the home and the investment goals that it offsets are removed from consideration in building the actively managed investment portfolio. Parents may, for example, wish to pass on to their children the wealth necessary to purchase a house and meet this goal through their own home ownership. Other investors may view the residence as a source of funding to meet future healthcare and housing costs.

Lifestyle changes often dictate selling a large, primary family residence and moving into a more manageable property or living arrangement (e.g., as an individual or couple matures, or as children move away to start their own lives and families). An increasingly popular option for older individuals in Western Europe and the United States is to use the value of the primary residence to fund the costs of living in a managed care facility. Generally, these facilities provide members with progressive levels of healthcare and personal assistance, making it possible to continue living independently.

Alternatively, many individuals plan to retire in their primary residence. The IPS should recognize and discuss financial risks and liquidity issues created by a concentration of net worth in the investor's residence. Although the residence is typically considered to be a long-term, illiquid holding, it can also be the source of significant short-term losses and cash flow problems. Financial engineers continue to develop products and techniques that allow individuals better access to their home equity (current market value, less any debt associated with the home) and better control over their exposure to fluctuations in property values. Some products, such as "reverse mortgages" and other annuity plans, have initially proven to be costly and illiquid. Newer financial vehicles are on the horizon, however, that may efficiently allow homeowners to "lock in" the current equity value of their home. In one such product (Robert Shiller's "macro securities"), hedges are built on the notion of swaps, in which two parties can exchange the returns of home appreciation for a static interest rate return.[3] Any decline in home value would be paid by the counterparty in exchange for the static rate of return.

Factoring the primary residence into a formal retirement plan is an uncertain proposition. Real estate returns vary with location, and the investor's holding period can be difficult to predict. Nonetheless, if the primary residence is treated as part of the investment portfolio, the advisor can use models for forecasting regional real estate inflation rates to approximate future values. Such models can be useful but will not capture the short-term dynamics of real estate markets.

The Inger Family   It appears that Peter and Hilda can afford to build their second residence. Nonetheless, they should bear in mind that the two homes will constitute 16 percent of their net worth. Peter and Hilda's primary residence has a current market value of approximately €1,200,000 and could serve in the future as a source of funds.

4.2.2 Time Horizon

The investment time horizon has already been seen to play an important role in setting return objectives and defining liquidity constraints. No universal definition of "long-term" or "short-term" exists, however, and discussion is often left in relative rather than absolute terms. In many planning contexts, time horizons greater than 15 to 20 years can be viewed as relatively long term, and horizons of less than 3 years as relatively short term. Between 3 years and 15 years, there is a transition from intermediate to long term that different investors may perceive differently.

A second issue relating to the investment time horizon is whether the investor faces a single- or multistage horizon. Certain investor circumstances, such as an elderly investor with limited financial resources, are consistent with a single-stage time horizon. Given the unique nature and complexity of most individual investors' circumstances, however, the time horizon constraint most often takes a multistage form.

"Stage-of-life" classifications, as discussed earlier, often assume that the investment time horizon shortens gradually as investors move through the various stages of life. Although this assumption may often be true, it is not always. Once the primary investors' needs and financial security are secure, the process of setting risk and return objectives may take place in the context of multigenerational estate planning. The advisor's clients may be advanced in years yet be planning for their grandchildren; it may be the grandchildren's personal circumstances that determine the investment portfolio's goals and time horizon.

Peter and Hilda are extremely secure, assuming that the sale of IngerMarine is successful. They have expressed a desire to provide financial security for three generations and clearly have a long-term and probably multistage time horizon.

---

3 See Shiller (2003).

4.2.3 *Taxes*

The issue of taxes is perhaps the most universal and complex investment constraint to be found in private portfolio management. Taxation of income or property is a global reality and poses a significant challenge to wealth accumulation and transfer. Although tax codes are necessarily country specific, the following general categories are widely recognized:

- **Income Tax**

  Income tax is calculated as a percentage of total income, often with different rates applied to various levels of income. Wages, rent, dividends, and interest earned are commonly treated as taxable income.

- **Gains Tax**

  Capital gains (profits based on price appreciation) resulting from the sale of property, including financial securities, are often distinguished from income and taxed separately. In many countries, the tax rate for capital gains is lower than the corresponding income tax; a minimum holding period between purchase and sale is sometimes required.

- **Wealth Transfer Tax**

  A wealth transfer tax is assessed as assets are transferred, without sale, from one owner to another. Examples of wealth transfer taxes include "estate" or "inheritance" taxes paid at the investor's death and "gift" taxes paid on transfers made during the investor's lifetime.

- **Property Tax**

  Property tax most often refers to the taxation of real property (real estate) but may also apply to financial assets. Such taxes are generally assessed annually, as a percentage of reported value. Although straightforward in concept, property taxes present challenges with regard to valuation and compliance.

Taxation varies greatly across regions and continents, but marginal tax rates of 50 percent are not uncommon. With tax burdens of such magnitude, clearly the individual investor must approach investments and financial planning from an after-tax perspective. Exhibit 6 illustrates the degree of variation in top marginal tax rates that can exist internationally at a given point in time.

Exhibit 6   Top Marginal Tax Rates

Country	Income Tax (%)	Gains Tax (%)	Wealth Transfer Tax (%)
Brazil	27.5	15.0	8.0
Canada (Ontario)	46.4	23.2	0.0
Chile	40.0	17.0	25.0
China (PRC)	45.0	20.0	0.0
Egypt	32.0	0.0	0.0
France	48.1	27.0	60.0
Germany	42.0	50.0	50.0
India	30.0	20.0	0.0
Israel	49.0	25.0	0.0
Italy	43.0	12.5	0.0
Japan	37.0	26.0	70.0
Jordan	25.0	0.0	0.0
Korea	35.0	70.0	50.0

(continued)

Exhibit 6	(Continued)		
Country	**Income Tax (%)**	**Gains Tax (%)**	**Wealth Transfer Tax (%)**
Mexico	30.0	30.0	0.0
New Zealand	39.0	0.0	25.0
Pakistan	35.0	35.0	0.0
Philippines	32.0	32.0	20.0
Russian Federation	35.0	30.0	40.0
South Africa	40.0	10.0	20.0
Taiwan	40.0	0.0	50.0
United Kingdom	40.0	40.0	40.0
United States	35.0	35.0	47.0

Note: Rates shown are subject to periodic change and do not fully reflect the complexity of the tax codes from which they were taken; additional regional taxes may also apply. This exhibit should not be used for tax planning purposes.
Source: "The Global Executive," Ernst & Young, 2005.

Taxes affect portfolio performance in two ways. When taxes are paid at the end of a given measurement period, portfolio growth is simply reduced by the amount of tax. When the same tax is assessed periodically throughout the measurement period, growth is further reduced: Funds that would otherwise compound at the portfolio growth rate are no longer available for investment. Exhibit 7 illustrates the effect of taxes on portfolio performance. In Example A, a periodic tax of 25 percent, similar to an annual income tax, is applied against investment returns over five years. In Example B, a tax of 25 percent is applied against the cumulative investment return at the end of a five-year holding period, similar to a capital gains tax. The difference in ending portfolio values demonstrates the benefit of deferring tax payments.

Tax strategies are ultimately unique to the individual investor and the prevailing tax code. Although the details of tax planning often involve complex legal and political considerations, all strategies share some basic principles.

Exhibit 7	**Effect of Taxes on Portfolio Performance**				
	Example A: *Periodic 25% Tax*				
Year	**Beginning Value**	**Returns[a]**	**Tax (25%)**	**Ending Value**	**Cumulative Gain**
1	100,000	10,000	(2,500)	107,500	7,500
2	107,500	10,750	(2,688)	115,563	15,563
3	115,563	11,556	(2,889)	124,230	24,230
4	124,230	12,423	(3,106)	133,547	33,547
5	133,547	13,355	(3,339)	143,563	**43,563**
	Example B: *Cumulative 25% Tax*				
Year	**Beginning Value**	**Returns[a]**	**Tax**	**Ending Value**	**Cumulative Gain**
1	100,000	10,000	n/a	110,000	10,000
2	110,000	11,000	n/a	121,000	21,000
3	121,000	12,100	n/a	133,100	33,100

| Exhibit 7 | (Continued) |

Example B: _Cumulative 25% Tax_

Year	Beginning Value	Returns[a]	Tax	Ending Value	Cumulative Gain
4	133,100	13,310	n/a	146,410	46,410
5	146,410	14,641	n/a	161,051	61,051
		Less 25% Tax (15,263)		(15,263)	(15,263)
				145,788	**45,788**

[a] Annual return: 10%.

Tax Deferral For the long-term investor, periodic tax payments severely diminish the benefit of compounding portfolio returns. Many tax strategies, therefore, seek to defer taxes and maximize the time during which investment returns can be reinvested. (Exhibit 7 demonstrated the value of tax deferral in general.) A portfolio strategy focusing on low turnover, for example, extends the average investment holding period and postpones gains taxes.

Loss harvesting, another tax reduction strategy, focuses on realizing capital losses to offset otherwise taxable gains without impairing investment performance. Low turnover and loss harvesting strategies are representative of a general portfolio policy that strives for a low rate of capital gains realization, resulting in deferred tax payments.

Tax Avoidance The ideal solution is to avoid taxes when legally possible.[4] A number of countries have introduced special purpose savings accounts, such as Peter Inger's RSA account, that may be exempt or deferred from taxation. Tax-exempt bonds may be available as alternative investment vehicles. Estate planning and gifting strategies may allow the investor to reduce future estate taxes by taking advantage of specific tax laws.

Tax-advantaged investment alternatives typically come at a price, however, paid in some combination of lower returns, reduced liquidity, and diminished control.

- Tax-exempt securities typically offer lower returns or involve higher expenses (including higher transaction costs) relative to taxable alternatives, and they are attractive only when the following relationship holds (ignoring differential transaction costs): $R_{\text{Tax-free}} > [R_{\text{Taxable}} \times (1 - \text{Tax rate})]$.

- Liquidity is reduced in tax-sheltered savings accounts when a minimum holding period is required or when withdrawals are limited to specific purposes.

- The investor must often relinquish or share the direct ownership of assets placed in tax-advantaged partnerships or trusts.

Tax Reduction If taxes cannot be avoided entirely, opportunities may remain to reduce their impact. When income tax rates exceed the capital gains tax rate, as they do in a number of countries (see Exhibit 6), a portfolio manager may emphasize securities and investment strategies whose investment returns are recognized as gains rather than income (a portfolio "tilt," for example, toward low-dividend-paying stocks). Because the gains tax is assessed only at the time of sale, such strategies may also benefit from tax deferral as well as the lower tax rate. If only _net_ gains are taxed, a policy to actively

---

4 The term "tax avoidance" is typically used in reference to the legal pursuit of tax efficient investment strategies; the term "tax evasion" typically describes an illegal attempt to circumvent tax liability.

realize offsetting losses ("loss harvesting") will reduce reported gains. To achieve port-folio tax efficiency, a manager may use a variety of additional strategies, an increasing number of which are made possible through the use of derivatives.[5]

Wealth Transfer Taxes   Wealth transfer strategies belong perhaps more to the world of tax- and estate-planning attorneys than to the realm of portfolio management. As a practical matter, however, investment advisors should have a working knowledge of estate planning principles, as it is often the advisor who first recognizes the investor's need for estate planning and makes the necessary recommendation to seek legal counsel.

Multiple variables potentially influence the timing of personal wealth transfers, including the investor's net worth, time horizon, and charitable intentions, as well as the age, maturity, and tax status of the beneficiaries. Generally speaking, strategies for addressing wealth transfers focus on either the timing or the legal structure (partner-ships, trusts, etc.) of the transfer. The possible legal structures for a wealth transfer are necessarily country specific. Timing of wealth transfers, however, involves the more universal principles of tax avoidance, tax deferral, and maximized compound returns.

Transfer at Death.   If the investor pursues no other strategy, a wealth transfer tax may be assessed at death (often referred to as an estate tax or death tax). In this scenario, the transfer tax has been deferred for as long as possible, retaining maximum financial flexibility for the individual and maximizing the final value of the investment portfolio. In a multigeneration estate plan, however, this strategy may not minimize transfer taxes.

Early Transfers.   Accelerated wealth transfers and philanthropic gifting may be desirable when the investor wishes to maximize the amount of his or her estate, after taxes, that is passed on to individuals or organizations. Early gifting of higher-growth assets into the hands of a younger generation may shelter the subsequent growth of those assets from transfer taxes when the investor ultimately dies. Logically, earlier transfers to younger beneficiaries offer the greatest tax deferral. Because assets transferred to children will quite possibly be taxed again when the children die, it may be advantageous to make gifts directly to grandchildren, effectively skipping a generation of transfer taxes. Note that some tax regimes may differentiate among recipients, taxing gifts made to family members, for example, at lower rates than gifts made to other parties.

The benefit of early wealth transfers is largely determined by tax codes and life expectancies. Additional issues to consider before making a permanent transfer include 1) the amount of retained wealth needed to ensure the financial security of the primary investor; 2) possible unintended consequences of transferring large amounts of wealth to younger, potentially less mature beneficiaries; and 3) the probable stability or vol-atility of the tax code. Early transfers implicitly assume that the current tax structure will remain relatively constant through time. If an early gift is made and the transfer tax is later abolished, refunds are unlikely.

4.2.4 Legal and Regulatory Environment

In the context of portfolio management for individual investors, legal and regulatory constraints most frequently involve taxation and the transfer of personal property ownership. Legal and regulatory constraints vary greatly from country to country and change frequently. Achieving investment objectives within the constraints of a given jurisdiction frequently requires consultation with local experts, including tax accountants and estate planning attorneys. Whatever a portfolio manager's level of legal and regulatory understanding, she must be careful to avoid giving advice that

---

5 See Brunel (2002).

would constitute the practice of law (the role of a licensed attorney). To the extent that the manager is acting in a fiduciary capacity (e.g., employed as trustee of a trust), prudent investor rules may apply, depending on the legal jurisdiction.

The Personal Trust   The use of trusts to implement investment and estate planning strategies is well established in English and American law, and a basic familiarity with the vocabulary of trusts is often useful in other jurisdictions as well. Typically, a trust is a legal entity established to hold and manage assets in accordance with specific instructions.

The term "personal trust" refers to trusts established by an individual, who is called the "grantor." The trust is a recognized owner of assets and can be subject to taxation in much the same manner that individuals are taxed. To form a trust, the creator (grantor) drafts a trust document defining the trust's purpose and naming a trustee who will be responsible for oversight and administration of the trust's assets. The trustee may or may not be the same person as the grantor. Many banks have "trust departments" that provide trustee services, including trust administration, investment management, and custody of assets. "Trust companies" are non-bank providers of trust services that have been granted trust powers by a government or regulatory body; these companies may or may not be owned by a bank.

The trust is funded when the grantor transfers legal ownership of designated assets to the trust. The assets of the trust can include a wide variety of items that the grantor owns, such as investment securities, residential or commercial real estate, farm or timber land, notes, precious metals, oil and gas leases, and collectibles. The valuation, marketability, and restrictions on sale of such assets can present challenges for the trustee trying to prudently manage the trust's holdings.

Personal trusts are not in and of themselves an investment strategy but rather an important tool for implementing certain aspects of an investment strategy (e.g., gifting). The appeal of personal trusts lies in the flexibility and control with which the grantor can specify how trust assets are to be managed and distributed, both before and after the grantor's demise. The two basic types of personal trusts, revocable and irrevocable, differ largely with respect to the issue of control. In a revocable trust, any term of the trust can be revoked or amended by the grantor at any time, including those terms dealing with beneficiaries, trustees, shares or interests, investment provisions, and distribution provisions. Revocable trusts are often used in place of a will or in combination with a will, because of their tax planning efficiency and the generally lower legal expenses associated with transferring ownership of personal property at the time of the grantor's death. Because the grantor retains control over the trust's terms and assets, she also remains responsible for any tax liabilities, such as income and gains taxes, generated by the trust's assets; trust assets remain subject to any wealth transfer tax due after the grantor's demise (often referred to as estate taxes or death taxes). Upon the grantor's death, the trust can typically no longer be amended; in accordance with the terms of the trust, trust assets either continue under management by a trustee or are distributed outright to the trust's beneficiaries.

In an irrevocable trust, the terms of management during the grantor's life and the disposition of assets upon the grantor's death are fixed and cannot be revoked or amended. The creation of an irrevocable trust is generally considered to be an immediate and irreversible transfer of property ownership, and a wealth transfer tax, sometimes called a gift tax, may have to be paid when the trust is funded. US tax treatment of irrevocable trusts is similar to the tax treatment of individuals. The trust, not the grantor, is responsible for tax liabilities generated by trust assets and for filing its own tax return. The grantor retains no control or ownership interest in the trust, and the trust's assets are no longer considered part of the grantor's estate.

The framework for investment decision-making within a trust can vary significantly, but ultimate responsibility for investment oversight resides with the trustee (or co-trustees, if the trust document names multiple trustees). In revocable trusts, the trustee is often the grantor, who may or may not wish to personally manage the investment portfolio. As trustee of a revocable trust, the grantor may 1) appoint an investment manager, who then acts as an "agent" for the trustee; 2) amend the trust document to include a co-trustee with investment responsibility; or 3) manage the investment process directly. In the first two scenarios, the grantor may require that the agent or co-trustee obtain prior approval from the grantor before executing individual transactions. Requiring such prior approval can present difficulties from an investment management perspective, as no party has full authority to act. Upon the death of the grantor/trustee, the trust passes authority on to the successor trustee or co-trustees (named in the trust document), who then have responsibility for managing the assets according to the terms of the trust.

The Family Foundation   Civil law countries, as found in continental Europe, are characterized by the existence of family foundations. Similar to an irrevocable trust, the foundation is an independent entity, often governed by family members. Such foundations can be part of a multigeneration estate plan and often serve as a vehicle for introducing younger family members to the process of managing family assets.

There are many examples of trusts and foundations with customized terms of distribution. It is important to keep in mind, however, that trusts, foundations, and similar structures are only instruments with which to implement an underlying investment, estate-planning, or tax-saving strategy. Following are examples of how the Ingers might use such instruments:

■ **Gifting to Grandchildren**

Jürgen is currently too young to receive large, direct gifts, but an irrevocable trust might be established for his benefit. The trustee would disburse funds from the trust, in accordance with conditions specified in the trust document by the Ingers. The terms for distribution might limit early access, or allow funding only for specific purposes, such as education expenses. As previously mentioned, generation-skipping gifts may reduce wealth-transfer taxes.

■ **Gifting to Children**

Although the Ingers are eager to provide for the financial security of their children, they may be reluctant to entrust Hans and Christa with the management of large, unconditional transfers of family wealth. Christa does not seem to have the necessary investment skills or experience, and Hans' appetite for risk-taking may leave his parents uneasy. As an alternative to direct transfers, the Ingers could create a trust or foundation and structure the terms of distribution such that lifetime support is assured. The trust or foundation might be instructed to distribute funds based on reasonable need, as defined by the Ingers, or as the children reach specific ages and stages of life.

■ **Gifting with Retained Interest**

Various options exist for creating hybrid structures that provide immediate support for one party but ultimately distribute their assets to a second party. The Ingers might consider a trust in which they retain an ownership interest in any income generated by the trust but give up control over the trust's assets. All income would be distributed to Peter and Hilda, making them the income beneficiaries of the trust. When the income beneficiaries die or have no further claim on income, the trust's remaining assets will be distributed to remaindermen, which might be charities, foundations, or other individuals, including the Ingers' children. Such trusts are generally irrevocable and treated as a deferred gift to the remaindermen. Transfer taxes on the gift's present value may have to be paid at the time the trust is created. When the remainder beneficiaries are charities or foundations, such arrangements may be referred to as a "charitable remainder trust."

The conflicting needs and interests of income beneficiaries and remaindermen may present the trustee of an irrevocable trust with portfolio management challenges. Trust beneficiaries will often pressure the trustee to favor either current income or long-term growth, depending on their beneficial interest. Income beneficiaries will typically desire that the trustee seek to maximize current income through the selection of higher income-producing assets. Remainderman beneficiaries will favor investments with long-term growth potential, even if this reduces current income. The trustee has the responsibility to consider the needs of both groups, under guidelines and criteria provided by the trust document. Although many older trust documents commonly define income as "interest, dividends and rents," the trend is to adopt a total return approach, consistent with modern portfolio management, that allows distributions from realized capital gains as well as traditional "income" sources.

Jurisdiction   Individual investors may enjoy a limited degree of flexibility in determining the jurisdiction in which their income and assets will be taxed. Some countries have both national and regional tax codes. By choosing to live in a region with low tax rates, the investor may be able to reduce his tax liability. Generally speaking, however, all investment returns (including "offshore" investments) are subject to taxation in the investor's country of citizenship or residence. The same is true for trusts, which are taxed in accordance with their "situs" (locality under whose laws the trust operates).

"Offshore" investments and trusts in "tax friendly" countries typically offer some measure of enhanced privacy, asset protection, and estate planning advantages, as well as possible opportunities to reduce tax liabilities. If tax reduction is the investor's only concern, however, an alternative domestic tax strategy may prove more efficient. Again, investors are generally required to declare and pay taxes on returns received from offshore investments, regardless of whether return data are disclosed by the host country.

4.2.5 *Unique Circumstances*

Not surprisingly, individual investors often present their investment advisors with a wide range of unique circumstances that act to constrain portfolio choices. Such constraints might include guidelines for social or special purpose investing, assets legally restricted from sale, directed brokerage arrangements, and privacy concerns. It is also appropriate to list here any assets held outside the investment portfolio and not otherwise discussed in the IPS.

In the Ingers' case, a unique circumstance exists in the self-imposed limitation on acceptable investments. In the 1960s, Peter and several of his friends lost money in equity investment schemes. Since that time, he has had a bias against putting his money in the stock market. Peter does feel quite comfortable with investments in real estate, however, and mentions that he has always been quite successful and comfortable investing in real estate projects. After several "educational" discussions, Peter still insists that he wants only a limited exposure to common stock investments.

4.2.6 *Peter and Hilda Inger's Investment Policy Statement*

Using all of the information she has gathered about Peter and Hilda Inger, Jourdan formulates an investment policy statement for them. Exhibit 8 displays the IPS.

| Exhibit 8 | Investment Policy Statement Prepared for Peter and Hilda Inger |

I. Background

Peter and Hilda Inger own and operate IngerMarine, a producer of luxury pleasure boats sold worldwide. The Ingers are eager to convert their equity stake in IngerMarine to cash and have received bids indicating probable proceeds to Peter and Hilda of €52 million, net of taxes. They consider everyone in their family to be financially secure and wish to preserve that security.

The Ingers' family consists of their son Hans, daughter Christa, and grandson Jürgen. Hans is a senior vice president at IngerMarine, specializing in design. Christa is an artist and a single mother to Jürgen.

II. Return Objectives

Longer term, the Ingers wish to assure not only their own financial security and standard of living but that of their children as well. The investment portfolio must replace Peter's salary, which currently covers the couple's annual expenses and gifting. It should also provide a return sufficient to offset the effect of inflation (assumed to approximate 3 percent annually) on what will ultimately be their children's inheritance.

Required return[a]	1.17%
Expected inflation	3.00%
Return objective	4.17%

[a] Expected cash flow requirement in Year 2 divided by investable assets (€493,949/€42,340,438).

III. Risk Tolerance

Ability

Following the sale of IngerMarine, the Ingers' investment portfolio will be able to accommodate considerable volatility without endangering its ability to meet their financial objectives. Given Peter and Hilda's cash flow circumstances, their likely wealth position after the IngerMarine sale, and their postretirement objectives, their ability to take risk appears to be "above average."

Willingness

The Ingers are relatively conservative by nature. Personality typing of the Ingers identifies Peter as "methodical" and Hilda as "individualist." Peter seems to have managed IngerMarine with a bias toward low debt and stable earnings rather than rapid expansion. The Ingers have historically held a large portion of their liquid assets in money market accounts. Furthermore, the Ingers do not want a portfolio value decline of more than 10 percent in nominal terms in any given 12-month period. Their willingness to take risk is generally "below average."

To reconcile the portfolio's considerable ability to accommodate risk and the Ingers' apparent preference for lower risk, their overall risk tolerance is described in this policy statement as "moderate" or "average."

IV. Constraints

Liquidity

The Ingers have multiple short- to intermediate-term liquidity constraints:

- Construction of a second home (next one to three years)   € 7,000,000
- Probable investment in the magazine *Exteriors* (within one year)   € 5,000,000
- Emergency reserve   € 1,000,000
- Annual expenses (estimated to rise with inflation)   € 500,000
- Annual support for grandson (estimated to rise with inflation)   € 15,000

- Illiquid holding: IngerMarine currently represents a disproportionately large and illiquid part of the Ingers' net worth.

- Illiquid holding: After the sale of IngerMarine and the construction of their second home, the Ingers will have approximately 16 percent of their net worth committed to personal residences.

Time Horizon

Aside from the liquidity events listed above, the Ingers have a long-term, multistage time horizon.

Taxes

The Ingers are subject to their country's tax code and wish to pursue strategies that maximize the wealth passed on to their children.

Legal and Regulatory Environment

Any Retirement Savings Accounts created by the Ingers must be managed in compliance with prevalent fiduciary standards for diversification and prudence.

Unique Circumstances

- The critical component of Peter and Hilda's retirement plan is the disposition of IngerMarine stock to a willing buyer. This situation should be continually monitored to ensure that the assumptions made in any plan remain valid.

- The Ingers' second home will represent an illiquid portion of their total net worth. They have discussed the possible risks and have decided to not consider the home as part of their actively managed investment portfolio. The second home will not carry a mortgage.

- Estate Planning Considerations: 1) *Gifts to children.* The Ingers will consider various means of tax-efficiently securing their children's financial security, including outright gifts and the creation of special purpose trusts or foundations. 2) *Charitable gifts.* In addition to outright gifts, the Ingers will consider special purpose trusts or foundations, naming selected charities as remaindermen and family members as income beneficiaries.

- The complex family changes that are about to occur suggest the need for increased flexibility in whatever investment strategy is adopted, to accommodate potentially frequent and abrupt shifts in attitudes and circumstances.

- The Ingers want only limited exposure to common stock investments.

- The Ingers want to maintain a fixed long-term holding of €500,000 in gold bullion.

5   AN INTRODUCTION TO ASSET ALLOCATION

In establishing a strategic asset allocation policy, the advisor's challenge is to find a set of asset-class weights that produce a portfolio consistent with the individual investor's return objective, risk tolerance, and constraints. This task must be completed from a taxable perspective, taking into consideration 1) after-tax returns, 2) the tax consequences of any shift from current portfolio allocations, 3) the impact of future rebalancing, and 4) asset "location." The issue of asset location results from the individual investor's ownership of both taxable and tax-deferred investment accounts—clearly, nontaxable investments should not be "located" in tax-exempt accounts.

In the balance of the reading, we will illustrate the basic concepts of asset allocation for individual investors with a new case study, followed by a continuation of the Inger case. The reading concludes with a discussion of probabilistic analysis, as applied to individual investor asset allocation and retirement planning.

5.1   Asset Allocation Concepts

This section illustrates how to arrive at an appropriate strategic asset allocation (or set of approximately equivalent allocations) through a process of elimination. Investment objectives and constraints must be formulated prior to addressing asset allocation.

Example 1 introduces a new case study and provides the background information needed to establish asset allocation guidelines for a new private client, Susan Fairfax. The discussion then returns to Peter and Hilda Inger, formulating a strategic asset allocation appropriate to the Ingers' IPS.

EXAMPLE 1

Asset Allocation Concepts (1)

Susan Fairfax is president of Reston Industries, a US-based company whose sales are entirely domestic and whose shares are listed on the New York Stock Exchange. The following additional facts reflect her current situation:

- Fairfax is single and 58 years old. She has no immediate family, no debts, and does not own a residence. She is in excellent health and covered by Reston-paid health insurance that continues after her expected retirement at age 65.

- Her base salary of $500,000 a year, inflation-protected, is sufficient to support her present lifestyle but can no longer generate any excess for savings.

- She has $2,000,000 of savings from prior years held in the form of short-term instruments.

- Reston rewards key employees through a generous stock-bonus incentive plan, but the company provides no pension plan and pays no dividend.

- Fairfax's incentive plan participation has resulted in her ownership of Reston stock worth $10 million (current market value). The stock was received tax-free but is subject to tax at a 35 percent rate (on entire proceeds) if sold. She expects to hold the Reston stock at least until her retirement.

- Her present level of spending and the current annual inflation rate of 4 percent are expected to continue after her retirement.

- Fairfax is taxed at 35 percent on all salary, investment income, and realized capital gains. Her composite tax rate is assumed to continue at this level indefinitely.

Fairfax's orientation is patient, careful, and conservative in all things. She has stated that an annual after-tax real total return of 3 percent would be completely acceptable to her, if it were achieved in a context whereby an investment portfolio created from her accumulated savings was unlikely to decline by more than 10 percent in nominal terms in any given 12-month period.

Working with Fairfax, HH Advisors (HH) created the following draft version of an investment policy statement.

Investment Policy Statement for Susan Fairfax

Overview

Ms. Fairfax is 58 years old and has seven years until her planned retirement. She has a fairly lavish lifestyle but few financial worries: Her salary pays all current expenses, and she has accumulated $2 million in cash equivalents from savings in previous years (the "Savings Portfolio"). Her health is excellent, and her employer-paid health insurance coverage will continue after retirement. She has sought professional advice to begin planning for her investment future, a future that is complicated by ownership of a $10 million block of company stock. The stock is listed on the NYSE, pays no dividends, and has a zero-cost basis for tax purposes. All salary, investment income (except interest on municipal bonds), and realized capital gains are taxed to Ms. Fairfax at a 35 percent rate. This tax rate and a 4 percent annual inflation rate are expected to continue into the future. Ms. Fairfax would accept a 3 percent real, after-tax return from the investment portfolio to be formed from her Savings Portfolio, if that return could be obtained with only modest downside risk (i.e., less than a 10 percent annual decline). She describes herself as being conservative in all things.

Objectives

- **Return Requirement**

  Ms. Fairfax's need for portfolio income begins seven years from now, when her salary stops on the day she retires. The interim return focus for her investment portfolio (to be created from the Savings Portfolio) should be on growing the portfolio's value in a way that provides protection against loss of purchasing power. Her 3 percent real, after-tax return preference implies a gross total return requirement of at least 10.8 percent, assuming her investments are fully taxable (as is the case now) and assuming 4 percent inflation and a 35 percent tax rate. For Ms. Fairfax to maintain her current lifestyle, she must generate $500,000 × $(1.04)^7$, or $658,000, in annual, inflation-adjusted income when she retires. If the market value of Reston's stock does not change, and if she has been able to earn a 10.8 percent return on the investment portfolio (or 7 percent nominal after-tax return = $2,000,000 × $(1.07)^7$ = $3,211,500), she should accumulate $13,211,500 by retirement age. To generate $658,000, a return on $13,211,500 of approximately 5.0 percent is needed. If she sells her position in Reston Industries leaving $(1 - 0.35)(\$10,000,000)$ + $3,211,500 = $9,711,500 to invest, a return of $658,000/$9,711,500 = 6.8 percent is needed.

- **Risk Tolerance**

Ms. Fairfax has a below-average *willingness* to take risk, as evidenced by her statement that in any given year, she does not want to experience a decline of more than 10 percent in the value of the investment portfolio. This desire indicates that her portfolio should have below-average risk exposure to minimize its downside volatility. A below-average willingness is also suggested by her generally careful and conservative orientation. Her overall wealth position, however, suggests an above-average *ability* to take risk. Because of her preferences and the nondiversified nature of the total portfolio, an average to below-average risk tolerance objective is appropriate for the portfolio.

It should be noted that truly meaningful statements about the risk of Ms. Fairfax's total portfolio are tied to assumptions about the volatility of Reston's stock (if it is retained) and about when and at what price the Reston stock will be sold. Because the Reston holding constitutes 83 percent of Ms. Fairfax's total portfolio, it will largely determine the large risk she is likely to experience as long as the holding remains intact.

Constraints

■ **Time Horizon**

Ms. Fairfax has a multistage time horizon. The first stage is the intermediate-term period, seven years, until her retirement. The second stage is relatively long term, representing Ms. Fairfax's life expectancy of perhaps 30 years or more. During the first stage, Ms. Fairfax should arrange her financial affairs in preparation for the balance of the second stage, a retirement period of indefinite length. Of the two horizons, the second horizon is the dominant one because it is during this period that her assets must fulfill their primary function of funding her expenses, in an annuity sense, in retirement.

■ **Liquidity**

With liquidity defined either as income needs or as cash reserves to meet emergency needs, Ms. Fairfax's immediate liquidity requirement is minimal. She has $500,000 of salary available annually, healthcare costs are not a concern, and she has no planned needs for cash from the portfolio.

■ **Taxes**

Ms. Fairfax's taxable income (salary, taxable investment income, and realized capital gains on securities) is taxed at a 35 percent rate. Careful tax planning and coordination of tax policy with investment planning is required. All else equal, investment strategies should seek to maximize after-tax income and defer the realization of taxable gains. Sale of the Reston stock will have sizeable tax consequences because Ms. Fairfax's cost basis is zero; special planning will be needed for this sale. Ms. Fairfax may want to consider some form of charitable giving, either during her lifetime or at death. She has no immediate family, and no other potential gift or bequest recipients are known.

■ **Laws and Regulations**

Ms. Fairfax should be aware of and abide by all laws and regulations relating to her "insider" status at Reston and her holding of Reston stock. Although no trust instrument is in place, if Ms. Fairfax's future investing is handled by an investment advisor, the responsibilities associated with the Prudent Person Rule will come into play, including the responsibility for investing in a diversified portfolio.

■ **Unique Circumstances and/or Preferences**

Clearly, the value of the Reston stock dominates Ms. Fairfax's portfolio value. A well-defined exit strategy must be developed for the stock as soon as is practical and appropriate. If the stock's value increases, or at least does not decline before the holding is liquidated, Ms. Fairfax's present lifestyle can be sustained after retirement. A significant and prolonged setback for Reston Industries, however, could have disastrous consequences for the portfolio. Such circumstances would require a dramatic downscaling of Ms. Fairfax's lifestyle or generation of alternate sources of income to maintain her current lifestyle. A worst-case scenario might be characterized by a 50 percent drop in the market value of Reston's stock and a subsequent sale of the stock, with proceeds subject to a 35 percent tax. The net proceeds from such a sale would be $10,000,000 × 0.5 × (1 − 0.35) = $3,250,000. When added to the Savings Portfolio, Ms. Fairfax's total portfolio value would be $5,250,000. For this portfolio to generate $658,000 in income, a 12.5 percent return would be required.

Ms. Fairfax will need to seek legal estate planning assistance, especially if she wishes to establish a gifting program.

Synopsis

The policy governing investments in Ms. Fairfax's Savings Portfolio shall emphasize realizing a 3 percent real, after-tax return from a mix of high-quality assets representing, in aggregate, no more than average, and preferably below average, risk. Ongoing attention shall be given to Ms. Fairfax's tax planning and legal needs, her progress toward retirement, and the value of her Reston stock. The Reston stock holding is a unique circumstance of decisive significance; corporate developments should be monitored closely, and protection against the effects of a worst-case scenario should be implemented as soon as possible.

In setting asset allocation guidelines for Ms. Fairfax, one of the constraints that HH Advisors must address is her concern regarding negative portfolio returns. So-called "safety-first" rules[6] provide a means of reasonably approximating and controlling downside risk; HH uses the following safety-first guideline in establishing an asset allocation policy for Ms. Fairfax.

If:

■ the portfolio has an important or dominant equity component,

■ the portfolio does not make significant use of options, and

■ the investment horizon for the shortfall risk concern is not short term;

Then:

the normal distribution may reasonably be used as an approximate model of portfolio returns.

Fama (1976) and Campbell, Lo, and MacKinlay (1997), for example, provide evidence about the normal distribution as applied to US common stocks. A 2.5 percent probability of failing to meet a return threshold may be acceptable for many clients.

---

6 Elton, Gruber, Brown, and Goetzmann (2003) and DeFusco et al. (2004) discuss safety-first rules.

For a normal distribution of returns, the probability of a return that is more than two standard deviations below the mean or expected return is approximately 2.5 percent. If the client is more (less) risk averse, the advisor can choose a larger (smaller) number for standard deviation. Therefore, if we subtract two standard deviations from a portfolio's expected return and the resulting number is above the client's return threshold, the client may find the resulting portfolio acceptable. If the resulting number is below the client's threshold, the portfolio may be unsatisfactory. Of course, the client may have other or different downside risk objectives than the two-standard-deviation approach we have used to illustrate this concept.

Once return and risk objectives and constraints have been established, an advisor sometimes will include a statement of the client's strategic asset allocation as part of the IPS. HH now turns to the task of establishing an appropriate strategic asset allocation for the investment portfolio to be created from Ms. Fairfax's existing savings (the "Savings Portfolio"). An HH analyst has developed the five potential asset allocations presented in Exhibit 9 and Exhibit 10. The analyst has commented that there is more uncertainty in the expectational data for REITs than for small- or large-cap US stocks.

Exhibit 9   Proposed Asset Allocation Alternatives

Asset Class	Projected Total Return (%)	Expected Standard Deviation (%)	Allocation				
			A (%)	B (%)	C (%)	D (%)	E (%)
Cash equivalents	4.5	2.5	10	20	25	5	10
Corporate bonds	6.0	11.0	0	25	0	0	0
Municipal bonds	7.2	10.8	40	0	30	0	30
Large-cap US stocks	13.0	17.0	20	15	35	25	5
Small-cap US stocks	15.0	21.0	10	10	0	15	5
International stocks (EAFE)	15.0	21.0	10	10	0	15	10
Real estate investment trusts (REITs)	10.0	15.0	10	10	10	25	35
Venture capital	26.0	64.0	0	10	0	15	5
Total			100	100	100	100	100

Summary Data	Allocation				
	A	B	C	D	E
Expected total return	9.9%	11.0%	8.8%	14.4%	10.3%
Expected after-tax total return	7.4%	7.2%	6.5%	9.4%	7.5%
Expected standard deviation	9.4%	12.4%	8.5%	18.1%	10.1%
Sharpe ratio	0.574	0.524	0.506	0.547	0.574

Exhibit 10	Asset Allocation Alternatives: Nominal and Real Expected Returns				
	Allocation				
Return Measure	**A (%)**	**B (%)**	**C (%)**	**D (%)**	**E (%)**
Nominal expected return	9.9	11.0	8.8	14.4	10.3
Expected real after-tax return	3.4	3.2	2.5	5.4	3.5

The process of selecting the most satisfactory from among several potential strategic asset allocations, both in the case of Susan Fairfax and for individual investors generally, consists of the following steps:

1 Determine the asset allocations that meet the investor's return requirements. In carrying out this step, the investment advisor should compare expected returns for the different asset allocations on a basis consistent with the IPS. The policy statement might, for example, set return requirements in real, after-tax terms. In that case, the advisor would adjust for the effects of taxes and expected inflation before deciding which allocations meet the investor's return requirement.

2 Eliminate asset allocations that fail to meet quantitative risk objectives or are otherwise inconsistent with the investor's risk tolerance. For example, an investor may have risk objectives related to the expected standard deviation of return, worst-case return, or any of several other downside risk concepts (as is true for Fairfax). On a long-term basis, an individual investor will be unable to apply an asset allocation that violates a risk objective.

3 Eliminate asset allocations that fail to satisfy the investor's stated constraints. For example, an investor may have a liquidity requirement that is appropriately met by holding a certain level of cash equivalents, and allocations must satisfy that constraint. Unique circumstances may also make certain allocations unacceptable to the investor.

4 Evaluate the expected risk-adjusted performance and diversification attributes of the asset allocations that remain after Steps 1 through 3 to select the allocation that is expected to be most rewarding for the investor.

Example 2 applies these four steps to the Fairfax case.

EXAMPLE 2

Asset Allocation Concepts (2)

■ **Step 1: Return Requirement**

Fairfax has stated that she is seeking a 3 percent real, after-tax return. Exhibit 9 provides nominal, pretax figures, which HH must adjust for both taxes and inflation to determine which portfolios meet Fairfax's return guideline. A simple approach is to subtract the municipal bond return component from the stated return, then subject the resulting figure to a 35 percent tax rate and add back tax-exempt municipal bond income. This calculation produces a nominal, after-tax return, from which the expected 4 percent per year inflation rate is subtracted to arrive at the real, after-tax return. For example, Allocation A has an expected real after-tax return of 3.4 percent, calculated by $[0.099 - (0.072 \times 0.4)] \times (1 - 0.35) + (0.072 \times 0.4) - 0.04 = 0.034 = 3.4$ percent.

Alternately, the return can be calculated by multiplying the taxable returns by their allocations, summing these products, adjusting for the tax rate, adding the result to the product of the nontaxable (municipal bond) return and its allocation, and deducting the inflation rate from this sum. For Allocation A, $[(0.045 \times 0.10) + (0.13 \times 0.2) + (0.15 \times 0.1) + (0.15 \times 0.1) + (0.1 \times 0.1)] \times (1 - 0.35) + (0.072 \times 0.4) - (0.04) = 0.035 = 3.5$ percent.

Exhibit 10 presents the allocations' expected nominal returns—without adjustment for either inflation or taxes—and their expected real after-tax returns calculated by the first of the above approaches. From Exhibit 10, the HH analyst notes that Allocations A, B, D, and E meet Fairfax's real, after-tax return objective of 3 percent a year.

▪ **Step 2: Risk Tolerance**

Fairfax has stated that a worst-case nominal return of –10 percent in any 12-month period would be acceptable. As discussed above, the expected return less two times the portfolio risk (expected standard deviation) is a reasonable baseline measure of shortfall risk. If the resulting number is above the client's threshold return level, the criterion is met. Two of the remaining four allocations—A and E—meet the risk tolerance criterion.

Parameter	Allocation				
	A (%)	B (%)	C (%)	D (%)	E (%)
Expected return	9.9	11.0	8.8	14.4	10.3
Exp. standard deviation	9.4	12.4	8.5	18.1	10.1
Worst-case return	–8.9	–13.8	–8.2	–21.8	–9.9

▪ **Step 3: Constraints**

Portfolios A and E both meet the stated constraints of Fairfax and neither is eliminated in this step.

▪ **Step 4: Risk-Adjusted Performance and Diversification Evaluation**

The recommended allocation is A. The allocations that are expected to meet both the minimum real, after-tax objective and the maximum risk tolerance objective are A and E. Both allocations have similar Sharpe ratios and expected real after-tax returns. Both A and E have large exposures to municipal bonds; Allocation E, however, has a large position in REIT stocks, whereas Allocation A's counterpart large equity allocation is to a diversified portfolio of large- and small-cap domestic stocks. Allocation A provides greater diversification through its large and small stock representation, as opposed to the specialized nature of REIT stocks. Furthermore, because of the great uncertainty in the expectational data for REIT stocks compared with small- and large-cap stocks, we can be more confident in selecting Allocation A that Fairfax's return and risk objectives will be met. Therefore, HH Advisors specifies Allocation A as Fairfax's strategic asset allocation.

The Susan Fairfax case in Examples 1 and 2 presented a process for selecting the strategic asset allocation most appropriate to her objectives and constraints. Example 3 contrasts the asset allocation problem of Peter and Hilda Inger to that of Fairfax.

EXAMPLE 3

Asset Allocation for Peter and Hilda Inger

To recap some important facts presented in the family's IPS, the Ingers have average risk tolerance in general but are relatively averse to common stock investments as a result of Peter's prior negative experience. Peter, however, has always been successful and comfortable investing in real estate projects (even those constituting greater overall risk than corresponding equity investments). Also, the Ingers do not wish to experience a loss greater than 10 percent, in nominal terms, in any given 12-month period. The Ingers' required return was calculated as their estimated disbursements, including taxes, beginning in Year 2, divided by their net worth at the end of Year 1 (€493,949/€42,340,438 = 1.17 percent). Adding expected annual inflation of 3 percent, the Ingers' stated return objective is 4.17 percent.

The critical component of Peter and Hilda's retirement plan is the disposition of IngerMarine stock to a willing buyer. If the sale is not realized, their investment objectives and the associated strategic asset allocation will both require review. We have discussed certain principles of asset allocation for individual investors and illustrated their application in previous examples. In terms of the IPS and asset allocation, what similarities and contrasts would an investment advisor observe in applying the methods used for Fairfax in Examples 1 and 2 to the Ingers? Among the key observations are the following:

- **Risk Tolerance and Return Objective**

  In consultation with the client, the investment advisor needs to develop an IPS prior to embarking on asset allocation. The client's risk tolerance and return objective are important parts of an IPS, and any asset allocation must be appropriate for these objectives. The Ingers want a chosen asset allocation to satisfy a downside risk constraint of −10 percent, just as in the Fairfax case. Yet because the Ingers' objective of a 1.17 percent real, after-tax return is less than one half of Fairfax's in magnitude, all else being equal we would expect a wider variety of asset allocations to satisfy the Ingers' requirements.

- **Asset Class Selection**

  As with Fairfax, the Ingers' investment advisor must establish an appropriate set of asset classes. The asset classes in Exhibit 9 have a US bias. Eurozone equities and fixed-income asset classes for the Ingers would play a similar role to US equities and US fixed income classes for Fairfax, because the Ingers' consumption is in euros. US equities represent a substantial proportion of the market value of world equities, and one might expect them to play a meaningful role in the Ingers' portfolio. The advisor would need to respect Peter's aversion to holding equities, however. On the other hand, because of Peter's prior experience and success with real estate projects, the Ingers might include more than one real estate investment asset type among those permissible for investment. The inclusion of a wide array of asset classes brings diversification benefits, as long as portfolio risk and expected return characteristics remain consistent with the investment policy statement. Emerging Markets, Commodities, and Private Capital Ventures are examples of asset classes that may be strong diversifiers but that also have higher volatility and less liquidity than traditional equity and fixed-income investments. Like Fairfax, the Ingers are taxable investors; if possible in their domestic market, the Ingers should probably also include tax-exempt investments as a permissible asset class.

- **Taxation and Asset Allocation Simulation**

  As in the Fairfax case, the Ingers' advisor should make an asset allocation decision in real, after-tax terms. This observation raises the point that expected after-tax returns for the Ingers will be computed using a tax rate different from Fairfax's, and such returns would incorporate their own expectations concerning future inflation rates.

  Taxes present one of the more vexing challenges in asset allocation for private wealth clients, because taxes depend heavily on the regulatory environment and the investor's unique set of financial circumstances. In modeling asset allocation scenarios, the advisor must address the question of whether to use after-tax return assumptions for individual asset classes or to instead use pretax assumptions and apply taxes to the resulting investment outcomes. Running simulations using after-tax return assumptions can be a daunting task—listed below are some of the hurdles in configuring asset allocation scenarios using after-tax estimates.

  - **Location**

    After-tax risk and return assumptions will be influenced by an investment's "location." After-tax returns on common stocks located in a tax-sheltered retirement account, for example, may differ distinctly from the return on common stocks located in an unsheltered account. Consequently, an advisor may need to break down the traditional asset classes into multiple, location-specific subclasses, each with its own risk and return profile.

  - **Tax Conventions**

    Differing tax treatment of investment returns, depending for example on holding period or method of dissolution, may again create multiple risk and return characteristics for a given asset class. Securities held for a required minimum time period may be taxed at different, often more favorable rates. Assets ultimately gifted to charity or family members may be taxed favorably or not at all.

  - **Investment Instruments**

    Investment securities whose tax characteristics are easily recognizable and predictable today may change dramatically over time, through legislative initiative or tax authority interpretations.

5.2 Monte Carlo Simulation in Personal Retirement Planning

Monte Carlo simulation is described in detail in the reading on asset allocation. Here we focus on its applicability to personal retirement planning. With the introduction of Monte Carlo simulation methodologies, the technology of retirement planning for individuals now rivals that of corporate pension planning. Monte Carlo analysis is computer and data intensive, so its availability for personal retirement planning at affordable cost is a direct result of the availability of inexpensive computing power. Such methodologies are now readily available to individual investors and their investment managers, from a variety of vendors.[7]

7 Wei Hu and Robert L. Young, CFA, of Financial Engines Inc. made important contributions to our presentation of Monte Carlo simulation for retirement planning in this section.

Monte Carlo simulation is the process by which probability "distributions" are arrayed to create path-dependent scenarios to predict end-stage results.[8] The methodology is useful when trying to forecast future results that depend on multiple variables with various degrees of volatility. Its use in projecting retirement wealth is valuable because the prediction of future wealth depends on multiple factors (e.g., investment returns, inflation, etc.), each with a unique distribution of probable outcomes. Monte Carlo simulation is generally superior to steadystate, or deterministic, forecasting because it incorporates the consequences of variability across long-term assumptions and the resulting path dependency effect on wealth accumulation. Merely using long-term averages for capital market returns or inflation assumptions oversimplifies their variability and leads to the clearly unrealistic implication of linear wealth accumulation. There is also an inherent assumption when using deterministic forecasting that performance in future periods will more or less replicate historical performance. Monte Carlo estimation, in contrast, allows for the input of probability estimates over multiperiod time frames and generates a probability distribution of final values rather than a single point estimate. This approach allows the investment advisor to view projections of possible best- and worst-case scenarios and leads to better financial planning over long time frames.

The ultimate objective of probabilistic approaches, such as Monte Carlo simulation, for investment planning is to improve the quality of managers' recommendations and investors' decisions. A brief look at the distinction between traditional deterministic analysis and probabilistic analysis reveals how the latter approach seeks to achieve that objective. In both approaches, the individual supplies a similar set of personal information, including age, desired retirement age, current income, savings, and assets in taxable, tax deferred, and tax-exempt vehicles. In a deterministic analysis, single numbers are specified for interest rates, asset returns, inflation, and similar economic variables. In a Monte Carlo or probabilistic analysis, a probability distribution of possible values is specified for economic variables, reflecting the real-life uncertainty about those variables' future values.

Suppose an individual investor is 25 years away from her desired retirement age. A deterministic retirement analysis produces single number estimates of outcomes for stated objectives, such as retirement assets and retirement income at the end of 25 years. Using the same inputs, a Monte Carlo analysis produces probability distributions for those objective variables by tabulating the outcomes of a large number (often 10,000) of simulation trials, each trial representing a possible 25-year experience. Each simulation trial incorporates a potential blend of economic factors (interest rates, inflation, etc.), in which the blending reflects the economic variables' probability distributions.

Consequently, whereas deterministic analysis provides a yes/no answer concerning whether the individual will reach a particular goal for retirement income, or perhaps retirement wealth, mirroring a single set of economic assumptions, a Monte Carlo analysis provides a probability estimate, as well as other detailed information, that allows the investor to better assess risk (for example, percentiles for the distribution of retirement income). Thus Monte Carlo analysis is far more informative about the risk associated with meeting objectives than deterministic analysis. The investor can then respond to such risk information by changing variables under her control. An advisory module may present a range of alternative asset allocations and the associated probabilities for reaching goals and objectives.

---

8 Path dependency exists when the outcome in a given period is influenced or constrained by the outcomes of prior events.

A probabilistic approach conveys several advantages to both investors and their investment advisors. First, a probabilistic forecast more accurately portrays the risk–return tradeoff than a deterministic approach. Until recently, advisors nearly exclusively used deterministic projections to inform their recommendations and communicate with their clients. Unfortunately, such projections cannot realistically model how markets actually behave. The probability of observing a scenario in which the market return is constant each year is effectively zero. Fundamentally, deterministic models answer the wrong question. The relevant question is not "How much money will I have if I earn 10 percent a year?" but rather "Given a particular investment strategy, what is the likelihood of achieving 10 percent a year?" By focusing on the wrong question, deterministic models can fail to illustrate the consequences of investment risk, producing, in effect, a misleading "return–return" tradeoff in investors' minds whereby riskier strategies are always expected to produce superior long-term rewards.

In contrast, a probabilistic forecast vividly portrays the actual risk–return tradeoff. For example, an investor considering placing a higher percentage of his portfolio in equities might be told that the average forecast return of the S&P 500 Index is 13 percent. Given an average forecast money market return of 5 percent, it may seem obvious that more equity exposure is desirable. This choice, however, should take into account the risk that the S&P 500 will not achieve its average return every year. Moreover, the median simulation outcome of the S&P 500, using the average return of 13 percent, is likely to be substantially lower because of return volatility. For example, a 20-year forecast of $1,000 invested in the S&P 500, using a riskless average return of 13 percent, yields ending wealth of $11,500. If a simulation is performed assuming normally distributed returns with an annual standard deviation of 20 percent, the median wealth after 20 years is only $8,400. In addition, a simulation-based forecast shows that there is substantial downside risk: The fifth percentile of wealth after 20 years is only approximately $2,000, even before adjusting for inflation.

A second benefit of a probabilistic approach is that a simulation can give information on the possible tradeoff between short-term risk and the risk of not meeting a long-term goal. This tradeoff arises when an investor must choose between lowering short-term volatility on one hand and lowering the portfolio's long-term growth because of lower expected returns on the other hand.

Third, as already discussed, taxes complicate investment planning considerably by creating a sequential problem in which buy and sell decisions during this period affect next-period decisions through the tax implications of portfolio changes. Through its ability to model a nearly limitless range of scenarios, Monte Carlo analysis can capture the variety of portfolio changes that can potentially result from tax effects.

Finally, an expected value of future returns is more complicated than an expected value of concurrent returns, even in the simplest case of independent and normally distributed returns. For concurrent returns, the expected portfolio return is simply the weighted sum of the individual expected returns, and the variance depends on the individual variances and covariances, leading to the benefits of diversification with lower covariances. In this case, the $1 invested is simply divided among several investment alternatives. The future return case, however, involves a multiplicative situation; for example, the expected two-period return is the product of one plus the expected values of the one-period returns, leading to the importance of considering expected geometric return. As Michaud (1981) demonstrates, the expected geometric return depends on the horizon of the investment. The stochastic nature of the problem can be summarized by recognizing that the $1 invested now will then be reinvested in the next period and possibly joined by an additional $1 investment. This scenario clearly differs from the simple one-period case of spreading the dollar among several asset classes. Again, Monte Carlo analysis is well suited to model this stochastic process and its resulting alternative outcomes.

Monte Carlo simulation can be a useful tool for investment analysis but like any investment tool it can be used either appropriately or inappropriately. What should investors and managers know about a particular Monte Carlo product in order to be confident that it provides reliable information? Unfortunately, not all commercially available Monte Carlo products generate equally reliable results, so users should be aware of product differences that affect the quality of results.

First, any user of Monte Carlo should be wary of a simulation tool that relies only on historical data. History provides a view of only one possible path among the many that might occur in the future. As previously mentioned, it is difficult to estimate the expected return on an equity series using historical data, because the volatility of equity returns is large in relation to the mean. For example, suppose we are willing to assume that the expected return of the S&P 500 is equal to the average historical return. Annual data from 1926 through 1994 would yield an average return of 12.16 percent. Adding just five more years of data, however, would produce an average return of 13.28 percent. For a 20-year horizon, this relatively small adjustment in the input data would lead to a difference of more than 20 percent in ending wealth, given returns every year that were equal to the assumed average.

Second, a manager who wants to evaluate the likely performance of a client's portfolio should choose a Monte Carlo simulation that simulates the performance of specific investments, not just asset classes. Although asset class movements can explain a large proportion of, for example, mutual fund returns, individual funds can differ greatly in terms of their performance, fees, fund-specific risk, and tax efficiency. Failing to recognize these factors can yield a forecast that is far too optimistic. As an example of how much fees can affect performance, consider the case of a hypothetical S&P 500 index fund that charges an annual fee of 60 basis points; expected return is 13 percent with annual standard deviation of 20 percent and normally distributed returns, and capital gains are taxed at 20 percent. A Monte Carlo simulation shows that a $1,000 investment will grow to a median after-tax wealth of $6,200 after 20 years, if that fund pays no short-term distributions. In contrast, an investor with access to an institutional fund that charges only 6 basis points will see her after-tax wealth grow to a median of $6,800 after 20 years.

Third, any Monte Carlo simulation used for advising real-world investors must take into account the tax consequences of their investments. Monte Carlo simulation must and can be flexible enough to account for specific factors such as individual-specific tax rates, the different treatment of tax-deferred versus taxable accounts, and taxes on short-term mutual fund distributions. To understand the importance of short-term income distributions, take the previous example of the institutionally priced index fund. If the same fund were to pay half of its annual return as a short-term distribution taxed at a rate of 35 percent, the $6,800 median wealth after 20 years would shrink to just $5,600.

Certainly, no forecasting tool is perfect, and Monte Carlo simulation has drawbacks that create challenges in relying on it solely as a window to the future. Inputting distributions in determining probability outcomes for the simulations can be biased by historical perspective and the perceptions of the analyst. The process can be quite rigorous and still produce estimates that vary widely from actual results.

SUMMARY

This reading has presented an overview of portfolio management for individual investors, including the information-gathering process, situational and psychological profiling of clients, formulation of an investment policy statement, strategic asset allocation, and the use of Monte Carlo simulation in personal retirement planning.

▪ Situational profiling seeks to anticipate individual investors' concerns and risk tolerance by specifying the investor's source of wealth, measure or adequacy of wealth in relationship to needs, and stage of life.

▪ Psychological profiling addresses human behavioral patterns and personality characteristics and their effect on investment choices. It is particularly important in assessing risk tolerance.

▪ Underlying behavioral patterns often play an important role in setting individual risk tolerance and return objectives.

▪ Based on their responses to a questionnaire, individual investors may be classified into descriptive personality types, such as *cautious*, *methodical*, *spontaneous*, or *individualist*.

▪ Using the results of situational and psychological profiling, and the financial information gathered in the interviewing process, an advisor can formulate an investment policy statement.

▪ A carefully formulated IPS serves as the keystone to the relationship between investor and investment advisor. The process of creating an IPS mirrors the process of portfolio management. The policy statement reconciles investment goals with the realities of risk tolerance and investment constraints, resulting in operational guidelines for portfolio construction and a mutually agreed-upon basis for portfolio monitoring and review. By necessity, the investor and advisor must discuss the construction of an IPS in a linear fashion. In practice, the process is dynamic, similar to solving simultaneously for multiple variables.

▪ The return objective for an investment portfolio must ultimately be made consistent with the investor's risk tolerance and the portfolio's ability to generate returns. The traditional division of return requirements between "income" and "growth" objectives may seem intuitive, but these terms blur the distinction between return goals and risk tolerance. The "total return" approach seeks to identify a portfolio return that will meet the investor's objectives without exceeding the portfolio's risk tolerance or violating its investment constraints.

▪ Risk tolerance reflects both an investor's ability and willingness to accept risk. Ability to accept risk is a probabilistic assessment of the investment portfolio's ability to withstand negative investment outcomes and still meet the investor's objectives. Willingness to accept risk is a more subjective assessment of the investor's propensity for risk taking. Because many individuals are unfamiliar with the quantitative terminology of risk tolerance, the investment advisor may use psychological or situational profiling to anticipate client attitudes toward risk.

▪ Investment constraints include the following:

1 *Liquidity.* Liquidity needs may be categorized as ongoing expenses, emergency reserves, and negative liquidity events. Liquidity is the ease and price certainty with which assets can be converted into cash. Because assets with stable prices and low transaction costs are generally low-risk investments, an increasing need for liquidity will constrain the investment portfolio's ability to accept risk. Significant illiquid holdings and their associated

risks should be documented. For many investors, the home or residence represents a large percentage of total net worth and is relatively illiquid. Although the primary residence may be viewed as offsetting long-term needs for care and housing, it should be discussed as a source of investment risk and as a source of funding for future cash flow needs. The investor and advisor should together thoroughly review the risks associated with any concentration of net worth. Large "positive" liquidity events should also be documented, even though they will not act as a constraint.

2 *Time horizon.* The investor's time horizon also constrains his ability to accept risk; shorter investment horizons allow less time to make up portfolio losses. The time horizon constraint may be categorized as short term, intermediate term, or long term and as single stage or multistage. With sufficient assets and multigenerational estate planning, even older investors may retain a long-term investment perspective.

3 *Taxes.* The basic principles of tax deferral, avoidance, and reduction underlie all tax-driven portfolio strategies, but individual solutions are highly country specific and client specific. Taxes relevant to portfolio management generally fall into four major categories: income, gains, wealth transfer, and property.

4 *Legal and regulatory environment.* The investment portfolio's legal and regulatory environment is ultimately country and client specific. A basic knowledge of English and American trust law is often valuable, however, as the terminology is widely recognized and the framework widely applied.

5 *Unique circumstances.* The IPS should capture all unique investment considerations affecting the portfolio. Unique circumstances might include guidelines for social investing, trading restrictions, and privacy concerns.

■ As a general rule, only certain asset allocations will be consistent with the client's return objectives, risk tolerance, and investment constraints. The advisor can use a process of elimination to arrive at an appropriate long-term strategic allocation.

■ For individual investors, investment decisions, including asset allocation, are made on an after-tax basis. This is a key distinction in contrast to tax-exempt institutions.

■ Monte Carlo simulation has certain advantages over deterministic approaches: It more accurately portrays risk–return trade-offs, can illustrate the trade-offs between the attainment of short-term and long-term goals, provides more realistic modeling of taxes, and is better suited to assessing multiperiod effects.

PRACTICE PROBLEMS

The following information relates to Questions 1–8

Father (Peter), mother (Hilda), son (Hans), and daughter (Christa) and her child (Jürgen). Peter is the founder and majority owner of IngerMarine. To answer the questions, additional relevant information on the Ingers may be found in the reading.

Christa estimates that her revised annual living expenses, including a new studio and apartment, will average €132,500 (excluding Jürgen's educational costs). If necessary, she could combine her apartment and studio to reduce spending by €32,500. She does not want her financial security to be dependent on further gifting from her parents and is pleased that, after the sale of IngerMarine, she will be able to meet her new living expenses with proceeds from art sales (€50,000) and the expected total return of the proposed investment portfolio (€82,500). Because of the uncertainty of art sales, Christa plans to establish an emergency reserve equal to one year's living expenses. Her after-tax proceeds from the sale of IngerMarine are expected to be €1,200,000 × (1 − 0.15) = €1,020,000. She also holds €75,000 in balanced mutual funds and €25,000 in a money market fund. Christa intends to reevaluate her policy statement and asset allocation guidelines every three years.

1   Discuss Christa's liquidity requirements.

2   Determine Christa's return requirement and evaluate whether her portfolio can be expected to satisfy that requirement if inflation averages 3 percent annually and she reduces her annual living expenses to €100,000 by combining her apartment and studio.

3   Explain why an analysis of Christa's investment policy statement might become necessary before the next three-year review.

Hans' increasingly irresponsible lifestyle has become a burden to his parents. Hans was recently arrested for reckless driving—he crashed his car into a restaurant, causing considerable damage and injuring a patron. As a result of Hans' behavior, Peter has placed him on probationary leave of absence from IngerMarine but will allow him to retain his annual salary of €100,000. The restaurant patron is suing Hans for €700,000 in damages, and the restaurant owner estimates that it will take €500,000 to repair damages to his building. Hans' insurance will cover costs to a maximum of only €200,000.

4   Assess the impact of these events on Hans' liquidity and his personal financial statement. What course of action should he pursue?

5   Assess Hans' probable future ability to assume risk, based on information about his background and current living situation.

Peter and Hilda are considering an investment of €1,000,000 in one of the following investment funds. Their tax rates on income and capital gains are 25 percent and 15 percent, respectively.

Investment	Projected Income (%)	Projected Price Appreciation (%)	Projected Turnover (%)
High-growth stock fund	2.0	12	75
Equity value fund	2.5	10	25
Municipal bond fund	5.0 (tax free)	2	15

6 Evaluate each investment fund based only on its after-tax return.

> Note: Capital gains tax = Price appreciation × 15% × Turnover rate.

Since the original evaluation described in the reading, IngerMarine has experienced a catastrophic event from which it cannot recover. Damage claims resulting from a design flaw are expected to leave IngerMarine bankrupt and its stock worthless. Peter's pension is also lost.

7 Assess the probable impact on Peter's and Hilda's return requirement.

8 Assess the probable impact on Peter's and Hilda's portfolio constraints.

---

9 James Stephenson, 55 years old and single, is a surgeon. He has accumulated a $2.0 million investment portfolio with a large concentration in small-capitalization US equities. During the last five years, his portfolio has averaged a 20 percent annual total return on investment. Stephenson's current portfolio of $2.0 million is invested as shown in Exhibit 1.

Exhibit 1   Summary of Stephenson's Current Portfolio

	Value ($)	Percent of Total (%)	Expected Annual Return (%)	Annual Standard Deviation (%)
Short-term bonds	200,000	10	4.6	1.6
Domestic large-cap equities	600,000	30	12.4	19.5
Domestic small-cap equities	1,200,000	60	16.0	29.9
Total portfolio	2,000,000	100	13.8	23.1

His newly hired financial advisor, Caroline Coppa, has compiled the following notes from her meetings with Stephenson:

> Stephenson hopes that long term, his investment portfolio will continue to earn 20 percent annually. For the remainder of this year, he would like to earn a return greater than the 5 percent yield to maturity currently available from short-term government notes. When asked about his risk tolerance, he described it as "average." He was surprised when informed that US small-cap portfolios have historically experienced extremely high volatility.

> Stephenson does not expect to retire before age 70. His current annual income from his surgical practice is $250,000, which is more than sufficient to meet his current yearly expenses of $150,000. Upon

retirement, he plans to sell his surgical practice and use the proceeds to purchase an annuity to cover his post-retirement cash flow needs. He could not state any additional long-term goals or needs.

Stephenson's income and realized capital gains are taxed at a 30 percent rate. No pertinent legal or regulatory issues apply. He has no pension or retirement plan but does have sufficient health insurance for post-retirement needs.

Stephenson soon expects to receive an additional $2.0 million from an inheritance and plans to invest the entire amount in an index fund that best complements the current portfolio. Coppa is evaluating the four index funds shown in Exhibit 2 for their ability to produce a portfolio that will meet the following two criteria relative to the current portfolio:

- maintain or enhance expected return;
- maintain or reduce volatility.

Each fund is invested in an asset class that is not substantially represented in the current portfolio.

Exhibit 2   Index Fund Characteristics

Index Fund	Expected Annual Return (%)	Expected Annual Standard Deviation (%)	Correlation of Returns with Current Portfolio
A	15	25	+0.80
B	11	22	+0.60
C	16	25	+0.90
D	14	22	+0.65

A Formulate the following elements of Stephenson's investment policy statement and justify your response for each element with two arguments:

   i. Return objective.

   ii. Risk tolerance.

   iii. Liquidity requirements.

   iv. Time horizon.

B State which fund Coppa should recommend to Stephenson. Justify your choice by describing how your chosen fund best meets both of the criteria set forth by Coppa. (No calculations are required.)

10 Robert Taylor, 50 years old and a US resident, recently retired and received a $500,000 cash payment from his employer as an early retirement incentive. He also obtained $700,000 by exercising his company stock options. Both amounts are net of tax. Taylor is not entitled to a pension; however, his medical expenses are covered by insurance paid for by his former employer. Taylor is in excellent health and has a normal life expectancy.

Taylor's wife died last year after a long illness, which resulted in devastating medical expenses. All their investments, including a home, were liquidated to fully satisfy these medical expenses.

Taylor has no assets other than the $1,200,000 cash referenced above, and he has no debts. He plans to acquire a $300,000 home in three months and insists on paying cash given his recent adverse experience with creditors. When presented with investment options, Taylor consistently selects the most conservative alternative.

After settling into his new home, Taylor's living expenses will be $2,000 per month and will rise with inflation. He does not plan to work again.

Taylor's father and his wife's parents died years ago. His mother, Renee, is 72 years old and in excellent physical health. Her mental health, however, is deteriorating and she has relocated to a long-term care facility. Renee's expenses total $3,500 per month. Her monthly income is $1,500 from pensions. Her income and expenses will rise with inflation. She has no investments or assets of value. Taylor, who has no siblings, must cover Renee's income shortfall.

Taylor has one child, Troy. Troy and a friend need funds immediately for a start-up business with first-year costs estimated at $200,000. The partners have no assets and have been unable to obtain outside financing. The friend's family has offered to invest $100,000 in the business in exchange for a minority equity stake if Taylor agrees to invest the same amount.

Taylor would like to assist Troy; however, he is concerned about the partners' ability to succeed, the potential loss of his funds, and whether his assets are sufficient to support his needs and to support Renee. He plans to make a decision on this investment very soon. If he invests $100,000 in Troy's business, he insists that this investment be excluded from any investment strategy developed for his remaining funds.

With the above information, portfolio manager Sarah Wheeler prepared the investment policy statement for Taylor shown in Exhibit 3.

Exhibit 3	Robert Taylor Investment Policy Statement
Return objective	• Income requirement is $2,000 monthly.
	• Total return requirement is 2.7% annually ($24,000/$900,000).
Risk tolerance	• Substantial asset base and low return requirement provide ample resources to support an aggressive, growth-oriented portfolio.
Time horizon	• Client is 50 years old, recently retired, and in excellent health.
	• Time horizon exceeds 20 years.
Liquidity needs	• $300,000 is needed in three months for purchase of home.
	• Modest additional cash is needed for normal relocation costs. $100,000 may be needed for possible investment in son's business.
	• A normal, ongoing cash reserve level should be established.
Tax concerns	• There is little need to defer income.
	• Mother's expenses may have an effect.

(continued)

Exhibit 3   (Continued)

Legal and regulatory factors	• No special considerations exist.
Unique circumstances	• Client desires to support mother.
	• Client insists that any investment in son's business be excluded from long-term planning.
	• Client has strong aversion to debt.

A Evaluate the appropriateness of Taylor's investment policy statement with regard to the following objectives:

   i. Return requirement.

   ii. Risk tolerance.

   iii. Time horizon.

   iv. Liquidity requirements.

After revising the investment policy statement and confirming it with Taylor, Wheeler is now developing a long-term strategic asset allocation for Taylor. Wheeler will use the following revised information to recommend one of the allocations in Exhibit 4.

- Taylor has decided to invest $100,000 in his son's business but still insists that this investment be disregarded in making his allocation decision.

- Taylor's total cash flow needs have changed to $4,200 a month.

- The available asset base is $800,000.

- Wheeler estimates that the inflation rate will be 1 percent next year.

- Taylor is determined to maintain the real value of his assets because he plans to set up a charitable foundation in the future.

- Taylor insists on taking no more risk than absolutely necessary to achieve his return goals.

- The expected annual nominal risk-free rate of return is 3%.

Exhibit 4   Potential Long-Term Strategic Asset Allocations

	Allocation			
	A	**B**	**C**	**D**
Asset Class Weighting				
Stocks	20%	40%	60%	80%
Bonds	75%	55%	35%	15%
Cash	5%	5%	5%	5%
Total	100%	100%	100%	100%
Expected Annual				
Return	6.7%	7.5%	8.2%	9.1%
Standard deviation	9.0%	11.5%	15.3%	19.0%
Potential for Growth				
Asset growth	Very low	Low	Moderate	High
Income growth	Very low	Low	Moderate	High

Exhibit 4 (Continued)

	Allocation			
	A	**B**	**C**	**D**
Current income	High	High	Low	Very low
Stability	Very high	High	Moderate	Low

> **B** Select the strategic asset allocation that is most appropriate for Taylor and justify your selection with two supporting reasons related to the revised information shown above.

11 Mark and Andrea Mueller, US residents, are reviewing their financial plan. The Muellers, both 53 years old, have one daughter, 18 years old. With their combined after-tax salaries totaling $100,000 a year, they are able to meet their living expenses and save $25,000 after taxes annually. They expect little change in either their incomes or expenses on an inflation-adjusted basis other than the addition of their daughter's college expenses. Their only long-term financial goal is to provide for themselves and for their daughter's education. The Muellers both wish to retire in 10 years.

Their daughter, a talented musician, is now entering an exclusive five-year college program. This program requires a $50,000 contribution, payable now, to the college's endowment fund. Thereafter, her tuition and living expenses, to be paid entirely by the Muellers, are estimated at $40,000 annually.

The Mueller's personal investments total $600,000, and they plan to continue to manage the portfolio themselves. They prefer "conservative growth investments with minimal volatility." One-third of their portfolio is in the stock of Andrea's employer, a publicly traded technology company with a highly uncertain future. The shares have a very low-cost basis for tax purposes. The Muellers, currently taxed at 30 percent on income and 20 percent on net realized capital gains, have accumulated losses from past unsuccessful investments that can be used to fully offset $100,000 of future realized gains.

In 10 years, Mark will receive a distribution from a family trust. His portion is now $1.2 million and is expected to grow prior to distribution. Mark receives no income from the trust and has no influence over, or responsibility for, its management. The Muellers know that these funds will change their financial situation materially but have excluded the trust from their current financial planning.

> **A** Construct the objectives and constraints portion of an investment policy statement for the Muellers, addressing each of the following:
>
>   **i.** Return objective.
>
>   **ii.** Risk tolerance.
>
>   **iii.** Time horizon.
>
>   **iv.** Liquidity requirements.
>
>   **v.** Tax concerns.
>
>   **vi.** Unique circumstances.

Ten years have passed. The Muellers, now both aged 63, will retire this year. The distribution from Mark's family trust will occur within the next two weeks. The Muellers' current circumstances are summarized below:

Personal Circumstances and Assets

- Pension income will total $100,000 a year and will not increase with inflation.
- Annual expenses will total $180,000 initially and will increase with inflation.
- Inflation is expected to be 2 percent annually.
- Their personal investments now total $1,000,000 (excluding trust distribution).
- The Muellers will rely on this $1,000,000 portfolio to support their lifestyle and do not wish to reduce their level of spending.
- The Muellers have health problems and neither is expected to live more than 10 years. All health care expenses will be covered by employer-paid insurance.
- The Muellers' daughter is now financially independent, and the Muellers' sole investment objective is to meet their spending needs.
- The Muellers are not concerned with growing or maintaining principal. The income deficit may be met with both investment income and by invading principal.

Trust Distribution Assets

- The trust distribution totals $2,000,000 and will occur within the next two weeks. No tax liability is created by the distribution.
- The Muellers will maintain separate accounts for their personal assets and the trust distribution.
- They do not plan to withdraw income or principal.
- Tax liabilities produced by these assets will be paid from this portfolio.
- The Muellers plan to donate these assets to an arts society when the surviving spouse dies. They have made a minimum pledge of $2.6 million toward construction of a new building.
- An after-tax annual return of 5.4 percent is required over five years to meet the minimum pledge.
- The Muellers are concerned only that a minimum gift of $2.6 million is available. The Muellers assume that at least one of them will live at least five years and that neither will live more than 10 years.

Alternative portfolios for the Muellers' consideration appear in Exhibit 5.

Exhibit 5

Asset Allocation	Portfolio			
	A (%)	B (%)	C (%)	D (%)
Domestic large-cap stocks	14	30	40	30
Domestic small-cap stocks	3	5	10	25
Foreign stocks	3	5	10	25
Intermediate-term fixed income	70	60	30	20
Cash equivalents	10	0	10	0
Total	100	100	100	100
Expected annual return[a]	4.2	5.8	7.5	8.5
Annual standard deviation	6.0	8.0	13.0	18.0

[a] Nominal after-tax returns.

    B   Select and justify with three reasons the most appropriate of the four portfolios from Exhibit 5 as an asset allocation for the Muellers' $1,000,000 in personal assets.

    C   Select and justify with three reasons the most appropriate of the four portfolios from Exhibit 5 as an asset allocation for the Muellers' $2,000,000 in trust distribution assets.

12 John Mesa, CFA, is a portfolio manager in the Trust Department of BigBanc. Mesa has been asked to review the investment portfolios of Robert and Mary Smith, a retired couple and potential clients. Previously, the Smiths had been working with another financial advisor, WealthMax Financial Consultants (WFC). To assist Mesa, the Smiths have provided the following background information:

Family: We live alone. Our only daughter and granddaughter are financially secure and independent.

Health: We are both 65 years of age and in good health. Our medical costs are covered by insurance.

Housing: Our house needs major renovation. The work will be completed within the next six months, at an estimated cost of $200,000.

Expenses: Our annual after-tax living costs are expected to be $150,000 for this year and are rising with inflation, which is expected to continue at 3 percent annually.

Income: In addition to income from the Gift Fund and the Family Portfolio (both described below), we receive a fixed annual pension payment of $65,000 (after taxes), which continues for both of our lifetimes.

Financial Goals: Our primary objective is to maintain our financial security and support our current lifestyle. A secondary objective is to leave $1 million to our grandchild and $1 million to our local college. We recently completed the $1 million gift to the college by creating a "Gift Fund." Preserving the remaining assets for our granddaughter is important to us.

Taxes: Our investment income, including bond interest and stock dividends, is taxed at 30 percent. Our investment returns from price appreciation (capital gains) are taxed at 15 percent, at the time of sale. We have no other tax considerations.

General Comments: We needed someone like WFC to develop a comprehensive plan for us to follow. We can follow such a plan once it is prepared for us. We invest only in companies with which we are familiar. We will not sell a security for less than we paid for it. Given our need for income, we invest only in dividend-paying stocks.

Investments: We benefit from two investment accounts:

- The Gift Fund ($1 million) represents our gift to the college. During our lifetimes, we will receive fixed annual payments of $40,000 (tax free) from the Gift Fund. Except for the annual payments to us, the Gift Fund is managed solely for the benefit of the college—we may not make any other withdrawals of either income or principal. Upon our deaths, all assets remaining in the Gift Fund will be transferred into the college's endowment.

- The Family Portfolio ($1.2 million) represents the remainder of our lifetime savings. The portfolio is invested entirely in very safe securities, consistent with the investment policy statement prepared for us by WFC as shown in Exhibit 6.

Exhibit 6	WFC Investment Policy Statement for Smith Family Portfolio

The Smith Family Portfolio's primary focus is the production of current income, with long-term capital appreciation a secondary consideration. The need for a dependable income stream precludes investment vehicles with even modest likelihood of losses. Liquidity needs reinforce the need to emphasize minimum-risk investments. Extensive use of short-term investment-grade investments is entirely justified by the expectation that a low-inflation environment will exist indefinitely into the future. For these reasons, investments will emphasize US Treasury bills and notes, intermediate-term investment-grade corporate debt, and select "blue chip" stocks with assured dividend distributions and minimal price fluctuations.

To assist in a discussion of investment policy, Mesa presents four model portfolios used by BigBanc; Exhibit 7 applies the bank's long-term forecasts for asset class returns to each portfolio.

Exhibit 7	BigBanc Model Portfolios						

Asset Class	Total Return	Yield	Portfolios			
			A	B	C	D
US large-cap stocks	13.0%	3.0%	0%	35%	45%	0%
US small-cap stocks	15.0	1.0	0	5	15	0
Non-US stocks	14.0	1.5	0	10	15	10
US corporate bonds (AA)	6.5	6.5	80	20	0	30
US Treasury notes	6.0	6.0	0	10	5	20
Non-US government bonds	6.5	6.5	0	5	5	0
Municipal bonds (AA)[a]	4.0	4.0	0	10	0	10
Venture capital	20.0	0.0	0	0	10	25
US Treasury bills	4.0	4.0	20	5	5	5
Total			100%	100%	100%	100%
After-tax expected return			4.2%	7.5%	13.0%	6.4%
Sharpe ratio			0.35	0.50	0.45	0.45
After-tax yield			4.2%	2.9%	1.9%	3.3%
Expected inflation: 3.0%						

[a] Tax exempt.

A Prepare and justify an alternative investment policy statement for the Smiths' Family Portfolio.

B Describe how your IPS addresses three specific deficiencies in the WFC investment policy statement.

C Recommend a portfolio from Exhibit 7 for the Family Portfolio. Justify your recommendation with specific reference to:

　　i. three portfolio characteristics in Exhibit 7 other than expected return or yield; and

　　ii. the Smiths' return objectives. Show your calculations.

13 Louise and Christopher Maclin live in London, United Kingdom, and currently rent an apartment in the metropolitan area. Christopher Maclin, aged 40, is a supervisor at Barnett Co. and earns an annual salary of £80,000 before taxes. Louise Maclin, aged 38, stays home to care for their newborn twins. She recently inherited £900,000 (after wealth-transfer taxes) in cash from her father's estate. In addition, the Maclins have accumulated the following assets (current market value):

- £5,000 in cash;
- £160,000 in stocks and bonds;
- £220,000 in Barnett common stock.

The value of their holdings in Barnett stock has appreciated substantially as a result of the company's growth in sales and profits during the past ten years. Christopher Maclin is confident that the company and its stock will continue to perform well.

The Maclins need £30,000 for a down payment on the purchase of a house and plan to make a £20,000 non-tax deductible donation to a local charity in memory of Louise Maclin's father. The Maclins' annual living expenses are £74,000. After-tax salary increases will offset any future increases in their living expenses.

During discussions with their financial advisor, Grant Webb, the Maclins express concern about achieving their educational goals for their children and their own retirement goals. The Maclins tell Webb:

- They want to have sufficient funds to retire in 18 years when their children begin their four years of university education.
- They have been unhappy with the portfolio volatility they have experienced in recent years. They state that they do not want to experience a loss in portfolio value greater than 12 percent in any one year.
- They do not want to invest in alcohol and tobacco stocks.
- They will not have any additional children.

After their discussions, Webb calculates that in 18 years the Maclins will need £2 million to meet their educational and retirement goals. Webb suggests that their portfolio be structured to limit shortfall risk (defined as expected total return minus two standard deviations) to no lower than a negative 12 percent return in any one year. Maclin's salary and all capital gains and investment income are taxed at 40 percent and no tax-sheltering strategies are available. Webb's next step is to formulate an investment policy statement for the Maclins.

A **i.** Formulate the risk objective of an investment policy statement for the Maclins.

   ii. Formulate the return objective of an investment policy statement for the Maclins. Calculate the pre-tax rate of return that is required to achieve this objective. Show your calculations.

B Formulate the constraints portion of an investment policy statement for the Maclins, addressing *each* of the following:

   i. Time horizon.

   ii. Liquidity requirements.

   iii. Tax concerns.

   iv. Unique circumstances.

Note: Your response to Part B should not address legal and regulatory factors.

SOLUTIONS

1 Need for cash:

Ongoing expenses: €132,500/year

Emergency reserve: €132,500

Anticipated income: €50,000/year art sales

€82,500/year expected total return on portfolio (subject to risk)

€1,020,000 after taxes from sale of IngerMarine

The after-tax proceeds from the imminent sale of IngerMarine well exceed Christa's anticipated needs for cash for the coming year (2 × €132,500 = €265,000). Thus her liquidity needs are currently met. Because portfolio returns are risky and her anticipated annual income of €132,500 just covers her annual cash needs, however, Christa may face a challenge in the form of liquidity requirements at some point in the future.

2 After the sale of IngerMarine, Christa's portfolio will have a market value of roughly €1,120,000, taking account of the after-tax proceeds from the sale of IngerMarine (€1,020,000), her balanced mutual funds (€75,000), and her money market fund (€25,000). Her expected portfolio return is €82,500, equal to a 7.4 percent rate of return. Her required real return, if she reduces her spending by combining her apartment and studio, is €50,000 (art sales of €50,000 less €100,000 expenses), or 4.5 percent as a rate of return on her portfolio.

Because the portfolio's expected return of 7.4 percent translates to a real return of approximately 4.4 percent (7.4 percent less 3 percent inflation), the portfolio is *not* expected to meet the return requirement of 4.5 percent.

3 Portfolio guidelines and investment policy should be reviewed whenever a significant change occurs in the underlying assumptions of the policy statement. At Christa's portfolio performance reviews, the need for an interim reevaluation of the policy statement should always be considered. Possible triggers for a policy statement review might include the following:

● A change in personal circumstances affecting risk–return objectives or portfolio constraints. Examples could include an increase in expected income from nonportfolio sources, uninsured health problems, or marriage.

● A change in market conditions affecting long-term risk–return relationships among asset classes. Examples could include a shift in outlook for inflation and global political changes.

● New investment markets or vehicles. Examples could include markets made accessible through commingled investment funds and Retirement Saving Accounts.

● A change in tax laws. An example could be elimination of the capital gains tax.

● A severe performance shortfall, sufficient to jeopardize the portfolio's ability to meet expense needs in excess of income from other sources.

4 Hans' reckless actions will significantly reduce his portfolio. Hopefully this incident will make him aware of his financial vulnerability and the long-term consequences of his actions. The potential costs of the accident have created an immediate need for liquidity. Currently, Hans has a diversified equity portfolio valued at €200,000 and cash of €100,000. If he has not already done so, he

should immediately use the cash to retain an attorney for his upcoming legal challenges. He should also make his financial advisor aware of his situation and instruct him or her to establish a high level of portfolio liquidity. Hans may need to convert a portion of his IngerMarine holdings to cash, if he can, and should notify his father of this possibility. Alternatively, Hans may be able to obtain a loan using IngerMarine shares as collateral. If the IngerMarine holdings cannot be monetized, Hans may be able to borrow against the equity in his home.

5   In light of the auto accident, Hans must reassess his investment portfolio. Assuming that the legal challenges against him are successful, he stands to lose €1,000,000 in savings (after insurance). In addition, his legal fees may be large, resulting in a further decline in net worth. His salary has not been reduced, but depending on the outcome of his legal troubles, he may face job termination. His investment personality profile classified Hans as a spontaneous risk-taker, and his propensity to engage in riskier investing will have to be reevaluated. Even though Hans is young, his ability to take risk has been severely curtailed by the recent incident. His net worth may be reduced by as much as half, and he faces the potential loss of his current income. Hans will now need to consider rebuilding his life, engaging in lower-risk investing until his contingent liabilities are settled.

6   Peter and Hilda are subject to a flat tax of 25 percent on all income and a capital gains tax of 15 percent. The analysis below presents comparative after-tax returns. Even though the High Growth Stock Fund maintains high portfolio turnover, its return is high enough to provide superior after-tax performance. Of course, a complete investment evaluation should also address the relative risk of each investment alternative. The High Growth Stock Fund is quite likely to have high portfolio volatility, and this factor must also be considered before a final decision is made.

After-Tax Investment Evaluation

Investment Vehicle	High-Growth Stock Fund (€)	Equity Value Fund (€)	Municipal Bond Fund (€)
Investment	1,000,000	1,000,000	1,000,000
Projected income	20,000	25,000	50,000
Projected price appreciation	120,000	100,000	20,000
Projected income tax liability	(5,000)	(6,250)	0
Projected capital gains tax liability[a]	(13,500)	(3,750)	(450)
Net investment gains	**121,500**	**115,000**	**69,550**

[a] Gains tax liability = Price appreciation × 15% × Turnover rate

7   Remaining investment portfolio:

Stocks	€750,000
Bonds	1,000,000
Cash	1,000,000
Gold	500,000
	€3,250,000

Additional resources:

Hilda's trust distribution	€75,000/year
House	€1,200,000
Peter's RSA	€50,000

The goal of replacing Peter's €500,000 salary has become a "desired" portfolio return that is clearly not realistic. Peter and Hilda must now reconsider the return that they will "require" in order to meet their basic financial goals. The required return must be reconcilable with their new investment constraints and ability to assume risk. Before reaching an achievable return objective, Peter and Hilda will have to address some difficult decisions regarding their future lifestyle and long-term goals. Possible changes might include the following:

- postpone retirement;
- attempt to rebuild IngerMarine;
- return to the workforce as consultants or salaried employees;
- sell home;
- curtail gifting programs;
- cancel plans for second home;
- cancel investment in *Exteriors* magazine;
- liquidate Hilda's design company.

8 Portfolio Constraints

- *Liquidity.* The Ingers' short-term liquidity needs have clearly increased. Because spending commitments are sometimes difficult to curtail, Peter and Hilda may need to withdraw as much as €500,000 in the coming year from their remaining assets, to pay for expenses previously covered by Peter's salary. Fortunately, the Ingers have an emergency reserve of cash and bullion equivalent to approximately three years' salary.

  The Ingers must ultimately reconcile their ongoing liquidity needs, as well as targeted liquidity events, with their remaining net worth. Left unchanged, the increased liquidity requirements will require an increasing allocation to investments with lower volatility and lower return. At the same time, withdrawals will begin to outstrip returns, leaving the Ingers' portfolio in a deteriorating situation.

- *Time horizon.* Peter and Hilda's investment time horizon has been shortened, as the increased need to secure their own financial future has left them less able to approach portfolio risk from a multigenerational perspective. Their joint life expectancy, however, would reasonably warrant a portfolio time horizon that is still long term (20 to 25 years or more).

- *Taxes.* Tax rates remain unchanged for the Ingers, although their tax burden will decline with the loss of Peter's income. Their business loss from IngerMarine may be available to offset future investment gains.

- *Regulatory environment.* The regulatory environment is unchanged.

- *Unique circumstances.* It would be appropriate to note the bankruptcy of IngerMarine and any consequences it might have for portfolio management, such as the allocation of portfolio assets to build a new family business.

9 A i. *Return objective.* Stephenson's expressed desire for 20 percent average annual return is unrealistic. Coppa should counsel Stephenson on the level of return he can reasonably expect from the financial markets over long time periods and to define an achievable return objective.

Nevertheless, Stephenson's circumstances support an above-average return objective that emphasizes capital appreciation. This formulation is justified by the following:

- Because Stephenson has a sizable asset base and ample income to cover his current spending, focus should be on growing the portfolio.

- Stephenson's low liquidity needs and long time horizon support a long-term capital appreciation approach.

- Stephenson is in the consolidation phase of his life cycle and does not rely on the portfolio to meet living expenses.

Stephenson stated that he wants a return in excess of 5.0 percent for the remainder of the year. This short-term goal needs to be considered to the extent possible but should not be a significant factor in the IPS, which focuses on the client's long-term return objective.

ii. *Risk tolerance.* Stephenson has an above-average risk tolerance.

- Although Stephenson describes his risk tolerance as "average," his current investment portfolio indicates an apparent above-average willingness to take risk.

- His financial situation (large current asset base, ample income to cover expenses, lack of need for liquidity or cash flow, and long time horizon) indicates an above-average ability to assume risk.

iii. *Liquidity requirements.* Stephenson's liquidity needs are low.

- Stephenson has no regular cash flow needs from the portfolio because the income from his medical practice meets all current spending needs.

- No large, one-time cash needs are stated. It would be appropriate, however, to keep a small cash reserve for emergencies.

iv. *Time horizon.* Stephenson's time horizon is long term and consists of two stages:

- time until retirement, which he expects to be 15 years; and

- his lifetime following retirement, which could range from 15 to 20 years.

B Fund D represents the single best addition to complement Stephenson's current portfolio, given his selection criteria. First, Fund D's expected return (14.0 percent) has the potential to increase the portfolio's return somewhat. Second, Fund D's relatively low correlation coefficient with his current portfolio (+0.65) indicates that it will provide larger diversification benefits than any of the other alternatives except Fund B. The result of adding Fund D should be a portfolio with about the same expected return and somewhat lower volatility compared with the original portfolio.

The three other funds have shortcomings in either expected return enhancement or volatility reduction through diversification benefits:

- Fund A offers the potential for increasing the portfolio's return but is too highly correlated to provide substantial volatility reduction benefits through diversification.

- Fund B provides substantial volatility reduction through diversification benefits but is expected to generate a return well below the current portfolio's return.

- Fund C has the greatest potential to increase the portfolio's return but is too highly correlated to provide substantial volatility reduction benefits through diversification.

10 A   **i.** The IPS's *return objective* section is inadequate.

- Although Wheeler accurately indicates Taylor's personal income requirement, she has not recognized the need to support Renee.

- Wheeler does not indicate the need to protect Taylor's purchasing power by increasing income by at least the rate of inflation over time.

- Wheeler does not indicate the impact of income taxes on the return requirement.

- Wheeler calculates required return based on assets of $900,000, appropriately excluding Taylor's imminent $300,000 liquidity need (house purchase) from investable funds. However, Taylor may invest $100,000 in his son's business. If he does, Taylor insists this asset be excluded from his plan. In that eventuality, Taylor's asset base for purposes of Wheeler's analysis would be $800,000.

- Assuming a $900,000 capital base, Wheeler's total return estimate of 2.7 percent is lower than the actual required after-tax real return of 5.3 percent ($48,000/$900,000).

ii. The *risk tolerance* section is inappropriate.

- Wheeler fails to consider Taylor's below-average willingness to assume risk as exemplified by his aversion to loss, his consistent preference for conservative investments, his adverse experience with creditors, and his desire not to work again.

- Wheeler fails to consider Taylor's below-average ability to assume risk, which is based on his recent life changes, the size of his capital base, high personal expenses versus income, and expenses related to his mother's care.

- Wheeler's policy statement implies that Taylor has a greater willingness and ability to accept volatility (higher risk tolerance) than is actually the case. Based on Taylor's need for an after-tax return of 5.3 percent, a balanced approach with both a fixed-income and growth component is more appropriate than an aggressive growth strategy.

iii. The *time horizon* section is partially appropriate.

- Wheeler accurately addresses the long-term time horizon based only on Taylor's age and life expectancy.

- Wheeler fails to consider that Taylor's investment time horizon is multistage. Stage 1 represents Renee's life expectancy, during which time Taylor will supplement her income. Stage 2 begins at Renee's death, concluding Taylor's need to supplement her income, and ends with Taylor's death.

iv. The *liquidity* section is partially appropriate.

- Wheeler addresses potential liquidity events.

- Wheeler fails to specifically consider ongoing expenses ($2,000/ month for Taylor's living expenses and $2,000/month to support his mother) relative to expected portfolio returns.

- The reference to a "normal, ongoing cash reserve" is vague. The reserve's purpose and size should be specified.

B   Allocation B is most appropriate for Taylor. Taylor's real-return annual return requirement is 6.3 percent, based on his cash flow (income) needs ($50,400 annually), to be generated from a current asset base of $800,000. After adjusting for expected annual inflation of 1.0 percent, the nominal requirement becomes 7.3 percent. To grow to $808,000 ($800,000 × 1.01), the portfolio must generate $58,400 ($50,400 + $8,000) in the first year ($58,400/$800,000 = 7.3%).

Allocation B meets Taylor's minimum return requirement. Of the possible allocations that provide the required minimum real return, Allocation B also has the lowest standard deviation of returns (i.e., the least volatility risk) and by far the best Sharpe ratio. In addition, Allocation B offers a balance of high current income and stability with moderate growth prospects.

Allocation A has the lowest standard deviation and best Sharpe ratio but does not meet the minimum return requirement when inflation is included in that requirement. Allocation A also has very low growth prospects.

Allocation C meets the minimum return requirement and has moderate growth prospects but has a higher risk level (standard deviation) and a lower Sharpe ratio, as well as less potential for stability, than Allocation B.

11 A The Muellers' investment policy statement should include the following objectives and constraints:

   i. *Return objective.* The Mueller's return objective should reflect a total return approach that combines capital appreciation and capital preservation. After retirement, they will need approximately $75,000 (adjusted for inflation) annually to maintain their current standard of living. Given the Muellers' limited needs and asset base, preserving their financial position on an inflation-adjusted basis may be a sufficient objective. Their long life expectancy and undetermined retirement needs, however, lead to the likely requirement for some asset growth over time, at least to counter any effects of inflation.

   Although the Muellers wish to exclude the future trust distribution from their current planning, that distribution will substantially increase their capital base and dramatically alter the return objective of their future IPS, primarily by reducing their needed return level.

   ii. *Risk tolerance.* The Muellers are in the middle stage of the investor life cycle. Their income (relative to expenses), total financial resources, and long time horizon give them the ability to assume at least an average, if not an above-average, level of investment risk. Their stated preference of "minimal volatility" investments, however, apparently indicates a below-average willingness to assume risk. The large realized losses they incurred in previous investments may contribute to their desire for safety. Also, their need for continuing cash outflow to meet their daughter's college expenses may temporarily and slightly reduce their risk-taking ability. In sum, the Muellers' risk tolerance is average.

   Two other issues affect the Muellers' ability to take risk. First, the holding of Andrea's company stock represents a large percentage of the Mueller's total investable assets and thus is an important risk factor for their portfolio. Reducing the size of this holding or otherwise reducing the risk associated with a single large holding should be a priority for the Muellers. Second, the future trust distribution will substantially increase their capital base and thus increase their ability to assume risk.

   iii. *Time horizon.* Overall, the Muellers' ages and long life expectancies indicate a long time horizon. They face a multistage horizon, however, because of their changing cash flow and resource circumstances. Their time horizon can be viewed as having three distinct stages: the next five years from now (some assets, negative cash flow because of their daughter's college expenses), the following five years (some assets, positive cash flow), and beyond 10 years (increased assets from a sizable trust distribution, decreased income because they plan to retire).

iv. *Liquidity.* The Muellers need $50,000 now to contribute to the college's endowment fund. Alternatively, they may be able to contribute $50,000 of Andrea's low-cost-basis stock to meet the endowment obligation. In addition, they expect the regular annual college expenses ($40,000) to exceed their normal annual savings ($25,000) by $15,000 for each of the next five years. This relatively low cash flow requirement of 2.7 percent ($15,000/$550,000 asset base after $50,000 contribution) can be substantially met through income generation from their portfolio, further reducing the need for sizable cash reserves. Once their daughter completes college, the Muellers' liquidity needs should be minimal until retirement because their income more than adequately covers their living expenses.

v. *Tax concerns.* The Muellers are subject to a 30 percent marginal tax rate for ordinary income and a 20 percent rate for realized capital gains. The difference in the rates makes investment returns in the form of capital gains preferable to equivalent amounts of taxable dividends and interest.

Although taxes on capital gains would normally be a concern to investors with low-cost-basis stock, this is not a major concern for the Muellers because they have a tax loss carryforward of $100,000. The Muellers can offset up to $100,000 in realized gains with the available tax loss carryforward without experiencing any cash outflow or any reduction in asset base.

vi. *Unique circumstances.* The large holding of the low-basis stock in Andrea's company, a "technology company with a highly uncertain future," is a key factor to be included in the evaluation of the risk level of the Muellers' portfolio and the future management of their assets. In particular, the family should systematically reduce the size of the investment in this single stock. Because of the existence of the tax loss carryforward, the stock position can be reduced by at least 50 percent (perhaps more depending on the exact cost basis of the stock) without reducing the asset base to pay a tax obligation.

In addition, the trust distribution in 10 years presents special circumstances for the Muellers, although they prefer to ignore these future assets in their current planning. The trust will provide significant assets to help meet their long-term return needs and objectives. Any long-term investment policy for the family must consider this circumstance, and any recommended investment strategy must be adjusted before the distribution takes place.

B *Personal portfolio.* Portfolio A is the most appropriate portfolio for the Muellers. Because their pension income will not cover their annual expenditures, the shortfall will not likely be met by the return on their investments, so the 10 percent cash reserve is appropriate. As the portfolio is depleted over time, it may be prudent to allocate more than 10 percent to cash equivalents. The income deficit will be met each year by a combination of investment return and capital invasion.

Now that their daughter is financially independent, the Muellers' sole objective for their personal portfolio is to provide for their own living expenses. Their willingness and need to accept risk is fairly low. Clearly, there is no need to expose the Muellers to the possibility of a large loss. Also, their health situation has considerably shortened their time horizon. Therefore, a 70 percent allocation to intermediate-term high-grade fixed-income securities is warranted.

The income deficit will rise each year as the Muellers' expenses rise with inflation, but their pension income remains constant. The conservative 20 percent allocation to equities should provide diversification benefits and some protection against unanticipated inflation over the expected maximum 10-year time horizon.

Portfolio B, the second-best portfolio, has no cash reserves, so it could not meet the Muellers' liquidity needs. Also, although it has a higher expected return, Portfolio B's asset allocation results in a somewhat higher standard deviation of returns than Portfolio A.

Portfolios C and D offer higher expected returns but at markedly higher levels of risk and with relatively lower levels of current income. The Muellers' large income requirements and low risk tolerance preclude the use of Portfolios C and D.

C *Trust distribution portfolio.* Portfolio B is the most appropriate for the trust assets. Portfolio B's expected return of 5.8 percent exceeds the required return of 5.4 percent, and the required return will actually decline if the surviving spouse lives longer than five years. The portfolio's time horizon is relatively short, ranging from a minimum of 5 years to a maximum of 10 years. The Muellers' sole objective for this money is to adequately fund the building addition. The portfolio's growth requirements are modest, and the Muellers have below-average willingness to accept risk. The portfolio would be unlikely to achieve its objective if large, even short-term losses were absorbed during the minimum five-year time horizon. Except for taxes, no principal or income disbursements are expected for at least five years; therefore, only a minimal or even zero cash reserve is required. Accordingly, an allocation of 40 percent to equities to provide some growth and 60 percent to intermediate-term fixed-income to provide stability and capital preservation is appropriate.

There is no second-best portfolio. Portfolio A's cash level is higher than necessary, and the portfolio's expected return is insufficient to achieve the $2,600,000 value within the minimum value in five years. Portfolio C has a sufficient expected return, but it has a higher cash level than is necessary and, more importantly, a standard deviation of return that is too high given the Muellers' below-average risk tolerance. Portfolio D has a sufficient return and an appropriate cash level but a clearly excessive risk (standard deviation) level. Portfolios C and D share the flaw of having excessive equity allocations that fail to recognize the relatively short time horizon and that generate risk levels much higher than necessary or warranted.

12 A To prepare an appropriate IPS, a manager should address the Smiths' return objective, risk tolerance, and constraints.

Return objective. To achieve its objectives, the Family Portfolio must provide for after-tax distributions equal to the difference between the Smiths' expenses and their fixed income payments. To maintain its real value, the portfolio must also grow at a rate that offsets inflation's impact on the Smiths' total expenses, including those currently covered by the fixed pension and Gift Fund payments.

A secondary objective is the gifting of $1 million to the Smiths' granddaughter. Because the Family Portfolio will be worth $1 million after the renovation of their house, the Smiths need no further capital growth to reach their nominal goal. To maintain its real value, the portfolio must have growth at least equal to the rate of inflation.

Risk tolerance. The Smiths are in a relatively late stage of the investor life cycle, and their comments suggest a conservative bias or below-average willingness to accept risk. In light of their long-term goals and current financial security, however, the Smiths have the ability to accommodate moderate portfolio volatility.

In the short term, the consequences of an adverse investment outcome are limited; the Smiths could use principal from the Family Portfolio to cover occasional performance shortfalls. They are thus able to accommodate some measure of short-term volatility in return for greater long-term expected returns. In extreme circumstances, the Smiths could modify or forgo their secondary objective of leaving $1 million to their granddaughter.

The consequences of an adverse portfolio outcome in the long term, however, could be serious. Depending on the length of their remaining lifetimes and the growth rate of their expenses, the Smiths could seriously deplete the corpus of the Family Portfolio and jeopardize their financial security.

The Smiths' comments imply that they have spent a lifetime saving and building a "safe" collection of income-oriented investments. Their desire to preserve market value and the WealthMax Financial Consultants (WFC) policy statement's emphasis on secure investments suggest that they may fall, at least partially, into the "cautious" category, a group with below-average risk tolerance.

Time horizon. The Family Portfolio should have an intermediate to slightly longer-term investment horizon.

The Smiths' joint life expectancy, at 65 years of age, is still substantial. Because their objective of financial security is well provided for in the short term (see discussion of risk tolerance), the Smiths can afford to focus more on the long-term aspects of that objective.

To the extent that the Smiths emphasize the objective of leaving $1 million to their granddaughter in their planning, a longer-term time horizon would be warranted.

Liquidity requirements. The Smiths' current annual living costs ($150,000 after taxes) are being met, which allows them to address longer-term growth objectives. The Smiths must plan for the upcoming expense of renovating their home. Their Family Portfolio should anticipate the renovation costs by holding a reserve of at least $200,000 in highly liquid, short-term funds.

Laws and regulations. No special legal or regulatory problems are apparent.

Tax concerns. The Smiths must pay a higher tax on dividends and interest than on capital gains. All else being equal, therefore, they prefer portfolio returns in the form of capital gains rather than equivalent amounts of taxable investment income.

Unique circumstances. Establishment of the Gift Fund had increased the Smiths' dependence on fixed payments. As a consequence of this increased exposure to the eroding effects of inflation, the Smiths' long-term financial security is significantly reduced.

Synopsis. The Smiths may not fully appreciate the impact of inflation and taxes on their financial security. The Family Portfolio can meet their immediate needs, but it is unlikely to grow at the same rate as disbursements. Depending on how long the Smiths live, the secondary objective of giving $1 million to their granddaughter may not be fully attainable, even in nominal terms.

B   Rather than a true policy statement, the WFC statement is a compendium of opinions and assertions that may or may not be supportable by evidence and may or may not be appropriate to the Smiths' specific situation. WFC's statement fails to:

- identify specific return requirement;
- consider inflation;
- consider the Smiths' willingness and ability to accept risk;
- consider the Smiths' investment time horizon;
- specify the Smiths' liquidity requirements;
- address the possibility of legal and regulatory constraints;
- consider tax concerns; and
- consider possible unique circumstances.

C   **i.** Portfolio B is an appropriate recommendation based on three portfolio characteristics other than expected return and yield: diversification, efficiency (Sharpe ratio), and risk.

- Diversification across asset classes contributes to portfolio efficiency and is a desirable portfolio characteristic. Portfolio B appears to be the most broadly diversified.

- Efficiency, as measured by return for each unit of risk (Sharpe ratio), is a desirable portfolio characteristic. Portfolio B dominates the other portfolios on this criterion.

- Risk is an attribute that must be constrained to fit the Smiths' fiscal and psychological tolerance levels. The 85 percent allocation to equities and venture capital in Portfolio C entails relatively high risk. Portfolio B, which is more balanced between fixed-income and equity markets, is better suited to the Smiths' below-average risk profile.

ii. Meeting the Smiths' return objectives in the first year will require an after-tax total return of 7.5 percent on the $1 million remaining in the Family Portfolio after their house renovation. The Family Portfolio must accommodate a disbursement of $45,000 and grow at a rate that offsets the impact of inflation:

Expenses		($150,000)
Sources of funds		
Pension (after tax)	65,000	
Gift Fund (after tax)	40,000	105,000
Family Portfolio disbursement (after tax)		45,000
		$150,000
Required return		
Disbursement ($45,000)	4.50%	
Inflation	3.00%	
Total	7.50%	

Subsequent distributions from the Family Portfolio will increase at a rate substantially higher than inflation (to offset the lack of growth in $105,000 of fixed pension and Gift Fund payments):

	Year 1	Year 2	Change
Expenses (3% growth)	$150,000	$154,500	3%
Portfolio distribution	$45,000	$49,500	10%

Portfolios B and C both have expected returns that meet the Smiths' projected disbursements in Year 1. Portfolio C's expected return is closer to that necessary to meet their objective over a longer time frame. However, Portfolio C's level of risk is too high given the Smiths' risk tolerance. Although Portfolio C should allow the Smiths to both fund their lifetime real income needs and leave $1 million to their grandchild, the risk in Portfolio C may endanger both their income and the bequest.

The Smiths' advisor should select Portfolio B based on its appropriate risk level and conformity with the Smiths' constraints. As a consequence of Portfolio B's probable inability to meet the Smiths' long-term spending needs, however, principal invasion may be necessary, and the secondary objective of giving $1 million, even in nominal terms, to their granddaughter may be forfeited.

13 A **i.** The Maclins' overall risk objective must consider both willingness and ability to take risk:

Willingness. The Maclins have a below-average willingness to take risk, based on their unhappiness with the portfolio volatility they have experienced in recent years and their desire not to experience a loss in portfolio value in excess of 12 percent in any one year.

Ability. The Maclins have an average ability to take risk. Although their fairly large asset base and long time horizon in isolation would suggest an above-average ability to take risk, their living expenses of £74,000 are significantly higher than Christopher's after-tax salary of £80,000(1 − 0.40) = £48,000, causing them to be very dependent on projected portfolio returns to cover the difference and thereby reducing their ability to take risk.

Overall. The Maclins' overall risk tolerance is below average, as their below-average willingness to take risk dominates their average ability to take risk in determining their overall risk tolerance.

ii. The Maclins' return objective is to grow the portfolio to meet their educational and retirement needs as well as to provide for ongoing net expenses. The Maclins will require annual after-tax cash flows of £26,000 (calculated below) to cover ongoing net expenses and will need £2 million in 18 years to fund their children's education and their retirement. To meet this objective, the Maclins' pretax required return is 7.38 percent, which is determined below.

The after-tax return required to accumulate £2 million in 18 years beginning with an investable asset base of £1,235,000 (calculated below) and with annual outflows of £26,000 is 4.427 percent, which when adjusted for the 40 percent tax rate, results in a 7.38 percent pretax return [4.427%/(1 − 0.40) = 7.38%].

Christopher's annual salary	£80,000
Less: Taxes (40%)	−32,000

(continued)

Living expenses	−74,000
Net annual cash flow	−£26,000
Inheritance	900,000
Barnett Co. common stock	220,000
Stocks and bonds	160,000
Cash	5,000
Subtotal	£1,285,000
Less one-time needs:	
Down payment on house	−30,000
Charitable donation	−20,000
Investable asset base	£1,235,000

Note: No inflation adjustment is required in the return calculation because increases in living expenses will be offset by increases in Christopher's salary.

B The Maclins' investment policy statement should include the following constraints:

  i. *Time horizon.* The Maclins have a two-stage time horizon, because of their changing cash flow and resource needs. The first stage is the next 18 years. The second stage begins with their retirement and the university education years for their children.

  ii. *Liquidity requirements.* The Maclins have one-time immediate expenses totaling £50,000 that include the deposit on the house they are purchasing and the charitable donation in honor of Louise's father.

  iii. *Tax concerns.* A 40 percent tax rate applies to both ordinary income and capital gains.

  iv. *Unique circumstances.* The large holding of the Barnett Co. common stock represents almost 18 percent of the Maclins' investable asset base. The concentrated holding in Barnett Co. stock is a key risk factor of the Maclins' portfolio, and achieving better diversification will be a factor in the future management of the Maclins' assets.

  The Maclins' desire not to invest in alcohol and tobacco stocks is another constraint on investment.

Taxes and Private Wealth Management in a Global Context

by Stephen M. Horan, PhD, CFA, CIPM, and
Thomas R. Robinson, PhD, CFA

Stephen M. Horan, PhD, CFA, CIPM, is at CFA Institute (USA). Thomas R. Robinson, PhD, CFA, is at CFA Institute (USA).

LEARNING OUTCOMES

Mastery	The candidate should be able to:
☐	a. compare basic global taxation regimes as they relate to the taxation of dividend income, interest income, realized capital gains, and unrealized capital gains;
☐	b. determine the effects of different types of taxes and tax regimes on future wealth accumulation;
☐	c. calculate accrual equivalent tax rates and after-tax returns;
☐	d. explain how investment return and investment horizon affect the tax impact associated with an investment;
☐	e. discuss the tax profiles of different types of investment accounts and explain their impact on after-tax returns and future accumulations;
☐	f. explain how taxes affect investment risk;
☐	g. discuss the relation between after-tax returns and different types of investor trading behavior;
☐	h. explain the benefits of tax loss harvesting and highest-in/first-out (HIFO) tax lot accounting;
☐	i. demonstrate how taxes and asset location relate to mean–variance optimization.

INTRODUCTION

1

Private wealth managers have the basic goal of maximizing after-tax wealth subject to a client's risk tolerance and portfolio constraints. Portfolio managers can add value in a number of ways, such as buying undervalued securities, selling overpriced securities, and improving asset allocations. This is challenging in highly efficient markets where informational advantages are difficult to exploit as market participants compete with each other in search of abnormal returns. Managing a portfolio efficiently from a tax perspective, however, is a reasonable goal in almost all markets. In most economies around the world, taxes have a significant impact on net performance and affect an adviser's understanding of risk for the taxable investor. Tax rates, particularly those for high-net-worth (HNW) individuals, are non-trivial and typically affect returns more than portfolio management costs.

Despite a long history of high tax rates on investment returns, most modern portfolio theory is grounded in a pretax framework. This phenomenon is understandable because most institutional and pension portfolios are tax-exempt. As more wealth becomes concentrated with individuals, it is important to examine the impact of taxes on risk and return characteristics of a portfolio and wealth accumulation. The purpose of this reading is to outline basic concepts that serve as the foundation for building tax-aware investment models that can be applied in a global environment.

The approach developed here is valuable for several reasons. First, it can be applied in a broad range of circumstances representing different taxing jurisdictions, asset classes, and account types. Second, it can provide a framework with which advisers can better communicate the impact of taxes of portfolio returns to private clients and develop techniques to improve their after-tax performance. Third, tax codes change over time. The models developed here provide the adviser a framework to manage changes should they occur.

2 OVERVIEW OF GLOBAL INCOME TAX STRUCTURES

Tax structures (the specifics of how governments collect taxes) are determined by national, regional, and local jurisdictions in order to meet governmental funding needs. Major sources of government tax revenue include:

- *Taxes on income.* These taxes apply to individuals, corporations, and often other types of legal entities. For individuals, income types can include salaries, interest, dividends, realized capital gains, and unrealized capital gains, among others. Income tax structure refers to how and when different types of income are taxed.

- *Wealth-based taxes.* These include taxes on the holding of certain types of property (e.g., real estate) and taxes on the transfer of wealth (e.g., taxes on inheritance).

- *Taxes on consumption.* These include sales taxes (which are taxes collected in one step from the final consumer on the price of a good or service) and value-added taxes (which are collected in intermediate steps in the course of producing a good or service but borne ultimately by the final consumer).

This reading's focus will be on the taxes that most directly affect tax planning for investments, specifically taxes on investment income to individuals and, secondarily, wealth-based taxes.

In many cases, the tax system is used to encourage or discourage certain activities (for example, investing in domestic companies or encouraging retirement savings). Tax structures vary globally and can change as the needs and objectives of the governmental jurisdiction change. In such a dynamic environment, the investment manager needs to understand the impact of different tax structures on investment returns and wealth. Rather than delineate specific country tax rules, this reading provides a framework for managers to understand and implement investment strategies in a dynamic environment where different tax environments may apply to different clients and tax environments can change over time.

2.1 International Comparisons of Income Taxation

We reviewed the taxation of different types of income, particularly investment income, around the world in order to summarize the major tax regimes.[1] The review was based on data from over 50 countries as reported in the Deloitte Touche Tohmatsu International Business Guides, which were available during the summer of 2007. This summary provided the basis for our discussion of the common elements of individual income taxation around the world and our classification of different countries into general income tax regimes.

2.2 Common Elements

In most tax jurisdictions, a tax rate structure applies to ordinary income (such as earnings from employment). Other tax rates may apply to special categories of income such as investment income (sometimes referred to as capital income for tax purposes). Investment income is often taxed differently based on the nature of the income: interest, dividends, or capital gains and losses. Most of the countries examined in our review have a progressive ordinary tax rate structure. In a progressive rate structure, the tax rate increases as income increases. For example:

Taxable Income (€)		Tax on	Percentage on Excess
Over	Up to	Column 1	Over Column 1
0	15,000	—	23
15,000	28,000	3,450	27
28,000	55,000	6,960	38
55,000	75,000	17,220	41
75,000		25,420	43

In such an environment, if an individual has taxable income of €60,000, the first €15,000 is taxed at 23 percent; the next €13,000 (i.e., from €15,000 to €28,000) is taxed at 27 percent; and so on. The amount of tax due on taxable income of €60,000 would be €17,220 + 0.41(€60,000 − €55,000) or €19,270. This would represent an average tax rate of €19,270/€60,000 or 32.12 percent. In tax planning for investments, it is useful to think about how much tax would be paid on additional income, known as the marginal tax rate. The marginal rate, or rate on the next €1 of income, would be 41 percent in this example. This taxpayer could have €15,000 more in income before moving into the next tax bracket (a new marginal rate of 43 percent). Some countries do not have a progressive tax system and instead impose a flat tax. In a flat tax structure, all taxable income is taxed at the same rate. For example, at the time of this writing, Russia had a flat tax rate of 13 percent.

Many countries provide special tax provisions for interest income. These special provisions included an exemption for certain types of interest income (for example, Argentina exempted interest income from Argentine banks for residents), a favorable tax rate on interest income (for example, Italy taxed some interest income at 12.5 percent even though the minimum marginal rate is 23 percent), or an exclusion

---

[1] The guides are available at www.deloitte.com and are updated on a rotational basis. As a result, some data may not be current as of the summer of 2007.

amount where some limited amount of interest income is exempt from tax (for example, Germany provided such an exclusion). Some fixed income instruments are indexed for inflation and this inflation adjustment may not be subject to taxation in some jurisdictions. Unless special provisions exist, interest income, including inflation adjustments, is taxed at the tax rates applicable to ordinary income (ordinary rates).

Similarly, dividend income may have special provisions. In some cases there are exemptions, special tax rates, or exclusions as described above for interest income. In other cases, there may be provisions for mitigating double taxation because dividends are a distribution of company earnings and the company may have already paid tax on the earnings. Tax credits can be used to mitigate the effects of double taxation. For example, the dividend can be taxed at ordinary rates but the individual is entitled to a credit for a portion of the taxes paid by the company (referred to as "franking" in some jurisdictions such as Australia). As with interest income, absent special rules dividend income is taxed at ordinary rates.

Finally, capital gains (losses) may have special provisions or rates. These often vary depending upon how long the underlying investment has been held. Generally, long term gains are treated more favorably than short term gains. Long term is defined differently in different jurisdictions; for example, in the data examined, we observed required holding periods of six months, one year, two years, and five years. Special provisions observed included total exemption of capital gains or long-term capital gains from taxation (for example, Austria exempted long-term gains), exemption of a certain percentage of gains from taxation (for example, Canada exempted 50 percent of gains), a favorable tax rate on capital gains (for example, Brazil provided a flat 15 percent rate for capital gains), or indexing the cost of the investment for inflation (for example, India permitted inflation indexing for some investments). In some cases, countries provided more favorable provisions for domestic companies or companies traded on a local exchange (sometimes applied to both dividend income and capital gains). In most cases, only realized gains were taxed (when the investment was sold). In rare cases, countries impose a tax on unrealized gains (appreciation of the investment prior to sale) either annually, upon exiting the country to relocate domicile, or upon inheritance.[2]

EXAMPLE 1

Tax Rates

Vanessa Wong is a new client living in a jurisdiction with a progressive tax rate structure. She expects to have taxable ordinary income of €70,000 this year. The tax rate structure in her jurisdiction is as follows:

Taxable Income (€)		Tax on	Percentage on Excess
Over	Up to	Column 1	Over Column 1
0	30,000	—	20
30,000	60,000	6,000	30
60,000	90,000	15,000	40
90,000		27,000	50

1 Wong's marginal tax rate is *closest* to:

A 35%.

---

2 In other cases upon inheritance the recipient receives a "step-up in basis" such that for tax purposes the value on the date of death is used to compute any future gain or loss.

B 40%.

C 50%.

2 Wong's average tax rate is *closest* to:

A 27%.

B 35%.

C 40%.

Solution to 1:

B is correct. Wong's marginal tax rate is 40 percent. Because Wong's income is over €60,000 but below €90,000, her next €1 of income would be taxed at 40 percent.

Solution to 2:

A is correct. Wong's tax liability would be €15,000 + 0.40 (€70,000 − €60,000) = €19,000. With a tax liability of €19,000 and taxable income of €70,000, her average tax rate would be about 27 percent (€19,000/€70,000).

2.3 General Income Tax Regimes

Each country's income tax structure can be classified as either progressive or flat. Income tax regimes can be further distinguished based on the taxation of investment returns in taxable accounts. Interest income is either taxed at ordinary rates or at favorable rates under special provisions. In this review, interest income is considered to be taxable at ordinary rates unless significant exceptions apply. Similar classifications were used for dividends and capital gains. Seven different tax regimes were observed in the sample of countries examined. Exhibit 1 classifies common elements of tax regimes and is further explained below.

- *Common Progressive Regime*: This regime has progressive tax rates for ordinary income, but favorable treatment in all three investment income categories: interest, dividends, and capital gains. This was the most common regime observed. Even though categorized as "common," there is variation within this regime with some countries treating some interest income as ordinary and other interest income as tax exempt, while other countries provide for exemption or special treatment for all interest.

- *Heavy Dividend Tax Regime*: This regime has a progressive tax system for ordinary income and favorable treatment for some interest and capital gains but taxes dividends at ordinary rates.

- *Heavy Capital Gain Tax Regime*: This regime has a progressive tax system for ordinary income and favorable treatment for interest and dividends, but taxes capital gains at ordinary rates. Only one such country was observed.

- *Heavy Interest Tax Regime*: This regime has a progressive tax system for ordinary income and favorable treatment for dividends and capital gains, but taxes interest income at ordinary rates.

- *Light Capital Gain Tax Regime*: This regime has a progressive tax system for ordinary income, interest, and dividends, but favorable treatment of capital gains. This was the second most commonly observed regime.

Exhibit 1   Classification of Income Tax Regimes

Regime	1 – Common Progressive	2 – Heavy Dividend Tax	3 – Heavy Capital Gain Tax	4 – Heavy Interest Tax	5 – Light Capital Gain Tax	6 – Flat and Light	7 – Flat and Heavy
Ordinary Tax Rate Structure	Progressive	Progressive	Progressive	Progressive	Progressive	Flat	Flat
Interest Income	Some interest taxed at favorable rates or exempt	Some interest taxed at favorable rates or exempt	Some interest taxed at favorable rates or exempt	Taxed at ordinary rates	Taxed at ordinary rates	Some interest taxed at favorable rates or exempt	Some interest taxed at favorable rates or exempt
Dividends	Some dividends taxed at favorable rates or exempt	Taxed at ordinary rates	Some dividends taxed at favorable rates or exempt	Some dividends taxed at favorable rates or exempt	Taxed at ordinary rates	Some dividends taxed at favorable rates or exempt	Taxed at ordinary rates

Exhibit 1   (Continued)

Regime	1 – Common Progressive	2 – Heavy Dividend Tax	3 – Heavy Capital Gain Tax	4 – Heavy Interest Tax	5 – Light Capital Gain Tax	6 – Flat and Light	7 – Flat and Heavy
Capital Gains	Some capital gains taxed favorably or exempt	Some capital gains taxed favorably or exempt	Taxed at ordinary rates	Some capital gains taxed favorably or exempt	Some capital gains taxed favorably or exempt	Some capital gains taxed favorably or exempt	Taxed at ordinary rates
Example Countries	Austria	Argentina	Colombia	Canada	Australia	Kazakhstan	Ukraine
	Brazil	Indonesia		Denmark	Belgium	Russia	
	China	Israel		Germany	India	Saudi Arabia	
	Czech Republic	Venezuela		Luxembourg	Kenya	(Zakat)	
	Finland			Pakistan	Mexico		
	France				New Zealand		
	Greece				Norway		
	Hong Kong				Spain		
	Hungary				Switzerland		
	Ireland				Taiwan		
	Italy				Turkey		
	Japan						
	Latvia						
	Malaysia						
	Netherlands						
	Nigeria						
	Philippines						
	Poland						
	Portugal						
	Singapore						
	South Africa						
	Sweden						
	Thailand						
	United Kingdom						
	United States						
	Vietnam						

Sources: Classified based on information provided in International Business Guides from Deloitte Touche Tohmatsu (available at www.deloitte.com) and online database of worldwide taxation provided by PricewaterhouseCoopers (www.taxsummaries.pwc.com).

■ *Flat and Light Regime*: This regime has a flat tax system and treats interest, dividends, and capital gains favorably.

■ *Flat and Heavy Regime*: This regime has a flat tax system for ordinary income, dividends, and capital gains. It does not have favorable treatment for dividends and capital gains, but has favorable treatment for interest income.

2.4 Other Considerations

In addition to the different tax regimes in which different types of income are taxed at possibly different rates, there are other important dimensions in tax planning for investments. Some countries permit the use of tax deferred retirement accounts. A tax deferred account

■ defers taxation on investment returns within the account;

■ may permit a deduction for contributions;

■ may occasionally permit tax free distributions.

On the other hand, a few countries impose a wealth tax on accumulations on a periodic basis which reduces after-tax returns and accumulations similar to income taxes.

In the next section we will examine how taxes affect after-tax returns and accumulations. We also examine the impact of tax deferred accounts and wealth taxes. In a later section we will discuss planning opportunities suitable for the various tax regimes.[3]

---

3   AFTER-TAX ACCUMULATIONS AND RETURNS FOR TAXABLE ACCOUNTS

Taxes on investment returns have a substantial impact on performance and future accumulations. This section develops models to estimate the tax impact on future accumulations in various tax environments. These models enable the investment adviser to evaluate potential investments for taxable investors by comparing returns and wealth accumulations for different types of investments subject to different tax rates and methods of taxation (accrued annually or deferred).

3.1 Simple Tax Environments

As the preceding analysis of global tax regimes suggests, investment returns can be taxed in a number of different ways. This section begins with some straightforward methods that illustrate basic concepts and serve as building blocks for more complex environments.

All but four of the countries studied in the tax regime analysis have a progressive income tax system.[4] The discussion in this section assumes uniform marginal tax rates based on the investor's current tax bracket which is effectively flat for some range of income. Models that accommodate multiple tax brackets grow in complexity very quickly. Also, investors are often subject to a single rate on the margin, limiting the usefulness of an analysis based on multiple tax brackets. Finally, much of the intuition and analysis that is derived in a flat tax framework applies in a setting with multiple tax brackets.

---

3 Gift, death, or estate taxes are also imposed in some jurisdictions. These are not addressed in this reading.
4 Countries with a flat tax include the Ukraine, Russia, Kazakhstan, and Saudi Arabia.

3.1.1 *Returns-Based Taxes: Accrual Taxes on Interest and Dividends*

One of the most straightforward methods to tax investment returns is to tax an investment's annual return at a single tax rate, regardless of its form. Accrual taxes are levied and paid on a periodic basis, usually annually, as opposed to deferred taxes that are postponed until some future date. Most of the countries examined above tax interest income on an accrual basis annually, either at ordinary rates or at favorable rates as the result of special provisions. Germany, Greece, Canada, Colombia, and the United States, for example, tax most interest income at ordinary rates, although some interest income may receive favorable tax treatment. Japan, China, Finland, the Czech Republic, and the United Kingdom tax interest income at a special fixed rate. Dividends, like interest income, are typically taxed in the year they are received, albeit often at different rates.

When returns are subject to accrual taxes, the after-tax return is equal to the pretax return, r, multiplied by $(1 - t_i)$ where t_i represents the tax rate applicable to investment income. For the purposes of this section, we consider an investment with a return that is entirely taxed at a single uniform rate.

The amount of money accumulated for each unit of currency invested after n years, assuming that returns (after taxes at rate t_i are paid) are reinvested at the same rate of return, r, is simply

$$FVIF_i = [1 + r(1 - t_i)]^n \tag{1}$$

Equation 1 is simply a future value interest factor (FVIF) based on an after-tax return. For example, €100 invested at 6 percent per annum for ten years in an environment in which returns are taxed each year at a rate of 30 percent will accumulate to be €100[1 + 0.06(1 − 0.30)]^{10} = €150.90. Had returns not been taxed, this investment would have grown to €100[1 + 0.06(1 − 0.00)]^{10} = €179.08, a difference of €28.18. Notice that taxes reduce the potential gain on investment by (€179.08 − €150.90)/ (€179.08 − €100.00) = €28.18/€79.08 = 35.6 percent, which is more than the ordinary income tax rate. This suggests that the tax drag on capital accumulation compounds over time when taxes are paid each year. (Tax drag refers to the negative effect of taxes on after-tax returns.) By contrast, when taxes on gains are deferred until the end of the investment horizon, the tax rate equals the tax drag on capital accumulation as we shall see in the next section.

Exhibit 2 illustrates the impact of taxes on capital growth for various investment horizons and rates of return and demonstrates several conclusions. First, when investment returns are taxed annually, the effect of taxes on capital growth is greater than the nominal tax rate as noted above. Second, the adverse effects of taxes on capital growth increase over time. That is, the proportional difference between pretax and after-tax gains grows as the investment horizon increases. Third, the tax drag increases as the investment return increases, all else equal. Fourth, return and investment horizon have a multiplicative effect on the tax drag associated with future accumulations. Specifically, the impact of returns on the tax effect is greater for long investment horizons, and the impact of investment horizon is greater for higher returns because figures in the bottom right corner change more rapidly than figures in the upper left corner.

Exhibit 2	Proportion of Potential Investment Growth Consumed by Annual Taxes on Return							
	Investment Horizon in Years (n)							
r (%)	**5**	**10**	**15**	**20**	**25**	**30**	**35**	**40**
2	0.308	0.319	0.330	0.340	0.351	0.362	0.373	0.384
4	0.317	0.338	0.359	0.381	0.403	0.425	0.447	0.469

(continued)

Exhibit 2   (Continued)

r (%)	Investment Horizon in Years (n)							
	5	10	15	20	25	30	35	40
6	0.325	0.356	0.389	0.421	0.454	0.486	0.518	0.549
8	0.333	0.375	0.418	0.461	0.503	0.545	0.584	0.622
10	0.341	0.393	0.446	0.499	0.550	0.598	0.643	0.684
12	0.348	0.411	0.474	0.535	0.593	0.646	0.694	0.737
14	0.356	0.429	0.501	0.569	0.633	0.689	0.739	0.781
16	0.364	0.446	0.526	0.601	0.669	0.727	0.776	0.818
18	0.371	0.462	0.551	0.631	0.701	0.760	0.808	0.848

Note: The calculations assume a 30 percent annual tax rate on investment returns.

Conceptually, this framework could apply to securities, such as fixed-income instruments or preferred stock, in which most or possibly all of the return is subject to annual taxes. This is an oversimplification, of course, but we will address that concern below.

EXAMPLE 2

Accrual Taxes

Vladimir Kozloski is determining the impact of taxes on his expected investment returns and wealth accumulations. Kozloski lives in a tax jurisdiction with a flat tax rate of 20 percent which applies to all types of income and is taxed annually. Kozloski expects to earn 7 percent per year on his investment over a 20 year time horizon and has an initial portfolio of €100,000.

1   What is Kozloski's expected wealth at the end of 20 years?
2   What proportion of potential investment gains were consumed by taxes?

Solution to 1:

$$FV = €100,000 \times FVIF_i$$
$$= €100,000 \times [1 + 0.07(1 - 0.20)]^{20}$$
$$= €297,357.$$

Solution to 2:

Ignoring taxes, $FV = €100,000 [1 + 0.07]^{20} = €386,968$. The difference between this and the after tax amount accumulated from above is €89,611. The proportion of potential investment gains consumed by taxes was €89,611/€286,968 = 31.23 percent.

3.1.2 Returns-Based Taxes: Deferred Capital Gains

Another straightforward method of taxing returns is to focus on capital gains, the recognition of which can usually be deferred until realized, instead of interest income and dividends, which are generally taxable each year. A portfolio of non-dividend-paying stocks could fall under this type of framework. The analysis of global tax systems in the previous section indicates that it is very rare for unrealized investment gains to be taxed, so this implicit deferral mechanism has nearly universal application.

If the tax on an investment's return is deferred until the end of its investment horizon, n, and taxed as a capital gain at the rate t_{cg}, then the after-tax future accumulation for each unit of currency can be represented in several ways, including the following:

$$FVIF_{cg} = (1 + r)^n - [(1 + r)^n - 1]t_{cg} \qquad \text{(2a)}$$

$$FVIF_{cg} = (1 + r)^n(1 - t_{cg}) + t_{cg} \qquad \text{(2b)}$$

The first term of Equation 2a represents the pretax accumulation. The bracketed term is the capital gain (i.e., future accumulation less the original basis), while the entire second term represents the tax obligation on that gain. Viewed differently, the first term of Equation 2b represents the future accumulation if the entire sum (including the original basis) were subject to tax. The second term returns the tax of the untaxed cost (also known as cost basis or basis) associated with the initial investment.

For example, €100 invested at 6 percent for ten years in an environment in which capital gains are taxed at the end of that time at a rate of 30 percent will accumulate to be €100[(1 + 0.06)^{10}(1 − 0.30) + 0.30] = €155.36. Notice that this sum is greater than the €150.90 accumulated in the previous example using Equation 1, where returns are taxed annually at the same rate. This comparison illustrates the value of tax deferral.

Notice, as well, that the after-tax investment gain equals the pretax investment gain multiplied by one minus the tax rate. That is, €55.36 = €79.08 × (1 − 0.30). Whereas the tax drag on after-tax accumulations subject to annual accrual taxes compounds over time, the tax drag from deferred capital gains is a fixed percentage regardless of the investment return or time horizon. In other words, when deferral is permitted, the proportion of potential investment growth consumed by taxes is always the same as the tax rate, 30 percent in this case, which is less than that presented in Exhibit 2 when there was annual taxation.

Because the tax drag in Exhibit 2 increases with the investment return and time horizon, the value of a capital gain tax deferral also increases with the investment return and time horizon. One implication of the value of tax deferral is that investments taxed on a deferred capital gain basis can be more tax efficient (i.e., tax advantaged) than investments with returns that are taxed annually, all else equal, even if the marginal tax rate on the two is the same. Moreover, the difference compounds over time. The tax regime analysis from Exhibit 1 reveals that relatively few jurisdictions tax components of equity returns (dividends and capital gains) more heavily than interest income. There are rare exceptions where dividends (but usually not capital gains) are taxed to a greater extent than interest (such as the Heavy Dividend Tax Regime countries in Exhibit 1). Moreover, even if the tax rate on deferred capital gains is greater than the tax rate on interest income, the value of the deferral can more than offset a lower tax rate on annually taxed income, especially over time.

Exhibit 3 illustrates the value of tax deferral and its compounding effects more generally by presenting the ratio of after-tax accumulation in a deferred capital gain regime to after-tax accumulation in a regime in which returns are taxed annually. For example, with a 6 percent annual return, 20-year time horizon and a 30 percent tax rate, the accumulation of €100 in a deferred capital gain environment, is €100[(1 + 0.06)^{20}(1 − 0.30) + 0.30] = €254.50. In an annual taxation environment, it is €100[1 + 0.06(1 − 0.30)]^{20} = €227.70. Therefore, a deferred capital gain environment accumulates €254.50/€227.70 = 1.118 times the amount accumulated in an annual taxation environment. The relative accumulations can be substantially larger when gains are deferred for long time horizons, especially for high returns. It is important to note, however, that the advantages of tax deferral can be offset or even eliminated if securities taxed on an accrual basis have greater risk-adjusted returns.

Exhibit 3	Ratio of Future Accumulations: Accumulation in a Deferred Capital Gain Environment to Accumulation in an Annual Taxation Environment

	Investment Horizon in Years (n)							
r (%)	5	10	15	20	25	30	35	40
2	1.001	1.004	1.008	1.015	1.023	1.033	1.045	1.058
4	1.003	1.014	1.031	1.056	1.086	1.123	1.165	1.213
6	1.007	1.030	1.067	1.118	1.181	1.257	1.346	1.447
8	1.012	1.050	1.113	1.198	1.305	1.432	1.582	1.754
10	1.018	1.075	1.169	1.294	1.453	1.644	1.871	2.136
12	1.025	1.104	1.232	1.405	1.624	1.892	2.214	2.598
14	1.033	1.137	1.303	1.529	1.818	2.177	2.616	3.149
16	1.041	1.172	1.380	1.666	2.035	2.500	3.080	3.799
18	1.050	1.210	1.464	1.814	2.273	2.862	3.612	4.561

Note: The calculations assume a 30 percent annual tax rate on investment returns and a 30 percent tax rate on deferred capital gains.

In many countries, the rate applied to capital gains is lower than the rate applied to interest income. In such cases, the investor gets a dual benefit from returns in the form of capital gains: deferral of taxation and a favorable tax rate when gains are realized. The capital gain tax rate may also vary depending on the holding period. Longer holding periods may receive a lower tax rate to encourage long-term rather than short-term investment. Australia, for example, taxes short-term gains (i.e., holding period less than 12 months) at ordinary rates. Only half the gains on assets held for more than 12 months are taxed, however, making the effective long-term capital gain tax rate half of the rate on ordinary income. In such cases the investor gets a dual benefit; deferral of taxation and a favorable rate on realized gains. The holding period can vary. Belgium and the Czech Republic, for example, require a five-year holding period to receive preferential tax treatment on capital gains.

EXAMPLE 3

Deferred Capital Gains

Assume the same facts as in Example 2. Kozloski invests €100,000 at 7 percent. However, the return comes in the form of deferred capital gains that are not taxed until the investment is sold in 20 years hence.

1 What is Kozloski's expected wealth at the end of 20 years?

2 What proportion of potential investment gains were consumed by taxes?

Solution to 1:

$$FV = €100{,}000 \times FVIF_{cg} = €100{,}000 \times [(1 + 0.07)^{20}(1 - t) + t]$$
$$= €100{,}000 \times [(1 + 0.07)^{20}(1 - 0.20) + 0.20] = €329{,}575.$$

> **Solution to 2:**
>
> Ignoring taxes, FV = €100,000 $[1 + 0.07]^{20}$ = €386,968. The difference between this and the after-tax amount accumulated from above is €57,393. The proportion of potential investment gains consumed by taxes was €57,393/€286,968 = 20.0 percent. This result compares favorably to the potential investment gains consumed by taxes in Example 2.

3.1.3 *Cost Basis*

In taxation, cost basis is generally the amount that was paid to acquire an asset. It serves as the foundation for calculating a capital gain, which equals the selling price less the cost basis. The taxable gain increases as the basis decreases. In consequence, capital gain taxes increase as the basis decreases. In some circumstances, this basis may be adjusted under tax regulations or carry over from another taxpayer. The previous capital gains examples assume that cash is newly invested so that the cost basis was equal to the current market value. That is, the tax liability at the end of the investment horizon is based on the difference between the pretax ending value and the current market value today.

In many cases, an investment being evaluated today was purchased some time ago and has a cost basis that is different from the current market value. If a security has risen in value since its initial purchase, the cost basis may be less than its current market value. Cost basis affects an investment's after-tax accumulation because it determines the taxable capital gain. Specifically, the after-tax cash flow from liquidation increases as the cost basis increases, holding all else equal. Put differently, an investment with a low cost basis has a current embedded tax liability because, if it were liquidated today, capital gain tax would be owed even before future capital growth is considered. Newly invested cash has no such current tax liability.

If the cost basis is expressed as a proportion, B, of the current market value of the investment, then the future after-tax accumulation can be expressed by simply subtracting this additional tax liability from the expression in either Equation 2a or 2b. In other words,

$$FVIF_{cgb} = (1 + r)^n (1 - t_{cg}) + t_{cg} - (1 - B)t_{cg} \qquad \textbf{(3a)}$$

Notice that if cost basis is equal to the initial investment, then $B = 1$ and the last term simply reduces to Equation 2b. The lower the cost basis, however, the greater the embedded tax liability and the lower the future accumulation. Distributing and canceling terms produces

$$FVIF_{cgb} = (1 + r)^n (1 - t_{cg}) + t_{cg} B \qquad \textbf{(3b)}$$

This form resembles Equation 2b, and the last term represents the return of basis at the end of the investment horizon. The lower the basis, the lower is the return of basis. For example, suppose an investment has a current market value of €100 and a cost basis of €80. The gain when realized will be subject to a capital gains tax of 30 percent. The cost basis is equal to 80 percent of the current market value of €100. If it grows at 6 percent for 10 years, the future after-tax accumulation is €100 $[(1.06)^{10}(1 - 0.30) + (0.30)(0.80)]$ = €149.36, which is €6 less than the €155.36 accumulation that would result if the basis were equal to €100. The €6 difference represents the tax liability associated with the embedded capital gain.

EXAMPLE 4

Cost Basis

Continuing with the facts in Examples 2 and 3, Kozloski has a current investment with a market value of €100,000 and cost basis of €80,000. The stock price grows at 7 percent per year for 20 years.

1 Express the cost basis as a percent of the current market value.

2 What is Kozloski's expected wealth after 20 years?

Solution to 1:

Cost basis/Current market value = B = €80,000/€100,000 = 0.80.

Solution to 2:

$$
\begin{aligned}
FV &= €100,000 \times FVIF_{cbg} \\
&= €100,000 \times [(1 + 0.07)^{20}(1 - 0.20) + 0.20(0.80)] \\
&= €325,575.
\end{aligned}
$$

This amount is €4,000 smaller than Kozloski's expected wealth in Example 3, in which it was assumed that the cost basis equaled the current market value.

3.1.4 *Wealth-Based Taxes*

Some jurisdictions impose a wealth tax, which is applied annually to a specific capital base. Often the wealth tax is restricted to real estate investments (e.g., Australia, Singapore, Belgium, Germany, and the United Kingdom). In other countries, it is levied on aggregate assets including financial assets above a certain threshold (e.g., Colombia). If limited to real estate holdings, the tax may be levied at the federal level or a municipal level. In any case, the wealth tax rate tends to be much lower than capital gains or interest income rates because it applies to the entire capital base—i.e., principal and return—rather than just the return.

The expression for an after-tax accumulation subject to a wealth tax is therefore different from the previous scenarios in which only incremental gains are taxed. If wealth is taxed annually at a rate of t_w, then after n years each unit of currency accumulates to

$$
FVIF_w = [(1 + r)(1 - t_w)]^n \tag{4}
$$

For example, if wealth capital is taxed at 2 percent, then €100 invested at 6 percent for ten years will grow to $[(1.06)(1 - 0.02)]^{10}$ = €146.33. Because the form of a wealth tax differs from the form of taxes on either investment returns or deferred capital gains, this figure is not comparable to the previous two examples. This figure is substantially less than the pretax accumulation of €179.08, however. In other words, the two percent wealth tax consumed 41.4 percent of the investment growth that would have accrued over ten years in the absence of a wealth tax (i.e., (€79.08 − €46.33)/€79.08).

Exhibit 4 illustrates the impact of a wealth tax on investment growth for various rates of return and investment horizons. Because wealth taxes apply to the capital base, the absolute magnitude of the liability they generate (measured in units of currency) is less sensitive to investment return than taxes based on returns. Consequently, the proportion of investment growth that it consumes decreases as returns increase. Viewed differently, a wealth tax consumes a greater proportion of investment growth when returns are low. In fact, when returns are flat or negative, a wealth tax effectively reduces principal. Like the previous two types of taxes, however, the wealth tax consumes a greater share of investment growth as the investment horizon increases.

Exhibit 4	Proportion of Investment Growth Consumed by Wealth Taxes							
	Investment Horizon in Years (n)							
r (%)	**5**	**10**	**15**	**20**	**25**	**30**	**35**	**40**
4	0.540	0.564	0.588	0.611	0.635	0.657	0.679	0.700
6	0.380	0.414	0.449	0.483	0.517	0.550	0.583	0.614
8	0.301	0.341	0.382	0.423	0.464	0.505	0.544	0.581
10	0.253	0.298	0.344	0.390	0.437	0.482	0.526	0.567
12	0.222	0.270	0.320	0.371	0.421	0.470	0.517	0.560
14	0.200	0.250	0.304	0.358	0.412	0.464	0.512	0.557
16	0.183	0.237	0.293	0.350	0.406	0.460	0.510	0.556
18	0.171	0.226	0.285	0.345	0.403	0.458	0.508	0.555

Note: The calculations assume a 2 percent annual wealth tax.

EXAMPLE 5

Wealth Tax

Olga Sanford lives in a country that imposes a wealth tax of 1.0 percent on financial assets each year. Her €400,000 portfolio is expected to return 6 percent over the next ten years.

1   What is Sanford's expected wealth at the end of ten years?
2   What proportion of investment gains was consumed by taxes?

Solution to 1:

$$FV = €400,000[(1.06)(1 - 0.01)]^{10} = €647,844.$$

Solution to 2:

Had the wealth tax not existed, $FV = €400,000(1.06)^{10} = €716,339$. This sum represents a €316,339 investment gain compared to a €247,844 gain in the presence of the wealth tax. Therefore, the one percent wealth tax consumed 21.65 percent of the investment gain (i.e., (€316,339 – €247,844)/€316,339).

3.2 Blended Taxing Environments

The discussion in the previous section is an oversimplification because each model assumes that investment gains were taxed according to only one of a number of possible taxes. In reality, portfolios are subject to a variety of different taxes depending on the types of securities they hold, how frequently they are traded, and the direction of returns. The different taxing schemes mentioned above can be integrated into a single framework in which a portion of a portfolio's investment return is received in the form of dividends (p_d) and taxed at a rate of t_d; another portion is received in the form of interest income (p_i) and taxed as such at a rate of t_i; and another portion is taxed as realized capital gain (p_{cg}) at t_{cg}. The remainder of an investment's return is unrealized capital gain, the tax on which is deferred until ultimately recognized at the end of the investment horizon.[5] These return proportions can be computed by simply dividing each income component by the total dollar return.

EXAMPLE 6

Blended Tax Environment

Zahid Kharullah has a balanced portfolio of stocks and bonds. At the beginning of the year, his portfolio has a market value of €100,000. By the end of the year, the portfolio was worth €108,000 before any annual taxes had been paid, and there were no contributions or withdrawals. Interest of €400 and dividends of €2,000 were reinvested into the portfolio. During the year, Kharullah had €3,600 of realized capital gains. These proceeds were again reinvested into the portfolio.

1   What percentage of Kharullah's return is in the form of interest?

2   What percentage of Kharullah's return is in the form of dividends?

3   What percentage of Kharullah's return is in the form of realized capital gain?

4   What percentage of Kharullah's return is in the form of deferred capital gain?

Solution to 1:

p_i = €400/€8,000 = 0.05 or 5 percent.

Solution to 2:

p_d = €2,000/€8,000 = 0.25 or 25 percent.

Solution to 3:

p_{cg} = €3,600/€8,000 = 0.45 or 45 percent.

Solution to 4:

Unrealized gain = €8,000 − €400 − €2,000 − €3,600 = €2,000. Expressed as a percentage of return, €2,000/€8,000 = 0.25, or 25 percent. The unrealized gain is the portion of investment appreciation that was not taxed as either interest, dividends, or realized capital gain.

In this setting, the annual return after realized taxes can be expressed as

$$r^* = r(1 - p_i t_i - p_d t_d - p_{cg} t_{cg})$$

In this case, r represents the pre-tax overall return on the portfolio. From the preceding example, note that the pre-tax return was 8 percent [(€108,000/€100,000) − 1], however there would be taxes due on the interest, dividends and realized capital gains. The effective annual after-tax return, r^*, reflects the tax erosion caused by a portion of the return being taxed as ordinary income and other portions being taxed as realized capital gain and dividends. It does not capture tax effects of deferred unrealized capital

---

5 Capital gains are almost always taxed when recognized. Some countries, such as Denmark and Australia, however, impose an exit tax on some unrealized gains for residents who become non-residents. In Canada, capital gains are taxed at death as if realized unless the property is transferred to a surviving spouse.

gains. One can view this expression as being analogous to the simple expression in which after-tax return equals the pretax return times one minus the tax rate. The aggregate tax rate has several components in this case, but the intuition is the same.[6]

EXAMPLE 7

Blended Tax Environment: After Tax Return

Continuing with the facts in Example 6, assume that dividends and realized capital gains are taxed at 15 percent annually while interest is taxed at 35 percent annually.

1 What is the annual return after realized taxes?

2 Assuming taxes are paid out of the investment account, what is the balance in the account at the end of the first year?

Solution to 1:

$$r^* = r(1 - p_i t_i - p_d t_d - p_{cg} t_{cg})$$
$$= 8\%[1 - (0.05 \times 0.35) - (0.25 \times 0.15) - (0.45 \times 0.15)]$$
$$= 7.02\%$$

Solution to 2:

Using the income data from above,

Income Type	Income Amount (€)	Tax Rate (%)	Tax Due (€)
Interest	400	35	140
Dividends	2,000	15	300
Realized capital gains	3,600	15	<u>540</u>
Total tax due			980

After paying taxes there would be €107,020 in the account (€108,000 − €980). Note that this is consistent with the 7.02 percent return computed for the first question.

A portion of the investment return has avoided annual taxation, and tax on that portion would then be deferred until the end of the investment horizon. Holding the tax rate on capital gains constant, the impact of deferred capital gain taxes will be diminished as more of the return is taxed annually in some way as described above. Conversely, as less of the return is taxed annually, more of the return will be subject to deferred capital gains. One can express the impact of deferred capital gain taxes using an effective capital gain tax rate that adjusts the capital gains tax rate gain t_{cg} to reflect previously taxed dividends, income, or realized capital gains. The effective capital gains tax rate can be expressed as[7]

$$T^* = t_{cg}(1 - p_i - p_d - p_{cg})/(1 - p_i t_i - p_d t_d - p_{cg} t_{cg})$$

---

6 This expression could be expanded to incorporate any number of different taxable components, such as a different rate for short term capital gains or special treatment of certain types of taxable income. The general principle is that a portfolio can generate return in different forms, each of which may be taxed differently.
7 Horan and Peterson (2001) and Horan (2002) provide more thorough developments of these expressions.

The adjustment to the capital gains tax rate takes account of the fact that some of the investment return had previously been taxed as interest income, dividends, or realized capital gain before the end of the investment horizon and will not be taxed again as a capital gain.

The future after-tax accumulation for each unit of currency in a taxable portfolio can then be represented by

$$FVIF_{Taxable} = (1 + r^*)^n(1 - T^*) + T^* - (1 - B)t_{cg} \qquad \text{(5)}$$

Although this formulation appears unwieldy, $(1 + r^*)^n(1 - T^*) + T^*$ is analogous to the after-tax accumulation for an investment taxed entirely as a deferred capital gain in Equation 3. The only difference is that r^* is substituted for r, and T^* is substituted for t_{cg} in most places.[8]

Different assets and asset classes generate different amounts of return as interest income, dividends, or capital gain, and will thus have different values for p_i, p_d, and p_{cg}. Moreover, Equation 5 can replace the equations introduced in the previous sections.[9] For example, the return on a hypothetical taxable bond with no capital appreciation or depreciation over the course of a tax year might be taxed entirely at ordinary rates so that $p_i = 1$, $p_d = 0$, and $p_{cg} = 0$. If the cost basis is equal to market value (i.e., $B = 1$), the expression for the after-tax future value simply reduces to $[1 + r(1 - t_i)]^n$.

On the other hand, the return for a passive investor with a growth portfolio of non-dividend paying stocks and no portfolio turnover may be entirely tax-deferred such that $p_d = 0$, $p_i = 0$ and $p_{cg} = 0$, and the future value reduces to $(1 + r)^n(1 - t_{cg}) + t_{cg}$. The return for an active investor with a similar growth portfolio might be composed entirely of realized long-term capital gains and taxed annually at t_{cg} in which case $p_d = p_i = 0$ and $p_{cg} = 1$, and the after-tax future value is $[1 + r(1 - t_{cg})]^n$.

Most accounts conform to none of these extremes, but can be accommodated by simply specifying the proper distribution rates for interest income, dividends, and capital gain. It is useful then to have an understanding of how investment style affects the tax-related parameters (e.g., p_i, p_d, and p_{cg}).

EXAMPLE 8

Blended Tax Environment: Future Long Term Accumulation

Continuing with the facts in the previous example, assume there is a five-year investment horizon for the account. Annual accrual taxes will be paid out of the account each year with the deferred tax on previously unrealized capital gains paid at the end of the five-year horizon. The account is rebalanced annually. Consider a €100,000 portfolio with the return and tax profile listed in Panel A of Exhibit 5. What is the expected after-tax accumulation in five years?

Exhibit 5   Hypothetical Tax Profile

Panel A: Tax Profile		
	Annual Distribution Rate (p)	Tax Rate (T)
Ordinary Income (i)	5%	35%
Dividends (d)	25%	15%

---

8 Although Equation 5 ignores the wealth tax, it could be modified to incorporate it.

9 Equation 5 does not replace the equation for the wealth tax. It can be modified, however, to do so.

Exhibit 5 (Continued)		

Panel A: Tax Profile		
	Annual Distribution Rate (p)	Tax Rate (T)
Capital Gain (cg)	45%	15%
Investment Horizon (n)		5 years
Average Return (r)		8%
Cost Basis		€100,000

Panel B: Intermediate Accumulation Calculations	
Annual after-tax return (r^*)	7.02%
Effective capital gains tax rate (T^*)	4.27%

In this case, 25 percent of the return is composed of dividends; 5 percent is composed of realized short-term capital gains; and 45 percent is composed of realized long-term gains. These figures imply that the remaining 25 percent (i.e., $1 - 0.05 - 0.25 - 0.45$) of portfolio returns are deferred capital gains and not taxed until the end of the investment horizon.

The annual return after realized taxes, r^*, is $0.08[1 - (0.05)(0.35) - (0.25)(0.15) - (0.45)(0.15)] = 7.02$ percent as computed previously. This figure reflects the annual return after having accounted for the tax drag imposed by annually levied taxes on the portion of return composed of elements like dividends, interest, and realized capital gains. It does not take into account, however, tax obligations from gains not yet realized; that effect is considered in the effective capital gains tax rate, T^*, which equals $0.15[(1 - 0.05 - 0.25 - 0.45)/(1 - 0.05 \times 0.35 - 0.25 \times 0.15 - 0.45 \times 0.15)] = 0.15(0.25/0.8775) = 4.27$ percent. The figure is relatively low in this example because a relatively small proportion of return, 25 percent, is subject to deferred capital gains tax.

Because the cost basis and the current market value portfolio are both €100,000, the cost basis expressed as a percent of current market value is 1.00. Substituting these intermediate results into Equation 5, the expected future accumulation of the portfolio in 5 years equals $€100,000[(1 + r^*)^n(1 - T^*) + T^* - (1 - B)t_{cg}] = €100,000[(1.0702)^5(1 - 0.0427) + 0.0427 - (1 - 1.00)0.15] = €138,662$.

3.3 Accrual Equivalent Returns and Tax Rates

Because returns can come in various forms and be taxed in various ways, an overall understanding of the impact of taxes on return can be obscure. A useful way to summarize the impact of taxes on portfolio returns is to calculate an accrual equivalent after-tax return. Conceptually, an accrual equivalent after-tax return is the tax-free return that, if accrued annually, produces the same after-tax accumulation as the taxable portfolio.[10] For example, in the previous example Kharullah's €100,000 portfolio earned an 8 percent return before taxes and will grow to €138,662 over a 5 year period after accrued and deferred taxes are considered. The tax-free return that will accumulate

---

[10] This term is coined by Poterba (2000).

€138,662 over 5 years is the accrual equivalent return. The difference between the accrual equivalent return and the taxable return of 8 percent is a measure of the tax drag imposed on the portfolio.

An analogous way to measure tax drag is with the accrual equivalent tax rate. An accrual equivalent tax rate finds the annual accrual tax rate (of the simple form described in Section 3.1.1) that would produce the same after-tax accumulation as a tax system based in whole or in part on deferred realized gains (such as those described in Sections 3.1.2 or 3.2). Both these concepts recognize that deferring taxes through unrealized gains does not eliminate the tax liability but moves its payment through time.

3.3.1 *Calculating Accrual Equivalent Returns*

Calculating accrual equivalent returns is straightforward. In the previous example, the €100,000 portfolio has an after-tax accumulation 5 years hence of €138,662. The accrual equivalent return is found by solving for the return that equates the standard future value formula to the after-tax accumulation and solving for the return. In this example, we solve the following equation for R_{AE}:

$$€100,000(1 + R_{AE})^5 = €138,662$$

The accrual equivalent return, R_{AE}, is 6.756 percent. Notice that this rate is less than the annual return after realized taxes, r^*, of 7.02 percent because the accrual equivalent return incorporates the impact of deferred taxes on realized gains as well as taxes that accrue annually. The accrual equivalent return is always less than the taxable return, r. It approaches the annual return after realized taxes, however, as the time horizon increases. This phenomenon demonstrates the value of tax deferral. The value of deferral in this example is relatively modest, however, because only 25 percent of the tax obligation associated with the return is assumed to be deferred. If more of the return is in the form of deferred gains, the value of the deferral increases.

3.3.2 *Calculating Accrual Equivalent Tax Rates*

The accrual equivalent tax rate is derived from the accrual equivalent return. It is the hypothetical tax rate, T_{AE}, that produces an after-tax return equivalent to the accrual equivalent return. In our example, it is found by solving for T_{AE} in the following expression:

$$r(1 - T_{AE}) = R_{AE} \tag{6}$$

In the blended tax regime example, $0.08(1 - T_{AE}) = 0.06756$. Solving for T_{AE}, the accrual equivalent tax rate is therefore, 0.1555 or 15.55 percent. This rate is much lower than the marginal tax rate on ordinary income and only slightly higher than the favorable rate on dividends and capital gains in this example because a relatively small portion (i.e., 5 percent) of the portfolio's return is generated from highly taxed income. Most of the return receives preferential tax treatment in either the form of a reduced rate for dividends or a reduced rate on realized capital gains combined with valuable deferral for unrealized gains. As a result, investments with this tax profile are relatively tax efficient. The accrual equivalent tax rate would increase if either the return had a larger component taxed at ordinary rates, or if dividends and capital gains received less favorable treatment. In either case, R_{AE} would be smaller, implying a higher value of T_{AE} for a given level of pretax return r in Equation 6.

The accrual equivalent tax rate can be used in several ways. First, it can be used to measure the tax efficiency of different asset classes or portfolio management styles. Second, it illustrates to clients the tax impact of lengthening the average holding periods of stocks they own. Third, it can be used to assess the impact of future tax law changes. If the client's tax rate is likely to change in the future, the manager can determine the impact of the expected change on the accrual equivalent tax rate. The future tax rate could change for several reasons such as tax law changes, changes in client circumstances, or the client taking advantage of tax rules designed to encourage certain behaviors such as charitable contributions which may be deductible in some tax regimes.

EXAMPLE 9

Accrual Equivalent Return

We extend Example 3 with the same facts repeated here: Vladimir Kozloski is determining the impact of taxes on his expected investment returns and wealth accumulations. Kozloski lives in a tax jurisdiction with a flat tax rate of 20 percent, which applies to all types of income and is taxed annually. He expects to earn 7 percent per year on his investment over a 20-year time horizon and has an initial portfolio of €100,000. The 7 percent return is expected to come from deferred capital gains, which are not taxed until sold in 20 years. Kozloski's expected wealth at the end of 20 years is:

$$FV = €100,000 \times FVIF_{cg} = €100,000 \times [(1 + 0.07)^{20}(1 - 0.2) + 0.2]$$
$$= €329,575$$

1 What is the accrual equivalent return?
2 What is the accrual equivalent tax rate?

Solution to 1:

$$€100,000(1 + R_{AE})^{20} = €329,575$$

$$R_{AE} = 6.1446 \text{ percent}$$

Kozloski would be just as well off if he could find a tax-free investment earning 6.1446 percent.

Solution to 2:

$$0.07(1 - T_{AE}) = 0.061446$$

$$T_{AE} = 12.22 \text{ percent}$$

This rate is lower than the stated tax rate on dividends because there is an advantage from the deferral of taxes.

TYPES OF INVESTMENT ACCOUNTS

4

The previous section examined models for taxable accounts in which the tax profile was determined by the asset class and/or the portfolio management style. The impact of taxes on future accumulations often depends heavily on the type of account in which assets are held. Many countries have account structures with different tax profiles designed to provide some relief to the taxable investor. These structures are often intended to encourage retirement savings, but may also accommodate savings for health care and education. Most industrialized and developing countries have tax incentives to encourage retirement savings. An international survey of 24 industrialized and developing countries commissioned by the American Council for Capital Formation

(ACCF) indicates that tax-advantaged savings accounts are offered to taxpayers by two-thirds of the countries surveyed, including Australia, Canada, Germany, Italy, the Netherlands, and the United Kingdom.[11]

Most types of investment accounts can be classified into three categories. The first type is taxable accounts. Investments to these accounts are made on an after-tax basis and returns can be taxed in a variety of ways as discussed in the previous section. A second class of accounts can be called tax-deferred accounts, or TDAs. Contributions to these accounts may be made on a pretax basis (i.e., tax-deductible), and the investment returns accumulate on a tax-deferred basis until funds are withdrawn at which time they are taxed at ordinary rates. As such, these accounts are sometimes said to have front-end loaded tax benefits. All but one of the countries in the ACCF study have some kind of retirement account that permits tax deductible contributions. In Canada they are called Registered Retirement Savings Plans (RRSPs), and in the United States some are called Individual Retirement Accounts (IRAs). In some countries, like Australia and Chile, individuals are mandated to contribute a fixed proportion of their income to these accounts. Many types of defined contribution pension plans, whether sponsored by the state or an employer, fall into this category. Argentina, for example, offers citizens the option to make contributions to a public pension fund company.

A third class of accounts has back-end loaded tax benefits. These accounts can be called tax-exempt (at least on a forward-looking basis) because although contributions are not deductible, earnings accumulate free of taxation even as funds are withdrawn, typically subject to some conditions. An example is the Roth IRA in the United States.

4.1 Tax-Deferred Accounts

Assets held in a TDA accumulate on a tax deferred basis. Tax is owed when funds are withdrawn at the end of an investment horizon at which time withdrawals are taxed at ordinary rates or another rate, T_n, prevailing at the end of the investment horizon. The future after-tax accumulation of a contribution to a TDA is therefore equal to

$$FVIF_{TDA} = (1 + r)^n (1 - T_n) \tag{7}$$

The form of Equation 7 is similar to the future value interest factor when tax is based entirely on capital gains that are recognized at the end of the investment horizon with a cost basis equal to zero (see Equation 3).

4.2 Tax-Exempt Accounts

Tax-exempt accounts have no future tax liabilities. Earnings accumulate without tax consequence and withdrawals create no taxable event. Therefore, the future accumulation of a tax-exempt account is simply

$$FVIF_{TaxEx} = (1 + r)^n \tag{8}$$

Potential insights are available in comparing Equations 7 and 8. First, we notice that $FVIF_{TDA} = FVIF_{TaxEx}(1 - T_n)$, which means that future after-tax accumulation of assets held in a tax deferred account are less than the after-tax accumulation of the same assets when held in a tax-exempt account regardless of the type of asset (assuming equivalent returns). Put simply, assets in a TDA have a built-in tax liability whereas assets in a tax-exempt account do not. It can be shown that the value of an asset held in a TDA measured on an after-tax basis is therefore equal to $(1 - T_n)$ times the value

---

11 American Council for Capital Formation, "An International Comparison of Incentives for Retirement Saving and Insurance" (June 1999).

of the same asset held in a tax-exempt account. The taxing authority essentially owns T_n of the principal value of a TDA, regardless of the type of asset held in it, leaving the investor effectively owning only $(1 - T_n)$ of the principal.

EXAMPLE 10

Comparing Accumulations of Account Types

Extending Examples 2 and 3, recall that Vladimir Kozloski lives in a tax jurisdiction with a flat tax rate of 20 percent which applies to all types of income. Kozloski expects to earn 7 percent per year on his investment over a 20 year time horizon and has an initial portfolio of €100,000. Assume that Kozloski has the following current investments:

1 €100,000 invested in a taxable account earning 7 percent taxed annually

2 €100,000 invested in a taxable account earning 7 percent deferred capital gains (cost basis = €100,000)

3 €100,000 invested in a tax deferred account earning 7 percent

4 €100,000 invested in a tax exempt account earning 7 percent

Compute the after-tax wealth for each account at the end of 20 years assuming all assets are sold and accounts liquidated at the end of 20 years and assuming a tax rate of 20 percent.

Solution to 1:

$$FVIF = €100,000[1 + 0.07(1 - 0.20)]^{20} = €297,357$$

Solution to 2:

$$FVIF = €100,000[(1 + 0.07)^{20}(1 - 0.20) + 0.20] = €329,575$$

Solution to 3:

$$FVIF = €100,000[(1 + 0.07)^{20}(1 - 0.20)] = €309,575$$

Solution to 4:

$$FVIF = €100,000[(1 + 0.07)^{20}] = €386,968$$

4.3 After-Tax Asset Allocation

The notion that a TDA is worth $(1 - T_n)$ times an otherwise equivalent tax-exempt account has implications for after-tax asset allocation, which is the distribution of asset classes in a portfolio measured on an after-tax basis. Consider, for example, an investor with €1,500,000 worth of stock held in a TDA and €500,000 of bonds held in a tax-exempt account as displayed in Exhibit 6. Withdrawals from the TDA account will be taxed at 40 percent. A traditional view of asset allocation based on pretax values would suggest the investor has €2,000,000 of assets, 75 percent of which are allocated in stocks and 25 percent of which are allocated in bonds. In after-tax terms, however, the total portfolio is worth only €1,400,000 because the TDA has a built-in tax liability of €600,000, money the investor cannot spend. Moreover, because the investor is holding stock in the TDA, her after-tax equity exposure is less than a pretax analysis would suggest. Specifically, the after-tax equity allocation is only 64.3 percent rather than 75 percent.[12]

Exhibit 6	Simple Example of After-Tax Asset Allocation				
Account Type	Asset Class	Pretax Market Value (€)	Pretax Weights (%)	After-Tax Market Value (€)	After-Tax Weights (%)
TDA	Stock	1,500,000	75	900,000	64.3
Tax-Exempt	Bonds	500,000	25	500,000	35.7
Total Portfolio		2,000,000	100	1,400,000	100

Note: Withdrawals at the end of the investment horizon are assumed to be taxed at a rate of 40 percent.

This simple example excludes taxable accounts and does not depend on an investor's time horizon. However, the after-tax value of taxable accounts may depend on an investor's time horizon, which can be difficult to estimate and may change over time. Therefore, estimating an investor's time horizon presents a potential impediment to incorporating after-tax asset allocation in portfolio management. Another challenge is improving client awareness, understanding, and comfort with asset allocation from an after-tax perspective. Suppose an adviser increases pretax equity exposure to achieve a target after-tax asset allocation. Her client may have difficulty accepting the notion of after-tax asset allocation, especially in a bear market when the extra equity exposure would hinder performance.

4.4 Choosing Among Account Types

A euro invested in a tax-exempt account always has a higher after-tax future value than a euro invested in a TDA, all else equal. Based on this, one may infer that it is always better to save in a tax-exempt account instead of a TDA. That conclusion would be premature, however, because the comparison overlooks the fact that contributions to TDAs are often tax-deductible whereas contributions to the tax-exempt accounts considered here generally are not.

Let's compare after-tax future values of contributions of a *pretax* euro to a tax-exempt account and a TDA. Because contributions to a tax-exempt account are taxable, a pretax investment is reduced by taxes such that the after-tax investment is $(1 - T_0)$, where T_0 is the tax rate applicable to the initial pretax contribution. The future value of a pretax dollar invested in a tax-exempt account is therefore $(1 - T_0)(1 + r)^n$. This expression reflects that taxes reduce the initial investment. The future value of a pretax dollar invested in a TDA is $(1 + r)^n(1 - T_n)$ because withdrawals are taxed at T_n. The only difference between the equations is the beginning and ending tax rates. The tax-exempt account is taxed at today's rate, T_0, while the TDA is eventually taxed at the tax rate in the withdrawal year, T_n. Therefore, comparing the attractiveness of the two types of accounts reduces to comparing the tax rate today to the expected tax rate when funds are withdrawn. If the prevailing tax rate when funds are withdrawn is less than the tax rate when they are invested, the TDA will accumulate more after-tax wealth than the tax-exempt account, and vice versa.

---

[12] Reichenstein (1998, 2001, 2006, 2007) and Horan (2007a and 2007b) develop the concept of after-tax asset allocation in more detail.

For example, consider an investor currently in the 40 percent tax bracket who is willing to forego €1,200 of spending this year. He could invest €2,000 pretax dollars in a TDA or €1,200 after taxes in a tax-exempt account. Both investments will reduce this year's spending by €1,200 because the €2,000 TDA contribution would reduce this year's taxes by €800. He invests in an asset that earns a 5 percent annual return for ten years. Assuming his tax rate is unchanged, in ten years, the TDA will be worth €2,000$(1.05)^{10}$(1 − 0.40) = €1,955 after taxes. The tax-exempt account will be worth €1,200$(1.05)^{10}$ = €1,955, the same as the TDA.

In this example, he could invest €2,000 in the TDA or €1,200 in the tax-exempt account; a contribution limit did not affect his choice of account type. However, annual contribution limits are usually expressed as a set amount whether the contribution is made with pretax or after-tax funds. A €2,000 contribution of after-tax funds to a tax-exempt account is effectively a larger contribution than a €2,000 contribution of pretax funds to a TDA. As a result, the tax-exempt account allows the investor to put more after-tax funds in a tax-sheltered account than a TDA, all else equal. Horan (2003, 2005) developed a more general approach that incorporates contribution limits in the balance of considerations.

Suppose, however, that the investor's tax rate upon withdrawal will be 20 percent, which is lower than his current tax rate. The future value of the €1,200 contribution to tax-exempt accumulation is unchanged at €1,955, but the TDA accumulation increases to €2,606 or 2,000$(1.05)^{10}$(1 − 0.20) making the TDA the better choice. The decision would be reversed if the tax rate at withdrawal exceeds the current tax rate.

EXAMPLE 11

Choosing Among Account Types

Bettye Mims would like to invest for retirement and is willing to reduce this year's spending by €3,000. She will invest €3,000 *after taxes* this year and is in a 25 percent tax bracket, which is the top marginal tax rate in her jurisdiction. Mims is considering three types of accounts but would invest in the same portfolio which is expected to have a pre-tax return of 6 percent annually. If invested in a taxable account the income would be taxed each year at the same 25 percent rate.

Assuming Mims will make a single contribution today and withdraw all funds—paying any necessary taxes in 30 years—which of the following accounts will result in the largest after-tax accumulation?

- *Account A*. A taxable account with an initial investment of €3,000.

- *Account B*. A tax deferred account, where Mims can make a €4,000 tax deductible contribution (a €3,000 after tax cost to Mims).

- *Account C*. A tax exempt account, where a €3,000 contribution is not deductible.

Solution:

The taxable account would accumulate €11,236 after taxes:

For A, $FVIF$ = €3,000$[1 + 0.06(1 − 0.25)]^{30}$ = €11,236

The tax deferred account would accumulate €17,230 after taxes:

For B, $FVIF$ = €4,000$[(1 + 0.06)^{30}(1 − 0.25)]$ = €17,230

The tax exempt account would also accumulate €17,230 after taxes:

For C, $FVIF$ = €3,000$[(1 + 0.06)^{30}]$ = €17,230

> Both B and C achieve the same after-tax accumulation assuming her tax rates in the contribution year and withdrawal year are the same.

5   TAXES AND INVESTMENT RISK

It is fairly obvious that taxes reduce returns. Less obvious is the impact of taxes on investment risk. A fundamental premise regarding taxes and risk is that, by taxing investment returns, a government shares risk as well as return with the investor. Because the returns on assets held in TDAs and tax-exempt accounts are not currently taxed, investors bear all of the risk associated with returns in these accounts. Even in the case of TDAs in which the government effectively owns T_n of the principal, the variability of an investor's return in relation to the current after-tax principal value is unaffected by the tax on withdrawals.[13]

Because the returns on assets held in taxable accounts are typically taxed annually in some way, investors bear only a fraction of the risk associated with these assets. Suppose asset returns are taxed entirely as ordinary income at a rate of t_i. If the standard deviation of pretax returns is σ, returns are fully taxed at ordinary rates (and all investment losses can be recognized for tax purposes in the year they are incurred), then the standard deviation of after-tax returns for a taxable account is $\sigma(1 - t_i)$. That is, an investor bears only $(1 - t_i)$ of the pretax risk.

This concept is best demonstrated by way of example. Consider a €100,000 investment with an expected return of 10 percent, which is taxed annually at 40 percent. A three-state probability distribution of equally likely outcomes is presented in Exhibit 7. The standard deviation of pretax returns is 12.25 percent. The after-tax accumulations one year hence and the after-tax returns are presented in the last two columns.[14]

		Pretax Accumulation (€)	**Pretax Return (%)**	**After-Tax Accumulation (€)**	**After-Tax Returns (%)**
Exhibit 7	**Simple Example of Investment Risk and Taxes**				
Outcome	**Prob.**				
Good	1/3	125,000	25	115,000	15
Average	1/3	110,000	10	106,000	6
Bad	1/3	95,000	−5	97,000	−3
Exp. Value		110,000	10	106,000	6
Std. Dev. (σ)			12.25		7.35

Note: Investment returns are assumed to be taxed at a rate of 40 percent in the year they are earned.

---

13 For example, the after-tax accumulation of €1 in a TDA that earns a pretax return of r for n years is $(1 + r)^n(1 - T_n)$. The euro can be conceptually separated into $(1 - T_n)$ of the investor's funds plus T_n, the taxing authority's portion of the current principal. The investor's portion grows tax exempt from $(1 - T_n)$ today to $(1 + r)^n(1 - T_n)$ at withdrawal.

14 Readers will recognize that this analysis assumes symmetry in the tax system. That is, the €5,000 pretax loss in the bad state is partially offset by a €2,000 tax deduction in the same way a pretax gain is partially offset by a tax liability. Some jurisdictions do not build this symmetry into the tax code or may at least place restrictions on the amount of losses that can be used to reduce taxes. These complexities are not considered here.

The standard deviation of after-tax returns equals 7.35 percent, which also equals $0.1225(1 - 0.40)$. In other words, taxes absorbed t_{oi} of the pretax volatility; the after-tax volatility is $(1 - t_{oi})$ of the pretax volatility. As a result, the taxes not only reduce an investor's returns, but also absorb some investment risk. This concept has implications for portfolio optimization discussed below.

To see how taxes affect after-tax risk in a portfolio context, consider an investor with 50 percent of her wealth invested in equities and 50 percent invested in fixed income, both held in taxable accounts. The equity has a pretax standard deviation of 20 percent and is relatively tax-efficient such that all returns are taxed each year at a 20 percent tax rate. The fixed income is also taxed annually but at a 40 percent rate with pretax volatility of 5 percent. If the two asset classes are perfectly correlated, the pretax portfolio volatility is $0.50(0.20) + 0.50(0.05) = 0.125 = 12.5$ percent. On an after-tax basis, however, portfolio volatility is $0.50(0.20)(1 - 0.20) + 0.50(0.05)(1 - 0.40) = 0.095 = 9.5$ percent. This example illustrates that annually paid taxes reduce portfolio volatility.[15]

Alternatively, suppose that the equity is held in a taxable account and the fixed income is held in a tax-exempt account like those described in the previous section. In this case, the investor absorbs all of the bond volatility in the tax-exempt account, and the new portfolio volatility is $0.50(0.20)(1 - 0.20) + 0.50(0.05) = 0.105 = 10.5$ percent. After-tax volatility increased from the previous measure of after-tax volatility of 9.5 percent because one of the assets (bonds) became tax sheltered. The government therefore absorbed less investment risk through taxes, and the investor is left bearing more investment risk.

IMPLICATIONS FOR WEALTH MANAGEMENT

6

The concepts introduced above have several important implications for financial analysts and portfolio managers. The value created by using investment techniques that effectively manage tax liabilities is sometimes called tax alpha. This section briefly discusses some opportunities for considering taxation in the management of individual's portfolios and tax-planning opportunities to maximize the after-tax accumulation of wealth.

6.1 Asset Location

In most tax regimes, a security's asset class determines its tax profile when held in taxable accounts. Interest income on fixed income securities are often taxed differently from capital gains on stocks, for example. We have also seen how the account structure (e.g., TDAs or tax-exempt accounts) can override this tax treatment. Further, investments in TDAs and tax-exempt accounts are limited such that investors may not place all of their investments in these types of accounts. Investors, therefore, often have multiple types of accounts (e.g., taxable, TDAs, and tax-exempt) when tax advantaged accounts are permitted. An interaction exists between deciding what assets to own and in which accounts they should be held. The choice of where to place specific assets is called the asset location decision. It is distinct from the asset allocation decision.

---

15 The arithmetic is somewhat more complicated when the two assets are not perfectly correlated in which case one would use the standard expression for the volatility of a two security portfolio, $\sigma_p = (w_a^2 \sigma_a^2 + w_b^2 \sigma_b^2 + 2w_a w_b \rho \sigma_a \sigma_b)^{1/2}$. The general point that taxes reduce portfolio volatility remains unaffected.

A well designed portfolio not only prescribes a proper asset allocation but simultaneously tells the portfolio manager the proper location for those assets. This section presents some valuable intuition and general guidance derived from the literature.

Much of the intuition is based on an arbitrage argument developed for corporate pension fund policy by Black (1981) and Tepper (1980). Suppose contributions to a pension plan are tax-deductible and the returns on pension assets are exempt from tax, much like a TDA for an individual investor. The basic idea behind the arbitrage argument is that a company should place assets that would otherwise be heavily taxed assets within the tax shelter of the pension fund, and locate more lightly taxed securities outside the pension fund. If this strategy causes the allocation of the heavily taxed asset held in the pension fund to be too high, an offsetting short position in the heavily taxed asset outside the pension fund can offset the excessive exposure in the pension fund.

For example, suppose bonds are more heavily taxed than equity. Moreover, suppose filling a company's pension fund with bonds causes an excessive allocation to bonds. The company can borrow (i.e., short bonds) outside the pension fund and invest the proceeds in equities. In this way, lending (i.e., investing in bonds) in the pension fund offsets borrowing outside the pension fund, allowing the company to achieve the desired overall asset allocation. The exact amount of borrowing required to offset the fixed-income investment in the pension fund depends on the tax rate and how assets are taxed, but the concept remains the same.

This same logic applies to individual investors. That is, investors would place in TDAs and tax-exempt accounts those securities that would otherwise be heavily taxed if held in taxable accounts (e.g., securities subject to high tax rates and/or annual taxation). The taxable account would hold lightly taxed assets (e.g., securities subject to low rates and/or tax deferral). For example, suppose an investor has €100,000 in tax-deferred accounts and €25,000 in taxable accounts as in Exhibit 8. As suggested, the €100,000 of bonds is placed in the TDA, and €25,000 of stock is placed in the taxable account, creating a pretax bond allocation of 80 percent. Suppose that the target pretax allocation is 60 percent bonds and 40 percent stocks. The investor would borrow €25,000 and purchase additional stock in the taxable account for a total of €50,000 stock. The overall asset allocation is €75,000 bonds and €50,000 stock, which attains the target allocation of 60 percent bonds and 40 percent stock.[16]

Exhibit 8	Simple Example of Asset Location					
Account Type	Asset Class	Existing Pretax Market Value (€)	Existing Pretax Allocation (%)	Asset Class	Target Pretax Market Value (€)	Target Pretax Allocation (%)
TDA	Bond	100,000	80	Bond	100,000	80
Taxable	Stock	25,000	20	Stock	50,000	40
				Short Bond	(25,000)	(20)
Total		125,000	100		125,000	100

---

[16] In this example, asset allocation is expressed in pretax terms. Technically, the asset location question should be solved jointly with asset allocation because changing locations changes asset allocation in after-tax terms. We abstract from that complexity in this example and the following examples for illustrative ease.

There are limitations to this basic arbitrage argument. Investors may face restrictions on the amount and form of borrowing. For instance, the tax arbitrage argument assumes that investors can borrow and lend at the same rate in whatever amounts they wish. In reality, this is not the case. Investors are undoubtedly subject to borrowing costs that are greater than the yield on a bond of similar risk. At least a portion of the tax gains from the arbitrage are therefore consumed by this rate differential. Moreover, behavioral constraints can limit implementation because some investors are apprehensive about borrowing money (i.e., shorting bonds) to manage their retirement portfolio.

In addition, investors may face liquidity constraints (e.g., margin requirements or withdrawal penalties from TDAs and tax-exempt accounts) that would make the arbitrage strategy costly. For example, margin rules may preclude investors from borrowing as much as the arbitrage strategy would suggest or force them to borrow at rates in excess of the bond returns in the TDA. In some jurisdictions investors face penalties for withdrawing assets held in a TDA or tax-exempt account prior to a particular date. If the equity in a taxable account suffers a substantial decline in value, an investor may be forced to liquidate assets in the tax-deferred account to finance consumption, which may trigger an early withdrawal penalty for some investors. These constraints may make strictly executing the arbitrage strategy costly or impossible.

In these cases, asset location is still important. If there are constraints to borrowing in the taxable account then the investor may hold €25,000 in stocks in the taxable account. In the TDA, she could hold €75,000 in bonds and €25,000 in stocks in the TDA. This would achieve the target allocation, while following the location preference in the absence of borrowing.

Separately, suppose she has borrowing constraints and needs €5,000 as a cash reserve in her taxable account. She could hold €20,000 in stocks and €5,000 in cash in the taxable account. In the TDA, she could hold €70,000 in bonds and €30,000 in stocks, which would achieve her target asset allocation. In each example, she follows the asset location preference to the extent possible, while satisfying her other constraints and target asset allocation.

Some jurisdictions exempt municipal bond interest or other types of interest from taxes. In this case, it could conceivably make sense to place tax-free municipal bonds in a taxable account and more heavily taxed stock in the TDA. The yield on tax-free bonds, however, is generally much lower than those on taxable bonds so that in a well functioning market their after-tax returns are approximately equal. This yield concession is a significant disadvantage to placing low yielding tax-free bonds in a taxable account and equity in a TDA. In most instances the yield concession more than offsets the value of sheltering equity returns from taxes. As a result, it is generally better to follow the general strategy of locating bonds in TDAs and equity in taxable accounts.[17]

The tax regime governing the investor determines the relative importance of asset location. In a regime where all income is taxed annually (including unrealized capital gains) and at the same rates, asset location would not matter. As noted earlier, however, these regimes are rare. In most regimes the individual tax structure should be examined to determine which assets are taxed annually and highly versus those that are tax deferred or taxed lightly. Additionally, investment style impacts how an asset or asset class is taxed. For example, active management (discussed further below) or a covered call strategy for an equity portfolio may eliminate the ability to defer taxes.

Of course, taxes are only one of many factors that go into the asset location decision. Others include behavioral constraints, access to credit facilities, age, time horizon, and investment availability. Another factor is planned holding period. If the investor has two accounts—a tax deferred account and a taxable account—that contain funds intended for retirement, then they would both have long term objectives and locating

---

17 See Dammon, Spatt, and Zhang (2004).

assets based on their taxation makes sense. However, if the tax deferred account contains retirement funds and the taxable account contains funds held for short term needs, it may not be appropriate to locate assets based strictly on their taxation. The asset allocation should be appropriate to the client's time horizon for each account.

6.2 Trading Behavior

The tax burden for many asset classes, such as equities when held in taxable accounts, depends on an investor's trading behavior or that of the mutual fund held by an investor. Consider four types of equity investors. The first type is a *trader* who trades frequently and recognizes all portfolio returns in the form of annually taxed short term gains. This equity management style may subject investment returns to tax burdens similar to those applied to interest income thereby eroding possible tax efficiencies associated with equities. An *active investor*, who trades less frequently so that gains are longer term in nature, may receive more favorable tax treatment.[18] The *passive investor* passively buys and holds stock. The *exempt investor* not only buys and holds stocks, but he never pays capital gains tax.[19] Optimal asset allocation and asset location for each of these investors is likely to differ.

For example, suppose these four individuals invest €1,000 in non-dividend paying stocks that earn 8 percent annually for 20 years. They live in a country that taxes capital gains realized within a year at 40 percent and gains realized after at least one year at 20 percent. The after-tax accumulations and accrual equivalent tax rates are listed in Exhibit 9.

Exhibit 9   Future Accumulations for Different Types of Investors

Investor Type	Future Accumulation (€)	Expression (€)	Accrual Equivalent Return (%)	Accrual Equivalent Tax Rate (%)
Trader	2,554	$1,000[1 + 0.08(1 - 0.4)]^{20}$	4.8	40.0
Active Investor	3,458	$1,000[1 + 0.08(1 - 0.2)]^{20}$	6.4	20.0
Passive Investor	3,929	$1,000[(1.08)^{20}(1 - 0.2) + 0.2]$	7.1	11.5
Exempt Investor	4,661	$1,000(1.08)^{20}$	8.0	0.0

Holding all else constant, the trader accumulates the least amount of wealth, and the tax exempt investor accumulates the most. The active and passive investors fall in between. This comparison illustrates that trading behavior affects the tax burden on stocks (and other assets that provide capital gain appreciation) when held in taxable accounts.

Research suggests that active managers must earn greater pretax alphas than passive managers to offset the tax drag of active trading.[20] Other research suggests that mutual fund rankings change significantly depending on whether performance is measured on a pretax or after-tax basis.[21] Therefore, it is important for the taxable investor to consider the impact of taxes on after-tax returns. Generally, for assets held in taxable accounts, portfolio turnover generates taxable gains that might otherwise

---

18 Examples include Australia, Belgium, Denmark, Germany, Japan, Latvia, Luxemburg, the United Kingdom, and the United States.
19 Some jurisdictions permit capital gains tax to be avoided by making charitable contributions or passing assets to an estate upon death.
20 See, for example, Jeffrey and Arnott (1993).
21 See, for example, Dickson and Shoven (1993).

be deferred. Because a number of countries have lower long-term capital gains tax rates for investment held beyond a particular holding period, higher portfolio turnover also foregoes preferential tax treatment associated with longer holding periods and lower turnover.

It is important to note that although locating highly taxed assets in tax sheltered accounts can add value for investors, a proper investment management strategy remains more important than the proper asset location strategy. That is, optimally locating assets in TDAs and taxable accounts cannot overcome the negative impact of a poor investment strategy that either produces a negative pretax alpha or is highly tax inefficient.[22]

6.3 Tax Loss Harvesting

Although the previous section indicates that active management can create a tax drag, not all trading is necessarily tax inefficient. While jurisdictions allow realized capital losses to offset realized capital gains, limitations are often placed on the amount of net losses that can be recognized or the type of income it can offset (e.g., short-term capital gains, long-term capital gains, or ordinary income). Canada, for example, only allows tax deductible losses up to the level of realized taxable gains. Realized losses in excess of realized gains may be used to offset gains realized within the last three years. Realized losses beyond that point can be carried forward and applied against gain realized at some future date.

Regardless of the specific tax rules the opportunity to recognize a loss that offsets some kind of taxable gain in a given tax year can create value. The practice of realizing a loss to offset a gain or income—and thereby reducing the current year's tax obligation—is called tax loss harvesting.

EXAMPLE 12

Tax Loss Harvesting: Current Tax Savings

Eduardo Cappellino has a €1,000,000 portfolio held in a taxable account. The end of the 2008 tax year is approaching and Cappellino has recognized €100,000 worth of capital gains. His portfolio has securities that have experienced €60,000 of losses. These securities have not yet been sold and their losses are therefore unrecognized. Cappellino could sell these securities and replace them with similar securities expected to earn identical returns.[23] The federal government taxes capital gains at 20 percent.

1 Without making any further transactions, how much tax does Cappellino owe this year?

2 How much tax will Cappellino owe this year if he sells the securities with the €60,000 loss?

3 How much tax will Cappellino save this year if he sells the securities with the €60,000 loss?

Solution to 1:

Capital gain tax = 0.20 × €100,000 = €20,000.

---

22 See Reichenstein (2001).
23 Realizing losses by selling and buying similar securities may be subject to certain restrictions by the government or taxing authority.

Solution to 2:

If Cappellino realizes €60,000 of losses, the net gain will be reduced to €40,000. New capital gain tax = 0.20 × (€100,000 − €60,000) = €8,000.

Solution to 3:

Tax Savings = €20,000 − €8,000 = €12,000.

It is important to understand that the tax savings realized in a given tax year from tax loss harvesting overstates the true gain. Selling a security at a loss and reinvesting the proceeds in a similar security effectively resets the cost basis to the lower market value, potentially increasing future tax liabilities. In other words, taxes saved now may be simply postponed. The value of tax loss harvesting is largely in deferring the payment of tax liabilities.[24]

EXAMPLE 13

Tax Loss Harvesting: Tax Deferral

In the previous example, the securities with an unrealized loss have a current market value of €110,000 and cost basis of €170,000 (an unrealized loss of €60,000). Cappellino could:

Option A   Hold the securities with the unrealized loss, or

Option B   Sell the securities in 2008 and replace them with securities offering the same return.

Next tax year (2009), the securities increase in value to €200,000 and the securities are sold regardless of which option Cappellino chooses.

1   Calculate Cappellino's 2009 tax liability if he holds the securities until year end 2009.

2   Calculate Cappellino's 2009 tax liability if he recognizes the loss today in 2008, replaces them with securities offering the same return, and realizes the capital gain at year end 2009.

3   Compare the total two-year tax liability under both options using the 2008 tax liability computed in Example 12, in which the 2008 tax liability was €20,000 if the loss was not realized and €8,000 if the loss was realized.

Solution to 1:

Capital gain tax = 0.20(€200,000 − €170,000) = €6,000.

Solution to 2:

If Cappellino recognizes the loss in 2008 and replaces the securities, the basis will be reset to €110,000 from €170,000.

Capital gain tax in 2009 = 0.20(€200,000 − €110,000) = €18,000.

---

24 In cases where securities receive a step up in basis upon inheritance or are gifted to charity, the government will never recapture the current year tax savings, greatly increasing the harvesting value to the investor. Furthermore, in the United States the value of a built-in capital loss is lost at death. For example, someone could realize a $1,000 loss before death and save taxes. But the asset sold immediately after his death would not benefit from this tax loss.

Solution to 3:

The two-year tax liability for both options is the same:

	2008 (€)	2009 (€)	Total (€)
Option A	20,000	6,000	26,000
Option B	8,000	18,000	26,000

Although the two-year tax liability does not change, an advantage of tax loss harvesting is pushing a portion of the tax liability into subsequent years.

A subtle benefit of tax loss harvesting is that recognizing an already incurred loss for tax purposes increases the amount of net-of-tax money available for investment. Realizing a loss saves taxes in the current year, and this tax savings can be reinvested. This technique increases the amount of capital the investor can put to use.

EXAMPLE 14

Tax Loss Harvesting: Adding Net-of-Tax Principal

In the previous example, suppose Cappellino reinvests the 2008 tax savings if he sells the securities with an unrealized loss of €60,000. His two options are therefore:

Option A   Hold the securities, or

Option B   Sell the securities, and reinvest the proceeds and the tax savings in nearly identical securities.

In 2009, the securities experience an 81.81 percent increase regardless of which option Cappellino chooses.

1   Calculate the securities' pretax value next year if he holds the securities.

2   Calculate the securities' pretax value next year if he recognizes the loss, and reinvests the proceeds and the tax savings in nearly identical securities.

3   What will the after-tax value be under both options if the securities are sold the next year?

Solution to 1:

FV = €110,000(1.8181) = €200,000 (approximately).

Solution to 2:

If Cappellino replaces the securities and invests the tax savings of €12,000, the invested capital will become €110,000 + €12,000 = €122,000.

FV = €122,000(1.8181) = €221,808.

Solution to 3:

The new capital gain tax for Option B at the end of the next tax year is 0.20(€221,808 − €122,000) = €19,962.

	Pretax (€)	Tax (€)	After-Tax (€)
Option A	200,000	6,000	194,000
Option B	221,808	19,962	201,846

Another advantage of tax loss harvesting is increasing the net-of-tax capital invested in the portfolio.

A concept related to tax loss harvesting is using highest-in, first-out (HIFO) tax lot accounting to sell a portion of a position. When positions are accumulated over time, lots are often purchased at different prices. Depending on the tax system, investors may be allowed to sell the highest cost basis lots first, which defers realizing the tax liability associated with lots having a lower cost basis.

Opportunities to create value through tax loss harvesting and HIFO are greater in jurisdictions with high tax rates on capital gains. Studies have shown that a tax loss harvesting program can yield substantial benefits. Although cumulative tax alphas from tax loss harvesting increase over time, the annual tax alpha is largest in the early years and decreases through time as deferred gains are ultimately realized.[25] The complementary strategies of tax loss harvesting and HIFO tax lot accounting have more potential value when securities have relatively high volatility, which creates larger gains and losses with which to work.

The previous section suggests that active trading creates a tax drag on portfolio performance. A certain amount of trading activity is required, however, to harvest tax losses if a portfolio contains unrealized losses. That is, tax-efficient management of stocks in taxable accounts does not require passive management. It requires passively allowing gains to grow unharvested, but actively realizing losses.

Harvesting losses is not always an optimal strategy. For example, in cases where an investor is currently in a relatively low tax rate environment and will face higher tax rates on gains in a subsequent period (either because her tax bracket will increase or because tax rates generally are increasing) the best strategy may be to defer harvesting losses. Doing so would offset gains that will be taxed relatively lightly compared to subsequent gains if tax rates will increase.[26] Likewise, one might want to liquidate low basis stock (lowest in, first out or LIFO) if the current tax rate is temporarily low.

6.4 Holding Period Management

The tax regime analysis earlier in the reading indicated that many jurisdictions encourage long-term investing (or equivalently discourage short-term trading) by reducing tax rates on long-term gains. The required holding period varies, of course. Depending on the magnitude of gain from waiting, short-term trading can be difficult to justify on an after-tax basis. If short-term gains are taxed at 40 percent and long-term gains are taxed at 20 percent, then 20 percent (i.e., 40 percent less 20 percent) of an investor's gains are dictated by the holding period.

Exhibit 10 shows the relative benefit of gains subject to a lower tax rate. Using a twelve-month holding period requirement for a long-term capital gain tax of 20 percent versus a short-term capital gain tax of 40 percent, the table assumes that the entire return is taxed each year. For example, consider an 8 percent return over ten years. If returns are completely taxed each year as long term gains at 20 percent, €100 will grow to €100[1 + 0.08(1 − 0.20)]^{10} = €185.96. If returns are completely taxed as short-term gains at 40 percent, the accumulation is €100[1 + 0.08(1 − 0.40)]^{10} =

---

25 See, for example, Berkin, Ye, and Arnott (2001), Stein (2004b), and Berkin and Ye (2003).
26 See Stein (2004a) for further discussion.

€159.81. The ratio between the two figures is €185.96/€159.81 = 1.164. The benefit of realizing long-term gains in lieu of short-term gains is substantial, especially for long investment horizons and higher returns.

Exhibit 10	Ratio of Future Accumulations: Accumulation Using Long-Term Capital Gains Tax Rate to Accumulation Using Short-Term Capital Gains Tax Rate							
	Investment Horizon in Years (n)							
r(%)	**5**	**10**	**15**	**20**	**25**	**30**	**35**	**40**
2	1.020	1.040	1.061	1.082	1.104	1.126	1.148	1.171
4	1.040	1.081	1.124	1.168	1.215	1.263	1.313	1.365
6	1.059	1.122	1.189	1.259	1.334	1.413	1.496	1.585
8	1.079	1.164	1.255	1.354	1.461	1.575	1.699	1.833
10	1.098	1.206	1.324	1.453	1.596	1.752	1.924	2.112
12	1.117	1.248	1.394	1.557	1.739	1.943	2.170	2.425
14	1.136	1.290	1.466	1.665	1.892	2.149	2.441	2.773
16	1.155	1.333	1.540	1.778	2.053	2.371	2.738	3.162
18	1.173	1.377	1.615	1.896	2.224	2.610	3.062	3.593

Note: Capital gains are assumed to be taxed each year. Short-term gains are taxed at a rate of 40 percent. Long-term gains are taxed at 20 percent.

The penalty associated with realizing short-term gains in this environment can be viewed from a different perspective. An investment earning a 10 percent pretax return subject to a long term rate yields 8 percent after-tax [i.e., $0.10 \times (1 - 0.20)$]. A 13.33 percent pretax return taxed as a short-term gain is necessary to produce the same result [e.g., $0.08/(1 - 0.40)$]. In other words, the pretax return must be one-third greater to produce the same after-tax result. It can be quite difficult to generate enough pretax alpha to overcome the effect of taxes on short capital gains in these types of tax environments.

Another aspect of holding period management is more tactical in terms of which tax year the tax is due. If a taxpayer subject to taxation on a calendar year basis is contemplating an asset sale in December, it may be wise to defer the sale until January if there is a built-in capital gain or sell the asset in December if there is a built-in loss. Of course the timing of taxation is not the only consideration. The attractiveness of this investment relative to alternative investments must be considered.

EXAMPLE 15

Long-Term Gain

Gretel Hazburger is considering two different portfolio strategies. The first is a hyper-active market-timing trading strategy that is expected to yield a pretax return of 12 percent. All gains will be recognized each year and taxed at the short term capital gain rate of 50 percent. Alternatively, a less active tactical asset allocation trading strategy is expected to yield a pretax return of 10 percent. All gains will be recognized each year but classified as long term and taxed at 30 percent.

1   Which strategy is likely to produce a better after tax return?

2   What pretax return is required on the market timing strategy to produce the same after-tax return as the tactical asset allocation strategy?

Solution to 1:

After-tax return to market timing = 0.12(1 − 0.50) = 0.06 = 6 percent.
After-tax return to tactical asset allocation = 0.10 (1 − 0.30) = 0.07 = 7 percent.
The tactical asset allocation strategy produces a better return.

Solution to 2:

Required return for market timing = 0.07/(1 − 0.50) = 0.14 = 14 percent.

6.5 After-Tax Mean–Variance Optimization

We have seen how basic principles of measuring asset allocation in a pretax environment do not necessarily apply in a more economically relevant after-tax environment. The same is true for portfolio optimization techniques. That is, pretax efficient frontiers may not be reasonable proxies for after-tax efficient frontiers. It is beyond the scope of this reading to develop specific after-tax mean–variance optimization (MVO) methods. However, an important concept supporting those methods is that the same asset held in different types of accounts is essentially a distinct after-tax asset because it will produce different after-tax accumulations. In other words, an investor optimizing between two different asset classes (e.g., stocks and bonds) across two types of accounts (e.g., taxable and tax deferred accounts) has four different after-tax assets to allocate—stocks or bonds in each of the two accounts.

After recognizing that important insight, an important element in developing an after-tax MVO model is to substitute accrual equivalent returns, like those introduced above, for pretax returns in developing return expectations. Similarly, a portfolio manager would substitute the asset's after-tax standard deviation of returns for pretax standard deviations in the optimization algorithm.

The optimization process must include some constraints. For example, an optimization algorithm cannot allocate more to a tax deferred account than the funds that are available in that account. Specific investment options may also be constrained in some types of accounts. For example, privatized retirement accounts in certain countries may limit investors' options to certain types of securities. In sum, however, standard portfolio optimization practices can be adapted to consider the impact of taxes on investment returns and risk.

SUMMARY

Taxes can have a significant impact on investment returns and wealth accumulation, and managing taxes in an investment portfolio is one way advisers can add value. Taxes come in various forms and each country has its own tax code. Nonetheless, many jurisdictions share some common salient features, and many of those common elements can be identified. This allows one to define regimes that include countries with similar rules of taxation and to build models that capture the salient features of these regimes. That is the approach taken here and the resulting analysis suggests the following:

- Taxes on investments can take at least three primary forms as discussed here. They can be based on:
  - returns—accrued and paid annually;
  - returns—deferred until capital gains are recognized;
  - wealth—accrued and paid annually.
- The impact of taxes on wealth accumulation compounds over time.
- Deferred taxes on capital gains have less impact on wealth accumulation than annual tax obligations for the same tax rate.
- An investment with a cost basis below its current market value has an embedded tax liability that may reduce future after-tax accumulations.
- Wealth taxes apply to principal rather than returns and in consequence wealth tax rates tend to be much lower than returns-based tax rates.
- Investments are typically subject to multiple forms of taxation. The specific exposure depends on the asset class, portfolio management style, and type of account in which it is held.
- An accrual equivalent after-tax return is the tax-free return that, if accrued annually, produces a given after-tax accumulation.
- An accrual equivalent tax rate is the annually accrued tax rate that, when applied to the pretax return, produces a given after-tax accumulation.
- Sometimes the type of investment account overrides the tax treatment of an investment based on its asset class.
- Tax-deferred accounts allow tax-deductible contributions and/or tax-deferred accumulation of returns, but funds are taxed when withdrawn.
- Tax-exempt accounts do not allow tax-deductible contributions, but allow tax-exempt accumulation of returns even when funds are withdrawn.
- By taxing investment returns, a taxing authority shares investment risk with the taxpayer. As a result, taxes can reduce investment risk.
- The practice of optimally placing particular asset classes in particular types of accounts is called asset location.
- Tax loss harvesting defers tax liabilities from current to subsequent periods and permits more after-tax capital to be invested in current periods.
- When short-term gains are taxed more heavily than long-term gains, it can be difficult for a short-term trading strategy to generate enough alpha to offset the higher taxes associated with short term trading.
- Traditional mean–variance optimization can be modified to accommodate after-tax returns and after-tax risk.
- Otherwise identical assets held in different types of investment accounts should be evaluated as distinct after-tax assets.
- An after-tax portfolio optimization model that optimizes asset allocation also optimizes asset location.

PRACTICE PROBLEMS

The following information relates to Questions 1–7

Alan Jackson has a new client, Aldo Motelli, who expects taxable ordinary income (excluding investments) of €200,000 this tax year. Motelli currently has €250,000 in a taxable investment account for which his main objective is retirement in 15 years. He is considering making the maximum investment of €10,000 in a new type of tax deferred account permitted in his country of residence. The contribution would be deductible and distributions are expected to be taxed at a 20 percent rate when withdrawn. The income tax structure of his country is:

Taxes on Ordinary Income			
Taxable Income (€)		Tax on	Percentage on Excess
Over	Up to	Column 1 (€)	Over Column 1
0	20,000	—	10
20,000	40,000	2,000	15
40,000	60,000	5,000	20
60,000	80,000	9,000	25
80,000	100,000	14,000	30
100,000		20,000	35

Taxes on Investment Income

Interest	10% flat rate
Dividends	10% flat rate
Realized capital gains	10% flat rate

1 What is Motelli's average tax rate on ordinary income?

   A   22.5%.

   B   27.5%.

   C   35.0%.

2 If Motelli's current investment account of €250,000 is invested in an asset which is expected to earn annual interest of 6.5 percent and no capital gains, what is his expected after tax accumulation in 15 years?

   A   €578,664.

   B   €586,547.

   C   €642,960.

3 What is the accrual equivalent return assuming the facts in Question 2?

   A   5.85%.

   B   6.50%.

   C   7.22%.

4 If Motelli's current investment account of €250,000 is invested in an investment which is expected to earn a return of 7.5 percent, all of which are deferred capital gains, what is his expected after-tax accumulation in 15 years? The account's market value is equal to its cost basis.

A €640,747.

B €665,747.

C €690,747.

5 If Motelli's current investment account of €250,000, has a cost basis of €175,000, and is invested in an investment which is expected to earn a return of 7.5 percent, all of which are deferred capital gains, what is his expected after tax accumulation in 15 years?

A €673,247.

B €683,247.

C €690,747.

6 How much after-tax wealth would Motelli accumulate assuming the same facts as in Question 4 except that 50 percent of all capital gains are recognized each year?

A €640,747.

B €665,747.

C €678,158.

7 Assuming an annual return of 7.5 percent, what would be the after-tax wealth accumulated in 15 years for a single current contribution to the TDA? Assume the contribution would be deductible but taxed at the end of 15 years at a 20 percent tax rate.

A €23,671.

B €23,965.

C €29,589.

---

8 Sam Nakusi is managing a balanced portfolio of fixed income and equity securities worth £1,000,000. The portfolio's pretax expected return is 6.0 percent. The percentage of return composed of interest, dividends and realized capital gain as well as the associated tax rates are listed below. Assume the portfolio's cost basis equals market value.

Hypothetical Tax Profile and Example		
Tax Profile	**Annual Distribution Rate (p)**	**Tax Rate (T)**
Interest (i)	20%	35%
Dividends (d)	30%	15%
Capital gain (cg)	40%	25%

What is the expected future accumulation in 15 years assuming these parameters hold for that time period?

A £1,930,929.

B £1,962,776.

C £1,994,447.

9 In the previous question, recalculate the expected accumulation assuming the portfolio's costs basis is equal to £700,000.

A   £1,373,943.

B   £1,962,776.

C   £1,887,776.

10   Gloria Vander is pursuing a buy-and-hold equity strategy on non-dividend paying stocks. She expects her €400,000 portfolio to experience no turnover over the next 10 years but expects to liquidate it at that time. The cost basis is currently equal to market value. If Vander expects an 8 percent pretax return and capital gains are taxed at 20 percent, what is her accrual equivalent return over that time period?

A   6.40%.

B   6.78%.

C   4.60%.

11   What is the accrual equivalent tax rate in the previous question?

A   15.25%.

B   20.00%.

C   84.75%.

12   Peter Cavuto lives in a country that imposes a wealth tax of 0.5 percent on financial assets each year. His €500,000 portfolio is expected to return 5 percent per year over the next twenty years. Assuming no other taxes, what is Cavuto's expected wealth at the end of twenty years?

A   €1,200,100.

B   €1,205,857.

C   €1,326,649.

13   A client has funds in a tax deferred account and a taxable account. Which of the following assets would be *most appropriate* in a taxable account in a Flat and Heavy Tax Regime, in which dividends and capital gains are taxed at ordinary rates and interest income is tax exempt? Assume that all assets are held in a client's overall portfolio.

A   Bonds.

B   Actively traded stocks.

C   High dividend paying stocks.

14   John Kaplan and Anna Forest both have €100,000 each split evenly between a tax deferred account and a taxable account. Kaplan chooses to put stock with an expected return of 7 percent in the tax-deferred account and bonds yielding 4 percent in the taxable account. Forest chooses the reverse, putting stock in the taxable account and bonds in the tax deferred account. When held in taxable account, equity returns will be taxed entirely as deferred capital gains at a 20 percent rate, while interest income is taxed annually at 40 percent. The tax rate applicable to withdrawals from the tax deferred account will be 40 percent. Cost basis is equal to market value on asset held in taxable account.

Kaplan's and Forest's Asset Location		
Tax Profile	Kaplan (€)	Forest (€)
Taxable Account	50,000 bonds	50,000 stock
Tax deferred Account	50,000 stock	50,000 bonds
Total (Before-tax)	100,000	100,000

What is Kaplan's after-tax accumulation after 20 years?

A   €196,438.

   B €220,521.

   C €230,521.

15 In the previous question, what is Forest's after-tax accumulation after 20 years?

   A €196,438.

   B €220,521.

   C €230,521.

16 What is the after-tax asset allocation for the following portfolio if withdrawals from the TDA will be taxed at 40 percent?

Account	Pretax Market Value (€)	Asset Class
TDA	200,000	Bonds
Tax-exempt	80,000	Stock
Total	280,000	

   A 71.4% bonds; 28.6% stock.

   B 50% bonds; 50% stock.

   C 60% bonds; 40% stock.

17 Lorraine Newman is evaluating whether to save for retirement using a TDA or a tax-exempt account. The TDA permits tax-deductible contributions but withdrawals will be taxed at 30 percent. The tax-exempt account permits tax-free accumulation and withdrawals but contributions are taxable at a 40 percent tax rate. Assuming contribution limits do not affect Newman's choice of accounts, which account should she choose?

   A TDA.

   B Tax-exempt.

   C The choices are the same.

18 Which of the following assets would be most appropriate to locate in a tax deferred account in a Heavy Interest Tax Regime assuming all assets are held in a client's overall portfolio?

   A Low dividend paying stock.

   B Tax exempt bonds.

   C Taxable bonds.

19 Consider a portfolio that is generally appreciating in value. Active trading is most likely to be *least* attractive in a:

   A taxable account.

   B tax deferred account.

   C tax exempt account.

20 Jose DiCenzo has some securities worth €50,000 that have a cost basis of €75,000. If he sells those securities and can use the realized losses to offset other realized gains, how much can DiCenzo reduce his taxes in the *current* tax year assuming capital gains are taxed at 30 percent?

   A €7,500.

   B €15,000.

   C €17,500.

21 In the previous question, suppose DiCenzo sells the securities in the current tax year and replaces them with securities having the same returns. He will then sell the new securities in the next tax year. What is the total tax savings assuming DiCenzo does *not* reinvest the tax savings?

A €0.

B €7,500.

C €15,000.

22 Tax loss harvesting is most effective when:

A there are few similar investment opportunities for the security with the loss.

B the taxpayer is currently in a relatively high tax environment.

C the taxpayer is currently in a relatively low tax environment.

SOLUTIONS

1 B is correct. Motelli's tax liability on ordinary income is €20,000 (on the first €100,000, third column of table, last row) + (€200,000 − €100,000) × 0.35, or €55,000. The average tax rate on ordinary income is €55,000/€200,000, or 27.5 percent.

2 B is correct. The after tax wealth accumulation for annually taxable income is

$$FVIF_i = [1 + r(1 - t_i)]^n$$
$$FV = €250,000 \times FVIF_i = €250,000 \times [1 + 0.065(1 - 0.10)]^{15}$$
$$= €586,547$$

3 A is correct. The accrual equivalent return is found by the following equation:

$$€250,000(1 + R_{AE})^{15} = €586,547$$

$$R_{AE} = 5.85\%$$

4 C is correct. The after tax wealth accumulation for deferred capital gains is

$$FVIF_{cg} = (1 + r)^n(1 - t_{cg}) + t_{cg}$$
$$FVIF_{cg} = €250,000 \times [(1 + 0.075)^{15}(1 - 0.1) + 0.1] = €690,747$$

5 B is correct. The after tax wealth accumulation for deferred capital gains is

$$FVIF_{cg} = (1 + r)^n(1 - t_{cg}) + t_{cg} - (1 - B)t_{cg}$$
$$FVIF_{cg} = €250,000 \times [(1 + 0.075)^{15}(1 - 0.1) + 0.1 - (1 - 0.70)(0.10)] = €683,247$$

6 C is correct.

$$r^* = r(1 - p_{cg}t_{cg})$$
$$= 0.075(1 - (0.5)(0.10)) = 0.075(1 - 0.05) = 0.07125$$
$$T^* = t_{cg}(1 - p_{cg})/(1 - p_{cg}t_{cg})$$
$$= 0.10[(1 - 0.5)/(1 - 0.5 \times 0.10)] = 0.052632$$
$$FVIF_{Taxable} = (1 + r^*)^n(1 - T^*) + T^* - (1 - B)t_{cg}, B = 1$$
$$FV = €250,000 \times [(1 + 0.07125)^{15}(1 - 0.052632) + 0.052632]$$
$$= €678,158$$

7 A is correct.

$$FVIF_{TDA} = (1 + r)^n(1 - T_n)$$
$$FVIF = €10,000[(1 + 0.075)^{15}(1 - 0.20)] = €23,671$$

8 B is correct.

$$r^* = r(1 - p_d t_d - p_i t_i - p_{cg}t_{cg})$$
$$= 0.06*[1 - (0.30)(0.15) - (0.20)(0.35) - (0.40)(0.25)]$$
$$= 0.0471 \text{ or } 4.71 \text{ percent}$$
$$T^* = t_{cg}(1 - p_d - p_i - p_{cg})/(1 - p_d t_d - p_i t_i - p_{cg}t_{cg})$$
$$= t_{cg}(1 - 0.30 - 0.20 - 0.40)/[1 - (0.30)(0.15) - (0.20)(0.35) - (0.40)(0.25)]$$
$$= 0.0318$$
$$FVIF_{Taxable} = £1,000,000[(1 + r^*)^n(1 - T^*) + T^*]$$

$$= £1,000,000[(1 + 0.0471)^{15}(1 - 0.0318) + 0.0318]$$
$$= £1,962,776$$

9   C is correct.

$$B = £700,000/£1,000,000 = 0.70$$

$$
\begin{aligned}
FV_{Taxable} &= £1,000,000[(1 + r^*)^n(1 - T^*) + T^* - (0.25)(1 - 0.70)] \\
&= £1,000,000[(1 + 0.0471)^{15}(1 - 0.0318) + 0.0318 - 0.075] \\
&= £1,887,776
\end{aligned}
$$

10   B is correct.

$$
\begin{aligned}
FV_{cg} &= €400,000[(1 + r)^n(1 - t_{cg}) + t_{cg}] \\
&= €400,000[(1 + 0.08)^{10}(1 - 0.20) + 0.20] \\
&= €770,856
\end{aligned}
$$

Solving for the rate set equates €770,856 with its present value of €400,000

$$€770,856 = €400,000(1 + R_{AE})^{10}$$
$$R_{AE} = 0.0678 \text{ or } 6.78 \text{ percent}$$

11   A is correct.

$$r(1 - T_{AE}) = R_{AE}$$
$$0.08(1 - T_{AE}) = 0.0678$$
$$T_{AE} = 0.1525 \text{ or } 15.25 \text{ percent}$$

12   A is correct.

$$FVIF_w = [(1 + r)(1 - t_w)]^n$$
$$FV = €500,000[(1.05)(1 - 0.005)]^{20} = €1,200,100$$

13   A is correct. Tax-exempt assets are not appropriate for tax deferred accounts. In a Flat and Heavy Tax Regime, dividends and capital gains are taxed at ordinary rates and are not the best choices for taxable accounts.

14   A is correct. The taxable account will accumulate to

$$
\begin{aligned}
FV_i &= €50,000[1 + r(1 - t_i)]^n \\
&= €50,000[1 + 0.04(1 - 0.4)]^{20} \\
&= €80,347
\end{aligned}
$$

The tax deferred account will accumulate

$$
\begin{aligned}
FV_{TDA} &= €50,000(1 + r)^n(1 - T_n) \\
&= €50,000(1.07)^{20}(1 - 0.40) \\
&= €116,091
\end{aligned}
$$

Total = €196,438

15   C is correct. The taxable account will accumulate to

$$
\begin{aligned}
FV_{cg} &= €50,000[(1 + r)^n(1 - t_{cg}) + t_{cg}] \\
&= €50,000[(1.07)^{20}(1 - 0.20) + 0.20] \\
&= €164,787
\end{aligned}
$$

The tax deferred account will accumulate

$$FV_{TDA} = €50,000(1 + r)^n(1 - T_n)$$

$$= \text{€}50{,}000(1.04)^{20}(1 - 0.40)$$

$$= \text{€}65{,}734$$

$$\text{Total} = \text{€}230{,}521$$

16 C is correct. The after-tax value of the TDA account is €200,000(1 − 0.40) = €120,000. The after-tax value of the tax-exempt account is €80,000. The total after-tax value of the portfolio is €200,000. Stock represents €80,000/€200,000 = 40 percent of the total, whereas bonds represent €120,000/€200,000 = 60 percent of the total.

17 A is correct. The future accumulation of the TDA is $(1 + r)^n(1 - 0.30)$, whereas the future accumulation of the tax-exempt account is $(1 + r)^n(1 - 0.40)$. Therefore, the TDA will accumulate more wealth.

18 C is correct. In this regime, interest would be taxed heavily and is most appropriate for a tax deferred account.

19 A is correct. Active trading would generate annually taxed income and is most appropriate for a tax-exempt account, all else equal. If a portfolio contains unrealized losses, however, a certain amount of trading activity is required to harvest tax losses. That is, tax-efficient management of stocks in taxable accounts does not require passive management. It requires passively allowing gains to grow unharvested, but actively realizing losses.

20 A is correct. DiCenzo has a €75,000 − €50,000 = €25,000 unrealized loss. Assuming that realizing this loss will decrease his taxable gains by the same amount, his tax bill in the current year will be reduced by 0.30 × €25,000 = €7,500.

21 A is correct. Assuming DiCenzo does not reinvest the tax savings, tax loss harvesting does not reduce the total tax paid over time. It only defers taxes because recognizing the loss resets the cost basis to a lower figure which will ultimately increase the gain realized late by the same amount. Tax loss harvest can augment return by postponing tax liabilities. Reinvesting the current year's tax savings increases the after-tax principal investment, which can augment the value of tax loss harvesting further.

22 B is correct. Tax loss harvesting is best used when tax rates are relatively high.

Estate Planning in a Global Context

by Stephen M. Horan, CFA, CIPM, and Thomas R. Robinson, CFA

Stephen M. Horan, PhD, CFA, CIPM, is at CFA Institute (USA). Thomas R. Robinson, PhD, CFA, is at CFA Institute (USA).

LEARNING OUTCOMES

Mastery	The candidate should be able to:
☐	**a.** discuss the purpose of estate planning and explain the basic concepts of domestic estate planning, including estates, wills, and probate;
☐	**b.** explain the two principal forms of wealth transfer taxes and discuss effects of important non-tax issues, such as legal system, forced heirship, and marital property regime;
☐	**c.** determine a family's core capital and excess capital, based on mortality probabilities and Monte Carlo analysis;
☐	**d.** evaluate the relative after-tax value of lifetime gifts and testamentary bequests;
☐	**e.** explain the estate planning benefit of making lifetime gifts when gift taxes are paid by the donor, rather than the recipient;
☐	**f.** evaluate the after-tax benefits of basic estate planning strategies, including generation skipping, spousal exemptions, valuation discounts, and charitable gifts;
☐	**g.** explain the basic structure of a trust and discuss the differences between revocable and irrevocable trusts;
☐	**h.** explain how life insurance can be a tax-efficient means of wealth transfer;
☐	**i.** discuss the two principal systems (source jurisdiction and residence jurisdiction) for establishing a country's tax jurisdiction;
☐	**j.** discuss the possible income and estate tax consequences of foreign situated assets and foreign-sourced income;
☐	**k.** evaluate a client's tax liability under each of three basic methods (credit, exemption, and deduction) that a country may use to provide relief from double taxation;
☐	**l.** discuss how increasing international transparency and information exchange among tax authorities affect international estate planning.

1 INTRODUCTION

Estate planning is a critical component of wealth management for private clients. Translating the goals of an individual or family into effective legal and tax-efficient solutions can be a challenging task, which requires an intimate knowledge of, among other things, the tax and inheritance laws in a particular jurisdiction. The challenge is often magnified when a client has family members, assets, or income in multiple jurisdictions. Increasingly, high-net-worth individuals (HNWI) and families have these types of international interests.

Identifying the real needs of HNWI is crucial for the portfolio management and estate planning process. The issues are broad and differentiated. For example, non-taxable concerns for HNWI include succession and inheritance planning, business succession, charitable intentions, asset gathering and identification, asset protection and preservation, managing risks of divorce, "living" wills, privacy, second families, special assets like art, "toys," and more. Depending on the home country, forced heirship, political risk, kidnapping and security, and confidentiality could also be elements to consider in estate planning.

The wealth manager can add value to the advisor–client relationship by understanding salient tax and inheritance planning issues in a client's home country as well as those in other jurisdictions affecting the client's welfare. Professional tax and legal assistance is typically required to conceive, draft, and execute an estate plan or a particular solution within that plan because the field of estate planning falls largely outside the purview of the wealth manager. As such, this reading should not be considered legal advice or interpreted as a substitute for it. It is important, however, for the wealth manager to understand fundamental estate planning principles to identify issues that deserve attention and to integrate the solutions into an overall estate plan. This reading provides a framework for understanding generic tax and non-tax estate planning considerations in both a domestic and cross-border context. It also explores various approaches that different jurisdictions use to structure rules of wealth transfer.

On one hand, the complexity is daunting. On the other hand, a basic understanding of the landscape creates opportunities to develop valuable solutions to common problems. The approach developed here is valuable for several reasons. First, it can be applied in a variety of jurisdictions. The terminology used is intended to be generic and have international interpretation, but the local lexicon may vary from one jurisdiction to the next. Second, it provides an international perspective that advisors can use to counsel clients with a multi-jurisdictional footprint. Third, it provides a framework advisors can use to communicate tax and succession planning considerations to private clients and develop techniques to address the needs and objectives of such clients. Finally, inheritance laws and tax codes in many jurisdictions are fluid. They change over time as governments use them to affect social and economic objectives. The framework developed in this reading will help the advisor manage those changes and understand their impact should they occur.

DOMESTIC ESTATE PLANNING: SOME BASIC CONCEPTS

2.1 Estates, Wills, and Probate

An **estate**[1] is all of the property a person owns or controls. The property in one's estate may consist of financial assets (e.g., bank accounts, stocks, bonds, or business interests), tangible personal assets (e.g., artwork, collectibles, or vehicles), immovable property (e.g., residential real estate or timber rights), and intellectual property (e.g., royalties).

An estate might exclude, however, assets that a settlor transferred to an irrevocable trust during his or her lifetime as a gift, which would be considered an example of a lifetime gratuitous transfer, also known as an *inter vivos* gift. This is discussed in more detail below. It is important to note that the elements of an estate can differ for legal and tax purposes. For example, assets transferred to a trust may no longer be considered to be legally owned by the trust settlor, or the person giving the assets to the trust, whereby the trustee of the trust becomes the legal owner of the trust assets. The assets may be considered the settlor's assets for tax purposes, however, depending on applicable tax law and the trust structure.

Estate planning is the process of preparing for the disposition of one's estate (e.g., the transfer of property) upon death and during one's lifetime. It may involve making arrangements for other personal matters, as well, such as burial arrangements and end-of-life medical instructions should one become incapacitated. It can require the counsel of a variety of professionals including financial, legal, and taxation.

The core document most closely associated with an estate plan is a will or testament. A **will** (or testament) outlines the rights others will have over one's property after death. A testator is the person who authored the will and whose property is disposed of according to the will. **Probate** is the legal process to confirm the validity of the will so that executors, heirs, and other interested parties can rely on its authenticity. A decedent without a valid will or with a will that does not dispose of their property is considered to have died **intestate**. In that case, a court will often decide on the disposition of assets under applicable intestacy laws during the probate process.

Some individuals may wish to avoid probate. Court fees may be sizable, and the process can cause a delay in the transfer of assets to intended beneficiaries. A will can be challenged, and its contents are often a matter of public record, which may concern some wealthy families as it can cause embarrassment or divulge sensitive financial information. Moreover, many problems can arise in probate when multiple jurisdictions are involved. In some instances, probate can be avoided or its impact limited by holding assets in other forms of ownership, such as joint ownership (e.g., joint tenancy with right of survivorship), living trusts, or retirement plans. Through these structures, ownership of property is transferred to beneficiaries without the need for a will and hence the probate process can be avoided or substantially reduced.

Property in an estate can be held in a variety of ways including sole ownership, joint ownership, partnership, trust, or through life insurance. Assets held in **sole ownership** are typically considered part of a decedent's estate. The transfer of their ownership is dictated by the decedent's will (or, in the absence of their disposition under the decedent's will, applicable intestacy law) through the probate process. In some jurisdictions, assets held in **joint ownership with right of survivorship** automatically transfer to the surviving joint owner or owners, as the case may be, outside the probate process. The transfer of assets held in trust and the payout of death benefit

---

1 Terminology will vary from jurisdiction to jurisdiction depending upon the legal structure of the jurisdiction. The term "estate" comes from common law. Legal structures such as common law are described further.

proceeds under a life insurance policy depend on the terms of the trust deed and the provisions of the life insurance contract, respectively. Trusts, life insurance, and other similar planning techniques can, therefore, transfer assets outside the probate process and can be important estate planning tools.

2.2 Legal Systems, Forced Heirship, and Marital Property Regimes

A country's legal system can affect the disposition of a will. For example, common law jurisdictions, such as the United Kingdom and the United States, generally allow a **testator** (i.e., a person who makes a will) testamentary freedom of disposition by will; that is, the right to use their own judgment regarding the rights others will have over their property after death. Most civil law countries place restrictions on such disposition.

Civil law, which is derived from Roman law, is the world's predominant legal system. In civil law states, judges apply general, abstract rules or concepts to particular cases. **Common law** systems, which usually trace their heritage to Britain, draw abstract rules from specific cases. The distinction is arguably analogous to the distinction between deductive and inductive reasoning. Put differently, in civil systems law is developed primarily through legislative statutes or executive action. In common law systems, law is developed primarily through decisions of the courts.

Countries following **Shari'a**, the law of Islam, have substantial variation, but are more like civil law systems especially in regard to estate planning. In addition to the law of the land, Muslims may wish to consider guidance on inheritance provided by Shari'a or Islamic law. Because Shari'a is often not the law of the land in most countries, including many countries where a majority of the population is Muslim, those who wish to follow Islamic guidance on inheritance are usually able to do so through the making of a will, as long as the contents of the will are not in conflict with the concerned law of the land.

Appendix A presents a comparison of non-tax issues related to estate planning for 37 jurisdictions including the legal system of each.[2] Compiled by LawInContext, Appendix A shows that 22 of the 37 jurisdictions have civil law regimes, which are common in Europe, South America, and some larger Asian countries.

The legal concept of a trust is unique to the common law. A trust is a vehicle through which an individual (called a settlor) entrusts certain assets to a trustee (or trustees) who manages the assets. Civil law countries may not recognize foreign trusts. In fact, twelve of the 22 civil law jurisdictions, including France and Germany, do not recognize trusts at all.

Ownership, like other legal principles in civil law, is a precise concept tempered by statutes that place certain limitations on the free disposition of one's assets. Under **forced heirship rules**, for example, children have the right to a fixed share of a parent's estate. This right may exist whether or not the child is estranged or conceived outside of marriage. Wealthy individuals may attempt to move assets into an offshore trust governed by a different domicile to circumvent forced heirship rules. They may alternatively attempt to reduce a forced heirship claim by gifting or donating assets to others during their lifetime to reduce the value of the final estate upon death. In a number of jurisdictions, however, "clawback" provisions bring such lifetime gifts back into the estate to calculate the child's share. If the assets remaining in the estate are not sufficient to cover the claim, the child may be able to recover his or her forced share

---

2 None of the referenced appendixes are included or assigned as part of the curriculum. For those interested in further study, all three appendixes have been made available online under the heading "Supplemental Materials" at www.cfainstitute.org.

from the donees who received the lifetime gifts.[3] Twenty-five of the 37 jurisdictions in Appendix A have forced heirship rules of some variety, creating a common estate planning consideration.

Spouses typically have similar guaranteed inheritance rights under civil law forced heirship regimes. In addition, spouses have marital property rights, which depend on the marital property regime that applies to their marriage. For example, under **community property regimes**, each spouse has an indivisible one-half interest in income earned during marriage. Gifts and inheritances received before and after marriage may still be retained as separate property. Upon death of a spouse, the property is divided with ownership of one-half of the community property automatically passing to the surviving spouse. Ownership of the other half is transferred by the will through the probate process.

In **separate property regimes**, prevalent in civil law countries, each spouse is able to own and control property as an individual, which enables each to dispose of property as they wish, subject to a spouse's other rights. Italian forced heirship rules, for example, apply to the decedent's community and separate property. It is noteworthy that, in many civil law countries, couples can elect the marital property regime that will apply to their property. The marital property regimes of each of the 37 jurisdictions are summarized in Appendix A.

EXAMPLE 1

Community Property and Forced Heirship

Philippe and Helena Berelli live in a community property regime with their two children. The community property regime entitles a surviving spouse to receive one-half of the community property after the first spouse's death. There are also forced heirship laws in their country that entitle a spouse to one-third of the total estate and the children are entitled to split one-third of the total estate. After their marriage, Philippe received an inheritance that was retained as separate property and is worth €200,000 today. The remainder of the estate is considered community property. Suppose Philippe passes away today with a total estate of €800,000 and wishes to bequeath €300,000 to his surviving mother.

1 What is the minimum that Helena should receive?

2 What is the minimum amount the children should receive under forced heirship rules?

3 May Philippe bequeath €300,000 to his mother?

Solution to 1:

Helena is entitled to the greater of her share under community property or forced heirship rules. Under community property, she is entitled to receive one-half of the community property, or 0.50(€800,000 − €200,000) = €300,000. Under forced heirship rules she is entitled to one-third of the total estate, or (1/3)(€800,000) = €266,667. Therefore, Helena is entitled to €300,000.

Solution to 2:

The children are collectively entitled to receive one-third of the total estate equal to €266,667, or €133,333 for each child.

---

3 See Hayton (2003).

> **Solution to 3:**
>
> Philippe is able to freely dispose of the remainder, which is €800,000 − €300,000 − €266,667 = €233,333. Therefore, Philippe is unable to bequeath €300,000 to his mother, but may bequeath the remainder of €233,333.

2.3 Income, Wealth, and Wealth Transfer Taxes

An important part of estate planning is an understanding of how (or whether) assets are taxed when their ownership is transferred at or before death. In general, taxes are levied in one of four general ways:[4]

1 Tax on income
2 Tax on spending
3 Tax on wealth
4 Tax on wealth transfers

Taxes on income can be levied at different rates for a variety of income categories such as compensatory income, investment income, etc. Appendix B provides a brief description of income taxes (excluding separate capital gains tax regimes, if any), as well as wealth and gratuitous transfer taxes in 37 different jurisdictions.[5] Almost all jurisdictions in Appendix B, with the exception of the Bahamas, Cayman Islands, and the United Arab Emirates, impose income taxes.

Investment income is typically taxed in several possible ways. It can be taxed annually on either an accrual or cash basis as income or gains are received. Alternatively, tax can be deferred until the gain on an asset is ultimately recognized upon the sale or disposition of the asset. Horan and Robinson (2008) review the investment tax regimes of over 50 developed economies and discuss their investment implications in detail.

Taxes on spending normally take the form of sales taxes where a tax is applied to certain types of purchases. These can be applied at the time of purchase or periodically through some computation of consumption.

Wealth-based taxes can come in several forms. A jurisdiction may levy taxes annually on the principal value of real estate, financial assets, tangible assets, etc. Tax based on one's comprehensive wealth is often referred to as **net worth tax or net wealth tax**. According to Appendix B, only seven of the 37 jurisdictions covered in the appendix impose such wealth taxes. The economic implications of wealth-based taxes are different from taxes on investment returns because the asset's entire capital base (less liabilities associated with the relevant asset), rather than only incremental gains, is subject to tax. These implications are discussed in greater detail elsewhere.[6]

Taxes on wealth transfers are the purview of estate planning and will be a focus of this reading.[7] The two primary forms of taxes on wealth transfers correspond to the primary ways of transferring assets: gifting assets during one's lifetime, and bequeathing assets upon one's death through a will or via some other structure.

---

4 This categorization is based primarily on Wilcox, Horvitz, and diBartolomeo (2006) and Horvitz (2008), and corresponds closely with Bronson, Scanlan, and Squires (2007).

5 See Horan and Robinson (2008) for further details on global income tax regimes including capital gains taxes.

6 See, for example, Wilcox, Horvitz, and diBartolomeo (2006), Horan and Robinson (2008), Horvitz (2008).

7 Wilcox, Horvitz, and diBartolomeo (2006) categorize estate or inheritance taxes as a wealth-based tax, but we and others (including Horvitz 2008) categorize it as a transfer tax because the ownership of inherited assets is transferred to heirs and it is this transaction that is taxed. In addition, an inheritance tax is typically levied once rather than repeatedly as is the case for most wealth-based taxes.

In an estate planning context, lifetime gifts are sometimes referred to as **lifetime gratuitous transfers**, or *inter vivos* transfers, and are made during the lifetime of the donor. The term "gratuitous" refers to a transfer made with purely donative intent, that is, without expectation of anything in exchange. Gifts may or may not be taxed depending on the jurisdiction. Where gift tax applies, taxation may also depend on other factors such as the residency or domicile of the donor, the residency or domicile of the recipient, the tax status of the recipient (e.g., nonprofits), the type of asset (moveable versus immovable), and the location of the asset (domestic or foreign).

Bequeathing assets or transferring them in some other way upon one's death is referred to as a **testamentary gratuitous transfer**. The term "testamentary" refers to a transfer made after death. From a recipient's perspective, it is called an inheritance. Similar to lifetime gifts, the taxation of testamentary transfers (transfers at death) may depend upon the residency or domicile of the donor, the residency or domicile of the recipient, the type of asset (moveable versus immovable), and the location of the asset (domestic or foreign).

Taxes on wealth transfer may be applied to the transferor or the recipient. For example, in the case of testamentary gratuitous transfers, some jurisdictions impose an estate tax that is generally on the liability of the transferor (or more precisely, the estate of the transferor). Other jurisdictions impose liability for wealth transfer taxes on the recipient, often referred to as an inheritance tax.[8] These taxes may be applied at a flat rate or based on a progressive tax rate schedule, where the tax rate increases as the amount of wealth transferred increases. Often the tax is applied after the deduction of a statutory allowance. The tax rate may also depend on the relationship between transferor and recipient. Transfers to spouses, for instance, are often tax exempt.

EXAMPLE 2

UK Inheritance Tax Example

Paul Dasani, an unmarried individual, passed away in November 2008. Dasani was a resident of London at the time of his death and had a total estate valued at £600,000. His children are the beneficiaries of the estate. The United Kingdom imposes an inheritance tax threshold on estates valued above £312,000 in 2008. The tax is payable by the trustee of the estate out of estate assets at a rate of 40 percent on the amount over the statutory allowance of £312,000.

What is the amount of inheritance tax payable?

Solution:

The inheritance tax is computed as:

Estate value	£600,000
Less threshold	(£312,000)
Excess	£288,000
Rate on excess	40%
Inheritance tax	£115,200

---

8 As noted earlier, terminology differs from jurisdiction to jurisdiction, and the terms *estate tax* and *inheritance tax* are sometimes used interchangeably.

EXAMPLE 3

Progressive Estate Tax Example

Ya-wen Chao passed away in a jurisdiction with progressive estate tax rates as provided in the table below. After all applicable exemptions, Chao had a taxable estate of €2,000,000. What is Chao's estate tax?

Taxable Estate (€)	Tax Rate (%)
Up to 600,000	2
600,001–1,500,000	4
1,500,001–3,000,000	7
3,000,001–4,500,000	11
4,500,001–6,000,000	15
6,000,001–10,000,000	20
10,000,001–15,000,000	26
15,000,001–40,000,000	33
40,000,001–100,000,000	41
Over 100,000,000	50

Solution:

The estate tax is computed as:

Tax on first 600,000 (2%) =	€12,000
Tax on next 900,000 (4%) =	36,000
Tax on remaining 500,000 (7%) =	35,000
Total estate tax	€83,000

3   CORE CAPITAL AND EXCESS CAPITAL

Developing an estate plan that will sustain a family and their descendants over multiple generations is a challenging task. A mathematical reality is that the sheer number of family members has a tendency to grow exponentially from one generation to the next as members of subsequent generations propagate, often doubling from one generation to the next.

To put the problem into perspective, consider the case of a 60-year-old couple with no bequest motive; that is, no specific desire to transfer wealth to their children or beyond. One of their likely concerns is how much they can spend from their portfolio without depleting their resources before the end of their lifetimes, which probably means sustaining wealth for at least another 30 years. Estimates vary, but researchers place the sustainable spending rate between 3.5 percent and 6 percent of the initial portfolio value, assuming that spending increases by the inflation rate in subsequent years.[9] To many, these values are surprisingly modest and illustrate how easily a family can adopt a spending rate that is unsustainable, especially over a time horizon that extends beyond one generation. This challenge of sustaining wealth over multiple

---

9 See, for example, Bengen (1994, 1996, 1997), Guyton (2004), Milevsky and Robinson (2005), Spitzer and Singh (2006), Spitzer, Strieter, and Singh (2007), Stout and Mitchell (2007).

generations is magnified as the number of family members grows. Exacerbating the problem further is the potential erosion caused by taxes each time assets are transferred from one generation to the next.

Difficulties also arise when managing the conflicting interests within and across generations. The first generation's wealth transfer goals are often informed by the character, maturity, and circumstances of the individuals involved. In any case, the starting point in developing an estate plan is deciding how much wealth to transfer and whether to transfer wealth to future generations, philanthropic causes, or elsewhere. The answer to this question begins with an understanding of the spending needs of the first generation.

Wilcox, Horvitz, and diBartolomeo (2006) developed the notion of a life balance sheet, which is a comprehensive accounting of an investor's assets and liabilities, both explicit and implied. Explicit assets consist of financial assets (e.g., stocks and bonds), real estate, and other property that can be readily liquidated. A notable implied asset for many is the present value of one's employment capital, often referred to as **human capital** or **net employment capital**. Expected pension benefits are another implied asset that, although non-tradable, provide specific value to the investor.[10]

On the right-hand side of the life balance sheet are an investor's liabilities. Explicit liabilities, such as mortgages or margin loans, are fairly obvious entries. Less obvious are implied liabilities that represent the capitalized value of the investor's desired spending goals. These goals may include providing for a secure retirement, funding children's education, providing a safety reserve for emergencies, or earmarking seed capital for business ventures. The amount of capital required to fund spending to maintain a given lifestyle, fund these goals, and provide adequate reserves for unexpected commitments is called **core capital**.

An investor with more assets than liabilities on the life balance sheet has more capital than is necessary to fund their lifestyle and reserves and therefore has **excess capital** that can be safely transferred to others without jeopardizing the investor's lifestyle.[11] Exhibit 1 presents a hypothetical life balance sheet with assets listed on the left-hand side. Notice that the capitalized value of the investor's college funding obligations, retirement spending, and safety reserve, is represented by the implied liabilities on the right-hand side of the hypothetical balance sheet.

---

10 Wilcox, Horvitz, and diBartolomeo (2006) and Ibbotson, Milevsky, Chen, and Zhu (2006) discuss human capital and its relation to life cycle planning in more detail.

11 Wilcox, Horvitz, and diBartolomeo (2006) refer to this excess capital as "discretionary wealth."

Exhibit 1   Hypothetical Life Balance Sheet

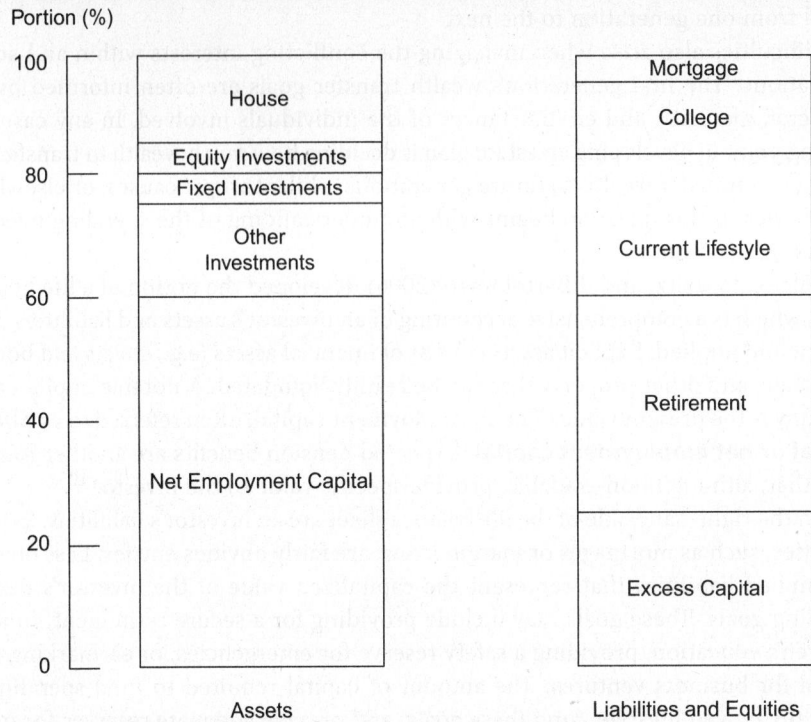

Portion (%)

Assets column (bottom to top):
- Net Employment Capital
- Other Investments
- Fixed Investments
- Equity Investments
- House

Liabilities and Equities column (bottom to top):
- Excess Capital
- Retirement
- Current Lifestyle
- College
- Mortgage

Axis labels: 0, 20, 40, 60, 80, 100

Assets   Liabilities and Equities

Source: Adapted from Wilcox, Horvitz, and diBartolomeo (2006), p.18.

3.1 Estimating Core Capital with Mortality Tables

The amount of core capital needed to maintain an investor's lifestyle in a probabilistic sense can be estimated in a number of ways. First, it is important to incorporate the effects of inflation, particularly over long time horizons. One can either forecast nominal spending needs discounting them to the present values using nominal discount rates, or forecast real spending needs discounting them using real discount rates. The two approaches are indistinguishable.

The most straightforward way of calculating core capital is to calculate the present value of anticipated spending over one's remaining life expectancy. One problem with this approach is that, by definition, an investor has a significant probability of living past their remaining life expectancy because life expectancy is an average that has substantial variation. Estimates of core capital based on life expectancy will fall short of what is actually required in a great many cases.[12]

Another approach is to calculate expected future cash flows by multiplying each future cash flow needed by the probability that such cash flow will be needed, or **survival probability**. When more than one person is relying on core capital (e.g., two

---

12 See Wilcox (2008) for a more thorough discussion.

spouses), the probability of survival in a given year is a joint probability that either the husband or the wife survives. Specifically, the probability that either the husband or the wife survives equals:

$$p(\text{Survival}) = p(\text{Husband survives}) + p(\text{Wife survives}) \\ -p(\text{Husband survives}) \times p(\text{Wife survives}) \quad (1)$$

assuming their chances of survival are independent of each other. The present value of the spending need is then equal to:

$$PV(\text{Spending need}) = \sum_{j=1}^{N} \frac{p(\text{Survival}_j) \times \text{Spending}_j}{(1+r)^j} \quad (2)$$

The numerator is the expected cash flow in year j, that is, the probability of surviving until that year times the spending in that year should the person survive.

For example, consider Ernest and Beatrice Webster, ages 79 and 68, respectively. Their individual probabilities of survival are shown in Columns 3 and 5 of Exhibit 2. Over the next year, Ernest has approximately a 93.6 percent chance of survival, while the younger Beatrice has a 98.3 percent chance of survival.[13] The chance of either one of them surviving, however, is greater than either of their individual probabilities of survival. Specifically, the combined probability that either or both survive for the first year is $0.9989 = 0.9355 + 0.9831 - 0.9355 \times 0.9831$. This figure is represented in Column 6.

Exhibit 2 Example of Core Capital Calculation for Ernest and Beatrice Webster

	Ernest		Beatrice		Combined	Annual	Expected	Discounted
Year (1)	Age (2)	p(Survival) (3)	Age (4)	p(Survival) (5)	p(Survival) (6)	Spending (7)	Spending (8)	Value (9)
1	80	0.9355	69	0.9831	0.9989	500,000	499,457	489,664
2	81	0.8702	70	0.9649	0.9954	515,000	512,654	492,747
3	82	0.8038	71	0.9457	0.9893	530,450	524,800	494,531
4	83	0.7339	72	0.9249	0.9800	546,364	535,443	494,666
5	84	0.6686	73	0.9025	0.9677	562,754	544,581	493,244
6	85	0.6001	74	0.8785	0.9514	579,637	551,476	489,695
7	86	0.5327	75	0.8526	0.9311	597,026	555,893	483,938
8	87	0.4674	76	0.8252	0.9069	614,937	557,682	475,976
9	88	0.4048	77	0.7958	0.8785	633,385	556,412	465,580
10	89	0.3459	78	0.7646	0.8460	652,387	551,947	452,789
11	90	0.2912	79	0.7311	0.8094	671,958	543,909	437,446
12	91	0.2414	80	0.6952	0.7688	692,117	532,095	419,553
13	92	0.1968	81	0.6582	0.7254	712,880	517,156	399,778
14	93	0.1576	82	0.6173	0.6776	734,267	497,573	377,098
15	94	0.1239	83	0.5775	0.6298	756,295	476,345	353,931
16	95	0.0955	84	0.5340	0.5785	778,984	450,638	328,265

(continued)

---

13 It is worth noting that survival probabilities change each year. They are conditioned on one surviving until a particular age. For example, Ernest is currently 79 years old and has an 87.02% chance of surviving two more years until age 81. Moving forward one year, if Ernest survives until age 80, his chances of surviving until age 81 increase because he has already made some progress in that direction. Therefore, the probabilities change from one year to the next and will warrant updating.

Exhibit 2   (Continued)

Year (1)	Ernest Age (2)	Ernest p(Survival) (3)	Beatrice Age (4)	Beatrice p(Survival) (5)	Combined p(Survival) (6)	Annual Spending (7)	Expected Spending (8)	Discounted Value (9)
17	96	0.0720	85	0.4894	0.5262	802,353	422,165	301,494
18	97	0.0532	86	0.4441	0.4736	826,424	391,431	274,064
19	98	0.0373	87	0.3987	0.4211	851,217	358,456	246,055
20	99	0.0262	88	0.3538	0.3707	876,753	325,053	218,751
21	100	0.0180	89	0.3100	0.3224	903,056	291,161	192,101
22	101	0.0000	90	0.2679	0.2679	930,147	249,204	161,195
23	102	0.0000	91	0.2281	0.2281	958,052	218,569	138,607
24	103	0.0000	92	0.1912	0.1912	986,793	188,652	117,289
25	104	0.0000	93	0.1575	0.1575	1,016,397	160,043	97,551
26	105	0.0000	94	0.1273	0.1273	1,046,889	133,275	79,643
27	106	0.0000	95	0.1009	0.1009	1,078,296	108,795	63,739
28	107	0.0000	96	0.0783	0.0783	1,110,645	86,937	49,935
29	108	0.0000	97	0.0594	0.0594	1,143,964	67,905	38,238
30	109	0.0000	98	0.0439	0.0439	1,178,283	51,764	28,578
31	110	0.0000	99	0.0317	0.0317	1,213,631	38,452	20,812
32	111	0.0000	100	0.0000	0.0000	1,250,040	—	—
						Total		9,176,955

The Websters' inflation-adjusted annual spending needs are calculated based on their current spending of €500,000 per year and are increased annually using a 3 percent real growth rate (that is, 3 percent annual spending growth after inflation). The Websters' *expected* spending need each year is presented in the column labeled *Expected Spending* (Column 8). It is calculated as the product of their joint survival probability and their required spending for that year (*Annual Spending*, Column 7). Each year's expected spending is discounted back to the present, using in this case a real risk-free discount rate of 2.0 percent. The sum of each year's present value of expected spending represents the investor's core capital. In this case, Ernest and Beatrice Webster have core capital spending needs of about €9,176,955.[14]

This approach can be modified by conditioning each year's spending based on each spouse's expected survival. For example, if Ernest were to pass away, Beatrice's independent spending needs may be lower than what would have been required if Ernest were also alive. Alternatively, her spending need could be higher. Estimates vary and would certainly be affected by individual circumstances, but some economists estimate that two people can maintain the same living standard for 1.6 times the cost of one. Using this estimate, Beatrice could maintain the same lifestyle with 1/1.6 (or 62.5%) of the amount of spending if Ernest passed away.

In this approach, spending needs are discounted using the real risk-free rate to match the risk of the cash flows. To be sure, the cash flows are not without risk but their uncertainty is most likely unrelated to market risk factors that would be priced in a normal asset pricing model, making their beta equal to zero. One may argue that,

---

14 A more conservative approach is assuming that both Ernest and Beatrice survive throughout the forecast horizon provided, rather than assigning probabilities to their combined survival each year.

although mortality risk in this context is non-systematic, it is also non-diversifiable. However, mortality risk can be hedged with traditional life insurance allowing the individual to eliminate the non-systematic risk even if it is non-diversifiable. Therefore, discounting spending needs with the risk-free rate is appropriate.

It is tempting to discount spending needs using the expected return of the assets used to fund them. This would be problematic because the risk of the Websters' spending needs is fundamentally unrelated to the risk of the portfolio used to fund those needs. Merton (2007) draws this distinction in the context of a defined-benefit pension plan. He points out that using the expected return of pension fund assets to discount the liabilities they are intended to fund systematically under-prices those liabilities, and has contributed to the decline of defined-benefit pension plans. Another approach using Monte Carlo simulation with expected returns and volatility is discussed below.

3.1.1 Safety Reserve

This approach does not, however, fully account for the risk inherent in capital markets. For example, there is no guarantee that capital markets will produce returns greater than the risk-free rate even over long periods of time. Therefore, the present value of the Websters' spending needs underestimates their true core capital needs. One way to adjust for this underestimation is to augment core capital with a safety reserve designed to incorporate flexibility into the estate plan.[15] Incorporating flexibility in this way can be important for at least two reasons. First, it provides a capital cushion if capital markets produce a sequence of unusually poor returns that jeopardize the sustainability of the planned spending program. Second, it allows the first generation to increase their spending beyond that explicitly articulated in the spending program. In this way, the safety reserve addresses not only the uncertainty of capital markets, but the uncertainty associated with a family's future commitments.

The size of the safety reserve can be based on a subjective assessment of the circumstances. For example, Evensky (1997) advocates a safety reserve equal to two years of spending. His reasons are behavioral as well as practical. The reserve provides a psychological buffer between an investor and the volatility of capital markets. The investor perceives that their spending needs are unaffected by short-term capital market volatility and is better able to adhere to a particular investment strategy during turbulent markets.

EXAMPLE 4

Core Capital with Mortality Probabilities

Kenroy and Alicia Trudeau live in South Africa and are 64 and 61 years old, respectively. Their survival probabilities based on their current ages are listed in the table below. They would like to maintain annual spending of ZAR 1,000,000 on an inflation-adjusted basis. Inflation is expected to be 3 percent, and the nominal risk-free rate is 5 percent.

---

15 Wilcox (2008) proposes a more complex solution that accounts for the joint distribution of uncertain life spans and asset returns and that produces even more conservative estimates of core capital.

Year	Kenroy		Alicia	
	Age	p(Survival)	Age	p(Survival)
1	65	0.991	62	0.996
2	66	0.981	63	0.986
3	67	0.971	64	0.976

1 What is the probability that either Kenroy or Alicia will survive in each of the next three years?

2 What is the capitalized value of their core capital spending needs over the next three years?

Solution to 1:

The probability that either Kenroy or Alicia will survive is equal to the sum of their individual probabilities less the product of their individual probabilities.

$$p(\text{Joint survival}) = p(\text{Kenroy survives}) + p(\text{Alicia survives})$$
$$- p(\text{Kenroy survives})\,p(\text{Alicia survives})$$

For the next three years, the joint probability of survival is:

Year	Joint p(Survival)
1	0.9999
2	0.9997
3	0.9993

Solution to 2:

The capitalized value of their core capital spending needs equals the product of the joint probability of survival and the real spending need for each year discounted using the real risk-free rate. Alternatively, one may discount the nominal expected cash flow at the nominal risk-free rate. Using the first approach, the real cash flows will remain constant and be discounted at 2 percent (or 5 percent less 3 percent).[16]

Year	Annual Spending	Expected Spending	Discounted Value
1	1,000,000	999,960	980,360
2	1,000,000	999,730	960,910
3	1,000,000	999,300	941,670
			2,882,940

---

16 Two percent is an approximation. A more precise calculation is: $(1.05/1.03) - 1 = 1.94\%$.

3.2 Estimating Core Capital with Monte Carlo Analysis

Another approach to estimating core capital uses Monte Carlo analysis, a computer-based simulation technique that allows the analyst to forecast a range of possible outcomes based on, say, 10,000 simulated trials.[17] Rather than discounting future expenses, this approach estimates the size of a portfolio needed to generate sufficient withdrawals to meet expenses, which are assumed to increase with inflation. This approach more fully captures the risk inherent in capital markets than the mortality table approach described above. For example, one could forecast a particular path of portfolio values based on a hypothetical sequence of returns that conforms to the statistical properties associated with the portfolio's expected return. That particular path is one of an infinite set of possible outcomes. The analyst can then forecast another path based on the same set of statistical properties, which will lead to a different outcome. Repeating this procedure thousands of times provides a range of possible outcomes and an understanding of the risk of the portfolio.

One can incorporate recurring spending needs, irregular liquidity needs, taxes, inflation, and other factors into the analysis. In the context of calculating core capital, the wealth manager might estimate the amount of capital required to sustain a pattern of spending over a particular time horizon with, for example, a 95 percent level of confidence. That is, the analyst determines the core capital that sustains spending in at least 95 percent of the simulated trials. A higher level of confidence leads to larger estimates of core capital, and vice versa. The safety reserve may also be added to accommodate flexibility in the first generation's spending patterns. It need not be quite as large as that used in the mortality table method, however, because Monte Carlo analysis already captures the risk of producing a sequence of anomalously poor returns. In contrast to the mortality table method in which cash flows are discounted at the risk-free rate of return, the expected returns used in Monte Carlo analysis are derived from the market expectations of the assets comprising the portfolio.

Milevsky and Robinson (2005) developed a method to calculate sustainable spending rates that approximate those produced from a Monte Carlo simulation but without the need for simulation. Their analysis incorporates life-span uncertainty as well as financial market risk. Exhibit 3 presents an example of ruin probabilities (i.e., the probability of depleting one's financial assets before death) based on their analysis. For example, consider Mr. Harper, a single 65-year-old with the same €500,000 annual spending need as the Websters. He is willing to accept a 9 percent chance that his spending pattern may exhaust his portfolio before the end of his life (e.g., 91 percent level of confidence). This represents the probability of ruin, or the probability that his spending is unsustainable.

This analysis assumes the balanced portfolio has a mean arithmetic return of 5 percent and volatility of 12 percent. It also assumes that the spending rate is determined by the initial portfolio value and increased by the rate of inflation annually thereafter. Under these conditions, Mr. Harper can spend €4.00 for each €100 of core capital, or 4 percent of capital. The core capital required for Mr. Harper to spend €500,000 per year is therefore €12,500,000 = €500,000/0.04. If he is willing to accept a higher probability of failure, Mr. Harper will need less capital. For example, a 15.8 percent chance of Mr. Harper's spending outlasting his portfolio allows him to spend €5.00 for every €100, which requires only €10,000,000, or €500,000/0.05, of core capital.

Asset allocation affects the expected return and volatility of the portfolio, which in turn affects the sustainability of a given spending rate. Obviously, higher return improves sustainability and would require less core capital to generate the same

---

17 See Sharpe, Chen, Pinto, and McLeavey (2007) for a more detailed discussion of its applications within the context of a retirement portfolio. In addition, Bernstein (2008) presents Monte Carlo analysis in the larger context of estate planning.

Exhibit 3   Ruin Probability for Balanced Portfolio of 50 Percent Equity and 50 Percent Bonds

Retirement Age	Median Age at Death	Hazard Rate, λ (%)	Real Annual Spending per $100 of Initial Nest Egg								
			$2.00 (%)	$3.00 (%)	$4.00 (%)	$5.00 (%)	$6.00 (%)	$7.00 (%)	$8.00 (%)	$9.00 (%)	$10.00 (%)
Endowment	Infinity	0.00	6.7	24.9	49.0	70.0	84.3	92.5	96.6	98.6	99.4
50	78.1	2.47	1.8	6.4	14.0	24.0	35.2	46.3	56.8	66.0	73.8
55	83.0	2.48	1.8	6.3	14.0	24.0	35.1	46.2	56.7	65.9	73.7
60	83.4	2.96	1.5	5.2	11.6	20.1	29.9	40.1	50.0	59.1	67.2
65	83.9	3.67	1.1	4.0	9.0	15.8	24.0	32.8	41.8	50.5	58.5
70	84.6	4.75	0.8	2.8	6.3	11.4	17.6	24.7	32.2	39.8	47.2
75	85.7	6.48	0.5	1.7	3.9	7.2	11.4	16.3	21.9	27.8	33.9
80	87.4	9.37	0.3	0.9	2.0	3.8	6.2	9.1	12.5	16.3	20.5

Note: Mean arithmetic portfolio return = 5 percent; standard deviation of return = 12 percent; mean geometric portfolio return = 4.28 percent.
Source: Milevsky and Robinson (2005).

level of spending. Volatility must also be considered, however, because it decreases the sustainability of a spending program for at least two reasons. First, even in the absence of a spending rule, volatility decreases future accumulations. This concept can be illustrated by noting that future accumulations per unit of currency are equal to the product of one plus the geometric average return, or:

$$\mathrm{FV} = \left(1 + R_G\right)^N = \prod_{n=1}^{N}\left(1 + R_n\right)$$
$$= \left(1 + R_1\right)\left(1 + R_2\right)\left(1 + R_3\right)\ldots\left(1 + R_N\right)$$

(3)

where R_G is the geometric average return over period N. It is commonly referred to as the compounded return. The geometric average return is related to the arithmetic average return and its volatility in the following way:

$$R_G \cong r - \frac{1}{2}\sigma^2$$

(4)

where r is the arithmetic average return and σ is the volatility of the arithmetic return. According to Equation 4, higher volatility decreases the geometric average return and hence future accumulations, which in turn decreases sustainability. Another way to illustrate this point is to consider a €100 portfolio that experiences sequential returns of +50 percent followed by –50 percent. Although the arithmetic average of those returns is zero, the portfolio's value after two years is only €75. The €25 decline in value is due to the volatility of returns represented by the second term in Equation 4.

The second reason volatility decreases sustainability relates to the interaction of periodic withdrawals and return sequences. Equation 3 shows that future accumulations do not depend on the sequence of returns in the absence of periodic spending withdrawals. That is, the future value calculation is unchanged regardless of whether R_1 and R_2 (or any other two periodic returns) are reversed. Put differently, in the example of +50 percent and –50 percent returns, the ending value after two years is the same regardless of whether the portfolio returns are sequenced with the positive return first or last.

This independence disappears when withdrawals are introduced. Specifically, the sustainability of a portfolio is severely compromised when the initial returns are poor because a portion of the portfolio is being liquidated at relatively depressed values, making less capital available for compounding at potentially higher subsequent returns. If the portfolio in our example were to experience a €10 withdrawal at the end of each year, the portfolio would be worth €60 at the end of two years if the positive return occurs first but only €50 if the negative return occurs first. A fixed withdrawal program can be thought of as the opposite of dollar-cost averaging in which volatility has a positive effect on future accumulations, holding the expected return constant.

Several authors have examined the return-volatility trade-off on portfolio sustainability in the context of asset allocation. Diversification is particularly useful in this context because it reduces volatility without necessarily decreasing return. Not surprisingly, recommendations vary; but equity allocations between 30 percent and 75 percent of total portfolio value seem to maximize portfolio sustainability.

EXAMPLE 5

Core Capital with Monte Carlo Analysis

Sophie Zang is a recent widow, 55-years old, living in Singapore. Upon his passing, her husband's estate and life insurance proceeds provided a total of SGD 2,000,000 to maintain her lifestyle. With no children, Zang has no bequest motives but she has established a charitable remainder trust (CRT) upon which she will rely to maintain her lifestyle in real terms for the rest of her life, with the balance going to her favorite charity upon her death. Assume the trust's asset allocation conforms to the capital market expectations from Exhibit 3.

1 How much can Zang withdraw from the CRT if she wants to be at least 98 percent certain that the portfolio will last for the remainder of her life?

2 How much can Zang withdraw from the CRT if she is willing to be only 94 percent certain that the portfolio will last for the remainder of her life?

Solution to 1:

The 55-year old retirement age row in Exhibit 3 indicates that Zang's median age at death is approximately 83 years old, or 28 years away. However, she is as likely to live longer than age 83 as she is to die prior to age 83. To be at least 98 percent certain that she does not run out of money, Zang's maximum probability of exhausting her assets should not exceed 2 percent. A spending rate of $2 per $100 of assets has a ruin probability of 1.8 percent. So Zang can withdraw approximately $0.02 \times$ SGD 2,000,000 = SGD 40,000 with 98% certainty that the portfolio will last for the remainder of her life.

Solution to 2:

If Zang can tolerate a 6 percent failure rate, then she can withdraw almost 3 percent from the CRT annually on an inflation-adjusted basis, or $0.03 \times$ SGD 2,000,000 = SGD 60,000, according to Exhibit 3. A spending rate of SGD 3 per SDG 100 of assets has a ruin probability of 6.3 percent, which is very close to the stated failure rate of 6 percent.

4 TRANSFERRING EXCESS CAPITAL

The first generation's core capital implicitly determines their discretionary wealth, or excess capital, which equals their assets less their core capital. For example, if the Websters have €20,000,000 of capital to meet their spending and discretionary needs and their core capital is €9,200,000, then excess capital is €10,800,000. The challenge then becomes developing a plan to transfer this wealth that matches the Websters' goals (e.g., family, philanthropy), accounts for the tax implications, and provides the desired amount of control and flexibility. As Bronson, Scanlan, and Squires (2007) point out, "The possible legal structures for a wealth transfer are necessarily country specific. Timing of wealth transfers, however, involves the more universal principles of tax avoidance, tax deferral, and maximized compound return."

4.1 Lifetime Gifts and Testamentary Bequests

An obvious method of transferring discretionary wealth is to donate it immediately or during one's lifetime through a series of gratuitous transfers. In jurisdictions having an estate or inheritance tax, gifting has the advantage of lowering the value of the taxable estate, thereby lowering estate or inheritance taxes (except where under applicable law the value of the gift is added back to the estate for estate or inheritance tax purposes). To mitigate this tax minimization strategy, jurisdictions that impose estate or inheritance tax typically also impose gift or donation taxes.

4.1.1 *Tax-Free Gifts*

Some gifts can escape transfer tax by falling below periodic or lifetime allowances. South Africa, for example, allows taxpayers to make tax-free gifts of up to ZAR 100,000 per tax year. During their lifetime, UK taxpayers may make gifts up to £312,000 that escape inheritance tax. Germany has gift allowances for gifts to close family members. Each parent may make a €205,000 gift to a child (€410,000 total from both parents) every 10 years, allowing a substantial amount of wealth to be transferred over time.

Other exclusions or relief may apply, as well. In France, for instance, a 50 percent relief applies to gifts from donors less than 70 years old, and a 30 percent relief applies if the donor is between 70 and 80 years old.[18] It is therefore common to be able to transfer some assets by gift in a tax-efficient manner.

Even in jurisdictions with relatively small annual exclusions, a gifting program that is started early and implemented over long periods of time can transfer substantial wealth in a tax-efficient manner. In the United States, for example, a donor's annual gift exclusions are currently limited to US$13,000 per year (for 2009), per donee (e.g., a parent may annually transfer US$13,000 to each child or US$26,000 from both parents). Exhibit 4 shows that an annual gifting program of transferring US$13,000 per year tax free implemented over a 30-year period transfers over US$640,000 inflation-adjusted dollars at an 8 percent nominal return that is taxed at 25 percent annually with a 2.5 percent inflation rate (i.e., 5.5 percent real rate of return).[19] The dashed line in Exhibit 4 represents the accumulated value of the gifts themselves, excluding investment returns. After 30 years, gifts total US$390,000 = US$13,000 × 30. If the donor had kept this amount, any future appreciation would have increased the value in his estate and hence the estate tax liability. Assuming an 8 percent nominal pretax return that is subject to a 25 percent annual tax would add an additional US$305,000 of real appreciation (after adjusting for inflation), for a total value of US$695,000. A tax-efficient investment strategy that defers the 25 percent tax until the end of the investment horizon increases the accumulated sum to almost US$843,000. Because these figures are based on real inflation-adjusted returns, this sum represents the amount of capital that can be transferred in today's dollars, and can therefore be a sizable proportion of many estates. Obviously, the amount of real wealth that can be transferred without tax increases with the rate of real return and the time horizon.

---

18 LawInContext Private Banking Helpdesk.
19 Five and a half percent is an approximation. A more precise calculation is 1.08/1.025 − 1 = 5.36%.

Exhibit 4   Inflation-Adjusted Wealth Transferred

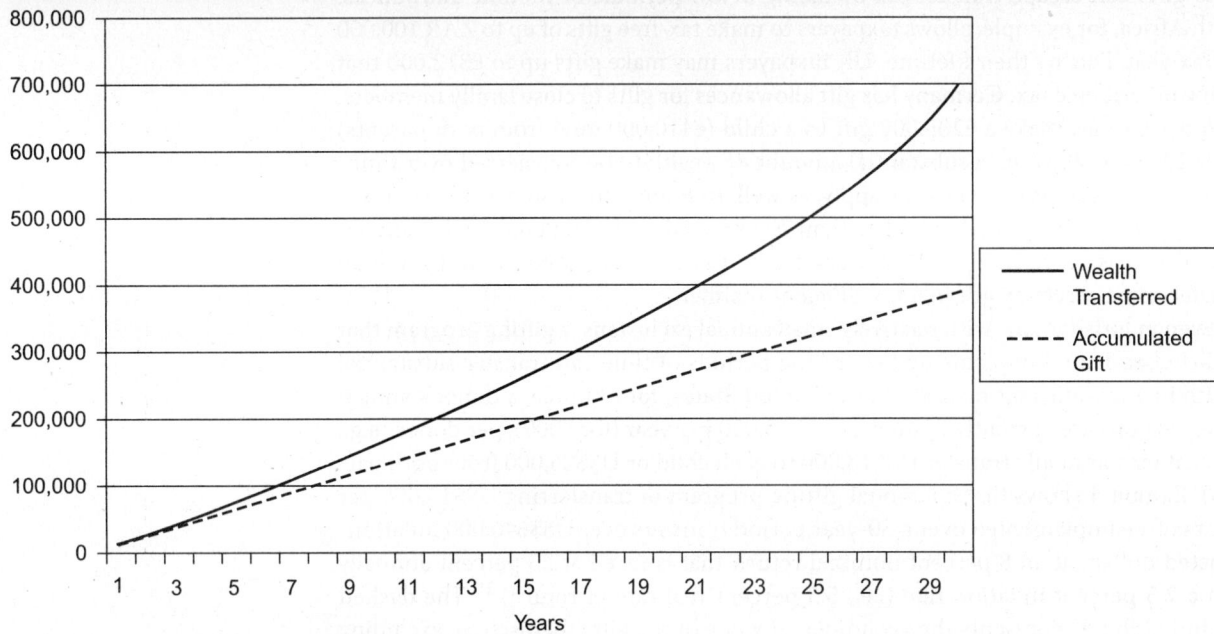

Note: Assumes a constant 5 percent real return.

The benefit of this strategy is that appreciation on gifted assets is effectively transferred to the donee without gift or estate tax. Importantly, appreciation on the gifted asset is likely still subject to tax on investment returns (e.g., dividends and capital gains) whether it remains in the donor's estate or is transferred to a donee. But if the tax-free gift had not been made and had remained in the estate, the appreciation on it would have been subject to estate or inheritance tax.

In general, the relative after-tax value of a tax-free gift made during one's lifetime compared to a bequest that is transferred as part of a taxable estate is

$$RV_{TaxFreeGift} = \frac{FV_{Gift}}{FV_{Bequest}} = \frac{\left[1 + r_g\left(1 - t_{ig}\right)\right]^n}{\left[1 + r_e\left(1 - t_{ie}\right)\right]^n \left(1 - T_e\right)} \tag{5}$$

where T_e is the estate tax if the asset is bequeathed at death; r_g and r_e are pretax returns to the gift recipient and the estate making the gift; t_{ig} and t_{ie} are the effective tax rates on investment returns on both the gift recipient and the estate making the gift; and n is the expected time until the donor's death at which point the asset would transfer and be subject to estate tax if it had not been gifted. The numerator is the future after-tax value of the tax-free gift. The denominator is the future after-tax value of a taxable transfer by bequest. The ratio is the relative value of making the tax-free gift compared to the bequest.

If the pretax return and effective tax rates are equal for both the recipient and donor, the relative value of the tax-free gift in Equation 5 simply reduces to $1/(1 - T_e)$. For example, consider the value of a €10,000 bequest in today's value subject to a 40 percent inheritance tax, netting €6,000 after tax. If the wealth is instead transferred as a tax-free gift without having to pay the 40 percent inheritance tax, the relative value of the tax-free gift is 1.67 times [i.e., $1/(1 - 0.40)$] as great as the taxable bequest, or €10,000 versus €6,000.

In the case of annual exclusions or allowances, individuals have the opportunity to transfer wealth without taxes each year. If these allowances or exclusions expire at the end of a tax year and do not accumulate over time, tax-free gifts not made in a particular tax year are lost opportunities to capture this value. It is, therefore, often beneficial for a family with wealth transfer goals to commence an early gifting program, which takes advantage of annual exclusions, where applicable.

4.1.2 Taxable Gifts

Opportunities to add value may even exist when a lifetime gift is taxable. In general, the value of making taxable gifts rather than leaving them in the estate to be taxed as a bequest, can be expressed as ratio of the after-tax future value of the gift and the bequest, or:

$$RV_{TaxableGift} = \frac{FV_{Gift}}{FV_{Bequest}} = \frac{\left[1 + r_g\left(1 - t_{ig}\right)\right]^n \left(1 - T_g\right)}{\left[1 + r_e\left(1 - t_{ie}\right)\right]^n \left(1 - T_e\right)} \tag{6}$$

where T_g is the tax rate applicable to gifts. It is important to note that this model assumes that the gift tax is paid by the recipient rather than the donor. We consider the alternative below.

If the after-tax returns associated with the gift and the asset to be bequeathed are identical, then the value of a taxable gift reduces to $(1 - T_g)/(1 - T_e)$. If the gift tax rate is less than the estate rate, gifting can still be tax efficient. For example, according to Appendix B, lifetime gratuitous transfers over £312,000 in the United Kingdom are taxed at 20 percent, while testamentary gratuitous transfers over £312,000 are taxed at 40 percent. The relative value of each pound of lifetime gift compared to each pound of bequest is therefore $1.33 = (1 - 0.20)/(1 - 0.40)$. Australia is another example in which the tax consequence of lifetime gifts can be less than the tax consequence of a testamentary bequest.

Opportunities to create value may even exist when the gift and estate tax rates are equal. As an illustration, in the Netherlands lifetime gifts and bequests are subject to the same progressive tax rate schedule, with tax rates ranging from 5 percent for smaller gifts to 68 percent for larger gifts (see Appendix B). Transferring wealth in smaller portions during one's lifetime, rather than transferring wealth in one large transaction when the owner dies, subjects each small transfer to a lower tax rate than one large transfer. Note that some jurisdictions, such as the United States, require a cumulative lifetime gift and estate tax computation that eliminates this benefit.

It is commonly believed that currently gifting assets that are expected to appreciate rather than bequeathing them later is more tax efficient because the future tax liability will be greater at death. If the donee pays the gratuitous transfer tax, however, the present value of the future inheritance tax obligation equals the gift tax. This balance of consideration changes if the donor pays tax, which is discussed in the next section. Similarly, many believe that transferring highly appreciating assets during one's lifetime and bequeathing lower return assets reduces transfer taxes. A valid comparison of the gift versus the bequest, however, requires the risk (and hence return) of the two to be held constant unless the high return asset is somehow valued below its intrinsic value, such as a valuation discount discussed later.

Alternatively, if a wealth manager is able to manage a family portfolio in the aggregate, and considers a family's overall asset allocation without being limited by constraints that dictate which types of assets must be held by which generation, then he or she may be able to place assets tax efficiently. If the return on the transferred assets will be taxed at a lower rate than if the assets were retained in the estate, the aggregate family portfolio can benefit because the numerator in Equation 6 will be greater than the denominator.

For example, consider a Japanese family contemplating a JPY 30 million lifetime gratuitous transfer in 2009. According to Appendix B, JPY 18 million can be transferred free of tax, but the remaining JPY 12 million transfer is subject to a 50 percent tax rate. The same 50 percent rate applies if the gift is delayed and transferred as a bequest, so no tax advantage related to transfer tax rates exists. However, if the recipient of the JPY 12 million gift had a lower marginal tax rate on investment returns (perhaps due to a progressive income tax schedule) of, say, 20 percent compared to the estate's marginal tax rate of, say, 50 percent, the gift can still create a tax advantage. Over a ten year horizon, the advantage for locating an asset with an 8 percent pretax return with the donee rather than the donor would be equal to:

$$RV_{TaxableGift} = \frac{FV_{Gift}}{FV_{Bequest}} = \frac{\left[1 + 0.08(1 - 0.20)\right]^{10}(1 - 0.50)}{\left[1 + 0.08(1 - 0.50)\right]^{10}(1 - 0.50)} = \frac{0.9298}{0.7401} = 1.256$$

That is, the lower 20 percent tax rate associated with the gift recipient will create 25.6 percent more wealth in 10 years than if the asset had remained in the estate and been taxed at 50 percent annually for 10 years.

Another common strategy for wealth managers managing an aggregate family portfolio is to gift assets with higher expected returns to the second generation or, in general, position assets with higher expected returns in the portfolios of the second generation, leaving the first generation to hold assets with lower expected returns. The additional expected growth of their assets escapes estate tax when the older generation passes on. Of course, assets with higher expected returns generally have higher return volatility, as well, so there is no guarantee that the second generation's portfolio will necessarily experience greater growth. But the strategy may nonetheless produce a better after-tax result on average.

Conceptually, the family portfolio can be balanced whether higher return/risk assets are held in second generation or first generation accounts. The wealth manager may need to make an adjustment, however, to ensure the after-tax risk is comparable between the two options. For example, consider a family with €4,000,000. €3,000,000 is held by the first generation (which is subject to a 40% estate tax) and €1,000,000 is held by the second generation (which will escape estate tax). Suppose further that the second generation holds bonds and the first generation holds equity as illustrated in Panel A of Exhibit 5.

Exhibit 5	Simple Example of After-Tax Asset Allocation					
Account Type	**Estate Tax Rate (%)**	**Asset Class**	**Pretax Market Value**	**Pretax Weights (%)**	**After-Tax Market Value**	**After-Tax Weights (%)**
Panel A: Bonds with Second Generation						
First Generation	40	Equity	€3,000,000	75	€1,800,000	64.3
Second Generation	0	Bonds	1,000,000	25	1,000,000	35.7
Total Portfolio			€4,000,000	100	€2,800,000	100
Panel B: Bonds with First Generation						
First Generation	40	Bonds	€1,000,000	25	€600,000	21.4
First Generation	40	Equity	2,000,000	50	1,200,000	42.9
Second Generation	0	Equity	1,000,000	25	1,000,000	35.7
Total Portfolio			€4,000,000	100	€2,800,000	100

Panel C: Bonds with First Generation and Asset Allocation Adjustment

Exhibit 5 (Continued)						
Account Type	**Estate Tax Rate (%)**	**Asset Class**	**Pretax Market Value**	**Pretax Weights (%)**	**After-Tax Market Value**	**After-Tax Weights (%)**
First Generation	40	Bonds	€1,666,667	41.7	€1,000,000	35.7
First Generation	40	Equity	1,333,333	33.3	800,000	28.6
Second Generation	0	Equity	1,000,000	25	1,000,000	35.7
Total Portfolio			€4,000,000	100	€2,800,000	100

A traditional view of asset allocation based on pretax values suggests the family has €4,000,000 of assets, 75 percent of which are allocated in stocks and 25 percent of which are allocated in bonds. In after-tax terms, however, the first generation's portfolio has a built-in tax liability of €1,200,000 because it will ultimately be subject to 40 percent tax. Therefore, the family portfolio is really only worth €2,800,000 after estate taxes. Moreover, the after-tax equity allocation is only 64.3 percent rather than 75 percent.[20]

Suppose the adviser were to locate equity with a higher expected return in the second generation portfolio so that its greater expected future growth escapes estate tax. The asset allocation may be unaffected based on pretax market values, but the after-tax asset allocation changes. For example, consider placing the €1,000,000 of bonds in the first generation portfolio as in Panel B of Exhibit 5. The pretax asset allocation is still 75 percent equity and 25 percent bonds. However, the after-tax asset equity allocation has increased from 64.3 percent to 78.6 percent because the estate tax decreases the bonds' after-tax value.

To hold the after-tax asset allocation constant, the wealth manager would increase the bond exposure until the after-tax asset allocation returns to its previous level. In this case, the family requires an additional €400,000/(1 − 0.40) = €666,667 of pretax bond exposure.

Long-term after-tax asset allocation is difficult to apply in countries such as France and Germany that regularly modify tax rates, rules, and entities.

4.1.3 *Location of the Gift Tax Liability*

The preceding discussion implicitly assumes that the tax liability associated with the lifetime gratuitous transfer in the numerator of Equation 6 is borne by the recipient. According to Appendix B, examples of jurisdictions that impose gift tax on the recipient include Colombia, Cyprus, Czech Republic, France, Germany, Italy, Japan, Netherlands, Russia, and Spain.

Other jurisdictions, such as Brazil, South Africa, and Switzerland, impose the tax liability on the donor. The distinction can be important for several reasons. First, a cross-border gift could result in both the donor and the recipient being taxed in their respective home countries. Second, if the tax liability is imposed on the donor's taxable estate rather than on the recipient, the tax benefit of the lifetime gift versus the bequest increases. Paying the tax liability from the donor's taxable estate decreases the size of the taxable estate and hence the ultimate estate tax (assuming the recipient's estate will either not be taxed or taxed at a lower rate). Gifting therefore becomes more

---

20 Horan and Robinson (2008), Reichenstein (1998, 2001, 2006, 2007), and Horan (2007a,b) develop the concept of after-tax asset allocation in more detail.

attractive from a tax perspective when the gift tax is paid by the donor. The relative after-tax value of the gift when the donor pays gift tax and when the recipient's estate will not be taxable (assuming $r_g = r_e$ and $t_{ig} = t_{ie}$) is:

$$RV_{TaxableGift} = \frac{FV_{Gift}}{FV_{Bequest}} = \frac{\left[1 + r_g\left(1 - t_{ig}\right)\right]^n \left(1 - T_g + T_g T_e\right)}{\left[1 + r_e\left(1 - t_{ie}\right)\right]^n \left(1 - T_e\right)} \qquad (7)$$

The last term in the second set of parentheses in the numerator, $T_g T_e$, represents the tax benefit from reducing the value of the taxable estate by the amount of the gift tax. In this way, allowing the transfer tax to be deducted from the taxable estate can be viewed as a partial gift tax credit.[21]

The size of the partial gift credit equals the size of the gift times $T_g T_e$. For example, consider Akio and Haruko Tochigi—a couple wishing to transfer JPY 100 million to their child. They have a JPY 500 million estate, most of which is taxable. Exhibit 6 illustrates the after-tax outcomes of a JPY 100 million gift made just prior to death or a JPY 100 million bequest made just after death, both of which would be subject to a 45 percent transfer tax. The gift reduces the size of the taxable estate to JPY 400 million, but the JPY 45 million gift tax further reduces the size of the taxable estate from JPY 400 million to JPY 355 million. Under the gifting strategy, the sum of the after-tax estate and gift is approximately JPY 295 million compared to only JPY 275 million for the bequest. As a result, the gift strategy saves JPY 100 million × 0.45 × 0.45 ≈ JPY 20 million in taxes. The economic impact of this difference grows as the time difference between the gift and bequest grows because of the compounding effect.

Exhibit 6 Illustration of Gift versus Bequest When Donor Pays Transfer Tax		
	Gift	**Bequest**
Gift	100	0
Gift Tax	45	0
Total Disbursement	145	0
Taxable Estate	355	500
Estate Tax	160	225
Net After-Tax Amount	195	275
After-Tax Estate plus Gift	295	275

Note: All amounts are in millions of JPY and rounded to the nearest million.

In some situations, the primary liability for the transfer tax may lie with the donor, but a secondary liability may rest on the recipient if the donor is unable to pay. The United Kingdom, for example, imposes gratuitous transfer tax liability on anyone with a vested interest in the gift. In addition to tax considerations, the location of the tax liability has potential implications for a recipient. For example, a recipient may receive an illiquid asset as a gift or bequest. If the recipient is responsible for the tax liability and has limited access to other liquid assets to pay that liability, then the recipient may face unintended liquidity constraints. In extreme cases, taxing authorities may take possession of the asset if the recipient is unable to pay.

---

21 Horvitz and Wilcox (2003) demonstrate this in the context of US estate tax law.

EXAMPLE 6

Gift and Estate Taxes

Philippe Zachary is 50 years old and resides in France. He is working with his wealth manager, Pierre Robé, to develop an estate planning strategy to transfer wealth to his second cousin, Etienne. Annual exclusions allow Zachary to make tax-free gifts of €20,000 per year, and gratuitous transfer tax liabilities are the responsibility of the recipient. Zachary notes that the relevant tax rate for bequests from the estate is likely to be 60 percent. He notes further, however, that gifts (in excess of the €20,000 exception mentioned above) made prior to age 70 enjoy 50 percent relief of the normal estate tax of 60 percent, for an effective tax rate of 30 percent. In addition, Etienne enjoys a low tax rate of 20 percent on investment income because he has relatively low income. Zachary, on the other hand, is subject to a 48 percent tax rate on investment income. Zachary is considering gifting assets that are expected to earn a 6 percent real return annually over the next 20 years.

1 Considering the first year's tax-free gift associated with the annual exclusion, how much of his estate will Zachary have transferred on an inflation-adjusted basis in 20 years without paying estate tax?

2 What is the relative value of the tax-free gift compared to the value of a bequest in 20 years?

3 Suppose Zachary wishes to make an additional gift that would be subject to gift tax. What would be the relative after-tax value of that taxable gift compared to a bequest 20 years later?

Solution to 1:

In 20 years, the future value (measured in real terms) equals €20,000 × [1 + 0.06(1 − 0.20)]^{20} = €51,080.56. Note that although the gift was not subject to a wealth transfer tax, its subsequent investment returns are nonetheless taxable at 20 percent.

Solution to 2:

The relative value of the tax-free gift compared to the bequest is

$$RV_{TaxFreeGift} = \frac{FV_{Gift}}{FV_{Bequest}} = \frac{\left[1 + 0.06(1 - 0.20)\right]^{20}}{\left[1 + 0.06(1 - 0.48)\right]^{20}(1 - 0.60)}$$

$$= \frac{2.5540}{0.7395} = 3.45$$

The gift is substantially more tax efficient in this case for three reasons. First, the gift is tax free and the bequest is heavily taxed. Second, if Etienne receives the gift, subsequent investment returns will be taxed at a much lower rate than if it is kept inside the estate. Third, the difference has time to compound over a relatively long period of time since the time horizon is 20 years.

Solution to 3:

In this case, the recipient is responsible for paying the gift tax at 30 percent, or half of the 60 percent estate tax. The relative value of the tax-free gift compared to a bequest subject to inheritance tax is:

$$RV_{TaxableGift} = \frac{FV_{Gift}}{FV_{Bequest}} = \frac{\left[1 + 0.06(1 - 0.20)\right]^{20}(1 - 0.30)}{\left[1 + 0.06(1 - 0.48)\right]^{20}(1 - 0.60)}$$

$$= \frac{1.7878}{0.7395} = 2.42$$

Although the gift is taxed, the after-tax value of the gift relative to the bequest is still quite large because the gift tax rate is low and because the gift is located in a lightly taxed place (i.e., with Etienne) for a long period of time.

4.2 Generation Skipping

Often, high-net-worth individuals have wealth transfer goals that extend beyond the second generation (i.e., their children). In these cases, transferring assets directly to the third generation (i.e., grandchildren) or beyond may reduce transfer taxes where permitted. In jurisdictions that tax gifts or bequests, transfers from the first generation to the second will be taxed. The same capital may be taxed again if it is transferred from the second to the third generation, and the second generation's estate is taxable. Transferring capital in excess of the second generation's needs for spending, safety, and flexibility, directly to the third generation can avoid a layer of this double taxation.

For example, consider Kenichi and Fumiko Kawaguchi, who have JPY 1,000,000,000 of first generation excess capital they would like to transfer to fulfill their goals of securing a sound financial future for their children and grandchildren. Suppose that core capital for their children amounts to JPY 800,000,000, leaving JPY 200,000,000 of excess capital for the second generation that can be transferred to the third generation. According to Appendix B, Japan imposes tax rates up to 50 percent on the recipient of a gift or inheritance. Suppose the second generation excess capital of JPY 200,000,000 is transferred twice—once from the first generation to the second in 10 years, and again from the second to the third generation 25 years beyond that. Its future value at a 5 percent real rate of return (e.g., 8 percent nominal return with 3 percent inflation) will be equal to:

$$JPY\ 200,000,000 \times \left[(1.05)^{10}(1 - 0.50)(1.05)^{25}(1 - 0.50)\right] = JPY\ 275,800,768$$

If the Kawaguchis instead transfer this sum directly to their grandchildren, the transfer is taxed only once and the future value is

$$JPY\ 200,000,000 \times \left[(1.05)^{35}(1 - 0.50)\right] = JPY\ 551,601,537$$

or twice as much as when the capital is taxed twice. In general, the relative value of skipping generations to transfer capital that is excess for both the first and second generations is $1/(1 - T_1)$ where T_1 is the tax rate of capital transferred from the first to the second generation.

In at least one jurisdiction (e.g., the United States), the taxing authorities discourage this strategy by imposing a special generation skipping transfer tax. This tax, in addition to the usual transfer tax, is imposed on transfers to, among others, grandchildren or subsequent generations and is intended to produce the same overall tax effect had the assets passed sequentially through two generations.

4.3 Spousal Exemptions

Most jurisdictions with estate or inheritance taxes (such as South Africa, the United Kingdom, and the United States) allow decedents to make bequests and gifts to their spouses without transfer tax liability. In these jurisdictions, gratuitous transfer tax exclusions also apply to smaller estates. In the case of the United Kingdom, estates less than £312,000 can pass without inheritance tax (see Appendix B). In these situations, it is worthwhile to note that a couple actually has two exclusions available—one for each spouse. As a result, it is often advisable to take advantage of the first exclusion when the first spouse dies by transferring the exclusion amount to someone other than the spouse.

For instance, consider Will and Samantha Quackenbush who have a £700,000 estate. If Will is the first to die and leaves the entire estate tax-free to his wife, Samantha, they have lost an opportunity to transfer £312,000 out of the taxable estate upon Will's death. If the £312,000 was excess capital that would likely be transferred to the next generation anyway, then transferring the £312,000 to the second generation upon Will's death will not trigger additional inheritance tax due to the exclusion and will reduce the taxable value of Samantha's estate to £388,000. In sum, even when assets can be transferred to a surviving spouse without tax consequences, it may be valuable to take advantage of any estate tax exclusions upon the death of the first spouse. Otherwise, the opportunity to use the exclusion to transfer wealth without tax consequences will be lost.

4.4 Valuation Discounts

Gift and estate taxes might also be mitigated by transferring assets that qualify for valuation discounts (or, in appropriate cases, structuring assets to qualify for such discounts). Typically, tax is levied on the fair market value of the asset being transferred, which is a straightforward determination in the case of cash or marketable securities. If shares in a privately held family business are being transferred, establishing fair market value is not obvious and requires a valuation according to some pricing model or models, which, in turn, requires assumptions. In addition to the inputs that must be estimated or forecasted to determine the intrinsic value of an otherwise similar publicly traded company, the valuation of privately held companies is often discounted at a higher cost of capital to reflect the lack of liquidity associated with their shares. Estimates of the average discount for lack of liquidity range from 20 percent to 25 percent of the value of an otherwise identical publicly traded company. The size of the discount tends to be inversely related to the size of the company and its profit margin.[22]

If the shares being transferred represent a minority interest in the privately held company, an additional discount is taken for lack of control associated with a minority interest. This valuation is distinct from, but not independent of, an illiquidity discount because positions of control are more marketable than minority positions that lack control. Minority interest discounts can be very large, ranging between 25 percent and 40 percent, but their interaction with illiquidity discounts is not additive. For example, if a stake in a privately held business warrants a 10 percent illiquidity discount and 15 percent lack of control discount, the combined discount may be a lower figure, such as 18 percent, rather than 25 percent.[23]

Transferring assets subject to valuation discount reduces the basis on which transfer tax is calculated, and hence the transfer tax. For this reason, HNWIs in some jurisdictions may intentionally create illiquidity and lack of control by placing assets in a

---

22 See, for example, Block (2007).
23 See Horvitz (2008).

family limited partnership (FLP). Rather than gift or bequeath the underlying assets, the first generation transfers minority interests in the FLP, which also is illiquid, to separate individuals. The lack of liquidity and control of an FLP structure may make it eligible for valuation discounts in some jurisdictions. In general, FLPs comprising cash and marketable securities will receive less of a discount than a privately held operating company.

FLPs may have non-tax benefits as well. By pooling the assets of multiple family members together, the family can gain access to certain asset classes requiring minimum investments (e.g., hedge funds, private equity, venture capital), which would be prohibitively large for the individual family members to invest in alone. An FLP also allows participating family members to share in a pro-rata fashion in the gains and losses of family investments. This equitable distribution of gains and losses can be an important consideration in some family dynamics.

4.5 Deemed Dispositions

Rather than impose an estate or inheritance tax on the amount of capital bequeathed at death, some countries treat bequests as **deemed dispositions**, that is, as if the property were sold. The deemed disposition triggers the realization of any previously unrecognized capital gains and liability for associated capital gains tax. The tax is therefore levied not on the principal value of the transfer, but only on the value of unrecognized gains, if any. According to Appendix B, Australia, Canada, and Colombia are examples of jurisdictions with deemed disposition regimes. Australia and Canada impose no gift taxes, making it potentially advantageous to gift highly appreciated assets that are not likely to be liquidated during one's lifetime anyway.

4.6 Charitable Gratuitous Transfers

Most jurisdictions provide two forms of tax relief for wealth transfers to not-for-profit or charitable organizations. First, most charitable donations are not subject to a gift transfer tax. Of the jurisdictions listed in Appendix B, only Belgium and South Africa impose a transfer tax on charitable gratuitous transfers. Second, most jurisdictions permit income tax deductions for charitable donations. Only four jurisdictions with income taxes listed in Appendix B do not offer income tax deductions for charitable donations. Therefore, families with philanthropic aspirations can transfer wealth very tax efficiently.

Charitable organizations may also be exempt from paying tax on investment returns, as well. Therefore, the early structuring of assets into a charitable organization allows investment returns to compound tax free, which has a significant impact on wealth accumulation especially over long time horizons. Therefore, the relative after-tax future value over n years of a charitable gift is compared to a taxable bequest as shown in Equation 8 below:

$$RV_{CharitableGift} = \frac{FV_{CharitableGift}}{FV_{Bequest}}$$

$$= \frac{\left(1 + r_g\right)^n + T_{oi}\left[1 + r_e\left(1 - t_{ie}\right)\right]^n\left(1 - T_e\right)}{\left[1 + r_e\left(1 - t_{ie}\right)\right]^n\left(1 - T_e\right)}$$

(8)

The first term in the numerator has no deduction for either gift tax or taxes on investment returns. The second term of the numerator represents the additional value created in the estate associated with the income tax deduction. T_{oi} is the tax rate on ordinary income and represents the current income tax benefit associated with a charitable transfer. The tax advantages of charitable giving allow the donor to either increase the charitable benefit associated with a given transfer of excess capital from the estate, or to use less excess capital to achieve a given charitable benefit.

EXAMPLE 7

Charitable Gifts

Continue with the example of Philippe Zachary in Example 6. France imposes an estate tax at rates of up to 60 percent, but qualifying charitable donations are not subject to inheritance tax. In addition, donations are eligible for income tax deductions at the same income tax rate of 48 percent, which also applies to investment income. What is the relative after-tax value of a charitable donation as compared to a taxable bequest?

Solution:

$$RV_{CharitableGift} = \frac{FV_{Gift}}{FV_{Bequest}}$$

$$= \frac{(1.06)^{20} + 0.48[1 + 0.06(1 - 0.48)]^{20}(1 - 0.60)}{[1 + 0.06(1 - 0.48)]^{20}(1 - 0.60)}$$

$$= \frac{3.5621}{0.7395} = 4.82$$

The relative value of the charitable gift is so large because the gift a) escapes estate tax, b) accrues investment returns free of taxes inside the tax-exempt organization, and c) provides Zachary with an income tax deduction.

ESTATE PLANNING TOOLS

5

The gratuitous transfers described above are often implemented through structures that either maximize tax benefit, produce a non-tax benefit, or both. Common estate planning tools include, among others, trusts (a common law concept), foundations (a civil law concept), life insurance, and companies. As noted earlier, partnerships may also be used in some circumstances. The structure of each has implications for how assets are controlled, whether they are protected from potential claims of future creditors, and how they are taxed. The availability of each of these tools and the tax and tax reporting ramifications to their use depends upon the jurisdiction or jurisdictions of relevance in the given case. Note that while foundations may have originated in civil law jurisdictions, they are also available in some common law jurisdictions. Similarly, trusts are recognized by some civil law jurisdictions.

5.1 Trusts

A trust is an arrangement created by a **settlor (or grantor)** who transfers assets to a trustee. The trust is a relationship in which the trustee holds and manages the assets for the benefit of the beneficiaries. As a result, the beneficiaries are considered to be the beneficial, not legal, owners of the trust assets. The terms of the trust relationship and the principles used by the trustee to manage the assets and distributions to the beneficiaries are outlined in the trust document. It is possible for the settlor of a trust to also be one of the beneficiaries.

Trusts can be categorized in many ways, but two dimensions are particularly important in understanding their character. First, a trust can be either revocable or irrevocable. In a **revocable trust** arrangement, the settlor (who originally transfers assets to fund the trust) retains the right to rescind the trust relationship and regain title to the trust assets. Under these circumstances, the settlor is generally considered to be the owner of the assets for tax purposes in many jurisdictions. As a result, the settlor is responsible for tax payments and reporting on the trust's investment returns. Additionally, the settlor's revocation power makes the trust assets vulnerable to the reach of creditors having claims against the settlor.

Alternatively, where the settlor has no ability to revoke the trust relationship, the trust is characterized as an **irrevocable trust**. In an irrevocable trust structure, the trustee may be responsible for tax payments and reporting in his or her capacity as owner of the trust assets for tax purposes. An irrevocable trust structure generally provides greater asset protection from claims against a settlor than a revocable trust.[24] In any event, both a revocable and an irrevocable trust structure can result in the transfer of assets to the beneficiaries without the time, expense, potential challenges, and publicity associated with probate because the settlor transfers legal ownership of the assets to the trustee and the transfer of those assets is dictated by the terms of the trust and not the settlor's will.

Second, trusts can be structured to be either fixed or discretionary. Distributions to beneficiaries of a **fixed trust** are prescribed in the trust document to occur at certain times or in certain amounts. For example, Maria Valez, a first generation wealth owner, may wish to make a large *inter vivos* transfer to her son, Conner, who is too young to manage the assets himself. Valez could fund a trust that directs the trustee to hold the assets until Conner's 21st birthday and begin making annual distributions of a specific amount over 10 years, at which time any remaining assets will be distributed to Conner. The trust is said to be fixed because the terms of the distributions are pre-determined in the trust documentation.

In contrast, if the trust document enabled the trustee to determine whether and how much to distribute based on Conner's general welfare and in the sole and uncontrolled discretion of the trustee, the trust would be called a **discretionary trust**. The settlor can make her wishes known to the trustee through language in the trust document and/or through a non-binding letter of wishes.

The legal concept of a trust is unique to the common law. Civil law countries may not recognize foreign trusts because it is a legal relationship, not a legal person. In fact, 12 of the 22 civil law jurisdictions in Appendix A do not recognize trusts.

5.1.1 *Control*

A common motivation for using a trust structure is to make resources available to a beneficiary without yielding complete control of those resources to them. For example, spendthrift trusts can be used to provide resources to beneficiaries who may be unable or unwilling to manage the assets themselves, perhaps because they are young, immature, or disabled. Or perhaps the settlor wishes assets to be used for particular purposes. In any case, the trust relationship can permit a settlor to transfer assets without the expense or publicity associated with probate, yet still retain control of those assets.

---

24 This is true provided the settlor was neither insolvent nor rendered insolvent when he settled the trust, and any such creditor claims arose after the trust settlement date.

5.1.2 *Asset Protection*

In general, creditors are unable to reach assets that an individual does not own. Just as an irrevocable trust can protect assets from claims against the settlor, as outlined above, discretionary trusts can protect assets from claims against the beneficiaries. Under a discretionary trust, the beneficiaries have no legal right to income generated by the trust or to the assets in the trust itself. Therefore, the creditors of the beneficiaries cannot reach the trust assets.

In the example on the previous page, suppose Maria Valez is concerned that Conner's new wife may divorce him and lay a claim on his trust assets in a divorce settlement. If the trust to which Conner is a beneficiary is discretionary, then his wife would be unable to lay claim to them because it is within the trustee's power to avoid making distributions to Conner. It is important to note that these structures must generally be established in advance of a claim, or even a pending claim, to effectively protect assets.

Trusts may also be used in circumstances where forced heirship laws permit the use of lifetime gifts and trusts to avoid the strict application of forced heirship rule. In fact, many countries specifically prohibit the application of forced heirship rules to trusts, making trusts an especially useful tool in this regard.

5.1.3 *Tax Reduction*

Trusts can be used to reduce taxes for either the settlor or the beneficiaries. Continuing the illustration above, suppose Valez creates an irrevocable trust such that she is no longer considered the owner of the assets held in the trust for tax purposes. The income generated by the trust assets may be taxed at a lower rate inside the trust than if they were owned by Valez for several possible reasons. In many countries, income is commonly taxed according to a progressive tax schedule (see Horan and Robinson 2008). A progressive tax rate schedule applied to trust income or beneficiary distributions may allow either the trust or beneficiary to apply taxable income to lower tax brackets unavailable to Valez whose income may be taxed at relative high rates.[25] Moreover, if an irrevocable trust is structured as discretionary, a trustee can consider a beneficiary's tax situation to decide whether or not to make a distribution in a particular tax period to the beneficiary. Alternatively, a settlor may create a trust in a jurisdiction with a low tax rate or even no taxes. As is the case with any trust planning technique, this strategy requires a consideration of the tax systems governing the settlor and beneficiary in their home country, which is discussed in more detail in Section 6.2.

The tax laws of some jurisdictions allow tax planning with the use of a trust in which assets are successfully transferred for estate tax purposes, but not for income tax purposes. That is, the assets are no longer part of the settlor's estate, but the income generated from the assets remains taxable to the settlor. In this way, assets can be successfully transferred from a settlor to a beneficiary under a gifting strategy and avoid estate tax. However, the income generated by the assets would nonetheless be taxable to the settlor, thereby further reducing the size of the settlor's taxable estate over time.[26] Section 4.1.3 discusses the value of locating the tax liability with the donor. A similar concept applies to the location of the income tax liability on trust asset returns.

---

25 In some jurisdictions, however, the progressive rate schedule applicable to trusts may be more compressed than that which applies to individuals. It is therefore important to determine and compare the rate structure that applies to individuals and trusts in the individual case.

26 See Brunel (2002) for a more thorough discussion of these structures.

5.2 Foundations

A foundation is a legal entity available in some jurisdictions. Foundations are typically set up to hold assets for a particular purpose—such as to promote education or for philanthropy. When set up and funded by an individual or family and managed by its own directors, it is called a private foundation. Similar to trusts, foundations survive the settlor, allow the settlor's wishes to be followed after the settlor's death, and can accomplish the same types of objectives as a trust (control, avoidance of probate, asset protection, and tax minimization). A foundation is based on civil law and, unlike a trust, is a legal person. Often, the choice of a trust or foundation depends on a client's residence or nationality.

5.3 Life Insurance

In creating a trust, a settlor divests himself of assets by transferring them to a trustee for the benefit of beneficiaries, creating potential advantages regarding how the assets are controlled, protected, and taxed. Life insurance is another planning tool in which the policy holder transfers assets (called a **premium**) to an insurer who, in turn, has a contractual obligation to pay death benefit proceeds to the beneficiary named in the policy. As is the case with trusts, insurance can produce tax and estate planning benefits. It can be a useful alternative to a trust in circumstances where the trust relationship is not recognized under applicable law or its legal and tax consequences are uncertain, such as some civil law countries common in Europe and South America that do not recognize trusts.

From a tax perspective, life insurance is afforded beneficial tax treatment in many jurisdictions. Death benefit proceeds paid to life insurance beneficiaries are tax exempt in many jurisdictions and, in some cases, no tax reporting consequences arise. In addition, premiums paid by the policy holder are typically neither part of the policy holder's taxable estate at the time of his or her death, nor subject to a gratuitous transfer tax.[27] Therefore, it may be possible to transfer money or other assets through life insurance without tax consequence. Life insurance can also offer income tax advantages in jurisdictions that allow any cash value in the policy to build tax deferred. A life insurance contract can also include provisions that allow a surrender or withdrawal (or partial surrender or withdrawal) of policy value during the policy term, as well as a loan facility, which, in some jurisdictions, can be made with advantageous tax consequences to the policy holder.

Tax authorities in many countries recognize these advantages and typically require that life insurance be properly structured to avoid abuse. For example, most jurisdictions require a certain minimum level of risk before a life insurance policy will be treated as such. Other laws mandate that the policy holder must typically have an insurable interest in the life assured to be a valid life insurance contract.

In addition to possible tax benefits, life insurance effectively allows assets to transfer to the policy holder's beneficiaries without the time, expense, potential challenges, and publicity associated with probate. Premiums paid by the policy holder are no longer part of the policy holder's estate at the time of death, and death benefit proceeds under a life insurance contract pass directly to policy beneficiaries outside the probate process. While this is also true of trusts, insurance is recognized in almost every country and generally regarded with less suspicion by tax authorities.

---

27 In some jurisdictions the value of the policy may attract gratuitous transfer tax exposure to the policy holder, insured, or beneficiaries; it is therefore important in the individual case to determine the tax consequences of life insurance to the parties.

Many wealth owners also use life insurance to help heirs pay inheritance tax triggered by the wealth owner's death. In other words, life insurance is a liquidity planning technique in that it can generate liquidity to pay gratuitous transfer tax. It is, therefore, especially valuable if an inheritance of illiquid assets creates a liquidity crisis for the heir as discussed in Section 4.1.3. In addition, life insurance policies can be used to transfer assets outside forced heirship rules, which normally do not apply to life insurance proceeds.

Life insurance policies can also offer asset protection in their own right or in combination with a trust. Premiums paid for life insurance are generally outside the reach of creditors' claims against the policy holder. Additionally, an insurance policy can assign a discretionary trust as the policy beneficiary. In this way, the use of life insurance in combination with a trust may be useful if the ultimate beneficiaries (i.e., beneficiaries of the trust) are unable to manage the assets themselves (e.g., in the case of minors, disabilities, or spendthrifts).

5.4 Companies and Controlled Foreign Corporations

Companies may also be a useful tool in which to place assets. For example, a **controlled foreign corporation** (CFC) is a company located outside a taxpayer's home country and in which the taxpayer has a controlling interest as defined under the home country law. A possible benefit of placing income generating assets in a CFC is that tax on earnings of the company may be deferred until either the earnings are actually distributed to shareholders or the company is sold or shares otherwise disposed. In addition, a CFC may be established in a jurisdiction that does not tax the company or its shareholders.

Many countries have CFC rules designed to prevent taxpayers from avoiding the taxation of current income by holding assets in a CFC. CFC rules can be triggered if a taxpayer owns more than, say, 50 percent of the foreign company's shares, although the ownership threshold will vary from one jurisdiction to the next. CFC rules may also look beyond direct ownership of CFC shares and consider beneficial ownership in a trust, for example, or even ownership attributed to related parties, such as a taxpayer's family members. Therefore, CFC rules may tax shareholders of a CFC on the company's earnings as if the earnings were distributed to shareholders even though no distribution has been made. This treatment of earnings is called a **deemed distribution**.

CROSS-BORDER ESTATE PLANNING

6

Individuals and families with business and personal interests in more than one country face special estate planning challenges. A family with assets located in multiple jurisdictions may have difficulty passing ownership of those assets upon the wealth owner's death. For example, income generated by assets located outside an investor's home country may be taxed in both the country where the income originates and the home country of the wealth owner. Passing ownership of overseas assets upon death may also be difficult and may trigger multiple tax liabilities from both the home country and country in which the asset is located.

Even when assets are located within a single jurisdiction, passing their ownership to heirs located outside the country through a will, gifting technique, or other strategy can be legally complex and may pose certain tax considerations. This section discusses some of these cross-border estate planning issues.

6.1 The Hague Conference

A legal document created in one country may not necessarily enjoy legal recognition in another country. The **Hague Conference on Private International Law** is an intergovernmental organization that works toward the convergence of private international law.[28] Its 69 members consist of countries and regional economic integration organizations, like the European Community (see Exhibit 7). The Conference has developed a series of conventions, or multilateral treaties, that have addressed a variety of international issues, including those related to cross-border transactions. The purpose is to simplify or standardize processes and facilitate international trade. Members of the Conference may or may not ratify a particular convention. Ratification by a country implies a legal obligation to apply the convention within its borders. Non-member countries may participate, as well, by electing to accede to be bound by the treaty, a process that sometimes requires acceptance by states already a party to the convention.

Exhibit 7	Members of the Hague Conference		
Albania	The European	The former	Serbia
Argentina	Community	Yugoslav	Slovakia
Australia	Finland	Republic of	Slovenia
Austria	France	Macedonia	South Africa
Belarus	Georgia	Malaysia	Spain
Belgium	Germany	Malta	Sri Lanka
Bosnia and	Greece	Mexico	Suriname
Herzegovina	Hungary	Monaco	Sweden
Brazil	Iceland	Montenegro	Switzerland
Bulgaria	India	Morocco	Turkey
Canada	Ireland	Netherlands	Ukraine
Chile	Israel	New Zealand	United Kingdom
China	Italy	Norway	of Great
Croatia	Japan	Panama	Britain and
Cyprus	Jordan	Paraguay	Northern
Czech Republic	Republic	Peru	Ireland
Denmark	of Korea	Poland	United States of
Ecuador	Latvia	Portugal	America
Egypt	Lithuania	Romania	Uruguay
Estonia	Luxembourg	Russian	Venezuela
		Federation	

Source: Hague Conference on International Private Law (www.hcch.net).

Because the typical form of a will can vary substantially from one state to the next, their recognition from one jurisdiction to the next can be especially troublesome. The Hague Convention of the Conflict of Laws Relating to the Form of Testamentary Dispositions addresses this particular issue and has been ratified by 39 countries, including most developed nations, but notably excluding the United States. Under this convention, a will is valid in the participating jurisdictions if it is consistent with the internal law associated with:

■ the place the will was made;

---

[28] More detailed information is available at www.hcch.net.

- the nationality, domicile, or habitual residence of the testator; or
- the location of immovable assets covered under the will.

Some participating countries have exceptions, however. Therefore, separate wills for different jurisdictions may be required, especially in relation to real estate.

An important area in which the Hague Conference affects wealth management is in relation to trusts. Common law jurisdictions recognize trusts, but civil law jurisdictions may not. The Hague Convention of the Law Applicable to Trusts and on Their Recognition is designed to harmonize the recognition of the trust relationship. By ratifying or acceding to this convention, a participating country recognizes the existence and validity of trusts with a written trust instrument as long as they have the following characteristics (outlined in Article 2 of the convention):

A The assets constitute a separate fund and are not a part of the trustee's own estate.

B Title to the trust assets stands in the name of the trustee or in the name of another person on behalf of the trustee.

C The trustee has the power and the duty, in respect of which he is accountable, to manage, employ, or dispose of the assets in accordance with the terms of the trust and the special duties imposed upon him by law.

Twelve countries participate in this convention. Nonetheless, a participating country may view ownership and beneficial interests related to trust relationships in various ways, which may limit some of their advantages. It is important for a wealth manager to know whether a trust will be recognized in the way it is intended by authorities in the countries of relevance to the trust relationship.

6.2 Tax System

Taxable claims for a particular country are based on its jurisdiction claim, that is, the conceptual framework that determines the basis for taxing income or transfers. A country that taxes income as a source within its borders is said to impose **source jurisdiction**, also referred to as a **territorial tax system**.[29] This jurisdiction is derived from the relationship between the country and the source of the income. Countries imposing income tax exercise source jurisdiction.

Countries may also impose tax based on residency, called **residence jurisdiction**, whereby all income (domestic and foreign sourced) is subject to taxation. In this case, the jurisdiction is derived from the relationship between the country and the person receiving the income. Most countries use a residential tax system.

According to Appendix B, only three of the 37 jurisdictions surveyed with income taxes have territorial-based systems (Hong Kong, Singapore, and Taiwan).

6.2.1 Taxation of Income

Although our primary concern will relate to gratuitous transfer taxes either on or before death for estate planning purposes, the basic concepts relate to income taxes equally well. Persons subject to residence jurisdiction are taxed on their worldwide income. Most countries impose residence jurisdiction on noncitizen residents, but not citizens who are non-resident in the jurisdiction. The United States is a notable exception given that both citizens (regardless of where resident) and residents are subject to US taxation on their worldwide income and estates.

---

29 Arnold and McIntyre (2002), p. 21. Much of the discussion in this and the following section is based on this reading.

There is no international standardized residency test that applies to individuals. Therefore, residency tests differ between countries. In determining residency, tax authorities may consider subjective standards, such as the extent of an individual's social, familial, and economic ties to the jurisdiction; e.g., whether the individual maintains a dwelling in the country, whether the individual has income producing activities in the country, etc. The tax authorities may also consider objective standards to determine residency, such as the number of days of physical presence the individual has within the country during the relevant tax period. High-net-worth individuals may want to acquire or avoid residency in a particular country, depending on the country's tax burden. It is critical to understand the tax residency rules in the relevant countries to achieve the objectives of such individuals.

For example, UK residents are considered non-domiciled in the United Kingdom if they do not form an intention to permanently remain in the United Kingdom. These resident, non-domiciliaries (RNDs) are taxed only on income sourced in the United Kingdom. Non-UK income is only subject to UK tax when it is remitted (or deemed remitted) to the United Kingdom. The UK RND tax regime is considered to be a very attractive regime for HNW RNDs when compared to tax regimes imposing tax based on residence. RNDs in the United Kingdom may therefore choose to locate assets outside the United Kingdom in countries having advantageous tax regimes, such as Singapore or Hong Kong, and avoid remittances (or deemed remittances) to the United Kingdom.

6.2.2 *Taxation of Wealth and Wealth Transfers*

Like income, wealth and wealth transfers may be subject to tax based on source or residence principles. The source principle taxes wealth economically sourced in a specific country, such as real estate. Eight of the 37 jurisdictions in Appendix B impose a wealth tax beyond that often imposed on real property (Colombia, France, Hungary, India, Mexico, Netherlands, Spain, and Switzerland). The residence principle, should it apply, would tax worldwide wealth with some exceptions, such as real estate situated abroad.

Gifts and bequests may be subject to different tax treatments depending on the tax regime of the donor's country, recipient's country, and the location of the asset being transferred. For example, the source principle would tax assets that are economically sourced or transferred within a particular country, whereas the residence principle would impose transfer tax on all assets transferred by a donor.

Again, the United States is unique in this regard. Not only does the United States impose estate tax on the worldwide assets of its citizens (regardless of where resident) and residents, it also imposes estate tax on non-US individuals holding assets situated in the United States, including US real estate, movable property located in the United States, and security holdings (public or private) of US companies. This may cause some asset transfers to be taxed twice by two different jurisdictions, but many estate tax treaties (discussed below) and, where available, foreign estate tax credits, can eliminate or mitigate this conflict.[30] This illustrates, however, that individuals need to be aware of the wealth transfer tax rules of the countries tied to the assets they hold.

6.2.3 *Exit Taxation*

In an effort to mitigate their income, wealth, and estate taxes, HNWIs may sometimes choose to renounce their citizenship in one country and expatriate to another country. To offset the lost tax revenue from such repatriation, some countries impose a so-called "exit tax" on individuals giving up their citizenship or residency. Seven of the 37 jurisdictions listed in Appendix B impose an exit tax (Australia, Canada, Germany, Israel,

---

30 See Marcovici (2007).

Netherlands, Sweden, and the United States). Exit taxation is generally not applicable for capital moving between EU countries, but could apply to capital moving outside the EU. In most cases, the exit tax amounts to a tax on unrealized gains accrued on assets leaving the taxing jurisdiction. This approach is called a deemed disposition. The exit tax may also include an income tax on income earned over a fixed period after expatriation, called a "shadow period."

6.3 Double Taxation

The interaction of country tax systems can result in tax conflicts in which two countries claim to have taxing authority over the same income or assets. This conflict can relate to either income tax or estate/inheritance tax and arise in a number of ways. For example, two countries may claim residence of the same individual, subjecting the individual's worldwide income to taxation by both countries. This situation represents a **residence–residence conflict**.

Alternatively, two countries may claim source jurisdiction of the same asset (i.e., **source–source conflict**). This conflict can arise, for example, on income from a company situated in Country A but managed from Country B. Both countries may claim that the company income is derived from their jurisdiction.

In other situations, an individual in Country A may be subject to residence jurisdiction and, therefore, taxation on worldwide income. Some of the individual's assets may be located in Country B, which exercises source jurisdiction on those assets, creating a **residence–source conflict**. For example, a US citizen owning Singapore situated real estate would be subject to US income tax and Singapore income tax on rental income from the property. Residence–source conflicts are the most common source of double taxation and the most difficult to avoid through tax planning without a separate mechanism for relief that can mitigate or eliminate double taxation through either foreign tax credit provisions or double taxation treaties. Because a source country is commonly viewed to have primary jurisdiction to tax income within its borders, the residence country is typically expected to provide double taxation relief if any is provided.

6.3.1 *Foreign Tax Credit Provisions*

A residence country may choose to unilaterally provide its taxpayers relief from residence-source conflicts within its own tax code using one or more of the following methods: credit method, exemption method, or deduction method.

In the **credit method**, the residence country reduces its taxpayers' domestic tax liability for taxes paid to a foreign country exercising source jurisdiction. The credit is limited to the amount of taxes the taxpayer would pay domestically, which completely eliminates double taxation. Under this method the tax liability equals the greater of the tax liability due in either the residence or source country.

$$T_{CreditMethod} = Max[T_{Residence}, T_{Source}] \qquad (9)$$

For example, suppose a residence country imposes a 50 percent tax on world-wide income but offers a relief for tax paid on foreign-sourced income via the credit method. If the foreign government taxes the foreign-sourced income at 40 percent, the taxpayer will pay a 50 percent tax rate (e.g., Max[50 percent, 40 percent]). Of the total, 40 percent is paid to foreign authorities and 10 percent is paid to the domestic authorities.

In the **exemption method**, the residence country imposes no tax on foreign-source income by providing taxpayers with an exemption, which, in effect, eliminates the residence–source conflict by having only one jurisdiction impose tax. The tax liability under the exemption method is simply the tax imposed at the foreign source, or:

$$T_{ExemptionMethod} = T_{Source} \qquad (10)$$

In the previous example, the tax liability would be 40 percent, all of which is collected by the foreign taxing authority. Only the few jurisdictions using territorial-based tax systems (Hong Kong, Singapore, Taiwan, and Thailand) have adopted the exemption method.

Under the **deduction method**, the residence country allows taxpayers to reduce their taxable income by the amount of taxes paid to foreign governments in respect of foreign-source income (i.e., provides a tax deduction rather than a credit or exemption). The taxpayer is still responsible for both taxes, but the aggregate liability is less than the sum of the two with the residence country reducing the size of its percentage claim by the product of the two tax rates. The tax rate under the deduction method is therefore equal to:

$$
\begin{aligned}
T_{DeductionMethod} &= T_{Residence} + T_{Source}\left(1 - T_{Residence}\right) \\
&= T_{Residence} + T_{Source} - T_{Residence}T_{Source}
\end{aligned}
\tag{11}
$$

It is clear from this equation that the deduction method results in a higher tax liability than either the credit or exemption method. Using rates from the previous example, the total tax liability equals 70 percent = 0.50 + 0.40 − (0.50 × 0.40). In this case, the source country receives 40 percent and the residence country receives 30 percent [i.e., 0.50 − (0.50 × 0.40)]. The residence country makes a partial concession recognizing the primacy of source jurisdiction.

The diagonal of double taxation matrix in Appendix C lists jurisdictions that have foreign tax credit relief provisions in their domestic tax code. The small case letters indicate whether the provisions apply to income (*i*), gift (*g*), or estate (*e*) taxes. The United States, for example, provides domestic relief for income and estate taxes, but not gift taxes. Therefore, by way of example, a US resident may choose to delay an *inter vivos* wealth transfer of an asset situated in another country with a gift tax (which would not receive double taxation relief under a double taxation treaty) until the death of the donor at which time it would receive estate tax relief under the United States foreign estate tax credit. France provides foreign tax credit provisions for gift and estate taxes but not for income taxes, whereas Spain provides provisions for all three types of taxes.

It is important to note that the term "foreign tax credit provision" in this context does not imply that the country applies the credit method in providing its relief. It could apply the exemption, deduction method, or some other method. Very few countries, however, have credit provisions based purely on the exemption or credit method.

6.3.2 Double Taxation Treaties

Relief from double taxation may be provided through a double taxation treaty (DTT) rather than domestic tax laws (i.e., foreign tax credit, deduction or exclusion provisions). Tax treaties, of which there are over 2,000 in effect, are intended to facilitate international trade and investment by eliminating double taxation. By limiting source jurisdiction, DTTs resolve residence–source conflicts that are the most frequent cause of double taxation. Virtually all modern tax treaties are based on the OECD (Organisation for Economic Co-operation and Development) Model Treaty.[31] The OECD Model Treaty sanctions the exemption and credit method to resolve residence-source conflicts.

With regard to investment income, the OECD Model Treaty endorses the notion that interest income and dividend income have their source in the country of the entity paying the interest or dividend. This type of investment income is taxed through a withholding from the source country. The OECD Model Treaty strongly endorses that withholding tax rates paid to the source country for dividends (paid to other

---

31 See www.oecd.org/dataoecd/52/34/1914467.pdf.

persons) and interest, be limited to 15 percent and 10 percent, respectively; but higher withholding rates are common. Additional tax may be owed to the residence country if the credit or deduction method is used. These relatively low rates are intended to allow tax revenue sharing between the source and residence country.

By contrast, capital gains are taxed in the seller's country of residence. Gains on immovable property, however, are typically taxed in the source country where the property is located.

In addition to residence–source conflicts, DTTs resolve residence–residence conflicts. A resident is taxable in a particular country "by reason of his domicile, residence, place of management or any other criterion of similar nature."[32] Should these criteria give rise to a "dual resident taxpayer," the OECD model outlines tie-breakers in the following order based on the location of an individual's:

1 permanent home

2 center of vital interests

3 habitual dwelling

4 citizenship[33]

DTTs typically do not resolve source–source conflicts.

A detailed OECD Commentary aids the interpretation of the OECD Model Treaty. The legal status of OECD Commentary and Model Treaty regarding the interpretation of tax treaties is ambiguous. The Vienna Convention on the Law Treaties, which governs the interpretation of all treaties (not just tax treaties), states that supplemental means of interpretation can only confirm meaning that is inferred from the treaty itself and other agreements between the parties unless these agreements produce an absurd result. In this regard, the OECD commentary provides guidance regarding the interpretation of double tax treaties, but is not binding.

As is the case with double taxation relief under domestic provisions, the nature of the relief under a DTT can be either through the credit, exemption, or deduction method, although the OECD model endorses the credit and exemption methods. Switzerland, for example, usually applies the exemption method in its treaties. It applies the credit method, however, for foreign-source taxes in countries with which it does not have a DTT. Appendix C summarizes the DTTs in existence between 37 jurisdictions as of September 2008. The upper-case letters I, G, and E, refer to treaties for income taxes, gift taxes, and estate taxes, respectively, between the entity listed in the row and the entity listed in the column. For example, France has a DTT covering income, gift, and estate taxes with Sweden. The French treaty with Spain covers only income taxes, but because both countries provide foreign tax credit provisions in their domestic tax codes for gift and estate tax (see the small letters down the diagonal), individuals may nonetheless be able to avoid or mitigate double taxation. Most DTTs relate to income taxes partly because many jurisdictions (15 of 37 in this sample) do not have estate taxes, eliminating the need for an estate DTT. In any case, a taxpayer must qualify as a resident under the terms of the treaty to be eligible for its benefits.

EXAMPLE 8

Double Taxation Credit Provisions

Boris Yankevich is a citizen and resident of Country A and has investments in Country B. The tax rates on investment income and bequests for both countries are listed below. Country A has a residence-based tax system and Country B

---

32 Article 4(1) of the OECD Model Treaty.
33 Article 4(2) of the OECD Model Treaty.

has a source jurisdiction on income generated within its borders. Country A and Country B have a double tax treaty (DTT) to address this residence–source conflict.

	Country A (%)	Country B (%)
Investment Income Tax	25	40
Estate Tax	50	30

1 What is Yankevich's tax rate on investment income under the DTT if it provides for the credit method? How much is remitted to Country A and how much is remitted to Country B?

2 What is Yankevich's tax rate on bequests under the DTT if it provides for the exemption method?

3 What is Yankevich's tax rate on bequests under the DTT if it provides for the deduction method?

Solution to 1:

Under the credit method, $T_{CreditMethod} = \text{Max}[T_{Residence}, T_{Source}]$. Therefore, $T_{CreditMethod} = \text{Max}[0.25, 0.40] = 40$ percent. In this case, 40 percent is remitted to Country B. Nothing is remitted to Country A because it provides Yankevich with a credit for his entire domestic tax liability.

Solution to 2:

Under the exemption method, the resident country relinquishes the tax jurisdiction, so that the tax rate on bequests would be only 30 percent, all of which is remitted to Country B.

Solution to 3:

Under the deduction method, Yankevich receives a home country tax deduction (rather than a credit) for estate taxes paid to Country B. In this case:

$$T_{DeductionMethod} = T_{Residence} + T_{Source} - T_{Residence}T_{Source}$$
$$= 0.50 + 0.30 - (0.50 \times 0.30) = 0.65$$

Country A receives 35 percent, and Country B receives 30 percent.

6.4 Transparency and Offshore Banking

A wealth management advisor can often create value for a client or family by developing an estate plan that minimizes taxes. In that regard, it must be emphasized that a distinction exists between tax avoidance (sometimes referred to as "tax minimization") and tax evasion. **Tax avoidance** is developing strategies that conform to both the spirit and the letter of the tax codes of jurisdictions with taxing authority. **Tax evasion**, on the other hand, is the practice of circumventing tax obligations by illegal means such as misreporting or not reporting relevant information to tax authorities.

International wealth management is occasionally characterized as the practice of placing assets in jurisdictions with bank secrecy laws to avoid detection by taxing authorities in an individual's home country. Income on these "undeclared funds" would therefore escape taxation by the home country that might otherwise impose a tax obligation if the income were reported. Recent private banking scandals have highlighted this practice. Although such behavior is not appropriate, banking secrecy may provide legitimate benefits in the form of security, privacy, intra-family dynamics, and politics. Moreover, offshore banking centers (such as those in London, New York,

Paris, Zurich, Luxembourg, Singapore, and Hong Kong) can be an efficient way to provide financial services to clients residing in other countries. So, offshore banking should not be equated with tax evasion.

Information exchange between tax authorities, however, is becoming increasingly fluid and increasingly exposing tax evasion strategies predicated on bank secrecy.[34] Marcovici (2007) outlines regulatory and other trends that contribute to this growing trend toward transparency. For example, in an effort to enforce the taxation of worldwide income on its residents and citizens, the United States demanded that banks around the globe provide the names of beneficial owners of all US securities whether the owners were US or non-US citizens. Fearing that the United States could share this ownership information with authorities in the home country of their non-US customers, most banks agreed to become Qualified Intermediaries (QIs). In exchange for not being required to categorically supply the names of beneficial owners of US securities, QIs agree to document this information for all their customers and provide information about US customers upon request. In this way, QIs are able to preserve the confidentiality of their non-US customers but are still required to gather information that could be shared with the US authorities.

Similarly, the European Union Savings Directive (EUSD) is a system to collect tax on interest payments made in one EU country for the benefit of an individual in another EU country. Under the EUSD system, EU members agree to automatically exchange information with each other with the exception of Austria, Belgium, and Luxembourg. These countries apply a tax at the source and transfer the respective proportion of the pooled tax revenues to the EU country of residency of the concerned EU national.

Other trends are also contributing to the increasing rate of information exchange between jurisdictions. In some cases authorities collect information from credit card companies about individuals who use credit cards in their country, whether or not they are citizens of that country. This information can then be shared with the individual's home country. Tax treaties not only provide relief from double taxation, but may also provide for far-reaching exchange of information between countries.

In sum, estate planning strategies designed around an understanding of the economics of taxation and law are likely to provide lasting benefit for wealthy individuals and families. Families that build wealth management plans on a foundation of bank secrecy and of "hiding the money" impose archaic and potentially costly structures on subsequent generations, who will likely be operating in a more transparent and compliant legal and tax environment. Moreover, these structures pass on values that may not match subsequent generations' attitudes toward integrity, compliance, and transparency.

SUMMARY

Estate planning is a multidisciplinary endeavor that involves the intersection of tax, law, and finance. An understanding of the primary legal, tax, and financial issues affecting clients can help wealth managers effectively and strategically create tax-efficient wealth transfer strategies that meet clients' needs and objectives. The major points of this reading include:

- Assets in an estate can have ownership transferred by virtue of the type of ownership (e.g., sole versus joint), a will, or a trust.

---

34 See Marcovici (2007) for a more thorough discussion of the regulatory climate on which this section is largely based.

- Probate is the process by which a will is validated and can be relied on by interested parties.

- A country's legal system can limit the freedom of a testator to dispose of assets as he or she sees fit (e.g., forced heirship, community property rules, etc.).

- The two primary ways of transferring ownership of assets are lifetime gratuitous transfers (i.e., gifts) and testamentary gratuitous transfers (i.e., bequests).

- A wealth transfer strategy involves estimating an individual's or a family's core capital and excess capital.

- Core capital is the amount of capital required to maintain a given lifestyle and provide adequate reserves for unexpected commitments and can be estimated using mortality tables or Monte Carlo analysis.

- Excess capital represents assets above and beyond core capital that can be safely transferred without jeopardizing the first generation's lifestyle.

- Tax-free gifts that fall below periodic or lifetime allowances can be an effective means of minimizing estate tax, especially if a gifting program is developed early.

- Opportunities for tax-efficient gifting programs also exist when lifetime gifts are taxed, especially when the gift tax is paid by the donor rather than by the recipient.

- Transferring capital in excess of a second generation's need for spending, safety, and flexibility directly to the third generation or beyond (i.e., generation skipping) can help to minimize taxes where permitted.

- Taxpayers in jurisdictions with both spousal exemptions and exclusions for smaller estates in effect have two estate exclusions available—one for each spouse.

- Tax efficiencies are possible using valuation discounts and charitable gratuitous transfer strategies.

- Common estate planning tools include trusts, foundations, insurance, and companies, each of which can provide benefits related to asset control, protection from creditors, and taxation.

- The control and protection trusts offer, whether structured as revocable or irrevocable, can provide flexibility as well as legal validity.

- Families with an international footprint face special issues relating to the drafting and recognition of legal documents, such as wills and trusts.

- The taxing authority of a country is determined by its tax system (e.g., source versus residence) and may conflict with the tax authority of another country.

- Jurisdictional claims based on source or residency can conflict with source jurisdictions typically given primacy.

- Double taxation conflicts can be resolved through either foreign tax credit provisions of the home country or double taxation treaties with other countries.

- The ability of locating undeclared funds in offshore savings accounts and other offshore structures to avoid detection by home country tax authorities is being eroded by trends toward an increase in information exchange and transparency across countries; compliant, tailored, tax-efficient strategies are key to meet the needs and objectives of clients and of their successor generations.

PRACTICE PROBLEMS

1 The drawing up of a will is an area of estate planning that requires an individual to have a clear understanding of the tax and succession (or inheritance) laws of any jurisdiction of relevance to the testator. Although an individual may elect to draw up a will, the validity of the will could be subject to various challenges in the probate process. In addition, probate may create sizeable court fees as well as unwelcome publicity and a delay in the distribution of assets. Describe how an individual can attempt to reduce or even avoid the impact of:

A probate.

B forced heirship.

2 After a lengthy career as a metallurgical engineer, Greg Pearsall recently retired at age 70 and is looking forward to spending retirement with his wife Christine, who is 75 years old. Although both Greg and Christine are now retired, they would prefer to maintain their present lifestyle which currently requires annual spending of $75,000 in real terms. Inflation is expected to be 6 percent, and the nominal risk-free rate is 10 percent. The Pearsalls' survival probabilities for the next five years based on their current age are listed in the table below.

| | Greg | | Christine | |
Year	Age	p(Survival)	Age	p(Survival)
1	71	0.9660	76	0.8235
2	72	0.9371	77	0.7996
3	73	0.9152	78	0.7727
4	74	0.8883	79	0.7208
5	75	0.8544	80	0.6919

A What is the probability that either Greg or Christine will survive over each of the next five years?

B Is it appropriate to use the expected return of the assets used to fund their spending needs when calculating the capitalized value of the Pearsalls' core capital spending needs? Why or why not?

C What is the capitalized value of the Pearsalls' core capital spending needs over the next five years?

3 As part of their estate, Tony and Eleanor Hall currently own a $2.5 million portfolio of equities and bonds that has an average annual pretax return of 10 percent. The Halls' after-tax return on the portfolio is 7 percent (the tax rate is 30 percent). Due to the rapid deterioration in their health, the Halls are considering transferring the $2.5 million portfolio to their eldest grandchild, Joe, during the current financial year. By transferring their investment portfolio directly to their grandson, the Halls are attempting to reduce the transfer taxation effect of their inheritance. Although $1.5 million can be transferred tax free, local jurisdiction requires that the remaining $1 million transfer be subject to a 30 percent tax rate, which is Joe's responsibility as donee. The Halls have consulted with their financial planner as they are uncertain whether the 30 percent tax rate would also apply if their gift to their grandson is delayed and transferred as a bequest five years from today. Their grandson currently pays a marginal tax rate of 25 percent.

A Discuss the effectiveness of the Halls' generation skipping strategy.

B Calculate the relative after-tax value of the Hall's $1 million gift (above and beyond the $1.5 million exclusion) to their grandson. Assume the $1 million transfer is subject to 30 percent tax whether it takes place today or is delayed and transferred as a bequest in five years.

C Given that the $1 million transfer is subject to 30 percent tax whether it takes place today or is delayed and transferred as a bequest in five years, is there any advantage in delaying payment of the gift by five years?

4 After five decades of living in Country A, a wealthy entrepreneur, Andrew Lloyd, has recently retired and taken up residency in Country B. Although he now lives in Country B, Lloyd has retained a number of investment properties in Country A. The investment income tax rate is 45 percent and 30 percent in Country A and Country B, respectively.

A Define source and residence tax as two possible primary tax systems of Country A and Country B.

B Discuss three potential double taxation conflicts that could arise due to Lloyd's new residency in Country B.

C Calculate Lloyd's tax rate liability under the following three methods providing for double taxation relief, assuming scenarios where either country claims source or residence jurisdiction:

   i. Credit method.

   ii. Exemption method.

   iii. Deduction method.

SOLUTIONS

1 A There is often a desire to avoid probate as court fees may be sizable, and the process can cause a delay in the transfer of assets to intended beneficiaries. A will can be challenged, and its contents are often a matter of public record, which may concern some wealthy families as it may cause embarrassment or divulge sensitive financial information. Moreover, many problems can arise in probate when multiple jurisdictions are involved. In some instances, probate can be avoided or its impact limited by holding assets in joint ownership (e.g., joint tenancy with right of survivorship), living trusts, retirement plans, or life insurance strategies. Through these structures, ownership transfers without the need for a will, and hence the probate process can be avoided.

B Under civil law, ownership is a precise concept that is tempered by statutes that place certain limitations on the free disposition of one's assets. Under forced heirship rules, for example, children have the right to a fixed share of a parent's estate. This right may exist whether or not the child is estranged or conceived outside of marriage. Forced heirship in civil law countries may reduce or eliminate the need for a will. Wealthy individuals may attempt to move assets into an offshore trust governed by a different domicile to circumvent forced heirship rules. Spouses typically have similar guaranteed inheritance rights under civil law forced heirship regimes. In addition, spouses have marital property rights, which depend on the marital property regime that applies to their marriage. Individuals can attempt to reduce or avoid forced heirship by:

- moving assets into an offshore trust governed by a different jurisdiction;

- gifting or donating assets to others during their lifetime to reduce the value of the final estate upon death; or

- purchasing life insurance, which can move assets outside of realm of forced heirship provisions.

Such strategies, however, may be subject to "clawback" provisions that provide a basis for heirs to challenge these solutions in court.

2 A Greg and Christine Pearsall's joint survival probabilities are equal to the sum of their individual probabilities less the product of their individual probabilities, calculated as follows:

$$p(\text{Joint survival}) = p(\text{Greg survives}) + p(\text{Christine survives})$$
$$-p(\text{Greg survives})p(\text{Christine survives})$$

For each of the next five years, their joint probability of survival is:

Year	Joint p(Survival)
1	0.9940
2	0.9874
3	0.9807
4	0.9688
5	0.9551

B It is not appropriate to use the expected return of the assets used to fund spending needs to calculate the capitalized value of their core capital needs, because the risk of the Pearsalls' spending needs is unrelated to the risk of the investment portfolio used to fund those needs. Although the annual spending cash flows are not riskless, a risk-free rate should be used to calculate the present value of the cash flows as their uncertainty is unrelated to market risk factors that would be priced in a normal asset pricing model, making their beta equal to zero.

C The capitalized value of their core capital needs equals the product of the joint probability of survival and the real spending need for each year discounted using the real risk-free rate. The real risk-free rate is calculated as follows:

$$\text{Real risk-free rate} = \left[(1 + \text{Nominal risk-free rate}) \div (1 + \text{Inflation rate}) - 1 \right]$$

$$3.7736\% = \left[(1 + 0.10) \div (1 + 0.06) - 1 \right]$$

Year	Annual Spending	Expected Spending	Discounted Value
1	75,000	74,550	71,839
2	75,000	74,055	68,767
3	75,000	73,553	65,817
4	75,000	72,660	62,654
5	75,000	71,633	59,522
			$328,599

$$\text{Discounted value} = \frac{\text{Real spending} \times \text{Joint probability}}{(1 + \text{Real risk-free rate})^t}$$

Alternatively, annual spending can be adjusted for inflation and these nominal expected cash flows can be discounted at the nominal risk-free rate.

Year	Annual Spending	Expected Spending	Discounted Value
1	79,500	79,023	71,839
2	84,270	83,208	68,767
3	89,326	87,602	65,817
4	94,686	91,731	62,654
5	100,367	95,861	59,522
			$328,599

$$\text{Discounted value} = \frac{\text{Real spending} \times (1 + \text{Inflation})^t \times \text{Joint probability}}{(1 + \text{Risk-free rate})^t}$$

Greg and Christine Pearsall have core capital spending needs of $328,599 for the next five years.

3 A Transferring their investment portfolio assets directly to the third generation (grandson), the Halls may reduce transfer tax liabilities. In jurisdictions that tax gifts or bequests, transfers from the first generation to the second will be taxed. The same capital may be taxed again if it is transferred from the second to third generation and the second generation's estate is taxable.

Transferring capital in excess of the second generation's needs for spending, safety, and flexibility directly to the third generation can avoid a layer of this double taxation. However, in the United States, taxing authorities discourage this strategy by imposing a special generation skipping tax. This tax, in addition to the usual transfer tax, is imposed on transfers to grandchildren or subsequent generations and is intended to produce the same overall tax effect had the assets passed sequentially through two generations.

B

$$RV_{TaxableGift} = \frac{FV_{Gift}}{FV_{Bequest}}$$

$$= \frac{\left[1 + 0.10(1 - 0.25)\right]^5 (1 - 0.30)}{\left[1 + 0.10(1 - 0.30)\right]^5 (1 - 0.30)} = \frac{1.0049}{0.9818} = 1.02$$

C There is no advantage in delaying payment of the gift because their grandson has a lower marginal tax rate on investment returns compared to the estate's marginal tax rate; the gift still creates a tax advantage if donated today. As their grandson is subject to a lower tax rate of 25 percent, subsequent investment returns will be taxed at a lower rate than if it is kept inside the estate. As the calculation in Solution B indicates, 2 percent more wealth will be created in five years than if the portfolio had remained in the estate and been taxed at 30 percent annually. This analysis assumes that the gratuitous transfer tax is paid by the grandson rather than by the Halls.

4 A *Source tax system*: A jurisdiction that imposes tax on an individual's income that is sourced in the jurisdiction.

Residence tax system: A jurisdiction that imposes a tax on an individual's income based on residency whereby all income (domestic and foreign sourced) is subject to taxation.

B The interaction of countries' taxation jurisdictions can create tax conflicts in which Country A and B can claim to have authority to tax the same investment properties. This conflict can arise in three ways:

- *Residence–residence conflict*: If he were a resident of both countries, Country A and B would both claim residence of Mr. Lloyd, subjecting his worldwide income to taxation by both countries.

- *Source–source conflict*: Both Country A and B may claim source jurisdiction of the same investment properties as income from the investments that are in Country A, but managed from Country B.

- *Residence–source conflict*: Because Lloyd lives in Country B, but has investment properties in Country A, he may be subject to a combination of two taxation jurisdictions. As a resident of Country B he could be taxed on worldwide income; and if Country A exercises source jurisdiction on his assets, he will be taxed on these as well. In this case, the source country (Country A) is commonly viewed to have primary jurisdiction to tax income within its borders and the residence country (Country B) is expected to provide double taxation relief.

C i. In the credit method, the residence country reduces its taxpayers' domestic tax liability for taxes paid to a foreign country exercising source jurisdiction. The credit is limited to the amount of taxes the taxpayer would pay domestically, which completely eliminates double taxation. Under this method the tax liability equals the greater of the tax liability due in either the residence or source country.

If Country A claims source jurisdiction and Country B residence jurisdiction:

$$T_{CreditMethod} = \text{Max}[T_{Residence}, T_{Source}]$$

$$T_{CreditMethod} = \text{Max}[0.30, 0.45] = 45\%$$

In this case, Lloyd remits the entire 45 percent to Country A, which has the source claim.

If Country A were to exercise residence jurisdiction and Country B source jurisdiction, the effective tax rate is the same:

$$T_{CreditMethod} = \text{Max}[T_{Residence}, T_{Source}]$$

$$T_{CreditMethod} = \text{Max}[0.45, 0.30] = 45\%$$

However, Lloyd would remit 30 percent to Country B and apply that remittance toward Country A's 45 percent tax liability, effectively paying Country A 15 percent.

ii. Under the exemption method, the residence country imposes no tax on foreign-source income by providing taxpayers with an exemption, which, in effect, eliminates the residence–source conflict by having only one jurisdiction impose tax. The tax liability under the exemption method is simply the tax imposed at the foreign source, so the source tax rate prevails:

If Country A is the source country, Lloyd's tax rate is 45 percent.

If Country B is the source country, Lloyd's tax rate is 30 percent.

iii. Under the deduction method, the residence country allows taxpayers to reduce their taxable income by the amount of taxes paid to foreign governments in respect of foreign-source income (i.e., provides a tax deduction rather than a credit or exemption). The taxpayer is still responsible for both taxes, but the aggregate liability is less than the sum of the two taxes individually with the residence country reducing the size of its percentage claim by the product of the two tax rates.

$$T_{DeductionMethod} = T_{Residence} + T_{Source} - (T_{Residence}T_{Source})$$

<u>Country A: Residence jurisdiction and Country B: Source jurisdiction</u> = 0.45 + 0.30 − (0.45 × 0.30) = 0.6150

Country A receives 31.50% and Country B receives 30%

<u>Country A: Source jurisdiction and Country B: Residence jurisdiction</u> = 0.30 + 0.45 − (0.30 × 0.45) = 0.6150

Country A receives 45%, and Country B receives 16.50%

5

Private Wealth Management (2)

The wealth of many individuals and families is often concentrated in a limited number of financial securities, business holdings, or real estate properties. The sale of such holdings to allow diversification may create a substantial tax liability. Dealing with concentrated single asset positions is the subject of the first reading in this study session.

The second reading examines the dynamic mix of human and financial capital during an investor's lifetime and the challenge of meeting financial goals throughout that lifetime. It specifically addresses mortality and longevity risks by integrating insurance products into the asset allocation solution.

READING ASSIGNMENTS

Reading 11	Concentrated Single Asset Positions by Thomas J. Boczar, Esq., LL.M., CFA, and Nischal R. Pai, CFA
Reading 12	Lifetime Financial Advice: Human Capital, Asset Allocation, and Insurance by Roger G. Ibbotson, PhD, Moshe A. Milevsky, PhD, Peng Chen, PhD, CFA, and Kevin X. Zhu, PhD

Concentrated Single-Asset Positions

by Thomas J. Boczar, Esq., LL.M., CFA, and Nischal R. Pai, CFA

Thomas J. Boczar, Esq., LL.M., CFA, is at Intelligent Edge Advisors (USA). Nischal R. Pai, CFA (USA).

LEARNING OUTCOMES

Mastery	The candidate should be able to:
☐	a. explain investment risks associated with a concentrated position in a single asset and discuss the appropriateness of reducing such risks;
☐	b. describe typical objectives in managing concentrated positions;
☐	c. discuss tax consequences and illiquidity as considerations affecting the management of concentrated positions in publicly traded common shares, privately held businesses, and real estate;
☐	d. discuss capital market and institutional constraints on an investor's ability to reduce a concentrated position;
☐	e. discuss psychological considerations that may make an investor reluctant to reduce his or her exposure to a concentrated position;
☐	f. describe advisers' use of goal-based planning in managing concentrated positions;
☐	g. explain uses of asset location and wealth transfers in managing concentrated positions;
☐	h. describe strategies for managing concentrated positions in publicly traded common shares;
☐	i. discuss tax considerations in the choice of hedging strategy;
☐	j. describe strategies for managing concentrated positions in privately held businesses;
☐	k. describe strategies for managing concentrated positions in real estate;
☐	l. evaluate and recommend techniques for tax efficiently managing the risks of concentrated positions in publicly traded common stock, privately held businesses, and real estate.

1 INTRODUCTION

Frequently, the wealth of individuals and families is concentrated in an asset or group of assets that has played a role in their (or their forebears') accumulation of wealth. Wealth managers must be able to assist private clients with decisions concerning such positions. The three major types of "concentrated position in a single asset" (or "concentrated position") examined in this reading are (1) publicly traded stock, (2) a privately owned business, and (3) commercial or investment real estate.

Exhibit 1 shows that ownership interests in privately owned business enterprises constitute much of the wealth of private clients in many countries.

Exhibit 1	Percentage of Global Private Clients Who Derive Their Wealth from a Private Business, by Region

Clients (%)

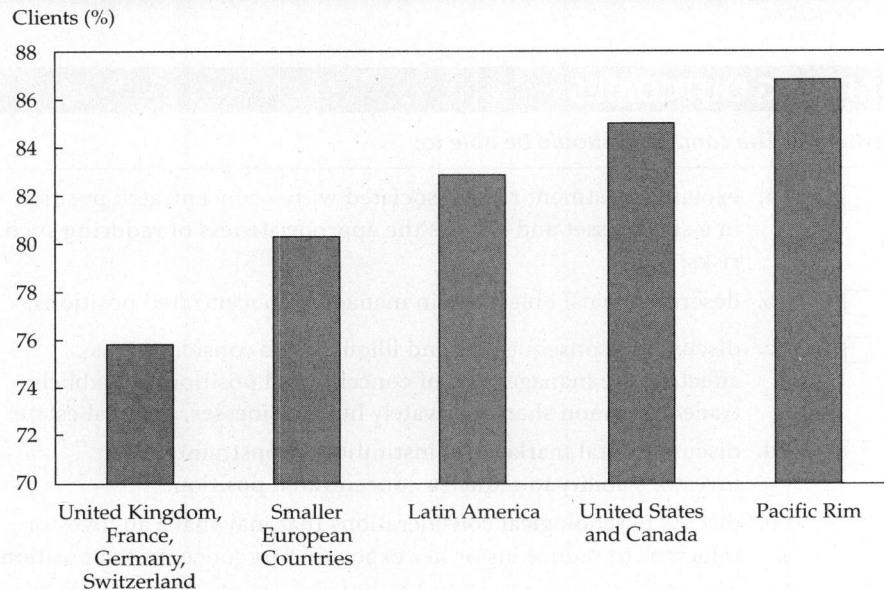

Source: VIP Forum, *Strictly Business: Strategies for Acquiring and Serving High-Net-Worth Business Owners* (Arlington, VA: Corporate Executive Board, 2005).

Concentrated positions sometimes make up a large share of a client's net worth. As the owner of a concentrated position ages, the asset may need to be sold or monetized to fund retirement needs, or for risk management purposes. (In general terms, to **monetize** something is to access its cash value without transferring ownership of it, as would be the case in a sale.)

Private clients often want to compare the potential results of continuing to hold these often illiquid assets with selling or monetizing them and reinvesting the proceeds in other asset classes. Wealth managers who understand their clients' finances and personal long-term objectives are ideally suited to play a key role in assisting them to chart an efficient path in handling their concentrated positions.

Creating a globally relevant reading in this field for generalists presents many challenges. Decisions concerning the treatment of concentrated single-asset positions must always be made in the context of a specific single market and tax code. The available means for attempting to achieve a given objective vary across markets, as do tax codes. We show problems that arise worldwide, but the contexts and questions addressed are often simplified. Frequently, US considerations are mentioned, but other markets are not ignored. This reading provides a familiarity with various recurring themes. Expertise in the field is needed to address real-life problems of concentrated positions. This reading is organized as follows. Section 2 provides an overview of concentrated positions, including how investors typically acquire these assets and the risks inherent in owning them. Section 3 discusses the general principles associated with managing the risk of a concentrated position. Sections 4, 5, and 6 focus on the range of strategies that are available to the owners of concentrated positions in a single stock, private business equity, and real estate, respectively, and Section 7 summarizes the key points of the reading.

CONCENTRATED SINGLE-ASSET POSITIONS: OVERVIEW

2

There is no universally accepted definition of what is meant by a concentrated position. Practically speaking, a concentrated position is one that makes up a significant portion of a private client's net worth. In practice, many wealth managers and fiduciaries consider 25% of a client's net worth to be a relevant threshold, although many use a higher or lower threshold.

Concentration within asset classes poses problems that need to be managed. For instance, a holding of a highly illiquid stock might constitute only a modest portion of a private client's net worth but might be a large percentage of his or her equity exposure. The equity component of the portfolio would then be undiversified and thus entail certain inherent risks. This type of concentration presents risks that also need to be managed.

A concentrated position is often a position that has been held by the private client for a long period, sometimes for decades, and that has greatly appreciated in value over its original cost (cost basis). It will often present tax, liquidity, or other considerations that make a simple sale problematic.

The three asset classes in which concentration risk most commonly arises are

- publicly traded single-stock positions,
- privately held businesses (including family-owned businesses), and
- investment real estate.

Publicly traded single-stock positions. There are a number of ways an investor can end up owning a concentrated stock position. The investor might have worked at a publicly traded company as an executive, perhaps for many years, and received company stock, options, or some other financial instrument that is convertible into company stock as part of his or her executive compensation.

It is also not unusual for the seller of a privately owned business to receive stock in lieu of cash if the acquirer is a publicly traded company. Under many tax regimes, including Japan, the United Kingdom, and the United States, it is possible to structure a purchase using stock without triggering an immediate taxable event. In these situations, the owner goes from holding a highly appreciated position in a privately held stock to a highly appreciated position in a publicly traded stock.

A concentrated position in a publicly traded stock can also come about because of a successful long-term buy-and-hold investing strategy or as a result of a private company that elects to go public through an initial public offering.

Privately owned businesses. Some successful privately owned businesses have been in existence for many years, with ownership passed down from one generation to the next. In other cases, an entrepreneur may have built a successful business in a much shorter period of time, a situation that is not uncommon in such industries as technology and social media.

Investment real estate. Commercial or industrial real estate often constitutes a significant portion of the value of a private business enterprise. It is also often held as a standalone investment by private clients, as in the case of real estate developers. Typically, real estate is held for a long-term period. It is not uncommon when selling or monetizing a business that the buyer does not wish to purchase the real estate component of the business (because, for example, the buyer may already have sufficient space to accommodate the purchased operations). In that case, the seller is left with a large real estate holding.

Concentrated positions in investment real estate could also be derived from inheritance, from a lack of other investment opportunities in certain jurisdictions (e.g., China in the 1990s and 2000s, when financial markets were still in their infancy), or from rapid price appreciation leading to a bubble (e.g., Japan—especially Tokyo—in the 1980s).

Of course, the holder of each of these types of assets might have received his or her ownership stake in the asset through either gifting or inheritance, which is quite common. Ownership of concentrated positions is not a challenge reserved exclusively for private clients. Entities such as trusts, estates, and foundations often hold concentrated positions as the result of a gift or bequest. Pension funds are sometimes exposed to a heavy allocation of the fund sponsor's company stock. Also, publicly traded companies sometimes hold a significant amount of shares of another publicly traded company for business or investment purposes.

2.1 Investment Risks of Concentrated Positions

The owners of concentrated positions face systematic risk and non-systematic risk, which can be company- or property-specific risk. Exposures to any of these risks may not be consistent with the individual's willingness and capacity to bear risk or may be suboptimal with respect to asset allocation.

This section focuses on describing these risks. However, return consequences of concentrated positions can also be important. Some concentrated positions may not be expected to earn fair risk-adjusted returns, for example. There may be large opportunity costs in holding under-performing company stock or non-income-producing land.

2.1.1 *Systematic Risk*

Systematic risk is the component of risk that cannot be eliminated by holding a well-diversified portfolio. The capital asset pricing model as practically implemented equates systematic risk to equity market risk. More recently developed asset pricing models identify multiple sources of systematic risk; for example, one model based on macroeconomic factors identifies business cycle risk (unexpected changes in the level of real business activity), inflation risk (unexpected changes in the inflation rate), and three other factors, including that part of equity market risk that is unexplained by macroeconomic factors. If the concentrated position has systematic risk exposures that are similar to those of the human capital of the owner of the concentrated position, the individual may be exposed to investment portfolio losses at the same time that job earnings are jeopardized. An example is the founder of a securities firm with a concentrated position in the firm's shares. In a bear market, the firm's earnings and the founder's compensation may be low at the same time that share returns are negative.

2.1.2 *Company-Specific Risk*

With respect to the ownership of a privately held business and publicly traded stock, we call specific risk **company-specific risk**. Company-specific risk is the non-systematic or idiosyncratic risk that is specific to a particular company's operations, reputation, and business environment. To describe it in another way, it is the possibility that the value of the company may decline because of an event that affects that company but not the industry or market as a whole. Having a concentrated position can expose an individual to an unacceptably high level of company-specific risk. A negative corporate event may result in essentially permanent and irrecoverable losses in wealth. All else equal, the level of company-specific risk is positively related to volatility of returns; company-specific risk can range from relatively low to high for small undiversified or unprofitable companies.

The concept and importance of company-specific risk with respect to a publicly traded company can perhaps best be highlighted through a real life example. During the 1990s, Enron Corporation was one of the most admired companies in the United States. A position in Enron shares returned over 27% per year from 1990 through September 2000, compared with 13% for the S&P 500 Index for the same time period. During this period, thousands of Enron employees participated in the company's defined contribution retirement plan and chose to invest in Enron stock. In January 2001, the retirement accounts were valued at US$2 billion, of which 62%, or US$1.24 billion, was invested in Enron shares even though the employees had the option to sell most of those shares tax free within the plan. Between January 2001 and January 2002, Enron's share price fell from about US$90 per share to zero. On the other hand, the S&P 500 Index declined by only 12% in the same time period.

The higher volatility associated with company-specific risk of single-stock holdings significantly lessens the benefit of higher expected capital accumulation over time. For example, Exhibit 2 compares investing a dollar in a single security having a zero cost basis and 40% volatility with the alternative of selling it, paying a 20% capital gains tax, and reinvesting the net proceeds of 80 cents in a diversified portfolio with a volatility of only 17%. Either alternative has an annual expected pretax return of 10%. Exhibit 2 illustrates the comparison at the end of a 20-year horizon.

Exhibit 2   Holding a Security vs. Outright Sale of a Security: Probability Distribution of After-Tax Liquidation Value

A. $1.00 in Single Security with Zero Cost Basis and 40% Volatility

Frequency (%)

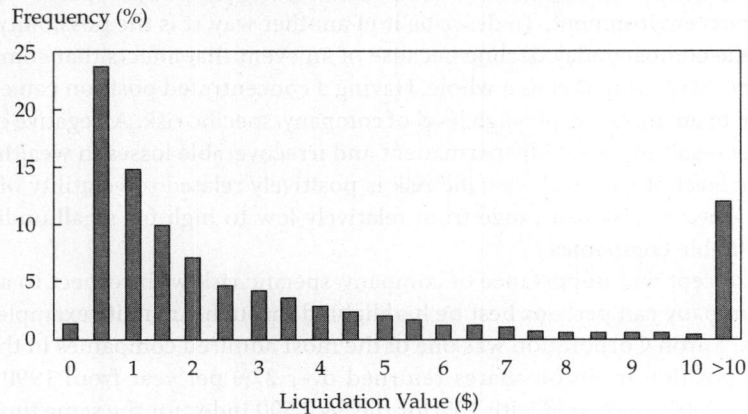

Liquidation Value ($)

B. $0.80 in Diversified Portfolio with $0.80 Cost Basis and 17% Volatility

Frequency (%)

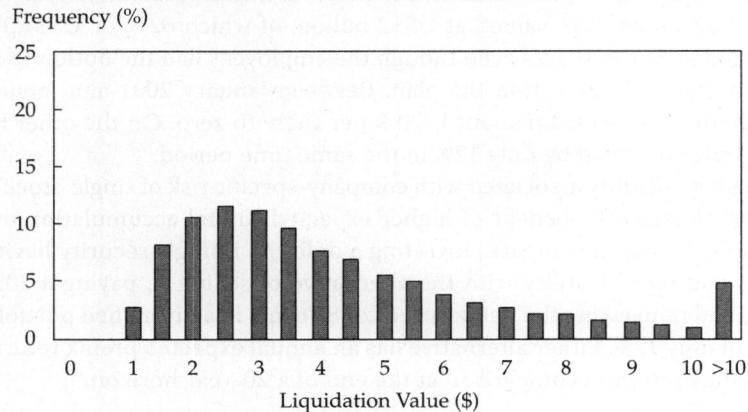

Liquidation Value ($)

Measure	A	B
Expected final value	$5.3	$4.2
Median value	$1.6	$3.3
Probability of $1 or less	39%	2%
Probability of $2 or less	57%	21%

Note: Annual expected return = 10%; dividends on stock = 0; dividends on diversified portfolio = 1.2%; horizon = 20 years; terminal liquidation.
Source: David M. Stein, "Taxes and Quantitative Portfolio Management," in *Developments in Quantitative Investment Models* (Charlottesville, VA: Association for Investment Management and Research, 2001).

Although the expected value (i.e., arithmetic average) is higher for the single stock, the median outcome is much higher for the diversified portfolio. Moreover, the diversified portfolio has a much smaller chance of suffering large losses. The diversified portfolio strategy has only a 2% chance of losing money, versus a 39% chance for the single stock. As this example illustrates, a "tax minimization" strategy may not be optimal.

2.1.3 *Property-Specific Risk*

Property-specific risk is the non-systematic risk that is specific to owning a particular piece of real estate. It is the possibility that the value of that property might fall because of an event that could affect that property but not the broader real estate market.

For instance, a potential environmental liability associated with a particular property might be discovered that significantly reduces the value of that property even though the broader real estate market and similar properties are increasing in value.

As another example, an investor might own a large office building that is leased out to a few investment-grade tenants for a long-term period. If the tenants decide not to renew their leases for an additional term when their lease terms expire, the owner may have a difficult time leasing the entire property to a few large investment-grade tenants. Instead, the owner may have to lease the property to a number of smaller tenants, which could take more time, and therefore, a good portion of the property might sit vacant for some time. Also, the new and smaller tenants might not be investment grade, thus increasing the credit risk that the owner must incur in order to fully lease out the building. These types of changes with respect to the tenants/occupancy could negatively affect the resale value of that property even though the broader real estate market and similar office properties are increasing in value.

GENERAL PRINCIPLES OF MANAGING CONCENTRATED SINGLE-ASSET POSITIONS

3

The following sections review certain basic principles that are germane to managing concentrated positions.

3.1 Objectives in Dealing with Concentrated Positions

The financial adviser should first and foremost help clients identify and define their objectives.

3.1.1 *Typical Objectives*

Irrespective of the form of the concentrated position—whether it is a privately owned business, investment real estate, or a concentrated position in publicly traded stock—there are three objectives that are frequently considered in discussions with the client.

Risk is reviewed and the appropriateness of risk reduction considered. Any adverse results from risk reduction (e.g., loss of control of a business) should be weighed against the benefits. With such qualifications, a frequent (if not universal) objective is to *reduce the risk of wealth concentration*. Psychological considerations are often at work to cause owners to seriously underestimate the riskiness of their concentrated position and significantly overestimate the value of that asset.

Cash flow needs should be identified. An appropriate strategy for monetization and/or risk reduction should be developed. Often, an objective is to *generate liquidity in order to diversify and satisfy spending needs*. Illiquid private business equity, investment real estate, and concentrated stock positions need to be transformed into cash. A replacement source of income then needs to be created to satisfy essential lifetime spending needs. Fulfilling legacy and charitable intentions are also drivers of liquidity needs along with other aspirational desires.

Another typical objective is to *optimize tax efficiency*, which can be accomplished by either structuring transactions involving concentrated positions so as not to trigger an immediate taxable event, or if a taxable event will be triggered, structuring the transaction in a manner that minimizes the tax the owner will incur.

3.1.2 *Client Objectives and Concerns*

There are many objectives that the owner of the concentrated position might wish to achieve. For instance, the concentrated position could be used in conjunction with gifting strategies to satisfy the owner's wealth transfer desires, such as leaving a legacy for the next generation or to satisfy his or her charitable intentions. The previous section indicated that risk reduction and diversification are common objectives. It is important to note that in order to achieve such objectives, it is *not* always appropriate for the owner to reduce or eliminate the concentration risk of a concentrated position.

With respect to concentrated stock positions, examples of objectives consistent with risk retention include the following:

- An executive might have received shares as part of his or her incentive compensation with the expectation or mandate that those shares be held for a long time period to motivate the executive to work hard as part of a team to grow the company and hopefully result in a much higher stock price in the future.
- The owner of a concentrated position might wish to *maintain effective voting control* of the company.
- The owner of a concentrated position might wish to *enhance the current income* of his or her stock position in the short term but in the long term still retain significant upside potential with respect to the stock.

With respect to privately owned businesses, the following are examples of client objectives:

- An entrepreneur might have recently founded a business, and it would be premature to sell that company because its growth phase has just begun.
- The owner of a mature and stable privately owned business might wish to maintain total control of the company.
- In return for years of prior service, the owner might wish to give senior management and other key employees the opportunity to eventually acquire control of the business.
- The business owner might have plans to pass control of the business to the next generation of his family.

With respect to investment real estate, examples of client objectives include the following:

- Maintain control because the property is an essential asset necessary for the successful operation of a business enterprise.
- Retain ownership in order to pass ownership of the real estate to the next generation.
- Benefit from a recent purchase or development through price appreciation.

3.2 Considerations Affecting All Concentrated Positions

Owners of concentrated positions face numerous constraints and obstacles that must be overcome in order for them to meet their primary and secondary objectives.

3.2.1 *Tax Consequences of an Outright Sale*

Concentrated positions are often highly appreciated versus their original cost. Therefore, simply selling the asset outright will usually trigger an immediate and sometimes significant taxable capital gain for the owner.

With respect to taxation, the tax cost basis is generally the amount that was paid to acquire an investment or capital asset. It serves as the foundation for calculating capital gain (or loss), which equals the selling price less the tax cost basis. For example, a share of stock bought for 10 monetary units and sold 20 years later for 100 monetary units would generate a capital gain of 90 monetary units.

In the case of concentrated positions, frequently the asset was acquired a long time ago and has a tax cost basis that is much lower than the current fair market value. The asset may therefore have a significant embedded capital gains tax liability.

The key point is that many, but by no means all, tax regimes throughout the world do impose a tax on capital gains.

Given that most families have accumulated the wealth represented by their concentrated positions through many years of hard work and calculated business risks, the fact that an outright sale of those assets would result in a tax obligation is often not psychologically palatable to the family. Therefore, deferring and, if possible, eliminating the capital gains tax is typically a primary objective for investors who own a concentrated position. There are a number of tools and strategies that can be used in many jurisdictions to achieve these objectives.

3.2.2 *Liquidity*

With the possible exception of concentrated positions in publicly traded stocks, concentrated positions are generally illiquid. This is especially true for the owners of privately owned businesses and investment real estate. Owners of concentrated publicly traded stock positions may also face this illiquidity if the trading volume of the company's shares is small relative to the size of the concentrated position or if the shareholder is an insider and the timing or amount of any sales is restricted by applicable securities laws and regulations.

The sale of private business equity does not resemble the sale of shares of publicly traded stock because the latter trade on established stock exchanges or public trading venues where there are publicly quoted bids and offers and usually many ready buyers and sellers. That is, there is no readily available market for a private company's shares. Rather, a buyer needs to be found for private business equity, and different classes of potential buyers may place a different value on the business. Therefore, the most important factors determining the amount that a business owner will receive when selling his or her business are ultimately the strategy that is employed and who the buyer is.

Direct ownership of investment real estate is also illiquid. A buyer needs to be found for a particular property, and different classes of potential buyers may place different values on that property.

Illiquidity in general acts as a constraint on the choice of strategies for dealing with a concentrated position.

3.3 Institutional and Capital Market Constraints

Various features of the institutional and capital market environment act as constraints on the choice of methods that may be effective in dealing with concentrated positions. Execution of any strategy is dependent on the governing law. The legal relationship that exists between the owners of a business depends on the type of entity that is being used (e.g., sole trader, partnership, limited partnership, or limited company, among other forms, in the United Kingdom), the laws governing that type of entity, and any documentation or agreements those laws require.

3.3.1 *Margin-Lending Rules*

Margin rules also present obstacles and additional complexity. Margin rules determine how much a bank or brokerage firm can lend against securities positions that their customers own. Various margin regimes exist throughout the world. They can be either rule based or risk based.

Under a *rule-based* system, the amount that can be borrowed against a security that the investor owns will depend on strict rules dealing with the use of the loan proceeds. If the purpose of the loan is to buy additional securities, the maximum loan proceeds are usually quite limited. For instance, in the United States, such a "purpose loan" is subject to a maximum of 50% of the value of the stock that is borrowed against even if that stock is completely hedged by a long put.

In contrast, portfolio margining is an example of a margin regime that is *risk based*. If an investor borrows against a stock that is completely hedged by a long put, the dealer will typically lend close to 100% of the put strike to the investor even if the investor wishes to purchase additional equity securities with the loan proceeds.

The implications of "portfolio margining," which is available in the United States and other countries, are powerful, especially for ultra-high-net-worth investors. These rules provide advisers with additional flexibility to achieve the desired economic and tax results.

Certain forms of secured lending, such as a **prepaid variable forward** (collar[1] and loan combined within a single instrument) in the United States, are considered "off-balance-sheet" debt and not subject to the margin rules. Such transactions are considered "sales" for margin rule purposes (so the margin rules do not apply and therefore there are no limitations on the use of proceeds) but are structured to not be sales for tax purposes (so capital gains taxes can be deferred or eliminated).

3.3.2 *Securities Laws and Regulations*

Company insiders and executives must often comply with a myriad of rules and regulations promulgated by governmental authorities. In most countries, such individuals, like any investor, cannot trade on material, non-public information. However, they typically must also comply with certain notice and disclosure/reporting requirements, and there may be specific limitations with respect to the timing and volume of sales or hedging transactions.

3.3.3 *Contractual Restrictions and Employer Mandates*

Beyond restrictions imposed by securities laws and regulations, contractual restrictions, such as initial public offering "lockups," and employer mandates and policies, such as a prohibition of trading during certain "blackout periods" (i.e., periods when insiders cannot sell their shares) can greatly restrict the flexibility of insiders and employees to either sell or hedge their shares. In the case of private companies especially, there might be a right of first refusal, meaning that equity holders cannot sell their investment to a third party without first giving other equity investors the right to buy the interest at the same price and under the same conditions that the third party is offering. In addition to the right held by the investors, the entity may also have a right of first refusal, which further reduces the liquidity of an investment holding.

3.3.4 *Capital Market Limitations*

Certain characteristics of the underlying stock ultimately determine the feasibility of hedging different concentrated positions and in what degree they can be hedged.

---

1 A collar is the combination of a long put (to limit potential losses) and a short call (to cap potential gains) below and above their respective strike prices.

The ability to borrow shares is critical because the dealer needs to manage the risk inherent in being a counterparty to the investor's hedge. Managing this risk is achieved by first locating and borrowing the shares and then selling those shares in the marketplace. Although the investor executing the hedging transaction with the dealer could make its long shares available for the dealer to borrow if the shares were not restricted in any manner, the tax authorities could potentially view the transaction effectively as a sale.

In addition, the *liquidity* of the stock is vital because the dealer will periodically adjust its hedge, either borrowing and shorting additional shares or buying back shares and covering some of its outstanding short position. The average daily trading volume of the stock is important, and the dealer will observe whether the shares have had a propensity to "spike" either up or down. Because of this, most dealers will not execute collars or use other hedging techniques with respect to shares of a company that has recently undergone an initial public offering (IPO) because the dealer wants to be able to observe an established trading history/pattern of the stock prior to entering into such a transaction.

3.4 Psychological Considerations[2]

Various psychological considerations of clients can effectively act as constraints or obstacles to dealing with concentrated positions. Financial advisers hear many different types of rationalizations from their clients for declining to take any action with respect to the concentrated stock positions they own. Following are some common explanations that wealth managers often encounter:

- "It would be terribly disloyal for me to sell the stock after having worked at the company for so many years and the company treated me so well. What would my former colleagues think of me?"

- "My peers will look down on me if I sell the stock."

- "My husband picked and owned this stock for many years and made me promise before he died that I wouldn't sell it."

- "I have a duty to pass on ownership of the business to subsequent generations."

Advisers need to identify the cognitive and emotional biases that are affecting their clients and then communicate effectively with their clients to overcome the sometimes irrational decisions caused by these biases.

3.4.1 *Emotional Biases*

A number of emotional biases can combine to negatively affect the decision making of holders of concentrated positions, including the following:

- Overconfidence and familiarity (illusion of knowledge)

- Status quo bias (preference for no change)

- Naïve extrapolation of past returns

- Endowment effect (a tendency to ask for much more money to sell something than one would be willing to pay to buy it)

- Loyalty effects

---

2 The discussion within this section draws heavily on the CFA Program Level III readings "The Behavioral Biases of Individuals" and "Behavioral Finance and Investment Processes."

When biases are emotional in nature, simply drawing them to the attention of the investor is unlikely to lead to a positive outcome; the investor may become defensive rather than receptive to considering alternatives.

To overcome emotional biases, it might be helpful to pose the question, if an equivalent sum to the value of the concentrated position were received in cash, how would you invest the cash? Often, the answer is to invest in a portfolio very different from the concentrated position. It may also prove useful to explore a deceased person's intent in owning the concentrated position and bequeathing it: Was the primary intent to leave the specific concentrated position because it was perceived as a suitable investment based on fundamental analysis, or was it to leave financial resources to benefit the heirs? Heirs who affirm the latter conclusion are more responsive to considering strategies to reduce the concentration risk. It should also prove useful to review the historical performance and risk of the concentrated position.

3.4.2 *Cognitive Biases*

A number of cognitive biases can combine to negatively affect the decision making of holders of concentrated positions, including the following:

- Conservatism (in the sense of reluctance to update beliefs)
- Confirmation (looking for what confirms one's beliefs)
- Illusion of control (the tendency to overestimate one's control over events)
- Anchoring and adjustment (the tendency to reach a decision by making adjustments from an initial position, or "anchor")
- Availability heuristic (the probability of events is influenced by the ease with which examples of the event can be recalled)

If cognitive errors are brought to the attention of the investor, he or she is likely to be more receptive to correcting the errors.

EXAMPLE 1

Constraints and the Concentrated Position Decision-Making Process

Zachary Sloan, CFA, serves as investment counsel for the Bailer family. Pierce Bailer was formerly the CEO of ABC Corp., a large public company, for over 20 years. During his tenure as CEO, Bailer accumulated a significant position in ABC Corp. stock. Bailer retired as CEO effective 1 January 2010 and continued to serve as a member of the board of directors until his term expired 31 December 2011. Bailer is currently 55 years old and healthy and has a life expectancy of 87 years. He is married to Brooke, who is also 55 and healthy.

Bailer currently owns a 3 million share position in ABC Corp. At the current market price, the position is worth $60 million and represents 80% of the Bailer family's total investment portfolio, which is worth $75 million. The other 20% of their portfolio is invested evenly in high-quality fixed-income securities and a diversified portfolio of equities. Bailer has owned the ABC Corp. shares for many years, and the shares have increased significantly in value over that time. In addition, the stock has always paid, and continues to pay, a fairly attractive dividend, currently yielding approximately 2%. The dividend covers most of the Bailer family's day-to-day living expenses. The tax cost basis of the ABC Corp. shares is close to zero, and the sale of the entire position would trigger a tax liability of approximately $9 million at a capital gains tax rate of 15%.

While Bailer was CEO, he was required by his employment contract and company policy to maintain a large position in ABC Corp. shares, and although occasional sales were permitted, sales and hedging transactions by executives and other employees were frowned upon and discouraged by the board of directors. In fact, it was company policy to encourage retirees to not sell their shares in order to protect the company against a hostile takeover because collectively the shareholder votes of the former employees might help stave off a takeover. In addition, until Bailer left the board of directors, he was deemed an "insider" and the securities laws and regulations limited the timing and amount of any sales or hedging activity. The country in which the Bailer family resides currently has a long-term capital gains tax rate of 15%. Because of the political situation in that jurisdiction and pending legislation, however, the capital gains tax rate is generally expected to increase significantly, very likely to 23%, effective 1 January of the following year. Also, in this jurisdiction, the shares would qualify for a "step-up" in tax cost basis upon the death of the owner. That is, upon inheritance of the shares, the recipient/beneficiary would receive a new tax cost basis equal to the value of the investment asset on the date of death. This new tax cost basis would then be used to compute any future gain or loss on the sale of the investment asset by the recipient/beneficiary.

Even though he no longer has any formal affiliation with ABC Corp., Bailer remains extremely loyal to ABC Corp., is a big fan of ABC Corp. stock, and follows the stock regularly. Although he has no better access to information about the company than any other investor, Bailer feels that he knows the company much better than other investors. Mrs. Bailer remembers that she and Pierce started their married life with a negative net worth and the family's net worth grew over time as Pierce's ABC Corp. position skyrocketed in value. Mrs. Bailer also realizes that for many years, the dividends paid on their ABC Corp. stake paid for a good portion of their living expenses.

Immediately following the expiration of Bailer's term as a member of the board of directors, Sloan suggested a meeting to discuss an alternative asset allocation framework.

1   Identify primary investment objectives for the Bailer family's concentrated single-asset position.

2   Identify primary constraints that might impede the Bailer family's ability to achieve their primary objectives.

3   On the basis of the information given, discuss what emotional and cognitive biases may affect decision making of Mr. and Mrs. Bailer.

Solution to 1:

The family owns a concentrated position in ABC Corp. shares that constitutes 80% of their investment portfolio. The first objective should be to significantly reduce the concentration risk. The second objective should be to generate liquidity in order to diversify while satisfying spending needs. The third objective should be to achieve the first two objectives in the most tax-efficient manner.

Solution to 2:

The income tax consequences of an outright sale are a primary constraint to fulfilling the primary investment need. If the entire position was sold this year, a capital gains tax of approximately $9 million would be incurred. However, if the position is sold on or after 1 January of the following year, a capital gains tax of approximately $13,800,000 would likely be incurred because of the anticipated increase in the capital gains tax rate—an increase of $4,800,000. Although the tax is a constraint, the fact that the tax will likely be considerably higher in the near future should be an impetus for Bailer to sell the ABC Corp. position this year and lock in the current capital gains tax before it increases. The step-up in tax cost basis the shares would receive if Bailer held them until his death should also be considered. However, Bailer's fairly long life expectancy of approximately 32 more years implies that the present value of the step-up is fairly low and should be greatly outweighed by the benefits of diversification over that long-term period.

Solution to 3:

The facts indicate that loyalty effects, overconfidence/familiarity (illusion of knowledge), and confirmation bias could be affecting Mr. Bailer, while status quo bias, naïve extrapolation of past returns, and anchoring and adjustment bias could be affecting Mrs. Bailer. Illiquidity is no longer an issue. For many years and until recently, Mr. Bailer was deemed an "insider" for securities law purposes and the timing and amount of any sales and hedging activity was restricted by applicable securities laws and regulations. In addition, for many years, he was bound by his employment contract and company policies to limit the sale and hedging of his ABC Corp. shares. However, these restrictions were completely eliminated when his term as a member of the board of directors ended.

3.5 Goal-Based Planning in the Concentrated-Position Decision-Making Process

Goal-based planning is one way to incorporate psychological considerations into asset allocation and portfolio construction that can be especially helpful for advisers to clients who own concentrated positions because it can highlight the consequences of selecting an asset allocation that is riskier than is appropriate for a particular investor.

A goal-based methodology expands the traditional Markowitz framework of diversifying market risk by incorporating several notional "risk buckets." Asset allocation, including concentrated positions, subsequently occurs within each risk bucket.[3]

The first risk bucket can be referred to as the **personal risk bucket**. Here, the goal is protection from poverty or a dramatic decrease in lifestyle. The desire is to achieve almost certainty of protection. Allocations to this bucket limit loss but yield below-market rates of return. This bucket is where the client would allocate his or her home (primary residence), certificates of deposit, Treasury bills, and other "safe haven" investments.

The second risk bucket can be referred to as the **market risk bucket**. Here, the objective is to maintain the current standard of living—to have a high likelihood of maintaining the current status quo. Allocations to this bucket provide average risk-adjusted market returns. This bucket is where the client would allocate his or her stock and bond portfolio.

The third risk bucket can be referred to as the **aspirational risk bucket**. Here, the goal is the opportunity to increase wealth substantially—to have the possibility of moving upward in the wealth spectrum. Allocations to this bucket are expected to yield above-market returns but with substantial risk of loss of capital. This bucket is where the client would allocate his or her concentrated positions, including privately owned businesses, investment real estate, concentrated stock positions, stock options, and the like.

---

3 For further reading on goal-based planning, see Ashvin Chhabra, "Beyond Markowitz: A Comprehensive Wealth Allocation Framework for Individual Investors," *Journal of Wealth Management*, vol. 7, no. 4 (Spring 2005) and Jean L.P. Brunel, "Goal-Based Wealth Management in Practice," *Journal of Wealth Management*, vol. 14, no. 3 (Winter 2011).

This type of risk allocation framework gives financial advisers a basis to sit down with a client and identify and highlight the significant risk that owners of concentrated positions are subject to. It may be the most effective way to open the conversation with a client about their concentrated positions because it can highlight when allocations to the personal risk and market risk buckets are not adequate.

In addition, concentrated-position owners need a touchstone for deciding whether to sell or monetize, and one useful metric might be whether the proceeds, when combined with the assets the owner already has outside the concentrated position, are at least sufficient to provide for the owner's lifetime spending needs. We can refer to this amount as the owner's **primary capital**, and it comprises allocations to his or her personal and market risk buckets. Ideally, the sale or monetization will generate even more than the primary capital requirement. We refer to this as the owner's **surplus capital**, which comprises allocations to his or her aspirational risk bucket.[4]

To determine whether the sale or monetization of the concentrated position can achieve financial independence for the owner, the financial adviser needs to work with the owner to answer five key questions:

1 What are the lifetime *spending needs and desires* of the client after the sale or monetization of the concentrated position?

2 How much capital will it take *today* to know that these spending needs and desires will be satisfied throughout the owner's lifetime with little or no chance of the investor running out of money (primary and surplus capital requirements)?

3 What is the current value of the concentrated position? Different strategies may result in significantly different values for the concentrated position.

4 What is the value of liquid and other assets that are available outside the concentrated position today—that is, how much capital does the owner have now outside the concentrated position?

5 Is the current value of the concentrated position under one or more of the monetization strategies that are available to the owner sufficient to "bridge the gap" between the capital the client currently has and his or her primary and surplus capital requirements?

For many concentrated-position owners, it's key to come away from a sale or monetization event with a transaction that has the highest likelihood of meeting at least their primary capital requirement. Generation of surplus capital puts the owner a step ahead.

If wealth managers have a holistic view of their clients' finances, an understanding of their personal long-term financial objectives, and expertise in investment management, they are well situated to assist their clients in determining their primary and surplus capital requirements. Goal-based planning works equally well with clients who own businesses, real estate, and concentrated stock positions. By using this approach, wealth managers can work with clients first to identify and highlight the concentration risk that each client faces and then to create a framework that should prove helpful in determining whether a sale or monetization event would cause the owner of the concentrated position to achieve financial goals. If it would, this approach may give the owner of the concentrated position the impetus to begin dealing with the emotional aspects of selling or monetizing the asset.

---

4 Similar to "surplus capital" is the concept of "discretionary wealth" in Jarrod Wilcox, "Harry Markowitz and the Discretionary Wealth Hypothesis," *Journal of Portfolio Management* (2003).

EXAMPLE 2

A Business Owner and the Concentrated-Position Decision-Making Process (1)

Bill Wharton is Fred Garcia's financial adviser. Garcia is 60 years old and is CEO of an aircraft parts business that he founded 30 years ago. For over a decade, Garcia's son had taken on increasingly important responsibilities, and Garcia's exit plan was to pass on the business to his son. His son's sudden decision to pursue other career opportunities was a shock to Garcia and provided the motivation for Garcia to consider selling or monetizing his business.

As Exhibit 3 portrays, Garcia owned a business worth $40 million, investment real estate consisting of an office building, warehouse, and land used by the business worth $5 million, a $3 million stock and bond portfolio, $1 million in cash, and an unmortgaged home worth $1 million. Garcia asked Wharton what he thought of his current financial picture.

Exhibit 3　Wealth Distribution Shown in Risk Buckets

"Personal" Risk 4% Protective Assets		"Market" Risk 6% Market Assets		"Aspirational" Risk 90% Aspirational Assets	
Home	$1,000,000	Equities	$1,500,000	Family Business	$40,000,000
Mortgage on Primary Residence	$0	Intermediate- and Long-Term Fixed Income	$1,500,000	Investment Real Estate	$5,000,000
Cash/Short-Term Treasury Bonds and Notes	$1,000,000				
Total	$2,000,000	Total	$3,000,000	Total	$45,000,000

1　Using a goal-based planning framework (i.e., personal, market, and aspirational risk buckets), identify and highlight the significant risk(s) that Garcia is currently facing.

Garcia agreed with Wharton that the current asset allocation seemed very aggressive for someone his age and that it might be time to make some changes. Garcia then asked Wharton what he felt the next step should be in terms of helping to decide whether selling or monetizing his business might make sense.

2　Using a goal-based planning framework, describe the initial step that Wharton should work through with Garcia to help determine whether selling or monetizing his business might make sense.

After carefully considering Garcia's lifetime spending needs, Garcia and Wharton determined that a primary capital requirement of $35 million should be more than sufficient to sustain Garcia's current lifestyle with very little or no risk of running out of capital during his lifetime, even after considering such potential factors as severe market shocks, tax rate increases, inflation, and an unexpectedly long life span. Later in the reading, after providing the tool set for addressing the problem of obtaining the needed primary capital amount, we will return to Garcia's needs in Example 6.

3 Explain how this knowledge—that the sale or monetization should meet Garcia's $35 million primary capital requirement—should be helpful to Garcia in making a decision as to whether to sell or monetize his business.

Solution to 1:

Garcia currently has 90% ($45 million out of the $50 million) of his wealth allocated to a family-run business and commercial real estate, which falls in his high-risk/high-return aspirational risk bucket. That level would qualify as excessive risk taking for someone over 60 years old, especially now that Garcia's son is no longer interested in taking over the business.

Solution to 2:

Wharton should work very carefully with Garcia to determine his lifetime spending needs. They should establish how much capital it would take today to know that Garcia's spending needs would be satisfied throughout Garcia's lifetime with little or no chance of Garcia running out of money. Put another way, they need to ascertain how much capital would need to be allocated to Garcia's personal and market risk buckets (his primary capital requirement).

Solution to 3:

This knowledge is important because Garcia now understands that the sale or monetization of his business should generate sufficient after-tax proceeds to allocate to his personal and market risk buckets to cover his lifetime spending needs and desires. Put another way, Garcia now knows that the sale or monetization of his business can enable him to achieve financial independence as he has defined it.

3.6 Asset Location and Wealth Transfers

The implications of **asset location** (what type of account an asset is held within) for the holders of concentrated positions should be considered. In most tax regimes, a security's asset class usually determines its tax profile when held in taxable accounts. For instance, interest income on fixed-income securities is often taxed differently from long-term capital gains on stocks.[5] However, the account structure can override the normal tax treatment. Therefore, a relationship exists between deciding what assets to own and in which accounts they should be held. The choice of where to place specific assets is often referred to as the *asset location decision*. It is distinct from the asset allocation decision. The tax regime governing the investor ultimately determines the relative importance of asset location. The concept of asset location and gifting strategies can often be used together to minimize transfer taxes with respect to concentrated positions.

A second tool for addressing concentrated positions is wealth transfers. Undertaking wealth transfer planning *early* in the ownership life of a concentrated position often enables the owner to shift future wealth with little or no transfer tax consequences. Which methods will work depends on the tax regime of the country the owner is subject to, the owner's age and family circumstances, whether he or she is charitably inclined, and whether the planning takes place before or after some value has accumulated.

---

5 Stephen M. Horan and Thomas R. Robinson, "Taxes and Private Wealth Management in a Global Context," Reading 11 of 2013 CFA Program Level III Curriculum.

Advisers who are able to work with clients *before* the concentrated position has appreciated greatly in value can have the most impact. At this point in time, the simplest strategies, such as direct gifts to family members, direct gifts to long-term trusts, and estate freeze strategies, typically add the most value. With the passage of time, after there has been some run-up in the concentrated position's value, wealth transfer tools tend to be less efficient, more complex, and more costly to implement—which underscores the importance of addressing this subject with the owners of concentrated positions as early as possible.

In addition to direct gifting, a valuable concept in wealth transfer planning is that of an early ownership transfer of an estate, or **estate tax freeze**. Here the goal is to transfer *future* appreciation to the next generation at little or no gift or estate tax cost. An estate tax freeze is a plan usually involving a corporation, partnership, or limited liability company in which the owners transfer a junior equity interest to the children that will receive most or all of the future appreciation of the enterprise. Any gift or wealth transfer tax is based on the current market value of the interest transferred; future appreciation of the equity position transferred will not be subject to gift or transfer tax. Estate tax freezes were initially used by closely held family businesses but were later expanded to include other concentrated positions, including publicly traded stocks and real estate.

The classic corporate estate tax freeze involves recapitalizing a closely held family-owned corporation. The older generation, who owns all of the stock of the corporation, exchanges their existing company stock for two newly issued classes of stock. One class is voting preferred; the other is non-voting common. The non-voting common stock is gifted to the next generation. The transaction is structured so that the value of the voting preferred shares is equal to the value of 100% of the corporation. In addition, the value of the preferred stock should not appreciate greatly because those shares pay a fixed rate and resemble a bond. Therefore, the common stock has only a nominal value and can be gifted to the next generation and trigger little or no gift tax. The future appreciation in the value of the corporation should benefit the common shareholders. None of the appreciation is subject to gift or estate tax until the common shares are passed by gift or bequest to the next generation. The parents retain control because all the voting power is held in the preferred shares. The United States, Canada, and Australia, among others, allow some form of a corporate estate tax freeze. Note that although not all jurisdictions allow corporate estate tax freezes, it is the concept that is important, and other techniques have been developed that accomplish the same objectives as the corporate estate tax freeze.

EXAMPLE 3

A Corporate Estate Tax Freeze

John and Barbara Wilson live in a country that imposes a current gift tax of 40% on the transfer of any property directly (or indirectly through trusts) from parents to children that exceeds $10 million during their lifetimes. The Wilsons have already used the $10 million exemption by making prior gifts to their children. The Wilsons own a business currently worth $10 million, but they believe the business is poised for explosive growth that will begin shortly. Their children are already involved with the business. The Wilsons eventually want to pass control of the business to their children, but at this point, they feel their children don't have the necessary experience to run the business, so the Wilsons would like to retain control. However, they would like the growth that is expected of the business to directly benefit their children, as contrasted with having that appreciation remain in their estate. Based only on the above information, address the following.

1 Would a direct gift of the company stock from the Wilsons to their children satisfy their objectives?

2 Would a direct gift of the company stock from the Wilsons to a trust set up for the benefit of their children satisfy their objectives?

3 Would a corporate estate tax freeze satisfy the Wilsons' objectives?

Solution to 1:

No. They would give up control of the company, which they don't want to do. Because they've already used their $10 million gift tax exemption, any further gifts would trigger an immediate 40% gift tax.

Solution to 2:

No, for roughly the same reasons stated in the Solution to 1. Although a trust could be set up such that voting control passes on to the children at a later date, a gift tax would still apply.

Solution to 3:

Yes. The Wilsons could recapitalize their company and keep new voting preferred stock (worth the current value of the company) and gift new non-voting common stock (with a current nominal value) to their children with little or zero gift tax due. The Wilsons retain control of the company, and all future appreciation of the company inures to the benefit of their children. Upon the Wilsons's retirement or death, the company can redeem their preferred shares and the common shares can be given voting rights.

Although the greatest opportunities for estate planning and wealth transfer occur before the concentrated position has significantly appreciated, there are techniques the owner can use *after* significant appreciation has occurred to minimize transfer taxes.

A common technique for gifting an interest in a concentrated position is to contribute the concentrated position to an entity such as a family limited partnership. For instance, the parents who own a concentrated position might contribute their concentrated position to a partnership in a manner that does not trigger a current taxable event. The parents retain the general partnership interest and therefore retain control of the partnership and the concentrated position within it. The parents gift the limited partnership interests to their children.

When a limited partnership interest is valued for transfer tax purposes, the value is typically less than a proportionate value of the assets held in the partnership. This discount arises because of two factors. First, there is a *lack of marketability*. Family limited partnership interests are typically restricted and are difficult, if not impossible, to sell outside the family; therefore, an unrelated buyer would very likely not be willing to pay the pro-rata value for the partnership interest. Second, because the general partner retains control, the limited partner's non-controlling *interest* is worth less because he has very little ability to influence management of the partnership and the underlying assets. Because of these two factors, the valuation of a limited partnership interest is often discounted from 10% to 40% of the value of the underlying assets. For instance, assuming a combined discount of 35%, a 20% interest in a $10 million concentrated position would be transferred at a gift tax valuation of $1.3 million (i.e., a 35% discount) instead of $2 million.

In addition to the gift tax savings at the time of transfer, substantial estate tax may be saved if the concentrated position appreciates further between the date of the gift and the date of the parent's death. In the above example, if the $10 million concentrated position appreciates to $30 million by the time the donor dies, the children will hold an interest worth $6 million but only $1.3 million will be subject to transfer taxes.

Finally, if the owner of the concentrated position is charitably inclined, there are a variety of gifting and asset location strategies that the owner might consider using to avoid triggering any tax (i.e., the capital gains tax on the appreciation), as well as any transfer taxes (i.e., gift and estate taxes).

3.7 Concentrated Wealth Decision Making: A Five-Step Process

Working with the owners of concentrated positions can be quite complex. The following five-step process, if applied systematically to each client holding a concentrated position, should help assure that services are delivered to each client using a uniform and consistent methodology with the result that each client should implement the plan of action or strategy that best satisfies their objectives given their particular circumstances.

Step 1   **Identify and establish objectives and constraints.** The objective (or combination of objectives) of the owner of the concentrated position should be identified, established, and put in written form. Constraints should be identified and their impact analyzed.

Step 2   **Identify tools/strategies that can satisfy these objectives.** All the tools and strategies that could be used to satisfy the owner's stated objectives subject to binding constraints need to be identified, while remembering that different techniques can often provide essentially the same economics.

Step 3   **Compare tax advantages and disadvantages.** The tax advantages and disadvantages of each tool/strategy should be compared.

Step 4   **Compare non-tax advantages and disadvantages.** The non-tax considerations of each alternative tool/strategy need to be thoroughly compared.

Step 5   **Formulate and document an overall strategy.** After weighing the tax and non-tax advantages and disadvantages of each alternative tool/strategy, the overall strategy that appears to best position the client to achieve his or her goals is selected.

These steps should be viewed as a dynamic process involving feedback loops so that when an element of the process or circumstance changes, the strategy may need to be adjusted.

4   MANAGING THE RISK OF CONCENTRATED SINGLE-STOCK POSITIONS

Diversification, one of the bedrock investment principles, seeks to balance risk and reward within a portfolio. A portfolio consisting of only a few stocks would not generally be considered prudent because of the risk from the concentrated position. The same reasoning applies to the holder of a concentrated position in a single stock.

To mitigate the risks of any concentrated position, be it publicly traded common stock, ownership of a private business, or ownership of real estate, there are several broad types of tools that can be used:

- Outright sale: Owners can sell the concentrated position, which gives them funds to spend or reinvest but often incurs significant tax liabilities.

- Monetization strategies: These provide owners with funds to spend or re-invest without triggering a taxable event. A loan against the value of a concentrated position is an example of a simple monetization strategy.

- Hedging the value of the concentrated asset: Derivatives are frequently used in such transactions.

Furthermore, a strategy can combine these elements. Exhibit 4 lists the tool set for managing single-stock positions. Selected tools will be discussed in more detail.

Exhibit 4   The Financial Tool Set for Managing a Single-Stock Position

I. Equity derivatives to hedge value:

  A Exchange-traded options (sometimes referred to as listed options)

  B Over-the-counter (OTC) derivatives

    1 Options

    2 Forwards

    3 Swaps

II. Borrowing to monetize the position:

  A Margin loans

  B Recourse and non-recourse debt[a]

  C Fixed- and floating-rate debt

  D Loans embedded within a derivative (e.g., a prepaid variable forward)

III. Other monetization:

  A Short sales against the box

  B Restricted stock sales

  C Public capital market–based transactions

    1 Debt exchangeable for common (DEC) offerings

  D Rule 10b5-1 plans and blind trusts (United States)

  E Exchange funds (United States)

---

[a] *Note*: Recourse with respect to a debt means there is a right to collect beyond what collateral provides in the event of default against the borrower or some other party.

Please note that the tool set listed above is specific to the United States; investors in other jurisdictions may or may not have access to all of these tools. It is also possible that tools other than those mentioned may be available in other jurisdictions.

4.1 Introduction to Key Tax Considerations

There are a variety of financial tools that investors can use to hedge to achieve a desired economic result. For instance, an investor can synthetically dispose of a stock by shorting the stock directly or, alternatively, by using options, swaps, forwards, or futures.

Although each produces the same economic result, they may not be taxed similarly. Although most tax regimes governing the taxation of financial instruments are comprehensive in nature, they are not always internally consistent.

In most jurisdictions, the basic tax rules applicable to financial products have developed over time in a somewhat piecemeal fashion. The usual process is that investors first innovate and create a new product and the tax authorities later respond. Financial engineers develop a product that begins to trade in the marketplace. Tax authorities soon realize there is no provision in the tax law that currently addresses this particular financial instrument, and they respond accordingly with a tax provision crafted to address this new product.

However, the drafters of such tax laws may not consider that investors might use several different tools to achieve the identical economic objective, so there could be significant differences in the tax treatment among these different tools because of the different provisions that govern them. This is certainly the case in the United States as well as for most other tax regimes.

If there is internal inconsistency of tax codes, there may be an opportunity for well-advised investors to reap substantial tax savings or reduce tax risk by selecting and implementing the *form* of a transaction that delivers the optimal economic and tax result.

4.2 Introduction to Key Non-Tax Considerations

There are certain considerations unrelated to taxation that investors and their advisers need to consider when deciding whether to use an exchange-traded instrument (i.e., options or futures) or an over-the-counter (OTC) derivative (i.e., forward sale or swap).

4.2.1 *Counterparty Credit Risk*

With respect to an OTC derivative, the investor incurs the credit risk of the single counterparty that he or she contracts with. With respect to exchange-traded instruments, because a clearinghouse (that is typically owned and jointly and severally backed by all its members) is the counterparty and guarantees the instrument, the investor incurs significantly less counterparty credit risk.

4.2.2 *Ability to Close Out Transaction Prior to Stated Expiration*

The investor can close out exchange-traded instruments prior to their stated maturity by acquiring exactly offsetting positions with any market participant. With respect to OTC derivatives, the investor can attempt to negotiate an early termination of a particular contract, but the counterparty can and usually does extract a concession in return for permitting early termination.

4.2.3 *Price Discovery*

By their very nature, exchange-traded instruments should achieve robust price discovery. In contrast, an OTC derivative is priced through negotiation with a single dealer, although fiduciaries and advisers should get bids from at least several dealers to ensure that reasonable price discovery has occurred. (Basic financial analysis of derivatives can independently provide a reasonableness benchmark for transaction prices.)

4.2.4 *Transparency of Fees*

Fees and expenses are more transparent in exchange-traded transactions. All commissions and fees must be identified on trade tickets, trade confirmations, and monthly statements. It is much easier for dealers to build their fees into OTC derivative transactions, especially such instruments as prepaid variable forwards, where the collar and loan are combined into a single instrument.

4.2.5 *Flexibility of Terms*

OTC derivatives give the investor maximum flexibility with respect to negotiating the key terms and conditions of any transaction. Exchange-traded instruments do not give investors the same degree of flexibility.

4.2.6 *Minimum Size Constraints*

Exchange-traded instruments typically have a smaller minimum than OTC derivatives. OTC derivatives have a minimum size that is typically around US$3 million.

4.3 Strategies

There are three primary strategies that investors use in the case of a concentrated position in a common stock:

- Equity monetization
- Hedging
- Yield enhancement

4.3.1 *Equity Monetization*

Investors holding a concentrated position can (1) hedge against a decline in the price of a stock, (2) defer the capital gains tax, and (3) generate liquidity (cash), which can be used to diversify, by implementing an equity monetization strategy.

Equity monetization generally refers to the transformation of a concentrated position into cash. Equity monetization usually refers to transactions that are designed to empower an investor to receive cash for their stock position through a manner other than an outright sale in a way that avoids triggering a current taxable event.

In addition to avoiding an immediate tax liability associated with an outright sale, there are other factors that might make the use of an equity monetization strategy attractive to a holder of a concentrated position, such as the following:

- The investor may be subject to a diverse array of securities law restrictions that are applicable to a sale of stock.

- The investor might own a large percentage of outstanding shares of the company and may not wish to cede control of the company or give the opportunity to another investor to acquire a large block of company shares.

- The investor may be subject to contractual provisions, such as an IPO lockup or an employment agreement or policy, that prohibit the sale of shares.

Equity monetization entails a two-step process:

- The *first step* is for the investor to remove a large portion of the risk inherent in the concentrated position. The process of hedging the concentrated stock position could be fraught with complex tax regulations. In the United States, for example, the IRS has been known to scrutinize hedging transactions closely, especially for ultra-high-net-worth individuals and families. Care should be taken in structuring the hedge such that the economic incentives (as well as disincentives) of holding the concentrated stock position are not, for practical purposes, eliminated.

- The *second step* is for the investor to borrow against the hedged position. In most instances, a high loan-to-value (LTV) ratio can be achieved because the stock position is hedged; the loan proceeds are then invested in a diversified portfolio of other investments.

4.3.1.1 Equity Monetization Tool Set

The four basic tools an investor can use to establish a short position in a stock are[6]

- a short sale against the box,
- a total return equity swap,
- options (forward conversion), and
- a forward sale contract or single-stock futures contract.

For instance, assume an investor owns 1 million shares of ABC Corp. stock and ABC Corp. shares are currently trading at $100 per share, so the investor is long $100 million of ABC Corp. shares. To establish an exactly offsetting short position in ABC Corp. shares, the investor could use any of the four techniques mentioned above and described below.

A **short sale against the box** involves shorting a security that is held long. In our example, the investor could borrow 1 million shares of ABC Corp. stock from a broker/dealer and then sell those shares in the marketplace, thus establishing a $100 million short position in ABC Corp. stock.

Because the investor is simultaneously long and short the same number of shares of the same stock, any future change in the stock's price will have absolutely no effect on the investor's economic position. Likewise, any dividends or other distributions that are received on the long shares are passed through to the lender of the shares that were sold to open the short position.

Because the long and short positions together constitute a riskless position, the investor will earn a money market rate of return on the $100 million position. The investor has economically transformed the risky ABC Corp. stock position into a riskless asset that will earn a money market rate of return.

Because the short sale against the box creates a riskless (i.e., devoid of price risk) position, margin rules typically allow the investor to borrow with a high loan to value (LTV) ratio against the position. It is usually possible to borrow up to 99% of the value of the stock that is hedged, and there are usually no limitations on the use of the proceeds. The proceeds are typically invested in a portfolio of securities and other investments to achieve diversification. The net cost of borrowing through a short sale against the box is quite low because the interest income earned on the completely hedged stock position greatly offsets the interest expense associated with the margin loan.

The short sale against the box is the least expensive technique that is available to hedge, monetize, and potentially defer the capital gains tax on a concentrated position. It is the "paradigm" among all hedging and monetization strategies. The strategy is less costly than the other tools that enable investors to establish a synthetic short position in a stock (i.e., swaps, options, and forwards/futures, discussed below) because a derivative dealer need not be involved. That is, there are typically fewer dealer fees involved in a short sale against the box versus synthetic short sales.

A **total return equity swap** is a contract for a series of exchanges of the total return on a specified asset in return for specified fixed or floating payments.

In our example, the investor and a derivative dealer could agree to an exchange of cash flows based on a $100 million notional amount of ABC Corp. shares as follows:

- The investor agrees to pay the dealer any appreciation on her ABC shares plus any dividends and other distributions received on her shares.
- In return, the dealer agrees to pay the investor any loss in the value of the ABC shares plus one-month Libor (less a dealer spread).

---

[6] Some of these tools may not be available in practice, depending on the jurisdiction.

Note the similarity to the short sale against the box. The investor is fully hedged and is earning a money market rate of return on the full value of the position. Because a derivative dealer is involved, the money market rate of return earned on the position would likely be slightly less than what would be earned on a short sale against the box position because of the larger dealer spread charged to implement the total return swap. Because the ABC Corp. stock position is completely hedged, monetization with a very high LTV ratio should be possible.

A **forward conversion with options** involves the construction of a synthetic short forward position against the asset held long. This strategy is based on the fact that the payoff of a short forward position is identical to the payoff of a long put and a short call on the same underlying asset.

In our example, the investor could buy ABC Corp. puts and sell ABC Corp. calls with the same strike price (i.e., $100) and the same termination date covering 1 million shares. By doing so, the investor has locked in a price of $100 no matter which way the stock moves. If the stock price goes to zero, the investor would exercise the puts, deliver her shares, and receive $100 from the dealer. If the stock price increased to $200, the calls would be exercised against the investor; she would deliver shares and receive $100 from the dealer.

Because the position created is riskless, a forward conversion should be priced in the marketplace to generate a money market rate of return for the investor. Because the ABC Corp. stock position is perfectly hedged, monetization with a very high LTV ratio should be possible.

An **equity forward sale contract** is a private contract for the forward sale of an equity position.

In our example, the investor could agree today to sell her ABC shares to a dealer three years from now. In return, the investor will receive the "forward price" from the dealer three years from now. A forward contract on an individual stock allows the investor to sell her stock at some future date at a guaranteed price (i.e., the forward price). If the market price is above the forward price at the termination of the contract, the investor will receive the forward price and will not participate in any market increase above that price.

Because the position created is riskless, a forward contract will generate a money market rate of return for the investor, which is reflected in the forward price. Because the ABC Corp. stock position is perfectly hedged, monetization with a very high LTV ratio should be possible.

To summarize, by using any of these four techniques, an owner of a concentrated position accomplishes the following:

- A riskless position is created by establishing a direct or synthetic short position covering the same amount of shares that she is long.

- A money market rate of return is generated on the full value of the long position.

- Borrowing against the hedged position with a very high LTV ratio is possible (it is similar to borrowing against a government bond).

- Borrowing is quite inexpensive because the income generated on the hedged position greatly offsets cost of borrowing.

- The borrowed proceeds can be invested in a diversified portfolio.

4.3.1.2 Tax Treatment of Equity Monetization Strategies
Equity monetization strategies allow an investor to transfer the economic risk and reward of a stock position without transferring the legal and beneficial ownership of that asset. Put another way, equity monetization can eliminate concentration risk and generate about the same amount of cash that would be generated by an outright sale. The basic premise in most

tax regimes is that economic gains (including unrealized gains on a stock position) do *not* constitute "income" and are therefore *not* subject to tax unless and until they are "realized."[7]

Historically, the concept of capital gain realization has been tied to the "sale or disposition" of appreciated securities. In the case of monetization transactions, there has been no actual transaction in the appreciated securities themselves. That is, there is no formal legal "connection" between the monetization transaction and the appreciated securities. The investor still owns the securities and, if the securities are viewed in isolation, remains fully exposed to the risk of loss and opportunity for profit associated with the securities. The investor can assert that entering into a monetization arrangement does not, as a matter of legal form, constitute a sale or disposition of the appreciated securities.

The *critical question* is whether an equity monetization strategy will be treated as a taxable event for tax purposes in a particular country. If the tax regime treats the long and short (or synthetically short) position separately for tax purposes, tax on the appreciation of the long position will be deferred. Put more succinctly, if the tax authorities of a country respect legal form over economic substance, which is typically the case, equity monetization techniques should not trigger an immediate taxable event.

A comprehensive comparative tax analysis of how different countries' tax systems deal with equity monetization strategies is beyond the scope of this reading. However, it is important that advisers, irrespective of the country where their client is domiciled, know how to appropriately appraise equity monetization strategies. Exhibit 5 broadly classifies the various tax regimes that exist in the world today. No matter which tax regime is being examined, certain questions should be asked and a certain process followed as investors and their advisers seek to ensure that the strategy that is used is the most tax efficient. Along these lines, working with the client's tax adviser to answer the following questions should help in selecting the tool that minimizes the tax cost to the client.

1   When unwinding or cash settling the hedge, if there is a gain generated by the hedge, is it short term or long term in nature? Long-term gain is generally preferred in many jurisdictions.

2   When unwinding or cash settling the hedge, are potential losses generated by the hedge short term or long term in nature, and is it currently deductible or instead added to the tax cost basis of the shares being hedged? Short-term loss and currently deductible are generally preferred.

3   If the contract is physically settled by delivering shares, is the gain short term or long term in nature? Long-term gain is usually better.

4   Are the carrying costs associated with monetization (i.e., interest expense or the equivalent) currently deductible or instead added to the tax cost basis of the shares being hedged? Current deductibility is preferred.

5   Does the hedge in any way affect the taxation of dividends or distributions received on the shares? No impact is preferred.

---

7 Paul Hayward, "Monetization, Realization and Statutory Interpretation," *Canadian Tax Journal*, vol. 51, no. 5 (2003).

Exhibit 5 Classification of Income Tax Regimes

Regime	1. Common Progressive	2. Heavy Dividend Tax	3. Heavy Capital Gains Tax	4. Heavy Interest Tax	5. Light Capital Gains Tax	6. Flat and Light	7. Flat and Heavy
Ordinary Tax Rate Structure	Progressive	Progressive	Progressive	Progressive	Progressive	Flat	Flat
Interest Income	Some interest taxed at favorable rates or exempt	Some interest taxed at favorable rates or exempt	Some interest taxed at favorable rates or exempt	Taxed at ordinary rates	Taxed at ordinary rates	Some interest taxed at favorable rates or exempt	Some interest taxed at favorable rates or exempt
Dividends	Some dividends taxed at favorable rates or exempt	Taxed at ordinary rates	Some dividends taxed at favorable rates or exempt	Some dividends taxed at favorable rates or exempt	Taxed at ordinary rates	Some dividends taxed at favorable rates or exempt	Taxed at ordinary rates
Capital Gains	Some capital gains taxed favorably or exempt	Some capital gains taxed favorably or exempt	Taxed at ordinary rates	Some capital gains taxed favorably or exempt	Some capital gains taxed favorably or exempt	Some capital gains taxed favorably or exempt	Taxed at ordinary rates
Example Countries	Austria, Brazil, China, Czech Republic, Finland, France, Greece, Hong Kong, Hungary, Ireland, Italy, Japan, Latvia, Malaysia, Netherlands, Nigeria, Philippines, Poland, Portugal, Singapore, South Africa, Sweden, Thailand, United Kingdom, United States, Vietnam	Argentina, Indonesia, Israel, Venezuela	Columbia	Canada, Denmark, Germany, Luxembourg, Pakistan	Australia, Belgium, India, Kenya, Mexico, New Zealand, Norway, Spain, Switzerland, Taiwan, Turkey	Kazakhstan, Russia, Saudi Arabia (Zakat)	Ukraine

Sources: Stephen Horan and Thomas Robinson, "Taxes and Private Wealth Management in a Global Context" (CFA Institute, 2009). Classification based on information provided in International Business Guides from Deloitte Touche Tohmatsu (available at www.deloitte.com) and online database of worldwide taxation provided by PricewaterhouseCoopers (www.taxsummaries.pwc.com).

4.3.2 *Lock In Unrealized Gains: Hedging*

Hedging is a useful strategy when the holder of a concentrated position would like to protect against downside risk but would also like to capture either unlimited or a significant amount of potential upside with respect to the stock. There are two major hedging approaches investors can consider:

▪ Purchase of puts

▪ Cashless, or zero-premium, collar

4.3.2.1 Purchase of Puts   Investors holding a concentrated position can purchase put options to (1) lock in a floor price, (2) retain unlimited upside potential, and (3) defer the capital gains tax.

Investors usually buy put options with a strike price that is either at or, more typically, slightly below the current price of the stock (that is, either "at-the-money" or slightly "out-of-the-money" puts). The investor pays an amount, referred to as the premium, to acquire the puts.

Conceptually, this is very similar to the payment of an insurance premium. In return, the investor is fully protected, subject to the credit risk of the counterparty, from any loss resulting from a decline of the stock price below the strike price of the put. The premium paid will vary depending on a number of factors, including the volatility of the stock, the strike price, and the maturity. The investor retains any dividends received and voting rights.

As an example, suppose an investor, Bill, owns shares of ABC Corp. that are currently trading at $100. ABC one-year put options with a strike price of $90 currently trade at $5, and Bill buys these puts. If the stock price has decreased below the $90 strike price at maturity, the puts can be exercised and Bill will deliver his long shares for $90 from the exercise of the puts. His total initial investment was $105—$100 in stock and $5 worth of puts. If ABC closes at or above $90 at expiration, the puts will expire worthless but Bill will have paid $5 for this "wasting" asset, which can be thought of as "term" insurance. The trade will make sense in retrospect only if the underlying stock price declines below $85 per share, assuming that no put was purchased.

The concept of combining a long stock position with a long put position is intuitively extremely appealing: downside protection with unlimited upside price participation. However, the out-of-pocket expenditure necessary to acquire puts can be significant. Therefore, investors often seek to lessen their out-of-pocket costs. Described below are a few ways for investors to accomplish this.

The most common way is to lower the strike price. An at-the-money put will cost considerably more than an out-of-the-money put. With an out-of-the-money put, the investor, in essence, "self-insures" down to the strike price. Of course, the lower the strike price, the greater the downside risk the holder retains.

Along similar lines, puts with a shorter maturity will cost less than puts with a longer maturity because the "term insurance" doesn't last very long.

Another popular strategy is to combine the purchase of put options with the sale of put options with a lower strike price and with the same maturity as the long puts, which is known as a "put spread." The idea is to lessen the cost of the long puts by selling puts to bring in some premium income in order to partially finance the purchase of the long puts. In this case, the investor will be protected from the strike price of the long put down to the strike price of the short put. However, below the strike price of the short put, the investor is fully exposed to further declines in the underlying stock price.

Another, less frequently used way to lessen the cost of put protection is to use a "knock-out" option. A knock-out put is an "exotic" option that can be acquired only through an over-the-counter dealer (i.e., these types of options are not traded on an exchange). This type of put is less expensive than a "plain vanilla" put because the protection "knocks out" or disappears before its stated expiration if the stock price increases to a certain level. The rationale for using knock-out puts is that once the stock price increases to a certain level, the downside protection of the put is no longer necessary. Such exotic options can be implemented only for fairly large positions (i.e., there is a high minimum size requirement among the OTC dealers).

However, by far the most common way for stockholders to reduce the out-of-pocket expenditure necessary to achieve the desired downside protection is to enter into a cashless, or zero-premium, collar, which is discussed in the next section.

4.3.2.2 Cashless (Zero-Premium) Collars   Investors holding a concentrated position can implement what is commonly referred to as a cashless, or zero-premium, collar to (1) hedge against a decline in the price of a stock, (2) retain a certain degree of upside potential with respect to the stock, and (3) defer the capital gains tax while avoiding any out-of-pocket expenditure. The investor retains any dividend income and voting rights.

Cashless collars are a very popular tool that investors around the globe frequently use to hedge their concentrated positions.

When structuring cashless collars, investors buy puts with a strike price that is either at or, more typically, slightly below the current price of the stock. The investor must pay a premium to acquire the puts and in return is fully protected (subject to the credit risk of the counterparty) from any loss should the stock price fall below the strike price of the puts.

Simultaneously, the investors sell calls with the same maturity with a strike price that is above the current price of the stock and in return receives premium income. The strike price of the calls is set at the level that brings in exactly the amount required to pay for the puts. In other words, the sale of the calls fully finances the purchase of the puts.[8] Note that investment risk is reduced but not eliminated.

Therefore, although the investor forfeits some of the upside potential of the underlying stock (i.e., the amount the stock price is above the call strike at maturity), by using a cashless collar, no out-of-pocket expenditure is required, and this is perceived to be a huge advantage by most investors and their financial advisers.

Consider again the investor who owns shares of ABC Corp. that are currently trading at $100. As before, ABC one-year puts with a strike price of $90 currently trade at $5. Suppose now that ABC one-year calls with a strike price of $120 currently trade at $5. The investor simultaneously sells the calls and buys the puts, with the $5 premium received for selling the calls fully financing the $5 premium paid to acquire the puts; therefore, no out-of-pocket expenditure is required.

If the stock price has increased above the $120 strike price at maturity, the calls will be exercised. In this case, Bill could deliver his long shares and receive $120 ($120 from the exercise of the calls plus the $5 call premium received less the $5 put premium paid).

If ABC closes between $90 and $120 at expiration, both the puts and calls will expire worthless and Bill will have paid the $5 put premium and received the $5 call premium. If the stock price decreases below the $90 strike price at maturity, the puts will be exercised. In this case, Bill could deliver his long shares and receive $90 ($90 from the exercise of the puts plus $5 from the sale of the calls less the $5 cost of the puts).

---

8 When using exchange-traded put and call options to implement a collar, in almost all cases, there will be two contracts involved: one involving the puts and another involving the calls. The purchase and sale of the puts and calls, respectively, can be executed on an option exchange simultaneously pursuant to what is referred to as a "spread order"—that is, without concern that the investor buys the puts without selling the calls (and vice versa). Nonetheless, on almost all exchanges, there will be two separate contracts involved: one for the puts and one for the calls.

The concept of a cashless collar is very appealing to many investors and advisers. Nevertheless, investors often look for ways to increase the upside potential that is retained.

The most common way to accomplish this is to lower the strike price of the put. The lower the strike price, the lower the premium required to pay for the put. Therefore, a call with a higher strike price can be sold to finance the put purchase, resulting in greater upside potential. Of course, the lower the strike price of the put, the greater the downside risk the holder retains.

Another popular strategy is to combine a "put spread" (described above) with the sale of a call of the same maturity. The idea is to lessen the cost of the long put by selling a put to bring in some premium income to partially finance the purchase of the long put. This, in turn, allows a higher strike price call to be sold in order to fully finance the net cost of the put spread. The investor will be protected from the strike price of the long put down to the strike price of the short put. However, the investor is fully exposed to declines of the underlying stock below the strike price of the short put. In return for taking this risk, the investor will have more upside potential than with a plain vanilla cashless collar.

Along the same lines, investors sometimes pay a portion of the put premium "out of pocket," which is often referred to as a "debit" collar. It allows a higher strike price call to be sold in order to finance the net cost of the put.

4.3.2.3 Prepaid Variable Forwards   A collar hedges the value of the concentrated position. The value of the concentrated position can concurrently be monetized by means of a margin loan. A prepaid variable forward (PVF) where the hedge and the margin loan are combined in one instrument achieves an identical economic result. The margin loan advanced to the client depends on the precise collar structure and its term. A PVF, in essence, is an agreement to sell a security at a specific time in the future with the number of shares to be delivered at maturity varying with the underlying share price at maturity. For example, an investor holding ABC Corp. shares currently trading at $100 might enter into a PVF requiring the dealer to pay the investor $88 up front in exchange for the right to receive a variable number of shares from the investor in three years pursuant to a preset formula that embodies the economics of a particular collar (e.g., a long put with a $95 strike and a short call with a $110 strike). The formula, in this case, would require the investor to deliver all its ABC Corp. shares if the price of ABC shares in three years is less than $95. If the price of ABC shares is greater than $95 but less than $110, the investor must deliver $95 worth of shares. If the price of ABC shares is above $110, the investor must deliver $95 worth of shares plus the value of the shares above $110.

Alternatively, a PVF can be cash settled. If the price of ABC shares is less than $95 three years from now, the investor will pay the dealer the then-current value of ABC shares in cash. If the price of ABC shares is between $95 and $110, the investor will pay the dealer $95 in cash. If the price of ABC shares is above $110, the investor will pay the dealer $95 plus the difference between the then-current price of ABC shares and $110. The investor could enter into another PVF to get the liquidity to satisfy its obligations under the original PVF. A PVF combines the economics of a collar and a borrowing against the underlying stock within a single instrument.

EXAMPLE 4

Hedging a Concentrated Position

Rachel LeMesurier recently retired from Denton Corp., where she experienced a long and successful tenure as a senior executive. During her 30-year career with Denton Corp., LeMesurier received a considerable portion of her compensation in the form of Denton Corp. shares. She currently owns 100,000 shares of Denton Corp. stock, which are currently trading at $40 per share.

LeMesurier has decided that she would like to hedge the risk of her $4 million position (= 100,000 shares × $40) in Denton stock. LeMesurier has been exploring various hedging alternatives with her financial adviser and feels that a cashless collar will give her the downside protection that she needs while still allowing her to participate to a certain extent should the price of Denton Corp. shares increase.

LeMesurier and her financial adviser know that there are two types of options: exchange traded and over the counter (OTC).

LeMesurier likes the transparency of exchange-traded options, as well as the fact that her counterparty will be a clearinghouse that is owned and guaranteed by all the exchange members as opposed to a single dealer, which means there is less counterparty risk when using exchange-traded options.

Currently, Denton Corp. one-year exchange-traded puts with a strike price of $36 are trading at a premium of $3 per share, and Denton Corp. one-year exchange-traded calls with a strike price of $48 are trading at a premium of $3 per share. Through her financial adviser, LeMesurier submits a spread order to simultaneously sell the calls and buy the puts covering her entire $4 million Denton Corp. stock position, with the $300,000 premium received for selling the calls fully financing the $300,000 premium required to purchase the puts.

The price of Denton Corp. shares traded in a range during most of the one-year period the collar was in place. On the expiration date of the collar, Denton Corp. shares closed at $42, and both the puts and calls expired worthless on that date.

In the country where LeMesurier is domiciled, like many other countries, the tax code does not treat all financial instruments that achieve the same economic result the same. The tax code in her country treats the call premium received on short calls as a current short-term capital gain whereas the premium paid to acquire puts is treated as a deferred long-term capital gain that merely increases the tax cost basis of the shares that were hedged.

1 Can this treatment result in a less-than-optimal tax result?

In the jurisdiction where LeMesurier is domiciled, OTC derivatives, including options, forwards, and swaps, are taxed more favorably than exchange-traded options. For instance, a forward contract or a swap could be used to achieve the same collar-like economics. By their very nature, the embedded call and put premiums are netted, and the economics of a long put/short call structure are built into a single contract, with the premiums automatically netted.

OTC options could also be used to implement a collar. Because the terms of such a collar are negotiated with a single dealer, the transaction could be structured and documented as a single contract, with the premiums effectively netted out. The trade confirmation for either type of collar will not show the cost of the call and put separately but will instead show a net cost of zero. Most option exchanges do not yet allow collars to be structured as a single contract.

2   Could OTC derivatives deliver a potentially more tax-efficient result than exchange-traded options?

3   Would there have been a cost to LeMesurier if she decided to implement her collar with OTC derivatives in lieu of exchange-traded options?

Solution to 1:

Yes. Because LeMesurier used exchange-traded options, she faces an immediate taxable gain on the expired calls. More specifically, the $300,000 premium LeMesurier received on the sale of the calls will be taxable in the year the options expired as a short-term capital gain.

However, because the tax code does *not* permit LeMesurier to deduct the $300,000 premium paid to acquire the puts in the year the options expired, the put premium instead increases her tax cost basis in her Denton Corp. shares. Therefore, LeMesurier gets the tax benefit of her loss on the puts only when she sells those shares, and she has no plans to sell her Denton Corp. shares.

Solution to 2:

Yes. If LeMesurier had used a collar based on OTC derivatives documented as a single instrument in lieu of exchange-traded options, she could have achieved a more tax-efficient result. Instead of being currently taxed on $300,000 of short-term capital gains and having deferred long-term capital losses of $300,000, which was added to her tax cost basis, LeMesurier could have had no taxable event at all had she used an OTC derivative and documented the collar properly.

Solution to 3:

Yes, the cost to LeMesurier of using an OTC derivatives–based collar in lieu of exchange-traded options is that the non-tax advantages (e.g., lower counterparty risk, transparency in pricing) of exchange-traded options are forfeited. However, many investors in LeMesurier's situation feel this is a fair price to pay for the enhanced tax efficiency that an OTC derivative–based collar documented as a single instrument can deliver in certain jurisdictions.

4.3.2.4 Choosing the Best Hedging Strategy   The tax characteristics of the shares or other instrument that is being hedged can help determine which strategy will deliver the optimal result for the client.

To illustrate, it is not unusual for employees to receive compensation in the form of either restricted company shares or various forms of employee options to acquire common shares of their employer in the future. Because these types of instruments are received as compensation for services rendered, tax regimes often tax these types of instruments differently from common shares that have been held as an investment asset for a long-term period by an investor. For instance, restricted shares and employee stock options are often treated in a manner similar to other forms of compensation income, such as salary and bonus. These types of "ordinary income" are often taxed at significantly higher rates than long-term capital gains income.

A key tax issue that arises when hedging restricted shares and employee stock options is the potential tax inefficiency that can result if the instrument being hedged and the tool that is being used to hedge it produce income and loss of a different character. This problem is called a **mismatch in character**.

For example, when an employee exercises employee stock options, any gains are typically treated like cash salary and bonus—that is, as ordinary income. In contrast, most derivative-based hedging tools give rise to capital gains or losses. Therefore, in some jurisdictions, the use of a derivative-based collar to hedge employee stock options can create the potential for ordinary income on one hand (i.e., the employee stock options) and capital losses on the other (i.e., the derivative-based hedge). That is, if the underlying stock continues to appreciate above the strike price of the employee stock option, the investor will have ordinary income on the stock option and a capital loss on the hedge. Unless the employee has capital gains from other sources, the loss may not be currently deductible because capital losses are generally deductible against capital gains, not against ordinary income.

EXAMPLE 5

Mismatch in Character

David Hawk, a senior executive at US-based Garner-Price Corp., receives a large portion of his compensation in the form of stock options. These options will be taxed as ordinary income upon their exercise. Hawk decides to hedge his employee stock options using an option-based collar. During the period the collar is in place, the employee stock options increased in value by $10 million above the strike price of the collar.

1 Taking no account of either potential tax implications or the net cost of the collar, has Hawk benefitted economically from this increase in value?

2 Explain the problem of "mismatch in character" in hedging.

3 Describe the mismatch in character that potentially affects Hawk.

Solution to 1:

Economically and taking no account of potential tax implications, Hawk has not benefited from this increase in value because the $10 million of additional income on his employee stock options is exactly offset by the $10 million loss on the collar.

Solution to 2:

A mismatch in character occurs when the gain or loss in the concentrated position and the offsetting loss or gain in hedge are subject to different tax treatments.

Solution to 3:

When the collar expires and Hawk exercises his employee stock options, he will have an additional $10 million of ordinary income and $10 million of capital losses from the collar, resulting in a mismatch in character between the employee stock option income (ordinary) and the losses on the hedge (capital). Unless he has sufficient capital gains, he won't be able to fully use those losses.

Therefore, while this option-based collar provided the desired economics (downside protection), it also resulted in $10 million of ordinary income in the current year with no offsetting deduction.

In Example 5, Hawk's strategy was subject to a mismatch in character that implied taxes would be payable at ordinary income rates. Is there a possible solution to this dilemma? That is, is it possible to avoid such a mismatch in character? The answer depends on the tax treatment of alternatives to the collar used. In the United States, Hawk could consider a swap that has the optionality of a collar embedded within it.

If the stock price rises above the embedded call strike, the investor will incur a loss on the swap. If the investor makes a payment to the dealer to terminate his obligation under the swap, depending on application of local tax law, the termination payment may or may not be treated as a deduction from ordinary income. With the appreciation of the employee stock options treated as ordinary income, if the loss on the swap is treated as a deduction from ordinary income, no mismatch in character would occur.

The key point is that the tax attributes and characteristics of the shares or other instrument that is being hedged can influence the decisions as to what hedging tool should be used and how the transaction should be documented.

4.3.3 *Yield Enhancement*

Investors can enhance the yield of a concentrated stock position while decreasing its volatility by writing covered calls against some or all of the shares.

Investors typically sell call options with a strike price that is above the current price of the stock and in return receive premium income. The amount of premium received will vary depending on a number of factors, including the volatility of the stock, the strike price, and the maturity. The investor retains any dividends received on the shares and voting rights.

The strategy effectively allows the investor to *establish a liquidation value* (the strike price) for the shares he or she writes call options against. However, the investor does retain full downside exposure to the shares (to the extent the stock price decreases by more than the premium received) and has capped the upside potential (the call strike price plus the premium received).

For example, suppose that Denton Corp. shares are currently trading at $100. Denton Corp.'s one-year call options with a strike price of $120 currently trade at $5, and Rachel LeMesurier sells these call options. If the stock price has increased above the $120 strike price at maturity, the calls will be exercised and LeMesurier will deliver her long shares. In that case, she will receive a total of $125: $120 upon the exercise of the calls and $5 from the initial sale of the calls. If Denton Corp. closes at or below $120 at expiration, the calls will expire worthless and LeMesurier will retain the $5 premium and the long shares. The end result is that LeMesurier is better off so long as the stock price at call expiration is below $125 (i.e., the strike price plus the call premium received).

Covered call writing is often viewed as attractive if the holder believes the stock will be stuck in a trading range for the foreseeable future. Covered call writing can be a good substitute for a structured selling program. Many financial advisers recommend that investors simply set multiple price targets today and sell a fixed number or percentage of their shares if and when the stock price reaches the previously established price targets. Essentially, the same economics can be achieved by entering into a covered call writing program (i.e., by selling call options with staggered maturities and strike prices), but the economics are considerably improved because the investor receives the call premium.

Perhaps the most significant benefit of implementing a covered call writing program, even if only on a portion of the concentrated position, is that it can *psychologically prepare the owner to dispose of those shares*.

4.3.4 *Other Tools: Tax-Optimized Equity Strategies*

Tax-optimized equity strategies seek to combine investment and tax considerations in making investment decisions. They start with the generic concept of tax efficiency and quantitatively incorporate dimensions of risk and return in the investment decision-making process. In the context of managing the risk of a concentrated stock position, these strategies are used in two primary ways: (1) as an index-tracking strategy with active tax management and (2) in the construction of completeness portfolios.

An index-tracking separately managed portfolio is funded by cash, from a partial sale of the investor's concentrated stock position, from the monetization proceeds derived from the hedged stock position, or a combination of any of these. The portfolio is quantitatively designed to track a broad-based market index (e.g., the S&P 500 Index) on a pre-tax basis, and outperform it on an after-tax basis. The goal from an investment-return perspective is not to perfectly replicate the benchmark but to track it closely. Furthermore, these strategies use opportunistic capital loss harvesting and gain deferral techniques that can be used by the holder of the concentrated stock position to sell a commensurate amount of stock without incurring any capital gains taxes.

In contrast, a completeness portfolio incorporates the risk characteristics of the concentrated stock position to build a portfolio such that the combination of the two portfolios tracks the broadly diversified market benchmark to the best extent possible. The completeness portfolio minimizes correlation with the concentrated stock by not including similar industry and sector bets. Capital loss harvesting in the completeness portfolio allows a concurrent sale of the concentrated stock position without a tax liability. Over time, the size of the concentrated stock position is whittled down to zero, whereas the completeness portfolio becomes an index-tracking one.

This strategy is certainly one way for an investor to diversify out of a concentrated position, but it does come with certain risks and costs.

First, and most importantly, this strategy is intended to be implemented over time, so the investor continues to retain the company-specific risk of the remaining, albeit a progressively diminishing, concentrated stock position.

Second, in a perfect world (that is, assuming the concentrated stock position does not decrease precipitously early on during this process and the index proxy manager performs well), the best possible result will be that the client moves from holding a single low-basis stock to holding a diversified portfolio of lower-basis (i.e., not current) stocks. Hence, when this diversified market portfolio needs to be liquidated, there could be a tax associated with it.

4.3.5 *Other Tools: Cross Hedging*

In certain circumstances, it may not be possible for an investor to directly hedge a position. For instance, the derivatives required to accomplish this task may not exist in the marketplace or may be prohibitively costly to execute or the securities laws may preclude an insider or affiliate from executing a hedging transaction. In such a case, the investor might wish to consider an indirect or **cross hedge** by using derivatives on a substitute asset with an expected high correlation with the investor's concentrated stock position.

After a careful analysis of a pool of securities with characteristics similar to the investor's stock position, a security or basket of securities could be selected that have the highest correlation with the investor's concentrated stock position. Another alternative would be to select a broad or targeted index that is investable to serve as the substitute asset.

By using a cross hedge, the investor is at least able to hedge market and industry risk. However, the investor retains all of the company-specific risk of the concentrated position.

Investors considering a cross hedge should probably limit themselves to purchasing puts on the proxy asset even though this will entail an out-of-pocket cost. If a cashless collar or short position is used, the investor is exposed to considerable risk should the concentrated stock position drop in value because of factors specific to that company while the proxy asset or index increases in value. In that case, if the proxy asset or index increases above the call strike or short-sale price, the investor is responsible for that amount when the stock position is down in value.

As always, all else being equal, the investor should use the derivative tool to implement the transaction that should deliver the desired economics in the most tax-efficient manner.

4.3.6 *Exchange Funds*

An exchange fund is an investment fund structured as a partnership in which the partners have each contributed their low-basis concentrated stock positions to the fund. Each partner (contributor to the fund) then owns a pro rata interest in the partnership potentially holding a diversified pool of securities. Participating in the exchange fund is not considered a taxable event; the partners' cost basis in the partnership units is identical to the cost basis of the contributed concentrated stock positions. For tax purposes, each partner must remain in the fund for a minimum of seven years, after which he or she has the option to redeem his or her interest in the partnership and receive a basket of securities at the discretion of the fund manager equal in value to the pro rata ownership of the partnership or continue his or her investment in the fund.

5   MANAGING THE RISK OF PRIVATE BUSINESS EQUITY

As Exhibit 1 depicted, although there is slight variation from region to region throughout the world, a high percentage of private clients derive their wealth from the ownership of a privately owned business. Indeed, owning or controlling a private company can be a very exciting and rewarding experience for its owners. However, as discussed previously, business owners are exposed to a significant degree of concentration risk and illiquidity. Furthermore, they often significantly underestimate the risks inherent in owning and managing their businesses and may overestimate the value of their businesses.

Before a discussion on the risk concentrations of owning a privately held business, it is important to note that sale or divestiture of that business can have many more motivations apart from risk management compared with someone who owns a concentrated stock position, for instance. Some of these other considerations might include the time and effort needed to manage the business, the potential or disposition of heirs to succeed the business owner, and a myriad of other human, emotional, and family issues. It is prudent for an adviser to be cognizant of these non-investment issues before educating the business owner of the risks of his or her concentration.

Business owners are often asset rich but relatively cash poor. That is, many private company owners have most of their personal net worth tied up in their businesses. The owners quite often would like to generate liquidity to diversify in other investments in order to reduce their concentration risk. But there is likely little or no liquidity among the existing shareholders, and in fact, there is likely a prohibition against selling shares to anyone other than the company or its existing shareholders.

As they age and approach retirement, many business owners come to appreciate the high risks they face in continuing to own and operate their businesses and realize they must soon sell or otherwise monetize their private business equity to fund their retirement lifestyles. In many cases, the owner's shares are likely to be highly appreciated versus their tax cost basis, and accessing meaningful liquidity can, and often does, trigger an immediate and sometimes significant taxable event. In addition, generating liquidity can, and often does, result in a loss of control or dilution of one's ownership stake. Exhibit 6 lists major tools for dealing with a concentrated business equity position.

Exhibit 6	The Financial Tool Set for Managing Private Business Equity

Strategies that are available to allow company owners to generate full or partial liquidity include

- Sale to third-party investor:
  - Strategic buyer
  - Financial buyer
  - Other investor
- Sale to insider:
  - Management (management buyout, or MBO)
  - Employees (employee stock ownership plan, or ESOP, in the United States)
  - Sale or transfer to next generation of family
- Recapitalization
- Divestiture of non-core assets (often real estate)
- Personal line of credit against company shares
- Initial public offering (IPO)

These strategies use different *sources of capital* that can include

- Senior debt
- Mezzanine debt (debt that is subordinate to other debt including senior debt)
- Equity

The conduciveness of the market for business sale and monetization transactions varies greatly over time. At any given point in time, many factors determine the attractiveness of the market from the seller's perspective, including

- Valuation level of target companies (at, above, or below historical norms)
- Tax rate applicable to a particular exit strategy
- Condition of the credit markets
- Level of interest rates
- Amount of buying power in the marketplace (strategic and financial buyers)
- Currency valuation

5.1 Profile of a Typical Business Owned by a Private Client

Most businesses owned and managed by private clients can be characterized as "middle-market" businesses. There is no universally accepted definition of the term "middle-market," but these are businesses that are privately owned and worth anywhere from $10 million to over $500 million.

The business often comprises the bulk of the owner's net worth. For instance, the private client might have a liquid portfolio of $3 million but own and manage a business that is worth $30 million. Real estate can often form a significant portion of the assets and value of the business. Alternatively, real estate may be held individually and leased to the business.

The business is typically the owner's primary source of income and a means to fulfill legacy and charitable objectives. It is also usually a source of pride and personal identity for the business owner.

5.2 Profile of a Typical Business Owner

It is very difficult to generalize regarding business owners, but there are some commonalities that are worth noting. The business and personal lives of business owners are usually entangled because of the demands of managing and operating the business. Family members and business partners are often involved. Long-term objectives can vary and often change quickly.

Owners often underestimate the risks inherent in running their businesses. There is also a tendency to overestimate the value of their enterprise. Often the business has been owned and managed by the family for many years or decades. The owner has probably received unsolicited inquiries from potential buyers in the past.

In many cases, a business owner may not have an exit plan in place. The owner may know little about the process that should be used in deciding whether, when, and how to sell, monetize, or otherwise transfer the business. Aging aside, an unforeseen event may trigger the owner into action. Such events can include

- an unsolicited inquiry or offer from a competitor,
- illness of the owner or a family member, or
- the realization that a son or daughter does not wish to work in the business.

5.3 Monetization Strategies for Business Owners

Most business owners and their financial advisers are not familiar with the range of strategies that can be used to monetize their private business equity. Rather, most incorrectly assume that it is a "sell or hold" decision. In addition, most believe it is a one-time decision. It is possible, by using certain techniques, to implement an exit plan that is staged or phased over time to generate liquidity in more than one event. Conditions in the capital markets and the merger and acquisition deal market will ultimately influence the attractiveness of these strategies, and these factors differ greatly over time.

5.3.1 *Sale to Strategic Buyers*

Strategic buyers are competitors or other companies involved in the same or a similar industry as the seller. Most strategic buyers tend to take a long-term view of their investments in other companies. Because of this fact, they will typically pay the highest price for a business because of potential revenue, cost, and other potential synergies.

Strategic buyers are usually quite active in the marketplace, executing "add-on" or "fill-in" acquisitions, many of which involve middle-market companies. Strategic buyers view these types of acquisitions as a low-risk way to enhance revenue and earnings growth and view them as especially attractive in a slow growth environment.

5.3.2 *Sale to Financial Buyers*

Private equity firms are often referred to as **financial buyers** or financial sponsors. Private equity firms typically raise funds from institutional investors which they manage within investment funds known as private equity funds. They are investment advisers. They make direct investments in mature and stable middle-market businesses. They look for companies that provide the opportunity for them to create significant value.

Private equity firms typically will not pay as high a price as a strategic buyer primarily because they do not have the same opportunity as strategic buyers to take advantage of financial and operational synergies. They target earning a high internal rate of return on their invested capital over a fairly short period of time, typically three to five years, at which time the company will ideally either be sold to a strategic buyer or go public. To achieve their return targets, private equity firms have to be careful to not overpay at the outset.

5.3.3 *Recapitalization*

A leveraged recapitalization is a strategy that is especially attractive to middle-market business owners who would like to reduce the risk of their wealth concentration and generate liquidity to diversify but who are not yet ready to exit entirely and have the desire to continue to grow their businesses.

A **leveraged recapitalization** is essentially a leveraging of a company's balance sheet, usually accomplished by working with a private equity firm. The private equity firm generally invests equity and provides or arranges debt with senior and mezzanine (subordinated) lenders.

The owner transfers a portion of her stock for cash and retains a minority ownership interest in the freshly capitalized entity. Doing so allows the owner to monetize a large portion of her business equity (typically 60–80%) and retain significant upside potential (20–40%) from that point forward. Because of the retained stake, the owner should remain highly motivated to grow the business.

From a tax perspective, the owner is typically taxed currently on the cash received. If structured properly, a tax deferral is achieved on the stock rolled over into the newly capitalized company. This strategy should be especially appealing to business owners who are considering cashing out in the near future and are domiciled in jurisdictions where tax rates are either scheduled to increase in the near future (such as Japan, at the time of writing) or viewed as likely to increase in the near future (such as the United States, at the time of writing).

The after-tax cash proceeds the investor receives could be deployed into other asset classes to help build a diversified portfolio.

A recapitalization is an example of a "staged" exit strategy in that it allows the owner to have two liquidity events, one up front and another typically within three to five years, when the private equity firm seeks to cash out its investment (which could be an IPO, a sale to a strategic or financial buyer, or another recapitalization). Because the owner is now partnering with a resource-rich private equity firm, the owner can focus on growing the business and will no longer have to personally guarantee bank debt. The owner does relinquish overall control of the company but may maintain day-to-day operating responsibility for the business and retains his or her title, salary, benefits, and reputation in the community as a successful entrepreneur.

Private equity firms are increasingly investing in middle-market companies. The recapitalization has become their vehicle of choice for doing so. For all these reasons, recapitalization is an attractive alternative to an outright sale to a third-party buyer.

5.3.4 *Sale to Management or Key Employees*

A group of senior managers or employees can acquire control of a business from the company owner through a management buyout (MBO).

For a sale to senior management or a group of key employees, the current owner knows the abilities of the key employees and the employees know the inner workings of the company. However, a serious risk is that these key employees may not, in fact, be successful entrepreneurs. That is, once the risk of owning and running the business is completely on their shoulders, they may not perform as hoped, and this is a huge uncertainty. For this reason, it is usually very difficult for senior managers and key employees to obtain financial backing from private equity firms and financial institutions; therefore, they usually cannot raise sufficient funds to make a serious cash offer. In most instances, the amount offered by management/employees rarely matches the sum offered by a third party if a third party is bidding.

As a result, in management buyout situations, the owner is often asked to finance a substantial amount of the purchase price in the form of a promissory note with a significant portion of the purchase price therefore deferred and sometimes contingent on the financial performance of the company. The negotiations often end when the owner sees the mix of consideration offered by the employees, typically a very low cash component and a large promissory note, and realizes the considerable risk he or she would be taking by selling to management/employees with unknown entrepreneurial capabilities and then acting as creditor to them.

Another important consideration is that because the owner is negotiating with people who work for him or her, a failed attempt to do an MBO has the potential to negatively affect the dynamics of the employer–employee relationship.

As a general rule of thumb, unless the owner has accumulated sufficient investable assets outside the business to sustain his or her desired lifestyle after the sale of the business, an owner should probably sell to key management/employees only if the pricing, terms, and conditions of their purchase offer matches or exceeds that of a third-party buyer.

5.3.5 Divestiture (Sale or Disposition of Non-Core Assets)

If a business owner is not yet ready to retire and wishes to continue to run the business but would like to generate some liquidity now in order to diversify, the owner may wish to sell or dispose of non-core assets. Non-core assets can be broadly defined as those that are not essential to the continued operation or growth of the company. This process is often referred to as a divestiture.

For instance, a company may be considering the possibility of exiting a certain line of business or closing a division that does not fit in with the future growth plans of the company, yet this business line or division may have value to a competitor. As another example, a company may hold real estate used for company operations that has a greater value in an alternative use. For example, agricultural real estate located near population centers may have a greater value when developed as residential or commercial property than in continued agricultural use.

5.3.6 Sale or Gift to Family Member or Next Generation

Private company owners can sell or transfer their business, usually through a combination of tax-advantaged gifting strategies, to a family member or members who are typically actively involved in the business.

Family members may not have the necessary capital to buy the business. It is difficult for family members to obtain the financial backing of private equity firms or financial institutions for the same reasons senior management has difficulty obtaining financing to implement an MBO. Family members usually cannot raise sufficient funds to make an acceptable cash offer. If a sale does occur, the owner may carry a significant portion (sometimes all) of the purchase price in the form of a promissory note.

Gifting strategies are often used to transfer ownership to the next generation. However, unless the owner has accumulated sufficient investable assets outside the business to sustain his or her desired lifestyle without regard to the business, gifting might not be feasible.

5.3.7 Personal Line of Credit Secured by Company Shares

The owner might consider arranging a personal loan secured by his or her shares in the private company. This option is usually completely overlooked, yet it can be an attractive alternative to the other strategies.

One of the key benefits is that this type of borrowing should not cause an immediate taxable event to the company or the owner if structured properly. This technique basically uses corporate debt capacity (assuming it is available) to avoid a taxable stock sale or dividend.

The transaction is usually structured with a "put" arrangement back to the company to make the lender comfortable. The company can support this put obligation either through its existing credit arrangement or with a standby letter of credit issued for this specific purpose.

The exercise of the put to the company as a source of repayment of the loan would likely be considered a taxable event to the business owner. Also, at some point the debt will need to be repaid.

In the interim, the owner maintains full ownership and control of the company, has access to cash to diversify his or her concentration risk, and avoids triggering a taxable event. In addition, in most jurisdictions, the interest expense paid on the loan proceeds should be currently deductible for tax purposes.

5.3.8 Going Public through an Initial Public Offering

An initial public offering (IPO) is possible if the company is in an industry deemed attractive by investors and has a history of steady and significant growth.

The costs associated with going public are significant, although the pricing received in numerous instances more than offsets these costs. Importantly, the privacy and authority that many private business owners find attractive and have come to take for granted are eliminated. The owner will be the CEO and an employee of a publicly traded company and will be subject to significant scrutiny. Any and all decisions are open for the investment community to question. The necessity and pressure to meet short-term quarterly revenue and earnings expectations of the investment community cannot be overstated.

As a general rule, if the owner's objective is to exit from the company in the near term, an IPO is not a viable exit strategy. Rather, an IPO should be viewed as a financing tool that can be used to grow and take the company to a new level, assuming the owner wishes to remain actively involved in the company at least for the foreseeable future.

5.3.9 Employee Stock Ownership Plan

In some countries, legislation has been enacted that makes it attractive for a business owner to sell some or all of his or her company shares to certain types of pension plans.

For instance, in the United States, an employee stock ownership plan (ESOP) is a qualified retirement plan (i.e., a form of pension plan) that can be created by the company and is allowed to buy some or all of the owner's shares of company stock.

In a version known as a leveraged ESOP, if the company has borrowing capacity, the ESOP borrows funds (typically from a bank) to finance the purchase of the owner's shares.

US tax rules permit the deferral of the capital gains tax for a sale of stock to an ESOP, which can be an attractive benefit to the owner. However, this deferral benefit is available only to the shareholders of "Subchapter C" corporations, the details of which are beyond the scope of this reading.

The tax deferral benefit, combined with a possible step-up in basis at death (i.e., the elimination of tax on the capital gains), can make this strategy quite compelling for the owners of a Subchapter C corporation.

An ESOP is another example of a staged or phased exit strategy in that the company owner does not have to sell all of his or her shares to the ESOP. By using an ESOP, the owner can partially diversify his or her holdings, in a tax-advantaged manner, and diversify while retaining control of the company and maintaining upside potential in the retained shares.

Despite several potential disadvantages, including setup and maintenance costs, the strategy of selling shares to an ESOP, where it is a feasible strategy, can be attractive.

5.4 Considerations in Evaluating Different Strategies

In evaluating different strategies, the objective should be to maximize the after-tax proceeds that are available to the business owner to re-invest as opposed to simply maximizing the sales price. Astute transactional tax planning and structuring is extremely important and can result in significant tax savings for the owner.

The strategies described above may result in different values for the company that is being sold or monetized. The sale of private business equity differs from the sale of shares of publicly traded stock, where the shares trade on an established stock exchange and there are ready buyers and sellers. Rather, a market needs to be created for private business equity, and the potential buyers discussed above may place different values on the business and different equity interests therein. Therefore, the most important factor determining the amount that the business owner will receive after monetizing the business is the strategy that is ultimately used. As stated previously, a strategic buyer will typically pay the highest amount for a business.

The bulk of the consideration received by the business owner pursuant to a sale or monetization transaction is typically paid up front, but it is not uncommon for a portion of the purchase price, sometimes a significant portion, to be deferred or even to be contingent upon the occurrence of certain future events. For instance, the seller might lend the buyer a portion of the purchase price. Another example is when the seller and buyer agree to bridge the gap between what they each feel the company is worth by using an "earn-out." With respect to an earn-out, the payout is based on the company meeting or exceeding certain milestones, such as revenue or earnings targets. If the targets are met, the seller receives the post-closing payment (which may have been held in escrow). Therefore, when considering the "sale price," one must consider how much is paid up front in cash (or stock) and how much is deferred or contingent (and how likely it is that it will actually be received). As indicated, after-tax amounts are relevant to decision making. Example 6 builds on Example 2.

EXAMPLE 6

A Business Owner and the Concentrated-Position Decision-Making Process (2)

Recall that Fred Garcia had been persuaded by his financial advisor, Bill Wharton, that a sale to a strategic buyer or a recapitalization would satisfy his primary capital requirement of $35 million. Wharton then introduced Garcia to an investment banking firm to explore all exit strategies. The following facts were established:

- The government in Garcia's country is expected to increase the tax rate on capital gains, effective the following year.

- Garcia wants to spend more time with his family.

- Garcia is very attached to his identity as CEO of an aircraft business.

- Garcia believes that if his company had a capital infusion, his company would be positioned to triple its earnings within several years.

The financial data are shown from Exhibit 3, repeated here.

Exhibit 3	Wealth Distribution Shown in Risk Buckets (repeated)				
"Personal" Risk **4%** **Protective Assets**		**"Market" Risk** **6%** **Market Assets**		**"Aspirational" Risk** **90%** **Aspirational Assets**	
Home	$1,000,000	Equities	$1,500,000	Family Business	$40,000,000
Mortgage on Primary Residence	$0	Intermediate- and Long-Term Fixed Income	$1,500,000	Investment Real Estate	$5,000,000
Cash/Short-Term Treasury Bonds and Notes	$1,000,000				
Total	$2,000,000	Total	$3,000,000	Total	$45,000,000

1 Discuss which factors favor a sale to a strategic buyer and which factors favor a recapitalization.

Suppose that Garcia decides on a recapitalization. Garcia receives 80% of the value of the company in cash from a private equity firm, taxed at the current 15% capital gains tax rate. Investment real estate is included in the transaction. Assume that $10 million of proceeds are added to Garcia's personal risk bucket and the remaining balance of proceeds is added to his market risk bucket. The private equity firm shares Garcia's optimism about the potential growth of the company and is ready to extend debt financing to it on favorable terms.

2 A Calculate the (after-tax) amount monetized by the recapitalization and the value of his stake in the business immediately after recapitalization.

B Explain the meaning of primary capital in this context. Evaluate whether the amount monetized, combined with his existing portfolio, meets Garcia's requirement for $35 million in core capital. Justify your answer.

3 Describe a likely management objective of the recapitalized company.

Solution to 1:

These facts favor a sale to a strategic buyer:

■ In a sale, Garcia would be relieved of the day-to-day pressure of owning and running the business and therefore have more time to spend with his family.

■ A sale to a strategic buyer would generally realize the highest current proceeds. A sale now would avoid the expected higher tax rate.

These facts favor a recapitalization:

■ Garcia would retain his highly valued identity as CEO of his firm.

■ A recapitalization could raise capital that would allow the expansion to realize a major increase in earnings and value of the company within a relatively short time frame.

Solutions to 2:

A Sales price × Percent of equity sold × (1 − Tax rate) = $45 million × 0.80 × (1 − 0.15) = $30.6 million, which is the amount monetized. The value of Garcia's 20% stake is $9 million before any possible valuation discounts for the lack of control or limited marketability of the shares.

B Primary capital is the sum of the personal risk bucket and the market risk bucket. Yes, the recapitalization will meet Garcia's primary capital needs. The personal risk bucket becomes $2 million + $10 million = $12 million. That leaves $30.6 million − $10 million = $20.6 million. The market risk bucket is $3 million + $20.6 million = $23.6 million. Primary capital is $12 million + $23.6 million = $35.6 million. Exhibit 7 diagrams the allocation of Garcia's wealth after the recapitalization with some assumed asset allocations of the invested proceeds.

Exhibit 7

"Personal" Risk 27% Protective Assets		"Market" Risk 53% Market Assets		"Aspirational" Risk 20% Aspirational Assets	
Home	$1,000,000	Equities	$6,000,000	20% Interest in Recapitalized Business	$9,000,000
Mortgage on Primary Residence	$0	Intermediate- and Long-Term Fixed Income	$6,000,000		
Inflation Indexed Treasury bonds	$5,000,000	Alternative Investments	$11,600,000		
Cash/Short-Term Treasury Bonds and Notes	$6,000,000				
Total	$12,000,000	Total	$23,600,000	Total	$9,000,000

Note how Garcia's risk allocations have changed: 27% to personal risk, 53% to market risk, and only 20% to aspirational risk based on the new after-tax portfolio value of $44.6 million. Note also, however, that Garcia's net worth on paper has declined 10.8%, from $50.0 million to $44.6 million, as a result of gains realization and portfolio realignment decisions.

Solution to 3:

With the capital the private equity firm may add through a debt infusion, if growth expectations are realized, the private equity firm may seek to exit from its investment by either going public or selling out to a strategic buyer several years down the road. This second exit could be very profitable for Garcia.

EXAMPLE 7

Short Sale against the Box

Sam Smith, age 73, is the founder and 100% owner of ScreenTime, Inc., a technology company. The investment banker of Peak Products, Inc., a publicly traded competitor, has approached Smith with a two-pronged offer to buy. Smith engages the investment banker, Beverly Capital (BC), to evaluate Peak's offer. Other pertinent facts are as follows:

■ One offer is $300 million, all cash, for all of Smith's shares.

■ A second offer is $350 million in Peak shares in exchange for all of Smith's shares, with no cash consideration.

■ The capital gains tax rate is 25%.

■ BC advises that, as structured, the second offer qualifies as a tax-free stock swap (i.e., a type of business sale transaction that does *not* trigger an immediate taxable event). The tax cost basis that Smith has in ScreenTime shares, essentially zero, would become his tax cost basis in Peak shares transferred to the Peak shares.

■ Although referred to as a tax-free stock swap, the actual result is a deferral of the capital gains tax. That is, a taxable gain would occur if and when Smith sold his Peak shares.

■ Smith is domiciled in a country where the current tax regime allows for a stepped-up basis in shares held at the time of the investor's death. That is, upon Smith's death, the Peak shares received by Smith's estate or beneficiaries would receive a tax cost basis equal to fair market value on the date of Smith's death. Thus, at death, accrued gains permanently escape income taxation.

■ Smith is unwilling to bear the risk of holding Peak shares. Suppose that if Smith accepts a tax-free stock swap, he is able to sell the Peak shares short against the box. He would realize 99% of the value of the Peak shares with no limitations on the use of proceeds. The after-tax cost to access the proceeds would be locked in at 30 bps per year. Smith would be able to keep the position in place indefinitely.

1 Discuss the implication of Smith's unwillingness to bear the risk of the Peak shares.

2 Determine the value of the all-cash offer.

3 Determine the value of the tax-free stock swap offer with immediate sale of the Peak shares.

4 Determine the value of the tax-free stock swap offer with a short sale against the box.

5 Recommend a strategy to Smith.

Solution to 1:

The implication is that Smith needs to consider the all-cash offer, the tax-free stock swap offer with immediate sale of Peak shares, or the tax-free stock swap offer along with a long-term hedging strategy to remove the risk of Peak shares.

Solution to 2:

The all-cash offer is worth $300 million × (1 − 0.25) = $225 million.

Solution to 3:

The tax-free stock swap offer with immediate sale of Peak shares is worth $350 million × (1 − 0.25) = $262.5 million (assuming the block of stock can be sold without any adverse price impact and ignoring the cost to sell the Peak shares).

Solution to 4:

This strategy monetizes 0.99 × $350 million = $346.5 million at a cost of 0.0030 × $346.5 million = $1.04 million per year.

Solution to 5:

The tax-free stock swap offer in exchange with short selling against the box realizes the greatest value for Smith. The 25% capital gains tax will be indefinitely deferred, and if the shares are held until death, the capital gains tax will be eliminated because the Peak shares will receive a step-up in basis upon Smith's death. At that point, Smith's estate could close the short position, and no tax would be due. With Smith well into his 70s, the present value of the step-up in basis should be fairly high.

6   MANAGING THE RISK OF INVESTMENT REAL ESTATE

Real estate can constitute a significant portion of the value of a business. It can also be held as a stand-alone investment. Real estate can also constitute a significant portion of a private client's net worth.

Real estate owners are often exposed to a significant degree of concentration risk and illiquidity. In addition, real estate owners may underestimate those risks and overestimate the value of their properties.

Real estate owners may want to generate liquidity to diversify and reduce their concentration risk. Especially as they age and approach retirement, real estate owners may better recognize the risks inherent in owning real estate and the benefits of selling or otherwise monetizing their property to fund their retirement.

The owner's property is likely to have been held for a long period and to be highly appreciated versus its original tax cost basis. Accessing meaningful liquidity may trigger recognition of a tax liability.

Various forms of debt and equity financing are the primary capital markets tools that investors use to facilitate monetization events involving their real estate investments. Mortgage financing can be recourse or non-recourse and can be either fixed rate or floating rate. The conduciveness of the market for investment real estate sale and monetization transactions varies over time. At any given time, numerous factors determine the attractiveness of the market from the seller's perspective including the following:

- Current valuation of real estate relative to historical levels and future expectations
- Tax rate applicable to a particular property and transaction
- Condition of the credit markets and lending conditions
- Level of interest rates

6.1 Monetization Strategies for Real Estate Owners

As for private businesses, the strategies that real estate owners can use to monetize their properties include exit plans that are staged or phased to generate liquidity in more than one event. Real estate monetization decisions should never be motivated solely for tax reasons. The business or investment rationale for the transaction needs to make sense. If it does, then the next step is to explore the most tax-efficient execution.

6.1.1 *Mortgage Financing*

Besides an outright sale, which is the most common strategy, the use of mortgage financing is the next most common technique investors use to lower concentration in a particular property and generate liquidity to diversify asset portfolios without triggering a taxable event.

Consider an investor who owns a high-quality, income-producing property with a fair market value of $10 million. Suppose that the property has a tax cost basis close to zero. An outright sale of the property, given a capital gains tax rate of 25%, would result in the investor receiving $7.5 million in after-tax proceeds from the sale. The investor would have no further benefit if the property increased in value in the future.

As an alternative to an outright sale, the owner might obtain a fixed-rate mortgage against the property. He could seek to set the LTV (loan to value) ratio at the point where the net rental income generated from the property equaled the fixed mortgage payment (composed of interest expense and amortization of the loan principal). Assuming this cash flow–neutral LTV ratio is 75%, the investor could monetize $7.5 million of the real estate's value with no limitations on the use of the loan proceeds. The proceeds could be invested in a liquid, diversified portfolio of securities. The loan proceeds will not be taxed because they are not "income" for tax purposes. In addition, the net rental income derived from the property exactly covers the cost of servicing the debt and other expenses of the property, so the net income from the real estate is zero. Therefore, there are no income tax consequences from the transaction. If the value of the real estate increases over time, the investor will be able to borrow more against the property without triggering a taxable event.

If the investor is able to structure the borrowing as a *non-recourse loan* (meaning that the lender's only recourse upon an event of default is to look to the property that was mortgaged to the lender), the investor has economically acquired the equivalent of a put issued by the lender with a strike price of $7.5 million that has been 100% monetized, thereby reducing her concentration risk in the property.

Borrowing against appreciated, income-producing real estate, especially on a non-recourse basis, can be an attractive technique to effectively "realize" unrealized real estate gains. In lieu of selling the asset outright to realize the gain and trigger an immediate taxable event, the owner can often borrow against the property to access the same or a similar amount of proceeds that a sale would have generated but without paying any tax—and often with a net cost of carry close to zero—while capturing 100% of any increase in the property's value.

6.1.2 *Real Estate Monetization for the Charitably Inclined*

The implications of asset location for taxable investors can be significant. Asset location is not a concept that is applicable only to securities. Rather, asset location is important for concentrated positions, including real estate. For instance, financial advisers serve many clients who are charitably inclined, and there are many tools and techniques that can be used under different tax regimes to achieve their philanthropic goals that involve asset location.

In the United States, if a client would like to build a significant endowment fund over the next few years and allow the assets to grow tax free until grants are made, the use of a **donor-advised fund** (DAF) can deliver a very attractive result. For example, suppose an investor owns a rental property that is worth $2 million. The investor wants to endow a named professorship at the university from which he graduated several years ago. The amount needed to fund the professorship is $3 million. Especially if the investor believes that the property's growth prospects are less compelling than those of some other asset classes (e.g., publicly traded securities), the investor might decide to contribute the property directly to a DAF. If the property is then sold by the DAF to be invested in those more promising investments, there will not be an immediate taxable event. The appreciation forever escapes taxation. Nor are the accumulated depreciation deductions taken by the investor ever "recaptured." Therefore, the full $2 million would be available to invest and manage. Importantly, those proceeds grow tax free because the DAF qualifies as a charitable organization. In addition, the investor would qualify for an immediate $2 million charitable contribution deduction with a potential value of $700,000, given an applicable 35% income tax rate.[9] When the target of $3 million is reached, the DAF could then fund the professorship at his alma mater.

Similarly, in most common law jurisdictions, a tax-exempt charitable trust would achieve the same purpose as a DAF. The trust would have a defined and charitable purpose, the contributor would receive a tax deduction from the donation to trust, and the trust would not be taxed on property sale proceeds or investment income emanating from the property.

6.1.3 Sale and Leaseback

A **sale and leaseback** is a transaction wherein the owner of a property sells that property and then immediately leases it back from the buyer at a rental rate and lease term that is acceptable to the new owner and on financial terms that are consistent with the marketplace. In a typical transaction, a corporation will sell its real estate asset(s) to another party, which could be a real estate investment trust (REIT) or an institutional or private investor, and then lease the property back at a rental rate based on current market conditions.

The primary goal of a sale and leaseback is to raise capital or free up the owner's equity (that is invested in the property) for other uses while retaining use of the facility. When credit markets tighten (as they did throughout the world in 2008), sale and leasebacks may still be available for raising capital for business owners who are occupants of office buildings, manufacturing facilities, and industrial warehouse facilities.

The potential benefits of a sale and leaseback include the following:

1 It provides a source of capital to distribute to shareholders.

2 It provides 100% of the value of the asset compared with traditional mortgage debt financing, which rarely exceeds 75% unless the tenant is investment grade from a credit perspective. However, a taxable event is triggered and the after-tax proceeds will be less than 100% unless the company has a capital loss that can shield the gain from taxation.

3 The owner can redeploy the capital into the core focus of the business, and doing so may yield greater returns than would be generated by real estate investment.

4 Any debt that was associated with the real estate is removed from the balance sheet.

5 There is typically complete rental payment deductibility for tax purposes, meaning that rental payments under a sale and leaseback structure are typically 100% deductible against the company's taxable income, versus only the interest expense component of a mortgage payment. Sale and leasebacks have flexible lease terms—usually 10–20 years with built-in renewal options.

---

9 Any unused deduction can be carried forward for an additional five years.

In sum, for individuals who wish to monetize their real estate assets to fund a liquidity event for shareholders, to invest the capital in their core business, or to use it for other strategic purposes, a sale and leaseback can be an attractive financing alternative to traditional lending sources.

6.1.4 *Other Real Estate Monetization Techniques*

There are many real estate monetization techniques that are available but are outside the scope of this reading, including joint ventures, condominium structures, and sales of buildings with the seller retaining control through a long-term ground lease. In the United States, it is possible to implement what is referred to as a "monetizing tax-free exchange," which effectively allows a holder of an appreciated property to hedge, monetize, and defer and eventually eliminate the capital gains tax.[10]

EXAMPLE 8

Refinancing or Sale Leaseback?

Albert Lee is the owner of a medium-size business and is seeking to raise capital to facilitate the growth of the business. Lee wishes to either (1) sell and leaseback or (2) refinance his free and clear warehouse to raise capital. The warehouse is worth $5 million. Assume the following facts:

- By refinancing, Lee can achieve an LTV ratio of 75% and raise $3.75 million. By using a sale and leaseback, Lee can raise, on a pre-tax basis, 100% of the value of the warehouse, or $5 million.

- The warehouse is owned by Lee, not by the business, and is not key to the success of the business.

- Lee has $1.5 million of capital loss carryforwards.

- The capital gains tax rate is 25%.

State and justify two reasons in favor of a sale and leaseback (to the corporation) rather than a refinancing.

Solution:

(1) Lee can realize $1.25 million more through a sale and leaseback. (2) The warehouse is not a key business asset.

If Lee refinances the warehouse, he can deduct the interest expense and defer the payment of any taxes. However, the maximum amount he can raise is $3.75 million = $5 million × (1 − 0.25). If the sale and leaseback is used, without any capital loss carryforwards, Lee would monetize $3.75 million, but he would also have to pay the capital gains tax. However, the $1.5 million in capital loss carryforwards could be used to fully offset the 25% capital gains tax of $1.25 million. Thus, a sale and leaseback would realize $5 million. Note that with a sale and leaseback, Lee can deduct the annual lease payment. If the warehouse was a key business asset, that would be a point in favor of refinancing, which would leave Lee with full ownership and control over the property. However, that is stated not to be the case.

---

[10] In the United States, a variation of the traditional 1031 tax-free exchange, a "*monetizing* 1031 exchange," can be attractive for investors who wish to hedge, monetize, and defer and possibly eliminate the capital gains tax on their real estate investment.

SUMMARY

Much of the wealth owned by private clients throughout the world is held in the form of concentrated single-asset positions (concentrated positions), which include concentrated positions in publicly traded stock, privately owned businesses, and investment real estate.

- Owners of concentrated positions can face significant investment risks, including systematic, company-specific, and property-specific risk. Concentrated positions are also typically illiquid.

- There are three primary objectives that concentrated position owners should address. The first is to reduce the risk of wealth concentration by diversifying asset holdings. The second is to generate sufficient liquidity within a portfolio to meet current and future spending needs. The third is to optimize tax efficiency.

- Investors face many constraints when managing a concentrated position, including the income tax consequences of an outright sale, the inherent illiquidity of concentrated positions, and psychological considerations, such as the existence of any cognitive or behavioral biases.

- The concept of asset location and gifting strategies can often be used together to minimize transfer taxes for concentrated positions. Advisers able to work with clients *before* the concentrated position has appreciated greatly in value can have the most impact. With the passage of time, after there has been some increase in the concentrated position's value, wealth transfer tools, while still useful, tend to be less efficient, more complex, and more costly to implement, which underscores the importance of planning the management of an owner's concentrated positions as early as possible.

- There are often several economically equivalent ways to hedge or monetize a concentrated single-stock position. Because tax regimes governing the taxation of financial instruments differ, the tax results might be disparate. Investors can reap substantial tax savings or reduce tax risk by selecting and implementing the *form* of a transaction that delivers the optimal tax result.

- When hedging a concentrated single-stock position, investors can use either exchange-traded instruments (i.e., options or futures) or over-the-counter (OTC) derivatives (i.e., options, forward sales, or swaps). Each has its own advantages and disadvantages.

- Equity monetization refers to the transformation of a concentrated stock position into cash. Equity monetization usually refers to transactions designed to generate cash through a manner other than an outright sale in a way that avoids triggering a current taxable event.

- Equity monetization entails a two-step process. The first step is to remove most of the risk of the concentrated position. That is, the investor establishes a nearly riskless position in the stock. The second step is for the investor to borrow against the hedged position. In most instances, a high loan-to-value (LTV) ratio is achieved because the stock position is hedged and the loan proceeds are then invested in a diversified portfolio of other investments.

- The four basic equity monetization tools are (1) short sales against the box, (2) total return equity swaps, (3) forward conversion with options, and (4) forward sale contracts or single-stock futures contracts.

- Most tax regimes respect the legal form of a transaction over economic substance, and therefore, equity monetization techniques, if structured properly, do not typically trigger an immediate taxable event.

- Investors who wish to hedge their concentrated single positions but want to retain some upside potential can consider the use of long puts and cashless collars.

- The economics of a collar can be achieved through a variety of derivative tools, including exchange-traded options, OTC options, forwards, and swaps. Because these tools may be taxed differently, the investor should use the tool that delivers the most tax-efficient result, which often involves avoiding a mismatch in character.

- Business owners may be asset rich but cash poor because many private company owners have most of their personal net worth tied up in their businesses. The owners often want to generate liquidity to diversify into other investments in order to reduce their concentration risk, but there is typically little or no liquidity among the existing shareholder base.

- The common assumption of business and real estate owners that the monetization decision is a "sell or hold" decision and a "once and done" decision is not correct; exit plans can be staged or phased over time to generate liquidity in more than one event.

- Different business monetization strategies often result in different values for the company that is being sold or monetized. Strategic buyers may place higher values on the business compared with financial buyers. Selling to employees is also a possibility, although usually the seller will have to finance a portion of the sale price.

- In business and real estate sale and monetization transactions, the objective should be to maximize the after-tax proceeds that are available to re-invest.

- In a leveraged recapitalization, a business owner partners with a private equity firm and transfers his or her stock for cash and a minority ownership interest in a freshly capitalized entity. The owner monetizes a large portion of his or her business equity (typically 60–80%) and retains significant ownership (20–40%) from that point forward. Because of the retained stake, the owner should remain highly motivated to grow the business.

- Borrowing against appreciated, income-producing real estate, especially on a non-recourse basis, can be an attractive technique to effectively "realize" unrealized real estate gains. In lieu of selling the asset outright to realize the gain and trigger an immediate taxable event, the owner can often borrow against the property to access a large fraction of the proceeds that a sale would have generated but without paying any tax. However, with borrowing, the investor still bears the economic risk of the underlying property.

PRACTICE PROBLEMS

John C. Hill, sole owner of JCH Equipment Leasing Co. (JCH), is evaluating a future sale of his company and approaches Mary Keller, a wealth adviser, for advice. Three discussions from their most recent meeting are shown in Exhibit 1.

Exhibit 1	Selected Discussions from Hill–Keller Meeting	
Discussion Number	**Speaker**	**Discussion**
1	Hill:	I would like to sell JCH in three to five years and use the proceeds to fund my retirement. Up to this point, I have reinvested the majority of the profits back into the business and have not accumulated any meaningful wealth outside the business.
	Keller:	The first thing we need to consider is the cyclical nature of the equipment leasing industry. Although the economy is expanding today, the stage of the business cycle three years from now is uncertain.
2	Hill:	I have several good employees, but I make all of the strategic operating decisions for the company. I take great pride in the stellar reputation of the company and have been reluctant to cede any meaningful control. I have started the process of looking for a person to assist with the day-to-day operations of the company.
	Keller:	Because you are the sole owner and chief operator of the business, you are exposed to the consequences of a negative corporate event that may result in essentially permanent losses in wealth.
3	Hill:	I believe the operating enterprise is worth $45 million. There is a good chance that a large acquirer would not want the real estate associated with it.
	Keller:	I am concerned about the rural location, size, tailored nature of the structure, and the old fuel tanks located behind the warehouse.

1   For each discussion, **identify** what type of investment risk is being discussed by Hill and Keller. **Justify** each choice. *Answer Question 1 in the Template provided below.*

		Template for Question 1	

Template for Question 1

Discussion	Investment Risk (circle one)	Justification
1	systematic non-systematic	
2	systematic non-systematic	
3	systematic non-systematic	

The following information relates to Questions 2–11

Hill refers his friend, Richard Morrison, the former CEO of Masury Bridge and Iron (MBI), to Keller to discuss his wealth goals. Keller meets with Morrison and gathers the following information:

- Richard Morrison is 50 years old and his spouse, Meredith, is 49 years old. Both are healthy and both expect to live at least an additional 40 years.

- The Morrisons have a 20-year-old son and would like to transfer 5% of their wealth to him during their lifetime.

- Richard Morrison retired two years ago and intends to spend his time serving on philanthropic boards; Meredith does not work.

- The Morrisons own 2 million shares of MBI, currently valued at $50 million, representing approximately 90% of their wealth.

- MBI is a large, publicly traded company, and the Morrisons' position equals approximately 1% of the total market capitalization.

- The Morrison family depends on dividends from MBI for their day-to-day living expenses.

- The cost basis of their MBI shares is close to zero, and the capital gains tax rate is 15%.

- Richard Morrison is loyal to MBI, follows the stock closely, believes he knows the company better than other investors, and expects the company to continue to be a good investment in the future just like it has been in the past.

- The Morrisons' *key objective* is to maintain their current standard of living during retirement.

2 **Identify** and **describe** *three* primary objectives Keller would typically discuss with clients in the Morrisons' position.

3 **State** and **discuss** *two* constraints on the Morrisons' ability to achieve their primary objectives using an outright sale of MBI shares.

4 **Explain** *three* emotional biases that may affect Richard Morrison's decision making.

Keller realizes that the Morrisons' decision making is influenced by psychological considerations and decides to use a goal-based planning approach. Keller constructs Exhibit 2 to simplify the discussion at their next scheduled meeting.

Exhibit 2	Morrison Family Wealth Distribution	
Personal Risk Bucket	**Market Risk Bucket**	**Aspirational Risk Bucket**
3% of Assets	**7% of Assets**	**90% of Assets**
Home: $1,110,061	Equities: $1,850,505	MBI Stock: $50,000,000
Cash/Short-term	Fixed Income: $1,800,404	
Investments: $556,606	Commodity: $237,980	
Total: $1,666,667	Total: $3,888,889	Total: $50,000,000

5 **Describe** Keller's use of goal-based planning to highlight the consequences of the Morrisons' selecting an asset allocation that is too risky.

6 **Determine** if the current wealth distribution is consistent with the Morrisons' stated key objective. **Justify** your response.

Keller tells the Morrisons:

> "Diversification is a bedrock investment principle, and there are several tools that can be used to mitigate the risk of a concentrated single stock position."

7 **Identify** and **describe** *three* tools Keller is referring to in the above statement.

Keller and Richard Morrison discuss several hedging techniques and Morrison makes the following statement:

> "I like the strategy that allows me to lock-in a floor price and retain unlimited upside potential."

8 **Identify** and **discuss** the hedging tool that Morrison is *most likely* referring to in the above statement.

9 **Explain** *one* drawback of this hedging strategy.

Keller also discusses a yield enhancement strategy and asks Morrison to establish a liquidation value at which he would be willing to sell 10% of his position in MBI.

10 **State** and **discuss** the tool Keller is *most likely* recommending to Morrison.

11 **Explain** *two* drawbacks to this strategy.

Keller and John C. Hill, the sole owner of JCH Equipment Leasing Co. (JCH), meet to further consider alternate strategies to achieve his objectives of selling JCH, diversifying his single asset concentration, minimizing taxes, and retiring within a 3–5 year time period. Hill believes that tax rates are likely to increase in the near future. In the course of a discussion with Hill, Keller recommends that Hill meet with a reputable "middle market" private equity firm to discuss a leveraged recapitalization strategy.

12 **Describe** a leveraged recapitalization strategy and **determine** if this strategy will accomplish Hill's objectives.

13 **Explain** *two* disadvantages to this exit plan.

SOLUTIONS

1

Discussion	Investment Risk (circle one)	Justification
1	~~systematic~~ non-systematic	Discussion 1 best describes systematic risk. Systematic risk is the component of risk that cannot be eliminated by holding a well-diversified portfolio. Systematic risk includes macroeconomic factors such as unexpected changes in the level of real business activity and unexpected changes in the inflation rate. Given the cyclical nature of the equipment leasing business and 3 to 5 year target horizon to sell the company, Hill's concentrated position in JCH is exposed to systematic risk.
2	systematic ~~non-systematic~~	Discussion 2 best describes non-systematic risk, or company-specific risk. This type of risk is specific to a particular company's operations, reputation, and business environment. Hill is the sole owner and chief operator of JCH (key person); therefore, his concentrated position exposes him to a decline in value of the company should he become unable to run the day-to-day operations. Such a negative corporate event may result in essentially permanent losses in wealth.
3	systematic ~~non-systematic~~	Discussion 3 best describes non-systematic risk, or property-specific risk. It is the risk that the value of a particular property might fall in value because of an event that could affect that property, but not the broader real estate market.

2 The typical objectives Keller would discuss include reducing the risk of wealth concentration, generating liquidity to diversify and satisfy spending needs, and achieving the prior objectives in a tax-efficient manner.

3 Two constraints that may inhibit the Morrisons from achieving their primary objective are the tax consequences of a sale and the attachment of Mr. Morrison to his company as an investment. With a cost basis of nearly zero, an outright sale in the current year would result in the Morrisons incurring a capital gains tax of approximately $7.5 million.

4 A number of emotional biases can negatively affect the decision-making of holders of concentrated positions. Specifically, Richard Morrison's decision to diversify may be negatively affected by loyalty effects, overconfidence/familiarity, and status quo/naïve extrapolation of past returns. The facts indicate that Mr. Morrison is extremely loyal to MBI (loyalty effect); he believes he knows the company better than other investors (overconfidence/familiarity); and he expects the company to continue to be a good investment as it has been in the past (status quo/naïve extrapolation of past returns).

5   Goal-based planning allows the adviser to incorporate psychological considerations into the asset allocation and portfolio construction process. This approach highlights the consequences of selecting an asset allocation that is riskier than is appropriate for a particular investor. A goals-based methodology extends the Markowitz framework of diversifying market risk by incorporating several notional "risk buckets." The first bucket is the *personal risk bucket,* which includes assets such as a personal residence, certificates of deposit, treasury securities, and other safe investments. The goal of this bucket is protection from poverty or a decrease in lifestyle. The second bucket is the *market risk bucket,* which includes assets such as stocks and bonds. The goal of this bucket is to maintain the current standard of living. The third bucket is the *aspirational risk bucket* and includes assets such as a privately owned business, commercial and investment real estate, and concentrated stock positions. The goal of this bucket is the opportunity to increase wealth substantially. This type of risk allocation framework would give Keller a basis to sit down with the Morrisons and identify the significant risk they face from their concentrated position and highlight that their allocations to the personal risk and market risk buckets are inadequate.

6   The Morrisons' current distribution of wealth is inconsistent with their stated objective of maintaining their current standard of living. The Morrison family portfolio has 90% of their wealth allocated to MBI stock, which falls into the high risk/high return aspirational risk bucket, and only 10% allocated to the personal risk and market risk buckets. A significantly greater allocation to the personal risk and market risk buckets combined with diversification of the single asset concentration (MBI) would be consistent with the stated goal of maintaining their current standard of living into retirement.

7   The three tools for addressing a concentrated position in a publicly traded common stock include outright sale, monetization, and hedging. With an outright sale, owners can sell the concentrated position, which gives them funds to meet a spending need or reinvest. An outright sale typically results in significant tax liabilities. Monetization strategies provide the owners with funds to spend or reinvest without triggering a taxable event. A loan against the value of a concentrated position is an example of a monetization strategy. The owner of a concentrated position can hedge the value of the concentrated position with derivatives. A long put position is an example of a hedge.

8   The hedging tool Morrison is most likely describing is a protective put position. The strategy is the combination of a long stock position and a long put position, which would provide downside protection (lock in a floor price) with unlimited upside participation. Morrison would buy put options equivalent to the number of shares to be hedged. The put options would have a strike price that is either at or, more typically, slightly below the current stock price. Morrison would pay an amount, referred to as the option premium, to acquire the puts. Conceptually, this is similar to the payment of an insurance premium. If the price of MBI falls below the strike price during the term of the option, the put option could be exercised at the strike price, providing downside protection. If the share price is above the strike price at maturity, Morrison would let the option expire and retain the upside.

A zero-premium collar would not accomplish Morrison's goal to lock in a floor price and retain unlimited upside potential. A cashless collar is established by buying puts and selling calls on the shares to be hedged. The long put protects the owner of the shares from any loss below the strike price of the puts. However, the investor forfeits some of the upside potential of the underlying stock. Like a cashless collar, a prepaid variable forward (PVF) would not accomplish Morrison's goal. A PVF combines the economics of a collar and borrowing against the underlying stock within a single instrument.

9 There are two potential drawbacks with this hedging strategy. The strategy requires an out-of-pocket expenditure to purchase the put options, which can be significant depending on a number of factors, including the volatility of the stock, the strike price, and maturity. Another potential drawback is the credit risk of the counterparty. Counterparty risk is greater for an over-the-counter (OTC) derivative because the investor incurs the credit risk of a single counterparty. With respect to exchange-traded instruments, because a clearinghouse is the counterparty and guarantees the instrument, the investor incurs significantly less counterparty risk.

10 Keller is most likely recommending writing covered calls against 10% of Morrison's shares in MBI. Morrison would sell call options with a strike price that is above the current price of MBI and in return receive premium income (yield enhancement) from the sale of the call options. The strategy effectively allows the investor to establish a *liquidation value* (the strike price) for the shares he/she writes call options against. If the stock price increases above the strike price at maturity, the calls will be exercised and Morrison will deliver his long shares. He would receive a total sum equal to the strike price of the calls and the premium from the initial sale of the calls. If MBI closes at or below the strike price at expiration, the calls will expire worthless and Morrison will retain the option premium and the long shares. One of the most significant benefits of implementing a covered call writing program is that it can psychologically prepare the owner to dispose of his/her shares.

11 There are two potential drawbacks with this strategy: The investor retains full downside exposure to the shares (to the extent the share price decreases by more than the premium received), and the upside potential is limited (the call strike price plus the premium received).

12 A leveraged recapitalization is a strategy that involves retooling a company's balance sheet in partnership with a private equity firm. A recapitalization strategy is a "staged" exit strategy, which allows the owner to have two liquidity events, one up-front and a second typically within a 3 to 5 year timeframe, when the private equity firm cashes out of the investment. The private equity firm generally invests equity capital and arranges debt with senior or subordinated lenders. The owner transfers his/her stock for cash and an ownership interest in the newly capitalized entity. This allows the owner to monetize a significant portion of his/her business equity (typically 60% to 80%) and retain significant upside potential with the remaining ownership (typically 20% to 40%). The after-tax proceeds the investor receives could be deployed into other asset classes to help build a diversified portfolio. Additionally, the retained stake motivates the owner to grow the business.

From a tax perspective, the owner is taxed currently on the cash received and typically receives a tax deferral on the stock rolled over into the new entity. This strategy would be appealing to a business owner considering selling a private business in the near future and residing in a jurisdiction where tax rates are scheduled to increase.

A leveraged recapitalization strategy appears to be appropriate to meet Hill's objectives. The strategy would allow Hill to reduce the risk of his wealth concentration, generate liquidity to diversify his single asset concentration, minimize his tax liability before tax rates increase, and retire in a 3–5 year time period.

13 There are two potential disadvantages to employing a leveraged recapitalization strategy. Private equity firms are financial buyers and, as such, they typically will not pay as high a price as strategic buyers because they do not have the same opportunity as strategic buyers to take advantage of financial and operating synergies. A second potential disadvantage is that the owner relinquishes control of the company.

Lifetime Financial Advice: Human Capital, Asset Allocation, and Insurance

by Roger G. Ibbotson, PhD, Moshe A. Milevsky, PhD, Peng Chen, PhD, CFA, and Kevin X. Zhu, PhD

Roger G. Ibbotson, PhD, is at Yale School of Management and Zebra Capital Management (USA). Moshe A. Milevsky, PhD, is at Schulich School of Business, York University, and IFID Centre (Canada). Peng Chen, PhD, CFA, is at Dimensional Fund Advisors (Singapore). Kevin X. Zhu, PhD, is at School of Accounting and Finance, Hong Kong Polytechnic University (Hong Kong).

LEARNING OUTCOMES

Mastery	The candidate should be able to:
☐	**a.** explain the concept and discuss the characteristics of "human capital" as a component of an investor's total wealth;
☐	**b.** discuss the earnings risk, mortality risk, and longevity risk associated with human capital and explain how these risks can be reduced by appropriate portfolio diversification, life insurance, and annuity products;
☐	**c.** explain how asset allocation policy is influenced by the risk characteristics of human capital and the relative relationships of human capital, financial capital, and total wealth;
☐	**d.** discuss how asset allocation and the appropriate level of life insurance are influenced by the joint consideration of human capital, financial capital, bequest preferences, risk tolerance, and financial wealth;
☐	**e.** discuss the financial market risk, longevity risk, and savings risk faced by investors in retirement and explain how these risks can be reduced by appropriate portfolio diversification, insurance products, and savings discipline;
☐	**f.** discuss the relative advantages of fixed and variable annuities as hedges against longevity risk;
☐	**g.** recommend basic strategies for asset allocation and risk reduction when given an investor profile of key inputs, including human capital, financial capital, stage of life cycle, bequest preferences, risk tolerance, and financial wealth.

Note:
Candidates should focus on the framework, concepts, and conclusions of this reading, rather than the specific formulas used to optimize investor utility.

OPTIONAL
SEGMENT

INTRODUCTION

We can generally categorize a person's life into three financial stages. The first stage is the growing up and getting educated stage. The second stage is the working part of a person's life, and the final stage is retirement. This reading focuses on the working and the retirement stages of a person's life because these are the two stages when an individual is part of the economy and an investor.

Even though this reading is not really about the growing up and getting educated stage, this is a critical stage for everyone. The education and skills that we build over this first stage of our lives not only determine who we are but also provide us with a capacity to earn income or wages for the remainder of our lives. This earning power we call "human capital," and we define it as the present value of the anticipated earnings over one's remaining lifetime. The evidence is strong that the amount of education one receives is highly correlated with the present value of earning power. Education can be thought of as an investment in human capital.

One focus of this reading is on how human capital interacts with financial capital. Understanding this interaction helps us to create, manage, protect, bequest, and especially, appropriately consume our financial resources over our lifetimes. In particular, we propose ways to optimally manage our stock, bond, and so on, asset allocations with various types of insurance products. Along the way, we provide models that potentially enable individuals to customize their financial decision making to their own special circumstances.

On the one hand, as we enter the earning stage of our lives, our human capital is often at its highest point. On the other hand, our financial wealth is usually at a low point. This is the time when we began to convert our human capital into financial capital by earning wages and saving some of these wages. Thus, we call this stage of our lives the "accumulation stage." As our lives progress, we gradually use up the earning power of our human capital, but ideally, we are continually saving some of these earnings and investing them in the financial markets. As our savings continue and we earn returns on our financial investments, our financial capital grows and becomes the dominant part of our total wealth.

As we enter the retirement stage of our lives, our human capital may be almost depleted. It may not be totally gone because we still may have Social Security and defined-benefit pension plans that provide yearly income for the rest of our lives, but our wage-earning power is now very small and does not usually represent the major part of our wealth. Most of us will have little human capital as we enter retirement but substantial financial capital. Over the course of our retirement, we will primarily consume from this financial capital, often bequeathing the remainder to our heirs.

Thus, our total wealth is made up of two parts: our human capital and our financial capital. Recognizing this simple dichotomy dramatically broadens how we analyze financial activities. We desire to create a diversified overall portfolio at the appropriate level of risk. Because human capital is usually relatively low risk (compared with common stocks), we generally want to have a substantial amount of equities in our financial portfolio early in our careers because financial wealth makes up so little of our total wealth (human capital plus financial capital).

Over our lifetimes, our mix of human capital and financial capital changes. In particular, financial capital becomes more dominant as we age so that the lower-risk human capital represents a smaller and smaller piece of the total. As this happens, we will want to be more conservative with our financial capital because it will represent most of our wealth.

Recognizing that human capital is important means that we also want to protect it to the extent we can. Although it is not easy to protect the overall level of our earnings powers, we can financially protect against death, which is the worst-case scenario. Most of us will want to invest in life insurance, which protects us against this mortality risk. Thus, our financial portfolio during the accumulation stage of our lives will typically consist of stocks, bonds, and life insurance.

We face another kind of risk after we retire. During the retirement stage of our lives, we are usually consuming more than our income (i.e., some of our financial capital). Because we cannot perfectly predict how long our retirement will last, there is a danger that we will consume all our financial wealth. The risk of living too long (from a financial point of view) is called "longevity risk." But there is a way to insure against longevity risk, which is to purchase annuity products that pay yearly income as long as one lives. Providing that a person or a couple has sufficient resources to purchase sufficient annuities, they can insure that they will not outlive their wealth.

This reading is about managing our financial wealth in the context of having both human and financial capital. The portfolio that works best tends to hold stocks and bonds as well as insurance products. We are attempting to put these decisions together in a single framework. Thus, we are trying to provide a theoretical foundation—a framework—and practical solutions for developing investment advice for individual investors throughout their lives.

In this reading, we review the traditional investment advice model for individual investors, briefly introduce three additional factors that investors need to consider when making investment decisions, and propose a framework for developing lifetime investment advice for individual investors that expands the traditional advice model to include the additional factors that we discuss in the reading.

The Changing Retirement Landscape

According to the "Survey of Consumer Finances" conducted by the US Federal Reserve Board (2004), the number one reason for individual investors to save and invest is to fund spending in retirement. In other words, funding a comfortable retirement is the primary financial goal for individual investors.

Significant changes in how individual investors finance their retirement spending have occurred in the past 20 years. One major change is the increasing popularity of investment retirement accounts (IRAs) and defined-contribution (DC) plans. Based on data from the Investment Company Institute, retirement assets reached $14.5 trillion in 2005. IRAs and DC plans total roughly half of that amount—which is a tremendous increase from 25 years ago. Today, IRAs and DC plans are replacing traditional defined-benefit (DB) plans as the primary accounts in which to accumulate retirement assets.

Social Security payments and DB pension plans have traditionally provided the bulk of retirement income in the United States. For example, the US Social Security Administration reports that 44 percent of income for people 65 and older came from Social Security income in 2001 and 25 percent came from DB pensions. As Figure 1 shows, according to Employee Benefit Research Institute reports, current retirees (see Panel B) receive almost 70 percent of their retirement income from Social Security and traditional company pension plans whereas today's workers (see Panel A) can expect to have only about one-third of their retirement income funded by these sources (see GAO 2003; EBRI 2000). Increasingly, workers are relying on their DC retirement portfolios and other personal savings as the primary resources for retirement income.

Figure 1   How Will You Pay for Retirement?

A. Current Workers

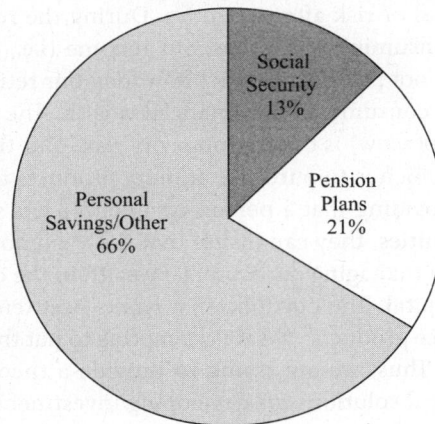

- Social Security 13%
- Pension Plans 21%
- Personal Savings/Other 66%

B. Current Retirees

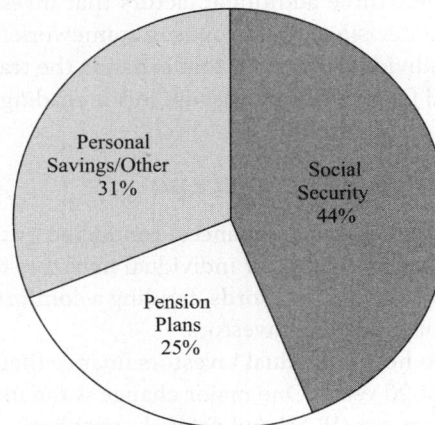

- Personal Savings/Other 31%
- Social Security 44%
- Pension Plans 25%

Source: Based on data from EBRI (2001).

The shift of retirement funding from professionally managed DB plans to personal savings vehicles implies that investors need to make their own decisions about how to allocate retirement savings and what products should be used to generate income in retirement. This shift naturally creates a huge demand for professional investment advice throughout the investor's life cycle (in both the accumulation stage and the retirement stage).

This financial advice must obviously focus on more than simply traditional security selection. Financial advisers will have to familiarize themselves with longevity insurance products and other instruments that provide lifetime income.

In addition, individual investors today face more retirement risk factors than did investors from previous generations. First, the Social Security system and many DB pension plans are at risk, so investors must increasingly rely on their own savings for retirement spending. Second, people today are living longer and could face much higher health-care costs in retirement than members of previous generations. Individual investors increasingly seek professional advice also in dealing with these risk factors.

Traditional Advice Model for Individual Investors

The Markowitz (1952) mean–variance framework is widely accepted in academic and practitioner finance as the primary tool for developing asset allocations for individual as well as institutional investors. According to modern portfolio theory, asset allocation is determined by constructing mean–variance-efficient portfolios for various risk levels.[1] Then, based on the investor's risk tolerance, one of these efficient portfolios is selected. Investors follow the asset allocation output to invest their financial assets.

The result of mean–variance analysis is shown in a classic mean–variance diagram. Efficient portfolios are plotted graphically on the *efficient frontier*. Each portfolio on the frontier represents the portfolio with the smallest risk for its level of expected return. The portfolio with the smallest variance is called the "minimum variance" portfolio, and it can be located at the left side of the efficient frontier. These concepts are illustrated in Figure 2, which uses standard deviation (the square root of variance) for the *x*-axis because the units of standard deviation are easy to interpret.

Figure 2   Mean–Variance-Efficient Frontier

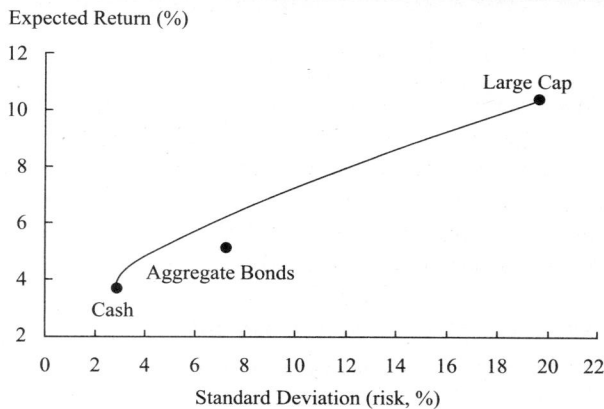

Note: "Large Cap" refers to large-capitalization stocks.

This mean–variance framework emphasizes the importance of taking advantage of the diversification benefits available over time by holding a variety of financial investments or asset classes. When the framework is used to develop investment advice for individual investors, questionnaires are often used to measure the investor's tolerance for risk.

Unfortunately, the framework in Figure 3 considers only the risk–return trade-off in financial assets. It does not consider many other risks that individual investors face throughout their lives.

---

1 In addition to Markowitz (1952), see Merton (1969, 1971).

Figure 3   Traditional Investment Advice Model

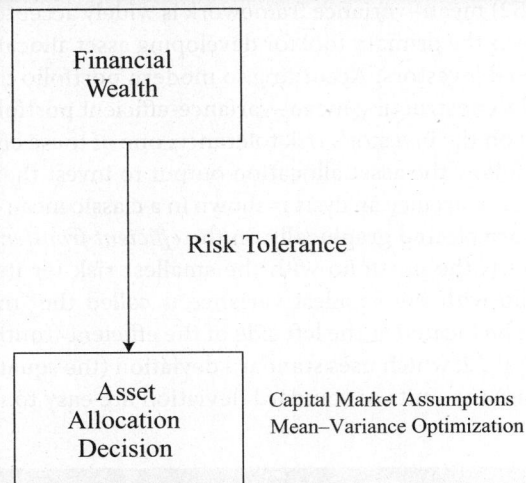

```
        ┌─────────────┐
        │  Financial  │
        │   Wealth    │
        └──────┬──────┘
               │
               │
          Risk Tolerance
               │
               ▼
        ┌─────────────┐
        │    Asset    │      Capital Market Assumptions
        │ Allocation  │      Mean–Variance Optimization
        │  Decision   │
        └─────────────┘
```

Three Risk Factors and Hedges

We briefly introduce three of the risk factors associated with human capital that investors need to manage—wage earnings risk, mortality risk, and longevity risk—and three types of products that should be considered hedges of those risks. Note that these risk factors, or issues, are often neglected in traditional portfolio analysis. Indeed, one of the main arguments in this monograph is that comprehensive cradle-to-grave financial advice cannot ignore the impact and role of insurance products.

Human Capital, Earnings Risk, and Financial Capital

The traditional mean–variance framework's concentration on diversifying financial assets is a reasonable goal for many institutional investors, but it is not a realistic framework for individual investors who are working and saving for retirement. In fact, this factor is one of the main observations made by Markowitz (1990). From a broad perspective, an investor's total wealth consists of two parts. One is readily tradable financial assets; the other is human capital.

Human capital is defined as the present value of an investor's future labor income. From the economic perspective, labor income can be viewed as a dividend on the investor's human capital. Although human capital is not readily tradable, it is often the single largest asset an investor has. Typically, younger investors have far more human capital than financial capital because young investors have a longer time to work and have had little time to save and accumulate financial wealth. Conversely, older investors tend to have more financial capital than human capital because they have less time to work but have accumulated financial capital over a long career.

One way to reduce wage earnings risk is to save more. This saving converts human capital to financial capital at a higher rate. It also enables the financial capital to have a longer time to grow until retirement. The value of compounding returns in financial capital over time can be very substantial.

And one way to reduce human capital risk is to diversify it with appropriate types of financial capital. Portfolio allocation recommendations that are made without consideration of human capital are not appropriate for many individual investors. To reduce risk, financial assets should be diversified while taking into account human capital assets. For example, the employees of Enron Corporation and WorldCom suffered from extremely poor overall diversification. Their labor income and their financial investments were both in their own companies' stock. When their companies collapsed, both their human capital and their financial capital were heavily affected.

There is growing recognition among academics and practitioners that the risk and return characteristics of human capital—such as wage and salary profiles—should be taken into account when building portfolios for individual investors. Well-known financial scholars and commentators have pointed out the importance of including the magnitude of human capital, its volatility, and its correlation with other assets into a personal risk management perspective.[2] Yet, Benartzi (2001) showed that many investors invest heavily in the stock of the company they work for. He found for 1993 that roughly a third of plan assets were invested in company stock. Benartzi argued that such investment is not efficient because company stock is not only an undiversified risky investment; it is also highly correlated with the person's human capital.[3]

Appropriate investment advice for individual investors is to invest financial wealth in an asset that is not highly correlated with their human capital in order to maximize diversification benefits over the entire portfolio. For people with "safe" human capital, it may be appropriate to invest their financial assets aggressively.

Mortality Risk and Life Insurance

Because human capital is often the biggest asset an investor has, protecting human capital from potential risks should also be part of overall investment advice. A unique risk aspect of an investor's human capital is mortality risk—the loss of human capital to the household in the unfortunate event of premature death of the worker. This loss of human capital can have a devastating impact on the financial well-being of a family.

Life insurance has long been used to hedge against mortality risk. Typically, the greater the value of human capital, the more life insurance the family demands. Intuitively, human capital affects not only optimal life insurance demand but also optimal asset allocation. But these two important financial decisions—the demand for life insurance and optimal asset allocation—have, however, consistently been analyzed *separately* in theory and practice. We have found few references in either the risk/insurance literature or the investment/finance literature to the importance of considering these decisions jointly within the context of a life-cycle model of consumption and investment. Popular investment and financial planning advice regarding how much life insurance one should carry is seldom framed in terms of the riskiness of one's human capital. And optimal asset allocation is only lately being framed in terms of the risk characteristics of human capital, and rarely is it integrated with life insurance decisions.

Fortunately, in the event of death, life insurance can be a perfect hedge for human capital. That is, term life insurance and human capital have a negative 100 percent correlation with each other in the "living" versus "dead" states; if one pays off at the end of the year, the other does not, and vice versa. Thus, the combination of the two provides diversification to an investor's total portfolio. The many reasons for considering these decisions and products jointly become even more powerful once investors approach and enter their retirement years.

Longevity Risk and the Lifetime-Payout Annuity

The shift in retirement funding from professionally managed DB plans to DC personal savings vehicles implies that investors need to make their own decisions not only about how to allocate retirement savings but also about what products should be used to

---

2 For example, Bodie, Merton, and Samuelson (1992); Campbell and Viceira (2002); Merton (2003).
3 Meulbroek (2002) estimated that a large position in company stock held over a long period is effectively, after accounting for the costs of inadequate diversification, worth less than 50 cents on the dollar.

generate income throughout retirement. Investors must consider two important risk factors when making these decisions. One is financial market risk (i.e., volatility in the capital markets that causes portfolio values to fluctuate). If the market drops or corrections occur early during retirement, the portfolio may not be able to weather the added stress of systematic consumption withdrawals. The portfolio may then be unable to provide the necessary income for the person's desired lifestyle. The second important risk factor is longevity risk—that is, the risk of outliving the portfolio. Life expectancies have been increasing, and retirees should be aware of their substantial chance of a long retirement and plan accordingly. This risk is faced by every investor but especially those taking advantage of early retirement offers or those who have a family history of longevity.

Increasingly, all retirees will need to balance income and expenditures over a longer period of time than in the past. One factor that is increasing the average length of time spent in retirement is a long-term trend toward early retirement. For example, in the United States, nearly half of all men now leave the workforce by age 62 and almost half of all women are out of the workforce by age 60. A second factor is that this decline in the average retirement age has occurred in an environment of rising life expectancies for retirees. Since 1940, falling mortality rates have added almost 4 years to the expected life span of a 65-year-old male and more than 5 years to the life expectancy of a 65-year-old female.

Figure 4 illustrates the survival probability of a 65-year-old. The first bar of each pair shows the probability of at least one person from a married couple surviving to various ages, and the second bar shows the probability of an individual surviving to various ages. For married couples, in more than 80 percent of the cases, at least one spouse will probably still be alive at age 85.

Figure 4   Probability of Living to 100

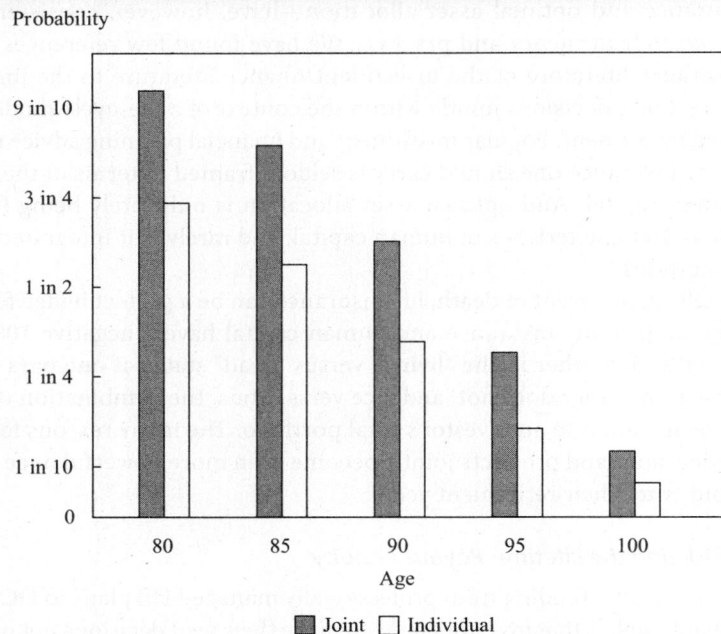

Source: Society of Actuaries, 1996 US Annuity 2000 table.

Longevity is increasing not simply in the United States but also around the world. Longevity risk, like mortality risk, is independent of financial market risk. Unlike mortality risk, longevity risk is borne by the investor directly. Also unlike mortality risk, longevity risk is related to income needs and so, logically, should be directly related to asset allocation.

A number of recent articles—for example, Ameriks, Veres, and Warshawsky (2001); Bengen (2001); Milevsky and Robinson (2005); Milevsky, Moore, and Young (2006)—have focused financial professionals' as well as academics' attention on longevity risk in retirement. A growing body of literature is trying to use traditional portfolio management and investment technology to model personal insurance and pension decisions. But simple retirement planning approaches ignore longevity risk by assuming that an investor need only plan to age 85. It is true that 85 is roughly the life expectancy for a 65-year-old individual, but life *expectancy* is only a measure of central tendency or a halfway point estimate. Almost by definition, half of all investors will exceed their life expectancy. And for a married couple, the odds are more than 80 percent that at least one spouse will live beyond this milestone. If investors use an 85-year life expectancy to plan their retirement income needs, many of them will use up their retirement resources (other than government and corporate pensions) long before actual mortality. This longevity risk—the risk of outliving one's resources—is substantial and is the reason that lifetime annuities (payout annuities) should also be an integral part of many retirement plans.

A lifetime-payout annuity is an insurance product that converts an accumulated investment into income that the insurance company pays out over the life of the investor.[4] Payout annuities are the opposite of life insurance. Consumers buy life insurance because they are afraid of dying too soon and leaving family and loved ones in financial need. They buy payout annuities because they are concerned about living too long and running out of assets during their lifetime.

Insurance companies can afford to provide this lifelong benefit by 1) spreading the longevity risk over a large group of annuitants and 2) making careful and conservative assumptions about the rate of return they will earn on their assets. Spreading or pooling the longevity risk means that individuals who do not reach their life expectancy, as calculated by actuarial mortality tables, subsidize those who exceed it. Investors who buy lifetime-payout annuities pool their portfolios together and collectively ensure that everybody will receive payments as long as each lives. Because of the unique longevity insurance features embedded in lifetime-payout annuities, they can play a significant role in many investors' retirement portfolios.

An Integrated Framework

This reading was inspired by the need to expand the traditional investment advice framework shown in Figure 3 to integrate the special risk factors of individual investors into their investment decisions. The main objective of our study was to review the existing literature and develop original solutions—specifically:

1   To analyze the asset allocation decisions of individual investors while taking into consideration human capital characteristics—namely, the size of human capital, its volatility, and its correlation with other assets.

---

4 In this reading, we use various terms synonymously to represent *lifetime-payout annuity*—lifetime annuity, payout annuity, and immediate annuity.

2 To analyze jointly the decision as to how much life insurance a family unit should have to protect against the loss of its breadwinner and how the family should allocate its financial resources between risk-free (bondlike) and risky (stocklike) assets within the dynamics of labor income and human capital.[5]

3 To analyze the transition from the accumulation (saving) phase to the distribution (spending) phase of retirement planning within the context of a lifecycle model that emphasizes the role of payout annuities and longevity insurance because of the continuing erosion of traditional DB pensions.

To summarize, the purpose here is to parsimoniously merge the factors of human capital, investment allocation, life insurance, and longevity insurance into a conventional framework of portfolio choice and asset allocation. We plan to establish a unified framework to study the total asset allocation decision in accumulation and retirement, which includes both financial market risk as well as other risk factors. We will try to achieve this goal with a minimal amount of technical modeling and, instead, emphasize intuition and examples, perhaps at the expense of some rigor. In some cases, we will provide the reader with references to more advanced material or material that delves into the mathematics of an idea.

We are specifically interested in the interaction between the demand for life insurance, payout annuities, and asset allocation when the correlation between the investor's labor income process and financial market returns is not zero. This project significantly expands our earlier works on similar topics.[6] First, we analyze portfolio choice decisions at both the preretirement stage and in retirement, thus presenting a complete life-cycle picture. Second, instead of focusing on traditional utility models, we explore lifetime objective functions and various computational techniques when solving the problem. Third, we include a comprehensive literature review that provides the reader with background information on previous contributions to the field.

The rest of the reading is organized into two general segments. This first segment investigates the advice framework in the accumulation stage. Then we analyze the impact of human capital on the asset allocation decision. Next, we present the combined framework that includes both the asset allocation decision and the life insurance decision. We present a number of case studies to illustrate the interaction between the two decisions and the effects of various factors.

The second segment investigates the retirement stage. We analyze the risk factors that investors face in retirement. We focus our discussion on longevity risk and the potential role that lifetime-payout annuities can play in managing longevity risk.

END OPTIONAL SEGMENT

1   HUMAN CAPITAL AND ASSET ALLOCATION ADVICE

In determinations of the appropriate asset allocation for individual investors, the level of risk a person can afford or tolerate depends not only on the individual's psychological attitude toward risk but also on his or her total financial situation (including the types and sources of income). Earning ability outside of investments is important in determining capacity for risk. People with high earning ability are able to take more

---

5 How much an investor should consume or save is another important decision that is frequently tied to the concept of human capital. In this reading, we focus on only the asset allocation and life insurance decisions; therefore, our model has been simplified by the assumption that the investor has already decided how much to consume or save. Our numerical cases assume that the investor saves a constant 10 percent of salary each year.

6 For example, Chen and Milevsky (2003); Huang, Milevsky, and Wang (2005); Chen, Ibbotson, Milevsky, and Zhu (2006).

risk because they can easily recoup financial losses.[7] In his well-known *A Random Walk Down Wall Street*, Malkiel (2004) stated, "The risks you can afford to take depend on your total financial situation, including the types and sources of your income exclusive of investment income" (p. 342). A person's financial situation and earning ability can often be captured by taking the person's human capital into consideration.

A fundamental element in financial planning advice is that younger investors (or investors with longer investment horizons) should invest aggressively. This advice is a direct application of the human capital concept. The impact of human capital on an investor's optimal asset allocation has been studied by many academic researchers. And many financial planners, following the principles of the human capital concept, automatically adjust the risk levels of an individual investor's portfolio over the investor's life stages. In this reading, we discuss why incorporating human capital into an investor's asset allocation decision is important. We first introduce the concept of human capital; then, we describe the importance of human capital in determining asset allocation. Finally, we use case studies to illustrate this role of human capital.

What Is Human Capital?

An investor's total wealth consists of two parts. One is readily tradable financial assets, such as the assets in a 401(k) plan, individual retirement account, or mutual fund; the other is human capital. Human capital is defined as the economic present value of an investor's future labor income. Economic theory predicts that investors make asset allocation decisions to maximize their lifetime utilities through consumption. These decisions are closely linked to human capital.

Although human capital is not readily tradable, it is often the single largest asset an investor has. Typically, younger investors have far more human capital than financial capital because they have many years to work and they have had few years to save and accumulate financial wealth. Conversely, older investors tend to have more financial capital than human capital because they have fewer years ahead to work but have accumulated financial capital. *Human capital should be treated like any other asset class;* it has its own risk and return properties and its own correlations with other financial asset classes.

Role of Human Capital in Asset Allocation

In investing for long-term goals, the allocation of asset categories in the portfolio is one of the most crucial decisions (Ibbotson and Kaplan 2000). However, many asset allocation advisers focus on only the risk–return characteristics of readily tradable financial assets. These advisers ignore human capital, which is often the single largest asset an investor has in his or her personal balance sheet. If asset allocation is indeed a critical determinant of investment and financial success, then given the large magnitude of human capital, one must include it.

Intuitive Examples of Portfolio Diversification Involving Human Capital

Investors should make sure that their total (i.e., human capital plus financial capital) portfolios are properly diversified. In simple words, investment advisers need to incorporate assets in such a way that when one type of capital zigs, the other zags. Therefore, in the early stages of the life cycle, financial and investment capital should be used to hedge and diversify human capital rather than used naively to build wealth.

---

7 Educational attainments and work experience are the two most significant factors determining a person's earning ability.

Think of financial investable assets as a defense and protection against adverse shocks to human capital (i.e., salaries and wages), not an isolated pot of money to be blindly allocated for the long run.

For example, for a tenured university professor of finance, human capital—and the subsequent pension to which the professor is entitled—has the properties of a fixed-income bond fund that entitles the professor to monthly coupons. The professor's human capital is similar to an inflation-adjusted, real-return bond. In light of the risk and return characteristics of this human capital, therefore, the professor has little need for fixed-income bonds, money market funds, or even Treasury Inflation-Protected Securities (real-return bonds) in his financial portfolio. By placing the investment money elsewhere, the total portfolio of human and financial capital will be well balanced despite the fact that if each is viewed in isolation, the financial capital and human capital are not diversified.

In contrast to this professor, many *students* of finance might expect to earn a lot more than their university professor during their lifetimes, but their relative incomes and bonuses will fluctuate from year to year in relation to the performance of the stock market, the industry they work in, and the unpredictable vagaries of their labor market. Their human capital will be almost entirely invested in equity, so early in their working careers, their financial capital should be tilted slightly more toward bonds and other fixed-income products. Of course, when they are young and can tolerate the ups and downs in the market, they should have some exposure to equities. But all else being equal, two individuals who are exactly 35 years old and have exactly the same projected annual income and retirement horizon should not have the same equity portfolio structure if their human capital differs in risk characteristics. Certainly, simplistic rules like "100 minus age should be invested in equities" have no room in a sophisticated, holistic framework of wealth management.

It may seem odd to advise future practitioners in the equity industry *not* to "put their money where their mouths are" (i.e., not to invest more aggressively in the stock market), but in fact, hedging human capital risks is prudent risk management. Indeed, perhaps with some tongue in cheek, we might disagree with famed investor and stock market guru Peter Lynch and argue that you should *not* invest in things you are familiar with but, rather, in industries and companies you know nothing or little about. Those investments will have little correlation with your human capital. Remember the engineers, technicians, and computer scientists who thought they knew the high-technology industry and whose human capital was invested in the same industry; they learned the importance of the human capital concept the hard way.

Portfolio allocation recommendations that do not consider the individual's human capital are not appropriate for many individual investors who are working and saving for retirement.

Academic Literature

In the late 1960s, economists developed models that implied that individuals should optimally maintain constant portfolio weights throughout their lives (Samuelson 1969, Merton 1969). An important assumption of these models was that investors have no labor income (or human capital). This assumption is not realistic, however, as we have discussed, because most investors do have labor income. If labor income is included in the portfolio choice model, individuals will optimally change their allocations of financial assets in a pattern related to the life cycle. In other words, the optimal asset allocation depends on the risk–return characteristics of their labor income and the flexibility of their labor income (such as how much or how long the investor works).

Bodie, Merton, and Samuelson (1992) studied the impact of labor income flexibility on investment strategy. They found that investors with a high degree of labor flexibility should take more risk in their investment portfolios. For example, younger investors may invest more of their financial assets in risky assets than older investors because the young have more flexibility in their working lives.

Hanna and Chen (1997) explored optimal asset allocation by using a simulation method that considered human capital and various investment horizons. Assuming human capital is a risk-free asset, they found that for most investors with long horizons, an all-equity portfolio is optimal.

In our modeling framework, which we will present in a moment, investors adjust their financial portfolios to compensate for their risk exposure to nontradable human capital.[8] The key theoretical implications are as follows: 1) younger investors invest more in stocks than older investors; 2) investors with safe labor income (thus safe human capital) invest more of their financial portfolio in stocks; 3) investors with labor income that is highly correlated with the stock markets invest their financial assets in less risky assets; and 4) the ability to adjust labor supply (i.e., higher flexibility) increases an investor's allocation to stocks.

Empirical studies show, however, that most investors do not efficiently diversify their financial portfolios in light of the risk of their human capital. Benartzi (2001) and Benartzi and Thaler (2001) showed that many investors use primitive methods to determine their asset allocations and many of them invest heavily in the stock of the company for which they work.[9] Davis and Willen (2000) estimated the correlation between labor income and equity market returns by using the US Department of Labor's "Current Occupation Survey." They found that human capital has a low correlation (−0.2 to 0.1) with aggregate equity markets. The implication is that the typical investor need not worry about his or her human capital being highly correlated with the stock market when making asset allocation decisions; thus, most investors can invest the majority of their financial wealth in risky assets.[10]

Empirical studies have also found that for the majority of US households, human capital is the dominant asset. Using the US Federal Reserve Board's 1992 "Survey of Consumer Finances," Lee and Hanna (1995) estimated that the ratio of financial assets to total wealth (including human capital) was 1.3 percent for the median household. Thus, for half of the households, financial assets represented less than 1.3 percent of total wealth. The 75th percentile of this ratio was 5.7 percent. The 90th percentile was 17.4 percent. In short, financial assets represented a high percentage of total wealth for only a small proportion of US households. The small magnitude of these numbers places a significant burden on financial advisers to learn more about their clients' human capital, which is such a valuable component of personal balance sheets.

Figure 5 shows the relationships among financial capital, human capital, other factors (such as savings and the investor's aversion to risk), and the asset allocation of financial capital.

---

8 See Merton (1971); Bodie, Merton, and Samuelson (1992); Heaton and Lucas (1997); Jagannathan and Kocherlakota (1996); Campbell and Viceira (2002).
9 Heaton and Lucas (2000) showed that wealthy households with high and variable business income invest less in the stock market than similarly wealthy households without that sort of business income, which is consistent with the theoretical prediction.
10 Although this might be true in aggregate, it can vary widely among individuals.

Figure 5   Human Capital and Asset Allocation

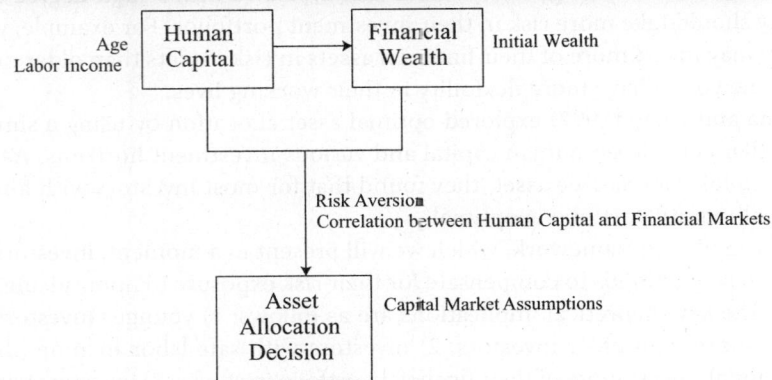

Human Capital and Asset Allocation Modeling

This section provides a general overview of how to determine optimal asset allocation while considering human capital. Human capital can be calculated from the following equation:

$$HC(x) = \sum_{t=x+1}^{n} \frac{E[h_t]}{(1 + r + v)^{t-x}} \qquad \text{(1)}$$

where

x = current age

$HC(x)$ = human capital at age x

h_t = earnings for year t adjusted for inflation before retirement and after retirement, adjusted for Social Security and pension payments

n = life expectancy

r = inflation-adjusted risk-free rate

v = discount rate[11]

In the model, we assume there are two asset classes.[12] The investor can allocate financial wealth between a risk-free asset and a risky asset (i.e., bonds and stocks). We assume the investor has financial capital W_t at the beginning of period t. The investor chooses the optimal allocation involving the risk-free asset and the risky asset that will maximize expected utility of total wealth, which is the sum of financial capital and human capital, $W_{t+1} + H_{t+1}$. We assume the investor follows the constant relative risk aversion (CRRA) utility function. In our case, it is

$$U = \frac{(W_{t+1} + H_{t+1})^{1-\gamma}}{1 - \gamma} \qquad \text{(2)}$$

for $\gamma \neq 1$ and

$$U = \ln(W_{t+1} + H_{t+1}) \qquad \text{(3)}$$

for $\gamma = 1$. In Equations 2 and 3, γ is the coefficient of relative risk aversion and is greater than zero.

---

11 The discount rate should be adjusted to the risk level of the person's labor income.

12 The model was inspired by an early model by Campbell (1980) that seeks to maximize the total wealth of an investor in a one-period framework. The total wealth consists of the investor's financial wealth and human capital. In this reading, we focus on the asset allocation decision for investors' financial capital instead of the life insurance decision in Campbell's paper.

In the model, labor income and the return of risky assets are correlated.

The investor's human capital can be viewed as a "stock" if both the correlation with a given financial market index and the volatility of labor income are high. It can be viewed as a "bond" if both correlation and volatility are low. In between these two extremes, human capital is a diversified portfolio of stocks and bonds, plus idiosyncratic risk.[13] We are quite cognizant of the difficulties involved in calibrating these variables that were pointed out by Davis and Willen (2000), and we rely on some of their parameters for our numerical examples in the following case studies.

Case Studies

In the cases, we look at some specific parameters and the resulting optimal portfolios. In the first case, we treat future labor income as certain (i.e., there is no uncertainty in the labor income). The model indicates that human capital in this case is a risk-free asset (as in the case of our professor). Then, we add uncertainty into consideration. Specifically, we treat human capital as a risky asset.

For example, let us assume that we have a male US investor whose annual income is expected to grow with inflation and there is no uncertainty about his annual income—which is $50,000. He saves 10 percent of his income each year. He expects to receive Social Security payments of $10,000 each year (in today's dollars) when he retires at age 65. His current financial wealth is $50,000, of which 40 percent is invested in a risk-free asset and 60 percent is invested in a risky asset. Finally, he rebalances his financial portfolio annually back to the initial portfolio allocation. Human capital was estimated by using Equation 1.

Financial capital for the examples, in contrast to human capital, can be easily parameterized on the basis of the evolution of returns over time. Table 1 provides the capital market assumptions that are used in this computation for this and other cases in this reading.

Table 1 Capital Market Return Assumptions		
Asset	Compounded Annual Return (%)	Risk (Standard Deviation) (%)
Risk free (bonds)	5	—
Risky (stocks)	9	20
Inflation	3	—

Note: These capital market assumptions are comparable to the historical performance of US stocks and bonds from 1926 to 2006, after adjusting for investment expenses the investor would have to pay. According to Ibbotson Associates (2006), the compounded annual return for that period was 10.36 percent for the S&P 500 Index (with a standard deviation of 20.2 percent), 5.47 percent for US government bonds, and 3.04 percent for inflation.

Figures 6 and 7 illustrate the relationships of financial capital, human capital, and total wealth (defined as the sum of financial capital and human capital) that investors might expect over their working (preretirement) years from age 25 to age 65. For example, under our assumptions and calculation of human capital, for a male

---

13 Note that when we make statements such as "this person's human capital is 40 percent long-term bonds, 30 percent financial services, and 30 percent utilities," we mean that the unpredictable shocks to future wages have a given correlation structure with the named subindices. Thus, as in our previous example, the tenured university professor could be considered to be a 100 percent real-return (inflation-indexed) bond because no shocks to his wages would be linked to any financial subindex.

investor who is 25 years old, Figure 6 shows that his human capital is estimated to be about $800,000; Figure 7 shows that it represents 94 percent of his total wealth and far outweighs his financial capital at that age. His financial capital is only $50,000. As the investor gets older and continues to make savings contributions, these monies plus the return from the existing portfolio increase the proportion of financial capital. At age 65, Figure 6 shows the human capital decreasing to $128,000 (to come from future Social Security payments) and the financial portfolio peaking just above $1.2 million.

Figure 6   Expected Financial Capital, Human Capital, and Total Wealth over Life Cycle with Optimal Asset Allocation

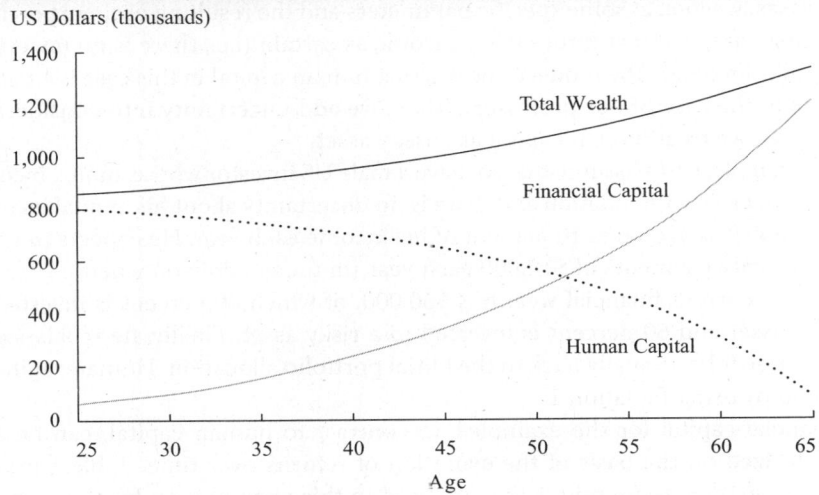

Figure 7   Financial Capital and Human Capital as Share of Total Wealth over Life Cycle

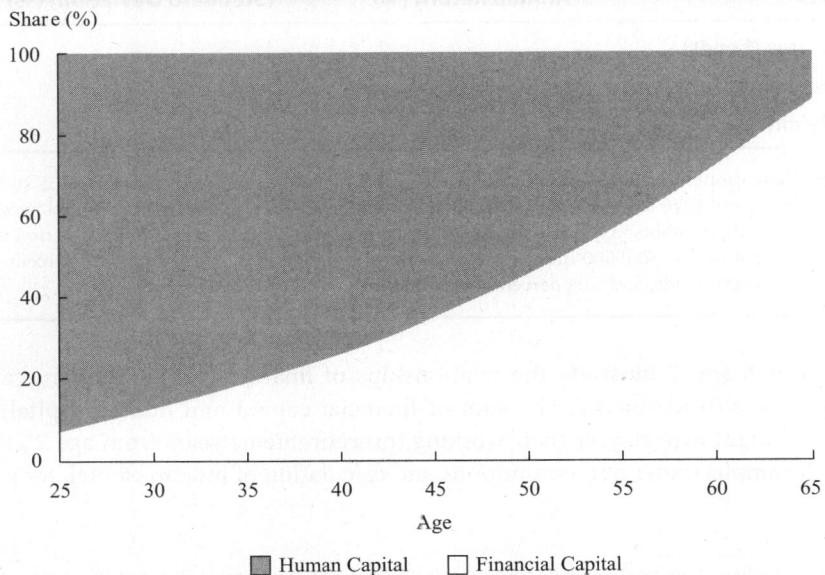

Case #1. Human Capital as a Risk-Free Asset

In this case, we assume that there is no uncertainty about the investor's annual income, so his human capital is a risk-free asset because it is the present value of future income. He is age 25 with annual income of $50,000 and current financial wealth of $50,000. The coefficient of relative risk aversion for this investor is assumed to be 5.5 (i.e., $\gamma = 5.5$).

Figure 8 shows the optimal asset allocation of this investor's financial capital from age 25 to 65. As can be seen, the allocation of financial wealth to risk-free assets increases over time. In other words, the investor increases allocations to the risk-free asset in order to maintain a desired risk exposure in the total wealth portfolio. Households will tend to hold proportionately less of the risk-free financial asset when young (when the value of human capital is large) and tend to increase the proportion of financial wealth held in the risk-free financial asset as they age (as the amount of human capital declines).

Figure 8 Case #1: Optimal Asset Allocation to the Risk-Free Asset over Life Cycle

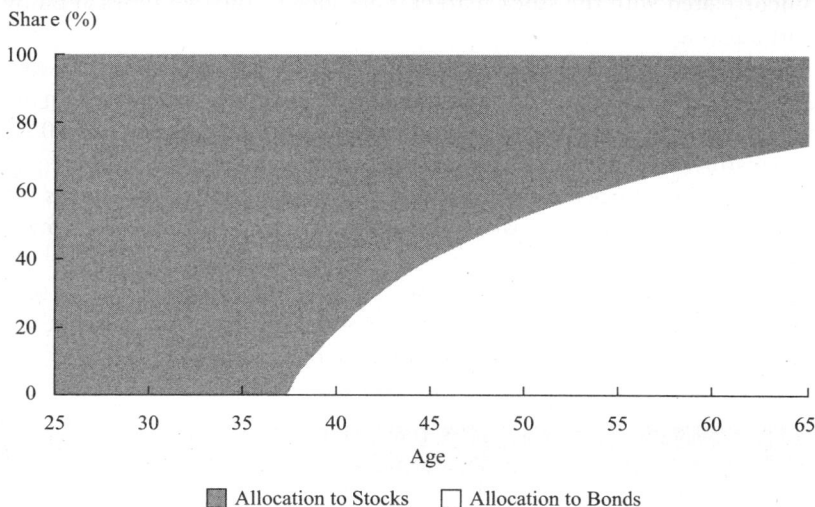

Note: Risk tolerance level at 5.5.

Now, let's analyze the risk exposure of the investor's total portfolio at different ages in this case. When considering human capital, to keep the desired risk exposure of his total portfolio at the level indicated by $\gamma = 5.5$, the investor will choose a 100 percent stock asset allocation because he already has 94 percent of his total wealth (represented by his human capital) invested in bonds. Investing 100 percent in stocks is the closest we can get his total portfolio to the target desired risk exposure level without borrowing. When the investor is 45, his total wealth consists of about 40 percent financial assets and 60 percent human capital; the asset allocation for his financial assets is about 60 percent stocks and 40 percent bonds. At age 65, he ends up with a financial portfolio of 27 percent stock and 73 percent bonds.

This simple example illustrates that when an investor's human capital is riskless, the investor should invest more in stocks than an investor closer to retirement, and when an investor gets older, his or her human capital will decrease and financial capital will increase. Thus, the investor should gradually scale back the amount invested in stocks.

Unfortunately, although investors are almost always given the discretion to change their allocations to various assets and account managers usually even maintain a website for this purpose, empirical studies (e.g., Ameriks and Zeldes 2001) suggest that only a small minority of investors actually make any adjustments.

Case #2. Human Capital as a Risky Asset

In Case #1, we assumed that human capital was 100 percent risk free. But only a small portion of investors would have this kind of "safe" human capital. Labor income is uncertain for most investors for a number of reasons, including the possibilities of losing one's job or being laid off. The uncertainty in labor income makes human capital a risky asset.

But the riskiness varies by individual; for example, a business owner, a stock portfolio manager, a stockbroker, and a schoolteacher have different risk profiles in their human capital. To incorporate human capital in total wealth, we need to consider the unique risk and return characteristics of each individual's human capital.

There are two basic types of risk for an investor's human capital. The first type can be treated as risk related to other risky assets (such as stocks). The second type is risk uncorrelated with the stock market. Let's look at the two types and how they affect optimal asset allocation.

To analyze the impact of the two types of human capital risk on the investor's allocation of financial capital, we constructed the following two scenarios. In Scenario 1, human capital is risky and highly correlated with the stock market ($\alpha_h = 0.2$, where α_h is the volatility of the shocks to the labor income, and $\rho_{hs} = 0.5$, where ρ_{hs} is the correlation between shocks to labor income and shocks to the risky asset's returns). In Scenario 2, human capital is risky but it is uncorrelated with the stock market ($\alpha_h = 0.2$ and $\rho_{hs} = 0$).

Figure 9 shows the optimal asset allocations of financial capital in the two scenarios. The assumptions used in Case #1 prevail except for the assumption about volatility and correlation between human capital and the stock market.

Figure 9   Case #2: Proportion of Risk-Free Asset in Scenarios 1 and 2

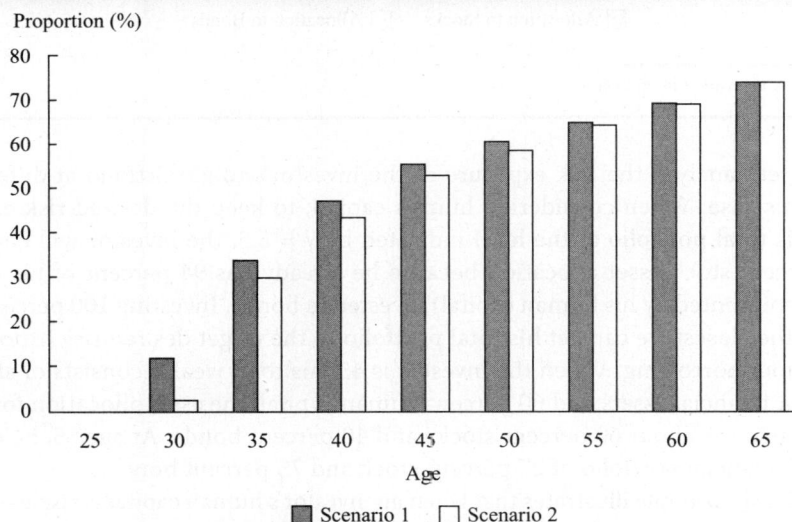

Let's start by analyzing the first type of risk (Scenario 1), in which the human capital risk is highly correlated with the risk of other risky financial assets. A simple example of this scenario would be the perfect correlation of labor income with the payoffs from holding the aggregate stock market—for example, a stockbroker or a stock portfolio manager. In this situation, our hypothetical investor will use his financial assets to balance his human capital risk. The stockbroker's human capital is far more sensitive to the stock market than a schoolteacher's. If a stockbroker and a schoolteacher have the same total wealth and similar risk tolerances, human capital theory recommends that the stockbroker invest a smaller portion of his financial assets in the stock market than the schoolteacher because the stockbroker has implicitly invested his human capital in the stock market. For young investors with equitylike human capital, the financial assets should be invested predominantly in fixed-income assets. Because the value of one's human capital declines with age, the share of risk-free assets in the stockbroker's portfolio will also decline and the share of risky assets in the portfolio of financial assets will rise until retirement.

Now, let's consider Scenario 2, in which the investor's labor income is risky but not correlated with the payoffs of the risky assets (i.e., is independent of financial market risk). In this case, the investor's optimal financial asset allocation follows, by and large, the same pattern as the case in which the investor's human capital is risk free—especially when the risk of human capital is small (variance in the income over time is small). The reason is that, similar to the risk-free asset, human capital is uncorrelated with financial market risk. When the risk of human capital increases, however, the investor should reduce overall risk in the financial portfolio. In other words, if your occupational income (and future prospects for income) is uncertain, you should refrain from taking too much risk with your financial capital.

Case #3. Impact of Initial Financial Wealth

The purpose of this case is to show the impact of different amounts of current financial wealth on optimal asset allocation. Assume that we hold the investor's age at 45 and set risk preference at a moderate level (a CRRA risk-aversion coefficient of 4). The correlation between shocks to labor income and risky-asset returns is 0.2, and the volatility of shocks to labor income is 5 percent. The optimal allocations to the risk-free asset for various levels of initial financial wealth are presented in Figure 10.

Figure 10   Case #3: Optimal Asset Allocation to the Risk-Free Asset at Various Financial Wealth Levels

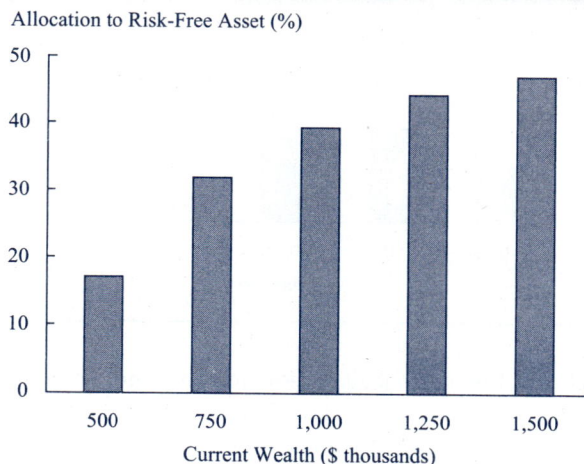

Figure 10 shows that the optimal allocation to the risk-free asset increases with initial wealth. This situation may seem to be inconsistent with the CRRA utility function because the CRRA utility function implies that the optimal asset allocation will not change with the amount of wealth the investor has. Note, however, that "wealth" here includes both financial wealth and human capital. In fact, this situation is a classic example of the impact of human capital on optimal asset allocation. An increase in initial financial wealth not only increases total wealth but also reduces the percentage of total wealth represented by human capital. In this case, human capital is less risky than the risky asset.[14] When initial wealth is low, human capital dominates total wealth and asset allocation. As a result, to achieve the target asset allocation of a moderate investor—say, an allocation of 60 percent to the risk-free asset and 40 percent to the risky asset—the closest allocation is to invest 100 percent of financial wealth in the risky asset because human capital is illiquid. As initial wealth rises, the asset allocation gradually approaches the target asset allocation that a moderately risk-averse investor desires.

In summary, for a typical investor whose human capital is less risky than the stock market, the optimal asset allocation is more conservative the more financial assets the investor has.

Case #4. Correlation between Wage Growth Rate and Stock Returns

In this case, we examine the impact of the correlation between shocks to labor income and shocks to the risky asset's returns. In particular, we want to evaluate asset allocation decisions for investors with human capital that is highly correlated with stocks. Examples are an investor's income that is closely linked to the stock performance of her employer's company or an investor's compensation that is highly influenced by the financial markets (e.g., the investor works in the financial industry).

Again, the investor's age is 45 and the coefficient of relative risk aversion is 4. The amount of financial capital is $500,000. The optimal asset allocations to the risk-free asset for various correlations are presented in Figure 11.

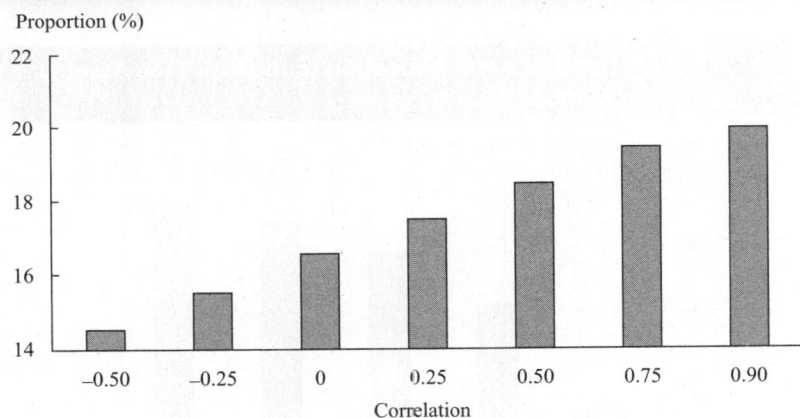

Figure 11   Case #4: Optimal Asset Allocation to the Risk-Free Asset at Various Correlation Levels

As Figure 11 shows, the optimal allocation becomes more conservative (i.e., more assets are allocated to the risk-free asset), with increasing correlation between income and stock market returns. One way to look at this outcome is that a higher correlation between human capital and the stock market results in less diversification and thus higher risk for the total portfolio (human capital plus financial capital). To reduce

---

14 In this case, income has a real growth rate of 0 percent and a standard deviation of 5 percent, yet the expected real return on stocks is 8 percent and the standard deviation for stock returns is 20 percent.

this risk, an investor must invest more financial wealth in the risk-free asset. Another way to look at this result is in terms of *certainty equivalents* (or utility equivalents) of wealth. The higher the uncertainty (or volatility), all else being equal, the lower the certainty-equivalent value. In utility terms, with increasing correlation and rising volatility, this investor is actually poorer!

Implications for Advisers

A financial adviser or consultant should be aware of the following issues when developing a long-term asset allocation plan for typical individual investors:

1 Investors should invest financial assets in such a way as to diversify and balance out their human capital.

2 A young investor with relatively safe human capital assets and greater flexibility of labor supply should invest more financial assets in risky assets, such as stocks, than an older investor should, perhaps even with leverage and debt. The portion of financial assets allocated to stocks should be reduced as the investor gets older. Also, if the stock market performs well, the investor's financial capital will grow, and again, the implication is to reduce the portion of financial assets invested in stocks.

3 An investor with human capital that has a high correlation with stock market risk should also reduce the allocation to risky assets in the financial portfolio and increase the allocation to assets that are less correlated with the stock market.[15]

In short, the risk characteristics of human capital have a significant impact on optimal financial portfolio allocation. Therefore, to effectively incorporate human capital into making the asset allocation decision, financial advisers and consultants need to determine 1) whether the investor's human capital is risk free or risky and 2) whether the risk is highly correlated with financial market risk.

SUMMARY

Human capital is defined as the present value of future labor income. Human capital—not financial assets—is usually the dominant asset for young and middle-aged people.

Many academic researchers have advocated considering human capital when developing portfolio allocations of an investor's financial assets. That is, investors should invest their financial assets in such a way as to diversify and balance their human capital.

In addition to the size of the investor's human capital, its risk–return characteristics, its relationship to other financial assets, and the flexibility of the investor's labor supply also have significant effects on how an investor should allocate financial assets. In general, a typical young investor would be well advised to hold an all-stock investment portfolio (perhaps even with leverage) because the investor can easily offset any disastrous returns in the short run by adjusting his or her future investment strategy, labor supply, consumption, and/or savings. As the investor becomes older, the proportion of human capital in total wealth becomes smaller; therefore, the financial portfolio should become less aggressive.

---

15 For example, all else being equal, alternative assets with low correlations with the stock market (e.g., commodities, certain hedge funds) can be attractive for these investors.

Although the typical US investor's income is unlikely to be highly correlated with the aggregate stock market (based on results reported by Davis and Willen 2000), many investors' incomes may be highly correlated with a specific company's market experience. Company executives, stockbrokers, and stock portfolio managers (whose labor income and human capital are highly correlated with risky assets) should have financial portfolios invested in assets that are little correlated with the stock market (e.g., bonds).

2   HUMAN CAPITAL, LIFE INSURANCE, AND ASSET ALLOCATION

In the first part of this reading, we discussed how human capital plays an important role in developing the appropriate investment recommendations for individual investors. In addition, recognition is growing among academics and practitioners that the risk and return characteristics of human capital (wage and salary profiles) should be taken into account when building portfolios for the individual investor. Therefore, we expanded the traditional investment advice framework to include not only an investor's financial capital but also human capital. To illustrate the effect of human capital in the expanded framework, we used case studies in which the human capital characteristics were quite different.

In this section, we study another (perhaps even more important) risk aspect of human capital—*mortality risk*.[16] And we further expand the framework developed previously to include the life insurance decision. We first explain the rationale for examining the life insurance decision together with the asset allocation decision. We develop a unified model to provide practical guidelines on developing optimal asset allocation and life insurance allocation for individual investors in their preretirement years (accumulation stage). We also provide a number of case studies in which we illustrate model allocations that depend on income, age, and tolerance for financial risk.

Life Insurance and Asset Allocation Decisions

A unique aspect of an investor's human capital is mortality risk—the family's loss of human capital in the unfortunate event of the investor's premature death. This risk is huge for many individual investors because human capital is their dominant asset.

Life insurance has long been used to hedge against mortality risk. Typically, the greater the value of the human capital, the more life insurance the family demands. Intuitively, human capital affects not only optimal asset allocation but also optimal life insurance demand. These two important financial decisions have consistently been analyzed separately, however, in theory and practice. We found few references in the literature to the need to consider these decisions jointly and within the context of a life-cycle model of consumption and investment. Popular investment and financial planning advice regarding how much life insurance one should acquire is never framed in terms of the riskiness of one's human capital. And the optimal asset allocation decision has only lately come to be framed in terms of the risk characteristics of human capital. Rarely is the asset allocation decision integrated with life insurance decisions.

---

16 This discussion is partly based on material in Chen, Ibbotson, Milevsky, and Zhu (2006).

Motivated by the need to integrate these two decisions in light of the risk and return characteristics of human capital, we have analyzed these traditionally distinct lines of thought together in one framework. These two decisions must be determined jointly because they serve as risk substitutes when viewed from an individual investor's portfolio perspective.

Life insurance is a perfect hedge for human capital in the event of death. Term life insurance and human capital have a negative 100 percent correlation with each other. If one pays off at the end of the year, then the other does not, and vice versa. Thus, the combination of the two provides great diversification to an investor's total portfolio. Figure 12 "updates" Figure 5 to illustrate the types of decisions the investor faces when jointly considering human capital, asset allocation, and life insurance decisions together with the variables that affect the decisions.

Figure 12   Relationships among Human Capital, Asset Allocation, and Life Insurance

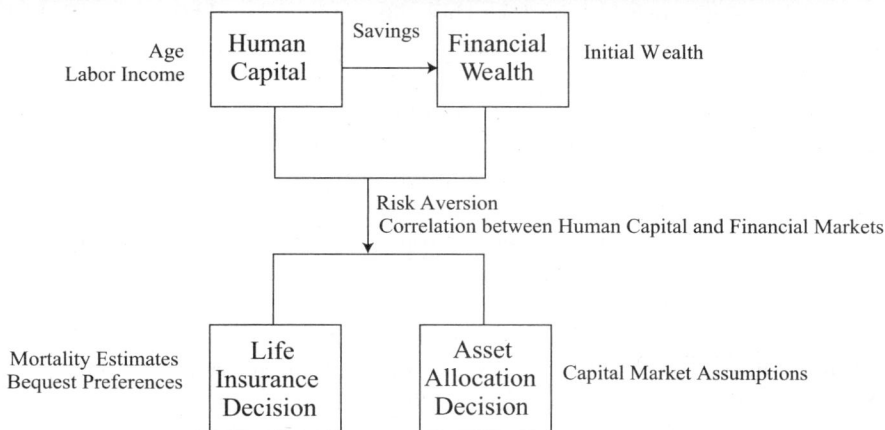

Human Capital, Life Insurance, and Asset Allocation

We have discussed the literature on human capital and asset allocation extensively to this point, so now we concentrate on the link between life insurance and human capital. A number of researchers have pointed out that the lifetime consumption and portfolio decision models need to be expanded to take into account lifetime uncertainty (or mortality risk). Yaari's 1965 paper is considered the first classical work on this topic. Yaari pointed out ways of using life insurance and life annuities to insure against lifetime uncertainty. He also derived conditions under which consumers would fully insure against lifetime uncertainty (see also Samuelson 1969; Merton 1969). Like Yaari, Fischer (1973) pointed out that earlier models either dealt with an infinite horizon or took the date of death to be known with certainty.

Theoretical studies show a clear link between the demand for life insurance and the uncertainty of human capital. Campbell (1980) argued that for most households, the uncertainty of labor income dominates uncertainty as to financial capital income. He also developed solutions based on human capital uncertainty to the optimal amount of insurance a household should purchase.[17] Buser and Smith (1983) used mean–variance analysis to model life insurance demand in a portfolio context. In deriving the optimal insurance demand and the optimal allocation between risky and

---

17 Economides (1982) argued in a corrected model that Campbell's approach underestimated the optimal amount of insurance coverage. Our model takes this correction into consideration.

risk-free assets, they found that the optimal amount of insurance depends on two components: the expected value of human capital and the risk–return characteristics of the insurance contract. Ostaszewski (2003) stated that life insurance—by addressing the uncertainties and inadequacies of an individual's human capital—is the business of human capital "securitization."

Empirical studies of life insurance adequacy have shown that underinsurance, however, is prevalent (see Auerbach and Kotlikoff 1991). Gokhale and Kotlikoff (2002) argued that questionable financial advice, inertia, and the unpleasantness of thinking about one's death are the likely causes.

Zietz (2003) has provided another excellent review of the literature on insurance.

Description of the Model

To merge considerations of asset allocation, human capital, and optimal demand for life insurance, we need a solid understanding of the actuarial factors that affect the pricing of a life insurance contract. Note that, although numerous life insurance product variations exist—such as term life, whole life, and universal life, each of which is worthy of its own financial analysis—we focus exclusively on the most fundamental type of life insurance policy—namely, the *one-year, renewable term policy*.[18]

On a basic economic level, the premium for a one-year, renewable term policy is paid at the beginning of the year—or on the individual's birthday—and protects the human capital of the insured for the duration of the year.[19] (If the insured person dies within that year, the insurance company pays the face value to the beneficiaries soon after the death or prior to the end of the year.) Next year, because the policy is renewable, the contract is guaranteed to start anew with new premium payments to be made and protection received.

In this section, we provide a general approach to thinking about the joint determination of the optimal asset allocation and prudent life insurance holdings.

We assume there are two asset classes. The investor can allocate financial wealth between a risk-free asset and a risky asset (i.e., bonds and stocks). Also, the investor can purchase a term life insurance contract that is renewable each period. The investor's objective is to maximize overall utility, which includes utility in the investor's "live" state and in the investor's "dead" state, by choosing life insurance (the face value of a term life insurance policy) and making an asset allocation between the risk-free and risky assets.[20] The optimization problem can be expressed as follows:

$$
\max_{(\theta_x, \alpha_x)} E\Big[(1 - D)\big(1 - \bar{q}_x\big)U_{alive}\big(W_{x+1} + H_{x+1}\big)
$$

$$
+ D\big(\bar{q}_x\big)U_{dead}\big(W_{x+1} + \theta_x\big)\Big]
$$

(4)

---

18 One-year, renewable term life insurance is used throughout this reading. Although an analysis is beyond the scope of this reading, we believe that all other types of life insurance policies are financial combinations of term life insurance with investment accounts, added tax benefits, and embedded options.

19 In this description, we are obviously abstracting somewhat from the realities of insurance pricing, but to a first-order approximation, the descriptions capture the essence of actuarial cost.

20 We assume that the investor makes asset allocation and insurance purchase decisions at the start of each period. Labor income is also received at the beginning of the period.

where

θ_x = amount of life insurance

α_x = allocation to the risky asset

D = relative strength of the utility of bequest

$\bar{q}_x$ = subjective probabilities of death at the end of the year $x + 1$ conditional on being alive at the age x

$1 - \bar{q}_x$ = subjective probability of survival

W_{x+1} = wealth level at age $x + 1$

H_{x+1} = human capital

and $U_{alive}(\bullet)$ and $U_{dead}(\bullet)$ are the utility functions associated with the alive and dead states.

We extend the framework of Campbell (1980) and Buser and Smith (1983) in a number of important directions. First, we link the asset allocation decision to the decision to purchase life insurance in one framework by incorporating human capital. Second, we specifically take into consideration the effect of the bequest motive (attitude toward the importance of leaving a bequest) on asset allocation and life insurance.[21] Third, we explicitly model the volatility of labor income and its correlation with the financial market. Fourth, we also model the investor's subjective survival probability.

Human capital is the central component that links both decisions. Recall that an investor's human capital can be viewed as a stock if both the correlation with a given financial market subindex and the volatility of the labor income are high. Human capital can be viewed as a bond if both the correlation and the volatility are low. In between those two extremes, human capital is a diversified portfolio of stocks and bonds, plus idiosyncratic risk. Again, we rely on some of the Davis–Willen (2000) parameters for our numerical case examples. It is important to distinguish between, on the one hand, correlations and dependence when considering human capital and aggregate stock market returns (such as return of the S&P 500 Index) and, on the other hand, correlations of human capital with individual securities and industries. Intuitively, a middle manager working for Dow Corning, for example, has human capital returns that are highly correlated with the performance of Dow Corning stock. A bad year or quarter for the stock is likely to have a negative effect on financial compensation.

The model has several important implications. First, as expressed in Equation 4, it clearly shows that both asset allocation and life insurance decisions affect an investor's overall utility; therefore, the decisions should be made jointly.[22] The model also shows that human capital is the central factor. The impact of human capital on asset allocation and life insurance decisions is generally consistent with the existing literature (e.g., Campbell and Viceira 2002; Campbell 1980). One of our major enhancements, however, is the explicit modeling of correlation between the shocks to labor income and financial market returns. The correlation between income and risky-asset returns plays an important role in both decisions. All else being equal, as the correlation between shocks to income and risky assets increases, the optimal allocation to risky assets declines, as does the optimal quantity of life insurance. Although the decline in allocation to risky assets with increasing correlation may be intuitive from a portfolio theory perspective, we provide precise analytic guidance on how it should be implemented. Furthermore, and contrary to intuition, we show that a higher correlation with

---

21 Bernheim (1991) and Zietz (2003) showed that the bequest motive has a significant effect on life insurance demand.

22 The only scenarios in which the asset allocation and life insurance decisions are not linked are when the investor derives his or her utility 100 percent from consumption or 100 percent from bequest. Both are extreme—especially the 100 percent from bequest.

any given subindex brings about the second result—that is, reduces the demand for life insurance. The reason is that the higher the correlation, the higher the discount rate used to estimate human capital from future income. A higher discount rate implies a lower amount of human capital—thus, less insurance demand.

Second, the asset allocation decision affects well-being in both the live (consumption) state and the dead (bequest) state whereas the life insurance decision affects primarily the bequest state. Bequest preference is arguably the most important factor, other than human capital, in evaluating life insurance demand.[23] Investors who weight bequest as more important (who have a higher *D)* are likely to purchase more life insurance.

Another unique aspect of our model is the consideration of subjective survival probability, $1 - \overline{q}_x$. The reader can see intuitively that investors with low subjective survival probability (i.e., those who believe they have a high mortality rate) will tend to buy more life insurance. This "adverse selection" problem is well documented in the insurance literature.[24]

Other implications are consistent with the existing literature. For example, our model implies that the more financial wealth one has—all else being equal—the less life insurance one demands. More financial wealth also indicates more conservative portfolios when human capital is "bondlike." When human capital is "stocklike," more financial wealth calls for more aggressive portfolios. Naturally, risk tolerance also has a strong influence on the asset allocation decision. Investors with less risk tolerance will invest conservatively and buy more life insurance. These implications will be illustrated in the case studies.

We emphasize at this point that our analysis completely ignores the nonhuman-capital aspects of insurance purchases. For example, a wide variety of estate planning, business succession, and tax minimization strategies might increase demand for insurance much more than the level we have derived in our models. These aspects are beyond the scope of our analysis.

Case Studies

To illustrate the predictions of the model, we analyze the optimal asset allocation decision and the optimal life insurance coverage for five different cases. We solve the problem via simulation.

For all five cases, we assumed the investor can invest in two asset classes. We used the capital market assumptions given in Table 1, which can be summarized as follows: compound annual geometric mean returns for bonds of 5 percent and for stocks of 9 percent, standard deviation of stock returns of 20 percent, and an inflation rate of 3 percent.

In these case studies, the investor is female. Her preference toward bequest is one-fourth of her preference toward consumption in the live state.[25] She has no special information about her relative health status (i.e., her subjective survival probability is equal to the objective actuarial survival probability). Her income is expected to grow with inflation, and the volatility of the growth rate is 5 percent.[26] Her real annual income is $50,000, and she saves 10 percent each year. She expects to receive a Social Security payment of $10,000 each year (in today's dollars) when she retires at age 65.

---

23 A well-designed questionnaire can help elicit individuals' attitudes toward bequest, even though a precise estimate may be hard to obtain.
24 The actuarial mortality tables can be taken as a starting point. Life insurance is already priced to take into account adverse selection.
25 That is, we set *D* equal to 0.2 in the model.
26 The salary growth rate and the volatility were chosen mainly to show the implications of the model. They are not necessarily representative.

Her current financial wealth is $50,000. She is assumed to follow constant relative risk aversion (CRRA) utility with a risk-aversion coefficient of γ. Finally, we assume that her financial portfolio is rebalanced and the term life insurance contract renewed annually.[27] These assumptions remain the same for all cases. Other parameters, such as initial wealth, will be specified in each case.

Case #1. Human Capital, Financial Asset Allocation, and Life Insurance Demand over the Lifetime

In this case, we assumed that the investor has a CRRA, γ, of 4. Also, the correlation between the investor's income and the market return of the risky asset is 0.20.[28] For a given age, the amount of insurance this investor should purchase can be determined by her consumption/bequest preference, risk tolerance, and financial wealth. Her expected financial wealth, human capital, and the derived optimal insurance demand over the investor's life from age 25 to age 65 are presented in Figure 13.

Figure 13　Case #1: Human Capital, Financial Asset Allocation, and Insurance Demand over Lifetime

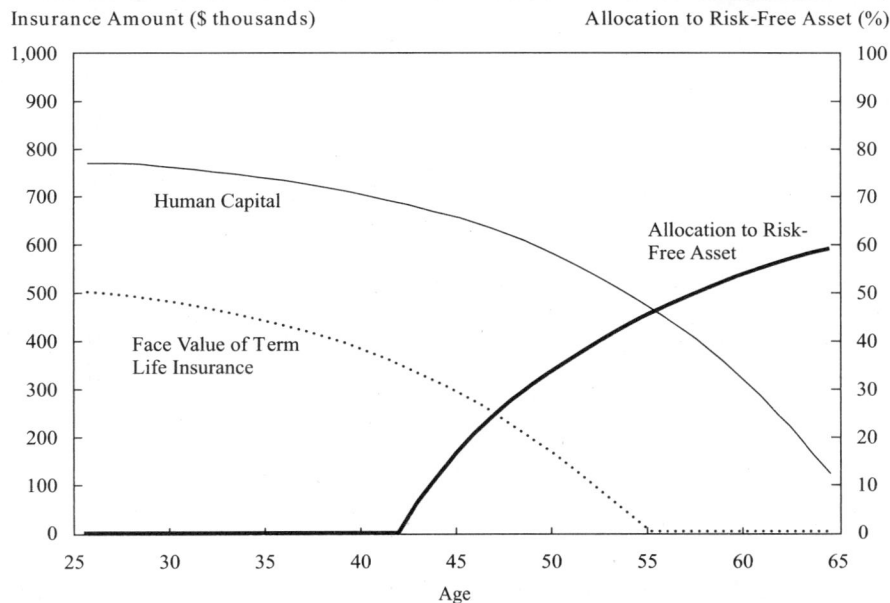

Several results of modeling this investor's situation are worth noting. First, human capital gradually decreases as the investor gets older and her remaining number of working years becomes smaller. Second, the amount of her financial capital increases as she ages as a result of growth of her existing financial wealth and the additional savings she makes each year. The allocation to risky assets decreases as the investor ages because of the dynamic between human capital and financial wealth over time. Finally, the investor's demand for insurance decreases as she ages. This result is not surprising because the primary driver of insurance demand is human capital, so the decrease in human capital reduces insurance demand.

---

27 The mortality and insurance loading is assumed to be 12.5 percent.
28 Davis and Willen (2000) estimated the correlation between labor income and equity market returns by using the US Department of Labor's "Current Occupation Survey." They found that the correlation between equity returns and labor income typically lies in the interval from –0.10 to 0.20.

These results appear to be consistent with conventional financial planning advice to reduce insurance holdings later in life, even though mortality risk itself has increased. In fact, one of the widespread misunderstandings about insurance, especially among young students of finance, is that a person needs large amounts of life insurance only when facing the greatest chance of death (i.e., only for older people). To the contrary, the magnitude of loss of human capital at younger ages is far more important than the higher probability of death at older ages.

Case #2. Strength of the Bequest Motive

This case shows the impact of the bequest motive on the optimal decisions about asset allocation and insurance. In this case, we assume that the investor is age 45 and has an accumulated financial wealth of $500,000. The investor has a CRRA coefficient of 4. The optimal allocations to the risk-free asset and insurance for various bequest preferences are presented in Figure 14.

Figure 14   Case #2: Optimal Insurance Demand and Allocation to the Risk-Free Asset by Strength of Bequest Preference

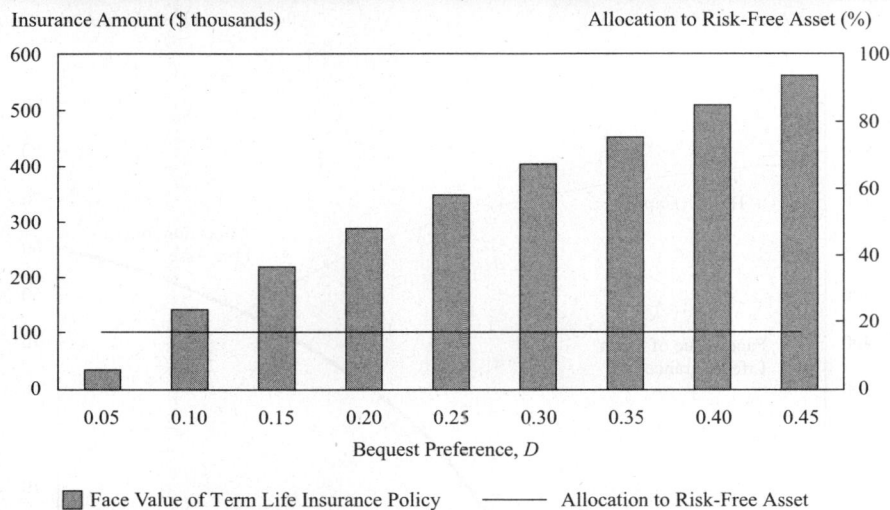

In this case, insurance demand increases as the bequest motive strengthens (i.e., as D gets larger). This result is expected because an investor with a strong bequest motive is highly concerned about her heirs and has an incentive to purchase a large amount of insurance to hedge the loss of human capital. In contrast, Figure 14 shows almost no change in the proportional allocation to the risk-free asset at different strengths of bequest motive. This result indicates that asset allocation is primarily determined by risk tolerance, returns on the risk-free and risky assets, and human capital. This case shows that the bequest motive has a strong effect on insurance demand but little effect on optimal asset allocation.[29]

---

[29] In this model, subjective survival probability and the bequest motive have similar impacts on the optimal insurance need and asset allocation. When subjective survival probability is high, the investor will buy less insurance.

Case #3. The Impact of Risk Tolerance

In this case, we again assume that the investor is age 45 and has accumulated financial wealth of $500,000. The investor has a moderate bequest preference level (i.e., $D = 0.2$). The optimal allocations to the risk-free asset and the optimal insurance demands for this investor for various risk-aversion levels are presented in Figure 15.

Figure 15   Case #3: Optimal Insurance Demand and Allocation to the Risk-Free Asset by Risk-Aversion Level

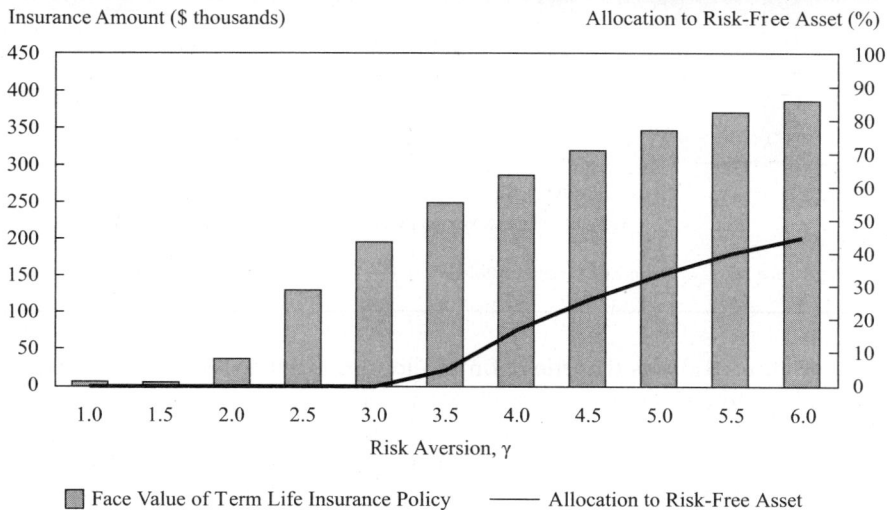

As expected, allocation to the risk-free asset increases with the investor's risk-aversion level—the classic result in financial economics. Actually, the optimal portfolio is 100 percent in stocks for risk-aversion levels less than 2.5. The optimal amount of life insurance follows a similar pattern: Optimal insurance demand increases with risk aversion. For this investor with moderate risk aversion (a CRRA coefficient of 4) and the human and financial assumptions that we have made, optimal insurance demand is about $290,000, which is roughly six times her current income of $50,000.[30] Therefore, conservative investors should invest more in risk-free assets and buy more life insurance than aggressive investors should.

Case #4. Financial Wealth

For this case, we hold the investor's age at 45 and her risk preference and bequest preference at moderate levels (a CRRA coefficient of 4 and bequest level of 0.2). The optimal asset allocation to the risk-free asset and the optimal insurance demands for various levels of financial wealth are presented in Figure 16.

---

30 This result is close to the typical recommendation made by financial planners (i.e., purchase a term life insurance policy that has a face value four to seven times one's current annual income). See, for example, Todd (2004).

Figure 16   Case #4: Optimal Insurance Demand and Allocation to the Risk-Free Asset by Level of Financial Wealth

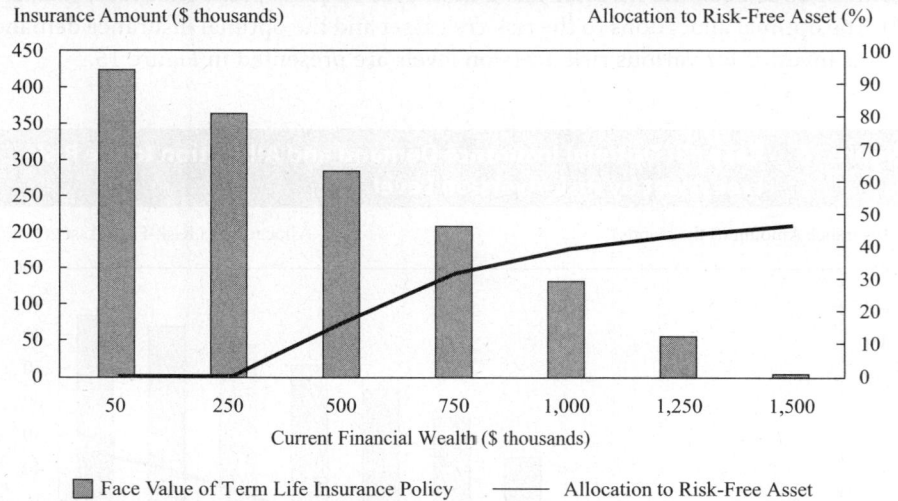

First, Figure 16 shows that the optimal allocation to the risk-free asset increases with initial wealth, which we discussed extensively earlier.

Second, optimal insurance demand decreases with financial wealth. This result can be intuitively explained through the substitution effects of financial wealth and life insurance. In other words, with a large amount of wealth in hand, one has less demand for insurance because the loss of human capital will have much less impact on the well-being of one's heirs. In Figure 16, the optimal amount of life insurance decreases from more than $400,000 when the investor has little financial wealth to almost zero when the investor has $1.5 million in financial assets.

In summary, for an investor whose human capital is less risky than the stock market, the more substantial the investor's financial assets are, the more conservative optimal asset allocation is and the smaller life insurance demand is.

Case #5. Correlation between Wage Growth Rate and Stock Returns

In this case, we want to evaluate the life insurance and asset allocation decisions for investors with a high correlation between the risky asset and the investors' income. This kind of correlation can happen when an investor's income is closely linked to the stock performance of the company where the investor works or when the investor's compensation is highly influenced by the financial market (e.g., the investor works in the financial industry).

Again, the investor's age is 45 and she has a moderate risk preference and bequest preference. Optimal asset allocation to the risk-free asset and insurance demand for various levels of correlations in this situation are presented in Figure 17.

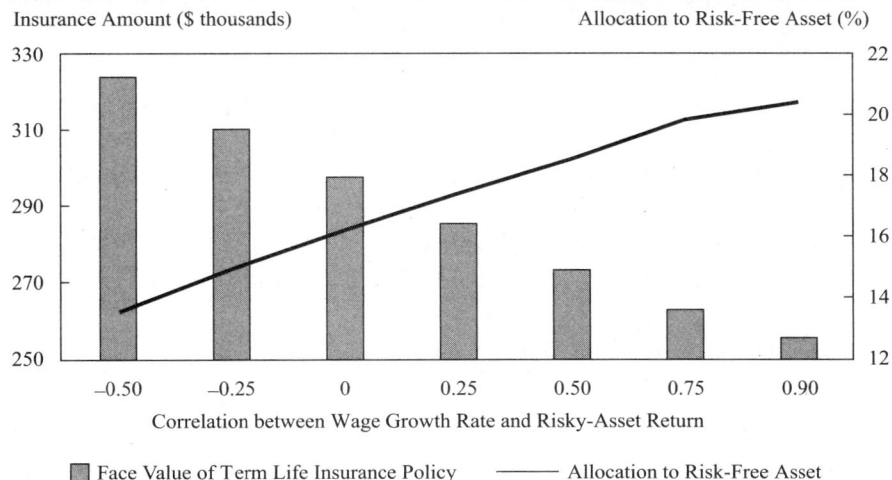

Figure 17   Case #5: Optimal Insurance Demand and Allocation to the Risk-Free Asset by Correlation Level

The optimal allocation becomes more conservative (i.e., more allocation is made to the risk-free asset) as income and stock market return become more correlated, which is similar to the results described earlier in this reading. The optimal insurance demand decreases as the correlation increases. Life insurance is purchased to protect human capital for the family and loved ones. As the correlation between the risky asset and the income flow increases, the *ex ante* value of human capital to the surviving family decreases. This lower valuation on human capital induces a lower demand for insurance. Also, less money spent on life insurance indirectly increases the amount of financial wealth the investor can invest, so the investor can invest more in risk-free assets to reduce the risk associated with her total wealth.[31]

Another way to think about these results is to consider the certainty (or utility) equivalent of risky human capital, which can be thought of as the economic present value of a cash flow stream. The higher the correlation with other financial assets and the higher the volatility of the cash flow stream, the lower the certainty equivalent value and, therefore, the lower the demand for insurance.

In summary, as wage income and stock market returns become more correlated, optimal asset allocation becomes more conservative and the demand for life insurance falls.

SUMMARY

We have expanded on the basic idea that human capital is a "shadow" asset class that is worth much more than financial capital early in life and that it also has unique risk and return characteristics. Human capital—even though it is not traded and is highly illiquid—should be treated as part of a person's endowed wealth that must be protected, diversified, and hedged.

We demonstrated that the correlation between human capital and financial capital (i.e., whether the investor resembles more closely a bond or a stock) has a noticeable and immediate effect on the investor's demand for life insurance—in addition to the

---

31 See Case #3 for a detailed discussion of the wealth impact.

usual portfolio considerations. Our main argument is that the two decisions—quantity of life insurance and asset allocation—cannot be solved in isolation. Rather, they are aspects of the same problem.

We developed a unified human capital-based framework to help individual investors with both decisions. The model provided several key results:

- Investors need to make asset allocation decisions and life insurance decisions jointly.

- The magnitude of human capital, its volatility, and its correlation with other assets significantly affect the two decisions over the life cycle.

- Bequest preferences and a person's subjective survival probability have significant effects on the person's demand for insurance but little influence on the person's optimal asset allocation.

- Conservative investors should invest relatively more in risk-free assets and buy more life insurance.

We presented five case studies to demonstrate the optimal decisions in different scenarios.

3　RETIREMENT PORTFOLIO AND LONGEVITY RISK

Thus far, we have studied human capital and its impact on asset allocation and life insurance decisions for investors in the accumulation stage (i.e., when people are generally saving money prior to retirement). Now we shift our attention to the retirement stage.

In this section, we investigate the risk factors that investors face when making decisions about saving for and investing their retirement portfolios. We illustrate the common mistakes that investors experience when making their asset allocation and spending decisions in retirement. Through the use of Monte Carlo simulation techniques, we illustrate the longevity risk that investors face and the potential benefits of including lifetime-payout annuities in retirement portfolios.

Three Risk Factors in Retirement

A typical investor has two goals in retirement. The primary goal is to ensure a comfortable life style during retirement. In other words, investors would like to enjoy roughly the same life style in retirement that they had before (or a better one). Second, they would like to leave some money behind as a bequest. Three important risks confront individuals when they are making saving and investment decisions for their retirement portfolios: 1) financial market risk, 2) longevity risk, and 3) the risk of not saving enough (spending too much). Part of the third risk is the risk of inflation.

Financial Market Risk

Financial market risk, or volatility in the capital markets, causes portfolio values to fluctuate in the short run even though they may appreciate in the long run. If the market drops or corrections occur early during retirement, the individual's portfolio may not be able to weather the stress of subsequent systematic withdrawals. Then, the portfolio may be unable to generate the income necessary for the individual's desired life style or may simply run out of money before the individual dies.

Investors often ignore financial market risk by assuming a constant rate of return from their retirement portfolio (i.e., no market volatility). As a result, they make inappropriate asset allocations and product selections. For an illustration of the impact of the constant-return assumption, consider the following case. Assume that a 65-year-old investor has $1 million invested in a 60 percent stock/40 percent bond portfolio (hereafter, 60/40).[32] He would like to have $75,000 a year worth of income in retirement. Social Security and his defined-benefit (DB) pension plan will provide about $25,000 of this annual retirement income. Thus, he needs his investment portfolio to generate $50,000 each year from age 65 for the remainder of his life. Assuming that the compounded annual nominal returns for stocks and bonds are, respectively, 9 percent and 5 percent, the estimated average compounded annual nominal return on the portfolio is 7.4 percent. We assume inflation to be 3.0 percent.

Figure 18 shows the wealth and income levels projected for the constant returns in this case.[33] If we assume that the future return is constant, each year the portfolio will generate a 6.14 percent compounded return after expenses and fees, or roughly 3.14 percent after inflation. The $1 million portfolio will be able to sustain a withdrawal of more than $50,000 a year in real terms for the investor's life expectancy and beyond. In other words, with constant returns, the investor will meet his income needs and not run out of money.

Figure 18   Projected Wealth

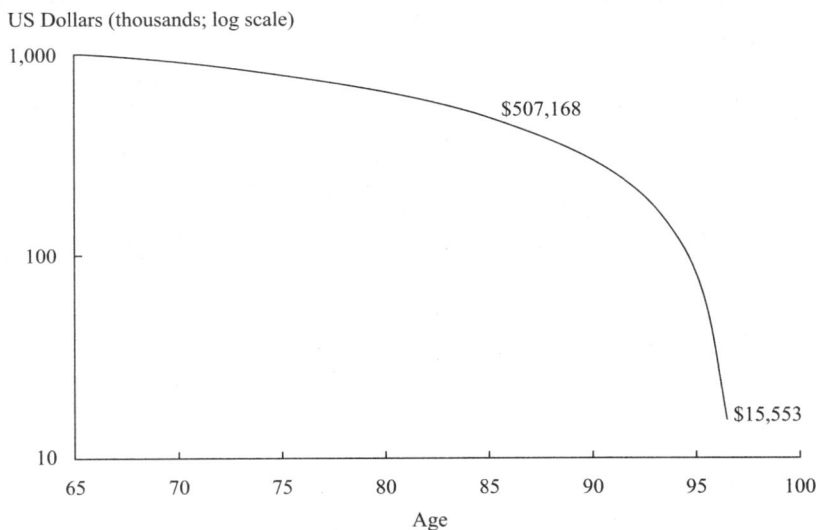

US Dollars (thousands; log scale)

Note: 65-year-old male investor; $1 million; 60/40 portfolio.

Market return, however, is not the same every year. In some periods, the portfolio returns will be much lower than 6.14 percent and may even be negative—as occurred in 2000, 2001, and 2002. So, although 6.14 percent may be a reasonable average assumption, it is unrealistic for the investor to make decisions based purely on the average return. Doing so underestimates the risk, and investors are generally risk averse by nature.

---

32 All dollar amounts presented in this section are in real dollars (i.e., inflation-adjusted amounts).
33 All illustrations in this study are net of fees and expenses. Fee amounts were obtained from Morningstar Principia as of March 2006. They are 1.26 percent for mutual funds and 2.40 percent for variable annuities.

To show the impact of the entire return spectrum, we used a Monte Carlo simulation. Monte Carlo simulation is a technique to evaluate the outcome of portfolios over time by using a large number of simulated possible future return paths. In this case, the returns were randomly generated from a normal distribution with a 6.14 percent compounded average return and a 13 percent standard deviation.[34]

Panel A of Figure 19 presents the Monte Carlo analysis results for the same case used in Figure 18. This analysis shows a 10 percent chance that this portfolio will be depleted by age 82, a 25 percent chance it will be depleted by age 88, and a 50 percent chance it will be depleted by age 95. When considered in light of the uncertain life spans of investors, this result reveals a much larger risk than many investors would accept. Panel B of Figure 19 shows the wealth produced by a nonannuitized 60/40 portfolio plus Social Security and DB plan payments of $25,000 a year.

Figure 19a	Nonannuitized Portfolio: Wealth

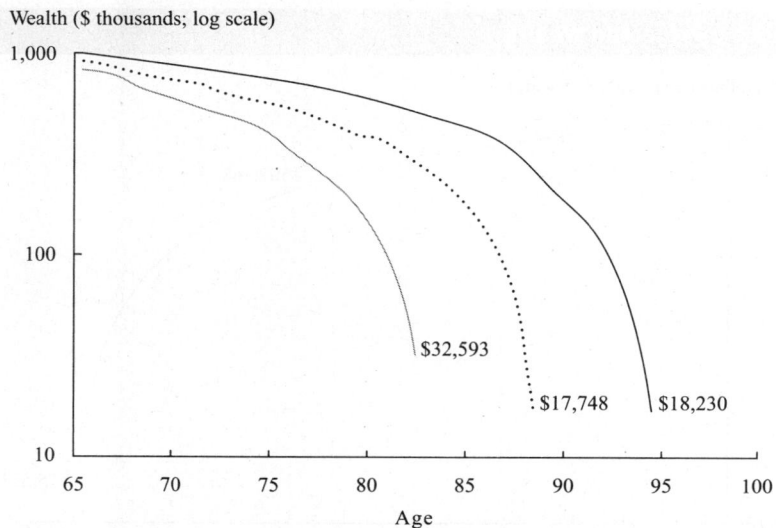

Wealth ($ thousands; log scale)

$32,593

$17,748 $18,230

Age

Figure 19b   Nonannuitized Portfolio: Annual Income

Income ($ thousands)

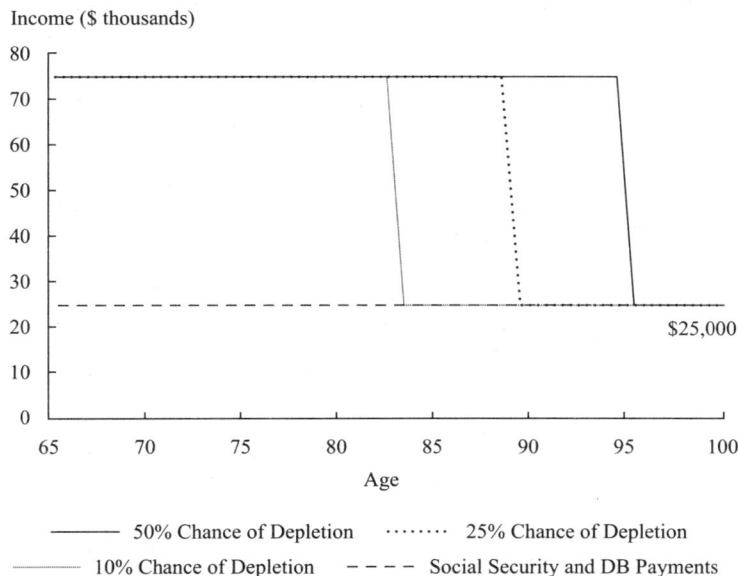

50% Chance of Depletion   .... 25% Chance of Depletion

10% Chance of Depletion   – – – – Social Security and DB Payments

Longevity Risk

Longevity risk is the risk of living longer than planned for and outliving one's assets. With life expectancies continuing to increase, retirees—especially those who retire early or have a family history of long lives—must be aware of the possibility of a long lifetime and adjust their plans accordingly.

Americans are living longer, on average, than ever before. The probability that an individual retiring at age 65 will reach age 80 is greater than 70 percent for females and greater than 62 percent for males. For a married couple, the odds reach nearly 90 percent that at least one spouse will live to age 70. As Figure 4 illustrated, in more than 80 percent of cases, at least one spouse will still be alive at age 85.

Simple retirement planning approaches ignore longevity risk by assuming the investor needs to plan only to age 85. It is true that 85 years is roughly the life expectancy for an individual who is 65 years old, but life expectancy is only the average estimate. Roughly half of investors will live longer than life expectancy. Therefore, investors who have used an 85-year life expectancy to plan their retirement income needs may find they have used up their retirement resources (other than government and corporate pensions) long before actual mortality. This longevity risk is substantial.

Risk of Spending Uncertainty

Investors may not save enough to adequately fund their retirement portfolios. Retirees are increasingly relying on investment income from their own portfolios, such as defined-contribution (DC) plans and individual retirement accounts, to fund their retirements. The ambiguity in this situation is that investors cannot determine exactly what they will earn between now and retirement. Moreover, they may not have the discipline to save adequately.

The evidence is that most investors do not save enough (Benartzi and Thaler 2001). A large proportion of investors do not even fund their 401(k) plans enough to use the match that their employers provide. If an employer provides a 50 percent match, then for each dollar an investor puts into her or his 401(k) plan, the employer puts in 50 cents. This immediate 50 percent "return" should not be given up by any rational employee, but it often is.

Although most savings can generate only normal capital market returns, savings are critical to meet retirement needs. To expect investment returns to compensate for a savings shortfall is not reasonable. To the contrary, investment returns allow the savings to multiply several times over the course of a retirement.

Controlling the Three Risks

Financial risk can be mitigated by using modern portfolio theory, which provides methods to reduce portfolio risk by capturing the long-term diversification benefits among investments. Insurance products can hedge away longevity risk. The risk of inadequate savings is primarily a behavioral issue.

For financial market risk, investors can turn to the rich literature and models of modern portfolio theory. Although financial market risk cannot be completely eliminated, investors can take advantage of the benefits of diversifying among various investments by following long-term asset allocation policies. The Markowitz mean–variance model is widely accepted as the gold standard for asset allocation.

Mean–variance optimization is a first step, but it considers only the risk and return trade-off in the financial market. It does not consider the longevity risk that people face during retirement.

DB pension plans provide longevity insurance by supplying their plan participants with income that cannot be outlived. In many cases, this income is also adjusted for inflation, which provides a further hedge against unexpected shocks to inflation. Fewer and fewer US workers, however, are being covered by DB plans.

Because living a long life means needing more resources to fund longer-term income needs, rational investors will have to turn to sources other than DB plans. One approach is to take on more financial risk, if the investor can tolerate the risk, in the hopes of gaining more return. This plan can be accomplished by selecting an aggressive asset allocation policy (typically by using more stocks than the usual 60 percent and/or by adding higher-risk assets, such as hedge funds).

Rational investors will also want to hedge away the financial aspect of longevity risk because this type of risk exposure offers no potential reward.[35] In other words, investors should be willing to pay an insurance premium to hedge away the longevity risk. This approach is similar to the concept of homeowner insurance, which protects against hazard to one's home. Lifetime annuities (payout annuities) provide investors with this type of longevity insurance. And lifetime annuities should be an integral part of many retirement plans precisely because of the real and substantial longevity risk—which should be treated just as seriously as the risks of disability, critical illness, and premature death.

Recently, behavioral economists have developed some innovative ways to help investors overcome the myopic behavior of spending today instead of saving for retirement. For example, Thaler and Benartzi (2004) pioneered the "Save More Tomorrow" (SMarT) program. SMarT takes advantage of the behavioral theory that people heavily weight current consumption over future (retirement) consumption. The program encourages workers to save some portion of their future *raises*, not their current income, in their 401(k) plans. In this plan, when they receive their raises, their savings rates go up but they still get to take home part of the extra compensation for immediate consumption. The plan is palatable because raises are in the future and people are less averse to trading future consumption for savings than to trading current consumption in order to save.

---

35 Living a long life is desirable, of course, from many aspects; we are focusing here only on the financial aspect of longevity.

Longevity Risk and Sources of Retirement Income

Social Security, DB pension plans, and personal savings (including DC savings) are the main sources of retirement income for Americans. In this section, we look closely at the effectiveness of various sources in managing longevity risk.

Social Security and DB Pension Plans

Traditionally, Social Security and DB pension plans have provided the bulk of retirement income. For example, the US Social Security Administration has reported that 39 percent of the income of persons 65 and older came from Social Security income in 2001 and 18 percent came from DB pensions (see GAO 2003). According to Employee Benefit Research Institute reports, current retirees receive about 60 percent of their retirement income from Social Security and traditional company pension plans, whereas today's workers can expect to have only about one-third of their retirement income funded by these sources (EBRI 2000).

Longevity insurance is embedded in US government-funded Social Security and DB pension benefits because the benefits are paid out for as long as the beneficiary (and, typically, the beneficiary's spouse) lives. In DB pension plans, the employer (as plan sponsor) agrees to make future payments during retirement and is responsible for investing and managing the pension plan assets, thus bearing the investment and longevity risks. Because a DB pension plan typically covers a large number of employees, the overall longevity risk of the plan is significantly mitigated for the employer.

In the past two decades, a shift has been going on from DB plans to DC plans.[36] Over the past 20 years, the percentage of private-sector workers who participate in a DB plan has decreased and the percentage of such workers who participate in a DC plan has consistently increased. Today, the majority of active retirement plan participants are in DC plans, whereas most plan participants were in DB plans 20–30 years ago.

DC Plans and Other Personal Savings

Because workers increasingly must rely on their DC retirement portfolios and other personal savings as their primary sources of retirement income, workers must now bear longevity risk. DC plans contain no promise by an employer or the government that money will be available during retirement.

In addition to being exposed to longevity risk as never before, today's workers who are saving for retirement through DC plans have to manage this risk themselves. Personal savings are used to fund retirement income in two ways. First, a retiree may receive a lump sum directly from the plan as a cash settlement and then invest and withdraw from the portfolio during retirement. This plan is typically referred to as a "systematic withdrawal strategy." Second, a retiree may receive a lump sum and preserve the assets by purchasing a lifetime annuity with some or all of the proceeds to provide a stream of income throughout retirement. This plan is typically referred to as "annuitization."

Annuitization and systematic withdrawals (from an invested portfolio) have different advantages and risks for retirees. A life annuity, whether received from an employer-sponsored pension plan or purchased directly through an insurance company, ensures that a retiree will not run out of income no matter how long he or she lives. If a retiree dies soon after purchasing an annuity, however, he or she will have received considerably less than the lump sum a systematic withdrawal strategy

---

36 The US Department of Labor has reported that private-sector employers sponsored only approximately 56,000 tax-qualified DB plans in 1998, down from more than 139,000 in 1979. The number of tax-qualified DC plans sponsored by private employers more than doubled over the same period—from approximately 331,000 to approximately 674,000 (see GAO 2003).

would provide. With payout annuities, the investor will also be unable to leave that asset as a bequest, and the income from the annuity may not be adequate to pay for unexpected large expenses.

Retiring participants who systematically withdraw lump sums have the flexibility of preserving or drawing down those assets as they wish, but they risk running out of assets if they live longer than expected, if assets are withdrawn too rapidly, or if the portfolio suffers poor investment returns. Payout annuities offer a means to mitigate much of the financial uncertainty that accompanies living to a very old age but may not necessarily be the best approach for all retirees. For example, an individual with a life-shortening illness might not be concerned about the financial needs that accompany living to a very old age.

Longevity Risk and Payout Annuities

Because mean–variance optimization addresses only the risk and return tradeoffs in the financial markets, we focus our attention on the importance of longevity insurance. We touch on the difference between fixed- and variable-payout annuities and then move on to address the proper allocation of retiree income between conventional financial assets and payout annuity products that help to manage longevity risk.

Living a long life means more resources are needed to fund longer-term income needs. On the one hand, rational investors may decide to take on more financial risk in hopes of gaining more return. On the other hand, rational investors would also want to hedge away the financial aspect of longevity risk because there is no potential financial reward for this type of risk exposure. In other words, investors should be willing to pay an insurance premium to hedge away longevity risk. Lifetime-payout annuities provide investors with this type of longevity insurance.

A lifetime-payout annuity is an insurance product that converts an accumulated investment into income that the insurance company pays out over the life of the investor. Payout annuities are the opposite of life insurance. Investors buy life insurance because they are afraid of dying too soon and leaving family and loved ones in financial need. They buy payout annuities because they are concerned about living too long and running out of assets during their lifetime. Insurance companies can provide this lifelong benefit by spreading the longevity risk over a large group of annuitants and making careful and conservative assumptions about the rate of return to be earned on their assets.

Spreading or pooling the longevity risk means that individuals who do not reach their life expectancy (as calculated by actuarial mortality tables) subsidize those who exceed it. Investors who buy lifetime-payout annuities pool their portfolios and collectively ensure that everybody will receive payments as long as they live. Because of the unique longevity insurance features embedded in lifetime-payout annuities, they can play a significant role in many investors' retirement portfolios.

The two basic types of payout annuities are fixed and variable. A fixed-payout annuity pays a fixed nominal dollar amount each period. A variable annuity's payments fluctuate in accord with the performance of the fortunes of the underlying investments chosen by the buyer of the annuity. Payments from a lifetime-payout annuity are contingent on the life span of the investor. Other payout options are available, however, that might guarantee that payments will be made for a specified period of time or might offer refund guarantees.

If an investor buys a life annuity from an insurance company, the investor is transferring the longevity risk to the insurance company, which is in a far better position than an individual to hedge and manage those risks. But of course, the investor pays a price. Should an investor self-insure against longevity risk?

Fixed-Payout Annuity

Figure 20 illustrates the payment stream from an immediate fixed annuity. With an initial premium or purchase amount of $1 million, the annual income payments for our 65-year-old male would be $6,910 a month, or $82,920 a year.[37] The straight line represents the annual payments before inflation. People who enjoy the security of a steady and predictable stream of income may find a fixed annuity appealing. The drawback of a fixed annuity, however, becomes evident over time. Because the payments are the same year after year, purchasing power is eroded by inflation as the annuitant grows older. The curved line in Figure 20 represents the same payment stream after taking into account a hypothetical 3 percent inflation rate.[38] Although the annuitant receives the same payment amount, that payment no longer purchases as much as it used to.

Figure 20   Income from Fixed Annuity

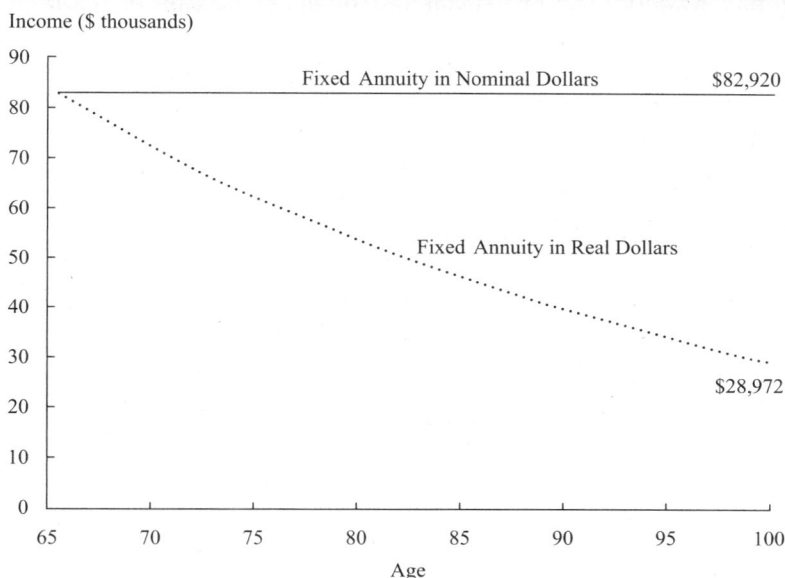

Despite the benefits of longevity insurance and fixed nominal payout amounts, a portfolio that consists solely of fixed lifetime annuities has several drawbacks. First, as noted, is decline in the value of the payments over time because of inflation. Second, one cannot trade out of the fixed-payout annuity once it has been purchased.[39] This aspect may be a problem for investors who need or prefer liquidity. Finally, when an investor buys a fixed annuity, the investor locks in payments based on the current interest rate environment. Payout rates from today's fixed-payout annuities are near historical lows because of current low interest rates. Our 65-year-old male might have received as much as $11,500 a month in the early 1980s in exchange for a $1 million initial premium. In 2003, that same $1 million bought only $6,689 a month. These

---

37 This rate is the quote obtained in July 2006 for a 65-year-old male living in Illinois with $1 million to spend. The quote was obtained from www.immediateannuities.com.
38 The average inflation rate in the United States from 1926 to 2006 was 3.04 percent.
39 Payout annuities are available that do allow the investor to withdraw money from them, but the investor typically has to pay a surrender charge or market value adjustment charge. Furthermore, this flexibility applies only during the period of the annuity when payments are guaranteed regardless of life status.

drawbacks do not mean that fixed annuities are a poor investment choice. On the contrary, as we will show, fixed annuities can be a crucial part of a well-diversified retirement income portfolio.

Variable-Payout Annuities

A variable-payout annuity is an insurance product that exchanges accumulated investment value for annuity units that the insurance company pays out over the lifetime of the investor. The annuity payments fluctuate in value depending on the investments held; therefore, disbursements also fluctuate. To understand variable-payout annuities, think of a mutual fund whose current net asset value (NAV) is $1 per unit. The unit fluctuates each day. On any given day in any given week, month, or year, the price may increase or decrease relative to the previous period. With a variable annuity, instead of receiving fixed annuity payments, the investor receives a fixed number of fund units. Each month, the insurance company converts the fund units into dollars based on the NAV at the end of the month to determine how much to pay the investor. Therefore, the cash flow from the variable-payout annuity fluctuates with the performance of the funds the investor chooses.

Figure 21 illustrates the annuity payment stream, in real terms, from a 60/40 portfolio and a life-only payment option in an immediate variable annuity. We conducted a Monte Carlo simulation to illustrate the various payment scenarios. The simulation was generated for the case of the same investor discussed earlier from historical return statistics for stocks, bonds, and inflation for 1926–2006; a $1 million initial portfolio; and a 3 percent assumed investment return (AIR).[40] The initial payment at age 65 is estimated to be $66,153 a year.[41] The three lines in the chart show the 10th, 25th, and 50th percentiles. As Figure 21 demonstrates, there is a 10 percent chance that annual inflation-adjusted annuity payments will fall below $17,300 if the investor reaches 100, a 25 percent chance that they will be around $32,000 or lower, and a 50 percent chance that they will fall below $57,000.

---

[40] The AIR is an initial interest rate assumption that is used to compute the amount of an initial variable annuity payment. Subsequent payments will either increase or decrease depending on the relationship of the AIR to the actual investment return.

[41] All initial payments for immediate payout annuities were obtained from www.immediateannuity.com on 12 June 2005 for an assumed 65-year-old female living in Illinois and a $100,000 premium.

Figure 21   Income from 100 Percent Immediate Variable Annuity

Income ($ thousands)

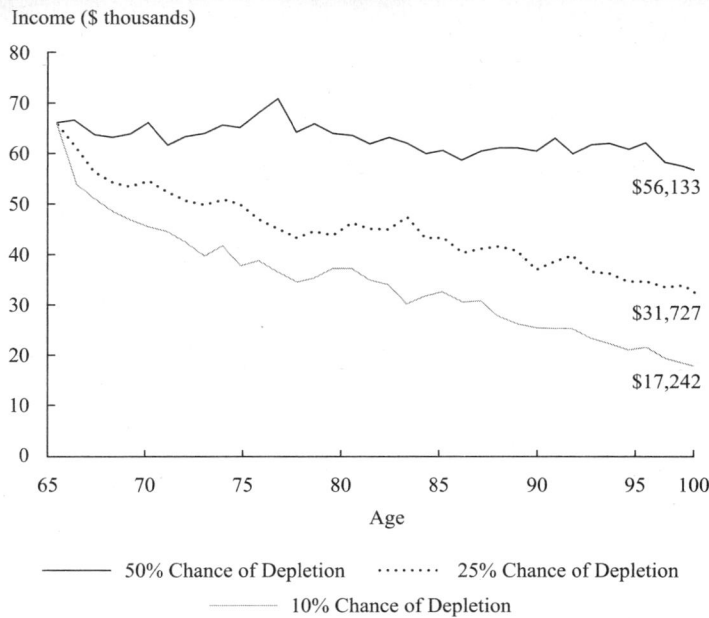

50% Chance of Depletion ········ 25% Chance of Depletion
10% Chance of Depletion

Asset Allocation, Payout Annuities, and Disciplined Savings

Figure 22 shows the probability of success for two retirement income strategies—one using 100 percent systematic withdrawal from a 60/40 portfolio without any lifetime annuity (as depicted in Figure 18) and a second strategy using a payout annuity (25 percent fixed annuitization, 25 percent variable annuitization) and 50 percent systematic withdrawal from the same 60/40 portfolio. The systematic withdrawal strategy with no annuity has a higher risk of causing the portfolio to fall short of funding the required income need. The probability of success begins to drop before age 80 and falls to a low of 42 percent by age 100. The combination strategy is a far better strategy for increasing the odds of meeting income goals over this investor's lifetime. Although the probability of not being able to meet the income goal 100 percent of the time remains, the shortfall comes at a later stage in life and the success rate remains the highest.

Figure 22   Probability of Meeting Income Goal: Payout Annuities vs. Systematic Withdrawal

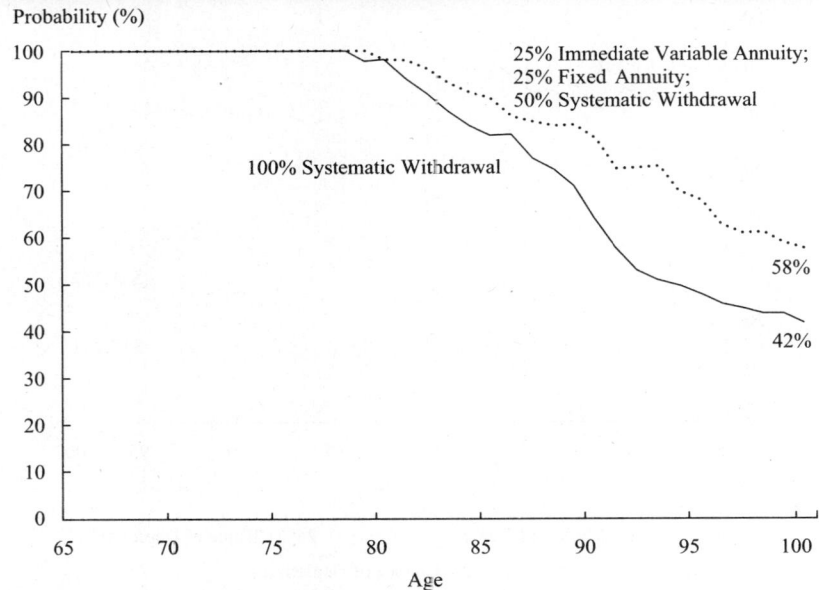

For retirees, such a combination of types of annuitization and systematic withdrawal could help manage the financial risks and the income needs they face during retirement.

SUMMARY

In this section, we presented the three risk factors that investors face when making retirement portfolio decisions: financial market risk, longevity risk, and the risk of spending too much (which includes inflation risk). We focused on the role that lifetime-payout annuities should play in a retirement portfolio to alleviate both financial market and longevity risks. First, we demonstrated that traditional wealth-forecasting techniques that use a constant-return assumption can lead investors to believe they face little or no risk in funding retirement income needs. We then used a Monte Carlo simulation to illustrate more realistically the market risks in systematic withdrawal from a mutual fund portfolio, and we compared the results of withdrawal strategies with the benefits of payout annuities. Our analysis made clear that combining immediate fixed and variable life annuities with conventional investment instruments, such as mutual funds, is the optimal solution to providing retirement income.

This section demonstrated that an immediate payout annuity is an effective way to manage longevity risk in retirement. Buying a lifetime-payout annuitization is not, however, an all-or-nothing decision; the investor can choose how much to allocate between mutual fund accounts and annuitization. Combining nonannuitized assets with annuitized assets can help investors manage financial market risk, longevity risk, and bequest desires.

PRACTICE PROBLEMS

The following information relates to Questions 1–4

1 Michael Smith, CFA, a financial advisor to several working professionals, gave a guest lecture on the analysis of human and financial capital as well as the important role human capital plays in a well-diversified investment portfolio. After the lecture, one of the students asked Smith to summarize the primary concepts.

Compare human capital with financial capital, and **explain** how to apply human capital to the construction of a well-diversified investment portfolio.

2 Smith is utilizing the following capital market return assumptions in his recommendations to his clients:

Asset	Compounded Annual Return	Standard Deviation (Risk)
AAA-rated government bonds	5%	---
Stocks	9%	20%

Smith is the financial advisor to Nancy Johnson and Michael Wu. Johnson is a 35-year old professor with a stable and secure annual income of $175,000. Wu is a 35-year old stockbroker with an income that averages $175,000 per annum and is highly correlated to risky asset returns. Johnson and Wu have comparable total wealth and exhibit moderate risk tolerance.

Recommend which of the following portfolio construction strategies are optimal for Johnson and Wu and **justify** the selections.

Allocation	Strategy A	Strategy B	Strategy C	Strategy D	Strategy E
Stocks	100%	80%	65%	20%	0%
AAA-rated government bonds	0%	20%	35%	80%	100%

3 Smith is the financial advisor to Steve Hernandez and Michael Lee. Hernandez is a 35-year old physician with an annual income of $200,000 and financial wealth of $250,000. Hernandez's financial wealth is expected to significantly increase to $1,000,000 over the next 2 months due to an inheritance. Michael Lee is a 35-year old equity trader with an average annual income of $200,000. Lee's income exhibits a 0.90 correlation to the performance of the S&P 500.

Recommend which of the following portfolio construction strategies are optimal for Hernandez and Lee and **justify** the selections.

Allocation	Strategy A	Strategy B	Strategy C	Strategy D	Strategy E
Stocks	100%	80%	65%	20%	0%
AAA-rated government bonds	0%	20%	35%	80%	100%

4   Smith is also the financial advisor to Mike Sanchez. Sanchez is a 40-year old corporate executive who wishes to leave a $1,000,000 bequest to each of his four children. His real annual income averages $200,000, and he saves 10% each year. He expects to receive pension payments equivalent to $50,000 current dollars each year when he retires at age 65. His current financial wealth is $1,500,000. Smith has concluded that Sanchez exhibits moderate risk aversion and has income that is moderately correlated with risky asset returns. Smith is contemplating making a recommendation for the purchase of life insurance to hedge against mortality risk. Smith recently gave a speech on high net worth investors' bequest motivation. During the speech, a member of the audience commented that she would recommend an increase in the purchase of risk-free assets as an investor's bequest motivation increases.

   i. **Discuss** how the ratio of financial to human capital changes as Sanchez approaches retirement.

   ii. **Explain** the change in Sanchez' demand for life insurance as he approaches retirement.

   iii. **Explain** the impact of the bequest motive and risk tolerance level on Sanchez' demand for life insurance.

   iv. **Evaluate** the recommendation of the audience member.

The following information relates to Questions 5–11

Max and Jan Sampson recently hired Jacob A. Depuy, CFA, a private wealth advisor at Sigma Ridge Investment Counselors, for financial advice. Specifically, the Sampsons have asked Depuy for a financial plan and for specific recommendations on how to best save for retirement, grow their current wealth, protect the remaining spouse should the other spouse fall ill or pass away, and leave an inheritance for their only son, Tom Sampson. For the purposes of this discussion, taxes are not considered. During an extensive introductory meeting, the Sampsons provided Depuy with the following information about their personal background and financial affairs:

   Comment 1   Max Sampson owns a small food distribution business that he started at age 18. Max is now 52 years old and spends all of his professional time involved in the distribution business. Max collects an annual salary of $75,000 per year, before taxes.

   Comment 2   The food distribution business was recently valued at $1,000,000 and is projected to increase in value by approximately 10% per year until retirement, at which point Max plans to sell the business to meet their future income needs.

Comment 3   Jan Sampson is a tenured professor at a local university. Jan is also 52 years old and collects an annual salary of $85,000 per year, before taxes.

Comment 4   Tom Sampson is 23 years old. Tom recently graduated with a degree in finance and just started a career in the financial services industry as a stockbroker. Tom collects an annual base salary of $35,000 per year, before taxes and does not plan to join the family food distribution business Max has requested that Depuy provide separate financial advice to Tom, based on Tom's individual circumstances. Tom is the sole heir of Max and Jan and he will receive an inheritance of their remaining assets.

Comment 5   Max and Jan plan to retire when they turn age 65. To date, they have collectively saved $400,000 which is invested in stocks. Jan will receive a monthly payment from her university's defined benefit plan at the time of her retirement. The payment will adjust with inflation.

Depuy also recorded the following notes while meeting with the Sampsons:

Note 1   Max stated that his investment risk tolerance is "moderately high."

Note 2   Max asked Depuy: "Beyond simply getting older, how can Jan and I lower our need to purchase life insurance?"

Note 3   Max also asked Depuy to explain the relationship between his job and term life insurance.

Note 4   Tom mentioned that he would like to follow in his mother's career path and eventually become a tenured finance professor.

Note 5   Jan stated that "Max and I are concerned about outliving our assets and running out of income to fund our retirement needs."

5   Taking into consideration Comments 1, 2 and 5 and Note 5, Depuy is *most likely* to recommend that Max and Jan increase their exposure to:

A   risky assets.

B   risk-free assets.

C   lifetime income instruments.

6   Taking into consideration only Comment 4, Depuy is *most likely* to recommend which of the following investments to Tom?

A   Bonds

B   Equities

C   Life insurance

7   Taking into consideration Comment 5, Depuy is *most likely* to consider Jan's human capital and retirement arrangement as having the properties of:

A   a fixed income bond.

B   a money market fund.

C   Treasury Inflation-Protected Securities.

8   Which of the following individuals *most likely* has the greatest exposure to human capital?

A   Max

B   Tom

C   Jan

9 If Tom makes the career change as indicated in Note 4, which of the following asset classes would he *most likely* increase in his overall asset allocation?

   A Bonds

   B Stocks

   C Risk-free assets

10 Which of the following statements is *least likely* to help Depuy answer the question Max asked in Note 3? Tom's job (human capital) and term life insurance:

   A pay off at identical moments.

   B are perfect hedges for each other.

   C provide 100% negative correlation.

11 Holding age constant, which of the following statements is Depuy's *most likely* response to Max's question in Note 2. Jan and Max can reduce their need for life insurance, by decreasing Max's:

   A human capital.

   B financial wealth.

   C investment risk tolerance.

SOLUTIONS

1 An investor's total wealth consists of two components. One is financial capital and the other is human capital. Human capital is defined as the present value of an investor's future labor income. Typically, younger investors have far more human capital than financial capital because they have many years to work and they have had few years to save and accumulate financial wealth. Investors should make sure that their total portfolios (i.e., human capital plus financial capital) are properly diversified. An investor's human capital can be viewed as "stocklike" if both the correlation to the financial markets and its volatility are high. It can be viewed as "bondlike" if both correlation to the financial markets and volatility are low. Initially, for a younger investor, if financial wealth is limited and human capital is "bondlike", it is appropriate to invest financial wealth predominantly in risky assets. As this investor's financial wealth increases relative to human capital (i.e., financial wealth increasingly dominates total wealth), a greater portion of financial wealth should be invested in the risk-free asset. For a younger investor, if financial wealth is limited and human capital is "stocklike", a greater portion of financial wealth should be invested in the risk-free asset. As this investor's financial wealth increases relative to human capital, a greater portion of financial wealth should be invested in the risky asset. With more financial wealth, balance is achieved by allocating a greater proportion to the asset(s) similar to human capital than would be indicated otherwise.

2 Strategy A is optimal for Johnson. In this scenario, Johnson's annual income is stable and secure, so her human capital is similar to a risk-free asset because it is the present value of relatively certain future income. When an investor's human capital is riskless, the investor should invest more in stocks. Given Johnson's age of 35, the optimal allocation to stocks is 100%. Johnson's human capital will decrease and financial capital will increase as she ages. She should gradually reduce the amount invested in stocks and increase the amount invested in the risk free asset over time.

Strategy C is optimal for Wu. There is uncertainty about Wu's annual income because it is highly correlated to risky asset returns. In this situation, he will use his financial assets to balance his human capital risk. Wu will invest a smaller portion of his financial assets in the stock market than would be indicated by his age because he has implicitly invested his human capital in the stock market. Given Wu's age of 35, the optimal allocation is 65% stocks and 35% risk free asset (AAA-rated bonds). A greater portion of his financial wealth will be allocated towards the risk free asset and less towards stocks over time.

3 Strategy C is optimal for Hernandez. The optimal allocation to the risk-free asset increases with initial wealth. Wealth is defined as both financial wealth and human capital. An increase in financial wealth not only increases total wealth but also reduces the percentage of total wealth represented by human capital. In this case, human capital is less risky than the risky asset. When initial wealth is low, human capital dominates total wealth. For a typical investor whose human capital is less risky than the risky asset, the optimal asset allocation is more conservative the more financial assets the investor has.

Strategy B is optimal for Lee. The optimal allocation of financial wealth becomes more weighted towards risk-free assets, than would otherwise be indicated based on age, as income and stock market returns become increasingly correlated. A higher correlation between human capital and the stock market results in less diversification and higher risk for the total portfolio. To reduce this risk, an investor must invest more financial wealth in the risk-free asset. At a 0.90 correlation between Lee's human capital and the stock market, the optimal allocation is 20% to the risk free asset and 80% to stocks. Lee's allocation of 80% to stocks is higher than might be expected given the correlation between his income and the S&P 500 because of behavioral factors. He is an equity trader and is likely to believe he knows stocks and to have a relatively high degree of risk tolerance. Assuming weaker correlations between his income and the S&P 500, the allocation to the risk free asset will be lower and allocation to stocks will be greater.

4   i. Human capital gradually decreases as Sanchez gets older and his remaining number of working years becomes smaller. The amount of his financial capital increases over time as a result of returns to his existing financial wealth and his additional contributions each year. Therefore, the ratio of financial to human capital increases as Sanchez approaches retirement. The allocation to risky assets decreases over time because of the dynamic between human capital and financial wealth.

    ii. Sanchez's demand for life insurance decreases over time. The primary driver of insurance demand is human capital so the decrease in human capital reduces insurance demand. It would not be in the investor's best interest to increase the amount of life insurance as he gets older.

    iii. Insurance demand increases as the bequest motive strengthens. An investor with a strong bequest motive is highly concerned about his heirs and is motivated to purchase insurance to hedge the loss of human capital and to provide a bequest. Insurance demand also increases with risk aversion and the allocation to risk-free assets increases with the investor's risk aversion level. Conservative investors are expected to invest more in risk-free assets and buy more life insurance than aggressive investors.

    iv. The audience member's recommendation is not correct. The bequest motive has a strong effect on insurance demand but little effect on optimal asset allocation. There is minimal change in the proportional allocation to the risk-free asset at different strengths of bequest motive. The result indicates that asset allocation is primarily driven by risk tolerance, returns on the risk-free and risky assets, and human capital.

5   B is correct. The allocation to risk-free assets should increase. The financial wealth of Jan and Max primarily consists of the food distribution business and stocks. Both of these are risky assets. As such, it would be wise to invest a greater proportion of the assets in risk-free assets. While Jan's human capital is bond-like, Max's human capital is more equity-like due to the relationship with the value of the business. Human capital is a lesser proportion of total wealth than it used to be. Therefore, increasing exposure to risk-free assets makes sense.

6   A is correct. Tom is a stockbroker, which means his human capital is risky and highly correlated with the stock market. As such, he will need to use his financial assets to balance his human capital risk; his human capital is sensitive to the stock market. Young investors with equity-like human capital should be invested predominantly in fixed-income assets. For most investors with long horizons, an all-equity portfolio is optimal. Tom's situation is different than that of most young investors because his financial services exposure means his human capital is highly correlated to the stock market.

7   C is correct. Jan's human capital as a professor and her pension resemble an inflation-adjusted, real-return bond. Treasury Inflation-Protected Securities are a specific form of an inflation-adjusted, real-return bond.

8   B is correct. Tom is the youngest and, though he will receive an inheritance, the amount is uncertain and he has not had time to build up his own financial capital. He has the longest period of earning in front of him and the present value of his future earnings is likely to be large relative to his financial capital. As such, he has the greatest exposure to human capital, in terms of overall asset allocation.

9   B is correct. Tom should increase his exposure to riskier assets. His income will no longer be correlated with financial markets after leaving the financial services industry, and given the greater stability in his income prospects as a professor, he would now have the willingness and capacity to assume more risk in his portfolio.

10   A is correct. In the event of death, term life insurance will pay off but human capital will no longer pay off because the income earner is no longer alive. In this respect, they do not pay off at the same time, and if human capital pays off, term life insurance will not as this means the income earner is still alive and working.

11   A is correct. The primary driver of insurance demand is human capital, so a decrease in human capital reduces insurance demand. The need for life insurance is driven by uncertainty and the magnitude of human capital. Higher human capital increases the need for life insurance.

6

Portfolio Management for Institutional Investors

Broadly defined, institutional investors include defined-benefit pension plans, defined-contribution plans, foundations, endowments, insurance companies, banks, and investment intermediaries. These institutions typically have a well-defined purpose or business model in which their investment portfolio plays a role. Each group faces a unique set of investment objectives and constraints.

The study session begins with an introduction of the concepts and practices important to determining the investment policy statement for an institutional investment management client. The second reading then examines the specific issue of asset/liability management in the context of defined-benefit pension plans. The implications for asset allocation and risk management are relevant, however, for a wide range of institutions that manage assets to fund anticipated liabilities.

READING ASSIGNMENTS

Reading 13	Managing Institutional Investor Portfolios by R. Charles Tschampion, CFA, Laurence B. Siegel, Dean J. Takahashi, and John L. Maginn, CFA
Reading 14	Linking Pension Liabilities to Assets by Aaron Meder, FSA, CFA, and Renato Staub, PhD

Note: The concepts and practices important to institutional investment management appear in many readings throughout the Level III study sessions.

Managing Institutional Investor Portfolios

by R. Charles Tschampion, CFA, Laurence B. Siegel, Dean J. Takahashi, and John L. Maginn, CFA

R. Charles Tschampion, CFA (USA). Laurence B. Siegel is at the CFA Institute Research Foundation (USA). Dean J. Takahashi (USA). John L. Maginn, CFA (USA).

LEARNING OUTCOMES

Mastery	The candidate should be able to:
☐	**a.** contrast a defined-benefit plan to a defined-contribution plan and discuss the advantages and disadvantages of each from the perspectives of the employee and the employer;
☐	**b.** discuss investment objectives and constraints for defined-benefit plans;
☐	**c.** evaluate pension fund risk tolerance when risk is considered from the perspective of the 1) plan surplus, 2) sponsor financial status and profitability, 3) sponsor and pension fund common risk exposures, 4) plan features, and 5) workforce characteristics;
☐	**d.** prepare an investment policy statement for a defined-benefit plan;
☐	**e.** evaluate the risk management considerations in investing pension plan assets;
☐	**f.** prepare an investment policy statement for a participant directed defined-contribution plan;
☐	**g.** discuss hybrid pension plans (e.g., cash balance plans) and employee stock ownership plans;
☐	**h.** distinguish among various types of foundations, with respect to their description, purpose, and source of funds;
☐	**i.** compare the investment objectives and constraints of foundations, endowments, insurance companies, and banks;
☐	**j.** discuss the factors that determine investment policy for pension funds, foundation endowments, life and non-life insurance companies, and banks;
☐	**k.** prepare an investment policy statement for a foundation, an endowment, an insurance company, and a bank;
☐	**l.** contrast investment companies, commodity pools, and hedge funds to other types of institutional investors;

(continued)

Managing Investment Portfolios: A Dynamic Process, Third Edition, John L. Maginn, CFA, Donald L. Tuttle, CFA, Jerald E. Pinto, CFA, and Dennis W. McLeavey, CFA, editors. Copyright © 2007 by CFA Institute.

1   INTRODUCTION

The two broad classes of investors active in capital markets internationally are individual and institutional investors. **Institutional investors** are corporations or other legal entities that ultimately serve as financial intermediaries between individuals and investment markets. Frequently representing large pools of money, institutional investors have attained great importance—in many cases dominance—in financial markets worldwide. Institutional investors have also made important contributions to the advancement of investment knowledge and techniques, spurred by the challenges of effectively managing large amounts of money.

Today, advances in portfolio theory, performance pressures, and an ever-increasing array of new investment instruments surround the institutional portfolio manager and both test and enhance the manager's skills. As the manager meets these challenges and pressures, he or she should reflect that behind all investment portfolios lie "flesh and blood" individuals whose financial wellbeing is affected by the manager's actions. News reports remind us that ethical lapses occur with serious consequences for both clients and errant portfolio managers. The client's interests must come first. Ethical conduct is the fundamental requirement for managing an institutional or any other type of portfolio.

This reading presents the portfolio management process from the perspective of five different groups of institutional investors: pension funds, foundations, endowments, insurance companies, and banks. These five classes cover a wide spectrum of investment policy considerations and are well suited to illustrating the challenges and complexity of the institutional portfolio manager's tasks.

We have organized this reading as follows. In Section 2 we present the background and investment setting of pension funds, which fall into two main types: defined benefit and defined contribution. For each of these types of pensions, we discuss the elements of formulating an investment policy statement (IPS)—the governing document for all investment decision-making. We follow the same pattern of presentation for foundations and endowments in Section 3, insurance companies in Section 4, and banks in Section 5. The final section summarizes the reading.

2   PENSION FUNDS

Pension funds contain assets that are set aside to support a promise of retirement income. Generally, that promise is made by some enterprise or organization—such as a business, labor union, municipal or state government, or not-for-profit organization—that sets up the pension plan. This organization is referred to as the **plan sponsor**.

Pension plans divide principally into one of two broad types, based on the nature of the promise that was made. They are either defined-benefit (DB) plans or defined-contribution (DC) plans. A **defined-benefit plan** is a pension plan that specifies the plan sponsor's obligations in terms of the benefit to plan participants. In contrast, a **defined-contribution plan** specifies the sponsor's obligations in terms of contributions to the pension fund rather than benefits to plan participants. There are also some hybrid types of plans (or *schemes*, as they often are called outside of North America), such as cash balance plans, that have characteristics of both DB and DC plans. A **cash balance plan** is a defined-benefit plan whose benefits are displayed in individual recordkeeping accounts. These accounts show the participant the current value of his or her accrued benefit and facilitate portability to a new plan.

It is useful to understand the distinctions between DB and DC plans in greater detail. A DB plan sponsor promises the organization's employees or members a retirement income benefit based on certain defined criteria. For example, a worker may be promised that for every year employed by the company, he or she will receive a certain fixed money benefit each month. Alternatively, a plan sponsor might promise to pay a certain percentage of some factor related to the employee's pay (e.g., final year, average of final five years, average of top 5 of last 10 years, etc.). The sponsor might also promise to adjust benefit payments for those already retired in order to reflect price inflation. Additionally, the plan may have a whole list of other plan provisions dealing with early retirement supplements, surviving spouse benefits, and so forth.

All DB plans share one common characteristic: They are promises made by a plan sponsor that generate a future financial obligation or "pension liability." The nature and behavior of this liability is uncertain and often complex; consequently, setting investment policy for DB plans presents unique challenges.

The sponsor's promise for DB plans is made for the retirement stage—what the employee will be able to withdraw. In contrast, the promise for DC plans is made for the current stage—what the plan sponsor will contribute on behalf of the employee. This contribution promise at its most basic might be a fixed percentage of pay that is put into the plan by the employer. Alternatively, it could be a contribution based on a formula tied to the profitability of the sponsor. It could also be a promise to match a certain portion of a participant's own contributions into the plan.

DC plans encompass arrangements that are 1) pension plans, in which the contribution is promised and not the benefit, and 2) **profit-sharing plans**, in which contributions are based, at least in part, on the plan sponsor's profits. We can also classify as DC plans the miscellaneous individual, private business, and governmental tax-advantaged savings plans in which the benefit is not promised and in which participants typically make contributions to the plans (for example, Individual Retirement Accounts, or IRAs). The common elements of all these plans are 1) a contribution is made into an account for each individual participant, 2) those funds are invested over time, 3) the plans are tax-deferred, and 4) upon withdrawal from the plan or reaching retirement, the participants receive the value of the account in either a lump sum or a series of payments.

The key differences between DC and DB plans are as follows:

- For DC plans, because the benefit is not promised, the plan sponsor recognizes no financial liability, in contrast to DB plans.

- DC plan participants bear the risk of investing (i.e., the potential for poor investment results). In contrast, in DB plans the plan sponsor bears this risk (at least in part) because of the sponsor's obligation to pay specified future pension benefits. DB plan participants bear early termination risk: the risk that the DB plan is terminated by the plan sponsor.

- Because DC plan contributions are made for individual participants' benefit, the paid-in contributions and the investment returns they generate legally belong to the DC plan participant.

- Because the records are kept on an individual-account basis, DC plan participants' retirement assets are more readily **portable**—that is, subject to certain rules, vesting schedules, and possible tax penalties and payments, a participant can move his or her share of plan assets to a new plan.[1]

From an investment standpoint, DC plans fall into two types:

- Sponsor directed, whereby much like a DB plan, the sponsor organization chooses the investments. For example, some profit-sharing plans (retirement plans in which contributions are made solely by the employer) are sponsor directed.

- Participant directed, whereby the sponsor provides a menu of diversified investment options and the participants determine their own personalized investment policy. Most DC plans are participant directed.

For a participant-directed DC plan, there is very little the institutional sponsor can do in the context of establishing a single investment policy allocation for the plans. Even for sponsor-directed DC plans, the investment policy is substantially less complex than for DB plans. We thus address DB plans first.

2.1 Defined-Benefit Plans: Background and Investment Setting

Defined-benefit plans have existed for a long time, with the first such corporate arrangement established in the United States by American Express in 1928. Today the incidence of DB plans varies internationally, although in recent years the overall use of DC plans has been increasing. In the United States, private defined-benefit plan assets stood at approximately $2.2 trillion as of the end of 2010. Judging by both the number of plan participants and the aggregate amount of plan assets, however, in the United States DC plans predominate. The increasing dominance of DC plans in the United States has been fueled chiefly by the growth of 401(k) plans in the corporate sector. In the United Kingdom, the DB model traditionally accounted for the majority of private sector schemes; more recently, only about 20 percent of private sector workers are covered by DB plans.[2] Elsewhere in Europe, DB plans continue to follow the basic pension model as well, although DC plans are increasingly accepted. Japanese private pensions are overwhelmingly defined-benefit, although Japanese companies now offer cash balance and DC plans as well.

Pension assets fund the payment of pension benefits (liabilities). Thus a pension plan's investment performance should be judged relative to the adequacy of its assets with respect to funding pension liabilities, even if it is also judged on an absolute basis. Understanding pension liabilities is important for knowledgeably setting investment policy.

The sponsor's plan actuary is a mathematician who has the task of estimating the pension liabilities. In addition to the specifics of defining benefits, the estimation of liabilities also involves projecting future workforce changes, determining wage and

---

1 Transfer of assets from a DB plan may be feasible; if so, it requires an actuary's calculations. For example, in Canada a terminated employee can request that the dollar value of his vested benefits in a DB plan (as determined by an actuary) be transferred to an individual registered retirement plan. In this context, **vested** means owned by the plan participant.

2 See www.pensions-institute.org/workingpapers/wp0821.pdf.

salary growth levels, estimating probabilities of early retirement elections, applying mortality tables, and other factors. The plan actuary's work provides the following key information to the plan sponsor.

First, an actuary will determine the liability's size and how its present value relates to the portfolio's existing asset size. The relationship between the value of a plan's assets and the present value of its liabilities is known as the plan's **funded status**. In a **fully funded plan**, the ratio of plan assets to plan liabilities is 100 percent or greater (a funded status of 100 percent or greater). The **pension surplus** equals pension plan assets at market value minus the present value of pension plan liabilities. In an **underfunded plan**, the ratio of plan assets to plan liabilities is less than 100 percent.

Three basic liability concepts exist for pension plans:

- **Accumulated benefit obligation (ABO).** The ABO is effectively the present value of pension benefits, assuming the plan terminated immediately such that it had to provide retirement income to all beneficiaries for their years of service up to that date (**accumulated service**). The ABO excludes the impact of expected future wage and salary increases.

- **Projected benefit obligation (PBO).** The PBO stops the accumulated service in the same manner as the ABO but projects future compensation increases if the benefits are defined as being tied to a quantity such as final average pay. The PBO thus includes the impact of expected compensation increases and is a reasonable measure of the pension liability for a going concern that does not anticipate terminating its DB plan. Funding status is usually computed with respect to the PBO.

- **Total future liability.** This is the most comprehensive, but most uncertain, measure of pension plan liability. Total future liability can be defined as the present value of accumulated *and* projected future service benefits, including the effects of projected future compensation increases. This financial concept can be executed internally as a basis for setting investment policy.

An actuary's work will also determine the split of the plan liability between retired and active **lives** (employees). This distinction will indicate two important factors:

- Because retirees are currently receiving benefits, the greater the number of retired lives, the greater the cash flows out of the fund each month, and thus the higher the pension fund's liquidity requirement. The portion of a pension fund's liabilities associated with retired workers is the **retired-lives** part; that associated with active workers is the **active-lives** part.

- Because the same mortality table is being applied to both active and retired plan beneficiaries, a plan with a greater percentage of retirees generally has a shorter average life or duration of future pension liabilities.

We now turn to developing the investment policy statement elements for a DB plan.

2.1.1 *Risk Objectives*

In setting a risk objective, plan sponsors must consider plan status, sponsor financial status and profitability, sponsor and pension fund common risk exposures, plan features, and workforce characteristics, as shown in Exhibit 1. (Risk tolerance, to review, is the willingness and ability to bear risk.)

Exhibit 1	Factors Affecting Risk Tolerance and Risk Objectives of DB Plans	
Category	**Variable**	**Explanation**
Plan status	Plan funded status (surplus or deficit)	Higher pension surplus or higher funded status implies greater risk tolerance.
Sponsor financial status and profitability	Debt to total assets Current and expected profitability	Lower debt ratios and higher current and expected profitability imply greater risk tolerance.
Sponsor and pension fund common risk exposures	Correlation of sponsor operating results with pension asset returns	The lower the correlation, the greater risk tolerance, all else equal.
Plan features	Provision for early retirement Provision for lump-sum distributions	Such options tend to reduce the duration of plan liabilities, implying lower risk tolerance, all else equal.
Workforce characteristics	Age of workforce Active lives relative to retired lives	The younger the workforce and the greater the proportion of active lives, the greater the duration of plan liabilities and the greater the risk tolerance.

The points in Exhibit 1 deserve comment. In principle, an overfunded pension plan can experience some level of negative returns without jeopardizing the coverage of plan liabilities by plan assets because the plan surplus acts as a cushion. Thus the sponsor's ability to assume investment risk in the plan increases with funded status, even though it may have no need to do so. An underfunded plan may increase the plan sponsor's willingness to take risk in an attempt to make the plan fully funded; however, all else equal, an underfunded plan has less ability to take risk because a funding shortfall already exists. Consequently, an underfunded plan must de-emphasize its willingness to take risk.

If a plan is not fully funded, the plan sponsor has an obligation to make contributions to the plan. The sponsor's financial strength and profitability can affect the sponsor's ability and willingness to make such contributions when needed. When the sponsor is financially weak, it has a reduced ability to fund shortfalls that might occur from unfavorable investment experience.[3] Further, when the sponsor's operating results are highly correlated with pension asset returns, the size of pension contributions may increase when the sponsor's operating results are weak.

Certain plan provisions may give participants options to speed up the disbursement of benefits, decreasing risk tolerance, all else equal. Older workforces mean shorter duration liabilities and higher liquidity requirements, implying lower risk tolerance in general. Also, for a plan with an older workforce, if the plan becomes underfunded, the company will have less time to generate and make contributions to the plan.

Example 1 illustrates some of these concepts.

---

3 Historically, in some countries such as Germany and the United Kingdom, DB pensions are not set up as separate entities and pension liabilities are set up as book reserves on a company's own balance sheet. In such cases, pension benefits are direct liabilities of the company. However, the European Union prescription that International Accounting Standards be adopted by companies listed within the EU is one of several forces at work reducing national differences.

EXAMPLE 1

Apex Sports Equipment Corporation (1)

George Fletcher, CFA, is chief financial officer of Apex Sports Equipment Corporation (ASEC), a leading producer of winter and water sports gear. ASEC is a small company, and all of its revenues come from the United States. Product demand has been strong in the past few years, although it is highly cyclical. The company has rising earnings and a strong (low debt) balance sheet. ASEC is a relatively young company, and as such its defined-benefit pension plan has no retired employees. This essentially active-lives plan has $100 million in assets and an $8 million surplus in relation to the projected benefit obligation. Several facts concerning the plan follow:

■ The duration of the plan's liabilities (which are all US-based) is 20 years.

■ The discount rate applied to these liabilities is 6 percent.

■ The average age of ASEC's workforce is 39 years.

Based on the information given, discuss ASEC's risk tolerance.

Solution:

ASEC appears to have above average risk tolerance, for the following reasons:

1 The plan has a small surplus (8 percent of plan assets); that is, the plan is overfunded by $8 million.

2 The company's balance sheet is strong (low use of debt).

3 The company is profitable despite operating in a cyclical industry.

4 The average age of its workforce is low.

The primary purpose of DB pension fund assets is to fund the payment of pension liabilities. DB plans share this characteristic with insurance companies and banks, as we shall later see. For all these investors, risk relative to liabilities is important and the asset/liability management (ALM) perspective on risk and on investing more generally is a primary concern. **Asset/liability management** is a subset of a company's overall risk management practice that typically focuses on financial risks created by the interaction of assets and liabilities; for given financial liabilities, asset/liability management involves managing the investment of assets to control relative asset/liability values. For a DB plan, one key ALM concept is the pension surplus, defined as pension assets at market value minus the present value of pension liabilities. DB plans may state a risk objective relative to the level of pension surplus volatility (i.e., standard deviation). Another kind of ALM risk objective relates to shortfall risk with respect to plan liabilities. (**Shortfall risk** is the risk that portfolio value will fall below some minimum acceptable level over some time horizon; it can be stated as a probability.) Shortfall risk may relate to achieving:

■ a funded status of 100 percent (or some other level) with respect to the ABO, PBO, or total future liability;

■ a funded status above some level that will avoid reporting a pension liability on the balance sheet under accounting rules; and

■ a funded status above some regulatory threshold level. Examples (in the United States) include:

- levels under the Employee Retirement Income Security Act (ERISA) that would trigger additional contribution requirements; and

- levels under which the Pension Benefit Guaranty Corporation (PBGC) would require additional premium payments.[4]

Other goals that may influence risk objectives include two that address future pension contributions:

■ Minimize the year-to-year volatility of future contribution payments.

■ Minimize the probability of making future contributions, if the sponsor is currently not making any contributions because the plan is overfunded.

The risk considerations given above interact with each other extensively. For example, for a plan to maintain its funded status, the plan sponsor may need to increase contributions. Prioritizing risk factors is an integral part of establishing the sponsor's risk objectives. In addition to risk objectives relative to liabilities and contributions (which are characteristic of DB investment planning), sponsors may state absolute risk objectives, as with any other type of investing.

EXAMPLE 2

Apex Sports Equipment Corporation (2)

George Fletcher now turns to setting risk objectives for the ASEC pension plan. Because of excellent recent investment results, ASEC has not needed to make a contribution to the pension fund in the two most recent years. Fletcher considers it very important to maintain a plan surplus in relation to PBO. Because an $8 million surplus will be an increasingly small buffer as plan liabilities increase, Fletcher decides that maintaining plan funded status, stated as a ratio of plan assets to PBO at 100 percent or greater, is his top priority.

Based on the above information, state an appropriate type of risk objective for ASEC.

Solution:

An appropriate risk objective for ASEC relates to shortfall risk with respect to the plan's funded status falling below 100 percent. For example, ASEC may want to minimize the probability that funded status falls below 100 percent, or it may want the probability that funded status falls below 100 percent to be less than or equal to 10 percent. Another relevant type of risk objective would be to minimize the probability that ASEC will need to make future contributions.

In summary, plan funded status, sponsor financial status, plan features, and workforce characteristics influence risk tolerance and the setting of risk objectives. The plan sponsor may formulate a specific risk objective in terms of shortfall risk, risk related to contributions, as well as absolute risk.

2.1.2 Return Objectives

A DB pension plan's broad return objective is to achieve returns that adequately fund its pension liabilities on an inflation-adjusted basis. In setting return objectives, the pension sponsor may also specify numerical return objectives. A pension plan must

---

[4] The PBGC is a US government agency that insures the vested DB pension benefits of beneficiaries of terminated DB plans. The premium rates charged by PBGC increase with the insured DB plan's level of unfunded vested benefits.

meet its obligations. For a DB pension plan, the *return requirement* (in the sense of the return the plan needs to achieve on average) depends on a number of factors, including the current funded status of the plan and pension contributions in relation to the accrual of pension benefits. If pension assets equal the present value of pension liabilities and if the rate of return earned on the assets equals the discount rate used to calculate the present value of the liabilities, then pension assets should be exactly sufficient to pay for the liabilities as they mature. Therefore, for a fully funded pension plan, the portfolio manager should determine the return requirement beginning with the discount rate used to calculate the present value of plan liabilities.[5] That discount rate may be a long-term government bond yield, for example. The pension fund's stated return desire may be higher than its return requirement, in some cases reflecting concerns about future pension contributions or pension income:

- **Return objectives relating to future pension contributions.** The natural ambitious or "stretch target" of any DB plan sponsor is to make future pension contributions equal zero. A more realistic objective for most is to minimize the amount of future pension contributions, expressed either on an undiscounted or discounted basis.

- **Return objectives related to pension income.** Both US Generally Accepted Accounting Principles (GAAP) and International Accounting Standards (IAS) incorporate accounting rules that address the recognition of pension expense in the corporate plan sponsor's income statement. The rules are symmetrical—that is, a well-funded plan can be in a position of generating negative pension expense, i.e. pension income. In periods of strong financial market performance, a substantial number of corporations will have pension income that is a measurable portion of total net income reported on the corporate plan sponsor's income statement. A sponsor in this position may have an objective of maintaining or increasing pension income.[6]

Just as risk tolerance increases with the duration of plan liabilities, in general, so may the stated return desire—within realistic limits. For example, if the plan has a young and growing workforce, the sponsor may set a more aggressive return objective than it would for a plan that is currently closed to new participants and facing heavy liquidity requirements.

It is worth noting that pension plan sponsors may manage investments for the active-lives portion of pension liabilities according to risk and return objectives that are distinct from those they specify for the retired-lives portion. Retired-lives benefits may be fixed in nominal terms—for example, based on a worker's final wages. For assets associated with such liabilities, return and risk objectives may be more conservative than for assets associated with liabilities for active lives, because active-lives liabilities will grow with inflation.

---

5 See Scanlon and Lyons (2006) for a detailed discussion of current issues related to return requirements.
6 In considering whether to adopt this as an objective, however, a plan sponsor must recognize that pension income is based on the *expected* future return on pension assets. Many analysts exclude pension income from measures of core or underlying earnings.

EXAMPLE 3

Apex Sports Equipment Corporation (3)

George Fletcher now addresses setting return objectives for ASEC. Because the plan is fully funded, Fletcher is proposing a return objective of 7.5 percent for the plan. Referring to the information in Examples 1 and 2, as well as to the above facts, answer the following questions.

1 State ASEC's return requirement.

2 State one purpose Fletcher might have in proposing a desired return of 7.5 percent.

3 Create and justify the return objective element of an investment policy statement for the ASEC pension plan.

Solution to 1:

The discount rate applied to finding the present value of plan liabilities is 6 percent. This discount rate is ASEC's return requirement.

Solution to 2:

Besides meeting pension obligations, Fletcher may have one of the following objectives in mind:

■ To minimize ASEC's future pension contributions.

■ To generate pension income (negative pension expense).

Solution to 3:

A statement such as the following is appropriate:

Return objectives

The primary return objective for the ASEC pension plan is to achieve a total return sufficient to fund its liabilities on an inflation-adjusted basis. The ASEC pension plan has a long-term growth orientation, with a total return objective of 7.5 percent per year.

Justification

In formulating a return objective for this essentially active-lives fund, considerations include:

■ The return requirement is 6 percent. The objectives are consistent with achieving at least this level of return and with meeting pension liabilities.

■ Because the plan has a long duration, little need for immediate liquidity, and a fully funded status, and because the sponsor's financial strength and profitability are strong, ASEC has above-average risk tolerance and can adopt an aggressive return objective. Thus a long-term growth orientation with a focus on capital appreciation, as well as a specific objective of 7.5 percent, appears to be appropriate.

In the next sections, we address the five broad categories of constraints.

2.1.3 Liquidity Requirement

A DB pension fund receives pension contributions from its sponsor and disburses benefits to retirees. The net cash outflow (benefit payments minus pension contributions) constitutes the pension's plan liquidity requirement. For example, a pension fund paying $100 million per month in benefits on an asset base of $15 billion, and receiving no sponsor pension contribution, would have an annual liquidity requirement of 8 percent of plan assets. During the year, the asset base would need to grow to $16.2 billion in order to meet the payout requirement without eroding the capital base. The following issues affect DB plans' liquidity requirement:

- The greater the number of retired lives, the greater the liquidity requirement, all else equal. As one example, a company operating in a declining industry may have a growing retired-lives portion placing increasing liquidity requirements on the plan.

- The smaller the corporate contributions in relation to benefit disbursements, the greater the liquidity requirement. The need to make contributions depends on the funded status of the plan. For plan sponsors that need to make regular contributions, young, growing workforces generally mean smaller liquidity requirements than older, declining workforces.

- Plan features such as the option to take early retirement and/or the option of retirees to take lump-sum payments create potentially higher liquidity needs.

EXAMPLE 4

Apex Sports Equipment Corporation (4)

Recall the following information from Example 1. ASEC is a relatively young company, and as such its defined-benefit pension plan has no retired employees. This essentially active-lives plan has $100 million in assets and an $8 million surplus in relation to the PBO. Several facts concerning the plan follow:

- The duration of the plan's liabilities (which are all US-based) is 20 years;
- The discount rate applied to these liabilities is 6 percent; and
- The average age of the workforce is 39 years.

Because of excellent recent investment results, ASEC has not needed to make a contribution to the pension fund in the most recent two years.

Based on the above information, characterize ASEC's current liquidity requirement.

Solution:

ASEC currently has no retired employees and is not making pension contributions into the fund, but it has no disbursements to cover. Thus, ASEC has had no liquidity requirements recently. Given that the average age of ASEC's workforce is 39 years, liquidity needs appear to be small for the near term as well.

When a pension fund has substantial liquidity requirements, it may hold a buffer of cash or money market instruments to meet such needs. A pension fund with a cash balance can gain equity market exposure by holding stock index futures contracts, or bond market exposure by holding bond futures, if it desires.

2.1.4 Time Horizon

The investment time horizon for a DB plan depends on the following factors:

- whether the plan is a going concern or plan termination is expected; and
- the age of the workforce and the proportion of active lives. When the workforce is young and active lives predominate, and when the DB plan is open to new entrants, the plan's time horizon is longer.

The overall time horizon for many going-concern DB plans is long. However, the horizon can also be multistage: for the active-lives portion the time horizon is the average time to the normal retirement age, while for the retired-lives portion, it is a function of the average life expectancy of retired plan beneficiaries.

EXAMPLE 5

Apex Sports Equipment Corporation (5)

Based on the information from Example 4, characterize the time horizon for ASEC's pension plan.

Solution:

On average, the plan participants are 39 years old and the duration of plan liabilities is 20 years. The "time to maturity" of the corporate workforce is a key strategic element for any DB pension plan. Having a younger workforce often means that the plan has a longer investment horizon and more time available for wealth compounding to occur. These factors justify ASEC adopting a relatively long time horizon for as long as ASEC remains a viable going concern.

2.1.5 *Tax Concerns*

Investment income and realized capital gains within private defined-benefit pension plans are usually exempt from taxation. Thus investment planning decisions at the level of the plan itself can generally be made without regard to taxes. Although corporate contribution planning involves tax issues, as do plan terminations and the form of distributions to beneficiaries, defined-benefit pension fund investment planning usually does not. However, Example 6 illustrates a case in which tax considerations do arise.

EXAMPLE 6

Taxation and Return Objectives

In 1997, the UK government abolished a rule that had allowed pension funds to receive dividends gross of tax (that is, tax free). Discuss the probable impact of the change on the prior return objectives of pension funds, given that pension schemes often invest in dividend-paying ordinary shares.

Solution:

Total return on ordinary shares is the sum of capital appreciation and dividend yield. After the rule change, the after-tax total return became less than pretax total return for dividend-paying shares, so a given prior (pretax) return target became less effective at the margin in funding liabilities.

2.1.6 *Legal and Regulatory Factors*

All retirement plans are governed by laws and regulations that affect investment policy. Virtually every country that allows or provides for separate portfolio funding of pension schemes imposes some sort of regulatory framework on the fund or plan structure. In the United States, corporate plans and multi-employer plans are governed by the Employee Retirement Income Security Act of 1974 (ERISA), although state and local government plans as well as union plans are not. State and local government plans are subject to state law and regulations that can differ from each other and also from ERISA. In the United States, union plans are subject to regulation under the

Taft–Hartley Labor Act. An important attribute of ERISA is that it preempts state and local law, so that those plans that are subject to it must deal with only a single body of regulation. Both ERISA and state law and regulations generally specify standards of care that pension plan sponsors must meet in making investment decisions.

A pension plan trustee is an example of a **fiduciary**, a person standing in a special relation of trust and responsibility with respect to other parties (from the Latin word *fiducia*, meaning trust). A trustee is legally responsible for ensuring that assets are managed solely in the interests of beneficiaries (for a pension, the pension plan participants). Depending on legal jurisdiction, fiduciaries are subject to various legal standards of care as they execute their responsibilities. Beneficiaries may attempt to recover their losses from fiduciaries that fail to meet appropriate standards of care.

In Canada, pension funds are regulated at the provincial level, but the Ontario Pension Commission has arguably set the standard with an ERISA-like body of regulation. In the United Kingdom, recent years have seen the work of blue ribbon panels such as the Free Commission and the Myner Commission become standards for guiding investment policy. European countries such as the Netherlands; Asia-Pacific nations including Australia, Japan, and Singapore; and Latin American countries such as Brazil, Chile, and Mexico are examples of countries having regulatory frameworks for employee pension and savings plans.

Historically in some major developed markets, the pension plan structure does not involve having to deal with investment policy issues. For example, France has a state-run scheme requiring plan sponsor organizations to contribute. But apart from the countries where funded plans are not used, it is important for the institutional practitioner to understand and apply the law and regulations of the entity having jurisdiction when developing investment policy.

2.1.7 *Unique Circumstances*

Although we cannot make general statements about unique circumstances, one constraint that smaller pension plans sometimes face relates to the human and financial resources available to the plan sponsor. In particular, investment in alternative investments (for example, private equity, hedge funds, and natural resources) often requires complex due diligence. (**Due diligence** refers to investigation and analysis in support of an investment action or recommendation; failure to exercise due diligence may sometimes result in liability according to various laws.)

Another unique circumstance for a plan might be a self-imposed constraint against investing in certain industries viewed as having negative ethical or welfare connotations, or in shares of companies operating in countries with regimes against which some ethical objection has been raised. Such ethical investment considerations have played a role in the investment policy of many public employee pension plans and some private company and union pension plans. Australian and several European regulators require that pension funds disclose whether they include ethical criteria in their decision-making processes. In the United Kingdom, such legislation (imposed in 1999) contributed significantly to the growth of socially responsible investing in pension plans.

To conclude, Example 7 shows how Apex Sports Equipment might formulate an investment policy statement that incorporates the analysis in Examples 1 through 5.

EXAMPLE 7

Apex Sports Equipment Corporation Defined-Benefit Plan Investment Policy Statement

Apex Sports Equipment Corporation (the "Company") operates in the recreation industry. The Company sponsors the Apex Sports Equipment Corporation Pension Plan (the "Plan"), the purpose of which is to accumulate assets in order to fund the obligations of the Plan. The Plan fiduciary is the Apex Sports Equipment Corporation Plan Investment Committee (the "Committee"). The Plan is an employer contributory defined-benefit pension plan covering substantially all full-time Company employees.

Purpose

The purpose of the Investment Policy Statement (the "Policy") is to provide clear guidelines for the management of plan assets. This Policy establishes policies and guidelines for the investment practices of the Plan. The Committee has reviewed and, on 21 April 2011, adopted this Policy. The Policy outlines objectives, goals, restrictions, and responsibilities in order that:

- the Committee, staff, investment managers, and custodians clearly understand the objectives and policies of the Plan;
- the investment managers are given guidance and limitations concerning the investment of the Plan's assets; and
- the Committee has a meaningful basis for evaluating the investment performance of individual investment managers, as well as evaluating overall success in meeting its investment objectives.

The Plan shall at all times be managed in accordance with all state and federal laws, rules, and regulations including, but not limited to, the Employee Retirement Income Security Act of 1974 (ERISA).

Identification of Duties and Investment Responsibilities

The Committee relies on staff and outside service providers (including investment managers and bank custodians) in executing its functions. Each entity's role as fiduciary must be clearly identified to ensure clear lines of communication, operational efficiency, and accountability in all aspects of operation.

Investment Committee

The Committee is responsible for managing the investment process. The Committee, with the assistance of staff, monitors the performance of investments; ensures funds are invested in accordance with Company policies; studies, recommends, and implements policy and operational procedures that will enhance the investment program of the Plan; and ensures that proper internal controls are developed to safeguard the assets of the Plan.

Investment Managers

Investment managers will construct and manage investment portfolios consistent with the investment philosophy and disciplines for which they were retained. They will buy and sell securities and modify the asset mix within their stated guidelines. The Committee believes that investment decisions are best made when not restricted by excessive limitations. Therefore, full discretion is delegated to investment managers to carry out investment policy within their stated guidelines. However, investment managers shall respect and observe the specific limitations, guidelines, attitudes, and philosophies stated herein and within any implementation guidelines, or as expressed in any written amendments. Investment managers are expected to communicate, in writing, any developments that may affect the Plan's portfolio to the Committee within five business days of occurrence. Examples of such events include, but are not limited to, the following:

- a significant change in investment philosophy;
- a change in the ownership structure of the firm;
- a loss of one or more key management personnel; and
- any occurrence that might potentially affect the management, professionalism, integrity, or financial position of the firm.

Bank Custodian

The bank trustee/custodian(s) will hold all cash and securities (except for those held in commingled funds and mutual funds) and will regularly summarize these holdings for the Committee's review. In addition, a bank or trust depository arrangement will be used to accept and hold cash prior to allocating it to the investment manager and to invest such cash in liquid, interest-bearing instruments.

Investment Goals and Objectives

The Plan's overall investment objective is to fund benefits to Plan beneficiaries through a carefully planned and well-executed investment program.

Return Objectives

The overall return objective is to achieve a return sufficient to achieve funding adequacy on an inflation-adjusted basis. Funding adequacy is achieved when the market value of assets is at least equal to the Plan's projected benefit obligation as defined in Statement of Financial Accounting Standards No. 87, as calculated by the Plan's actuary. The Plan has a total return objective of 7.5 percent per year. In addition, the Plan has the following broad objectives:

- The assets of the Plan shall be invested to maximize returns for the level of risk taken.
- The Plan shall strive to achieve a return that exceeds the return of benchmarks composed of various established indexes for each category of investment, in which the weights of the indexes represent the expected allocation of the Plan's investments over a three- to five-year time horizon.

Risk Objectives

- The assets of the Plan shall be diversified to minimize the risk of large losses within any one asset class, investment type, industry or sector distributions, maturity date, or geographic location, which could seriously impair the Plan's ability to achieve its funding and long-term investment objectives.
- The Plan's assets shall be invested such that the risk that the market value of assets falls below 105 percent of the Plan's projected benefit obligation in a given year is 10 percent or less.

Constraints

- The assets of the Plan shall maintain adequate liquidity to meet required benefit payments to the Plan's beneficiaries. The Plan currently and for the foreseeable future has minimal liquidity requirements.

- The Plan's assets shall be invested consistent with the Plan's long-term investment horizon.

- As a tax-exempt investor, the Plan shall invest its assets with a focus on total return without distinction made between returns generated from income and returns generated from capital gains.

Review Schedule

The Committee will review investment performance on a quarterly basis. This investment policy statement will be reviewed annually or more frequently as required by significant changes in laws or regulations, in the funded status of the Plan, or in capital market conditions.

Asset Allocation

The Committee believes that the level of risk assumed by the Plan is largely determined by the Plan's strategic asset allocation. The Committee has summarized the factors that should be considered in determining its long-term asset allocation as follows:

- the Plan's time horizon;

- the funded status of the Plan; and

- the Company's financial strength.

In establishing the long-run asset allocation for the Plan, the Committee will consider conservative long-run capital market expectations for expected return, volatility, and asset class correlations. The Plan's strategic asset allocation will be set out by the Committee in a separate strategic asset allocation document.

Rebalancing

The Committee is responsible for the Plan's asset allocation decisions and will meet to review target allocations as required based on market conditions, but at least every three years. Until such time as the Committee changes target allocations, the portfolio must periodically be rebalanced as a result of market value fluctuations. The Committee has delegated to staff the duty of implementing such rebalancing. After the Plan has reached its target equity allocation, the equity allocation shall be rebalanced to its equity target on a quarterly basis using index-based vehicles. Specific investment manager allocations will be rebalanced back to target on an annual basis. Staff will report rebalancing activity to the Committee.

2.1.8 Corporate Risk Management and the Investment of DB Pension Assets

A DB pension plan can potentially so significantly affect the sponsoring corporation's financial performance that the study of DB pension asset investment in relation to pension and corporate objectives has developed into a wide-ranging literature. Practically, we can make several observations. From a risk management perspective, the two important concerns are:[7]

- managing pension investments in relation to operating investments; and

- coordinating pension investments with pension liabilities.

---

7 See Haugen (1990). Coordinating pension liabilities with corporate liabilities has also been suggested as a risk management focus.

To explain the first concern, in Exhibit 1 we identified the correlation between sponsor operating results and pension asset returns as one variable to monitor in assessing risk tolerance. We explained that the lower the correlation, the greater the risk tolerance, all else equal. Assuming that business and pension portfolio risks are positively correlated, a high degree of operating risk would tend to limit the amount of risk that a pension portfolio could assume, and vice versa. Although we are concerned with the IPS, our view will be more rounded if we look at the different perspective of building the pension portfolio. One question to address in that regard is whether the pension portfolio diversifies risk relative to the sponsor's operating activities. All else equal, a portfolio that diversifies sponsor operational risk increases the chance that, if the sponsor needs to increase contributions to support the payment of plan pension benefits, the sponsor will be in a position to do so. Consider a portfolio with actively managed equity holdings that overweight the telecommunications sector. Such a portfolio would be less risky for a plan sponsor operating in the consumer staples sector, which has a relatively low correlation to telecom, than for one operating in a telecom-related technology sector (e.g., a supplier of DSL equipment to telephone companies).

With respect to the second concern, coordination, the plan manager's objective is to increase the probability that pension plan assets will be sufficient to fund pension plan benefits with the minimal requirement for additional contributions by the corporate plan sponsor. For a fully funded pension plan, the goal is to maintain the plan's funded status (pension surplus) relative to plan liabilities. Although both stated concerns are consistent from a comprehensive risk management perspective, asset/liability management approaches to portfolio construction emphasize managing investments relative to liabilities. From an ALM perspective, the characterization of risk in the IPS needs to be stated in *relative* terms. The emphasis shifts from the expected volatility of pension *assets* to the expected volatility of pension *surplus* and to probabilities concerning expected levels of funded status over appropriate time frames. In practice, we can use tools such as simulation to explore whether specific portfolios can be expected to satisfy such relative risk objectives. The volatility of surplus is lower if changes in the value of plan assets are positively correlated with changes in the value of plan liabilities. Because pension plan liabilities are interest rate sensitive, pension plan sponsors emphasizing an ALM approach tend to make more intensive use of interest-rate-sensitive securities (in particular, bonds) than would otherwise be the case.

2.2 Defined-Contribution Plans: Background and Investment Setting

Two broad types of defined-contribution plans are those where the investment of the assets is directed by the plan sponsor and those where the investment is participant-directed. Because setting investment policy for sponsor-directed plans is a simpler subset of the process for DB plans, here we will focus on participant-directed plans.

The principal investment issues for DC plans are as follows:

- **Diversification.** The sponsor must offer a menu of investment options that allows participants to construct suitable portfolios. For example, in the United States, Section 404(c) of ERISA establishes a safe harbor for DC plan sponsors against claims of insufficient or imprudent investment choice if the plan has 1) at least three investment choices diversified versus each other and 2) provision for the participant to move freely among the options. Sponsors of participant-directed DC plans frequently make available to participants sophisticated retirement planning tools such as Monte Carlo simulation to aid in decision-making.

▪ **Company Stock.** Holdings of sponsor-company stock should be limited to allow participants' wealth to be adequately diversified.

Even for participant-directed DC plans, the plan sponsor must have a written investment policy statement. The IPS documents the manner in which the plan sponsor is meeting the fiduciary responsibility to have an adequate process for selecting the investment options offered to plan participants as well as for periodically evaluating those options; furthermore, the establishment of an IPS may be legally mandated. DC plans, however, call for quite different IPSs than do DB plans. A DC investment policy statement establishes procedures to ensure that a myriad of individual investor objectives and constraints can be properly addressed. This can best be seen in a sample statement, an example of which follows.

2.2.1 *The Objectives and Constraints Framework*

In the DC setting, the plan sponsor does not establish objectives and constraints; rather, the plan participants set their own risk and return objectives and constraints. The plan sponsor provides educational resources, but the participant is responsible for choosing a risk and return objective reflecting his or her own personal financial circumstances, goals, and attitudes toward risk.

EXAMPLE 8

Participant Wanting to Make Up for Lost Time

A middle-aged man joined the participant-directed DC plan of BMSR five years ago. He had no previous retirement plan or asset base aside from home equity, and he states that he needs to take more risk than most people so that he can catch up. In fact, the participant's asset base, current income, and desired spending rate for retirement at age 65 all indicate that the participant needs a very high annual rate of return to deliver his desired retirement income.

1 Does the participant have a higher than average risk tolerance?

2 If the participant's risk objectives are not appropriate, would BMSR counsel him to change them?

Solution to 1:

No. This participant's ability to take risk is less than his willingness because of his small asset base and the limited time left until he needs to draw on his retirement assets; his risk tolerance is not above average.

Solution to 2:

BMSR would not counsel the participant because the plan is participant-directed. The employee needs to educate himself about the objectives and constraints framework as applied to individual investors.

EXAMPLE 9

Participant Early in Career

A 25-year-old plan participant joined BMSR recently. She is single and in good health. She has always been conservative and does not feel confident in her ability to choose funds for her retirement plan. She thinks that perhaps she should just put half in the money market fund and half in the large-capitalization value common stock fund. How do this participant's plan choices match her situation?

Solution:

Given her investment time horizon, she may benefit by increasing her willingness to take risk to match her ability to take risk. She could adopt a more aggressive risk stance while increasing diversification by moving money from the money market fund to a bond fund and/or another equity fund (for example, a growth-oriented fund). If her company offers an investor education program, this participant should attend so that she can explore the elements of assessing risk tolerance.

As mentioned, participants in DC plans bear the risk of investment results. As a consequence, an investment policy statement for a DC plan fulfills a much different role than an investment policy statement for a DB plan. For example, an IPS for a participant-directed DC plan is the governing document that describes the investment strategies and alternatives available to the group of plan participants characterized by diverse objectives and constraints. Such an IPS necessarily becomes an overall set of governing principles rather than an IPS for a specific plan participant. Example 10 provides sample excerpts from an investment policy statement for a participant-directed DC plan.

EXAMPLE 10

Investment Policy Statement for BMSR Company Defined-Contribution Plan

Purpose

The purpose of this Investment Policy Statement is to assist the members of the Retirement Policy Committee (RPC) in effectively establishing, monitoring, evaluating, and revising the investment program established for the defined-contribution plan (the Plan) sponsored by the BMSR-Company (BMSR). The authority for establishing this responsibility is by action of the BMSR Board of Directors at its 26 March 2002 meeting. The primary focuses of this Investment Policy Statement are as follows:

- Clearly distinguish among the responsibilities of the RPC, the Plan participants, the fund managers, and Plan trustee/recordkeeper selected by the RPC.

- Provide descriptions of the investment alternatives available to Plan participants.

- Provide criteria for monitoring and evaluating the performance of investment managers and investment vehicles (funds) relative to appropriate investment benchmarks.

- Provide criteria for manager/fund selection, termination and replacement.
- Establish effective communication procedures for the fund managers, the trustee/recordkeeper, the RPC, and the Plan participants.

RPC Roles and Responsibilities

The RPC's responsibilities, in carrying out this Investment Policy Statement, include:

- monitoring the fund objectives and selecting specific funds to be offered to the Plan participants to provide sufficient diversification possibilities;
- monitoring the investment performance, including fees, of funds made available to Plan participants and terminating and replacing funds when judicious and appropriate;
- assuring ongoing communications with, and appropriate educational resources for, the Plan participants;
- selecting, monitoring and, if necessary, recommending the replacement of the Trustee/Recordkeeper of the Plan; and
- assuring that the interest rate for Plan loans is in accordance with the provisions of the Plan.

Plan Participant Roles and Responsibilities

The responsibilities of plan participants include the allocation of Plan contributions and accumulations among the various fund choices made available and the obligation to educate themselves sufficiently in order to make appropriate allocations over their career or life span. A participant's appropriate asset allocation is a function of multiple factors, including age, income, length of time before retirement, tolerance for risk, accumulation objectives, retirement income replacement objectives, and other assets. To permit participants to establish savings and investment strategies to suit their individual needs, the Plan offers a number of investment alternatives with varying return and risk characteristics.

The participant is best positioned to make the individual decision on how to allocate assets among the investment alternatives. As such, the investment direction of employees' elective deferrals and contributions made by BMSR will be each individual participant's responsibility. It is also each individual participant's responsibility to reallocate assets among funds as personal circumstances change.

To help address the factors mentioned above, BMSR will provide information to participants regarding the investment alternatives and basic principles of investing. However, the dissemination of information and the provision of investment alternatives by BMSR do not constitute advice to participants.

The return/risk concept is basic to investments. Over time, investment alternatives offering higher expected returns will exhibit higher risk (e.g., volatility of returns or of principal values). The Plan offers a variety of investment choices in order to provide participants the opportunity to select return/risk strategies that meet their savings and investment objectives and to adequately diversify.

ERISA 404(c) Compliance

BMSR intends to comply with ERISA Section 404(c) regulations by, among other things, offering a broad, diversified range of investment choices; allowing transfers of funds between investment choices at least once every 90 days; and providing sufficient investment information to participants on a regular basis.

Selection of Investment Alternatives

The RPC's role is to provide participants with an array of investment choices with various investment objectives that should enable participants to invest according to their varying investment needs. The investment choices offered should represent asset classes with different risk and return characteristics and with sufficient diversification properties. The following asset classes have the investment characteristics currently desired:

- money market instruments;
- intermediate-term fixed-income instruments;
- intermediate-term Treasury Inflation-Indexed Securities;
- equity
  - large-cap growth
  - large-cap blend/core
  - large-cap value
  - mid-cap blend/core
  - small-cap blend/core
  - international;
- life-cycle mutual funds (funds customized for various retirement dates).

The criteria for selection and for replacement of funds include the following:

- The array of investment options should be chosen with the goal of permitting participants to diversify their investments and to align the risk of their investments to their risk tolerance.
- The funds must have reasonable fees, including advisor fees, 12(b)-1 fees, and other fees.
- Every fund must have a clearly articulated and explained investment strategy, accompanied by evidence that the strategy is followed over time.
- The funds' time-weighted returns and volatility of returns over at least the three (and preferably five) prior years must compare favorably with the performance of a passively-managed index with the same style (e.g., large-cap growth). This is the primary performance criterion.
- Funds selected must:
  - be managed by a bank, insurance company, investment management company, or investment advisor (as defined by the Registered Investment Advisers Act of 1940) that has had significant assets under management for at least 10 years and has exhibited financial stability throughout that period;
  - provide historical quarterly performance calculated on a time-weighted basis and reported net and gross of fees;
  - provide performance evaluation reports that illustrate the risk–return profile of the manager relative to passive indexes and other managers of like investment style; and
  - clearly articulate the investment strategy to be followed and document that the strategy has been successfully executed over time.
- Transfers among investment funds are permitted on at least a quarterly basis, thus fulfilling an ERISA 404(c) requirement.

Monitoring Investment Performance

The RPC will monitor each fund's return and risk performance on a quarterly basis relative to appropriate investment benchmarks. In the event a fund over a five-year time frame:

- underperforms a passively managed (index) fund with similar objectives (i.e., same style) or, alternatively,
- ranks worse than the 50th percentile in terms of investment performance relative to funds with similar investment objectives,

the RPC will review the fund to determine whether its performance has resulted from the fund manager, the style of management, or market volatility, and decide whether the fund should be eliminated from the menu of possible investment choices. The RPC will also consider the fund's performance over periods of more than five years, if available, before making a decision.

As noted above, the RPC will evaluate each fund's performance using a five-year time horizon. The RPC realizes that most investments go through cycles; therefore, at any given time a fund may encounter a time period in which the investment objectives are not met or when a fund fails to meet its expected performance target. The fund's performance should be reported in terms of an annualized time-weighted rate of return. As noted above, the returns should be compared to appropriate market indexes and to peer group universes for the most recent five-year (or longer) period.

In light of the evaluation of each fund's performance, the RPC has the authority to recommend the replacement or elimination of an investment objective or fund if, in the opinion of the RPC, the investment objective or fund does not, or is not expected to, meet the specified performance criteria; is no longer suited to the needs of the Plan participants; or if, in the sole opinion of the RPC, a more appropriate investment choice exists.

EXAMPLE 11

BMSR Committee Decision

A member of the RPC committee for BMSR is concerned about the small-cap growth fund. During the last two years, this fund has ranked in the top half of small-cap growth funds and has outperformed a passively managed small-cap growth benchmark. However, the fund has dropped in value far more than the overall market. The concerned member suggests that the RPC replace the fund. Do the IPS criteria support this suggestion?

Solution:

According to IPS guidelines, investment performance must be evaluated over time horizons longer than two years. The IPS also specifies a comparison to a passively managed benchmark with the same style rather than to the overall market. For these reasons, the IPS cannot support the suggestion that the fund be eliminated.

2.3 Hybrid and Other Plans

During the 1990s, many employers concluded that neither the traditional DB nor DC plan structure exactly met their pension plan objectives. Hybrid plans began to emerge that combined the features of DB and DC plans.[8] Examples of hybrid plans include cash balance plans, pension equity plans, target benefit plans, and floor plans. These plans sought to combine some of the most highly valued features of a DC plan (such as portability, administrative ease, and understandability by participants) with the highly valued features of a DB plan (such as benefit guarantees, years of service rewards, and the ability to link retirement pay to a percentage of salary). In this section, we discuss cash balance plans as one example of a hybrid plan as well as another important type of plan, the employee stock ownership plan (ESOP).

A cash balance plan is a DB plan, in that the employer bears the investment risk. To employees, however, it looks like a DC plan because they are provided a personalized statement showing their account balance, an annual contribution credit, and an earnings credit. The contribution credit is a percentage of pay based on age, while the earnings credit is a percentage increase in the account balance that is typically tied to long-term interest rates. In reality, the account balance is hypothetical because unlike in a DC plan, the employee does not have a separate account. Some plans allow investment choices among fixed-income and equity-based options, which introduces investment risk for the employee.

Cash balance plans usually are not start-up plans but rather are traditional DB plans that have been converted in order to gain some of the features of a DC plan. Some of these plans have come under criticism as being unfair to older workers with many years of service, who may have accrued higher retirement benefits under the DB plan than the cash balance plan offers. In response to this criticism, some companies have offered a "grandfather" clause to older workers, allowing them to choose between joining a new cash balance plan or continuing with an existing traditional DB plan.

Finally, most developed countries allow for retirement or other savings plans that encourage employees to become stockholders of their employer. These plans may be complex qualified plans that purchase stock in a DC pension plan with pretax money, or they may be simple savings plans that allow employees to buy stock personally with their after-tax pay. The acronym ESOP refers to an employee *stock* ownership plan (in the United States) or employee *share* ownership plan (United Kingdom). These are DC plans that invest all or the majority of plan assets in employer stock. ESOPs are DC plans because the contribution is set as a percentage of employee pay. The final value of the plan for the employee will depend on the vesting schedule, the level of contributions, and the change in the per-share value of the stock.

Although ESOPs all share the common goal of increasing employee ownership in a company, they vary widely from country to country in terms of regulation. Some ESOPs may sell stock to employees at a discount from market prices, while others may not. Some require employee contribution; others prohibit such. Some ESOP trusts may borrow to purchase large amounts of employer stock, while others must rely solely on contributions.

In addition to encouraging ownership of one's employer, ESOPs have been used by companies to liquidate a large block of company stock held by an individual or small group of people, avoid a public offering of stock, or discourage an unfriendly takeover by placing a large holding of stock in the hands of employees via the ESOP trust. Apart from his or her investment in the ESOP, a plan participant may have a major investment of human capital in the company by virtue of working for that company. Should the company fail, the participant might see the value of the ESOP investment

---

8 In 1985 only 1 percent of Fortune 100 companies offered a hybrid plan; by 2002 that fraction had grown to 33 percent. See Scanlan and Lyons (2006, p. 38).

sharply decline at the same time that he or she becomes unemployed. An important concern for ESOP participants is that their overall investments (both financial and **human capital**) reflect adequate diversification.[9]

FOUNDATIONS AND ENDOWMENTS

Foundations and endowments provide vital support for much of today's philanthropic and charitable activities. **Foundations** are typically grant-making institutions funded by gifts and investment assets. **Endowments**, on the other hand, are long-term funds generally owned by operating non-profit institutions such as universities and colleges, museums, hospitals, and other organizations involved in charitable activities.

Although both are created by donations, foundations and endowments usually develop differently over time. Private foundations typically are created and funded by a single donor to fund philanthropic goals. The investment portfolio provides the dominant source of revenue, and the purchasing power of its corpus is either maintained or eventually given away. In the United States, tax law essentially mandates minimum levels of annual spending for some types of foundations. By donating cash and securities, many of the world's great industrialists and financiers have created foundations that bear their name (e.g., the Ford, Rockefeller, and Gates foundations). Endowments, by contrast, are often built up over time by many individual gifts to the endowed institution. Spending distributions are determined by the beneficiary institution, supplementing other revenue sources such as tuition, grants, fees, or gifts for current use. Prominent endowments, such as those of Harvard, Yale, and Princeton universities, have grown along with their institutions over centuries.

In Sections 3.1 and 3.2, we discuss the investment objectives and constraints of foundations and endowments, respectively.

3.1 Foundations: Background and Investment Setting

Foundations provide essential support of charitable activity. In broad terms, four types of foundations exist: independent, company sponsored, operating, and community.[10] Exhibit 2 briefly describes the principal types of foundations in the United States, as distinguished by their purpose, sources of funds, and annual spending requirements.[11] Independent foundations, also referred to as private or family foundations, are grant-making organizations funded by an individual donor and generally required to pay out a minimum of 5 percent of assets annually. Company-sponsored foundations tend to have a short-term investment focus to facilitate philanthropic funding from the corporation to grantees. Operating foundations, much like endowments, provide income to support specific programs. Community foundations draw upon broad support for donations to fund a variety of grants. Most of the following discussion relates to independent (private and family) foundations, which represent the majority of investment assets in the foundation sector.

---

9 Many 401(k) plans, especially large ones, have company stock as an investment option. For participants in such plans, similar issues arise.

10 Community foundations are a prominent type of public charity (meeting tax code tests for public support) in the United States and are used to represent public charities as a group.

11 The international links at the Association of Charitable Foundations (www.acf.org.uk/linksinter.htm) are good starting points for researching the diversity of foundations worldwide.

Exhibit 2   Types of Foundations in the United States

Foundation Type	Description	Source of Funds	Decision-Making Authority	Annual Spending Requirement
Independent foundation (private or family)	Independent grant-making organization established to aid social, educational, charitable, or religious activities.	Generally an individual, family, or group of individuals.	Donor, members of donor's family, or independent trustees.	At least 5% of 12-month average asset value, plus expenses associated with generating investment return.
Company-sponsored foundation	A legally independent grant-making organization with close ties to the corporation providing funds.	Endowment and/or annual contributions from a profit-making corporation.	Board of trustees, usually controlled by the sponsoring corporation's executives.	Same as independent foundation.
Operating foundation	Organization that uses its resources to conduct research or provide a direct service (e.g., operate a museum).	Largely the same as independent foundation.	Independent board of directors.	Must use 85% of interest and dividend income for active conduct of the institution's own programs. Some are also subject to annual spending requirement equal to 3.33% of assets.
Community foundation	A publicly supported organization that makes grants for social, educational, charitable, or religious purposes. A type of public charity.	Multiple donors; the public.	Board of directors.	No spending requirement.

The most noteworthy aspect of foundations is that they can vary widely in their investment goals and time horizons. For example, a foundation may be the primary or even sole source of funding for a charitable program. In such a case, a stable, reliable flow of funds is extremely important because the program has few alternative sources of funding to make up the shortfall. On the other hand, many foundations give funding for numerous independent projects or programs for only a few years at most. Because such foundations are generally not those projects' primary means of support, the funded programs can handle drops in spending by the foundation relatively easily because funding reductions are less likely to critically disrupt their operations. Often, a foundation's mission may address a problem with a limited time horizon or an urgent need (e.g., a need resulting from a natural disaster or an environmental emergency).

Another distinctive characteristic of the foundation sector, as contrasted to endowments, is that most private and family foundations must generate their entire grant-making and operating budget from their investment portfolio for the following reasons: These institutions generally do not engage in fund-raising campaigns; they may not receive any new contributions from the donor; and they do not receive any public support. These unique conditions help to guide the investment approach taken by foundations. In addition, as mentioned earlier, private and family foundations are subject to a payout requirement that mandates a minimum level of spending, while university endowments and many other nonprofit institutions face no such requirement.

3.1.1 *Risk Objectives*

Because foundations' goals differ somewhat from those of traditional defined-benefit pension funds and other asset pools, foundations can have a higher risk tolerance. Pension funds have a contractually defined liability stream (the pension payments expected to be made to retirees); in contrast, foundations have no such defined liability. The desire to keep spending whole in real terms, or to grow the institution, is simply that: a desire. Foundation investment policy can thus be more fluid or creative, and arguably more aggressive, than pension fund policy.

It is also acceptable, if risky, for foundations to try to earn a higher rate of return than is needed to maintain the purchasing power of assets—in essence, seeking to make as much money as possible. Such behavior makes it possible for the institution to increase its grant-making over time because the funding needs of organizations supported by foundations are essentially unbounded.

3.1.2 *Return Objectives*

Foundations differ in their purposes, and so vary in their return objectives. Some foundations are meant to be short lived; others are intended to operate in perpetuity. For those foundations with an indefinitely long horizon, the long-term return objective is to preserve the real (inflation-adjusted) value of the investment assets while allowing spending at an appropriate (either statutory or decided-upon) rate. Such a policy, if successful, keeps spending constant in real terms, on average over time, achieving what is sometimes called intergenerational equity or neutrality: an equitable balance between the interests of current and future beneficiaries of the foundation's support.[12]

If we look at the 5 percent annual spending minimum for foundations as a benchmark and add 0.3 percent as a low-end estimate of investment management expenses (i.e., the cost of generating investment returns), we thus have calculated that the fund must generate a return of 5.3 percent, plus the inflation rate, to stay even in real terms. We can use 5.3 percent plus the expected inflation rate as a starting point for setting the return objective of a foundation. If the expected inflation rate is 2 percent, the minimum return requirement will be 7.3 percent. This additive formulation of the return objective is intuitive but approximate. The most precise formulation is multiplicative, which accounts for the effect of compounding in a multiperiod setting and results in a higher requirement. For our example, the multiplicative calculation is $(1.05)(1.003)(1.02) - 1.0 = 0.0742$, or 7.42 percent.

3.1.3 *Liquidity Requirements*

A foundation's liquidity requirements are anticipated or unanticipated needs for cash in excess of contributions made to the foundation. Anticipated needs are captured in the periodic distributions prescribed by a foundation's spending rate. In the United States, the spending policy of private foundations is dictated, at least as concerns the 5 percent annual minimum, by the Tax Reform Act of 1969 and subsequent amendments. Expenses associated with management of the foundation's investments do not count toward the payout requirement, so one must add this cost (conservatively, 0.3 percent annually) to the minimum that the foundation is required to spend. "Overhead" associated with grant making—for example, the salaries of program officers and other executives—does count toward the payout requirement.

---

12 Think of a school that spends so much on scholarships in the current time frame that the endowment becomes depleted. A generation hence, the school will be in a poor financial position to give scholarships or otherwise compete for good students and professors. Under such a policy, intergenerational neutrality is clearly defeated. The underlying philosophy is that a long-lived foundation, or endowment, should not favor one particular generation of would-be recipients over another. A similar tension exists in certain types of trusts that must balance the interests of life income beneficiaries and remaindermen (who receive the trust corpus after the death of the income beneficiaries).

To avoid erosion in the portfolio's real value over time, many foundations try to spend only the minimum or else set a maximum that only slightly exceeds the minimum. In addition, to avoid large fluctuations in their operating budget, foundations may use a smoothing rule. A **smoothing rule** averages asset values over a period of time in order to dampen the spending rate's response to asset value fluctuation.

The US Internal Revenue Service (IRS) allows carry-forwards and carry-backs, within limits, so that a foundation may avoid being penalized for underspending by spending more than 5 percent of assets in a subsequent year. Conversely, as a result of overspending in prior years, a foundation may be allowed to underspend in a subsequent year. Carry-forwards and carry-backs not only make smoothing rules workable but also allow a foundation to make a large grant in a single year without compromising the long-run soundness of its investment program.

The 5 percent payout requirement for private and family foundations, combined with the desire to maintain the portfolio's value in real terms, can be daunting. Foundation executives may disagree about whether the 5 percent spending requirement motivates an aggressive investment policy or a conservative one. Clearly, motivation refers to willingness to bear risk, but ability to bear risk must also be considered in determining a foundation's risk tolerance.

It is prudent for any organization to keep some assets in cash as a reserve for contingencies, but private and family foundations need a cash reserve for a special reason: They are subject to the unusual requirement that spending in a given fiscal year be 5 percent or more of the 12-month average of asset values *in that year*. One cannot, of course, know what this amount will be in advance, so one cannot budget for it. Instead, a well-managed foundation places some (say 10 percent or 20 percent) of its annual grant-making and spending budget in a reserve. This reserve may simply be in the form of not spending budgeted money until the year is mostly over and the 12-month average of asset values is known with greater certainty. In an "up" year for markets, this method may cause a rush of grants to be paid by the foundation at the end of the year, to avoid spending less than the minimum required amount. A year-end rush should be more acceptable to the foundation than the alternative that would occur without a reserve—overspending in flat or "down" market years.

3.1.4 *Time Horizon*

The majority of foundation wealth resides in private and other foundations established or managed with the intent of lasting into perpetuity. Our discussion has thus focused on strategies for preserving capital in real terms after spending. Some institutions, however, are created to be "spent down" over a predefined period of time; therefore, they pursue a different strategy, exhibiting an increasing level of conservatism as time passes. All else equal, investors often assume that a longer time horizon implies a greater ability to bear risk because a longer horizon affords them more time to recoup losses.

3.1.5 *Tax Concerns*

In the United States, income that is not substantially related to a foundation's charitable purposes may be classified as **unrelated business income** and be subject to regular corporate tax rates. For instance, a museum gift shop that sells artwork has business income related to its purposes; if it sells motorcycles, it has unrelated business income. Income from real estate is taxable as unrelated business income if the property is debt financed, but only in proportion to the fraction of the property's cost financed with debt.

In the United States, a private foundation must estimate and pay quarterly in advance a tax (currently set at 2 percent) on its net investment income. "Net investment income" includes dividends, interest, and realized capital gains, less the foundation's expenses related directly to the production of such income. The excise tax may be reduced to 1 percent if the charitable distributions for the year equal or exceed both

5 percent and the average of the previous five years' payout plus 1 percent of the net investment income. In creating this requirement, Congress hoped that foundations would translate their tax savings into increased charitable activities.

3.1.6 *Legal and Regulatory Factors*

Foundations may be subject to a variety of legal and regulatory constraints, which vary by country and sometimes by type of foundation. As one example, in the United States, the Internal Revenue Code (Section 4944) addresses private foundations, imposing a graduated series of excise taxes if a private foundation invests in a manner that jeopardizes the carrying out of its tax-exempt purposes. In the United States, many states have adopted the Uniform Management of Institutional Funds Act (UMIFA) as the primary legislation governing any entity organized and operated exclusively for educational, religious, or charitable purposes. We will present some of the details of UMIFA that concern investing activities when we address endowments.

3.1.7 *Unique Circumstances*

A special challenge faces foundations that are endowed with the stock of one particular company and that are then restricted by the donor from diversifying. The asset value of such an institution is obviously subject to the large market fluctuations attendant to any one-stock position.

With the permission of the donor, some institutions have entered into swap agreements or other derivative transactions to achieve the payoffs of a more diversified portfolio. Such a strategy achieves the donor's goal of retaining voting rights in the stock, while providing the foundation with a more stable asset value. Other institutions simply tolerate the fluctuations associated with a single-stock position.

Against the background of investment objectives and constraints for foundations, Example 12 illustrates how all these elements come together in an investment policy statement.

EXAMPLE 12

The Fund for Electoral Integrity

A group of major foundations has endowed a new organization, the Fund for Electoral Integrity, to supervise elections and political campaigns in countries undergoing a transition to democracy. The fund is headquartered in a developing country. It has received initial grants of $20 million, with $40 million expected to be received in further grants over the next three years. The fund's charter expressly decrees that the fund should spend itself out of existence within 10 years of its founding rather than trying to become a permanent institution. Determine and justify appropriate investment policy objectives and constraints for the Fund for Electoral Integrity.

Solution:

Risk Objective

Although the fund has a 10-year life, it is receiving donations over a period of years and it is also constantly spending money on programs. Thus, it can be assumed to have a five-year investment horizon on average and should *initially* adopt a conservative or below-average risk profile (a standard deviation of annual returns in the range of 5 percent to 7 percent).[13] Over the life of the fund, the

---

13 The standard deviation of annual returns on intermediate-term bonds typically falls in this range.

risk objective should gradually migrate to an even more conservative profile (standard deviation of 3 percent to 5 percent). The relatively short time horizon calls for a below-average risk tolerance. Both the risks inherent in markets and the fund's risk tolerance may change, so it is important to periodically review the investment policy and the portfolio from a risk management perspective. In making their investment recommendations, the board and investment committee should take the following into account:

- market risk (fluctuation in asset values);
- liquidity risk;
- political, regulatory, and legal risks;
- operations and control risks;
- any other risks that the board and investment committee deem relevant.

Return Objective

The fund's broad return objective is to earn the highest inflation-adjusted return consistent with the risk objective. At inception, the fund's return objective is to equal or better the total return of an average five-year maturity US Treasury note portfolio over a rolling four-year period.

Constraints

Liquidity

The fund must pay out roughly $6 million annually for 10 years.

Time Horizon

The fund has a 10-year time horizon.

Tax Concerns

The fund is a tax-exempt organization in the country in which it is organized.

Regulatory Factors

No special legal or regulatory factors impinge on the organization's ability to invest as it chooses.

Unique Circumstances

The fund has no constraints in the sense of prohibited investments.

3.2 Endowments: Background and Investment Setting

Endowments play a critical role in the vitality and success of today's charitable activity. As the long-term investment portfolios of nonprofit operating institutions, endowments provide a significant amount of budgetary support for universities, colleges, private schools, hospitals, museums, and religious organizations.

The term "endowment" has taken on two related but distinct meanings. As commonly understood, an endowment is simply the long-term investment portfolio of a charitable organization. Legally and formally, however, the term "endowment" refers to a permanent fund established by a donor with the condition that the fund principal be maintained over time. In contrast to private foundations, endowments are not subject to a specific legally required spending level.

Donors establish true endowments by making gifts with the stipulation that periodic spending distributions from the fund be used to pay for programs and that the principal value of the gift be preserved in perpetuity. Thus, true endowments are funds permanently restricted in terms of spending. Many schools and nonprofit organizations will supplement true endowments with voluntary savings in the form of quasi-endowments, sometimes referred to as funds functioning as endowment (FFE). Although designated as long-term financial capital, quasi-endowments have no spending restrictions; the institution may spend such funds completely. Because endowments are owned by nonprofit organizations, they generally are exempt from taxation on investment income derived from interest, dividends, capital gains, rents, and royalties.

Typically, the large investment pools commonly referred to as endowments consist of a variety of individual funds, including true endowments and FFEs. Each endowment fund is established with a specific indenture detailing the conditions and intended uses of the gifts. Although many endowment funds are unrestricted, meaning that endowment spending can be used for the general purposes of the beneficiary institution, others are restricted so that monies can be spent only for specified purposes. For instance, one restricted fund might support a professorship, while another fund might support student financial aid. Spending from these funds must be kept distinct and support only the specified use—money from a professorship endowment, for example, cannot be used to provide student aid.

Endowments are a vital source of funding for many charitable programs, and spending distributions should be substantial to support such programs' needs. Large fluctuations in year-to-year spending can disrupt the endowed institution's operating budget, finances and staffing. Therefore, spending distributions should be stable and reliable. Because donors establish endowment funds with the intention of funding an activity in perpetuity, recipient institutions generally operate with the fiduciary intent of preserving the fund's purchasing power. The nonprofit should not count on new gifts to supplement endowment funds whose value has been eroded by spending beyond investment returns. In summary, endowments should provide substantial, stable, and sustainable spending distributions.

Historically, prior to the 1970s, income provided the basis for determining an endowment's spending distributions. Institutions invested their endowments primarily in stocks, bonds and cash, and they spent the dividend and interest income. Unfortunately, in following such policies, endowment spending was not tied to the investment portfolio's total return after inflation. Institutions skewed portfolios toward high-yielding fixed-income instruments at the expense of equities in order to increase current endowment spending. Although high-quality bonds typically make their promised nominal payments, unanticipated inflation reduces those payments' real values below anticipated levels. Furthermore, shifts toward higher-yielding assets allowed increased portfolio spending but decreased an endowment's ability to generate adequate inflation-adjusted long-term returns.

Educated and encouraged by a seminal Ford Foundation report published in 1969, many endowed institutions adopted a new approach to determining spending based on the concept of total return.[14] As codified by UMIFA in 1972, income and capital gains (realized and unrealized) are now included in determining total return in the United States. Freed from the strictures of yield, institutions could determine endowment-spending levels as a percentage of an endowment's market value.

Today, most endowed institutions determine spending through policies based on total return as reflected in market values. A spending rule, by defining the amount of the distribution from the endowment available for spending, helps instill discipline into the budgeting and financial management process. A balanced budget is not a meaningful achievement if it results from pulling from the endowment whatever is needed to cover a deficit.

---

14 See Cary and Bright (1969) for more information.

Spending is typically calculated as a percentage, usually between 4 percent and 6 percent of endowment market value (endowments are not subject to minimum spending rates as are private foundations in the United States).[15] In calculating spending, endowments frequently use an average of trailing market values rather than the current market value to provide greater stability in the amount of money distributed annually. In computing such an average, the endowment manager may adjust historical market values to reflect inflation. A common, simple rule might call for spending 5 percent of the average of the past three years' ending market values of the endowment. One problem with this rule is that it places as much significance on market values three years ago as it does on more recent outcomes. Even if endowment values were relatively stable for the last two years, an extraordinary return three years ago could force a dramatic change in spending this year. A more refined rule might use a geometrically declining average of trailing endowment values adjusted for inflation, placing more emphasis on recent market values and less on past values. Examples of spending rules include the following:

- **Simple spending rule.** Spending equals the spending rate multiplied by the market value of the endowment at the beginning of the fiscal year.

  $$\text{Spending}_t = \text{Spending rate} \times \text{Ending market value}_{t-1}$$

- **Rolling three-year average spending rule.** Spending equals the spending rate multiplied by the average market value of the last three fiscal year-ends.

  $$\text{Spending}_t = \text{Spending rate} \times (1/3)[\text{Ending market value}_{t-1} + \text{Ending market value}_{t-2} + \text{Ending market value}_{t-3}]$$

- **Geometric smoothing rule.** Spending equals the weighted average of the prior year's spending adjusted for inflation and the product of the spending rate times the market value of the endowment at the beginning of the prior fiscal year. The smoothing rate is typically between 60 and 80 percent.

  $$\text{Spending}_t = \text{Smoothing rate} \times [\text{Spending}_{t-1} \times (1 + \text{Inflation}_{t-1})] + (1 - \text{Smoothing rate}) \times (\text{Spending rate} \times \text{Beginning market value}_{t-1})$$

Because most endowed institutions complete their budget planning process well before the endowment market value at the beginning of a fiscal year becomes known, it may be advisable to calculate spending from an endowment value based on a date in advance of the final budget process. The geometric smoothing rule description reflects this approach and uses the prior year's beginning, rather than ending, endowment market value.

3.2.1 Risk Objectives

An endowment's investment risk should be considered in conjunction with its spending policy and in the context of its long-term objective of providing a significant, stable, and sustainable stream of spending distributions. Spending policies with smoothing or averaging rules can dampen the transmission of portfolio volatility to spending distributions, allowing the institution to accept short-term portfolio volatility while striving for high long-term investment returns necessary to fund programs and maintain purchasing power. Endowments that do not use a smoothing rule may have less tolerance for short-term portfolio risk. Investment portfolios with very low volatility,

---

15 According to Swensen (2000), 90 percent of endowments spend between 4 percent and 6 percent of endowment market value annually.

or investment risk, usually provide low expected returns, which increases the risk of failing to achieve the endowment's goals of significant, stable, and sustainable spending. Low investment risk does not equate to low risk for meeting endowment objectives.

An institution's risk tolerance depends on the endowment's role in the operating budget and the institution's ability to adapt to drops in spending. If endowment income represents only a small portion of the budget, poor investment returns may have little impact on the bottom line. On the other hand, modest drops in endowment value may have serious consequences if endowment income contributes a large part of overall revenues. If the same market forces affect both its donor base and its endowment, an institution that relies heavily on donations for current income may see donations drop at the same time as endowment income. Large fixed expenditures such as debt service can aggravate damage inflicted by drops in endowment income.

On a short-term basis, an endowment's risk tolerance can be greater if the endowment has experienced strong recent returns and the smoothed spending rate is below the long-term average or target rate. In such a case, the endowment value could drop and spending might still increase the following year. On the other hand, endowment funds with poor recent returns and a smoothed spending rate above the long-term average run the risk of a severe loss in purchasing power. High spending rates can aggravate the erosion of the endowment's corpus at the same time that institution comes under pressure to cut operating expenses.

Because of the assumed positive relation between risk and return, a high required return objective and a willingness to meet relatively high spending needs often imply a high willingness to accept risk. On the other hand, short-term performance pressures will indicate a low willingness to accept risk. Despite their long-term investment mandate, endowment managers often come under pressure to perform well over relatively short-term time horizons for several reasons. Poor investment results may lead to reductions in the level of endowment spending. In addition, investment staff and trustees with oversight responsibility are evaluated formally or informally on relatively short time frames—often yearly. Many large endowments are highly visible; supporters and peers closely scrutinize their annual performance. Endowed institutions thus need to objectively assess and, if necessary, enhance their actual tolerance for short-term volatility before pursuing investment strategies that really are consistent with only a very long-term investment horizon.

3.2.2 Return Objectives

Endowments have high return objectives, reflecting the goal of providing a significant, stable and sustainable flow of income to operations. Endowments typically provide vital support of ongoing operations and programs, and distributions from endowment to operations should be as large as practical. An endowment manager must thus balance this objective of providing substantial resources to programs with the need to provide a stable flow. Erratic and volatile endowment distributions are unsuitable for programs with permanent staff or recurring expenses. Furthermore, an endowment must balance significant and stable spending objectives with the imperative to provide sustainable support—in other words, endowment funds should maintain their long-term purchasing power after inflation.

Endowments often need to generate relatively high long-term rates of return in order to provide a substantial flow of spending to institutions affected by rates of inflation above those of the general economy. The growth of higher education expenses in the United States is a case in point. Inflation for US higher education expenses has been generally above that for the broad economy such as the gross domestic product (GDP) deflator or for consumers as measured by the US Consumer Price Index (CPI). Since 1960, annual inflation for colleges and universities, as measured by the Higher Education Price Index (HEPI), averaged approximately 1 percentage point more than the CPI or the GDP deflator.[16] A major factor for this higher inflation rate is the difficulty of increasing faculty productivity without impairing the quality of education. For instance, colleges and universities cannot simply improve efficiency by increasing class size or student-to-faculty ratios. Because faculty compensation typically constitutes a majority portion of higher education operating budgets, many of the costs associated with increasing salaries cannot be offset by efficiency gains. In order to maintain long-term support of an academic program, therefore, a higher education institution must increase spending over time to adjust for inflation that is higher than the CPI or the GDP deflator.

The objective of providing a significant, stable, and sustainable flow of funds to support operating programs provides a useful framework for evaluating investment and spending policies. We may ask questions such as: How do the trade-offs of expected risk and returns relate to meeting endowment objectives? What spending policy makes sense for the institution? What long-term rate of spending can the portfolio support without unduly risking impairment of purchasing power? Conventional mean–variance analysis can help to suggest appropriate asset allocations. Computer simulations using Monte Carlo techniques can be extremely helpful in comparing and assessing investment and spending policies and their ability to meet endowment objectives. Monte Carlo techniques use random numbers to develop multiple, simulated time-series of annual returns given a portfolio's risk and return characteristics. Applying the spending rule to each time series, we can evaluate the interaction of investment choices and spending policy.

Monte Carlo simulations illustrate the effect of investment and spending policies on the likelihood that an endowment will provide a stable and sustainable flow of operating funds for an institution. How do various portfolios and spending rules affect the risk that the endowment will need to severely cut back on spending in the short term? How should the endowment's board set spending policies so as to support the objective of preserving the real purchasing power of the endowment? To answer these questions, an endowment must quantify risk measures. A severe drop in support for the operating budget might be defined as a real reduction of 10 percent from year to year. The risk of a dramatic decline in endowment purchasing power might be defined as the probability of more than a 50 percent real decline over a 50-year horizon. The specific pain threshold or downside risk tolerance would depend on the endowment's role with respect to operations and the endowed institution's ability to adapt to endowment spending declines.

Simulations can demonstrate several key aspects of the interaction of investment and spending policies on managing endowment risk. First, the endowment's spending rate must be lower than its expected rate of return in order to preserve purchasing power long term. For example, if an endowment has a 6 percent simple spending rate and 6 percent expected real returns with 12 percent annual standard deviation of returns, the probability that its purchasing power will fall by more than 50 percent over a 50-year period is 41 percent, according to Monte Carlo simulation. With the same portfolio return of 6 percent and a 5 percent simple spending rate, the long-term risk of such purchasing power impairment falls to 19 percent.

If returns had no volatility, an endowment could set spending at a rate that equated to the real return—that is, the nominal return net of inflation. Returns above spending would be reinvested to compensate for inflation, and the endowment would retain its purchasing power. With the introduction of volatility, however, the endowment's long-term purchasing power would be impaired more than 40 percent of the time

---

16 According to Research Associates of Washington.

according to the simulations. In order to achieve its objective of maintaining purchasing power, an endowment must keep its long-term average spending rate below its long-term expected real return.

From simulations, we can also observe that the risk of short-term disruptive spending may be reduced with a smoothing rule. For instance, there is a 17 percent risk of a 10 percent real drop in spending in any year with a simple 5 percent spending rule for an endowment with a 6 percent expected real return and 12 percent annual standard deviation of returns. With the same portfolio, a 70/30 smoothing rule (70 percent of last year's spending and 30 percent of 5% of last year's endowment market value) would reduce the risk of a short-term spending drop from 17 percent with a simple 5 percent rule to less than 3 percent.

Finally, a low-volatility, low-return portfolio increases the risk of an endowment failing to meet its objectives. For example, an endowment with a 5 percent spending target, a 70/30 smoothing rule, and a portfolio with a 5 percent real return and a 9 percent annual standard deviation of returns would lose half its purchasing power 34 percent of the time at the end of 50 years. Low investment risk does not equate to low risk of purchasing power impairment.

In summary, an endowment must coordinate its investment and spending policies. An endowment's returns need to exceed the spending rate to protect against a long-term loss of purchasing power. Calculating the return objective as the sum of the spending rate, the expected inflation rate, and the cost of generating investment returns can serve as a starting point for determining an endowment's appropriate return objective (analogous to the approach previously discussed for foundations). As is clear from Monte Carlo analysis in a multi-period setting, however, an endowment may need to set its return objective higher than the above starting point in order to preserve its purchasing power. In addition, an endowed institution should adopt a spending policy that appropriately controls the risk of long-term purchasing power impairment and dampens short-term volatility in spending distributions. Unlike foundations, endowments are not subject to specific payout requirements. The endowment can set a long-term spending rate consistent with its investment approach. Furthermore, spending policies can include a smoothing rule, which gradually adjusts to changes in endowment market values, to dampen the effects of portfolio volatility on spending distributions.

3.2.3 Liquidity Requirements

The perpetual nature and measured spending of true endowments limit their need for liquidity. They must, however, have cash to make spending distributions, to meet capital commitments, and to facilitate portfolio-rebalancing transactions. In addition to gifts, an endowment's investment yield, the normal sale of securities, and maturation of bonds meet much of its need for cash. Although the typical endowment maintains more liquidity than required, managers of quasi-endowments should monitor the potential for major capital projects, such as a planned capital outlay for the construction of a building.

In general, endowments are well suited to invest in illiquid, non-marketable securities given their limited need for liquidity. Care and discipline should be exercised in valuing non-marketable investments because endowments must use accurate market values estimates to determine spending, calculate performance, and establish unit values for funds entering and exiting pooled endowment portfolios.

3.2.4 Time Horizon

In principle, endowment time horizons are extremely long term because of the objective of maintaining purchasing power in perpetuity. Annual draws for spending, however, may present important short-term considerations, because endowments often use yearly market values to determine spending, and each annual withdrawal of capital has its specific time horizon. Such considerations, as well as planned decapitalizations (reductions in capital, e.g., to fund large projects) for quasi-endowments, may suggest a multistage time horizon, in certain cases.

3.2.5 *Tax Concerns*

Although taxation may vary by domicile internationally, taxes are not a major consideration for endowments, in general. In the United States, for example, endowments owned by non-profit organizations are exempt from taxation on investment income derived from interest, dividends, capital gains, rents, and royalties. Under certain circumstances, unrelated business taxable income (UBTI) from operating businesses or from assets with acquisition indebtedness may be subject to tax. In addition, a portion of dividends from non-US securities may be subject to withholding taxes that cannot be reclaimed or credited against US taxes.

3.2.6 *Legal and Regulatory Factors*

In the United States, few laws and regulations exist regarding the management and conduct of endowment funds. Most states have adopted UMIFA as the primary governing legislation for endowments. First promulgated in 1972, UMIFA authorizes a broad range of investments for endowments. It also allows for the delegation of investment responsibility to external advisors and managers, as well as for wide discretion in setting the compensation for such services.

An endowed institution's governing board must "exercise ordinary business care and prudence" in dealing with investments. UMIFA explicitly authorizes institutions to spend endowment investment gain as well as income. Endowment spending must, however, respect any use restriction imposed by the donor, and it should not include principal when an endowment fund's market value falls below its historical book value. In other words, only income may be spent when an endowment's market value is less than its original gift value.[17] This requirement can lead to disruptive spending patterns, particularly for new funds or funds with market value at or near book value. To maintain normal spending patterns, institutions may consider an accounting reclassification or transfer of unrestricted FFE to fulfill balance sheet requirements that the market value of an endowment fund not fall below its historical book value.

At the federal level, US endowed institutions must comply with tax and securities laws and reporting requirements. To achieve and maintain tax-exempt status under Section 501(c)(3) of the US Internal Revenue Code, an institution must ensure that no part of its net earnings inure or accrue to the benefit of any private individual. The code provides for intermediate sanctions in the form of excise taxes against individuals in a position to exercise substantial authority who engage in "excess benefit transactions" whereby they receive unreasonably high compensation or inappropriately derive private benefit from the tax-exempt organization. With little governmental oversight, endowed institutions must develop, maintain, and enforce clear guidelines and policies to prohibit improper behavior and manage conflicts of interest.

3.2.7 *Unique Circumstances*

Endowments vary widely in their size, governance, and staff resources, and thus in the investment strategies that they can intelligently and practically pursue. Endowments range from the very small, providing financial aid for a day care center, to the very large, supporting a major university. The responsibility of managing the endowment might fall to an unsophisticated board or to a collection of individuals knowledgeable about investments. Likewise, the investment staff responsible for managing and

---

17 A few states supplement UMIFA with this fiduciary standard of preserving the purchasing power of endowment values.

administering the endowment may be nonexistent or consist of many highly paid and experienced professionals. This wide variety in expertise and resources suggests that an endowment's specific circumstances may constrain the types of investments its board should consider.

Many large endowments have been leaders in adopting investments in alternative investments, such as private equities, real estate, natural resources, and absolute return strategies. These investments often require significant staff time and expertise to find, evaluate, select, and monitor. Because the **active management** component of returns in these alternative, less-efficient markets is extremely important to long-term success, endowments should have significant resources and expertise before investing in nontraditional asset classes.

Often, alternative investment funds in the United States will seek exemption from registration under the Investment Company Act of 1940 and accept capital commitments only from investors who are Qualified Purchasers. Generally, endowments must have at least $25 million of investments to qualify. In some instances, investments are placed privately without SEC registration and are limited to accredited investors with assets in excess of $5 million. Thus the resources and size of an endowment or foundation can dictate its universe of potential investments.

Some endowed institutions develop ethical investment policies that become constraints to help ensure that portfolio investment activity is consistent with the organization's goals and mores. These policies can guide portfolio managers in voting shareholder proxies on issues of social or political significance. In certain circumstances, such as apartheid in South Africa, ethical investment policies have been used in an attempt to foster change through shareholder resolutions and divestment. Other examples of socially responsible investing include the application of exclusion criteria related to child labor, gambling, tobacco, firearms, and violation of human rights. In Example 13, we show how investment objectives and constraints come together in the formulation of an investment policy statement for an endowment.

EXAMPLE 13

The City Arts School

The City Arts School (CAS) is an independent private school educating 500 children from 9th through 12th grade. Founded in 1920, it is located in a modest-sized city in the northeastern United States with a diverse socioeconomic and racial population. CAS has an outstanding reputation and draws students from the city and surrounding suburban communities. The school has an excellent program in the performing and visual arts; in addition, it offers a broad and innovative curriculum with small class sizes.

CAS has an annual operating budget of approximately $10 million, more than 90 percent of which goes to salaries and benefits for teachers and a small administrative staff. With conservative fiscal management, the school has built and maintained a fine campus over the years without the use of debt. Due to the limited availability of adjacent land or other space, the school is unlikely to expand in the foreseeable future. CAS's inflation rate has averaged 1 percent above that of the economy in general.

CAS has an endowment of $30 million, composed of $10 million for general unrestricted support, $10 million for financial aid, $5 million of small funds with various donor-specified use restrictions, and $5 million of unrestricted funds functioning as endowment.

The CAS board consists of 15 elected directors, each serving three-year terms. In addition, the head of the school serves on the board *ex officio*. The board delegates responsibility for investing the endowment to an investment committee that includes at least three board members as well as other members of the CAS community who can offer investment expertise and guidance. Investments are monitored and implemented by the school's business and operations manager.

Proposed Statement of Endowment Goals

The goal of the CAS Endowment (and funds that the board has designated as endowment) is to provide significant, stable, and sustainable funding to support the school's annual operating budget and specific donor-designated programs. Endowment funds will be invested with the objective of earning high, long-term returns after inflation without undue risk of permanently impairing the long-term purchasing power of assets or incurring volatile short-term declines in asset values or annual spending flows.

Spending Policy for Endowment

The goal of the CAS Endowment spending policy is to provide a sustainable, stable annual source of income from the endowment to the operating budget of CAS. The spending policy helps provide financial discipline to the school by providing a clear, unequivocal amount of annual funding from the endowment consistent with sustainable long-term operations.

Spending from the endowment (and funds designated as endowment by the board) shall be determined by a spending rule that smoothes the volatility of spending from year to year using a weighted-average formula. The formula takes into account spending from the prior year as well as the endowment's current market value. Spending for a fiscal year shall be calculated by adding 70 percent of the prior year's spending amount to 30 percent of the endowment market value at the beginning of the prior fiscal year times the policy spending rate of 4.5 percent.

$$\text{Spending for fiscal year } t = 70\% \times [\text{Spending for fiscal year } (t-1)] + 30\% \times [4.5\% \times \text{Endowment market value at beginning of fiscal year } (t-1)]$$

Adjustments will be made to incorporate the effects of new gifts, additions, or fund decapitalizations. Spending from new gifts or additions to the endowment in their first year shall be at the same rate as other endowment funds adjusted pro rata to reflect the partial year of inclusion in the endowment.

Given these goals for the endowment, specify appropriate objectives and constraints.

Solution:

Return Objectives

The goal of the CAS Endowment is to provide a significant annual distribution to support the school's programs while maintaining the fund's long-term purchasing power. In general, inflation for the school runs about 1 percent above that of the economy. Therefore, in order to maintain the fund's purchasing power with a 4.5 percent spending rate, net of investment management expenses the portfolio must generate a long-term return greater than 5.5 percent above a broad measure of inflation such as the US CPI.

Risk Objectives

CAS must address two primary risks in investing its endowment. As discussed above, CAS must protect the endowment's long-term purchasing power by generating real returns above spending. In the short term, the CAS Endowment should produce a reliable and somewhat stable flow of funding for programs. This short-term risk is tempered by CAS's spending rule, which smoothes distributions with a geometric moving average spending rate. In addition, endowment spending is not a very large part of the school's annual budget (less than 14 percent of revenues). Endowment spending could fall by as much as 20 percent and the impact on the budget would be less than 3 percent of revenues. CAS is debt free and has an above-average risk tolerance.

Constraints

Liquidity

Only a small percentage of the fund, approximately 4 or 5 percent, is spent each year, and the fund's historical gift value should remain invested and not spent. A portion of the CAS Endowment pool, however, is composed of funds functioning as endowment. The board, in extraordinary circumstances, may decide to spend the FFE because the monies are not permanently restricted.

Time Horizon

Endowment funds have an extremely long time horizon because they are expected to support activities in perpetuity.

Tax Concerns

CAS is a tax-exempt organization, and returns on its investments are not taxed in most circumstances. The school should carefully consider any investment or gift that generates UBTI, because such an item could dramatically increase tax reporting requirements.

Legal and Regulatory Factors

CAS's investments have very few legal and regulatory constraints. The school should, however, take precautions to avoid conflicts of interest, or the perception of conflicts, involving committee or board members. In addition to being poor and wasteful management, inappropriate transactions with individuals in a supervisory role may lead to sanctions and penalties under IRS regulations. In general, the school's financial and investment activities are under the purview of the state attorney general. Trustees are expected to act prudently, consistent with standards of sound business practice.

Unique Circumstances

CAS is a small school with limited administrative and investment resources. Its endowment portfolio, although meaningful to the school and its operations, is not of sufficient scale to support dedicated internal investment staffing. All investments should be managed externally. CAS should view skeptically any investment that requires extensive monitoring, a close long-term relationship with external investment managers, or a high degree of sophisticated expertise to manage properly. Similarly, CAS should be wary of investments that require a high degree of active management skill to generate satisfactory returns. The school does not have the resources to identify, evaluate, and monitor the top managers in specialized investment areas. Furthermore, the size of its portfolio will not support a diversified investment program in nontraditional alternatives such as private equity. Even an aggressive allocation of 20 percent would amount to only $6 million, barely enough to make a single commitment to a top-tier private equity investment fund.

The investment committee has a relatively high turnover, with members serving only three-year terms. CAS runs the risk that new committee members renounce some long-term investments and act hastily to liquidate or pull support from worthy but underperforming investments. This risk is greatest with volatile, unconventional investments that may require patience, fortitude, and a contrarian mindset to endure difficult market environments.

THE INSURANCE INDUSTRY

4

The economic significance of the insurance industry lies in its unique role as an absorber of personal and business risks. By providing financial protection, the industry plays a key role in a country's economic growth and development. Because of the risk aspects of the business and the contractual obligations to policyholders, the insurance industry's traditional investment practices have been characterized as conservative. As we will discuss later, however, insurers have shown increasing risk tolerance in recent years.

The insurance industry is complex but can be divided into three broad product categories: life insurance, health insurance, and property and liability insurance. For purposes of considering investment policy, it is sufficient to narrow the categories to life and non-life (casualty) insurance companies. This division is consistent with the major classifications established by the insurance regulatory bodies and some, if not most, taxing authorities in the world's industrialized countries.

Insurance companies, whether life or casualty, are established either as **stock companies** (companies that have issued common equity shares) or as **mutuals** (companies with no stock that are owned by their policyholders). Mutuals traditionally have played a major role in certain segments of the insurance industry, but stockholder-owned companies are now the primary form of entry into the industry. Many of the major mutual insurance companies in the United States, Canada, the United Kingdom, and continental Europe have completed or are in the process of **demutualizing** (converting to stock companies). Although the investment operations of mutual and stock companies differ only slightly, the differences between life and non-life insurers are substantial, as we illustrate in the following sections.

4.1 Life Insurance Companies: Background and Investment Setting

Exposure to interest-rate-related risk is one major characteristic of life insurers' investment setting. Besides fixed-income portfolio gains and losses related to interest rate changes, many life insurance company liabilities such as annuity contracts are interest rate sensitive. In addition, insurers also face the risk of disintermediation, which often becomes acute when interest rates are high.[18]

One type of disintermediation occurs when policyholders borrow against the accumulated cash value in insurance products such as ordinary life insurance.[19] US life insurance companies experienced unprecedented disintermediation in the early 1980s. As interest rates reached record high levels (in the mid to high teens) during that period, policyholders took advantage of the option to borrow some or all of the accumulated cash value in their policies at the below-market policy loan rates

---

18 Disintermediation occurs when individuals withdraw funds from financial intermediaries for deposit or investment in other financial intermediaries or investments offering a higher return (yield).

19 Ordinary life insurance (also called **whole life insurance**) is a type of policy that typically provides level death benefits for the whole of the insured's life. The premium is typically a level amount determined by such factors as the insured's sex and age at the time the policy is issued, and the cash value is based on the insurer's estimate of the expected return on the investments that fund policy reserves. In contrast, **term life insurance** provides death benefits for a specified length of time and accumulates little or no cash values.

(generally 5 to 9 percent) that were contractually defined in their insurance policies. The policy loan feature has long been considered an important life insurance policy provision. In the 1980s, the true cost of this option became clear to the industry, as cash available for investment at the then prevailing double-digit interest rates was siphoned off in part to fund policy loans. When interest rates are high, insurers also face another type of disintermediation: the risk that policyholders will surrender their cash value life insurance policies for their accumulated cash values, in order to reinvest the proceeds at a higher interest rate. As a result of these forces, insurers face marketplace pressures to offer competitive cash value accumulation rates or **credited rates** (rates of interest credited to a policyholder's reserve account).

These developments have made the liabilities of life insurers more interest rate sensitive than before and have tended to shorten the duration of liabilities. Policyholders are now more prone to exercise their option to surrender a life insurance policy or annuity contract as they seek the most competitive credited rates and/or policy benefits. Surrender rates triggered by interest rate changes are more difficult to predict than mortality rates and thus are the more critical variable for many interest-sensitive life insurance products. Shorter liability durations have necessitated the shortening of the duration of life insurance company portfolios, or at least those segments designed to fund these interest-rate-sensitive product liabilities.

Universal life, variable life, and variable universal life represent the insurance industry's response to disintermediation.[20] Companies developed these products to offset the competitive appeal of buying term insurance and investing the difference between term insurance premiums and the often higher premiums of ordinary life insurance policies. These new products provide life insurance buyers with a viable means of purchasing varying amounts of insurance protection along with an opportunity to save or invest at rates that vary with capital market and competitive conditions.

Exhibit 3 illustrates the growth of new individual life insurance forms in the United States, based on data provided by the American Council of Life Insurers. As the increase in term life insurance purchases demonstrates, there is a trend toward unbundling insurance risk management and investment management. To attract customers, each of the new policy forms must offer competitive rates of return.

Exhibit 3	Analysis of Life Insurance Purchases in the United States: Selected Years, 1978–2009				
	Percentage of Dollar Amount of Life Insurance Purchases				
Policy Type	**1978 (%)**	**1988 (%)**	**1999 (%)**	**2002 (%)**	**2009 (%)**
Term life	52	40	57	69	74
Whole life	45	30	13	10	26
Universal life	na	20	11	9	na
Variable life	na	9	19	12	na

---

20 Universal life insurance provides premium flexibility, an adjustable face amount of death benefits, and current market interest rates on the savings element. The universal life policyholder pays a specified amount for the insurance protection desired and can deposit funds in a savings account, for a fee. **Variable life insurance (unit-linked life insurance)** is a type of ordinary life insurance for which death benefits and cash values are linked to the investment performance of a policyholder-selected pool of investments held in a so-called separate account. **Variable universal life (flexible-premium variable life)** combines the flexibility of universal life with the investment choice flexibility of variable life.

Exhibit 3	**(Continued)**				
	Percentage of Dollar Amount of Life Insurance Purchases				
Policy Type	**1978 (%)**	**1988 (%)**	**1999 (%)**	**2002 (%)**	**2009 (%)**
Other	3	1	0	0	0
Total	100	100	100	100	100

na = not applicable.

Sources: Life Insurance Fact Book (1979, 1989, 2000, 2011) and *ACLI Survey* (2003).

4.1.1 *Risk Objectives*

An insurance company's primary investment objective is to fund future policyholder benefits and claims. Because of the economic importance of the insurance industry, the investment portfolio of an insurer (life or non-life) is looked upon from a public policy viewpoint as a quasi-trust fund. Accordingly, conservative fiduciary principles limit the risk tolerance of an insurance company investment portfolio. Confidence in an insurance company's ability to pay benefits as they come due is a crucial element in the economy's financial foundation. Therefore, insurance companies are sensitive to the risk of any significant chance of principal loss or any significant interruption of investment income.

To absorb some modest loss of principal, US life insurance companies are required to maintain an asset valuation reserve, a reserve established by the National Association of Insurance Commissioners (NAIC). Companies use specific NAIC-developed "quality tests" for each class of invested assets to determine the annual contributions to, and maximum amounts of, the reserve. The maximum reserve rates establish a substantial margin for absorbing investment losses. With a growing portfolio, however, a life company's asset valuation reserves may be inadequate. Surplus is thus vulnerable to write-downs if significant losses occur.[21]

Insurance regulators worldwide have been moving toward risk-based capital (RBC) requirements to assure that companies maintain adequate surplus to cover their risk exposures relating to both assets and liabilities. In the United States, RBC calculations are somewhat complex and attempt to allocate surplus in proportion to the asset and liability risk exposures of each insurance company. By subtracting the risk-based capital required from each company's total surplus, the regulators can estimate whether the company's surplus is sufficient. In addition, applying GAAP to both mutual and stock insurance companies requires the use of market valuation for most classes of assets and thus has increased balance sheet volatility. Absent a requirement that life insurance liabilities be marked to market, however, accounting statement implications may affect a company's risk tolerance in ways that are inconsistent with a market-based-valuation perspective of the company's risk exposure.

Asset/liability risk considerations figure prominently in life insurers' risk objectives, not only because of the need to fund insurance benefits but also because of the importance of interest-rate-sensitive liabilities. Examples of such liabilities are annuities and deposit-type contracts, such as GICs and funding agreements (stable-value instruments similar to GICs).

---

21 The excess of losses on assets over the assets' valuation reserve is a direct reduction in surplus. A **valuation reserve** is an allowance, created by a charge against earnings, to provide for losses in the value of the assets. **Surplus** is the net difference between the total assets and total liabilities of an insurance company; it is equivalent to policyholders' surplus for a mutual insurance company and stockholders' equity for a stock company.

The two aspects of interest rate risk are valuation concerns and reinvestment risk:

■ **Valuation concerns.** In a period of changing interest rates, a mismatch between the duration of an insurance company's assets and that of its liabilities can lead to erosion of surplus. Life insurance companies are particularly sensitive to the losses that can result during periods of rising interest rates from holding assets with an average duration that exceeds the average duration of liabilities. (Adding to insurers' concerns is the fact that the risk of disintermediation is greatest in such interest rate environments.) In these situations, the existence of valuation reserves alone may be insufficient to prevent a write-down of surplus, possibly creating a capital adequacy problem. Consequently, valuation concerns tend to limit insurers' risk tolerance.

■ **Reinvestment risk.** For many life insurance companies, especially those competing for annuity business, yet another risk factor can be significant—reinvestment risk. **Reinvestment risk** is defined as the risk of reinvesting coupon income or principal at a rate less than the original coupon or purchase rate. For annuity contracts on which no interest is paid until maturity (the terminal date) of the contract, the guarantee rate typically includes the insurance company's best estimate of the rate(s) at which interest payments will be reinvested. If a company does not carefully manage its asset and liability durations, an unexpected decline in interest rates can jeopardize the profitability of these contracts. Thus, controlling reinvestment risk is also an important risk objective.

Asset/liability management is the foundation for controlling both interest rate risk and liquidity for a life insurance company. Risk objectives addressing the mismatch of the duration of assets and liabilities are common.

Credit risk is also important in meeting insurance promises:

■ **Credit risk. Credit risk** represents another potential source of income loss for insurance companies, although credit analysis has long been considered one of the industry's strengths. Insurers seek to control this risk through broad diversification and seek adequate compensation for taking risk in terms of the expected return or interest rate spread when investing in various asset classes. Risk objectives may relate to losses caused by credit risk.[22]

Another risk consideration relates to uncertainty in the timing of receipt of cash flows:

■ **Cash flow volatility.** Loss of income or delays in collecting and reinvesting cash flow from investments is another key aspect of risk for which life insurance companies have low tolerance. Compounding (interest on interest) is an integral part of the reserve funding formula and a source of surplus growth. Actuaries assume that investment income will be available for reinvestment at a rate at least equal to an assumed (minimum return) rate. Controlling cash flow volatility is thus a risk objective.

---

[22] Recent changes in GAAP have further complicated the management of credit risk by US insurance companies. The Financial Accounting Standard 115 and subsequent interpretative documents require a permanent write-down of the value of securities that have experienced an "Other Than Temporary Impairment" (OTTI). This type of impairment in value is defined as an unrealized loss that results from the decline in the market value of a security below its cost for an extended period of time. This Standard has been controversial and most likely will undergo additional modification because it does not allow for any subsequent write-up in value if the credit quality of the issuer improves and is so recognized in the market value. Also, declines in market value below cost that are caused by an increase in interest rates may require a permanent write-down under the current interpretation of FAS 115.

Despite the above four risk-related considerations, competition has modified the traditional conservatism of life insurance companies, motivating them to accept and manage varying degrees of risk in pursuit of more competitive investment returns.

4.1.2 *Return Objectives*

Historically, a life insurance company's return requirements have been specified primarily by the rates that actuaries use to determine policyholder reserves, i.e., accumulation rates for the funds held by the company for future disbursement.[23] In effect, the rate either continues as initially specified for the life of the contract or may change to reflect the company's actual investment experience, according to the contract terms. Interest is then credited to the reserve account at the specified rate; this rate can thus be defined as the minimum return requirement. If the insurer fails to earn the minimum return, its liabilities will increase by an accrual of interest that is greater than the increase in assets. The shortfall is reflected in a decrease in surplus or surplus reserves, assuming the simplest case. The insurer, in short, desires to earn a positive net interest spread, and return objectives may include a desired net interest spread. (The **net interest spread** is the difference between interest earned and interest credited to policyholders.) Reserve funding adequacy is monitored carefully by management, regulatory commissions, and insurance rating agencies such as A.M. Best, as well as through the claims paying rating services initiated by Moody's Investors Service, Standard & Poor's Corporation, and Fitch Ratings.

In the mid to late 1980s, Japanese life insurance companies issued policies that guaranteed what proved to be unsustainable reserve crediting rates—and guaranteed those rates for as long as 10 years. With the sharp decline in interest rates, stock prices, and real estate values during the 1990s in Japan, these companies sustained unprecedented losses and consequent erosion of the surplus of the Japanese life insurance industry. These events provided an important lesson regarding the setting of return objectives, crediting rates, and guarantee periods in a volatile investment environment.

In the United States, with whole-life insurance policies, the minimum statutory accumulation rate for most life insurance contracts ranges between 3 and 5.5 percent. Thus, in the higher interest rate environment of the 1970s and 1980s, the spread between life insurance companies' return on new investments and even the return on their entire portfolio exceeded the minimum returns by a widening margin. But as growing investor sophistication and competition in insurance markets led to higher credited rates, and as interest rates declined in the 1990s and early 2000s, the net interest spread narrowed quickly and dramatically. As a result, US regulators have permitted minimum statutory accumulation rates to be reduced.

Consistently above-average investment returns should and do provide an insurance company with some competitive advantage in setting premiums. Life insurance companies have found that an improvement as small as 10 basis points (0.10 percent) in the total portfolio yield improves their competitive position and profitability significantly. Portfolio yields for most life portfolios, however, are more similar than different, as Exhibit 4 shows. To a large extent, this similarity reflects the role regulation plays in constraining the asset mix and quality characteristics of every life insurance company portfolio and the historical evolution of portfolio asset allocation in that regulatory environment.

---

23 Policyholder reserves are a balance sheet liability for an insurance company; they represent the estimated payments to policyholders, as determined by actuaries, based on the types and terms of the various insurance policies issued by the company.

Exhibit 4	Portfolio Yields of US Life Insurance Companies: Selected Years, 1975–2010			
	Major Life Insurance Companies			
	Industry Rate (%)	Prudential (%)	Lincoln National (%)	AXA Equitable-NY (%)
1975	6.44	6.47	6.98	6.22
1985	9.87	9.07	8.49	8.72
1995	7.90	7.47	7.87	6.88
2000	7.40	6.41	6.93	6.70
2004	5.93	5.55	5.82	6.23
2010	5.37	5.16	5.48	6.13

Note: Portfolio yield equals the ratio of net investment income (after expenses and before income taxes) to mean cash and invested assets.
Sources: Life Insurance Fact Book (2001); *Best's Insurance Reports* (2005) *Best's Review* (October, 2011).

Some companies have experimented with using total return rather than interest rate spread to measure their investment portfolios' performance and their products' profitability. When only the asset side of a balance sheet reflects market volatility, it is difficult to use total return measures. To the extent that comprehensive fair market value accounting standards are developed in the future, they will greatly enhance asset/liability management and performance and profitability measurement on a total return basis.

For companies selling annuity and guaranteed investment contracts, competitive investment returns have become necessary and spread margins are narrow. The annuity segment of the life insurance business has accounted for approximately two-thirds of total industry reserves for more than a decade (see Exhibit 5).

Exhibit 5	Reserves for Annuities and Guaranteed Investment Contracts for the US Life Insurance Industry: Selected Years, 1970–2009	
		Percentage of Total Reserves
	1970	26.6%
	1980	45.4
	1990	66.7
	2002	64.6
	2009	64.0

Source: Life Insurance Fact Book (2003, 2011).

For these lines of business, competition comes from outside as well as from within the industry. These competitive pressures create a dilemma for insurance companies. While insurance companies are required to control risk, many companies feel compelled to mismatch asset/liability durations or downgrade the credit quality of their investments in an attempt to achieve higher returns for competitive reasons.

Segmentation of insurance company portfolios has promoted the establishment of sub-portfolio return objectives to promote competitive crediting rates for groups of contracts. The major life insurance companies find themselves specifying return requirements by major line of business, the result being that a single company's investment policy may incorporate multiple return objectives.

Another dimension of return objectives for life insurance companies relates to the need to grow surplus to support expanding business volume. Common stocks, equity investments in real estate, and private equity have been the investment alternatives most widely used to achieve surplus growth. Life companies establish return objectives for each of these classes of equity investments to reflect historical and expected returns. Many life insurance companies are evaluating a variety of capital appreciation strategies, as well as financial leverage, to supplement the narrowing contribution to surplus from the newer product lines that are more competitive and have lower profit margins.

4.1.3 Liquidity Requirements

Traditionally, life insurance companies have been characterized as needing minimal liquidity. Except during the depression of the 1930s and the disintermediation of the early 1980s, annual cash inflow has far exceeded cash outflow. Thus, the need to liquidate assets has been negligible, reflecting the growing volume of business, the longer-term nature of liabilities, and the rollover in portfolio assets from maturing securities and other forms of principal payments. However, volatile interest rate environments and the ever-increasing importance of annuity products require that life companies pay close attention to their liquidity requirements. Otherwise, insurers may be forced to sell bonds at a loss to meet surrenders of insurance policies in periods of sharply rising interest rates. In assessing their liquidity needs, insurers must address disintermediation and asset marketability risk.

- **Disintermediation.** In the United States, on four different occasions in the past 40 years (1966, 1970, 1974, and 1979–1981), inflation and high interest rates have forced life insurance companies to take measures to accommodate extraordinary net cash outflows. Initially, policy loan drains in conjunction with heavy forward commitment positions forced some remedial but temporary changes in investment strategies. Likewise, the trend of policy surrenders caused 1) actuaries to reevaluate and reduce their estimates of the duration of liabilities and 2) portfolio managers to reduce the average duration of the portfolio and in some cases add to liquidity reserves.

  In a period of rising interest rates, a mismatch between the duration of an insurance company's assets and its liabilities can create a net loss if the assets' duration exceeds that of the liabilities. If disintermediation occurs concurrently, the insurer may need to sell assets at a realized loss to meet liquidity needs. Thus, an asset/liability mismatch can exacerbate the effects of disintermediation.

- **Asset marketability risk.** The marketability of investments is important to insure ample liquidity. Life insurance companies have traditionally invested some portion of their portfolios in less liquid investments, such as private placement bonds, commercial mortgage loans, equity real estate, and venture capital. Increasingly, liquidity considerations are constraining the percentage invested in these asset classes. Also, forward commitment activity has been slowed by liquidity considerations. Such commitments represent agreements by life insurance companies to purchase private placement bonds or mortgages, with part or all of the settlement typically delayed from 6 to 18 months. The traditional stability and growth of cash flow fostered this practice in the 1960s and

1970s, but volatile interest rates and disintermediation have undermined the predictability of life companies' cash flow. Forward committing has thus waned in importance in recent years.

The growth and development of the derivatives market has broadened the life insurance industry's ability to manage interest rate risk and reduced companies' need to hold significant liquidity reserves. Many companies also maintain lines of credit with banks for added liquidity.

4.1.4 *Time Horizon*

Life insurance companies have long been considered the classic long-term investor. Traditionally, portfolio return objectives have been evaluated within the context of holding periods as long as 20 to 40 years. Most life insurance companies have traditionally sought long-term maturities for bond and mortgage investments. In addition, life companies have found equity investments (real estate, common stocks, convertible securities, and venture capital) attractive because of their capital appreciation potential and inflation (purchasing power) risk protection.

One reason that life insurance companies have traditionally segmented their portfolios is the recognition that particular product lines or lines of business have unique time horizons and return objectives. For example, group annuities are generally written with maturities of 2 to 10 years. Therefore, many, if not most, of the assets funding those products have comparable maturities (or, more accurately, durations).

Asset/liability management practices have tended to shorten the overall investment time horizon of the typical life insurance company. Today, portfolio segments have differing time horizons, reflected in each segment's investment policies.

4.1.5 *Tax Concerns*

Unlike pension funds and endowments, insurance companies are tax-paying rather than wholly or partially tax-exempt investors. As commercial enterprises, they are subject to income, capital gains, and other types of taxes in the countries where they operate. The types and application of taxes differ by country, but in all cases, taxes mean that insurance companies must focus on after-tax returns in their investment activities.

In a very simplified context, life insurance companies' investment income can be divided into two parts for tax purposes: the policyholders' share (that portion relating to the actuarially assumed rate necessary to fund reserves) and the corporate share (the balance that is transferred to surplus). Under present US law, only the latter portion is taxed.

One very important tax consideration being watched carefully by the US life insurance industry relates to the tax treatment of the so-called inside buildup of cash values under a life insurance policy or annuity. The deferral of taxes on the accumulation of cash values within a life insurance contract has been a longstanding characteristic of such products. In the United States, Congress periodically reassesses the tax deferral of such inside buildup for life and annuity products. Tax law changes that would reduce or eliminate the tax deferral granted to the inside buildup would create significant competitive issues for the life insurance industry.

4.1.6 *Legal and Regulatory Factors*

Insurance is a heavily regulated industry. In the United States, state rather than federal regulation prevails. The lack of uniformity of state regulation and the cost of meeting the unique requirements imposed by 50 different states impose costs on insurers. Currently, state regulation pervades all aspects of an insurance company's operations—permitted lines of business, product and policy forms, authorized investments, and the like. The NAIC, whose membership includes regulators from all 50 states, promulgates insurance industry accounting rules and financial statement forms. In

1999, the US Congress passed the Financial Modernization Act, which essentially removed barriers to entry for banks, insurance companies, and investment brokerage firms that dated back to the Great Depression of the 1930s. Regulation of financial institutions in the United States is now more closely aligned with prevailing regulation in many other parts of the world. In Canada, regulation is federal, except for those companies doing business only within a specific province. At either level—federal or provincial—Canadian regulation is as pervasive as US regulation. In Japan, the Ministry of Finance regulates insurance companies, while in the United Kingdom, the Financial Services Authority has been the responsible governmental authority, with the Prudential Regulatory Authority (as a subsidiary of the Bank of England) expected to take over that role by the end of 2012.

The relevant insurance department or ministry audit procedures ensure compliance with the regulations of the state or country where the company is domiciled. In most cases, these regulations are the primary constraint affecting investment policy. Important concepts related to regulatory and legal considerations include eligible investments, the prudent investor rule, and valuation methods.[24]

- **Eligible investments.** Insurance laws determine the classes of assets eligible for investment and may specify the quality standards for each asset class. In the United States, for example, many states' insurance laws require that for a bond issue to be eligible for investment, its interest coverage ratio (earnings plus interest divided by interest) must meet minimum standards over a specified time period (e.g., 1.5 times coverage over each of the past five years) or minimum credit ratings. Generally, regulations specify the percentage of an insurance company's assets that may be invested in a specific class of eligible assets. For example, in the United States, most states limit the value (at cost) of life companies' common stock holdings to no more than 20 percent of total admitted assets. Non-US investments are also limited to some extent as a percentage of admitted assets in most states.

- **Prudent investor rule.** Although the scope of regulation is extensive, it is important to note that the prudent investor concept has been adopted in some US states. Replacing traditional "laundry lists" of approved investments with prudent investor logic simplifies the regulatory process and allows life insurance companies much needed flexibility to keep up with the ever-changing array of investment alternatives. New York's leadership in this area is important because, traditionally, regulations of this state have been the model for insurance regulation in the United States. Despite a major effort in the mid-1990s, however, no model law or universal investment standards have been adopted by all US states.

- **Valuation methods.** In the European Union, International Accounting Standards specify a set of valuation procedures. In the United States, uniform valuation methods are established and administered by the NAIC. In fact, the NAIC's *Security Valuation Book*, published at the end of each year, compiles the values or valuation bases to be used by insurance companies for portfolio securities. This book is the source of the valuation data listed in Schedule D of the annual statement that each company files with the insurance departments of the states in which it operates. Schedule D is an inventory of all bond and stock holdings at year-end and a recap of the year's transactions.

---

24 The scope of regulation is not limited to these areas. Many life insurance and annuity products have investment features. In the United States and the European Union, life insurance companies are subject to anti-money-laundering regulation to prevent the use of such products for illegal purposes.

In summary, regulation has a profound effect on both the risk and return aspects of a life insurance company portfolio, primarily because it constrains two critical aspects of portfolio management—asset allocation and the universe of eligible investments.

4.1.7 *Unique Circumstances*

Each insurance company, whether life or non-life, may have unique circumstances attributable to factors other than the insurance products it provides. These idiosyncrasies may further modify portfolio policies. The company's size and the sufficiency of its surplus position are among the considerations influencing portfolio policy.

To conclude, we provide a sample investment policy statement. Although the format and content of investment policy statements are unique to each insurance company, Example 14 represents a typical IPS for a stock life insurance company.[25]

EXAMPLE 14

Investment Policy Statement for a Stock Life Insurer

ABC Life Insurance Company ("the Company") underwrites and markets life insurance and annuity products. The Company is licensed to do business in all 50 US states. In recent years, the Company has expanded its operations outside the United States and now is licensed and doing business in one Asian and two European countries. The Company's total assets exceed $15 billion; the Company has surplus of more than $1 billion. Competition in its markets is increasing both from traditional insurance company competitors and more recently, from other financial institutions, such as banks and mutual funds. In response to this increased competition, the Company must take more risk and establish higher return objectives for its investment portfolio so as to maintain an adequate margin (spread) between its investment portfolio return and the weighted-average rates of return being credited to its interest-rate-sensitive life insurance policies and annuity contracts. The Company's investment objectives may be defined in terms of its return and risk objectives for each of the portfolio segments (for example, its real estate portfolio). The statement below reflects a common set of objectives that applies in whole or in part to each of the respective portfolio segments. Policy statements exist for each segment that contain details on segment-specific risk and return specifications. Capital market and insurance market conditions shape the achievement of these policy objectives.

Investment Philosophy

The assets of the Company should be invested to provide for the payment of all contractual obligations to policyholders and to contribute to the growth of surplus over the long-term. Therefore, the investment strategy will be based on prudent investment principles within the context of applicable insurance regulations. The strategy will seek to achieve the appropriate balance between: providing investment income to enhance profitability; maintaining liquidity and generating cash flow to meet all obligations; funding policyholder reserves within pricing strategies; and growing the value of surplus over time, thereby contributing to the Company's future growth.

---

25 A stock life insurance company is organized as a corporation owned by stockholders.

Investment Goals, Objectives and Constraints

The Company's investment goals and objectives will be stated in terms of return expectations and requirements and risk tolerance. The constraints under which the investment portfolio will be managed include liquidity considerations, time horizon, regulatory restrictions, tax considerations and unique requirements.

Return Objectives

The return objectives of the Company are twofold: a) earn a sufficient return to fund all policyholder liabilities and match or exceed the expected returns factored into the pricing of the Company's various products, and b) contribute to the growth of surplus through capital appreciation. The return objectives will be stated in terms of meeting or exceeding projected needs related to investment income, product pricing spreads, and total return. The return requirements may vary by portfolio segments that have been established for certain product lines or groupings of product lines.

Risk Tolerance

The risk tolerance of the Company is based on the competitive requirements of various product lines, asset/liability management factors, risk-based capital considerations, rating agency parameters and the responsibility to fulfill all short-term and long-term obligations to policyholders. Interest rate risk and credit (default) risk need to be monitored and managed to support the competitive position of the Company while providing for its long-term viability. The risk parameters may vary by segment.

Investment Constraints

The Company's investment constraints are defined in terms of the following factors, all or some of which may apply to specific portfolio segments.

Liquidity

The portfolio will be managed to meet the liquidity requirements so as to pay all benefits and expenses in a timely manner. Investment cash flows will be a primary source of liquidity, so as to minimize the need to hold lower yielding cash reserves. In addition, publicly traded securities will provide an additional source of liquidity.

Time Horizon

The Company is a long-term investor and will establish duration targets for the portfolio and any product segments based on appropriate asset/liability management specifications.

Tax

Income tax considerations determine the mix of investments that provides the most favorable after-tax returns. From time to time, operating conditions or corporate tax planning requirements may mandate the realization or postponement of capital gains.

Regulatory

All investments must qualify under the insurance code of the state in which the Company is domiciled and the nondomestic insurance companies' regulations in the countries in which the Company operates.

Unique Circumstance

The Company may invest in less liquid private placement bonds, commercial mortgage loans, real estate and private equity to enhance returns so long as liquidity requirements are not compromised.

Review Schedule

This policy statement will be reviewed at least annually by the Board of Directors and is subject to modification based on significant changes in insurance or tax regulations as well as significant changes in the Company's financial position and/or capital- or insurance-market conditions.

Asset Allocation

The Company's strategic allocation is designed to identify and authorize the strategies for achieving the objectives specified by the investment policy statement. The strategic asset allocation also recognizes the constraints (both regulatory and self-imposed) specified in the investment policy statement. The selection of authorized asset classes and their allocation percentages are recognized as key determinants of the success of the Company's investment activities. The strategic asset allocation will be set out in a separate document.

Rebalancing

Changes in market values and market conditions require periodic portfolio rebalancing on at least a quarterly (and in some cases a more frequent) basis. Cash flow, insofar as it is available, will be used to rebalance. It should be recognized that some asset classes, such as private placement bonds, private equity, commercial mortgage loans, and real estate, are less liquid than publicly traded securities. Therefore, under most conditions, these asset classes should not be allowed to exceed the target allocations specified in the strategic asset allocation.

Investment Responsibilities

The Board of Directors is responsible for overseeing the invested assets and the investment process of the Company. The Board will rely on both Company employees and/or external investment service providers for the ongoing management of the investment portfolio. Because of the number of parties involved, each entity's role must be identified to ensure operational efficiency, clear lines of communication and accountability in all aspects of the management of the investment portfolio of the Company.

Board of Directors

The Board of Directors approves the investment policy statement and asset allocation at least annually. At least quarterly, the Board will review the performance of the investment portfolio and review and approve all transactions for that quarter.

Investment Management Committee

The Investment Management Committee will be composed of investment and financial officers of the Company. They will have ongoing responsibility for the management of the investment portfolio. On a quarterly basis, the Investment Management Committee will review investment performance and cash flow requirements with the Board of Directors. On an annual basis, or when either the Company's financial condition or capital market conditions change, the Investment Management Committee will review the investment policy statement and asset allocation and recommend changes to the Board.

External Investment Advisors

With the approval of the Board of Directors, the Investment Management Committee may retain external investment consultants and advisors to assist in the management of the investment portfolio or subparts thereof. All external investment advisors will be expected to manage all or any part of the portfolio in conformity with the investment policy statement and asset allocation.

Custodian

The Investment Management Committee is authorized to retain the services of a regulated bank or trust company to safeguard the cash and invested assets of the Company. The custodian will also be responsible for the payment and collection of all investment funds.

4.2 Non-Life Insurance Companies: Background and Investment Setting

The second broad insurance category is the non-life (casualty) sector, which includes but is not limited to health, property, liability, marine, surety, and workers' compensation insurance. For purposes of considering investment policy, these non-life companies are really quite similar even though the products they sell are rather diverse. The investment policies of a non-life company differ significantly from those of a life insurance company, however, because the liabilities, risk factors, and tax considerations for non-life companies are distinctly different from those for life companies. For example:

- non-life liability durations tend to be shorter, and claim processing and payments periods are longer, than for life companies;

- some (but not all) non-life liabilities are exposed to inflation risk, although liabilities are not directly exposed to interest rate risk as those of life insurance companies; and

- in general, a life insurance company's liabilities are relatively certain in value but uncertain in timing, while a non-life insurance company's liabilities are relatively uncertain in both value and timing, with the result that non-life insurance companies are exposed to more volatility in their operating results.

As detailed in this section, the investment policies and practices of non-life insurance companies in the United States are evolving, with changes brought on by both operating considerations and new tax laws. In fact, tax planning has dominated the investment policy of non-life companies for decades, reflecting the cyclical characteristics of this segment of the insurance industry. For reasons described in the following pages, asset/liability management is receiving increased attention.

A unique aspect of the casualty insurance industry is what is often described as the "long tail" that characterizes the industry's claims reporting, processing, and payment structure.[26] Whereas life insurance is heavily oriented toward products sold to or for individuals, commercial customers account for a very large portion of the total casualty insurance market. The long tail nature of many types of liability (both individual and commercial) and casualty insurance claims arises from the fact that months and years may pass between the date of the occurrence and reporting of the claim and the actual payment of a settlement to a policyholder. Many casualty industry claims are the subject of lawsuits to determine settlement amounts. Furthermore, some of these claims require expert evaluation to determine the extent of the damages—for example, a fire in a major manufacturing plant or damage to an oceangoing vessel. Thus, the liability structure of a casualty insurance company is very much a function of the products that it sells and the claims reporting and settlement process for those types of products.

From an asset/liability management perspective, most casualty insurance companies traditionally have been classified as having relatively short-term liabilities, even though the spectrum of casualty insurance policies covers a wide range of liability durations.

---

26 "Long tail" refers to the possibly long time span between the liability-triggering event and the filing of a claim related to it.

One of the primary factors that limits the duration of a non-life company's assets is the so-called **underwriting (profitability) cycle**, generally averaging three to five years. These cycles typically result from adverse claims experience and/or periods of extremely competitive pricing. They often coincide with general business cycles and, in the low part of the cycle, frequently require companies to liquidate investments to supplement cash flow shortfalls.

Estimating the duration of a casualty insurance company's liabilities introduces a different set of issues than with life insurance liabilities. Using multiscenario and multifactor models, casualty actuaries attempt to capture 1) the underwriting cycle, 2) the liability durations by product line, and 3) any unique cash outflow characteristics. For non-life companies, business cycles and not interest rate cycles, per se, determine a company's need for liquidity through appropriate durations and maturities of assets.

4.2.1 Risk Objectives

Like life insurance companies, casualty insurance companies have a quasi-fiduciary role; thus the ability to meet policyholders' claims is a dominant consideration influencing investment policy. The risks insured by casualty companies, however, are less predictable. In fact, for companies exposed to catastrophic events—such as hurricanes, tornadoes, and explosions—the potential for loss may be significantly greater. Furthermore, casualty policies frequently provide replacement cost or current cost coverage; thus inflation adds to the degree of risk. In setting risk objectives, casualty companies must consider both cash flow characteristics and the common stock to surplus ratio.

- **Cash flow characteristics.** Not surprisingly, cash flows from casualty insurance operations can be quite erratic. Unlike life insurance companies, which historically have been able to project cash flows and make forward commitments, casualty companies must be prepared to meet operating cash gaps with investment income or maturing securities. Therefore, for the portion of the investment portfolio relating to policyholder reserves, casualty companies have low tolerance for loss of principal or diminishing investment income. Investment maturities and investment income must be predictable in order to directly offset the unpredictability of operating trends.

  Interestingly, no regulations require casualty insurance companies to maintain an asset valuation reserve, although risk-based capital requirements have been established in the United States. Regulators and rating agencies closely monitor the ratio of a casualty insurance company's premium income to its total surplus. Generally, this ratio is maintained between 2-to-1 and 3-to-1.

- **Common stock to surplus ratio.** Inflation worldwide has further reduced investment risk tolerance among many casualty insurers. In fact, volatile stock market conditions in the 1970s persuaded many casualty companies to reduce the percentage of surplus invested in common stock. Until then, it was not uncommon for a casualty insurance company to hold common stock investments equal to or greater than its total surplus. Regulators in the United States forced several major companies to liquidate large portions of their common stock holdings near the end of the 1974 bear market because of significant erosion of surplus. This liquidation impaired these companies' ability to increase volume and, in some cases, their ability to provide sufficient financial stability for existing volume of business.

  Essentially, the regulators gave such companies the option of reducing common stock holdings or of temporarily ceasing or curtailing the issuance of new policies. Needless to say, this experience reduced casualty companies' risk tolerance for the portion of the investment portfolio related to surplus. Unlike the life insurance industry, the casualty industry has almost no absolute limits imposed by regulation (in the United States, some states do limit commons stocks as a percentage of surplus). However, many casualty companies have adopted self-imposed limitations restricting common stocks at market value to some significant but limited portion (frequently one-half to three-quarters) of total surplus. During the bull market of the 1990s, many companies modified those self-imposed limits. Nevertheless, the attention paid to stock market risk exposure has prevented a repeat of the mid-1970s experience.

4.2.2 Return Objectives

Historically, most casualty insurance companies have not implicitly taken investment earnings into account when calculating premiums, in striking contrast to the accumulation rates long factored into life insurance premiums. For this reason, casualty insurance companies were once thought to be operating as if they were two separate organizations—an insurance company and an investment company operating a balanced fund (a fund holding a mixture of bonds and stocks). However, times have changed and the investment and operating functions are much more closely coordinated now. Factors influencing return objectives include competitive pricing policy, profitability, growth of surplus, tax considerations, and total return management.

- **Competitive policy pricing.** Low insurance policy premium rates, due to competition, provide an incentive for insurance companies to set high desired investment return objectives. The flip side is that high investment returns may induce insurance companies to lower their policy rates, even though a high level of returns cannot be sustained. In the late 1970s and early 1980s, for example, many casualty insurance companies, especially the larger ones, took advantage of the high interest rates being earned on new investments to lower insurance premiums or to delay the normal pass-through of cost increases to their customers. As a result of this strategy, casualty insurance premiums lagged the otherwise high rate of inflation that characterized the early 1980s. Once interest rates began to fall, projections of high investment returns became suspect. The operating margin decline that many casualty insurance companies experienced in the mid-1980s resulted, in part, from the mispricing of their products because of expected returns that did not materialize. The low interest rate and weak stock market environment of 2000–2002 reinforced the perception that insurers cannot rely on investment returns to cover underwriting losses and that underwriting quality and profitable pricing are important. Thus any influence of competitive policy pricing on a casualty company's return objectives needs to be assessed in light of well-thought-out capital market assumptions and the insurance company's ability to accept risk.

- **Profitability.** Investment income and the investment portfolio return are primary determinants of continuing profitability for the typical casualty company and, indeed, the industry. The underwriting cycle influences the volatility of both company and industry earnings. Return requirements for casualty companies are not framed in reference to a crediting rate for their policies; rather, casualty insurance portfolios are managed to maximize return on capital and surplus to the extent that prudent asset/liability management, surplus adequacy considerations, and management preferences will allow.

  Given the underwriting uncertainties inherent in the casualty insurance business, investment income obviously provides financial stability for the insurance reserves. In fact, investment earnings are expected to offset periodic underwriting losses (claims and expenses in excess of premium income) from the insurance side of the company. Most casualty insurance products are priced competitively, and thus casualty premium rates are generally not sufficiently ample or flexible to eliminate the loss aspects of the underwriting cycle. The insurance industry measures underwriting profitability using the "combined ratio," the percentage of premiums that an insurance company spends on claims and expenses. Over the past 25 years, the combined ratio for US-based non-life insurance companies has been above 100 percent, reflecting underwriting losses, in over 60 percent of the years.

▪ **Growth of surplus.** An important function of a casualty company's investment operation is to provide growth of surplus, which in turn provides the opportunity to expand the volume of insurance the company can write. As mentioned earlier, the risk-taking capacity of a casualty insurance company is measured to a large extent by its ratio of premiums to capital and surplus. Generally, companies maintain this ratio between 2-to-1 and 3-to-1, although many well capitalized companies have lower ratios. Casualty companies have invested in common stocks, convertible securities, and alternative investments to achieve growth of surplus. These investments' return and marketability characteristics fit well within the industry's underwriting cycles.

▪ **Tax considerations.** Over the years, non-life insurance companies' investment results have been very sensitive to the after-tax return on the bond portfolio and to the tax benefits, when they exist, of certain kinds of investment returns. In the United States, these returns have included dividend income (through the exclusion of a portion of the dividends received by one corporation on stock issued by another corporation), realized long-term capital gains, and tax-exempt bonds. US casualty insurance companies have historically favored the latter, especially when underwriting is profitable, to achieve the highest after-tax return. For many casualty companies, the flexibility to shift between taxable and tax-exempt bonds has long been an important consideration as a key element of managing and optimizing after-tax income through the operating loss carryback and carryforward provisions of the US tax code. Most companies have maintained some balance of taxable and tax-exempt bonds in their portfolios, shifting that mix as tax considerations warranted. Recent changes in the tax laws have diminished most of the tax benefits available to casualty insurance companies. Outside of the United States, tax-exempt securities for insurance companies either do not exist or are more limited in supply. For non-US insurance companies, therefore, taxes are even more of a constraint.

▪ **Total return management.** Active bond portfolio management strategies designed to achieve total return, rather than yield or investment income goals only, have gained popularity among casualty insurance companies, especially large ones. Because GAAP and statutory reporting require that realized capital gains and losses flow through the income statement, the decline in interest rates and increase in bond prices since 1982 have encouraged casualty insurance portfolio managers to trade actively for total return in at least some portion of their bond portfolios.

One of the most interesting characteristics of casualty insurance companies is that their investment returns vary significantly from company to company. This variation reflects 1) the latitude permitted by insurance regulations; 2) differences in product mix, and thus in the duration of liabilities; 3) a particular company's tax position; 4) the emphasis placed on capital appreciation versus the income component of investment return; and 5) the strength of the company's capital and surplus positions. Exhibit 6 illustrates this contrast.[27]

Exhibit 6	Pretax Portfolio Yields of US Casualty Insurance Companies: Selected Years, 1975–2009			
	Allstate (%)	CNA Financial (%)	State Farm (%)	Travelers (%)
1975	5.1	5.3	5.5	7.3
1985	6.8	9.7	8.2	7.2
1995	6.0	6.4	5.7	5.9
2000	5.5	6.4	6.0	6.8
2004	5.3	4.3	4.6	5.5
2009	3.8	5.3	3.9	4.7

Source: Best's Insurance Reports (2005); *Best's Review* (October, 2011).

4.2.3 *Liquidity Requirements*

Given the uncertainty of the cash flow from casualty insurance operations, liquidity has always been a paramount consideration for non-life companies, in sharp contrast with life insurance companies which face relatively certain cash flows, excluding policy loans and surrenders. In addition to its use in meeting cash flow needs, liquidity has also been a necessary adjunct of a casualty company's variable tax position. Historically, casualty companies have found it necessary to liquidate portions of their bond port-folios to increase tax-exempt income during periods of underwriting profits and to increase taxable income during periods of underwriting losses. Liquidity remains a necessity for casualty companies, providing portfolio flexibility under changing tax, underwriting, and interest rate conditions.

To meet its liquidity needs, the typical casualty company does several things related to the marketability and maturity schedule of its investments. Quite often it maintains a portfolio of short-term securities, such as commercial paper or Treasury bills, as an immediate liquidity reserve. In addition, it may also hold a portfolio of readily marketable government bonds of various maturities; maintain a balanced or laddered maturity schedule to ensure a sufficient rollover of assets; match some assets against seasonal cash flow needs; or concentrate some portion of its bond portfolio in higher-quality bonds that are generally more marketable. Needless to say, such attention to maturity and marketability complements the limited risk tolerance and further modifies the return objectives of casualty insurers.

4.2.4 *Time Horizon*

The time horizon of casualty insurance companies is a function of two primary factors. First, the durations of casualty liabilities are typically shorter than those of life insur-ance liabilities. Second, underwriting cycles affect the mix of taxable and tax-exempt bond holdings. Because the tax-exempt **yield curve** in the United States tends to be

---

27 Because insurers' portfolios are heavily weighted toward fixed income, the variation in yields for four major companies shown in Exhibit 6 provides evidence for variation in total returns (data for which are not readily available).

more positively sloped than the taxable curve, casualty companies find that they must invest in longer maturities (15 to 30 years) than the typical life company to optimize the yield advantage offered by tax-exempt securities (see Exhibit 7).

Exhibit 7	Comparison of Average Maturity of Bond Portfolios of Selected US Non-Life and Life Insurance Companies: Year-End 2004	
Company	**Average Maturity of Bond Portfolio (Years)**	
Casualty		
Allstate	13	
CNA Financial	14	
State Farm	7	
Travelers	7	
Life		
AXA Equitable-NY	11	
Lincoln National	9	
Prudential	8	

Source: Best's Insurance Reports (2005).

Differences in the average maturity of bond portfolios between casualty and life insurance companies may also reflect the companies' willingness to accept interest rate risk via asset/liability duration mismatches and trade at least some portion of their portfolios through a market or underwriting cycle.

In terms of common stock investments, casualty companies historically have been long-term investors, with growth of surplus being the primary return objective of their portfolios' stock portion. As noted earlier, realized gains and losses flow through the income statement. Currently, the long-term equity investor status of the industry has been modified by objectives related to current reported earnings that have in turn led to some additional turnover in the common stock portfolio and more active management of the total portfolio.

4.2.5 *Tax Concerns*

Tax considerations are a very important factor in determining casualty insurance companies' investment policy. Prior to changes in the tax law in 1986, US casualty insurance companies operated under a relatively simple and straightforward set of tax provisions. Under those laws, their investment policy was directed toward achieving the appropriate balance between taxable and tax-exempt income on one hand, and taking advantage of the lower capital gains tax rate and corporate dividend exclusion, where possible, on the other.

As a result of the 1986 changes, tax-exempt bond income became subject to tax for US casualty insurance companies. Applying the current tax provisions requires a series of calculations to determine the net tax being levied on tax-exempt bond income. Because the equations must factor in both the operating profit or loss characteristics of the casualty company and alternative minimum tax provisions of the code, a computer model is generally needed to determine the appropriate asset allocation, if any, between tax-exempt and taxable securities for both new purchases and existing holdings. The complexities and implications of the taxation of tax-exempt bond income for casualty companies are beyond the scope of this reading.

As in the life insurance industry, casualty insurers are likely to be subjected to further tax code modification, which increases uncertainty for the investment manager as to the tax consequences of certain portfolio activities or alternatives when measured over a long time horizon. Tax considerations also shape the investment policy of non-US casualty insurance companies. Portfolio managers typically work closely with the companies' tax advisors to measure and monitor the tax implications of various portfolio strategies.

4.2.6 *Legal and Regulatory Factors*

Although the insurance industry in general is heavily regulated, casualty company investment regulation is relatively permissive. On the one hand, classes of eligible assets and quality standards for each class are specified just as they are for life companies. In the United States, New York state law, which is considered the most restrictive, requires that assets equal to 50 percent of unearned premium and loss reserves combined be maintained in "eligible bonds and mortgages." Beyond these general restrictions, however, casualty insurance companies are permitted to invest the remainder of their assets in a relatively broad array of bonds, mortgages, stocks, and real estate, without restriction as to the amount invested in any particular asset class (except in certain states that limit common stock and/or real estate holdings).

A casualty company is not required to maintain an asset valuation reserve. In essence, then, the surplus of a casualty company reflects the full impact of increases and decreases in the market value of stocks. The United States, however, has recently established risk-based capital regulations for the casualty industry. US risk-based capital regulations for casualty insurers specify the minimum amount of capital that an insurer must hold as a function of the size and degree of the asset risk, credit risk, underwriting risk, and off-balance sheet risk that the insurer takes.[28]

4.2.7 *Determination of Portfolio Policies*

As in the case of life insurance companies, casualty companies' limited investment risk tolerance is the dominant factor in determining their investment policy. Because of contractual liabilities and difficulty in forecasting the cash flow from insurance operations, casualty companies seek some degree of safety from the assets offsetting insurance reserves. Indeed, casualty companies' willingness to assume investment risk with the assets offsetting surplus has been moderated, or is at least subject to more careful management, as a result of market volatility in recent years.

Over and above liquidity needs, which are clearly important, casualty insurance companies develop a significant portfolio of stocks and bonds and generate a high level of income to supplement or offset insurance underwriting gains and losses. Capital appreciation also builds the surplus base and supports additional investment in the business. The structure of a casualty company's bond portfolio between taxable and tax-exempt securities depends on the company's underwriting experience and current tax policy. A casualty company's investment and business operating policies and strategies must be closely coordinated given the volatility of both the capital markets and the casualty insurance markets.

To conclude, we provide a sample investment policy statement. The format and content of investment policy statements are of course unique to each insurance company; however, Example 15 details an investment policy statement for a typical casualty insurance company.

---

28 Asset risk addresses fluctuation in market value. **Credit risk** addresses probability of default. Underwriting risk arises from underestimating liabilities from business already written or inadequately pricing current or prospective business. Off-balance sheet risk addresses the risk from items not reflected in the balance sheet.

Investment Policy Statement for a Casualty Insurance Company

Cornish Casualty Insurance Company ("the Company") underwrites auto and homeowners insurance. The company is licensed to do business in all 50 US states. In recent years, the Company's business has been growing steadily, and its board of directors has approved a strategic plan for increasing its growth rate and profitability. The Company's total assets exceed $5 billion, and its surplus approaches $2 billion. The company is facing increased competition in its markets from companies selling auto and homeowners insurance through the Internet, as well as from other direct sellers. This competitive environment has focused the board and management's attention on increasing the after-tax return on the bond portfolio and enhancing the growth of surplus. The company's chief investment officer has been asked to revise the Company's investment policy statement to reflect the changes that will be necessary to meet the new growth targets. The CIO has revised the return and risk objectives for the overall portfolio and various portfolio segments. Following are the investment objectives and constraints under which the Company's investment portfolio will be managed.

Investment Philosophy

The assets of the Company should be invested to provide for the payment of all contractual obligations to policyholders and to contribute to the growth of surplus over the long-term. Therefore, the investment strategy will be based on prudent investment principles within the context of applicable insurance regulations. The strategy will seek to achieve the appropriate balance among the following: providing investment income to enhance profitability; maintaining liquidity and generating cash flow to meet all obligations; and growing the value of assets over time, thereby contributing to the Company's ability to write additional business and grow premium income.

Investment Goals, Objectives, and Constraints

The Company's investment goals and objectives will be stated in terms of return expectations and requirements and risk tolerance. The constraints under which the investment portfolio will be managed include liquidity considerations, time horizon, regulatory restrictions, tax considerations and unique requirements.

Return Objectives

The return objectives of the Company are threefold: a) earn a sufficient return to fund all policyholder liabilities, b) support the competitive pricing of all products, and c) contribute to the growth of surplus through capital appreciation. The return objectives will be measured in terms of meeting or exceeding projections of investment income and total return.

Risk Tolerance

The risk tolerance of the Company is based on the competitive requirements of various product lines, risk-based capital considerations, and the responsibility to fulfill all short-term and long-term obligations to policyholders. Credit (default) risk and stock market risk need to be monitored and managed so as to support the competitive position of the Company while providing for its long-term viability.

Investment Constraints

The Company's investment constraints can be defined in terms of the following factors.

Liquidity

The portfolio will be managed to meet the liquidity requirements to pay all benefits and expenses in a timely manner. Investment cash flows will be a primary source of liquidity, to minimize lower yielding cash reserves. In addition, publicly traded securities will provide an important additional source of liquidity.

Time Horizon

The Company is a long-term investor but will adjust the average maturity of the bond portfolio in line with the relative attractiveness of the after tax return on taxable versus tax-exempt bonds.

Tax

Tax considerations determine the optimal allocation within the bond portfolio between taxable and tax-exempt bonds. Tax considerations may also play a role in the realization of gains and losses for both the bond and stock portfolios.

Regulatory

All investments must qualify under the insurance law of the state in which the Company is domiciled.

Unique Circumstances

Private placement bonds are not authorized and investments in commercial mortgage loans and real estate are limited, due to liquidity considerations.

Review Schedule

This policy statement will be reviewed at least annually by the Board of Directors and is subject to modification based on significant changes in insurance or tax regulations as well as significant changes in the Company's financial position and/or capital or insurance market conditions.

[Other parts of the investment policy statement are omitted.]

BANKS AND OTHER INSTITUTIONAL INVESTORS

5

The final type of institutional investor that we discuss in detail is banks.

5.1 Banks: Background and Investment Setting

Banks are financial intermediaries involved in taking deposits and lending money. Nearly everywhere, however, the scope of banks' activities has evolved and widened over time, although distinct regional and national traditions remain. Western Europe and Canada follow the model of universal banking, in which traditional banking (involving deposit-taking and lending), securities underwriting, and insurance (in Europe) are organized under one corporate roof.[29] In this universal banking model, banks can provide one-stop shopping for financial services. In contrast to this model, in the 20th century the United States and Japan evolved regulatory separations between commercial

---

29 Bancassurance is the term that has developed to describe the sale of insurance by banks. As of 2004, more than 50 percent of life insurance is sold through banks in Spain, France, and Italy, and about 20 percent is sold through banks in the United Kingdom and Germany. Although banks in Japan have been permitted to sell insurance products since 2002 and in the United States since 1999, banks constitute a minor share of the insurance market in these countries.

banking and investment banking (security underwriting) activities. Gradually, this separation has eroded in the United States, as highlighted by the 1998 merger of Citicorp (a holding company that included Citibank) and Travelers Group (a holding company that included Travelers Insurance and Salomon Smith Barney) and by the Gramm-Leach-Bliley Act of 1999, which permits affiliations under a financial holding company structure. Nevertheless, important differences in regulatory constraints and business structures persist among banks internationally.

Banks' liabilities consist chiefly of time and demand deposits[30] (as much as 90 percent of total liabilities and capital for smaller banks) but also include purchased funds and sometimes publicly traded debt. The asset side of the balance sheet consists of loan and securities portfolios as well as an assortment of other assets. For Federal Deposit Insurance Corporation insured US commercial banks, in recent years loans and leases have represented on average slightly less than 60 percent of assets. Loans may include real estate, commercial, individual, and agricultural loans. Securities have represented about 20 percent of total assets; other assets (trading accounts, bank premises and fixed assets, and other real estate owned) have been about 15 percent; and cash and Federal funds have accounted for the remainder of assets.

Traditionally, a bank's portfolio of investment securities has been a residual use of funds after loan demand has been met. The securities portfolio nevertheless plays a key role in managing a bank's risk and liquidity positions relative to its liabilities. Consequently, a bank's asset/liability risk management committee (ALCO) is generally in charge of overseeing the bank's securities portfolio. Exhibit 8 sets a context for understanding a bank's ALCO's concerns. Although banks have fee and other non-interest sources of income, and, of course, non-interest expenses, interest revenues and costs are the chief financial variables affecting bank profitability. The quantity, duration, and credit quality of both the loan and securities portfolio affects a bank's interest revenues. On the market-value balance sheet, interest rate risk affects the market value of net worth representing the value of equity claims on the bank. Observing the bank's financial performance, the ALCO can make needed changes in assets and liabilities.

Exhibit 8   Elements of the ALM Process

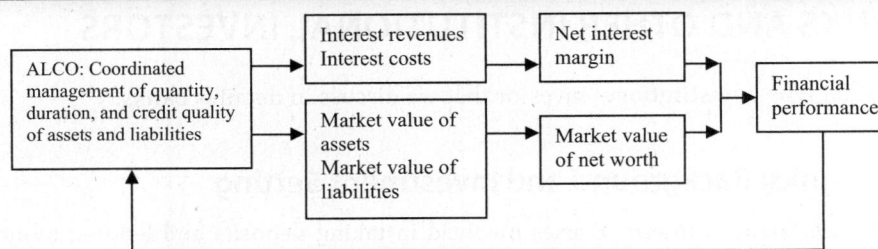

Some more detail is helpful. Among the profitability measures that the ALCO will monitor are the following:

- The **net interest margin**, already mentioned, equals net interest income (interest income minus interest expense) divided by average earning assets. Net interest margin is a summary measure of the net interest return earned on income-producing assets such as loans and bonds.[31]

- The **interest spread** equals the average yield on earning assets minus the average percent cost of interest-bearing liabilities. The interest spread is a measure of the bank's ability to invest in assets yielding more than the cost of its sources of funding.

Because both interest income and interest expense fluctuate in response to interest rate changes, net interest margin and interest spread are key indicators of a bank's ability to profitably manage interest rate risk. Among the risk measures the ALCO will monitor are the following:

- The **leverage-adjusted duration gap** is defined as $D_A - kD_L$, where D_A is the duration of assets, D_L is the duration of liabilities, and $k = L/A$, the ratio of the market value of liabilities (L) to the market value of assets (A). The leverage-adjusted duration gap measures a bank's overall interest rate exposure. For a positive interest rate shock (unexpected increase in rates), the market value of net worth will decrease for a bank with a positive gap; be unaffected for a bank with a zero gap (an immunized balance sheet); and increase for a bank with a negative gap.[32]

- Position and aggregate **Value at Risk (VaR)** are money measures of the minimum value of losses expected over a specified time period (for example, a day, a quarter, or a year) at a given level of probability (often 0.05 or 0.01). As a result of risk-based capital regulatory initiatives internationally, nearly all banks track this measure of exposure to large losses.

- Credit measures of risk may include both internally developed and commercially available measures such as CreditMetrics.

A bank's securities portfolio plays an important role in achieving its financial performance objectives. According to one survey, banks' objectives in managing securities portfolios include the following, listed in order of importance:[33]

- **To manage overall interest rate risk of the balance sheet.** In contrast to business, consumer, and mortgage loans, bank-held securities are negotiable instruments trading in generally liquid markets that can be bought and sold quickly. Therefore, securities are the natural adjustment mechanism for interest rate risk. For example, if the duration of equity is higher than desired, a bank can shorten it by shortening the maturity of its securities portfolio.

- **To manage liquidity.** Banks use their securities portfolios to assure adequate cash is available to them. The rationale for selling securities to meet liquidity needs is again the ready marketability of securities.

---

31 Earning assets include all assets that generate explicit interest income (plus lease receipts) but exclude discount instruments such as acceptances.

32 The change in the market value of net worth for an interest rate shock is approximately equal to the leverage-adjusted duration gap times the size of the bank (measured by A) times the size of the interest rate shock. Bankers also use other gap concepts in measuring interest rate risk. See Koch and MacDonald (2003).

33 BAI Foundation (1995).

- **To produce income.** Banks' securities portfolios frequently account for a quarter or more of total revenue.

- **To manage credit risk.** The securities portfolio is used to modify and diversify the overall credit risk exposure to a desired level. Banks frequently assume substantial credit risk in their loan portfolios; they can balance that risk by assuming minimal credit risk in their securities portfolio. Additionally, they can use the securities portfolio to diversify risk when the loan portfolio is not adequately diversified.

Banks also use their securities portfolios to meet other needs. For example, in the United States, banks must hold (pledge) government securities against the uninsured portion of deposits (an example of a **pledging requirement**—i.e., a required collateral use of assets).

Just as a bank's liabilities are interest-rate sensitive (as is its loan portfolio, on the asset side), a bank's security portfolios consist almost exclusively of fixed-income securities. This characteristic, as well as the bias toward low-credit risk holdings, is reinforced by regulatory constraints on securities holdings. Exhibit 9 gives the average asset class weights of US commercial banks' securities portfolios (because of rounding weights they do not sum to exactly 100). We note that Exhibit 9 does not show off-balance-sheet derivatives used to manage interest rate and credit risk.

The major trend in banks' securities holdings during the last 10 years or more has been the decline in holdings of tax-exempt bonds and the increase in holdings of mortgage-backed securities, which are included under corporate securities in Exhibit 9.

Exhibit 9	US Commercial Banks: Investment Securities Weights (Trading Account Not Included): Year-End 2009	
Asset Class		**All Commercial Banks (%)**
US Treasury securities		3
US government agency and corporate securities		51.4
Municipal securities		6.5
Asset-backed securities		6.6
Other domestic debt securities		21.1
Non-US debt securities		9.2
Equities		0.9

Source: 2011 *Financial Services Fact Book.*

5.1.1 *Risk Objectives*

As already emphasized, banks' risk objectives are dominated by ALM considerations that focus on funding liabilities. Therefore, risk relative to liabilities, rather than absolute risk, is of primary concern. Although banks would like to earn high interest margins, they must not assume a level of risk that jeopardizes their ability to meet their liabilities to depositors and other entities. Overall, banks have below-average risk tolerance as concerns the securities portfolio.

5.1.2 *Return Objectives*

A bank's return objectives for its securities portfolio are driven by the need to earn a positive return on invested capital. For the interest-income part of return, the portfolio manager pursues this objective by attempting to earn a positive spread over the cost of funds.

5.1.3 *Liquidity Requirements*

A bank's liquidity position is a key management and regulatory concern. Liquidity requirements are determined by net outflows of deposits, if any, as well as demand for loans.

5.1.4 *Time Horizon*

A bank's time horizon for its securities portfolio reflects its need to manage interest rate risk while earning a positive return on invested capital. A bank's liability structure typically reflects an overall shorter maturity than its loan portfolio, placing a risk management constraint on the time horizon length for its securities portfolio. This time horizon generally falls in the three- to seven-year range (intermediate term).

5.1.5 *Tax Concerns*

Banks' securities portfolios are fully taxable. In the United States prior to 1983, the full amount of interest used to finance the purchase of tax-exempt securities was tax deductible, and banks were major buyers of municipal bonds. Since 1986, such deductions have been completely disallowed for the purchase of most municipal bonds, and US banks' portfolios have been concentrated in taxable securities. In the United States since 1983 securities gains and losses affect net operating income. Thus realized securities losses decrease reported operating income, while securities gains increase reported operating income. According to some observers, this accounting treatment creates an incentive not to sell securities showing unrealized losses, providing a mechanism by which earnings can be managed.

5.1.6 *Legal and Regulatory Factors*

Regulations place restrictions on banks' holdings of common shares and below-investment-grade risk fixed-income securities. To meet legal reserve and pledging requirements banks may need to hold substantial amounts of short-term government securities. Risk-based capital (RBC) regulations are a major regulatory development worldwide affecting banks' risk-taking incentives. RBC requirements restrain bank risk-taking by linking the formula for required capital to the credit risk of the bank's assets, both on and off balance sheet. To illustrate this type of regulation, following the Basel Accord, in 1993 bank assets were placed in one of four risk categories involving risk weights of 0%, 20%, 50%, and 100%, respectively.[34] A risk weight of 100, for example, applied to most bank loans. That weight means that 100 percent of the loan is subject to the baseline minimum 8 percent capital requirement. Under Basel II, implemented in 2008, banks placed assets in risk-exposure categories involving weights of 0%, 20%, 50%, 100%, and 150%, respectively. In contrast to the original Basel Accord, Basel II accounted for credit-quality differences within a given security type. Basel III, agreed upon in 2010-11, further strengthened bank capital requirements and introduced new regulatory requirements on bank liquidity and leverage.

---

34 The Basel Accord, sponsored by the Bank for International Settlements, applies to the banks of a group of major industrialized countries.

5.1.7 *Unique Circumstances*

There are no common unique circumstances to highlight relative to banks' securities investment activities. That situation stands in contrast to banks' lending activities, in which banks may consider factors such as historical banking relationships and community needs, which may be viewed as unique circumstances.

Example 16 excerpts the investment policy statement of a hypothetical small commercial bank. We incorporated this reading's investment objectives and constraints framework in its format, and we included a section on authorized investments that typically is found in such documents. The IPS excerpts cover many of the major topics that would be included in an IPS for a typical US commercial bank (referred to as the "Bank").

EXAMPLE 16

Investment Policy Statement for a Commercial Bank

A. Purpose

The purpose of the investment policy statement (IPS) is to set forth the policies and procedures that govern the administration of all the Bank's investment activities. The Bank's Money Market Account is subject to additional constraints set forth in a later section of the IPS.

B. Responsibility

The Bank's Board of Directors (the "Board") is responsible for formulating and implementing investment policies. The Board delegates authority for making specific investments to the Bank's officers ("Management") designated in Exhibit A attached to this IPS, for investments consistent with this IPS. The Board also appoints an Investment Committee (the "Committee") to act as a liaison between the Board and Management and to carry out the following functions:

1 Monitor and review all investment decisions for compliance with the IPS and with federal and state regulations.

2 Review the IPS and recommend changes to it to the Board when appropriate.

C. Investment Objectives and Constraints

The primary purposes of the investment portfolio are to provide liquidity and to control the overall interest rate and credit risk exposures of the Bank. The portfolio will convert excess cash resulting from net deposit inflows and/or slack loan demand into earning assets. The portfolio will be drawn down when needed to meet net deposit outflows, loan demand, or other contingencies.

Return Requirements

The Bank will attempt to earn an average positive spread over the cost of funds.

Risk Objectives

▪ Because of the need to be able to satisfy depositor and other liabilities at short notice and taking account of the typical characteristics of its loan portfolio, the Bank's tolerance for interest rate, credit, and liquidity risk in its securities portfolio is below average.

▪ The yield on investments is secondary to liquidity and safety of principal.

▪ To limit the risk of loss as a result of an individual issuer default, the Bank will maintain adequate diversification in its holdings.

Tax

As a taxable corporation the Bank will appraise taxable and tax-exempt investments on an after-tax basis.

Regulatory

All investments must qualify under state and federal banking regulations governing the investment activities of the Bank.

Unique Circumstances

None.

D. Authorized Investments

The following investments are legally permitted by Federal Regulations and authorized by the Board.

1 US Treasury securities

2 US government agency and agency-guaranteed securities

3 Certificates of deposit and bankers acceptances

   a Insured CDs. Negotiable and nonnegotiable CDs of any domestic commercial bank or savings and loan association may be purchased.

   b Uninsured CDs. Investment in excess of $250,000 in the CDs of a single domestic bank may be made only in those banks shown on the Approved List (Exhibit B).

   c Eurodollar CDs. Investments may be made only in such CDs issued by banks on the Approved List.

   d Yankee CDs. Investments may be made only in such CDs issued by banks on the Approved List.

   e Banker's acceptances. Investments are limited to accepting banks on the Approved List.

   f Federal funds sold. Sales of federal funds may be made only to those institutions on the Approved List.

   g Repurchase agreements (repos).

     i. The term shall not exceed 30 days, although a continuous agreement (remaining in effect until cancelled) is allowed.

     ii. The securities acceptable for purchase under a repo are those issued by the US Treasury and agencies of the US government.

     iii. The institutions with which repos may be made are limited to those on the Approved List.

   h Reverse repurchase agreements (reverse repos). Reverse repos may be used so long as no more than 40 percent of the funds so obtained are used to purchase additional securities.

E. Maturity of Investments

To control the risk of loss resulting from an increase in the level of interest rates, Management is restricted to investments that mature within five years. This restriction does not apply to securities repurchased under the provisions of a repurchase agreement.

F. Diversification Requirements

1 US Treasury and agency securities. These may be held in unlimited quantities.

2 Securities not guaranteed by the US Government, its agencies, or instrumentalities are subject to an overall maximum 10% commitment at cost.

G. Unauthorized Transactions

1 Short sales.

2 Adjusted Trades. The Bank may not hide an investment loss by an adjusted trade—that is, selling a security at a fictitiously high price to a dealer and simultaneously buying another overpriced security from the same dealer.

[Exhibits and other sections omitted.]

5.2 Other Institutional Investors: Investment Intermediaries

As we define the term, institutional investors are financial intermediaries in various legal forms with relatively large amounts of money to invest. The institutional investors previously discussed in this reading (pension plans, foundations, endowments, insurance companies, and banks) have well-defined purposes besides investing. Banks take deposits and make loans, for example; pension plans have the specific purpose of providing retirement income.

Investment companies constitute another type of institutional investor that is important in financial markets. Investment companies include such investment vehicles as mutual funds (open-end investment companies), closed-end funds (closed-end investment companies), unit trusts, and exchange-traded funds. All these vehicles represent pooled investor funds invested in equity and fixed-income markets. Investment companies are pure investment vehicles in the sense that they have no other corporate purpose besides investing. We might aptly call them investment intermediaries. Each investment company selects its specific investment objectives and describes objectives, constraints, and costs in legally prescribed formats (e.g., a prospectus) and draws in funds from investors who are attracted to it for various portfolio purposes. Commodity pools serve similar purposes, but in futures rather than equity and fixed-income markets. Hedge funds are another type of investment vehicle that falls under the rubric of institutional investors. Hedge funds differ from investment companies in that they market to other institutional investors and to high-net-worth individuals exclusively; in addition, they are subject to fewer regulations.

One cannot generally characterize the investment objects and constraints of a given type of investment intermediary with the expectation that it will apply to all members of the group. Mutual funds, for example, cover the range of equity and fixed-income investment styles; one cannot characterize the return requirement and risk tolerance of "a mutual fund" in general, as we have done for other institutional investors such as life insurers. Readers who may be involved in managing equity or fixed-income mutual funds will find relevant guidance in the readings on equity portfolio management and fixed-income portfolio management, respectively.

Nonfinancial corporations (i.e., businesses), although not financial intermediaries, are major investors in **money markets** (markets for fixed-income securities with maturities of one year or less) to manage their cash positions. "Cash," of course, includes "liquid cash" such as funds held in demand deposits and very short-term money market securities, and "long-term" or "core" cash, which is invested in longer-term money market instruments. These investments are part of the corporate function of cash management, which typically falls under the responsibilities of an organization's corporate treasurer. For most companies, liquidity and safety of principal are paramount investment considerations in cash management. Companies with very large cash positions will actively manage the composition of the cash position relative to anticipated cash needs (including seasonal needs), nondomestic currency needs, and tax concerns. Cash management is an important function for all the institutional investors previously discussed as well as for governmental units.[35]

SUMMARY

This reading has described the investment contexts in which institutional investors operate. Our chief focus has been the development of an investment policy statement for defined-benefit pension plans, defined-contribution pension plans, endowments, foundations, life insurance companies, non-life insurance companies, and banks. We have discussed the specific considerations that enter into the development of appropriate return and risk objectives. We then addressed liquidity requirements, time horizon, tax concerns, legal and regulatory factors, and unique circumstances.

- The two major types of pension plan are defined-benefit (DB) plans and defined-contribution (DC) plans. A defined-benefit plan specifies the plan sponsor's obligations in terms of the benefit to plan participants. In contrast, a defined-contribution plan specifies the sponsor's obligations in terms of contributions to the pension fund rather than benefits to participants.

- DB pension assets fund the payment of pension benefits (liabilities). The investment performance of a DB plan should be judged relative to its adequacy in funding liabilities even if it is also judged on an absolute basis. The funded status of a DB plan is the relationship of the plan assets to the present value of plan liabilities, and is usually measured with respect to the projected benefit obligation (PBO) definition of plan liabilities.

- In setting a risk objective, DB plan sponsors need to consider plan funded status, sponsor financial status and profitability, sponsor and pension fund common risk exposures, plan features (such as provision for lump-sum distributions), and workforce characteristics.

- A DB pension plan's broad return objective is to achieve returns that adequately fund its pension liabilities on an inflation-adjusted basis. An appropriate return requirement for a fully funded plan is the discount rate applied to pension liabilities. The pension fund's stated return desire may be higher and may reflect considerations relating to reducing pension contributions or increasing pension income.

- For DB plans, liquidity requirements relate to the number of retired lives, the size of contributions in relation to disbursements, and plan features. Factors affecting the time horizon length include whether the plan is a going concern, the age of the workforce, and the proportion of retired lives.

- Defined-contribution plans fall into two types: those in which the plan sponsor sets investment policy, and those in which the plan participants individually set policy. The investment process for the sponsor-directed plans is a simpler version of the process for DB plans.

---

35 See Kallberg and Parkinson (1993) for more on cash management.

- For participant-directed DC plans, the principal issues are offering participants sufficient investment choices and avoiding inadequate diversification because of holdings of the sponsor company's stock.

- Hybrid pension plans combine features of DB and DC plans. A cash balance plan is a hybrid plan in which the promised benefit is shown as a balance in a participant-individualized statement. Another important type of hybrid plan is the Employee Stock Ownership Plan (ESOP), a type of DC plan entirely or primarily invested in the employer's stock.

- Foundations are grant-making institutions. Private foundations are typically subject to a payout requirement that specifies a minimum level of spending. Endowments are generally not subject to a legal spending requirement. Endowments typically provide vital support of ongoing operations and programs of institutions such as universities, hospitals, museums, and religious organizations.

- The return objective for most foundations (and endowments) can be stated as the sum of the annual spending rate, the cost of generating returns (managing assets), and the expected inflation rate. A multiplicative formulation of the components is more precise than an additive one in specifying the return level that should allow the foundation or endowment to preserve the inflation-adjusted value of assets over many periods.

- A foundation's investment policy can often be more risk tolerant than the investment policy of DB plans because foundation assets need not be managed with respect to a stream of legal liabilities, in general. Endowment risk tolerance often depends on the importance of the endowment to the supported institution's operating budget as reflected in the spending rate, and the use of a smoothing rule for spending, which dampens the portfolio's sensitivity to short-run volatility.

- A foundation or endowment's liquidity requirements come from both anticipated and unanticipated cash needs in excess of contributions received. Anticipated needs are captured in the periodic distributions prescribed by a foundation's or endowment's spending rate. Generally time horizons are long. A variety of legal and regulatory issues can affect a foundation or endowment's investment activities.

- Insurance companies play a role in absorbing personal and business risks. Insurers are broadly divided into life insurers and non-life insurers (casualty insurers); the two groups have distinct investment concerns.

- Historically, return requirements for life insurers have been tied to the interest rates used by actuaries to determine policyholder reserves or accumulation rates for the funds being held by a company for future disbursement. Actual return objectives have been less clearly defined but may relate to an interest rate spread concerning liabilities.

- Insurers have moved towards segmenting their portfolios in relation to associated liabilities and setting return objectives by major line of business. The result is that a single company's investment policy may incorporate multiple return objectives. Furthermore, many companies have established separate investment policies, and strategies, for each segment of their portfolios.

- Because of public policy concerns related to payment of insurance benefits, insurer portfolios are viewed as quasi-trust funds from a public policy perspective. As a result, conservative fiduciary principles limit the risk tolerance of both life and non-life insurers.

- As one consequence of the need for managing risk with respect to their contractual liabilities, insurers use a variety of asset/liability management techniques.

- Life insurance companies have valuation concerns (related to prescribed valuation reserves), reinvestment risk, credit risk, and cash flow volatility.

- The liquidity concerns associated with disintermediation of cash value policies, asset/liability mismatch, and asset marketability risk have increased insurers' traditionally relatively minimal liquidity requirements.

- Life insurers have been viewed as the classic long-term investor. As a result of portfolio segmentation, life insurers may establish relatively shorter time horizons for some portfolio segments (e.g., group annuities).

- As a regulated industry, life insurers face many regulatory and legal constraints including those relating to eligible investments, the prudent investor rule, and valuation methods.

- In contrast to life insurers, non-life insurers typically have shorter-term liabilities. The underwriting (profitability) cycle may require non-life insurers to liquidate investments to supplement cash flow shortfalls. For both of these reasons, non-life insurers have much shorter investment time horizons than do life insurers.

- Return requirements reflect competitive pricing policy, profitability concerns, and the requirement for a growing surplus to support the writing of new business.

- A bank's portfolio investments are a residual use of funds after loan demand has been met. The portfolio's overall objectives are to manage the interest rate risk of the balance sheet, manage liquidity, produce income, and manage credit risk. The bank's return objective is to earn a positive spread over the cost of funds. Banks typically have below-average risk tolerance, and liquidity is a key concern. Bank investment is subject to a range of legal and regulatory factors.

- Investment companies such as mutual funds as well as commodity pools and hedge funds are institutional investors that function as investment intermediaries. In contrast to other types of institutional investors, one cannot generalize about the investment objectives and constraints of these types of investors.

- Among institutional investors, ALM considerations are particularly important for DB pension funds, insurance companies, and banks.

PRACTICE PROBLEMS

1 **Worden Technology, Inc.**

Based in London, Worden Technology, Inc. is an established company with operations in North America, Japan, and several European countries. The firm has £16 billion in total assets and offers its employees a defined-benefit pension plan.

Worden's pension plan currently has assets of £8.88 billion and liabilities of £9.85 billion. The plan's goals include achieving a minimum expected return of 8.4 percent with expected standard deviation of return no greater than 16.0 percent. Next month, Worden will reduce the retirement age requirement for full benefits from 60 years to 55 years. The median age of Worden Technology's workforce is 49 years.

Angus Williamson, CFA, manages the pension plan's investment policy and strategic asset allocation decisions. He has heard an ongoing debate within Worden Technology about the pension plan's investment policy statement. Exhibit 1 compares two IPSs under consideration.

Exhibit 1	Investment Policy Statements	
	IPS X	**IPS Y**
Return requirement	Plan's objective is to outperform the relevant benchmark return by a substantial margin.	Plan's objective is to match relevant benchmark return.
Risk tolerance	Plan has a high risk tolerance because of the long-term nature of the plan and its liabilities.	Plan has a low risk tolerance because of its limited ability to assume substantial risk.
Time horizon	Plan has a very long time horizon because of its infinite life.	Plan has a shorter time horizon than in the past because of plan demographics.
Liquidity requirement[a]	Plan has moderate liquidity needs to fund monthly benefit payments.	Plan has minimal liquidity needs.

[a] Assume Worden will not contribute to its pension plan over the next several years.

Identify which investment policy statement, X or Y, contains the appropriate language for each of the following components of Worden Technology's pension plan:

  i. Return requirement.

  ii. Risk tolerance.

  iii. Time horizon.

  iv. Liquidity.

Justify your choice in each instance.

2 *LightSpeed Connections*

Hugh Donovan is chief financial officer of LightSpeed Connections (LSC), a rapidly growing US technology company with a traditional defined-benefit pension plan. Because of LSC's young workforce, Donovan believes the pension plan has no liquidity needs and can thus invest aggressively to maximize returns. He also believes that US Treasury bills and bonds, yielding 5.4 percent and 6.1 percent, respectively, have no place in a portfolio with such a long time horizon. His strategy, which has produced excellent returns for the past two years, has been to invest the portfolio as follows:

- 50 percent in a concentrated pool (15 to 20 stocks) of initial public offerings in technology and Internet companies, managed internally by Donovan;
- 25 percent in a small-capitalization growth fund;
- 10 percent in a venture capital fund;
- 10 percent in an S&P 500 index fund; and
- 5 percent in an international equity fund.

Working with LSC's Investment Committee, the firm's president, Eileen Jeffries, has produced a formal investment policy statement, which reads as follows:

> "The LSC Pension Plan's return objective should focus on real total returns that will fund its long-term obligations on an inflation-adjusted basis. The "time-to-maturity" of the corporate workforce is a key element for any defined pension plan; given our young workforce, LSC's Plan has a long investment horizon and more time available for wealth compounding to occur. Therefore, the Plan can pursue an aggressive investment strategy and focus on the higher return potential of capital growth. Under present US tax laws, pension portfolio income and capital gains are not taxed. The portfolio should focus primarily on investments in businesses directly related to our main business to leverage our knowledge base."

A Evaluate Donovan's investment strategy with respect to its effect on each of the following:

  i. LSC's pension plan beneficiaries.

  ii. Managing pension assets in relation to LSC's corporate strength.

B Evaluate LSC's investment policy statement in the context of the following:

  i. Return requirement.

  ii. Risk tolerance.

  iii. Time horizon.

  iv. Liquidity.

3 *Gwartney International*

US-based Gwartney International (GI) is a financially healthy, rapidly growing import/export company with a young workforce. Information regarding GI's defined-benefit pension plan (which is subject to ERISA) appears in Exhibits 2 and 3.

Exhibit 2

Asset Class	Actual and Target Allocation (%)	Prior-Year Total Return (%)
Large-capitalization US equities	35	10.0
Small-capitalization US equities	10	12.0
International equities	5	7.0
Total equities	50	
US Treasury bills (1-year duration)	10	4.5
US intermediate-term bonds and mortgage-backed securities (4-year duration)	17	1.0
US long-term bonds (10-year duration)	23	19.0[a]
Total fixed income	50	
Total	100	10.0

[a] Income element 7.0%; price gain element 12.0%.

Exhibit 3

Present value of plan liabilities	$298 million
Market value of plan assets	$300 million
Surplus	$2 million
Duration of liabilities	10 years
Actuarial return assumption	7.0%
GI board's long-term total return objective	9.0%

In accordance with GI policy, the plan discounts its liabilities at the market interest rate for bonds of the same duration. GI's risk objectives include a limitation on volatility of surplus.

Giselle Engle, the newly appointed chief financial officer, must explain to the board of directors why the surplus declined in a year when the actual investment return was 100 basis points more than the long-term objective stated by the board.

A Explain how the plan surplus could decline in a given year despite an actual return in excess of the long-term return objective.

B Explain the importance of an appropriate investment time horizon when setting investment policy for GI's corporate pension plan.

C Discuss the risk tolerance of GI's corporate pension plan.

4 *Food Processors, Inc.*

Food Processors, Inc. (FPI) is a mature US company with declining earnings and a weak balance sheet. Its defined-benefit pension plan (which is subject to ERISA) has total assets of $750 million. The plan is underfunded by $200 million by US standards—a cause for concern by shareholders, management, and the board of directors.

The average age of plan participants is 45 years. FPI's annual contribution to the plan and the earnings on its assets are sufficient to meet pension payments to present retirees. The pension portfolio's holdings are equally divided between large-capitalization US equities and high-quality, long-maturity US corporate bonds. For the purpose of determining FPI's contribution to the pension plan, the assumed long-term rate of return on plan assets is 9 percent per year; the discount rate applied to determine the present value of plan liabilities, all of which are US-based, is 8 percent. As FPI's Treasurer, you are responsible for oversight of the plan's investments and managers and for liaison with the board's Pension Investment Committee.

At the committee's last meeting, its chair observed that US stocks had relatively poor performance over the past decade. He then made a pointed comment: "Given this experience, and as there is a tendency for returns to revert to the mean, we seem to be overly conservative in using only a 9 percent future return assumption. Why don't we raise the rate to 10 percent? This would be consistent with the expectation of subsequent higher returns, would help our earnings, and should make the stockholders feel a lot better."

You have been directed to examine the situation and prepare a recommendation for next week's committee meeting. Your assistant has provided you with the background information shown in Exhibit 4.

Exhibit 4	Capital Markets Data			
Asset Class	**Total Return 1926–2010 (%)**	**Total Return 2001–2010 (%)**	**Annualized Monthly Standard Deviation 2001–2010 (%)**	**Consensus Forecast Total Return 2001–2010 (%)**
US Treasury bills	3.6	2.2	0.2	2.5
Intermediate-term Treasury bonds	5.4	5.6	5.4	5.0
Long-term Treasury bonds	5.5	6.6	13.5	6.0
US corporate bonds (AAA rated)	5.9	7.6	12.9	6.0
US common stocks (S&P 500)	9.9	1.4	16.9	8.5
US inflation rate (annual rate)	3.0	2.3	1.6	3.0

Source for Data: Ibbotson SBBI 2011 Classic Yearbook

Assume that consensus forecast total returns for bonds are at least approximately equal to the bonds' yields.

A   Explain what is meant when a pension plan is said to be "underfunded" and use FPI to illustrate.

B   Discuss the risk–return dilemma that FPI faces.

C   Explain a rationale for reducing the discount rate for determining the PV of plan liabilities from its current level of 8 percent.

D   Explain how the underfunded condition of FPI's plan would be affected if the discount rate were reduced to 7 percent from the current 8 percent.

5   *Medical Research Foundation*

The Medical Research Foundation (MRF), based in the United States, was established to provide grants in perpetuity. MRF has just received word that the foundation will receive a $45 million cash gift three months from now. The gift will greatly increase the size of the foundation's endowment from its current $10 million. The foundation's grant-making (spending) policy has been to pay out virtually all of its annual net investment income. Because its investment approach has been conservative, the endowment portfolio now consists almost entirely of fixed-income assets. The finance committee understands that these actions are causing the real value of foundation assets and the real value of future grants to decline because of inflation effects. Until now, the finance committee believed it had no alternative to these actions, given the large immediate cash needs of the research programs being funded and the small size of the foundation's capital base. The foundation's annual grants must at least equal 5 percent of its assets' market value to maintain MRF's US tax-exempt status, a requirement that is expected to continue indefinitely. The foundation anticipates no additional gifts or fundraising activity for the foreseeable future.

Given the change in circumstances that the cash gift will make, the finance committee wishes to develop new grant-making and investment policies. Annual spending must at least meet the 5 percent of market value requirement, but the committee is unsure how much higher spending can or should be. The committee wants to pay out as much as possible because of the critical nature of the research being funded; however, it understands that preserving the real value of the foundation's assets is equally important in order to preserve its future grant-making capabilities. You have been asked to assist the committee in developing appropriate policies.

A   Identify and discuss the three key elements that should determine the foundation's grant-making (spending) policy.

B   Formulate and justify an investment policy statement for the foundation.

6   *James Children's Hospital*

The James Children's Hospital (JCH), based in Washington, DC, has an operating budget of $15 million and has been operating at a budget surplus for the last two years. JCH has a $20 million endowment (JCHE) whose sole purpose is to provide capital equipment for the hospital. The endowment's long-term expected total return is 8.6%, which includes a 3.3% income component. JCHE has no minimum payout requirement and expects no future contributions. Traditionally, the JCHE board of directors has determined the annual payout based on current needs. Payouts have been rising steadily—to $1,375,000 two years ago and to $1,400,000 last year.

Michelle Parker, chief financial officer of JCHE, has asked the board's guidance in establishing a long-term spending policy for JCHE. She has received $1,600,000 in requests to buy equipment and is concerned about the inflation rate for medical equipment prices, which is 4%, versus 2.5% for the US Consumer Price Index.

A   Discuss the implications of the current pressure on JCHE to increase spending.

B   Discuss how JCHE's time horizon affects its risk tolerance.

C   Determine a long-term spending policy for JCHE, including a spending rate as a percentage of assets, and justify the policy.

7 *Donner Life Insurance*

Susan Leighton, treasurer for US-based Donner Life Insurance, has just joined the board of a charitable organization that has a large endowment portfolio. She is researching how the investment policy for an endowment differs from that of life insurance companies and has thus far reached the following conclusions:

A Both endowments and life insurance companies have aggressive return requirements.

B Endowments are less willing to assume risk than life insurance companies because of donor concerns about volatility and loss of principal.

C Endowments are less able to assume risk than life insurance companies because of expectations that endowments should provide stable funding for charitable operations.

D Endowments have lower liquidity requirements than life insurance companies because endowment spending needs are met through a combination of current income and capital appreciation.

E Both endowments and life insurance companies are subject to stringent legal and regulatory oversight.

Evaluate each of Leighton's statements in terms of accuracy and justify your conclusions.

8 *Hannibal Insurance Company*

US-based Hannibal Insurance Company sells life insurance, annuities, and guaranteed investment contracts (GICs) and other protection-based and savings-based products. The company has traditionally managed its investments as a single portfolio, neither segmenting the assets nor segregating the surplus. The following data describe the portfolio:

Exhibit 5 Hannibal Insurance Portfolio Data		
	Four Years Ago	**Last Year**
Assets (reserves and surplus portfolio)	$450 million	$500 million
Duration of assets	6.0 years	6.0 years
Liabilities	$390 million	$470 million
Estimated duration of liabilities	5.5 years	4.0 years

The company attributes the decline in the duration of its liabilities to increases in interest rates and the passage of time.

Hannibal's chief financial officer (CFO) has instructed the portfolio manager as follows: "The rapidly increasing popularity of our two-year fixed rate GIC product has increased our asset base substantially during the last year. Interest rates have been rising and will probably rise another 100 basis points this year. You should continue to take advantage of this situation by investing in higher-yielding, investment-grade, longer-duration bonds in order to maximize our spread and maintain a constant duration of the assets. This strategy will ensure the delivery of a competitive return to our customers."

A Judge the appropriateness of Hannibal's investment strategy as stated by the CFO. Prepare two arguments that support your position.

B Evaluate two factors that would affect liability duration for a life insurance company other than changes in interest rates and the passage of time. Relate the two factors to the specific situation at Hannibal. Assume stable mortality rates.

C Determine the suitability of the segmentation approach to portfolio management at Hannibal Insurance Company. Prepare three arguments that support your position.

D Contrast the return requirement of the surplus portfolio to the return requirement of policyholder reserves, in regard to US life insurance companies in general.

9 *Winthrop Bank*

Winthrop Bank is a commercial bank with operations in North America. Evaluate the effect of each of the following scenarios on the bank's investment objectives, constraints, or risk-taking ability.

A The target average maturity of loans is increased, with overall risk tolerance unchanged.

B The ALCO decides to increase Winthrop Bank's credit standards for loans although Winthrop Bank's overall risk tolerance is unchanged.

C Winthrop decides to sell its mortgage loans as soon as they are booked.

D More opportunities exist for expanding net interest margins with low risk in Winthrop's loan portfolio than in its securities portfolio.

SOLUTIONS

1 *Worden Technology, Inc.*

IPS Y and IPS X offer different components that are appropriate for Worden Technology's pension plan:

   i. *Return requirement.* IPS Y has the appropriate return requirement for Worden's pension plan. Because the plan is currently underfunded, the manager's primary objective should be to make it financially stronger. The risk inherent in attempting to maximize total returns would be inappropriate.

   ii. *Risk tolerance.* IPS Y has the appropriate risk tolerance for Worden's plan. Because of its underfunded status, the plan has a limited risk tolerance; a substantial loss in the fund could further jeopardize payments to beneficiaries.

   iii. *Time horizon.* IPS Y has the appropriate time horizon for Worden's plan. Although going-concern pension plans usually have long time horizons, the Worden plan has a comparatively short time horizon because of the company's reduced retirement age and relatively high median age of its workforce.

   iv. *Liquidity.* IPS X has the appropriate liquidity constraint for Worden's plan. Because of the early retirement feature starting next month and the age of the workforce (which indicates an increasing number of retirees in the near future), the plan needs a moderate level of liquidity to fund monthly payments.

2 *LightSpeed Connections*

   A **i.** Concentrating LSC's pension assets as Donovan has done subjects the plan beneficiaries to an extraordinarily high level of risk because of the high correlation between the market values of the portfolio and LSC's business results.

      ii. By concentrating the pension assets heavily in technology and Internet companies, Donovan has increased the company's risk as the pension plan's sponsor. LightSpeed now faces the prospect of having to provide additional funding to the pension plan at a time when the company's own cash flow and/or earnings position may be weakened. A more prudent approach would be to invest in assets expected to be less highly correlated with the company's market value, so in the event additional funding for the pension plan becomes necessary, it will be less likely to occur when LSC is in a weakened financial position.

   B **i.** The IPS drafted by Jeffries and the investment committee correctly identifies that the return requirement should be total return, with a need for inflation protection that is sufficient to fund the plan's long-term obligations. The IPS is weak in that it neglects to state a specific return requirement.

      ii. The IPS fails to address the pension plan's risk tolerance, one of the two main objectives of a complete investment policy statement. Consequently, the IPS does not provide the guidance on risk tolerance that would highlight the potential risk to the beneficiaries and the company of LSC's current aggressive investment strategy.

      iii. The IPS correctly addresses the time horizon constraint by stating that the assets are long-term in nature, both because of LSC's young workforce and the normal long-term nature of pension investing.

iv. The IPS fails to address the liquidity constraint; although liquidity is a minimal concern in this case, the IPS should nonetheless address that fact.

3 *Gwartney International*

A The amount of surplus will decline when the present value of plan liabilities rises faster than the market value of the assets. According to the information provided, GI's liabilities have a duration of 10 years, the same as US long-term bonds which returned a total of 19% for the previous year (7% income, 12% from capital gains associated with a decline in interest rates for the period). The decline in interest rates for long-term bonds translates into a lower discount rate for the plan's liabilities. The 12% gain in bonds implies that the plan's liabilities would have increased by the same amount. The combination of a 12% gain in liabilities and a 10% return on assets resulted in a decrease in the pension plan's surplus.

B Investment time horizon is a primary determinant of an investor's risk tolerance. GI has a young workforce with many years until retirement, indicating a long time horizon. GI should thus adopt a long investment horizon, allowing investment in higher-risk, higher-expected-return asset classes.

C The plan's risk tolerance embodies the plan sponsor's ability and willingness to absorb the consequences of adverse investment outcomes and/or prolonged subpar investment performance (i.e., its sensitivity to the possibility of being required to increase contributions at unpredictable times and intervals). The less risk an investor can tolerate, the less return will be achieved in the long run.

GI is financially healthy and growing. Given its financial health, the company has the ability to increase contributions when necessary. Because of GI's young workforce, the pension plan has a long time horizon, allowing for investment in riskier assets. The plan is also currently fully funded, and GI is financially strong. All these considerations point to GI having an above-average risk tolerance.

4 *Food Processors, Inc. (FPI)*

A In the United States, every ERISA-qualified defined-benefit pension plan has a projected benefit obligation, which represents the discounted present value of the retirement benefits that the plan is obligated by law to make, given certain assumptions about future rates of pay and workforce factors. If the plan assets at fair market value exceed the PBO, the plan is said to be overfunded. Conversely, if the value of the plan assets falls short of the PBO, the plan is said to be underfunded. Given that FPI's plan is underfunded by $200 million and its assets total $750 million, its PBO must be $950 million.

B FPI faces a dilemma. On the one hand, it needs to improve returns in order to "catch up" on its underfunding; this necessity implies that more risk should be taken. On the other hand, FPI cannot afford to have the underfunding become worse, which it would if FPI incurs more risk that does not produce higher returns in the short run. Alternatively, the company might be tempted, as the chair suggests, to raise the actuarial assumption of what future return levels will be, thereby making the asset base automatically more productive simply by declaring it to be so. Future returns, however, are generated not by actuaries or other individuals but by markets, by asset-class exposures within markets, and by long-term relationships between economic and market factors—all taking place in the context of funding, allocation, and payout decisions unique to FPI's pension plan.

Of primary importance is that the return expected must be consistent with the return the various alternative investment instruments available to the plan can reasonably offer in the long term.

C A US pension plan's discount rate is the rate applied in determining the present value of its pension obligations. Because pension liabilities are typically long term, the discount rate should bear some rational relationship to the long-term interest rates in the marketplace at the time of the calculation. The usual model for the discount rate is the rate at which high-quality, long-term bonds such as the long Treasury bond are quoted, reflecting consensus expectations of long-run inflation plus a real rate of return. Thus, a manager may decide to reduce the discount rate to make it consistent with current market yields for long-term Treasury bonds. Based on the consensus forecasts for long-term Treasury bonds and inflation shown in Exhibit 4, a discount rate of 6 to 7 percent would be reasonable. FPI is currently using an 8 percent discount rate, which is out of line with current capital market conditions. FPI should thus consider adopting a lower discount rate.

D Reducing the discount rate applied to FPI's PBO would have the effect of increasing the present value of FPI's pension benefit obligations. Because the market value of the assets available to liquidate this obligation remains unchanged, the underfunded situation would be made worse by a reduction in the discount rate. The size of the gap between the PBO and the value of the assets, now $200 million, would increase.

5 *Medical Research Foundation*

A Key elements that should determine the foundation's grant-making (spending) policy are as follows:

- average expected inflation over a long horizon;
- average expected nominal return on the endowment portfolio over the same long horizon; and
- the 5 percent of asset value payout requirement imposed by the tax authorities as a condition for ongoing tax exemption.

To preserve the real value of its assets and to maintain its spending in real terms, the foundation cannot pay out more, on average over time, than the average real return it earns from its portfolio net of investment management expenses. The portion of the total return representing the inflation rate must be retained and reinvested if the foundation's principal is to grow with inflation. Because of the minimum 5 percent spending policy mandated by tax considerations, the real return of the portfolio will have to equal or exceed 5 percent plus the cost of earning investment returns in order to preserve the foundation's tax-exempt status and maintain its real value of principal and future payouts.

B The new IPS should include the following components:

- *Return objective.* A total return approach is recommended to meet the foundation's objective of maintaining real value after grants. The required annual return shall be the sum of the spending rate plus the expected inflation rate.[1]

---

[1] This additive return objective is easy to understand; as discussed in the reading, a multiplicative return objective would be more precise.

- *Risk tolerance.* The adoption of a clear-cut spending policy will permit cash flows to be planned with some precision, adding stability to annual budgeting and reducing the need for liquidity. Based on its long time horizon, low liquidity needs, and (now) ample assets, the foundation's risk tolerance is above average.

- *Liquidity requirements.* Based on asset size and the predictable nature of cash payouts, liquidity needs are low.

- *Time horizon.* The foundation, with an unlimited lifespan, has a very long time horizon.

- *Tax considerations.* The foundation is tax-exempt under present US law as long as the annual minimum payout of 5 percent is met.

- *Legal and regulatory constraints.* The foundation is governed by the Uniform Management of Institutional Funds Act (UMIFA) as well as IRS regulations.

- *Unique circumstances.* None apply, other than those previously discussed.

6 *James Children's Hospital (JCH)*

A The current spending request of $1,600,000 represents $1,600,000/$20,000,000 = 0.08 or 8% of the value of the endowment. This level of spending is high given the endowment's long-term expected total return of 8.6 percent per year (in nominal terms) and expected 4 percent inflation rate for medical equipment prices. If such spending is permitted, the current beneficiaries of the JCHE (for example, the patients of JCH) may receive benefits at the expense of future beneficiaries, because the endowment is unlikely to be able to maintain its value in inflation-adjusted terms.

B JCHE has a perpetual time horizon; it can thus tolerate a higher risk level (in terms of volatility of returns) than a fund with a shorter time horizon. The higher risk tolerance results from the longer period available to make up for any market downturns. With a higher risk tolerance, JCHE can target a higher expected return.

C JCHE's long-term spending policy should balance the needs of current and future beneficiaries. Its spending policy should balance income needs and the need to build the payout stream to preserve purchasing power. JCHE balances these conflicting objectives only when future beneficiaries receive the same inflation-adjusted distribution that current beneficiaries receive. With zero real growth, intergenerational neutrality exists. Because market returns are variable, JCHE should use a smoothing mechanism that will apply the spending rate to a moving average of market value:

Expected total return	8.6%
– Inflation	–4.0
Real expected return	4.6
– Spending rate	–4.6
Expected real growth	0.0%
Recommended spending rate	4.6%

7 *Donner Life Insurance*

Leighton made both incorrect and correct statements about life insurance and endowment portfolios:

A *Both endowments and life insurance companies have aggressive return requirements* is an inaccurate statement. The return requirements of life insurance companies are first and foremost liability driven, matching assets with fixed obligations, and must be consistent with their conservative stance toward risk. Life insurance companies' return requirements also include, as an objective, the earning of a competitive return on the assets that fund surplus.

The return requirements of endowments, although subject to a range of risk tolerances, are driven by the endowment's spending rate, the need to preserve purchasing power, and the need to provide a growing financial contribution to the endowed organization.

B *Endowments are less willing to assume risk than life insurance companies because of donor concerns about volatility and loss of principal* is an inaccurate statement. Life insurance companies tend to have a lower tolerance for risk than endowments do. Confidence in a life insurance company's ability to pay its benefits (obligations) as they come due is a crucial element in the industry's financial viability. Life insurance companies thus are sensitive to the risk of any significant chance of principal loss or any significant interruption of investment income.

Endowments, by contrast, tend to have a higher tolerance for risk. Their long-term time horizons and predictable cash flows, relative to their spending rate requirements, enable them to pursue more aggressive strategies than life companies can.

C *Endowments are less able to assume risk than life insurance companies because of expectations that endowments should provide stable funding for charitable operations* is an inaccurate statement. Life insurance companies' ability to assume risk is circumscribed by their need to ensure the funding of liabilities to policyholders. The ALM focus of life insurance companies typically requires major holdings of bonds to offset the interest-sensitive nature of most life insurance liabilities. Regulations, including risk-based capital requirements, generally constrain the ability of life insurance companies to invest in higher risk assets.

In contrast, the main risk facing an endowment is loss of purchasing power over time. Endowments have very long time horizons and are not focused on funding liabilities. Therefore, endowments should be able to accept higher volatility than life insurance companies in the short term to maximize long-term total returns.

D *Endowments have lower liquidity requirements than life insurance companies because endowment spending needs are met through a combination of current income and capital appreciation* is an accurate statement. Life insurance companies face the need for liquidity as a key investment constraint, because life insurance products are promises to pay money depending on certain expected or unexpected events.

Endowments typically have low liquidity needs, except to fund periodic distributions and to cover emergency needs. Distributions are usually foreseeable and can usually be met from a combination of investment income and the sale of readily marketable securities.

E *Both endowments and life insurance companies are subject to stringent legal and regulatory oversight* is an inaccurate statement. Life insurance companies are subject to relatively rigorous legal and/or regulatory oversight with respect to their portfolio composition and investment strategies.

In contrast, endowments are relatively unburdened with legal and/or regulatory restraints, at least at the federal level in the United States, although some states do have specific rules and regulations regarding management of endowment assets.

8 *Hannibal Insurance Company*

A The investment strategy of Hannibal Insurance Company is inappropriate, because the company is ignoring interest rate risk and the strategy threatens both the surplus and policyholder reserves.

Hannibal's investment strategy has three key negative consequences. First, the company faces major interest rate risk, as evidenced by the duration mismatch. Second, a focus on short-duration products will accelerate the mismatch. Finally, the company has not generated sufficient reserves and surplus relative to liabilities, given the risks it faces; thus it is increasing its risk of insolvency.

Given the interest rate sensitivity of many life insurance products, controlling interest rate risk is one of the most challenging tasks facing portfolio managers in the insurance industry. Although tolerance for interest rate risk, or level of mismatch, varies from company to company, duration mismatch can become an acute problem in periods of rising interest rates. Meeting the return objective of earning a significant spread is important, but assets and liabilities must be managed in a way that offsets the effects of changes in interest rates.

Confidence in an insurance company's ability to meet its obligations is so vital to the company's survival that special care must be taken to avoid any significant losses of principal. Hannibal has taken on a substantial amount of interest rate risk in recent years. Continuing a spread-maximization strategy in the face of rising interest rates threatens the firm's financial stability.

The mismatch must be corrected. Continuing along the path outlined by the CFO will magnify the interest rate risk, which the CFO is ignoring because of the "increasing popularity" of a short-duration product. As the duration of the assets is held steady through the CFO's urging to invest in higher-yielding, longer-duration bonds, the duration of the liabilities will shrink. The CFO is focusing on a spread-maximization strategy and mistakenly relying on investment-grade securities to provide policyholder security. The real danger lies in another direction—namely the potential forced sale of assets, with sizable losses resulting from interest rate increases, to pay off short-duration liabilities.

The company has a relatively small surplus portfolio. Surplus is an indicator of an insurance company's financial health and is vital to expansion of the business. If interest rates continue to rise as expected, the market value of the portfolio assets will decline, which may wipe out the surplus and a portion of policyholder reserves. With the company unable to expand or meet its obligations, its viability becomes questionable.

B Two additional factors that affect liability duration for a life insurance company are 1) the duration of products sold and 2) policy surrenders and/or loans.

- The *duration of products sold* is a main driving force influencing the overall duration of liabilities. The extent to which a company directs marketing efforts toward short- or long-duration products will tilt overall duration. In this case, the company is placing a heavy emphasis on a two-year guaranteed investment contract product. The duration of this product will be much shorter than that of the overall portfolio.

Management indicates that this product is popular, with sales increasing in recent years. This increase, all else being equal, will contribute to a decline in the duration of liabilities.

■ Duration of liabilities is also driven by *policy surrender and/or loans*, either of which can be triggered by interest rate changes. Surrender rates triggered by interest rate changes are more difficult to predict than mortality rates and have become a critical variable for many life insurance companies. During periods of rising interest rates, policyholder redemptions accelerate as policyholders seek the most competitive rate. Such behavior would be typical in an environment in which "interest rates are rising and are expected to rise another 100 basis points." Accelerating surrenders could also influence an actuary to reduce the assumed duration of a company's liabilities.

C Because of the varied features in life and annuity contracts, most life insurance companies segment their portfolios to group liabilities with similar interest-rate-sensitivity characteristics. Portfolios are then constructed by segment in such a way that the most appropriate securities fund each product segment. This practice also recognizes that particular product lines have unique time horizons and return objectives and should be managed accordingly.

Segmentation would be appropriate at Hannibal because of the problems arising from the popularity of a short-duration product. The portfolio manager could construct a portfolio targeted to the liabilities created by this product. Three arguments for the segmentation approach could be chosen from the following. Segmentation:

■ aids in managing liabilities of similar characteristics;

■ assists in the selection of the most appropriate assets to fund product segments (liabilities);

■ aids in the management and/or measurement of interest rate risk and duration mismatch by product line;

■ provides a framework for meeting return objectives by product line;

■ provides for accurate measurement of the profitability of product lines and/or manager performance;

■ provides for the allocation of investment income by line of business;

■ provides for the measurement of risk-adjusted returns; and

■ facilitates accountability and allays regulatory concerns.

D The focus of the return requirement for policyholder reserves is on earning a competitive return on the assets used to fund estimated liabilities. Life insurance companies are considered spread managers, in that they manage the difference between the return earned on investments and the return credited to policyholders. Spread management can take various forms, such as a yield approach versus a total-return approach, but the objective remains the same.

The focus of the return requirement for the surplus is on long-term growth. An expanding surplus is an important indicator of financial stability and the base for building the lines of business. When selecting investments for the surplus portfolio, managers typically seek assets with the potential for capital appreciation, such as common stocks, venture capital, and equity real estate.

9 *Winthrop Bank*

    A   Because the loan portfolio is now subject to greater interest rate risk, although overall risk tolerance has not changed, the target maturity of the securities portfolio must be reduced to offset the loan portfolio's greater risk.

    B   Winthrop Bank should have more leeway to invest in below-investment-quality debt in its bond portfolio as a result.

    C   Winthrop's decision decreases the need for liquidity in its securities portfolio.

    D   The development suggests taking less risk in its securities portfolio.

Linking Pension Liabilities to Assets

by Aaron Meder, FSA, CFA, and Renato Staub, PhD

Aaron Meder, FSA, CFA, is at Legal & General Investment Management (United Kingdom). Renato Staub, PhD, is at William Blair Investment Management (USA).

LEARNING OUTCOMES

Mastery	The candidate should be able to:
☐	**a.** contrast the assumptions concerning pension liability risk in asset-only and liability-relative approaches to asset allocation;
☐	**b.** discuss the fundamental and economic exposures of pension liabilities and identify asset types that mimic these liability exposures;
☐	**c.** compare pension portfolios built from a traditional asset-only perspective to portfolios designed relative to liabilities and discuss why corporations may choose not to implement fully the liability mimicking portfolio.

Pension assets exist to defease[1] the benefit promises made by plan sponsors to participants and beneficiaries—the pension liability. It follows that pension investment policies should be set in a way that explicitly integrates the exposures of the pension liability. Excluding the liability's exposures from the analysis is like setting a soccer team's starting lineup without fully considering the opposing team. This is analogous to the traditional approach to pension investing, which has resulted in portfolios that may be appropriate in an asset-only framework but are exposed to unrewarded risk when evaluated relative to liabilities. Efficient investment policies can be designed and thus unrewarded risk avoided if the exposures of the liability are explicitly integrated into the investment framework.

---

1 Render void; offset.

The intent of this reading is twofold:

- Provide insight into modeling the pension liability, focusing on which fundamental and economic factors influence its evolution.

- Using the fundamental and economic factors that influence both assets and the pension liability we provide a framework to model assets and liabilities consistently.

While we focus on pension plans, the general framework put forth to link assets and liabilities via fundamental and economic factors is applicable to many situations where assets are set aside to defease a future obligation that has market related exposures. Thus, the framework can be generalized to insurance products, postretirement health benefits, or college savings plans.

1   INTRODUCTION

Some pension sponsors have not explicitly integrated the pension liability's fundamental and economic exposures into the investment policy decision. Instead, their process has focused on setting appropriate "asset-only" portfolios. Such a process may be the current paradigm because the plan's contribution requirement, accounting cost, and balance sheet are all currently based on a smoothed relationship between assets and liabilities, mitigating the impact of a mismatch between the two. Thus, many plan managers select portfolios from the asset-only efficient frontier, relying on the actuarial and accounting smoothing to keep the relationship between assets and liabilities relatively stable over the short horizon.

Selecting portfolios from an asset-only perspective implicitly assumes that the liability has no risk at all; at least none that is market related. By 'market related' we mean that the exposure is influenced by market related factors such as interest rates, inflation, or economic growth. However, pension liabilities, representing the present value of deferred wages, by their very nature are driven by economics and have many market related exposures. Not integrating these exposures can result in inefficient investment policies when measured versus liabilities, as they may be exposed to excessive and unrewarded risk relative to liabilities. Such unrewarded risk was masked by the bull market of the 1990s and subsequently unmasked by the storm of falling equity markets and interest rates that plagued the industry at the turn of the millennium. Couple this with the global pension regulatory environment trending towards unsmoothing pension assets and liabilities, and there is an increasing incentive to design investment policies that better integrate assets and liabilities.

Hence, in our investment framework, we allow for an *economic* liability.[2] This framework fundamentally changes the picture in that assets that mirror the economic liability (which becomes the investment benchmark), are considered low risk. Table 1 summarizes the fundamental difference between designing policies with an asset-only perspective versus a liability-relative perspective.

---

2 The concept of an economic liability is not new. There is much literature in support of an economic view of the liability. [9] Treynor, et al., (1976), [2] Bookstaber and Gold (1988), [1] Arnott and Bernstein (1988), [7] Ryan and Fabozzi (2002) and most recently [10] Waring (2004) are examples.

Table 1	Asset-Only and Liability-Relative Perspectives	
	Asset Only	**Liability Relative**
Liability exposures	None	Term structure, inflation, growth
Risk-free investment/ Benchmark	Cash	Liability mimicking asset portfolio
Low risk investments	Low correlation with assets	High correlation with liability

Clearly, in liability relative space the liability now takes center stage. Unfortunately, there is no investable asset that perfectly mimics the exposures of a pension liability. As a result, we must create the investment benchmark by constructing a portfolio of assets that best mimics the liability.

HOW TO DEFINE RISK?   2

Developing the appropriate investment benchmark depends on the relevant investment horizon for defining investment risk.

If the plan sponsor defines risk as the risk that assets will not hedge the liability *over the next year*, then we must focus on short-term market-related liability exposures. This has been the focus of most advisors by using a portfolio of long duration bonds to proxy the liability. This approach captures the liability's exposure to short-term changes of the term structure.

However, modeling the term structure exposure only captures part of the liability risk. Arnott and Bernstein (1988) state that "the size of pensions the corporation pays in future years will have little to do with today's level of long-term interest rates" and Bookstaber and Gold (1988) say "those who act as if the world were defined only by cash flows and interest rate exposure, duration and dedication, see only part of the asset/liability picture." Rather, in order to see the full picture of pension fund investment risk, one must also focus on the volatility of the estimated benefit payments themselves and how they change over time. An emphasis only on the short-term liability may be sensible for the relatively few financially weak companies with poorly funded plans. However, most companies are relatively healthy with well funded ongoing plans and have the ability to focus on both long and short horizons.

For the relatively healthy company with an ongoing plan, risk is both the short-term volatility of plan costs and the long-term risk of pension assets being insufficient to defease the liability. Hence, liability modeling must deal with both horizons, and in particular, it must address the question of what the liabilities will look like in the future and how can we best hedge them as they evolve.

PENSION LIABILITIES DECOMPOSED   3

Again, pension liabilities vary in value like assets, and in order to measure investment risk relative to liabilities, we must understand how assets and liabilities are related. To put our approach in perspective, we will focus on a hypothetical defined benefit plan of People Corporation Inc., which has a typical liability profile and typical plan provisions.

As for assets, the value of a liability can be determined in two steps:

■ estimating the expected benefit payments, i.e., the future cash outflows; and

■ discounting them. That is:

$$V_L = \sum_t \frac{B_t}{(1 + r_t)^t} \tag{1}$$

where V_L is the market value of the pension liability, B_t the benefit payment at time t, and r the appropriate discount rate. Liability risk is the volatility of its value and can be attributed to volatility in the discount rate and estimated benefit payments.

Consistent with asset pricing, the discount rate used for the economic liability must reflect the market related exposures of the benefit payments. For example, if the benefit payments increase with inflation then the investment benchmark would have a real rate bond component, and accordingly, the applicable discount rate should reflect the real rate bond risk premium used by the market to discount inflation linked cash flows.

Thus, we turn our attention to modeling the benefit payments and understanding their inherent fundamental and economic exposures, as these are what drive the interest rate used for discounting. Pension benefits are not known with certainty. They exhibit volatility attributable to volatility in wages, inflation, and many non-market-related factors; or growth attributable to future service costs, new entrants and other non-market-related factors.

The extent and causes of the uncertainty in pension benefits vary greatly by demographic group. Thus, modeling the variations in estimated benefits is easiest by decomposing the benefits into demographic groups whose benefit levels are driven by different exposures. These exposures are either market related or not. We address each in turn.

Market Related Exposures

1. *Inactive Participants*

These are the benefits attributable to participants currently receiving pension payments (retirees), or participants who are no longer working for the firm and are owed a benefit, but have not yet started receiving benefit payments (deferreds). The estimated benefit payments to this group are fixed, in a market related sense, unless they are indexed with inflation in order to protect the retiree's standard of living. Exhibit 1 shows People Corporation's estimated future inactive benefit payments.

Exhibit 1   Inactive Benefits

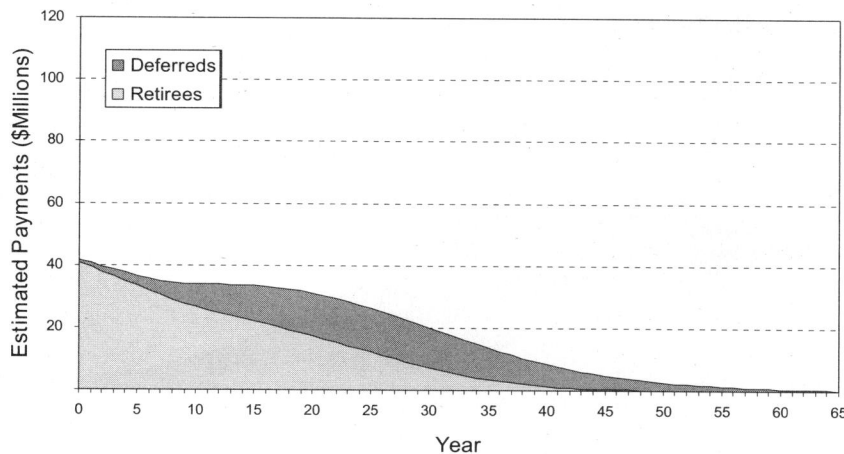

People Corporation's plan does not provide inflation indexing. Therefore the inactive benefit payments are fixed and hence the value of these benefit payments very "bond like" with the only market exposure being the exposure to the term structure. The portfolio of assets that best mimics such a liability is a bond portfolio whose cash flows match the estimated benefit payments. On the other hand, if the benefit payments are indexed with inflation, the benefit payments and thus the value of the liability will vary with the level of inflation. In this case, the investment benchmark is a mixture of real rate bonds and nominal bonds. If the plan provides full one for one inflation indexation the benchmark for this portion of the liability is 100% inflation linked bonds.

2. Active Participants

These are the estimated benefit payments associated with currently active employees. When modeling these benefit payments we slice the estimated benefit payments into two components: benefits attributable to past service rendered and wages earned (accrued benefits) and benefits attributable to future service and wages (future benefits).

2.1 Accrued Benefits   These are benefits attributable to past service rendered and past wages earned. Like inactive benefits, they are fixed in a market related sense unless they are indexed with inflation in order to protect the participant's standard of living. Consistent with People Corporation's inactive benefits, there is no inflation indexation and therefore the investment benchmark will consist of nominal bonds. The present value of these benefits plus the inactive benefits represents the plan's liability attributable to "accrued benefits." Exhibit 2 shows People Corporation's estimated benefit payments attributable to accrued benefits.

Exhibit 2	Accrued Benefits

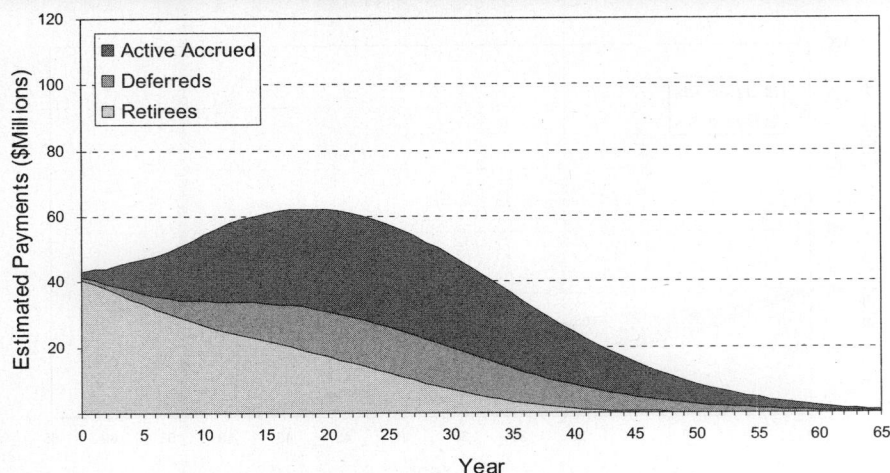

2.2 Future Benefits

2.2 Future Benefits Future benefits are benefits attributable to future wages to be earned, future service to be rendered, and future new entrants into the plan. These benefits drive the evolution of the liability over the long term, but they will have very little impact on the pension plan's overall liability in the short term. For many plans, these benefits will dominate the liability in 20 years. Therefore, to the extent that these benefits are funded (and therefore at risk of becoming unfunded) and capital market driven (hedgeable), they need to be considered today when determining the investment benchmark.

For frozen pension plans, the liability attributable to future benefits is zero and therefore doesn't need to be considered.[3] That is, for frozen plans the accrued benefit liability is the ultimate liability of the plan and has market exposures that are best mimicked by a combination of nominal and index-linked bonds.

2.2.1 Future Wages People Corporation's plan, along with many other plans, provides wage-related benefits. Assuming a certain rate of future wage increases, the actuary provides an estimate of benefit payments attributable to future wage increases. We will call the present value of these estimated benefit payments the "future wage liability." In many countries, the funding target is set equal to the accrued benefit liability plus future wage liability and therefore is the relevant investment benchmark. Using accounting nomenclature the accrued benefit liability plus the future wage liability is analogous to the projected benefit obligation in the United States under FAS 87 and the defined benefit obligation internationally under IAS19.

People Corporation assumes future wage increases of 4% per annum. These wage increases and the corresponding benefits are attributable to two economic forces: wage inflation and real wage growth. People Corporation assumes 2% wage inflation and 2% real wage growth. Exhibit 3 shows its estimated cash flows attributable to accrued benefits plus the future wage increases, split between future wage inflation and future real wage growth.

---

3 These are plans where the accrued benefits are frozen and no future accruals will be granted.

Exhibit 3   Accrued Benefits plus Future Wage Benefits

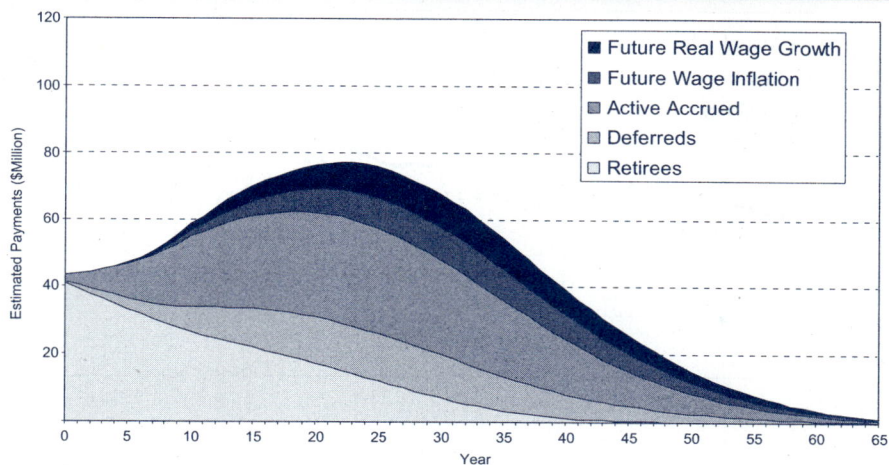

2.2.1.1 Future Wage Inflation   There is a long-term relationship between general inflation and wage inflation. Thus, cash flows of real rate bonds will vary similarly to the variations in the estimated benefit payments attributable to future wage inflation. However, People Corporation's wage inflation benefits for each active employee are only exposed to inflation until retirement. After retirement these benefit payments are fixed and no longer exposed to changes in inflation. As a result, a combination of real rate bonds and nominal bonds will be the investment benchmark for People Corporation's wage inflation liability.

2.2.1.2 Future Real Wage Growth   Real wage growth is linked with economic growth through labor's share of productivity increases. There is strong evidence for a stable share of labor in national income.[4] In other words, the real wage growth is linked with productivity increases. Dividends are also related to economic growth; therefore we expect a stable long-term relationship between the stock market and the GDP.[5] In order to portray this relationship, we regress the real US GDP on the real S&P 500 and find:[6]

---

4 See [8] Singer and Terhaar, p. 19.
5 More precisely, we expect the stock market to anticipate the economy.
6 The data series consists of annual observations.

Exhibit 4   GDP Regressed on the S&P 500

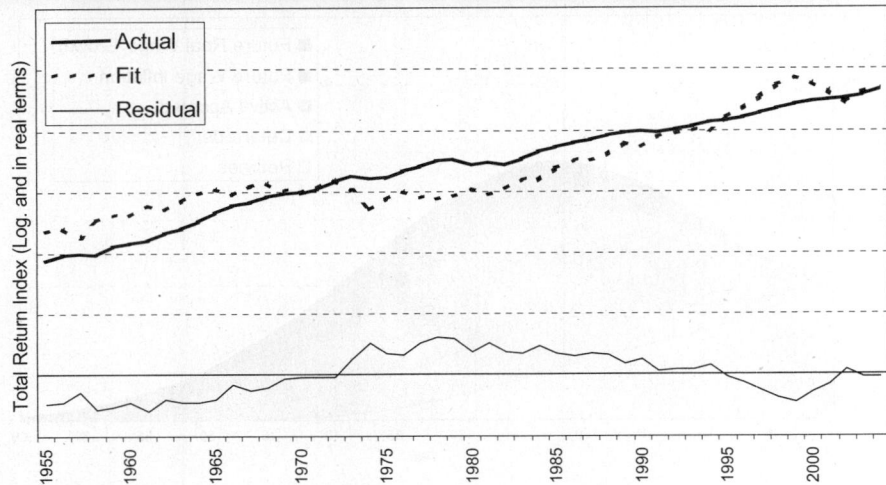

Very high t-statistics of 14 for the intercept and 27 for the slope, and an R^2 of 92% are evidence for a strong *long-term* relationship. However, this is not striking news, as there is much literature in support of this.[7]

Just like People Corporation's wage inflation benefits, its real wage growth benefits for each active employee are only exposed to real wage growth until retirement. After retirement these benefit payments are fixed and no longer exposed to changes in growth. As a result a combination of equities and nominal bonds will be the investment benchmark for People Corporation's real wage growth liability.

2.2.2 *Future Service Rendered*   To the extent that it is funded and hedgeable, we can expand our definition of the liability by including the benefit payments attributable to future service rendered. These are shown for People Corporation in Exhibit 5.

Exhibit 5   Estimated Benefit Payments: Accrued Benefits plus Future Wages plus Future Service

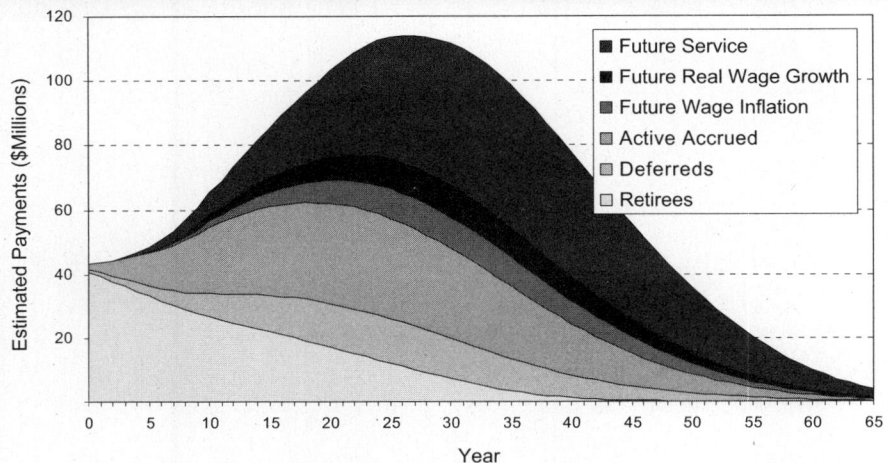

---

7 See for instance [3] Campbell, Lo, and MacKinlay, or [5] Fama and French.

Just like the volatility of future wage benefits, the volatility of future service benefits is linked to wage growth. As wages grow, the service accruals granted will be based on higher wages, and thus the corresponding benefit payment will be higher. But in reality this portion of the liability is often not included in the funding target and relatively uncertain. Hence, it should be excluded from the investment benchmark.

3. *Future Participants*

Finally, if appropriate, we can fully expand our definition of the liability and include the estimated benefits attributable to future new entrants. For a plan closed to new entrants, this liability is zero and for an ongoing plan this portion of the liability is rarely funded to any extent, and the corresponding benefits are the most uncertain of all the benefits we've discussed. As a result, they should be excluded from the investment benchmark.

For People Corporation, the relevant investment benchmark is the accrued benefit liability plus the future wage liability. Table 2 summarizes the market related exposures for each portion of this benchmark along with the corresponding liability mimicking assets.

Table 2 Market Related Exposures and Liability Mimicking Assets		
Portion of the Investment Benchmark	**Market Related Exposures**	**Liability Mimicking Assets**
Inactive	Term structure	Nominal bonds
Active—accrued	Term structure	Nominal bonds
Active—future wage	Inflation	Real rate bonds
	Growth	Equities
	Term structure	Nominal bonds

Non-Market Related Exposures: Liability Noise

As mentioned above, the estimated benefit payments have both market related and non-market related exposures. We call the uncertainty in benefit payments attributable to non-market related exposures "liability noise." There are two components of liability noise:

- plan demographic experience differing from the actuary's model given that the underlying probabilities are certain; and

- model uncertainty—the fact that the underlying probabilities are not certain (e.g., mortality rate change due to medical innovations).

If the probabilities underlying the actuary's model are certain, the main factor that drives liability noise is the number of participants. Statistical methods can be used to estimate this component of noise; the larger the plan's population the more closely experience will track the model.[8] By its very nature, however, model uncertainty is difficult to estimate. The extent and causes of the liability noise vary greatly by demographic groups. We address inactive participants and then active participants.

---

8 [6] Leibowitz, et al., (1991) estimates that this component of liability noise "would range from 2% to 3% for a small group ($10-million liability) to just a small fraction of 1% for a liability of $1 billion."

1. Inactive Participants

For retirees, liability noise is attributable to one major source. Embedded within the actuarial projection of benefit payments is a mortality assumption about the length of people's lives and hence the duration they will be receiving benefits. To the extent that mortality experience differs from what was assumed, the benefit payments will vary accordingly. If people live longer than assumed, benefit payments will be larger and vice versa. At this point in time there are few liquid assets whose cash flows are linked with mortality. Thus, mortality exposure is currently difficult to hedge. However, there are bonds under development where the coupons are inversely linked to mortality, and an index linked to US life expectancy has recently been developed.

In addition to longevity risk, a deferred's estimated benefits are based on an assumption about when the participant will retire and start receiving benefits. The sooner the participant elects to receive benefits the smaller the annual benefit the plan provides, as the participant is expected to receive it for a longer time. Thus, the uncertainty regarding the timing and amount of benefits coupled with mortality risk result in deferred liabilities being noisier and less hedgeable than retirees' liabilities.

2. Active Participants

In addition to a mortality assumption, active employees' estimated benefit payments are embedded with assumptions of withdrawal, disability, and retirement, and therefore are embedded with a large amount of uncertainty, much more so than those of retirees or deferreds. The estimated benefit payments for an employee who is many years away from retirement are based on a long string of probabilities and represent the actuary's best estimate regarding the plan's future obligation. Although we cannot hedge the noise, the greater the relative size of liability noise, the less hedgeable the liability.[9]

4 LINKING ASSETS AND LIABILITIES VIA FUNDAMENTAL FACTORS

As suggested above, pension liabilities have many market related and nonmarket related exposures. Based on the discussed exposures, we hypothesize that People Corporation's investment benchmark is some combination of nominal bonds, real rate bonds and equities. These are the cornerstone liability mimicking assets. The crucial question is: what is their appropriate combination? Using the economic and fundamental factors that underlie asset and liability values, we can formally link liabilities and assets and determine the investment benchmark.

We have demonstrated that the accrued benefit liability has primarily market related exposures to shifts in the discount rate, and thus the relevant factor is the term structure which entails the real rate, inflation, and a nominal bond premium. Further, the future wage liability is exposed to the change in wage level and thus economic growth and inflation. To the extent that the future wage liability is linked with economic growth, equity growth is a relevant factor as well. Finally, if the plan provides for some inflation indexation, the liability has some similarity with real rate bonds and thus is exposed to changes in the real rate bond premium.

On the other hand, the economic and fundamental factors underlying the cash flows provided by the assets are the real risk-free rate of return, the rate of inflation, the corresponding risk premia, and, in the case of equity, the rate of growth.

---

9 [6] Leibowitz, et al., (1991) claims that liabilities with noise in excess of 10% "offer little practical assistance in surplus management."

With these factors in mind we are ready for factor modeling. In a first step to that end, we determine the factors involved. The *Capital Asset Pricing Model* (CAPM) holds that an asset's fair return (expected return) entails the risk-free rate of return as a compensation for consumption deferral plus a risk premium commensurate with the asset's risk. Further, the risk-free rate can be disaggregated into the compensation for inflation and the real risk-free rate of return.

In practice, inflation is proxied by the change of the consumer price index (CPI), and the real risk-free rate is proxied by the T-bill return minus the inflation proxy. With regard to the risk premium, historical analysis, often combined with a forward-looking adjustment, helps to determine the risk premium as the difference between the asset's total return and the risk-free rate. Further, with regard to growth, we believe in a long-term relationship between the overall economy and the stock market.

Since assets and liabilities represent economic values, they can be modeled with the same underlying factors, as the above description implies. Table 3 shows our suggested factor covariance matrix, disaggregated into a correlation matrix and a column of standard deviations, i.e., it describes the relationships between the factors.[10]

Table 3   Factor Covariance Matrix

	Risk	Real Rate	Inflation	Growth	Equity Premium	Nominal Bonds Premium	Real Bonds Premium
Real Rate	0.80%	1.00		0.20	0.10	0.05	0.05
Inflation	0.80%		1.00	−0.10	0.20	0.20	
Growth	1.00%	0.20	−0.10	1.00	−0.10	0.10	0.05
Equity Premium	1.00%	0.10	0.20	−0.10	1.00	0.40	0.30
Nominal Bonds Premium	0.66%	0.05	0.20	0.10	0.40	1.00	0.85
Real Bonds Premium	0.40%	0.05		0.05	0.30	0.85	1.00

Setting Asset and Liability Sensitivities

The next step in the process requires setting the *sensitivities* of assets and liabilities versus the factors. The sensitivities describe how much the value of the assets and liabilities move in response to a move in the corresponding factor.

1 Assets

When determining the sensitivities of bonds it is useful to set up a model:

$$V_B = \sum_t \frac{CF_t}{(1 + r_t)^t} \qquad (2)$$

where CF are the cash flows and r is the discount rate. To the extent that the cash flows are fixed (as in the case of a nominal bond), the value is sensitive to changes in the real rate, inflation, and the nominal bond premium. If the cash flows are inflation linked as is the case with real rate bonds, then the bond will not be sensitive to changes in inflation since inflation affects the numerator and denominator in an offsetting way.

---

10 For a discussion of the parameters, see Appendix 14.

When modeling equities we utilize dividend discount models. For instance, according to the *Gordon Growth Model*, the intrinsic value of equity is:

$$V_E = \frac{D}{r - g}$$ (3)

where D is the annual dividend payment, r the discount rate, and g the growth rate of the dividends.

From these valuation formulas, we can derive the sensitivities versus the underlying factors. As an example, consider bonds with a maturity of five years and a par yield of 5.5%. If the actual short-term risk-free rate moves by 100 basis points, the yield of a 5-year bond usually moves by less since:

- the 5-year yield is a function of the *actual* short-term risk-free rate and all expected *future* short-term rates (i.e., the forward rates); and

- there is no information about the future short-term rates, as they are further out. Hence, the market assumes they are close to their average, i.e., it anticipates *mean-reversion*.

In Exhibit 6, the first case assumes that all expected future short-term rates move exactly by the same amount as the actual short-term risk-free rate, while the second case assumes that they still move in the same direction but by a decreasing amount the further out they are.

Exhibit 6   Bond Sensitivity vs. Risk-Free Rate

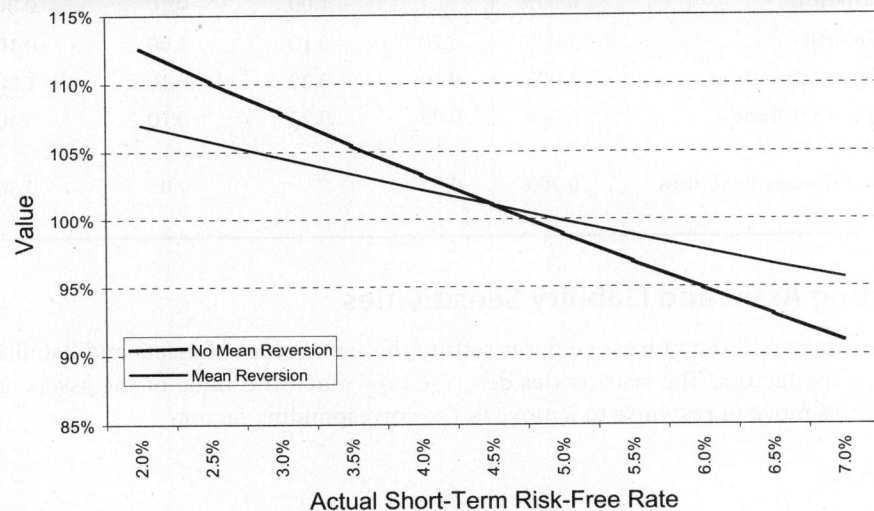

Specifically, the second case assumes mean reversion, while the first case does not. Since mean reversion mitigates the impact of a move of the actual short-term risk-free rate on the resulting discount rate, the corresponding bond value function is flatter than in the case of no mean reversion: we infer a decrease in bond value of approximately 2% in response to a 1% increase of the short term rate.

2 Liabilities

Since People Corporation's plan does not provide for inflation indexation, the accrued benefit liabilities' cash flows will be fixed in a market related sense. Visually the model for this portion of the liability looks identical to a bond.

$$V_{L-AB} = \sum_t \frac{B_t}{(1 + r_t)^t}$$

(4)

Essentially, we deal with a very long-term bond and hence, the key risk is a change in the discount rate.

People Corporation's future wage benefits are completely driven by wage inflation and real wage growth. In the case of s years till retirement, d years till demise and subsequent termination of the obligation, the intrinsic value of our future wage liability[11] is

$$V_{L-FW} = \frac{B}{r - g} \bullet \frac{\left((1 + g)^s - 1\right) \bullet \left((1 + r)^{d-s} - 1\right)}{(1 + r)^d}$$

(5)

where r is the discount rate of the liability, and g the rate of growth. Comparing this with the present value of equity (Equation 3), one will notice that the liability has the same core structure as equity but also includes a correction factor.

As mentioned earlier, future wage benefits can be bifurcated into two components—future wage inflation and future real wage growth. In a market-related sense, the future wage inflation is completely driven by the actual inflation between now and each active employee's retirement. If People Corporation's plan provided for inflation indexation, the cash flow stream would almost exactly mimic the cash flow stream of real rate bonds. But inflation linkage only exists between now and retirement. Therefore, for active participants the closer to retirement they are the more certain and similar to nominal bonds are the cash flows. We approximate the active population's time to retirement by using the average future service calculated by the actuary; for People Corporation's plan it is 11 years. Any change in inflation from the assumed rate (2% in People Corporation's case) would compound itself on average for 11 years if the change in inflation persisted that long. However, our model assumes that the market anticipates inflation to revert over the medium term, that is, in less than 11 years. Based on our model, inflation changes have very little impact on this portion of the liability.

Just like the future wage inflation, cash flows are not driven indefinitely by inflation. Future real wage growth only applies until retirement. Again, we use the average future service to approximate the sensitivity of these cash flows to changes in future real wage growth. The key difference here is that we expect changes in growth to persist longer than we assume for inflation, and this expectation is mirrored in a higher sensitivity.

With regard to the discount rate, we recognize that the cash flows in the case of future real wage growth are equity linked prior to retirement and fixed thereafter. As a result, the cash flows are similar to both equities and bonds, and thus their corresponding discount rate should reflect both the bond premium and the equity premium.

The sensitivity matrix turns out to be:

---

[11] For the derivation of Formula 5, see Appendix 14.

Table 4 Sensitivity Matrix

	Real Rate	Inflation	Growth	Equity Premium	Nominal Bonds Premium	Real Bonds Premium
Liability—Accrued Benefit	−200%	−200%			−1000%	
Liability—Wage Inflation	−200%				−500%	−500%
Liability—Wage Growth	−200%	−200%	1500%	−600%	−600%	
Equity	−500%	−200%	1000%	−1000%		
Nominal Bonds	−200%	−200%			−550%	
Real Bonds	−200%					−450%

The final piece of information we need is an estimate of the residual risks, liability noise in the case of liabilities. When estimating liability noise, we know that the accrued benefit is less noisy than the future wage liability and thus more hedgeable. However, the focus of the paper is not on quantifying the liability noise and for this example we assume People Corporation's liabilities have no residual risk.[12]

Results

At this point, we have all necessary ingredients to calculate the risks of assets and liabilities and their mutual correlations. Based on our parameters, we find:

Table 5 Derived Covariance Matrix

	Risk	Liability— Accrued Benefit	Liability— Wage Inflation	Liability— Wage Growth	Equity	Nominal Bonds	Real Bonds
Liability— Accrued Benefit	7.4%	1.00	0.94	0.32	0.31	0.98	0.73
Liability—Wage Inflation	5.4%	0.94	1.00	0.27	0.26	0.90	0.88
Liability—Wage Growth	17.6%	0.32	0.27	1.00	0.92	0.32	0.16
Equity	15.5%	0.31	0.26	0.92	1.00	0.35	0.25
Nominal Bonds	4.6%	0.98	0.90	0.32	0.35	1.00	0.75
Real Bonds	2.5%	0.73	0.88	0.16	0.25	0.75	1.00
Real Estate	9.2%	0.16	0.14	0.42	0.48	0.21	0.21

Most important, as the derived covariance matrix demonstrates, while the accrued benefit liability is highly correlated with nominal and real bonds, the future wage liability is highly correlated with equity. This is in line with our previous recommendation:

---

12 [4] Ezra (1991) estimates the noise for a liability consisting of accrued benefits and future wages to be 7%. This estimate is attained by modeling the liability as a bond.

accrued benefits can be hedged best with a combination of nominal and real bonds, and the most appropriate hedge for benefits due to future wages is dominated by equity; the reason for this is the joint growth component.

Recombining the decomposed liability and the corresponding mimicking assets we get the following liability mimicking asset portfolio for People Corporation's pension fund.

	Nominal Bonds	Real Rate Bonds	Equities
Liability mimicking asset portfolio	85%	5%	10%

The allocation of People Corporation's liability mimicking asset portfolio is representative of their typical pay related liability profile. However, the resulting allocation is sensitive to many liability structural factors including the proportion of the future wage liability to the overall liability, the degree of inflation indexation, and the status of the plan (e.g., ongoing, closed, or frozen). For example, if the fund was less mature and/or had a higher proportion of future wage liability there would be a higher allocation to equities. If the plan offered full one-for-one inflation indexation via a cost of living allowance (COLA), you would see the nominal bonds replaced with real rate bonds. And, if the plan was frozen and therefore no longer had any exposures to future wage growth, there would be no real rate bonds or equities, only nominal bonds.

Designing Investment Policies Relative to Liabilities

People Corporation could invest in this liability mimicking portfolio and this would be the low risk investment. This means that investing in this portfolio results in the best chance of tracking the liability as it grows and evolves over time. In addition, this is also the appropriate investment benchmark. If the return on the fund's assets beats the return on the liability mimicking asset portfolio, all stakeholders should be satisfied since the pension promises will be paid.

However, by definition, investing in the liability mimicking portfolio will not provide an expected return in excess of the liability and therefore future service benefits and benefits earned by future participants would be defeased by future cash contributions.

Often, this low risk strategy will be too expensive for plan sponsors to maintain over the long run. Therefore, in most cases, we do not recommend investing in the low risk portfolio, but only measuring investment risk against it. The challenge is to find the most efficient way to allocate more assets to "higher returning" asset classes such as equities while minimizing the amount of unrewarded risk taken versus the liability. This can be approached in two steps.

1 Hedge the liability. Derivatives can be used to synthetically represent the market-related exposures of the liability mimicking asset portfolio. For example, interest rate derivatives can be used to mimic the term structure exposure of the liability—the liability's largest risk factor. And, utilizing derivatives to hedge requires far less capital than cash investment, thus, freeing up capital to be invested in "higher returning" assets.

2 Focus the remaining capital on efficient return generation. This can be done within asset-only space because once the liability has been hedged assets should not be given "credit" for further hedging.

This liability relative approach often leads to different investment policies than the traditional asset-only approach. The traditional approach typically leads to 60%–70% equities with the remainder in short and immediate duration nominal bonds. The liability relative approach, on the other hand, leads to investing in long duration nominal bonds, real rate bonds, equities and derivatives to hedge the liability, with the remainder invested in well-diversified return focused component.

5   CONCLUSION

The recent poor performance of pension plan assets versus liabilities has called into question the traditional approach to measuring investment performance—the asset only framework. This has brought about an increasing emphasis on measuring pension fund performance relative to what really matters—the plan's liabilities. Utilizing this framework can help plans avoid unrewarded investment risk like that experienced at the beginning of the decade.

Measuring risk relative to liabilities requires modeling of the liability and understanding the liability's market related exposures. Many practitioners to date have taken an overly simplistic approach by modeling the liability as a short position in a long duration bond. Such an approach focuses on short-term changes in the term structure used to discount the expected benefit payments, but does not capture the expected benefit payments exposures to inflation and economic growth.

Given the long-term relationship between equity and the GDP, appropriate hedging of the obligation requires some equity exposure as well. Without a doubt, stock markets and the GDP do not constantly move in line, as the stock market is much more cyclical, but the cyclicality is around the GDP, and this is why we stress the long-term nature of this relationship.

The long-term relationship between the GDP and the equity market is important for considerations such as pension fund liabilities. Since pension liabilities represent deferred wages, the future value of benefit payments is exposed to future economic growth and inflation. Therefore, for the majority of plans, we believe that the low risk investment benchmark consists of mostly nominal and real rate bonds with the remainder in equities.

Capturing the liabilities' beta exposures to inflation and economic growth can be accomplished by employing a multifactor approach consistently to both assets and liabilities.

Ultimately, a liability is indeed more complicated than a long duration bond and factoring in exposures to economic growth and inflation allows for a more robust measurement of liability relative to investment risk and performance.

And, when most sponsors take investment risk relative to liabilities, this can be done most efficiently by first hedging the liability with the aid of derivatives and then focusing on efficient return generation.

APPENDIX 14

Derivation of Formula 5

Assume the accrued benefit equals B, but grows in line with economic growth of g. Further, there are s years till retirement and d years till demise and termination of the obligation.

Then the present value of an eternal benefit obligation attributable to future wage growth (this does not include the accrued benefit portion of the liability) starting in s years equals

$$V_{Ls} = \frac{B}{r-g} \bullet \frac{(1+g)^s - 1}{(1+r)^s} \qquad \qquad \textbf{(1)}$$

Next, the present value of the same eternal benefit obligation attributable to future wage growth (this does not include the accrued benefit portion of the liability) for s years till retirement but starting in d years equals

$$V_{Ld} = \frac{B}{r-g} \bullet \frac{(1+g)^s - 1}{(1+r)^d} \qquad \qquad \textbf{(2)}$$

The present value of a benefit obligation attributable to future wage growth, starting in s years and ending in d years equals the difference between 1 and 2.

$$V_L = V_{Ls} - V_{Ld}$$

or

$$V_{L-FW} = \frac{B}{r-g} \bullet \frac{\left((1+g)^s - 1\right) \bullet \left((1+r)^{d-s} - 1\right)}{(1+r)^d}$$

REFERENCES

Arnott, Robert D., and Peter L. Bernstein. 1988. "The Right Way to Manage Your Pension Fund." *Harvard Business Review*, (January–February)

Bookstaber, Richard, and Jeremy Gold. 1988. "In Search of the Liability Asset." *Financial Analysts Journal*, (January/February)

Campbell, John Y., Andrew W. Lo, and A. Craig MacKinlay. 1997. *The Econometrics of Financial Markets*. Princeton University Press, Chapter 7.

Ezra, D. Don. 1991. "Asset Allocation by Surplus Optimization," *Financial Analysts Journal*, (January–February).

Fama, Eugene, and Kenneth French. 1988. "Dividend Yields and Expected Stock Returns." *Journal of Financial Economics*, 22.

Leibowitz, Martin L., Stanley Kogelman, and Lawrence Bader. 1991. "Asset Performance and Surplus Control: A Dual Shortfall Approach." Salomon Brothers Inc., (July)

Ryan, Ronald J., and Frank J. Fabozzi. 2002. "Rethinking Pension Liabilities and Asset Allocation." *Journal of Portfolio Management*, (Summer)

Singer, Brian D., and Kevin Terhaar. 1997. "Economic Foundations of Capital Market Returns." Research Foundation of the Institute of Chartered Financial Analysts.

Treynor, Jack L., Patrick Regan, and William W. Priest, Jr. 1976. *The Financial Reality of Pension Funding Under ERISA*. Dow Jones-Irwin: Homewood, IL

Waring, M. Barton. 2004. "Liability-Relative Investing II." *Journal of Portfolio Management*, (Fall)

PRACTICE PROBLEMS

The following information relates to Questions 1–6

Gabriela Cardoso, CFA, is the managing director of the pension plan for Farima Bank (the "Company"). Headquartered in São Paulo, Brazil, it is the largest bank in South America. Cardoso has recently hired Paulo Silva to assist her in reevaluating the pension plan's investment portfolio.

In the past, the pension plan's investment portfolio has been constructed based on an asset-only framework rather than a liability-relative approach. In a discussion on switching to a liability-relative approach, Cardoso asks Silva to list the assumptions of an asset-only approach. Silva states the following are assumptions of an asset-only framework:

Assumption 1   There is no market-related liability risk.

Assumption 2   Liability exposures are limited to the term structure of interest rates.

Assumption 3   Low risk investments are those that have high correlations to liabilities.

Silva asks the Company's actuaries to develop an estimate of the Company's future pension payments. Currently, the Company pays a cost of living adjustment (COLA) on retiree pension payments, which is based on the local consumer price index (CPI). In order to reduce current costs, the Company is considering limiting the COLA to only payments to those who have already retired. Cardoso tells Silva to factor the COLA limitation into his estimate of the benefit payment that will be made 15 years from now.

Silva presents Exhibit 1, noting that approximately half of the future wage inflation liability is assumed to correlate closely to CPI and half of the future real wage growth is assumed to correlate closely with domestic equities:

Exhibit 1 Components of Estimated Future Benefit Payments in Year 15	
Liability Exposure	**Amount of Payment (in R\$* Millions)**
Retirees	10
Deferreds	5
Active Accrued	9
Future Wage Inflation	6
Future Real Wage Growth	2

*Brazilian real.

Cardoso next asks Silva to develop a liability mimicking portfolio based on the liability exposures for all future estimated pension payments in Year 15. She also asks him to identify the non-market factors that could have an impact on the Company's pension liability in Year 15. Silva lists the following non-market factors that he believes would be difficult if not impossible to mimic in an investment portfolio:

Factor 1 An increase in the Company retirees' savings rate.

Factor 2 A decrease in the number of participants versus projections.

Factor 3 Medical innovations resulting in changes to the mortality rate.

Cardoso notes the following characteristics of a low-risk investment for a pension fund:

Characteristic 1 A high correlation to pension liabilities.

Characteristic 2 A low correlation to other investment assets.

Characteristic 3 A low correlation to the term structure of interest rates.

Cardoso has one final request for Silva: develop strategies that will fully hedge the Company's market-related pension liability and reduce the expected cost of the plan to the Company (i.e., lower pension plan contributions in the future).

1 Which assumption of an asset-only approach stated by Silva is *most likely* correct?

   A Assumption 1.

   B Assumption 2.

   C Assumption 3.

2 Based on Exhibit 1, in a liability-mimicking portfolio, which of the following amounts is *closest* to the pension payments in Year 15 that could best be mimicked using real (inflation-indexed) bonds?

   A R$10 million.

   B R$12 million.

   C R$13 million.

3 Based on Exhibit 1, in a liability-mimicking portfolio, which of the following amounts is *closest* to the pension payments in Year 15 that could best be mimicked using nominal bonds?

   A R$13 million.

   B R$14 million.

   C R$18 million.

4 Which of the non-market factors listed by Silva would *least likely* have an impact on the Company's pension liability?

   A Factor 1.

   B Factor 2.

   C Factor 3.

5 Which of the characteristics of a low risk investment listed by Cardoso fits *most closely* to a liability-relative approach?

   A Characteristic 1.

   B Characteristic 2.

   C Characteristic 3.

6 Which of the following strategies will *most likely* satisfy Cardoso's final request? The Company should:

   A use derivatives to hedge the market-related pension liability and invest the remaining cash using an asset-only approach.

B use real and nominal bonds to hedge the market-related pension liability and invest the remaining cash in a well-diversified return-generating portfolio.

C use derivatives to hedge severe declines in the equity and bond markets and invest the remaining cash in a well-diversified return-generating portfolio.

The following information relates to Questions 7–11

Belgium-based Hendrik Goethals NV SA recently acquired two companies in the same industry: Locke-Berkeley PLC, based in the United Kingdom, and Prometheus Pyro, Inc., based in the United States. Both of the acquired companies have defined benefit pension plans. The portfolio manager of Locke-Berkeley uses the "liability-relative" perspective in constructing its pension portfolio, and the portfolio manager of Prometheus Pyro uses the "asset-only" perspective in constructing its pension portfolio. The CEO of Hendrik Goethals has called a meeting to review the pension plans of the new subsidiaries, and to consider whether it is advisable to adopt either the liability-relative perspective or the asset-only perspective for both portfolios. The managers of both portfolios provide profiles of their plans (see Exhibit 1).

At the meeting, the portfolio manager of Prometheus Pyro argues: "The asset-only perspective is best. Our approach carries more risk than the liability-relative approach used by Locke-Berkeley, but this increased risk is more than offset by our ability to generate returns in excess of the benefit payments and the change in pension liabilities related to past service, thereby decreasing the need for future cash contributions. By contrast, Locke-Berkeley's portfolio is limited to a return that simply mimics the change in the liabilities over time related to past service; the possibility of earning returns to cover a portion of future service benefits of active participants and benefits earned by future participants is ruled out by the very nature of their approach. That's one important reason many companies avoid the liability-relative approach used by Locke-Berkeley." The portfolio manager of Locke-Berkeley responds to these criticisms and argues for the superiority of the liability-relative approach.

After a vigorous discussion, the meeting is concluded. Within a week, the executives of Hendrik Goethals inform the portfolio managers that the decision is to have both plans follow the "liability-relative" approach. As a first step to implementing this change, the two portfolio managers meet to discuss what asset types; nominal rate bonds, real rate bonds, or equities, should be used to offset the liabilities associated with the specified participant groups within the Prometheus Pyro portfolio.

Exhibit 1	Selected Defined Benefit Pension Plan Data	
Plan characteristics	**Locke-Berkeley**	**Prometheus Pyro**
Assets (in millions)	£158	$257
Liabilities (in millions)	£166	$270
Average age of participants	52	58
Number of participants: active	275	408
Number of participants: retiree (inactive receiving benefits)	20	84

Exhibit 1   (Continued)

Plan characteristics	Locke-Berkeley	Prometheus Pyro
Number of participants: deferred (inactive not yet receiving benefits)	7	48
Benefits indexed to inflation?	No	Partially
Projected inflation rate	2.0% (UK)	2.0% (US)
Projected real GDP growth rate	2.5% (UK)	2.5% (US)

7   **List** *two* assets that would be used in the liability-mimicking portfolio to offset the liabilities associated with the specified participant groups in the Prometheus Pyro plan. **Justify** your choice of *each* listed asset by reference to the economic exposure of the related liabilities of each group.

PARTICIPANT GROUP	LIABILITY-MIMICKING ASSETS	JUSTIFICATION
Active		
Retiree		
Deferred		

8   **Identify** *two* non-market exposures that suggest the Prometheus Pyro plan has lower liability noise than the Locke-Berkeley plan. **Justify** *each* response.

9   **Explain** *one* significant advantage the approach used by Locke-Berkeley has over the approach used by Prometheus Pyro.

10   **Formulate** a strategy that the portfolio manager of Locke-Berkeley can use to provide an expected return in excess of pension liabilities, thus refuting a key claim of the portfolio manager of Prometheus Pyro.

11   **Identify** which portfolio is *most likely* to have a higher proportion of equities once Prometheus Pyro adopts the "liability-relative" approach already used by Locke-Berkeley. **Justify** your answer with *one* fact.

SOLUTIONS

1   A is correct. An asset-only approach assumes there is no market-related liability risk. An asset-only approach focuses only on the return and risk of the investment portfolio.

2   C is correct. All of the retiree benefits of R$10 million can be mimicked using real bonds to account for the CPI COLA as well as half of the R$6 million of future wage inflation [R$10 + (R$6 × 0.50) = R$13]. Only some of the future wage inflation is exposed to inflation because after retirement those benefit payments are fixed and no longer exposed to changes in inflation. Silva states that about half of the future wage inflation is assumed to correlate with CPI and thus can be mimicked using inflation-protected (real) bonds.

3   C is correct. All of the deferred benefits of R$5 million plus all of the active accrued benefits of R$9 million plus half of the future wage inflation and half of the real future wage growth can best be mimicked using nominal bonds whose cash flows match the estimated benefit payments. [R$5 + R$9 + (R$6 × 0.5) + (R$2 × 0.5)] = R$18.

4   A is correct. Changes in the retirees' savings rate have no impact on the Company's pension liability.

5   A is correct. The higher the correlation the investment has to the Company's pension liability, the more likely the Company will be to meet its pension obligations.

6   A is correct. The pension liability is fully hedged using derivatives (the first criterion) and the remaining cash is invested according to an asset-only approach that maximizes return while minimizing volatility with the expectation that the resulting return would be higher than the cost of the derivatives and thereby reduce the amount of future pension plan contributions (cost) by the Company (the second criterion).

7   The assets that would be used in a liability-mimicking portfolio to offset the liabilities associated with each group of participants is as follows:

PARTICIPANT GROUP	LIABILITY-MIMICKING ASSETS	JUSTIFICATION
Active	Nominal bonds Real rate bonds Equities	The liabilities, economic exposures, and corresponding assets associated with active participants are: ● Accrued benefits: — The term structure of these benefits is mimicked by nominal bonds. — The portion that is indexed to inflation is mimicked by real rate bonds. ● Future wage increases: — Future wage inflation is mimicked by real rate bonds. — Future real wage growth is mimicked by equities.
Retiree	Nominal bonds Real rate bonds	The liabilities associated with retirees are accrued benefits only:

PARTICIPANT GROUP	LIABILITY-MIMICKING ASSETS	JUSTIFICATION
		• The term structure of these benefits is mimicked by nominal bonds.
		• The portion that is indexed to inflation is mimicked by real rate bonds.
Deferred	Nominal bonds Real rate bonds	The liabilities associated with deferred participants are accrued benefits only:
		• The term structure of these benefits is mimicked by nominal bonds.
		• The portion that is indexed to inflation is mimicked by real rate bonds.

8 **A** Prometheus Pyro has significantly <u>more plan participants</u> than Locke-Berkeley (540 vs. 302). **Justification:** The larger a plan's population, the more closely the plan's experience will track the model. Thus, model uncertainty is reduced, which results in less liability noise.

B Prometheus Pyro has a <u>larger percentage of inactive participants</u> than Locke-Berkeley (24% = 132/540 vs. 9% = 27/302). **Justification:** The liability noise associated with inactive (i.e., retired and deferred) participants has only one major source: the longevity risk related to mortality assumptions. By contrast, the liability noise associated with active employees reflects not only longevity risk, but also risks related to withdrawal, disability, and retirement assumptions. These additional risks make the liability noise associated with active participants greater than the liability noise associated with inactive participants.

9 One advantage to the liability-relative approach used by Locke-Berkeley is that it considers the market related risk of the pension liabilities whereas the asset-only approach used by Prometheus Pyro does not. Pension liabilities, representing the present value of deferred wages, are driven by many market related exposures, such as interest rates, inflation and economic growth. Failing to integrate these exposures can result in inefficient investment policies when measured versus liabilities, as they may be exposed to excessive and unrewarded risk relative to liabilities. As a result, the liability-relative approach used by Locke-Berkeley has lower market-related risk because it better matches the risk of the pension assets with the risks of the pension liabilities.

10 Plan managers create an investment benchmark from assets that mimic the specific market related risks associated with the pension liabilities of each demographic group. Then managers use derivatives to hedge the market-related exposures of the liability-mimicking assets making up the investment benchmark. This is more efficient than investing in the low risk portfolio defined by the investment benchmark because the derivatives require far less capital, thus freeing up funds, which can then be used for efficient return generation within asset-only space once the liabilities have been hedged. The funds invested in this asset-only space allow the Locke-Berkeley plan to generate returns in excess of the pension liabilities, thereby decreasing the need for future cash contributions.

11 The Locke-Berkeley portfolio is most likely to have a higher proportion of equities for two reasons. One, equities mimic the liability associated with expected real wage growth, which only pertains to active participants. Locke-Berkeley has a higher percentage of active participants than Prometheus Pyro—91% =

275/302 vs. 76% = 408/540—thus Locke-Berkeley should have a higher proportion of equities. Two, Locke-Berkeley has a lower average participant age (52 vs. 58), which implies that a larger proportion of Locke-Berkeley's liability relates to future wage growth, and hence, real wage growth, which is offset with equities. (Note that the two portfolio managers project the same inflation rate and the same real GDP growth rate, so they share the same assumptions as to the rates of future wage inflation and future real wage growth.)

Glossary

Absolute return benchmark A minimum target return that an investment manager is expected to beat.

Absolute-return vehicles Investments that have no direct benchmark portfolios.

Accounting risk The risk associated with accounting standards that vary from country to country or with any uncertainty about how certain transactions should be recorded.

Accumulated benefit obligation (ABO) The present value of pension benefits, assuming the pension plan terminated immediately such that it had to provide retirement income to all beneficiaries for their years of service up to that date.

Accumulated service Years of service of a pension plan participant as of a specified date.

Active/immunization combination A portfolio with two component portfolios: an immunized portfolio which provides an assured return over the planning horizon and a second portfolio that uses an active high-return/high-risk strategy.

Active investment strategies An approach to investing in which the portfolio manager seeks to outperform a given benchmark portfolio.

Active-lives The portion of a pension fund's liabilities associated with active workers.

Active management An approach to investing in which the portfolio manager seeks to outperform a given benchmark portfolio.

Active/passive combination Allocation of the core component of a portfolio to a passive strategy and the balance to an active component.

Active return The portfolio's return in excess of the return on the portfolio's benchmark.

Active risk A synonym for tracking risk.

Actual extreme events A type of scenario analysis used in stress testing. It involves evaluating how a portfolio would have performed given movements in interest rates, exchange rates, stock prices, or commodity prices at magnitudes such as occurred during past extreme market events (e.g., the stock market crash of October 1987).

Ad valorem fees Fees that are calculated by multiplying a percentage by the value of assets managed; also called assets under management (AUM) fees.

Adaptive markets hypothesis (AMH) A hypothesis that applies principles of evolution—such as competition, adaptation, and natural selection—to financial markets in an attempt to reconcile efficient market theories with behavioral alternatives.

Adverse selection risk The risk associated with information asymmetry; in the context of trading, the risk of trading with a more informed trader.

Algorithmic trading Automated electronic trading subject to quantitative rules and user-specified benchmarks and constraints.

Allocation/selection interaction return A measure of the joint effect of weights assigned to both sectors and individual securities; the difference between the weight of the portfolio in a given sector and the portfolio's benchmark for that sector, times the difference between the portfolio's and the benchmark's returns in that sector, summed across all sectors.

Alpha Excess risk-adjusted return.

Alpha and beta separation An approach to portfolio construction that views investing to earn alpha and investing to establish systematic risk exposures as tasks that can and should be pursued separately.

Alpha research Research related to capturing excess risk-adjusted returns by a particular strategy; a way investment research is organized in some investment management firms.

Alternative investments Groups of investments with risk and return characteristics that differ markedly from those of traditional stock and bond investments.

Anchoring and adjustment An information-processing bias in which the use of a psychological heuristic influences the way people estimate probabilities.

Anchoring and adjustment bias An information-processing bias in which the use of a psychological heuristic influences the way people estimate probabilities.

Anchoring trap The tendency of the mind to give disproportionate weight to the first information it receives on a topic.

Angel investor An accredited individual investing chiefly in seed and early-stage companies.

Anomalies Apparent deviations from market efficiency.

Ask price The price at which a dealer will sell a specified quantity of a security. Also called *ask*, *offer price*, or *offer*.

Ask size The quantity associated with the ask price.

Aspirational risk bucket In goal-based portfolio planning, that part of wealth allocated to investments that have the potential to increase a client's wealth substantially.

Asset allocation reviews A periodic review of the appropriateness of a portfolio's asset allocation.

Asset covariance matrix The covariance matrix for the asset classes or markets under consideration.

Asset/liability management The management of financial risks created by the interaction of assets and liabilities.

Asset/liability management (ALM) approach In the context of determining a strategic asset allocation, an asset/liability management approach involves explicitly modeling liabilities and adopting the allocation of assets that is optimal in relationship to funding liabilities.

Asset location The type of account an asset is held within, e.g., taxable or tax deferred.

Asset-only (AO) approach In the context of determining a strategic asset allocation, an approach that focuses on the characteristics of the assets without explicitly modeling the liabilities.

Assurity of completion In the context of trading, confidence that trades will settle without problems under all market conditions.

Assurity of the contract In the context of trading, confidence that the parties to trades will be held to fulfilling their obligations.

Asynchronism   A discrepancy in the dating of observations that occurs because stale (out-of-date) data may be used in the absence of current data.

AUM fee   A fee based on assets under management; an ad valorem fee.

Automated trading   Any form of trading that is not manual, including trading based on algorithms.

Availability bias   An information-processing bias in which people take a heuristic approach to estimating the probability of an outcome based on how easily the outcome comes to mind.

Average effective spread   A measure of the liquidity of a security's market. The mean effective spread (sometimes dollar weighted) over all transactions in the stock in the period under study.

Back office   Administrative functions at an investment firm such as those pertaining to transaction processing, record keeping, and regulatory compliance.

Backtesting   A method for gaining information about a model using past data. As used in reference to VaR, it is the process of comparing the number of violations of VaR thresholds over a time period with the figure implied by the user-selected probability level.

Backwardation   A condition in the futures markets in which the benefits of holding an asset exceed the costs, leaving the futures price less than the spot price.

Balance of payments   An accounting of all cash flows between residents and nonresidents of a country.

Bancassurance   The sale of insurance by banks.

Barbell portfolio   A portfolio made up of short and long maturities relative to the investment horizon date and interim coupon payments.

Base   With respect to a foreign exchange quotation of the price of one unit of a currency, the currency referred to in "one unit of a currency."

Base-rate neglect   A type of representativeness bias in which the base rate or probability of the categorization is not adequately considered.

Basis   The difference between the cash price and the futures price.

Basis point value (BPV)   The change in the bond price for a 1 basis point change in yield. Also called *present value of a basis point* or *price value of a basis point (PVBP)*.

Basis risk   The risk resulting from using a hedging instrument that is imperfectly matched to the investment being hedged; in general, the risk that the basis will change in an unpredictable way.

Batch auction markets   Auction markets where multilateral trading occurs at a single price at a prespecified point in time.

Bayes' formula   A mathematical rule explaining how existing probability beliefs should be changed given new information; it is essentially an application of conditional probabilities.

Bear spread   An option strategy that involves selling a put with a lower exercise price and buying a put with a higher exercise price. It can also be executed with calls.

Behavioral finance   An approach to finance based on the observation that psychological variables affect and often distort individuals' investment decision making.

Behavioral finance macro   A focus on market level behavior that considers market anomalies that distinguish markets from the efficient markets of traditional finance.

Behavioral finance micro   A focus on individual level behavior that examines the behavioral biases that distinguish individual investors from the rational decision makers of traditional finance.

Benchmark   In an investments context, a standard or point of reference for evaluating the performance of an investment portfolio.

Best efforts order   A type of order that gives the trader's agent discretion to execute the order only when the agent judges market conditions to be favorable.

Beta   A measure of the sensitivity of a given investment or portfolio to movements in the overall market.

Beta research   Research related to systematic (market) risk and return; a way investment research is organized in some investment management firms.

Bid   The price at which a dealer will buy a specified quantity of a security. Also called *bid price*.

Bid–ask spread   The difference between the current bid price and the current ask price of a security.

Bid price   In a price quotation, the price at which the party making the quotation is willing to buy a specified quantity of an asset or security.

Bid size   The quantity associated with the bid price.

Binary credit options   Options that provide payoffs contingent on the occurrence of a specified negative credit event.

Block order   An order to sell or buy in a quantity that is large relative to the liquidity ordinarily available from dealers in the security or in other markets.

Bond-yield-plus-risk-premium method   An approach to estimating the required return on equity which specifies that required return as a bond yield plus a risk premium.

Bottom-up   Focusing on company-specific fundamentals or factors such as revenues, earnings, cash flow, or new product development.

Bounded rationality   The notion that people have informational and cognitive limitations when making decisions and do not necessarily optimize when arriving at their decisions.

Box spread   An option strategy that combines a bull spread and a bear spread having two different exercise prices, which produces a risk-free payoff of the difference in the exercise prices.

Broad market indexes   An index that is intended to measure the performance of an entire asset class. For example, the S&P 500 Index, Wilshire 5000, and Russell 3000 indexes for US common stocks.

Broker   An agent of a trader in executing trades.

Brokered markets   Markets in which transactions are largely effected through a search-brokerage mechanism away from public markets.

Bubbles   Episodes in which asset market prices move to extremely high levels in relation to estimated intrinsic value.

Buffering   With respect to style index construction, rules for maintaining the style assignment of a stock consistent with a previous assignment when the stock has not clearly moved to a new style.

Build-up approach   Synonym for the risk premium approach.

Bull spread   An option strategy that involves buying a call with a lower exercise price and selling a call with a higher exercise price. It can also be executed with puts.

Bullet portfolio   A portfolio made up of maturities that are very close to the investment horizon.

Business cycle   Fluctuations in GDP in relation to long-term trend growth, usually lasting 9–11 years.

Business risk   The equity risk that comes from the nature of the firm's operating activities.

Butterfly spread   An option strategy that combines two bull or bear spreads and has three exercise prices.

Buy side   Investment management companies and other investors that use the services of brokerages.

Buy-side traders   Professional traders that are employed by investment managers and institutional investors.

Calendar-and-percentage-of-portfolio   rebalancing   Monitoring a portfolio at regular frequencies, such as quarterly. Rebalancing decisions are then made based upon percentage-of-portfolio principles.

Calendar rebalancing   Rebalancing a portfolio to target weights on a periodic basis; for example, monthly, quarterly, semiannually, or annually.

Calmar ratio   The compound annualized rate of return over a specified time period divided by the absolute value of maximum drawdown over the same time period.

Cap   A combination of interest rate call options designed to hedge a borrower against rate increases on a floating-rate loan.

Cap rate   With respect to options, the exercise interest rate for a cap.

Cap weighting   See *capitalization weighting*.

Capital adequacy ratio   A measure of the adequacy of capital in relation to assets.

Capital allocation line   A graph line that describes the combinations of expected return and standard deviation of return available to an investor from combining an optimal portfolio of risky assets with a risk-free asset.

Capital flows forecasting approach   An exchange rate forecasting approach that focuses on expected capital flows, particularly long-term flows such as equity investment and foreign direct investment.

Capital market expectations   (CME) Expectations concerning the risk and return prospects of asset classes.

Capitalization weighting   The most common security weighting scheme in which constituents are held in proportion to their market capitalizations, calculated as price times available shares. Also known as *market value, market cap, or cap weighting*.

Caplet   Each component call option in a cap.

Carried interest   A private equity fund manager's incentive fee; the share of the private equity fund's profits that the fund manager is due once the fund has returned the outside investors' capital.

Carry trade   A trading strategy of borrowing in low-yield currencies and investing the borrowed amount in high-yield currencies.

Cash balance plan   A defined-benefit plan whose benefits are displayed in individual recordkeeping accounts.

Cash flow at risk   A variation of VaR that measures the risk to a company's cash flow, instead of its market value; the minimum cash flow loss expected to be exceeded with a given probability over a specified time period.

Cash flow matching   An asset/liability management approach that provides the future funding of a liability stream from the coupon and matured principal payments of the portfolio. A type of dedication strategy.

Cell-matching technique   (stratified sampling) A portfolio construction technique used in indexing that divides the benchmark index into cells related to the risk factors affecting the index and samples from index securities belonging to those cells.

Certainty equivalent   The maximum sum of money a person would pay to participate or the minimum sum of money a person would accept to not participate in an opportunity.

Chain-linking   A process for combining periodic returns to produce an overall time-weighted rate of return.

Cheapest-to-deliver   A bond in which the amount received for delivering the bond is largest compared with the amount paid in the market for the bond.

Civil law   A legal system derived from Roman law, in which judges apply general, abstract rules or concepts to particular cases. In civil systems, law is developed primarily through legislative statutes or executive action.

Claw-back provision   With respect to the compensation of private equity fund managers, a provision that specifies that money from the fund manager be returned to investors if, at the end of a fund's life, investors have not received back their capital contributions and contractual share of profits.

Closed-book markets   Markets in which a trader does not have real-time access to all quotes in a security.

Closeout netting   In a bankruptcy, a process by which multiple obligations between two counterparties are consolidated into a single overall value owed by one of the counterparties to the other.

Cobb-Douglas model   A production function (model for economic output) based on factors of labor and capital that exhibits constant returns to scale.

Cobb-Douglas production function   A production function (model for economic output) based on factors of labor and capital that exhibits constant returns to scale.

Cognitive dissonance   The mental discomfort that occurs when new information conflicts with previously held beliefs or cognitions.

Cognitive errors   Behavioral biases resulting from faulty reasoning; cognitive errors stem from basic statistical, information processing, or memory errors.

Collar   An option strategy involving the purchase of a put and sale of a call in which the holder of an asset gains protection below a certain level, the exercise price of the put, and pays for it by giving up gains above a certain level, the exercise price of the call. Collars also can be used to provide protection against rising interest rates on a floating-rate loan by giving up gains from lower interest rates.

Collateral return   The component of the return on a commodity futures contract that comes from the assumption that the full value of the underlying futures contract is invested to earn the risk-free interest rate. Also called *collateral yield*.

Collateralized debt obligation   A securitized pool of fixed-income assets.

Combination matching   A cash flow matching technique; a portfolio is duration-matched with a set of liabilities with the added constraint that it also be cash-flow matched in the first few years, usually the first five years. Also called *horizon matching*.

Commingled real estate funds (CREFs)   Professionally managed vehicles for substantial commingled (i.e., pooled) investment in real estate properties.

Commitment period   The period of time over which committed funds are advanced to a private equity fund.

Commodities   Articles of commerce such as agricultural goods, metals, and petroleum; tangible assets that are typically relatively homogeneous in nature.

Commodity trading advisors   Registered advisors who manage futures funds.

Common law   A legal system which draws abstract rules from specific cases. In common law systems, law is developed primarily through decisions of the courts.

Community property regime   A marital property regime under which each spouse has an indivisible one-half interest in property received during marriage.

Company-specific risk   The non-systematic or idiosyncratic risk specific to a particular company's operations, reputation, and business environment.

Completeness fund   A portfolio that, when added to active managers' positions, establishes an overall portfolio with approximately the same risk exposures as the investor's overall equity benchmark.

Confidence band   With reference to a quality control chart for performance evaluation, a range in which the manager's value-added returns are anticipated to fall a specified percentage of the time.

Confidence interval   An interval that has a given probability of containing the parameter it is intended to estimate.

Confirmation bias   A belief perseverance bias in which people tend to look for and notice what confirms their beliefs, to ignore or undervalue what contradicts their beliefs, and to misinterpret information as support for their beliefs.

Confirming evidence trap   The bias that leads individuals to give greater weight to information that supports an existing or preferred point of view than to evidence that contradicts it.

Conjunction fallacy   An inappropriate combining of probabilities of independent events to support a belief. In fact, the probability of two independent events occurring in conjunction is never greater than the probability of either event occurring alone; the probability of two independent events occurring together is equal to the multiplication of the probabilities of the independent events.

Conservatism bias   A belief perseverance bias in which people maintain their prior views or forecasts by inadequately incorporating new information.

Consistent growth   A growth investment substyle that focuses on companies with consistent growth having a long history of unit-sales growth, superior profitability, and predictable earnings.

Constant returns to scale   A characteristic of a production function such that a given percentage increase in capital stock and labor input results in an equal percentage increase in output.

Contango   A condition in the futures markets in which the costs of holding an asset exceed the benefits, leaving the futures price more than the spot price.

Contingent immunization   A fixed-income strategy in which immunization serves as a fall-back strategy if the actively managed portfolio does not grow at a certain rate.

Continuous auction markets   Auction markets where orders can be executed at any time during the trading day.

Contrarian   A value investment substyle focusing on stocks that have been beset by problems.

Controlled foreign corporation   A company located outside a taxpayer's home country and in which the taxpayer has a controlling interest as defined under the home country law.

Conversion factor   An adjustment used to facilitate delivery on bond futures contracts in which any of a number of bonds with different characteristics are eligible for delivery.

Convexity   A measure of how interest rate sensitivity changes with a change in interest rates.

Convexity adjustment   An estimate of the change in price that is not explained by duration.

Core capital   The amount of capital required to fund spending to maintain a given lifestyle, fund goals, and provide adequate reserves for unexpected commitments.

Core-plus   A fixed-income mandate that permits the portfolio manager to add instruments with relatively high return potential to core holdings of investment-grade debt.

Core–satellite   A way of thinking about allocating money that seeks to define each investment's place in the portfolio in relation to specific investment goals or roles.

Core-satellite portfolio   A portfolio in which certain investments (often indexed or semiactive) are viewed as the core and the balance are viewed as satellite investments fulfilling specific roles.

Corner portfolio   Adjacent corner portfolios define a segment of the minimum-variance frontier within which portfolios hold identical assets and the rate of change of asset weights in moving from one portfolio to another is constant.

Corner portfolio theorem   In a sign-constrained mean–variance optimization, the result that the asset weights of any minimum-variance portfolio are a positive linear combination of the corresponding weights in the two adjacent corner portfolios that bracket it in terms of expected return (or standard deviation of return).

Corporate governance   The system of internal controls and procedures used to define and protect the rights and responsibilities of various stakeholders.

Corporate venturing   Investments by companies in promising young companies in the same or a related industry.

Country beta   A measure of the sensitivity of a specified variable (e.g., yield) to a change in the comparable variable in another country.

Covered call   An option strategy involving the holding of an asset and sale of a call on the asset.

Credit default swap   A swap used to transfer credit risk to another party. A protection buyer pays the protection seller in return for the right to receive a payment from the seller in the event of a specified credit event.

Credit derivative   A contract in which one party has the right to claim a payment from another party in the event that a specific credit event occurs over the life of the contract.

Credit event   An event affecting the credit risk of a security or counterparty.

Credit forwards   A type of credit derivative with payoffs based on bond values or credit spreads.

Credit method   When the residence country reduces its taxpayers' domestic tax liability by the amount of taxes paid to a foreign country that exercises source jurisdiction.

Credit protection seller   With respect to a credit derivative, the party that accepts the credit risk of the underlying financial asset.

Credit risk   The risk of loss caused by a counterparty's or debtor's failure to make a timely payment or by the change in value of a financial instrument based on changes in default risk. Also called *default risk*.

Credit spread forward   A forward contract used to transfer credit risk to another party; a forward contract on a yield spread.

Credit spread option An option based on the yield spread between two securities that is used to transfer credit risk.

Credit spread risk The risk that the spread between the rate for a risky bond and the rate for a default risk-free bond may vary after the purchase of the risky bond.

Credit VaR A variation of VaR related to credit risk; it reflects the minimum loss due to credit exposure with a given probability during a period of time.

Credited rates Rates of interest credited to a policyholder's reserve account.

Cross-default provision A provision stipulating that if a borrower defaults on any outstanding credit obligations, the borrower is considered to be in default on all obligations.

Cross hedge A hedge involving a hedging instrument that is imperfectly correlated with the asset being hedged; an example is hedging a bond investment with futures on a non-identical bond.

Currency-hedged instruments Investment in nondomestic assets in which currency exposures are neutralized.

Currency overlay programs A currency overlay program is a program to manage a portfolio's currency exposures for the case in which those exposures are managed separately from the management of the portfolio itself.

Currency return The percentage change in the spot exchange rate stated in terms of home currency per unit of foreign currency.

Currency risk The risk associated with the uncertainty about the exchange rate at which proceeds in the foreign currency can be converted into the investor's home currency.

Currency swap A swap in which the parties make payments based on the difference in debt payments in different currencies.

Current credit risk The risk of credit-related events happening in the immediate future; it relates to the risk that a payment currently due will not be paid. Also called *jump-to-default risk.*

Cushion spread The difference between the minimum acceptable return and the higher possible immunized rate.

Custom security-based benchmark Benchmarks that are custom built to accurately reflect the investment discipline of a particular investment manager. Also called *strategy benchmarks* because they reflect a manager's particular strategy.

Custom security-based benchmarks Benchmarks that are custom built to accurately reflect the investment discipline of a particular investment manager. Also called *strategy benchmarks* because they reflect a manager's particular strategy.

Cyclical stocks The shares of companies whose earnings have above-average sensitivity to the business cycle.

Cyclically Adjusted P/E Ratio (CAPE) A price-to-earnings ratio in which the numerator (in a US context) is defined as the real S&P 500 price index and the denominator as the moving average of the preceding 10 years of real reported earnings on the S&P 500.

Day traders Traders that rapidly buy and sell stocks in the hope that the stocks will continue to rise or fall in value for the seconds or minutes they are prepared to hold a position. Day traders hold a position open somewhat longer than a scalper but closing all positions at the end of the day.

Dealer A business entity that is ready to buy an asset for inventory or sell an asset from inventory to provide the other side of an order. Also called *market maker.*

Decision price The prevailing price when the decision to trade is made. Also called *arrival price* or *strike price.*

Decision risk The risk of changing strategies at the point of maximum loss.

Deduction method When the residence country allows taxpayers to reduce their taxable income by the amount of taxes paid to foreign governments in respect of foreign-source income.

Deemed dispositions Tax treatment that assumes property is sold. It is sometimes seen as an alternative to estate or inheritance tax.

Deemed distribution When shareholders of a controlled foreign corporation are taxed as if the earnings were distributed to shareholders, even though no distribution has been made.

Default risk The risk of loss if an issuer or counterparty does not fulfill its contractual obligations.

Default risk premium Compensation for the possibility that the issue of a debt instrument will fail to make a promised payment at the contracted time and in the contracted amount.

Defaultable debt Debt with some meaningful amount of credit risk.

Defined-benefit plan A pension plan that specifies the plan sponsor's obligations in terms of the benefit to plan participants.

Defined-contribution plan A pension plan that specifies the sponsor's obligations in terms of contributions to the pension fund rather than benefits to plan participants.

Deflation A decrease in the general level of prices; an increase in the purchasing power of a unit of currency.

Delay costs Implicit trading costs that arise from the inability to complete desired trades immediately due to order size or market liquidity. Also called *slippage.*

Delivery option The feature of a futures contract giving the short the right to make decisions about what, when, and where to deliver.

Delta The relationship between the option price and the underlying price, which reflects the sensitivity of the price of the option to changes in the price of the underlying.

Delta hedge An option strategy in which a position in an asset is converted to a risk-free position with a position in a specific number of options. The number of options per unit of the underlying changes through time, and the position must be revised to maintain the hedge.

Delta hedging Hedging that involves matching the price response of the position being hedged over a narrow range of prices.

Delta-normal method A measure of VaR equivalent to the analytical method but that refers to the use of delta to estimate the option's price sensitivity.

Demand deposit A deposit that can be drawn upon without prior notice, such as a checking account.

Demutualizing The process of converting an insurance company from mutual form to stock.

Descriptive statistics Methods for effectively summarizing data to describe important aspects of a dataset.

Differential returns Returns that deviate from a manager's benchmark.

Diffusion index An index that measures how many indicators are pointing up and how many are pointing down.

Direct commodity investment   Commodity investment that involves cash market purchase of physical commodities or exposure to changes in spot market values via derivatives, such as futures.

Direct market access   Platforms sponsored by brokers that permit buy-side traders to directly access equities, fixed income, futures, and foreign exchange markets, clearing via the broker.

Direct quotation   Quotation in terms of domestic currency/foreign currency.

Discounted cash flow models   (DCF models) Valuation models that express the idea that an asset's value is the present value of its (expected) cash flows.

Discretionary trust   A trust structure in which the trustee determines whether and how much to distribute in the sole discretion of the trustee.

Disintermediation   To withdraw funds from financial intermediaries for placement with other financial intermediaries offering a higher return or yield. Or, to withdraw funds from a financial intermediary for the purposes of direct investment, such as withdrawing from a mutual fund to make direct stock investments.

Disposition effect   As a result of loss aversion, an emotional bias whereby investors are reluctant to dispose of losers. This results in an inefficient and gradual adjustment to deterioration in fundamental value.

Distressed debt arbitrage   A distressed securities investment discipline that involves purchasing the traded bonds of bankrupt companies and selling the common equity short.

Distressed securities   Securities of companies that are in financial distress or near bankruptcy; the name given to various investment disciplines employing securities of companies in distress.

Diversification effect   In reference to VaR across several portfolios (for example, across an entire firm), this effect equals the difference between the sum of the individual VaRs and total VaR.

Dividend recapitalization   A method by which a buyout fund can realize the value of a holding; involves the issuance of debt by the holding to finance a special dividend to owners.

Dollar duration   A measure of the change in portfolio value for a 100 bps change in market yields.

Domestic asset   An asset that trades in the investor's domestic currency (or home currency).

Domestic currency   The currency of the investor, i.e., the currency in which he or she typically makes consumption purchases, e.g., the Swiss franc for an investor domiciled in Switzerland.

Domestic-currency return   A rate of return stated in domestic currency terms from the perspective of the investor; reflects both the foreign-currency return on an asset as well as percentage movement in the spot exchange rate between the domestic and foreign currencies.

Donor-advised fund   A fund administered by a tax-exempt entity in which the donor advises on where to grant the money that he or she has donated.

Double inflection utility function   A utility function that changes based on levels of wealth.

Downgrade risk   The risk that one of the major rating agencies will lower its rating for an issuer, based on its specified rating criteria.

Downside deviation   A measure of volatility using only rate of return data points below the investor's minimum acceptable return.

Downside risk   Risk of loss or negative return.

Due diligence   Investigation and analysis in support of an investment action or recommendation, such as the scrutiny of operations and management and the verification of material facts.

Duration   A measure of the approximate sensitivity of a security to a change in interest rates (i.e., a measure of interest rate risk).

Dynamic approach   With respect to strategic asset allocation, an approach that accounts for links between optimal decisions at different points in time.

Dynamic hedge   A hedge requiring adjustment as the price of the hedged asset changes.

Earnings at risk (EAR)   A variation of VaR that reflects the risk of a company's earnings instead of its market value.

Earnings momentum   A growth investment substyle that focuses on companies with earnings momentum (high quarterly year-over-year earnings growth).

Econometrics   The application of quantitative modeling and analysis grounded in economic theory to the analysis of economic data.

Economic exposure   The risk associated with changes in the relative attractiveness of products and services offered for sale, arising out of the competitive effects of changes in exchange rates.

Economic indicators   Economic statistics provided by government and established private organizations that contain information on an economy's recent past activity or its current or future position in the business cycle.

Economic surplus   The market value of assets minus the present value of liabilities.

Effective duration   Duration adjusted to account for embedded options.

Effective spread   Two times the distance between the actual execution price and the midpoint of the market quote at the time an order is entered; a measure of execution costs that captures the effects of price improvement and market impact.

Efficient frontier   The graph of the set of portfolios that maximize expected return for their level of risk (standard deviation of return); the part of the minimum-variance frontier beginning with the global minimum-variance portfolio and continuing above it.

Electronic communications networks (ECNs)   Computer-based auctions that operate continuously within the day using a specified set of rules to execute orders.

Emerging market debt   The sovereign debt of nondeveloped countries.

Emotional biases   Behavioral biases resulting from reasoning influenced by feelings; emotional biases stem from impulse or intuition.

Endogenous variable   A variable whose values are determined within the system.

Endowment bias   An emotional bias in which people value an asset more when they hold rights to it than when they do not.

Endowments   Long-term funds generally owned by operating nonprofit institutions such as universities and colleges, museums, hospitals, and other organizations involved in charitable activities.

Enhanced derivatives products companies A type of subsidiary separate from an entity's other activities and not liable for the parent's debts. They are often used by derivatives dealers to control exposure to ratings downgrades. Also called *special purpose vehicles.*

Enterprise risk management An overall assessment of a company's risk position. A centralized approach to risk management sometimes called firmwide risk management.

Equal probability rebalancing Rebalancing in which the manager specifies a corridor for each asset class as a common multiple of the standard deviation of the asset class's returns. Rebalancing to the target proportions occurs when any asset class weight moves outside its corridor.

Equal weighted In an equal-weighted index, each stock in the index is weighted equally.

Equal weighting Security weighting scheme in which all constituents are held at equal weights at specified rebalancing times.

Equitized Given equity market systematic risk exposure.

Equity forward sale contract A private contract for the forward sale of an equity position.

Equity-indexed annuity A type of life annuity that provides a guarantee of a minimum fixed payment plus some participation in stock market gains, if any.

Equity monetization The realization of cash for an equity position through a manner other than an outright sale.

Equity *q* The ratio of a company's equity market capitalization divided by net worth measured at replacement cost.

Equity risk premium Compensation for the additional risk of equity compared with debt.

ESG risk The risk to a company's market valuation resulting from environmental, social, and governance factors.

Estate All of the property a person owns or controls; may consist of financial assets, tangible personal assets, immovable property, or intellectual property.

Estate planning The process of preparing for the disposition of one's estate (e.g., the transfer of property) upon death and during one's lifetime.

Estate tax freeze A plan usually involving a corporation, partnership, or limited liability company with the goal to transfer *future* appreciation to the next generation at little or no gift or estate tax cost.

Eurozone The region of countries using the euro as a currency.

Ex post alpha (or Jensen's alpha) The average return achieved in a portfolio in excess of what would have been predicted by CAPM given the portfolio's risk level; an after-the-fact measure of excess risk-adjusted return.

Excess capital An investor's capital over and above that which is necessary to fund their lifestyle and reserves.

Excess currency return The expected currency return in excess of the forward premium or discount.

Excess return The difference between the benchmark return and the portfolio return, which may be either positive or negative.

Exchange A regulated venue for the trading of investment instruments.

Exchange fund A fund into which several investors place their different share holdings in exchange for shares in the diversified fund itself.

Execution uncertainty Uncertainty pertaining to the timing of execution, or if execution will even occur at all.

Exemption method When the residence country imposes no tax on foreign-source income by providing taxpayers with an exemption, in effect having only one jurisdiction impose tax.

Exogenous shocks Events from outside the economic system that affect its course. These could be short-lived political events, changes in government policy, or natural disasters, for example.

Exogenous variable A variable whose values are determined outside the system.

Externality Those consequences of a transaction (or process) that do not fall on the parties to the transaction (or process).

Factor covariance matrix The covariance matrix of factors.

Factor-model-based benchmark Benchmarks constructed by examining a portfolio's sensitivity to a set of factors, such as the return for a broad market index, company earnings growth, industry, or financial leverage.

Factor-model-based benchmarks Benchmarks constructed by examining a portfolio's sensitivity to a set of factors, such as the return for a broad market index, company earnings growth, industry, or financial leverage.

Factor push A simple stress test that involves pushing prices and risk factors of an underlying model in the most disadvantageous way to estimate the impact of factor extremes on the portfolio's value.

Factor sensitivities In a multifactor model, the responsiveness of the dependent variable to factor movements. Also called *factor betas* or *factor loadings.*

Fallen angels Debt that has crossed the threshold from investment grade to high yield.

Fed model An equity valuation model that relates the earnings yield on the S&P 500 to the yield to maturity on 10-year US Treasury bonds.

Federal funds rate The interest rate on overnight loans of reserves (deposits) between US Federal Reserve System member banks.

Fee cap A limit on the total fee paid regardless of performance.

Fiduciary A person or entity standing in a special relation of trust and responsibility with respect to other parties.

Financial buyers Buyers who lack a strategic motive.

Financial capital As used in the text, an individual investor's investable wealth; total wealth minus human capital. Consists of assets that can be traded such as cash, stocks, bonds, and real estate.

Financial equilibrium models Models describing relationships between expected return and risk in which supply and demand are in balance.

Financial risk Risks derived from events in the external financial markets, such as changes in equity prices, interest rates, or currency exchange rates.

Fiscal policy Government activity concerning taxation and governmental spending.

Fixed annuity A type of life annuity in which periodic payments are fixed in amount.

Fixed-rate payer The party to an interest rate swap that is obligated to make periodic payments at a fixed rate.

Fixed trust A trust structure in which distributions to beneficiaries are prescribed in the trust document to occur at certain times or in certain amounts.

Flexible-premium variable life A type of life insurance policy that combines the flexibility of universal life with the investment choice flexibility of variable life. Also called *variable universal life.*

Floating-rate payer   The party to an interest rate swap that is obligated to make periodic payments based on a benchmark floating rate.

Floating supply of shares   The number of shares outstanding that are actually available to investors. Also called *free float*.

Floor   A combination of interest rate options designed to provide protection against interest rate decreases.

Floor broker   An agent of the broker who, for certain exchanges, physically represents the trade on the exchange floor.

Floorlet   Each component put option in a floor.

Forced heirship rules   Legal ownership principles whereby children have the right to a fixed share of a parent's estate.

Foreign assets   Assets denominated in currencies other than the investor's home currency.

Foreign currency   Currency that is not the currency in which an investor makes consumption purchases, e.g., the US dollar from the perspective of a Swiss investor.

Foreign-currency return   The return of the foreign asset measured in foreign-currency terms.

Formal tools   Established research methods amenable to precise definition and independent replication of results.

Forward conversion with options   The construction of a synthetic short forward position against the asset held long.

Forward discount   The forward rate less the spot rate, divided by the spot rate; called the forward discount if negative, and forward premium if positive. Also called *forward premium*.

Forward hedging   Hedging that involves the use of a forward contract between the foreign asset's currency and the home currency.

Forward rate bias   Persistent violation of uncovered interest rate parity that is exploited by the carry trade.

Foundations   Typically, grant-making institutions funded by gifts and investment assets.

Fourth market   A term occasionally used for direct trading of securities between institutional investors; the fourth market would include trading on electronic crossing networks.

Framing   An information-processing bias in which a person answers a question differently based on the way in which it is asked (framed).

Framing bias   An information-processing bias in which a person answers a question differently based on the way in which it is asked (framed).

Front office   The revenue generating functions at an investment firm such as those pertaining to trading and sales.

Front-run   To trade ahead of the initiator, exploiting privileged information about the initiator's trading intentions.

Full replication   When every issue in an index is represented in the portfolio, and each portfolio position has approximately the same weight in the fund as in the index.

Fully funded plan   A pension plan in which the ratio of the value of plan assets to the present value of plan liabilities is 100 percent or greater.

Functional duration   The key rate duration. Also called *multifunctional duration*.

Fund manager   The professional manager of separate accounts or pooled assets structured in a variety of ways.

Fund of funds   A fund that invests in a number of underlying funds.

Fundamental law of active management   The relation that the information ratio of a portfolio manager is approximately equal to the information coefficient multiplied by the square root of the investment discipline's breadth (the number of independent, active investment decisions made each year).

Fundamental weighting   Patented by Research Affiliates LLC, this scheme uses company characteristics such as sales, cash flow, book value, and dividends to weight securities.

Funded status   The relationship between the value of a plan's assets and the present value of its liabilities.

Funding currencies   The low-yield currencies in which borrowing occurs in a carry trade.

Funding ratio   A measure of the relative size of pension assets compared to the present value of pension liabilities. Calculated by dividing the value of pension assets by the present value of pension liabilities. Also referred to as the *funded ratio* or *funded status*.

Funding risk   The risk that liabilities funding long asset positions cannot be rolled over at reasonable cost.

Futures contract   An enforceable contract between a buyer (seller) and an established exchange or its clearinghouse in which the buyer (seller) agrees to take (make) delivery of something at a specified price at the end of a designated period of time.

Futures price   The price at which the parties to a futures contract agree to exchange the underlying.

Gain-to-loss ratio   The ratio of positive returns to negative returns over a specified period of time.

Gamblers' fallacy   A misunderstanding of probabilities in which people wrongly project reversal to a long-term mean.

Gamma   A numerical measure of the sensitivity of delta to a change in the underlying's value.

Global custodian   An entity that effects trade settlement, safekeeping of assets, and the allocation of trades to individual custody accounts.

Global investable market   A practical proxy for the world market portfolio consisting of traditional and alternative asset classes with sufficient capacity to absorb meaningful investment.

Global minimum-variance (GMV) portfolio   The portfolio on the minimum-variance frontier with smallest variance of return.

Gold standard currency system   A currency regime under which currency could be freely converted into gold at established rates.

Gordon (constant) growth model   A version of the dividend discount model for common share value that assumes a constant growth rate in dividends.

Government structural policies   Government policies that affect the limits of economic growth and incentives within the private sector.

Grinold–Kroner model   An expression for the expected return on a share as the sum of an expected income return, an expected nominal earnings growth return, and an expected repricing return.

Growth in total factor productivity   A component of trend growth in GDP that results from increased efficiency in using capital inputs; also known as technical progress.

Guaranteed investment contract   A debt instrument issued by insurers, usually in large denominations, that pays a guaranteed, generally fixed interest rate for a specified time period.

H-model   A variant of the two-stage dividend discount model in which growth begins at a high rate and declines linearly throughout the supernormal growth period until it reaches a normal growth rate that holds in perpetuity.

Hague Conference on Private International Law   An intergovernmental organization working toward the convergence of private international law. Its 69 members consist of countries and regional economic integration organizations.

Halo effect   An emotional bias that extends a favorable evaluation of some characteristics to other characteristics.

Hedge funds   A historically loosely regulated, pooled investment vehicle that may implement various investment strategies.

Hedge ratio   The relationship of the quantity of an asset being hedged to the quantity of the derivative used for hedging.

Hedged return   The foreign asset return in local currency terms plus the forward discount (premium).

Hedging   A general strategy usually thought of as reducing, if not eliminating, risk.

Herding   When a group of investors trade on the same side of the market in the same securities, or when investors ignore their own private information and act as other investors do.

High-water mark   A specified net asset value level that a fund must exceed before performance fees are paid to the hedge fund manager.

High yield   A value investment substyle that focuses on stocks offering high dividend yield with prospects of maintaining or increasing the dividend.

High-yield investing   A distressed securities investment discipline that involves investment in high-yield bonds perceived to be undervalued.

Hindsight bias   A bias with selective perception and retention aspects in which people may see past events as having been predictable and reasonable to expect.

Historical simulation method   The application of historical price changes to the current portfolio.

Holdings-based style analysis   An approach to style analysis that categorizes individual securities by their characteristics and aggregates results to reach a conclusion about the overall style of the portfolio at a given point in time.

Home bias   An anomaly by which portfolios exhibit a strong bias in favor of domestic securities in the context of global portfolios.

Home currency   See *domestic currency*.

Human capital   An implied asset; the present value of expected future labor income. Also called *net employment capital*.

Hybrid markets   Combinations of market types, which offer elements of batch auction markets and continuous auction markets, as well as quote-driven markets.

Hypothetical events   A type of scenario analysis used in stress testing that involves the evaluation of performance given events that have never happened in the markets or market outcomes to which we attach a small probability.

Illiquidity premium   Compensation for the risk of loss relative to an investment's fair value if an investment needs to be converted to cash quickly.

Illusion of control   A bias in which people tend to believe that they can control or influence outcomes when, in fact, they cannot. Illusion of knowledge and self-attribution biases contribute to the overconfidence bias.

Illusion of control bias   A bias in which people tend to believe that they can control or influence outcomes when, in fact, they cannot. Illusion of knowledge and self-attribution biases contribute to the overconfidence bias.

Immunization   An asset/liability management approach that structures investments in bonds to match (offset) liabilities' weighted-average duration; a type of dedication strategy.

Immunized time horizon   The time horizon over which a portfolio's value is immunized; equal to the portfolio duration.

Implementation shortfall   The difference between the money return on a notional or paper portfolio and the actual portfolio return.

Implementation shortfall strategy   A strategy that attempts to minimize trading costs as measured by the implementation shortfall method. Also called *arrival price strategy*.

Implied yield   A measure of the yield on the underlying bond of a futures contract implied by pricing it as though the underlying will be delivered at the futures expiration.

Incremental VaR   A measure of the incremental effect of an asset on the VaR of a portfolio by measuring the difference between the portfolio's VaR while including a specified asset and the portfolio's VaR with that asset eliminated.

Indexing   A common passive approach to investing that involves holding a portfolio of securities designed to replicate the returns on a specified index of securities.

Indifference curve analysis   A decision-making approach whereby curves of consumption bundles, among which the decision-maker is indifferent, are constructed to identify and choose the curve within budget constraints that generates the highest utility.

Indirect commodity investment   Commodity investment that involves the acquisition of indirect claims on commodities, such as equity in companies specializing in commodity production.

Inferential statistics   Methods for making estimates or forecasts about a larger group from a smaller group actually observed.

Inflation   An increase in the general level of prices; a decrease in the purchasing power of a unit of currency.

Inflation hedge   An asset whose returns are sufficient on average to preserve purchasing power during periods of inflation.

Inflation premium   Compensation for expected inflation.

Information coefficient   The correlation between forecast and actual returns.

Information-motivated traders   Traders that seek to trade on information that has limited value if not quickly acted upon.

Information ratio   The mean excess return of the account over the benchmark (i.e., mean active return) relative to the variability of that excess return (i.e., tracking risk); a measure of risk-adjusted performance.

Infrastructure funds   Funds that make private investment in public infrastructure projects in return for rights to specified revenue streams over a contracted period.

Initial public offering   The initial issuance of common stock registered for public trading by a formerly private corporation.

Input uncertainty   Uncertainty concerning whether the inputs are correct.

Inside ask   The lowest available ask price. Also called *market ask*.

Inside bid   The highest available bid price. Also called *market bid*.

Inside bid–ask spread   Market ask price minus market bid price. Also called *market bid–ask spread, inside spread*, or *market spread*.

Inside quote   Combination of the highest available bid price with the lowest available ask price. Also called *market quote*.

Inside spread   Market ask price minus market bid price. Also called *market bid–ask spread, inside bid–ask spread,* or *market spread.*

Institutional investors   Corporations or other legal entities that ultimately serve as financial intermediaries between individuals and investment markets.

Interest rate management effect   With respect to fixed-income attribution analysis, a return component reflecting how well a manager predicts interest rate changes.

Interest rate parity   A formula that expresses the equivalence or parity of spot and forward rates, after adjusting for differences in the interest rates.

Interest rate risk   Risk related to changes in the level of interest rates.

Interest rate swap   A contract between two parties (counter-parties) to exchange periodic interest payments based on a specified notional amount of principal.

Interest spread   With respect to banks, the average yield on earning assets minus the average percent cost of interest-bearing liabilities.

Internal rate of return   The growth rate that will link the ending value of the account to its beginning value plus all intermediate cash flows; money-weighted rate of return is a synonym.

Intestate   Having made no valid will; a decedent without a valid will or with a will that does not dispose of their property is considered to have died intestate.

Intrinsic value   The difference between the spot exchange rate and the strike price of a currency option.

Inventory cycle   A cycle measured in terms of fluctuations in inventories, typically lasting 2–4 years.

Inverse floater   A floating-rate note or bond in which the coupon is adjusted to move opposite to a benchmark interest rate.

Investment currencies   The high-yielding currencies in a carry trade.

Investment skill   The ability to outperform an appropriate benchmark consistently over time.

Investment style   A natural grouping of investment disciplines that has some predictive power in explaining the future dispersion of returns across portfolios.

Investment style indexes   Indices that represent specific portions of an asset category. For example, subgroups within the US common stock asset category such as large-capitalization growth stocks.

Investment universe   The set of assets that may be considered for investment.

Investor's benchmark   The benchmark an investor uses to evaluate performance of a given portfolio or asset class.

Irrevocable trust   A trust arrangement wherein the settlor has no ability to revoke the trust relationship.

J factor risk   The risk associated with a judge's track record in adjudicating bankruptcies and restructuring.

Joint ownership with right of survivorship   Jointly owned; assets held in joint ownership with right of survivorship automatically transfer to the surviving joint owner or owners outside the probate process.

Justified P/E   The price-to-earnings ratio that is fair, warranted, or justified on the basis of forecasted fundamentals.

Key rate duration   A method of measuring the interest rate sensitivities of a fixed-income instrument or portfolio to shifts in key points along the yield curve.

Knock-in/knock-out   Features of a vanilla option that is created (or ceases to exist) when the spot exchange rate touches a pre-specified level.

Lagging economic indicators   A set of economic variables whose values correlate with recent past economic activity.

Leading economic indicators   A set of economic variables whose values vary with the business cycle but at a fairly consistent time interval before a turn in the business cycle.

Legal/contract risk   The possibility of loss arising from the legal system's failure to enforce a contract in which an enterprise has a financial stake; for example, if a contract is voided through litigation.

Leverage-adjusted duration gap   A leverage-adjusted measure of the difference between the durations of assets and liabilities which measures a bank's overall interest rate exposure.

Leveraged floating-rate note   (leveraged floater) A floating-rate note or bond in which the coupon is adjusted at a multiple of a benchmark interest rate.

Leveraged recapitalization   A leveraging of a company's balance sheet, usually accomplished by working with a private equity firm.

Liability   As used in the text, a financial obligation.

Liability-based benchmark   A benchmark structured to accurately reflect the return required to meet the future obligations of an investor and to mimic the volatility of the liabilities.

Life annuity   An annuity that guarantees a monthly income to the annuitant for life.

Lifetime gratuitous transfer   A lifetime gift made during the lifetime of the donor; also known as *inter vivos* transfers.

Limit order   An instruction to execute an order when the best price available is at least as good as the limit price specified in the order.

Linear programming   Optimization in which the objective function and constraints are linear.

Liquidity   The ability to trade without delay at relatively low cost and in relatively large quantities.

Liquidity-motivated traders   Traders that are motivated to trade based upon reasons other than an information advantage. For example, to release cash proceeds to facilitate the purchase of another security, adjust market exposure, or fund cash needs.

Liquidity risk   Any risk of economic loss because of the need to sell relatively less liquid assets to meet liquidity requirements; the risk that a financial instrument cannot be purchased or sold without a significant concession in price because of the market's potential inability to efficiently accommodate the desired trading size.

Lock-up period   A minimum initial holding period for investments during which no part of the investment can be withdrawn.

Locked up   Said of investments that cannot be traded at all for some time.

Logical participation strategies   Protocols for breaking up an order for execution over time. Typically used by institutional traders to participate in overall market volumes without being unduly visible.

Longevity risk   The risk of outliving one's financial resources.

Loss-aversion bias   A bias in which people tend to strongly prefer avoiding losses as opposed to achieving gains.

Low P/E   A value investment substyle that focuses on shares selling at low prices relative to current or normal earnings.

M^2 A measure of what a portfolio would have returned if it had taken on the same total risk as the market index.

Macaulay duration   The percentage change in price for a percentage change in yield. The term, named for one of the economists who first derived it, is used to distinguish the calculation from modified duration. (See also *modified duration*).

Macro attribution   Performance attribution analysis conducted on the fund sponsor level.

Macro expectations   Expectations concerning classes of assets.

Managed futures   Pooled investment vehicles, frequently structured as limited partnerships, that invest in futures and options on futures and other instruments.

Managed futures funds   Pools of private capital managed by commodity trading advisors.

Manager continuation policies   Policies adopted to guide the manager evaluations conducted by fund sponsors. The goal of manager continuation policies is to reduce the costs of manager turnover while systematically acting on indications of future poor performance.

Manager monitoring   A formal, documented procedure that assists fund sponsors in consistently collecting information relevant to evaluating the state of their managers' operations; used to identify warning signs of adverse changes in existing managers' organizations.

Manager peer group   See *manager universe*.

Manager review   A detailed examination of a manager that currently exists within a plan sponsor's program. The manager review closely resembles the manager selection process, in both the information considered and the comprehensiveness of the analysis. The staff should review all phases of the manager's operations, just as if the manager were being initially hired.

Manager universe   A broad group of managers with similar investment disciplines. Also called *manager peer group*.

Market-adjusted implementation shortfall   The difference between the money return on a notional or paper portfolio and the actual portfolio return, adjusted using beta to remove the effect of the return on the market.

Market ask   The lowest available ask price.

Market bid   The best available bid; highest price any buyer is currently willing to pay.

Market bid–ask spread   Market ask price minus market bid price. Also called *inside bid–ask spread*, *inside spread*, or *market spread*.

Market cap weighting   See *capitalization weighting*.

Market fragmentation   A condition whereby a market contains no dominant group of sellers (or buyers) that are large enough to unduly influence the market.

Market impact   The effect of the trade on transaction prices. Also called *price impact*.

Market index   Represents the performance of a specified security market, market segment, or asset class.

Market integration   The degree to which there are no impediments or barriers to capital mobility across markets.

Market microstructure   The market structures and processes that affect how the manager's interest in buying or selling an asset is translated into executed trades (represented by trade prices and volumes).

Market model   A regression equation that specifies a linear relationship between the return on a security (or portfolio) and the return on a broad market index.

Market-not-held order   A variation of the market order designed to give the agent greater discretion than a simple market order would allow. "Not held" means that the floor broker is not required to trade at any specific price or in any specific time interval.

Market on close order   A market order to be executed at the closing of the market.

Market on open order   A market order to be executed at the opening of the market.

Market order   An instruction to execute an order as soon as possible in the public markets at the best price available.

Market oriented   With reference to equity investing, an intermediate grouping for investment disciplines that cannot be clearly categorized as value or growth.

Market quote   Combination of the highest available bid price with the lowest available ask price. Also called *inside quote*.

Market risk   The risk associated with interest rates, exchange rates, and equity prices.

Market risk bucket   In goal-based portfolio planning, that part of wealth allocated to investments intended to maintain the client's current standard of living.

Market segmentation   The degree to which there are some meaningful impediments to capital movement across markets.

Market spread   Market ask price minus market bid price. Also called *market bid–ask spread*, *inside spread*, or *inside bid–ask spread*.

Market value weighting   See *capitalization weighting*.

Marking to market   A procedure used primarily in futures markets in which the parties to a contract settle the amount owed daily. Also known as the *daily settlement*.

Mass affluent   An industry term for a segment of the private wealth marketplace that is not sufficiently wealthy to command certain individualized services.

Matrix prices   Prices determined by comparisons to other securities of similar credit risk and maturity; the result of matrix pricing.

Matrix pricing   An approach for estimating the prices of thinly traded securities based on the prices of securities with similar attributions, such as similar credit rating, maturity, or economic sector.

Maturity premium   Compensation for the increased sensitivity of the market value of debt to a change in market interest rates as maturity is extended.

Maturity variance   A measure of how much a given immunized portfolio differs from the ideal immunized portfolio consisting of a single pure discount instrument with maturity equal to the time horizon.

Maximum loss optimization   A stress test in which we would try to optimize mathematically the risk variable that would produce the maximum loss.

Mega-cap buy-out funds   A class of buyout funds that take public companies private.

Mental accounting bias   An information-processing bias in which people treat one sum of money differently from another equal-sized sum based on which mental account the money is assigned to.

Micro attribution   Performance attribution analysis carried out on the investment manager level.

Micro expectations   Expectations concerning individual assets.

Middle-market buy-out funds   A class of buyout funds that purchase private companies whose revenues and profits are too small to access capital from the public equity markets.

Midquote   The halfway point between the market bid and ask prices.

Minimum-variance frontier   The graph of the set of portfolios with smallest variances of return for their levels of expected return.

Minimum-variance hedge ratio   A mathematical approach to determining the optimal cross hedging ratio.

Mismatch in character   The potential tax inefficiency that can result if the instrument being hedged, and the tool that is being used to hedge it, produce income and loss of a different character.

Missed trade opportunity costs   Unrealized profit/loss arising from the failure to execute a trade in a timely manner.

Model risk   The risk that a model is incorrect or misapplied; in investments, it often refers to valuation models.

Model uncertainty   Uncertainty concerning whether a selected model is correct.

Modified duration   An adjustment of the duration for the level of the yield. Contrast with *Macaulay duration*.

Monetary policy   Government activity concerning interest rates and the money supply.

Monetize   To access an item's cash value without transferring ownership of it.

Money markets   Markets for fixed-income securities with maturities of one year or less.

Money-weighted rate of return   Same as the internal rate of return; the growth rate that will link the ending value of the account to its beginning value plus all intermediate cash flows.

Mortality risk   The risk of loss of human capital in the event of premature death.

Multifactor model   A model that explains a variable in terms of the values of a set of factors.

Multifactor model technique   With respect to construction of an indexed portfolio, a technique that attempts to match the primary risk exposures of the indexed portfolio to those of the index.

Multiperiod Sharpe ratio   A Sharpe ratio based on the investment's multiperiod wealth in excess of the wealth generated by the risk-free investment.

Mutuals   With respect to insurance companies, companies that are owned by their policyholders, who share in the company's surplus earnings.

Natural liquidity   An extensive pool of investors who are aware of and have a potential interest in buying and/or selling a security.

Net employment capital   See *human capital*.

Net interest margin   With respect to banks, net interest income (interest income minus interest expense) divided by average earning assets.

Net interest spread   With respect to the operations of insurers, the difference between interest earned and interest credited to policyholders.

Net worth   The difference between the market value of assets and liabilities.

Net worth tax or net wealth tax   A tax based on a person's assets, less liabilities.

Nominal default-free bonds   Conventional bonds that have no (or minimal) default risk.

Nominal gross domestic product   A money measure of the goods and services produced within a country's borders. Also called *nominal GDP*.

Nominal risk-free interest rate   The sum of the real risk-free interest rate and the inflation premium.

Nominal spread   The spread of a bond or portfolio above the yield of a Treasury of equal maturity.

Non-deliverable forwards   Forward contracts that are cash settled (in the non-controlled currency of the currency pair) rather than physically settled (the controlled currency is neither delivered nor received).

Nonfinancial risk   Risks that arise from sources other than the external financial markets, such as changes in accounting rules, legal environment, or tax rates.

Nonparametric   Involving minimal probability-distribution assumptions.

Nonstationarity   A property of a data series that reflects more than one set of underlying statistical properties.

Normal portfolio   A portfolio with exposure to sources of systematic risk that are typical for a manager, using the manager's past portfolios as a guide.

Notional principal amount   The amount specified in a swap that forms the basis for calculating payment streams.

Objective function   A quantitative expression of the objective or goal of a process.

Offer price   The price at which a counterparty is willing to sell one unit of the base currency.

Open market operations   The purchase or sale by a central bank of government securities, which are settled using reserves, to influence interest rates and the supply of credit by banks.

Open outcry auction market   Public auction where representatives of buyers and sellers meet at a specified location and place verbal bids and offers.

Operational risk   The risk of loss from failures in a company's systems and procedures (for example, due to computer failures or human failures) or events completely outside of the control of organizations (which would include "acts of God" and terrorist actions).

Opportunistic participation strategies   Passive trading combined with the opportunistic seizing of liquidity.

Optimization   With respect to portfolio construction, a procedure for determining the best portfolios according to some criterion.

Optimizer   A heuristic, formula, algorithm, or program that uses risk, return, correlation, or other variables to determine the most appropriate asset allocation or asset mix for a portfolio.

Option-adjusted spread (OAS)   The current spread over the benchmark yield minus that component of the spread that is attributable to any embedded optionality in the instrument.

Options on futures   Options on a designated futures contract. Also called *futures options*.

Options on physicals   With respect to options, exchange-traded option contracts that have cash instruments rather than futures contracts on cash instruments as the underlying.

Order-driven markets   Markets in which transaction prices are established by public limit orders to buy or sell a security at specified prices.

Ordinary life insurance   A type of life insurance policy that involves coverage for the whole of the insured's life. Also called *whole life insurance*.

Orphan equities investing   A distressed securities investment discipline that involves investment in orphan equities that are perceived to be undervalued.

Orphan equity   Investment in the newly issued equity of a company emerging from reorganization.

Output gap   The difference between the value of GDP estimated as if the economy were on its trend growth path (potential output) and the actual value of GDP.

Overall trade balance   The sum of the current account (reflecting exports and imports) and the financial account (consisting of portfolio flows).

Overbought   When a market has trended too far in one direction and is vulnerable to a trend reversal, or correction.

Overconfidence bias   A bias in which people demonstrate unwarranted faith in their own intuitive reasoning, judgments, and/or cognitive abilities.

Overconfidence trap   The tendency of individuals to overestimate the accuracy of their forecasts.

Oversold   The opposite of overbought; see *overbought*.

Pairs trade   A basic long–short trade in which an investor is long and short equal currency amounts of two common stocks in a single industry. Also called *pairs arbitrage*.

Panel method   A method of capital market expectations setting that involves using the viewpoints of a panel of experts.

Partial correlation   In multivariate problems, the correlation between two variables after controlling for the effects of the other variables in the system.

Partial fill   Execution of a purchase or sale for fewer shares than was stipulated in the order.

Participate (do not initiate) order   A variant of the market-not-held order. The broker is deliberately low-key and waits for and responds to the initiatives of more active traders.

Passive investment strategies   A buy-and-hold strategy to investing in which an investor does not make portfolio changes based upon short-term expectations of changing market or security performance.

Passive management   A buy-and-hold approach to investing in which an investor does not make portfolio changes based upon short-term expectations of changing market or security performance.

Passive traders   Traders that seek liquidity in their rebalancing transactions, but are much more concerned with the cost of trading.

Payment netting   A means of settling payments in which the amount owed by the first party to the second is netted with the amount owed by the second party to the first; only the net difference is paid.

Pension funds   Funds consisting of assets set aside to support a promise of retirement income.

Pension surplus   Pension assets at market value minus the present value of pension liabilities.

Percentage-of-portfolio rebalancing   Rebalancing is triggered based on set thresholds stated as a percentage of the portfolio's value.

Percentage-of-volume strategy   A logical participation strategy in which trading takes place in proportion to overall market volume (typically at a rate of 5–20 percent) until the order is completed.

Perfect markets   Markets without any frictional costs.

Performance appraisal   The evaluation of portfolio performance; a quantitative assessment of a manager's investment skill.

Performance attribution   A comparison of an account's performance with that of a designated benchmark and the identification and quantification of sources of differential returns.

Performance-based fee   Fees specified by a combination of a base fee plus an incentive fee for performance in excess of a benchmark's.

Performance evaluation   The measurement and assessment of the outcomes of investment management decisions.

Performance measurement   A component of performance evaluation; the relatively simple procedure of calculating an asset's or portfolio's rate of return.

Performance netting risk   For entities that fund more than one strategy and have asymmetric incentive fee arrangements with the portfolio managers, the potential for loss in cases where the net performance of the group of managers generates insufficient fee revenue to fully cover contractual payout obligations to all portfolio managers with positive performance.

Periodic auction markets   Auction markets where multilateral trading occurs at a single price at a prespecified point in time.

Permanent income hypothesis   The hypothesis that consumers' spending behavior is largely determined by their long-run income expectations.

Personal risk bucket   In goal-based portfolio planning, that part of wealth allocated to investments intended to protect the client from a drastic decrease in lifestyle.

Plan sponsor   The trustee, company, or employer responsible for a public or private institutional investment plan.

Pledging requirement   With respect to banks, a required collateral use of assets.

Point estimate   A single-valued estimate of a quantity, as opposed to an estimate in terms of a range of values.

Policy portfolio   A synonym of strategic asset allocation; the portfolio resulting from strategic asset allocation considered as a process.

Policyholder reserves   With respect to an insurance company, an amount representing the estimated payments to policyholders, as determined by actuaries, based on the types and terms of the various insurance policies issued by the company.

Political risk   The risk of war, government collapse, political instability, expropriation, confiscation, or adverse changes in taxation. Also called *geopolitical risk*.

Portable   Moveable. With reference to a pension plan, one in which a plan participant can move his or her share of plan assets to a new plan, subject to certain rules, vesting schedules, and possible tax penalties and payments.

Portable alpha   A strategy involving the combining of multiple positions (e.g., long and short positions) so as to separate the alpha (unsystematic risk) from beta (systematic risk) in an investment.

Portfolio segmentation   The creation of subportfolios according to the product mix for individual segments or lines of business.

Portfolio trade   A trade in which a number of securities are traded as a single unit. Also called *program trade* or *basket trade*.

Position a trade   To take the other side of a trade, acting as a principal with capital at risk.

Post-trade transparency   Degree to which completed trades are quickly and accurately reported to the public.

Potential output   The value of GDP if the economy were on its trend growth path.

Preferred return   With respect to the compensation of private equity fund managers, a hurdle rate.

Premium   Regarding life insurance, the asset paid by the policy holder to an insurer who, in turn, has a contractual obligation to pay death benefit proceeds to the beneficiary named in the policy.

Prepackaged bankruptcy   A bankruptcy in which the debtor seeks agreement from creditors on the terms of a reorganization before the reorganization filing.

Prepaid variable forward   A collar and loan combined within a single instrument.

Present value distribution of cash flows   A list showing what proportion of a portfolio's duration is attributable to each future cash flow.

Present value of a basis point (PVBP)   The change in the bond price for a 1 basis point change in yield. Also called *basis point value* (BPV).

Pretrade transparency   Ability of individuals to quickly, easily, and inexpensively obtain accurate information about quotes and trades.

Price discovery   Adjustment of transaction prices to balance supply and demand.

Price improvement   Execution at a price that is better than the price quoted at the time of order placement.

Price risk   The risk of fluctuations in market price.

Price uncertainty   Uncertainty about the price at which an order will execute.

Price value of a basis point   (PVBP) The change in the bond price for a 1 basis point change in yield. Also called *basis point value* (BPV).

Price weighted   With respect to index construction, an index in which each security in the index is weighted according to its absolute share price.

Price weighting   Security weighting scheme in which constituents are weighted in proportion to their prices.

Priced risk   Risk for which investors demand compensation.

Primary capital   Assets held outside a concentrated position that are at least sufficient to provide for the owner's lifetime spending needs.

Primary risk factors   With respect to valuation, the major influences on pricing.

Prime brokerage   A suite of services that is often specified to include support in accounting and reporting, leveraged trade execution, financing, securities lending (related to short-selling activities), and start-up advice (for new entities).

Principal trade   A trade with a broker in which the broker commits capital to facilitate the prompt execution of the trader's order to buy or sell.

Private equity   Ownership interests in non-publicly-traded companies.

Private equity funds   Pooled investment vehicles investing in generally highly illiquid assets; includes venture capital funds and buyout funds.

Private exchange   A method for handling undiversified positions with built-in capital gains in which shares that are a component of an index are exchanged for shares of an index mutual fund in a privately arranged transaction with the fund.

Private placement memorandum   A document used to raise venture capital financing when funds are raised through an agent.

Probate   The legal process to confirm the validity of a will so that executors, heirs, and other interested parties can rely on its authenticity.

Profit-sharing plans   A defined-contribution plan in which contributions are based, at least in part, on the plan sponsor's profits.

Projected benefit obligation (PBO)   A measure of a pension plan's liability that reflects accumulated service in the same manner as the ABO but also projects future variables, such as compensation increases.

Prospect theory   An alternative to expected utility theory, it assigns value to gains and losses (changes in wealth) rather than to final wealth, and probabilities are replaced by decision weights. In prospect theory, the shape of a decision maker's value function is assumed to differ between the domain of gains and the domain of losses.

Protective put   An option strategy in which a long position in an asset is combined with a long position in a put.

Proxy hedge   See *cross hedge*.

Proxy hedging   Hedging that involves the use of a forward contract between the home currency and a currency that is highly correlated with the foreign asset's currency.

Prudence trap   The tendency to temper forecasts so that they do not appear extreme; the tendency to be overly cautious in forecasting.

Public good   A good that is not divisible and not excludable (a consumer cannot be denied it).

Purchasing power parity   The theory that movements in an exchange rate should offset any difference in the inflation rates between two countries.

Pure sector allocation return   A component of attribution analysis that relates relative returns to the manager's sector-weighting decisions. Calculated as the difference between the allocation (weight) of the portfolio to a given sector and the portfolio's benchmark weight for that sector, multiplied by the difference between the sector benchmark's return and the overall portfolio's benchmark return, summed across all sectors.

Put spread   A strategy used to reduce the upfront cost of buying a protective put, it involves buying a put option and writing another put option.

Quality control charts   A graphical means of presenting performance appraisal data; charts illustrating the performance of an actively managed account versus a selected benchmark.

Quality option   With respect to Treasury futures, the option of which acceptable Treasury issue to deliver. Also called *swap option*.

Quantitative easing   A policy measure in which a central bank buys financial assets to inject a predetermined quantity of money in the financial system.

Quote-driven markets   Markets that rely on dealers to establish firm prices at which securities can be bought and sold. Also called *dealer markets*.

Quoted depth   The number of shares available for purchase or sale at the quoted bid and ask prices.

Rate duration   A fixed-income instrument's or portfolio's sensitivity to a change in key maturity, holding constant all other points along the yield curve.

Ratio spread   An option strategy in which a long position in a certain number of options is offset by a short position in a certain number of other options on the same underlying, resulting in a risk-free position.

Rational economic man   A self-interested, risk-averse individual who has the ability to make judgments using all available information in order to maximize his/her expected utility.

Re-base   With reference to index construction, to change the time period used as the base of the index.

Real estate   Interests in land or structures attached to land.

Real estate investment trusts (REITs)   Publicly traded equities representing pools of money invested in real estate properties and/or real estate debt.

Real option   An option involving decisions related to tangible assets or processes.

Real risk-free interest rate   The single-period interest rate for a completely risk-free security if no inflation were expected.

Rebalancing ratio   A quantity involved in reestablishing the dollar duration of a portfolio to a desired level, equal to the original dollar duration divided by the new dollar duration.

Recallability trap   The tendency of forecasts to be overly influenced by events that have left a strong impression on a person's memory.

Recession   A broad-based economic downturn, conventionally defined as two successive quarterly declines in GDP.

Reference entity   An entity, such as a bond issuer, specified in a derivatives contract.

Regime   A distinct governing set of relationships.

Regret   The feeling that an opportunity has been missed; typically an expression of *hindsight bias.*

Regret-aversion bias   An emotional bias in which people tend to avoid making decisions that will result in action out of fear that the decision will turn out poorly.

Regulatory risk   The risk associated with the uncertainty of how a transaction will be regulated or with the potential for regulations to change.

Reinvestment risk   The risk of reinvesting coupon income or principal at a rate less than the original coupon or purchase rate.

Relative economic strength forecasting approach   An exchange rate forecasting approach that suggests that a strong pace of economic growth in a country creates attractive investment opportunities, increasing the demand for the country's currency and causing it to appreciate.

Relative strength indicators   A price momentum indicator that involves comparing a stock's performance during a specific period either to its own past performance or to the performance of some group of stocks.

Remaindermen   Beneficiaries of a trust; having a claim on the residue.

Representativeness bias   A belief perseverance bias in which people tend to classify new information based on past experiences and classifications.

Repurchase agreement   A contract involving the sale of securities such as Treasury instruments coupled with an agreement to repurchase the same securities at a later date.

Repurchase yield   The negative of the expected percent change in number of shares outstanding, in the Grinold–Kroner model.

Resampled efficient frontier   The set of resampled efficient portfolios.

Resampled efficient portfolio   An efficient portfolio based on simulation.

Residence jurisdiction   A framework used by a country to determine the basis for taxing income, based on residency.

Residence–residence conflict   When two countries claim residence of the same individual, subjecting the individual's income to taxation by both countries.

Residence–source conflict   When tax jurisdiction is claimed by an individual's country of residence and the country where some of their assets are sourced; the most common source of double taxation.

Residue   With respect to trusts, the funds remaining in a trust when the last income beneficiary dies.

Resistance levels   Price points on dealers' order boards where one would expect to see a clustering of offers.

Retired-lives   The portion of a pension fund's liabilities associated with retired workers.

Returns-based benchmarks   Benchmarks constructed by examining a portfolio's sensitivity to a set of factors, such as the returns for various style indexes (e.g., small-cap value, small-cap growth, large-cap value, and large-cap growth).

Returns-based style analysis   An approach to style analysis that focuses on characteristics of the overall portfolio as revealed by a portfolio's realized returns.

Reverse optimization   A technique for reverse engineering the expected returns implicit in a diversified market portfolio.

Revocable trust   A trust arrangement wherein the settlor (who originally transfers assets to fund the trust) retains the right to rescind the trust relationship and regain title to the trust assets.

Risk budgeting   The establishment of objectives for individuals, groups, or divisions of an organization that takes into account the allocation of an acceptable level of risk.

Risk exposure   A source of risk. Also, the state of being exposed or vulnerable to a risk.

Risk premium approach   An approach to forecasting the return of a risky asset that views its expected return as the sum of the risk-free rate of interest and one or more risk premiums.

Risk profile   A detailed tabulation of the index's risk exposures.

Risk reversal   With respect to foreign exchange option strategies, one involving a long position in a call option and a short position in a put option.

Risk tolerance   The capacity to accept risk; the level of risk an investor (or organization) is willing and able to bear.

Risk tolerance function   An assessment of an investor's tolerance to risk over various levels of portfolio outcomes.

Roll return   The component of the return on a commodity futures contract that comes from rolling long futures positions forward through time. Also called *roll yield.*

Rolling return   The moving average of the holding-period returns for a specified period (e.g., a calendar year) that matches the investor's time horizon.

Sale and leaseback   A transaction wherein the owner of a property sells that property and then immediately leases it back from the buyer at a rate and term acceptable to the new owner and on financial terms consistent with the marketplace.

Sample estimator   A formula for assigning a unique value (a point estimate) to a population parameter.

Sample-size neglect   A type of representativeness bias in which financial market participants incorrectly assume that small sample sizes are representative of populations (or "real" data).

Sandwich spread   An option strategy that is equivalent to a short butterfly spread.

Satisfice   A combination of "satisfy" and "suffice" describing decisions, actions, and outcomes that may not be optimal, but are adequate.

Savings–investment imbalances forecasting approach   An exchange rate forecasting approach that explains currency movements in terms of the effects of domestic savings–investment imbalances on the exchange rate.

Scenario analysis   A risk management technique involving the examination of the performance of a portfolio under specified situations. Closely related to *stress testing.*

Seagull spread   An extension of the risk reversal foreign exchange option strategy that limits downside risk.

Secondary offering   An offering after the initial public offering of securities.

Sector/quality effect   In a fixed-income attribution analysis, a measure of a manager's ability to select the "right" issuing sector and quality group.

Security selection effect   In a fixed-income attribution analysis, the residual of the security's total return after other effects are accounted for; a measure of the return due to ability in security selection.

Segmentation   With respect to the management of insurance company portfolios, the notional subdivision of the overall portfolio into sub-portfolios each of which is associated with a specified group of insurance contracts.

Self-attribution bias   A bias in which people take personal credit for successes and attribute failures to external factors outside the individual's control.

Self-control bias   A bias in which people fail to act in pursuit of their long-term, overarching goals because of a lack of self-discipline.

Sell side   Broker/dealers that sell securities and make recommendations for various customers, such as investment managers and institutional investors.

Semiactive management   A variant of active management. In a semiactive portfolio, the manager seeks to outperform a given benchmark with tightly controlled risk relative to the benchmark. Also called *enhanced indexing* or *risk-controlled active management*.

Semivariance   A measure of downside risk. The average of squared deviations that fall below the mean.

Separate property regime   A marital property regime under which each spouse is able to own and control property as an individual.

Settlement date   The designated date at which the parties to a trade must transact. Also called *payment date*.

Settlement netting risk   The risk that a liquidator of a counterparty in default could challenge a netting arrangement so that profitable transactions are realized for the benefit of creditors.

Settlement risk   When settling a contract, the risk that one party could be in the process of paying the counterparty while the counterparty is declaring bankruptcy.

Settlor (or grantor)   An entity that transfers assets to a trustee, to be held and managed for the benefit of the trust beneficiaries.

Shari'a   The law of Islam. In addition to the law of the land, some follow guidance provided by Shari'a or Islamic law.

Sharpe ratio   A measure of risk-adjusted performance that compares excess returns to the total risk of the account, where total risk is measured by the account's standard deviation of returns. Also called *reward-to-variability*.

Short sale against the box   Shorting a security that is held long.

Shortfall risk   The risk that portfolio value will fall below some minimum acceptable level during a stated time horizon; the risk of not achieving a specified return target.

Shrinkage estimation   Estimation that involves taking a weighted average of a historical estimate of a parameter and some other parameter estimate, where the weights reflect the analyst's relative belief in the estimates.

Shrinkage estimator   The formula used in shrinkage estimation of a parameter.

Sign-constrained optimization   An optimization that constrains asset class weights to be nonnegative and to sum to 1.

Smart routing   The use of algorithms to intelligently route an order to the most liquid venue.

Smoothing rule   With respect to spending rates, a rule that averages asset values over a period of time in order to dampen the spending rate's response to asset value fluctuation.

Social proof   A bias in which individuals tend to follow the beliefs of a group.

Socially responsible investing   An approach to investing that integrates ethical values and societal concerns with investment decisions. Also called *ethical investing*.

Soft dollars   The use of commissions to buy services other than execution services. Also called *soft dollar arrangements* or *soft commissions*.

Sole ownership   Owned by one person; assets held in sole ownership are typically considered part of a decedent's estate. The transfer of their ownership is dictated by the decedent's will through the probate process.

Solow residual   A measure of the growth in total factor productivity that is based on an economic growth model developed by economist Robert M. Solow.

Sortino ratio   A performance appraisal ratio that replaces standard deviation in the Sharpe ratio with downside deviation.

Source jurisdiction   A framework used by a country to determine the basis for taxing income or transfers. A country that taxes income as a source within its borders imposes source jurisdiction.

Source–source conflict   When two countries claim source jurisdiction of the same asset; both countries may claim that the income is derived from their jurisdiction.

Sovereign risk   A form of credit risk in which the borrower is the government of a sovereign nation.

Spot return   The component of the return on a commodity futures contract that comes from changes in the underlying spot prices via the cost-of-carry model. Also called *price return*.

Spread duration   The sensitivity of a non-Treasury security's price to a widening or narrowing of the spread over Treasuries.

Spread risk   Risk related to changes in the spread between Treasuries and non-Treasuries.

Stale price bias   Bias that arises from using prices that are stale because of infrequent trading.

Static approach   With respect to strategic asset allocation, an approach that does not account for links between optimal decisions in future time periods.

Static hedge   A hedge that is not sensitive to changes in the price of the asset hedged.

Static spread   The constant spread above the Treasury spot curve that equates the calculated price of the security to the market price. Also called *zero-volatility spread*.

Stationary   A series of data for which the parameters that describe a return-generating process are stable.

Status quo bias   An emotional bias in which people do nothing (i.e., maintain the "status quo") instead of making a change.

Status quo trap   The tendency for forecasts to perpetuate recent observations—that is, to predict no change from the recent past.

Sterling ratio The compound annualized rate of return over a specified time period divided by the average yearly maximum drawdown over the same time period less an arbitrary 10 percent.

Stock companies With respect to insurance companies, companies that have issued common equity shares.

Stock index futures Futures contracts on a specified stock index.

Stops Stop-loss orders involve leaving bids or offers away from the current market price to be filled if the market reaches those levels.

Straddle An option strategy involving the purchase of a put and a call on the same underlying with the same exercise price and expiration date. If the put and call are held long, it is a long straddle; if they are held short, it is a short straddle.

Straight-through processing Systems that simplify transaction processing through the minimization of manual and/or duplicative intervention in the process from trade placement to settlement.

Strangle A variation on a straddle in which the put and call have different exercise prices; if the put and call are held long, it is a long strangle; if they are held short, it is a short strangle.

Strap An option strategy involving the purchase of two calls and one put.

Strategic asset allocation 1) The process of allocating money to IPS-permissible asset classes that integrates the investor's return objectives, risk tolerance, and investment constraints with long-run capital market expectations. 2) The result of the above process, also known as the policy portfolio.

Strategic buyers Buyers who have a strategic motive (e.g., realization of synergies) for seeking to buy a company.

Strategy benchmarks See custom security-based benchmarks.

Stratified sampling A sampling method that guarantees that subpopulations of interest are represented in the sample. Also called *representative sampling*.

Strike spread A spread used to determine the strike price for the payoff of a credit option.

Strip An option strategy involving the purchase of two puts and one call.

Structural level of unemployment The level of unemployment resulting from scarcity of a factor of production.

Structured note A variation of a floating-rate note that has some type of unusual characteristic such as a leverage factor or in which the rate moves opposite to interest rates.

Style drift Inconsistency in style.

Style index A securities index intended to reflect the average returns to a given style.

Stylized scenario A type of analysis often used in stress testing. It involves simulating the movement in at least one interest rate, exchange rate, stock price, or commodity price relevant to the portfolio.

Sunshine trades Public display of a transaction (usually high-volume) in advance of the actual order.

Support levels Price points on dealers' order boards where one would expect to see a clustering of bids.

Surplus The difference between the value of assets and the present value of liabilities. With respect to an insurance company, the net difference between the total assets and total liabilities (equivalent to policyholders' surplus for a mutual insurance company and stockholders' equity for a stock company).

Surplus capital Capital that is in excess of primary capital.

Surplus efficient frontier The graph of the set of portfolios that maximize expected surplus for given levels of standard deviation of surplus.

Survey method A method of capital market expectations setting that involves surveying experts.

Survival probability The probability an individual survives in a given year; used to determine expected cash flow required in retirement.

Survivorship bias Bias that arises in a data series when managers with poor track records exit the business and are dropped from the database whereas managers with good records remain; when a data series as of a given date reflects only entities that have survived to that date.

Swap rate The interest rate applicable to the pay-fixed-rate side of an interest rate swap.

Symmetric cash flow matching A cash flow matching technique that allows cash flows occurring both before and after the liability date to be used to meet a liability; allows for the short-term borrowing of funds to satisfy a liability prior to the liability due date.

Tactical asset allocation Asset allocation that involves making short-term adjustments to asset class weights based on short-term predictions of relative performance among asset classes.

Tactical rebalancing A variation of calendar rebalancing that specifies less frequent rebalancing when markets appear to be trending and more frequent rebalancing when they are characterized by reversals.

Tail value at risk (or conditional tail expectation) The VaR plus the expected loss in excess of VaR, when such excess loss occurs.

Target covariance matrix A component of shrinkage estimation; allows the analyst to model factors that are believed to influence the data over periods longer than observed in the historical sample.

Target semivariance The average squared deviation below a target value.

Target value The value that the portfolio manager seeks to ensure; the value that the life insurance company has guaranteed the policyholder.

Tax avoidance Developing strategies that minimize tax, while conforming to both the spirit and the letter of the tax codes of jurisdictions with taxing authority.

Tax efficiency The proportion of the expected pretax total return that will be retained after taxes.

Tax evasion The practice of circumventing tax obligations by illegal means such as misreporting or not reporting relevant information to tax authorities.

Tax-exempt bonds Bonds whose interest payments are in whole or in part exempt from taxation; they are typically issued by governmental or certain government-sponsored entities.

Tax premium Compensation for the effect of taxes on the after-tax return of an asset.

Tax risk The uncertainty associated with tax laws.

Taylor rule A rule linking a central bank's target short-term interest rate to the rate of growth of the economy and inflation.

Term life insurance A type of life insurance policy that provides coverage for a specified length of time and accumulates little or no cash values.

Territorial tax system   A framework used by a country to determine the basis for taxing income or transfers. A country that taxes income as a source within its borders imposes source jurisdiction.

Testamentary gratuitous transfer   The bequeathing or transfer of assets upon one's death. From a recipient's perspective, it is called an inheritance.

Testator   A person who makes a will.

Theta   The change in price of an option associated with a one-day reduction in its time to expiration; the rate at which an option's time value decays.

Tick   The smallest possible price movement of a security.

Time deposit   A deposit requiring advance notice prior to a withdrawal.

Time-series estimators   Estimators that are based on lagged values of the variable being forecast; often consist of lagged values of other selected variables.

Time to expiration   The time remaining in the life of a derivative, typically expressed in years.

Time value   The difference between the market price of an option and its intrinsic value, determined by the uncertainty of the underlying over the remaining life of the option.

Time-weighted average price (TWAP) strategy   A logical participation strategy that assumes a flat volume profile and trades in proportion to time.

Time-weighted rate of return   The compound rate of growth over a stated evaluation period of one unit of money initially invested in the account.

Timing option   With respect to certain futures contracts, the option that results from the ability of the short position to decide when in the delivery month actual delivery will take place.

Tobin's *q*   An asset-based valuation measure that is equal to the ratio of the market value of debt and equity to the replacement cost of total assets.

Top-down   Proceeding from the macroeconomy, to the economic sector level, to the industry level, to the firm level.

Total factor productivity (TFP)   A variable which accounts for that part of Y not directly accounted for by the levels of the production factors (K and L).

Total future liability   With respect to defined-benefit pension plans, the present value of accumulated and projected future service benefits, including the effects of projected future compensation increases.

Total rate of return   A measure of the increase in the investor's wealth due to both investment income (for example, dividends and interest) and capital gains (both realized and unrealized).

Total return   The rate of return taking into account capital appreciation/depreciation and income. Often qualified as follows: **Nominal** returns are unadjusted for inflation; **real** returns are adjusted for inflation; **pretax** returns are returns before taxes; **post-tax** returns are returns after taxes are paid on investment income and realized capital gains.

Total return analysis   Analysis of the expected effect of a trade on the portfolio's total return, given an interest rate forecast.

Total return equity swap   A swap contract that involves a series of exchanges of the total return on a specified asset or equity index in return for specified fixed or floating rate payments.

Total return swap   A swap in which one party agrees to pay the total return on a security. Often used as a credit derivative, in which the underlying is a bond.

Tracking risk   The condition in which the performance of a portfolio does not match the performance of an index that serves as the portfolio's benchmark. Also called *tracking error, tracking error volatility*, or *active risk*.

Trade blotter   A device for entering and tracking trade executions and orders to trade.

Trade settlement   Completion of a trade wherein purchased financial instruments are transferred to the buyer and the buyer transfers money to the seller.

Trading activity   In fixed-income attribution analysis, the effect of sales and purchases of bonds over a given period; the total portfolio return minus the other components determining the management effect in an attribution analysis.

Transaction exposure   The risk associated with a foreign exchange rate on a specific business transaction such as a purchase or sale.

Translation exposure   The risk associated with the conversion of foreign financial statements into domestic currency.

Transparency   Availability of timely and accurate market and trade information.

Treasury spot curve   The term structure of Treasury zero coupon bonds.

Twist   With respect to the yield curve, a movement in contrary directions of interest rates at two maturities; a nonparallel movement in the yield curve.

Type I error   With respect to manager selection, keeping (or hiring) managers with zero value-added. (Rejecting the null hypothesis when it is correct).

Type II error   With respect to manager selection, firing (or not hiring) managers with positive value-added. (Not rejecting the null hypothesis when it is incorrect).

Unconstrained optimization   Optimization that places no constraints on asset class weights except that they sum to 1. May produce negative asset weights, which implies borrowing or shorting of assets.

Underfunded plan   A pension plan in which the ratio of the value of plan assets to the present value of plan liabilities is less than 100 percent.

Underlying   An asset that trades in a market in which buyers and sellers meet, decide on a price, and the seller then delivers the asset to the buyer and receives payment. The underlying is the asset or other derivative on which a particular derivative is based. The market for the underlying is also referred to as the spot market.

Underwriting (profitability) cycle   A cycle affecting the profitability of insurance companies' underwriting operations.

Unhedged return   A foreign asset return stated in terms of the investor's home currency.

Unit-linked life insurance   A type of ordinary life insurance in which death benefits and cash values are linked to the investment performance of a policyholder-selected pool of investments held in a so-called separate account. Also called *variable life insurance*.

Universal life insurance   A type of life insurance policy that provides for premium flexibility, an adjustable face amount of death benefits, and current market interest rates on the savings element.

Unrelated business income   With respect to the US tax code, income that is not substantially related to a foundation's charitable purposes.

Unstructured modeling Modeling without a theory on the underlying structure.

Uptick rules Trading rules that specify that a short sale must not be on a downtick relative to the last trade at a different price.

Urgency of the trade The importance of certainty of execution.

Utility The level of relative satisfaction received from the consumption of goods and services.

Utility theory Theory whereby people maximize the present value of utility subject to a present value budget constraint.

Valuation reserve With respect to insurance companies, an allowance, created by a charge against earnings, to provide for losses in the value of the assets.

Value The amount for which one can sell something, or the amount one must pay to acquire something.

Value at risk (VaR) A probability-based measure of loss potential for a company, a fund, a portfolio, a transaction, or a strategy over a specified period of time.

Value-motivated traders Traders that act on value judgments based on careful, sometimes painstaking research. They trade only when the price moves into their value range.

Value weighted With respect to index construction, an index in which each security in the index is weighted according to its market capitalization. Also called *market-capitalization weighted*.

Variable annuity A life annuity in which the periodic payment varies depending on stock prices.

Variable life insurance A type of ordinary life insurance in which death benefits and cash values are linked to the investment performance of a policyholder-selected pool of investments held in a so-called separate account. Also called *unit-linked life insurance*.

Variable prepaid forward A monetization strategy that involves the combination of a collar with a loan against the value of the underlying shares. When the loan comes due, shares are sold to pay off the loan and part of any appreciation is shared with the lender.

Variable universal life A type of life insurance policy that combines the flexibility of universal life with the investment choice flexibility of variable life. Also called *flexible-premium variable life*.

Vega A measure of the sensitivity of an option's price to changes in the underlying's volatility.

Venture capital The equity financing of new or growing private companies.

Venture capital firms Firms representing dedicated pools of capital for providing equity or equity-linked financing to privately held companies.

Venture capital fund A pooled investment vehicle for venture capital investing.

Venture capital trusts An exchange-traded, closed-end vehicle for venture capital investing.

Venture capitalists Specialists who seek to identify companies that have good business opportunities but need financial, managerial, and strategic support.

Vested With respect to pension benefits or assets, said of an unconditional ownership interest.

Vintage year With reference to a private equity fund, the year it closed.

Vintage year effects The effects on returns shared by private equity funds closed in the same year.

Volatility Represented by the Greek letter sigma (σ), the standard deviation of price outcomes associated with an underlying asset.

Volatility clustering The tendency for large (small) swings in prices to be followed by large (small) swings of random direction.

Volume-weighted average price (VWAP) The average price at which a security is traded during the day, where each trade price is weighted by the fraction of the day's volume associated with the trade.

Volume-weighted average price (VWAP) strategy A logical participation strategy that involves breaking up an order over time according to a prespecified volume profile.

Wealth relative The ending value of one unit of money invested at specified rates of return.

Whole life insurance A type of life insurance policy that involves coverage for the whole of the insured's life. Also called *ordinary life insurance*.

Wild card option A provision allowing a short futures contract holder to delay delivery of the underlying.

Will A document associated with estate planning that outlines the rights others will have over one's property after death. Also called *testament*.

Within-sector selection return In attribution analysis, a measure of the impact of a manager's security selection decisions relative to the holdings of the sector benchmark.

Worst-case scenario analysis A stress test in which we examine the worst case that we actually expect to occur.

Yardeni model An equity valuation model, more complex than the Fed model, that incorporates the expected growth rate in earnings.

Yield beta A measure of the sensitivity of a bond's yield to a general measure of bond yields in the market that is used to refine the hedge ratio.

Yield curve The relationship between yield and time to maturity.

Yield curve risk Risk related to changes in the shape of the yield curve.

Yield to worst The yield on a callable bond that assumes a bond is called at the earliest opportunity.

Zero-cost collar A transaction in which a position in the underlying is protected from buying a put and selling a call with the premium from the sale of the call offsetting the premium from the purchase of the put. It can also be used to protect a floating-rate borrower against interest rate increases with the premium on a long cap offsetting the premium on a short floor.

Zero-premium collar A hedging strategy involving the simultaneous purchase of puts and sale of call options on a stock. The puts are struck below and the calls are struck above the underlying's market price.

Index